RURAL DEVELOPMENT AND INCLUSIVE GROWTH: LINKAGE AND IMPLICATIONS

RURAL DEVELOPMENT AND INCLUSIVE GROWTH

Linkage and Implications

Siddaraju V.G.

and

Ramesh

KALPAZ

ISBN: 978-93-5128-100-9

Price: ₹ 1500/-

Published by

Kalpaz Publications

C-30, Satyawati Nagar,
Delhi – 110052
E-mail: kalpaz@hotmail.com
Ph.: 9212142040

Laser Typesetting: Lucky Graphic, Delhi
Printed at: G. Print Process, Delhi

Cataloging in Publication Data—DK
Courtesy: D.K. Agencies (P) Ltd. <docinfo@dkagencies.com>

"Rural Development and Inclusive Growth: New Debates" (Conference) (2014 : University of Mysore)
Rural development and inclusive growth : linkage and implications / Siddaraju V.G. and Ramesh.
pages ; cm
Includes bibliographical references and index.
ISBN 9789351281009

1. Rural development—India—Congresses. 2. Rural development—Government policy—India—Congresses. I. Siddaraju, V. G., editor. II. Ramesh (Reader in law), editor. III. University of Mysore.host institution. IV. Title.

DDC 307.14120954 23

Contents

Foreword

The notion of rural development has undergone a lucid transformation during the last four decades as the focus has now shifted from technology-based agricultural production to the more embarked idea of inclusive rural development. Rural development is a course of action concerning foremost changes in rural social structures, popular attitudes of the people, national institutions, speedy economic growth, plummeting inequalities and eradicating absolute poverty.

Rural development is one of the foremost proportions of a sustainable development. In India, inclusive growth and development is a redoubtable confronted for the rural section of the society. As experts felt, it is an intricate to demarcate parameters of growth and development. Today, inclusive development focussing rural parts has vital significance, because it comprises national and nation-building issues. It is opined that the social element of inclusive rural development stressing the poor households be supposed to occur through the lessening down of the inequalities in social indicators, enhancing gender parity on condition that accessible social safety nets are meant tab for all in nearly marginalised groups of Indian rural society.

India is a country which saw more than 97 different rural development programmes in her just 65 years of independence! It means in an average one new programme per year! However, situation of rural lives has not yet speculatively developed. Development can be seen today, however, not up to the level of expectation. This is not an inclusive development. We need some more new instrumentals for speedy inclusive rural development of the country. Today emphasis is needed more on growth through technology determined interventions to shed light on various inclusive issues. Only the more recent effort is MGNREGP, which is an optimistic and a pertinent footstep towards inclusive rural development in the recent years.

Also, we need to frame more effectual land reforms establishing solid rural infrastructure, augmentation of valuable institutions, financial inclusion, more support for rural non-farm sectors for the speedy inclusive rural development today. Also, more concentration of land-ownership and the key role of certain dominant castes have been few hurdles in the way of Indian rural economic growth and poverty reduction in many states in India. In this context, I congratulate Prof. Ramesh and Dr Siddaraju V.G. faculties of Centre, for Study of Social Exclusion and Inclusive Policy, University of Mysore, Mysore for having done commendable work through editing this book. I hope this book will help in framing suitable rural policy initiatives in the future.

Prof K.S. Rangappa

Vice Chancellor,

University of Mysore,

Mysore

Preface

India's economy has grown at an impressive pace over the last two decades because of wide ranging structural reforms to open up the economy and make it more competitive. More recently, activity has slowed reflecting not only the weak global environment but also the emergence of strains created, by the pressure that rapid economic growth has put on energy, natural resources, infrastructure and skills. Making growth more inclusive and addressing widespread poverty is another key challenge for India. It requires sustained investment in people, especially in health and education and in transport and energy infrastructure. The 12th Five Year Plan was aimed to achieve "Faster, Sustainable and more Inclusive growth" in terms of benefits flowing through more employment and income to those sections of society, which have been bypassed by higher rates of economic growth witnessed in recent years. The recognition of the need for more inclusive growth by our planners is a welcome shift in emphasis from mere increase in growth rates to improvement in standards of living of those below the poverty line through increase in employment opportunities as well as better delivery systems.

Rural Development plays always the role of a decisive factor in nation's Development. Rural Development in India is one of the most important factors for the growth of the Indian economy. It has great significance for a country like India where majority of the population, 69 per cent (83.3 crore) live in rural areas while 31 per cent (37.7 crore) stay in urban areas (Census, 2011). The most deprived people live in India generally belong to the rural areas. The present strategy of rural development in India mainly focusses on poverty alleviation, better livelihood opportunities, provision of basic amenities and infrastructure facilities through innovative programmes of wage and self-employment. Rural development aims at improving rural people's livelihood in an equitable and sustainable manner, both socially and environmentally, through better access to assets (natural, physical, human, technological and social capital), and services, and control over productive capital (in its financial or economic and political forms) that enable them to improve their livelihoods on a sustainable and equitable basis. The basic objectives of Rural Development

Programmes have been alleviation of poverty and unemployment through creation of basic social and economic infrastructure, provision of training to rural unemployed youth and providing employment to marginal Farmers/ Labourers to discourage seasonal and permanent migration to urban areas besides the public partnership. The Government's policy and programmes have laid emphasis on poverty alleviation, generation of employment and income opportunities and provision of infrastructure and basic facilities to meet the needs of rural poor.

This is a collection of research papers, presented in the national level conference titled "Rural Development and Inclusive Growth: New Debates," conducted by the Centre for Study of Social Exclusion and Inclusive Policy (CSSEIP), University of Mysore, Karnataka held on 21st and 22nd August 2014. The Centre would like to thank the Indian Council of Social Science Research (ICSSR), New Delhi for its funding support and all contributors in this conference.

Editors

Dr Siddaraju V.G.
and
Dr Ramesh

Acknowledgements

The Editors of this discourse Dr Siddaraju V.G. and Dr Ramesh would like to convey their thanks to beloved Vice-Chancellor Prof. K.S. Rangappa for his constant encouragement and support. Both are also gratified to the Registrar for his logistic prop up. Both take this opportunity to express their heartfelt thanks to all the contributors, who have enriched the book by contributing their learned papers. The Editors were indebted to Dr Nanjunda DC and Dr Dinesha P T, faculty members of CSSEIP, University of Mysore for their valuable support. They acknowledge all others, who have supported and assisted directly and indirectly for completion of this work.

The Editors of this book are also indebted to the Kalpaz Publications, Delhi for publishing this edited volume.

List of Contributors from India

Ananad Gowda .Assistant Professor, Department of Post-Graduate Studies and Research in Political Science, Karnataka State Open University, Muktagangotri, Mysore, Karnataka.

Ananth S. Panth. Associate Professor, Mysore, Karnataka.

Arjun, R. Project Fellow, UGC-UPE Focus Area–II, University of Mysore, Mysore, Karnataka.

Appaji Gowda. Assistant Professor, Department of Anthropology, Karnataka State Open University, Mysore, Karnataka.

Ashoka. K.G. Assistant Professor, Department of Commerce, Alva's College Moodbidri, Dakshina Kannada, Karnataka.

Ashwini. H. Bidaralli. Assistant Professor, Department of Economics, Goverment First-Grade College, Shikaripura, Shimoga District, Karnataka.

Balraj M, Dos. in Commerce, Post-Graduate Satellite Centre, Chamarajanagara, Karnataka.

Chandrashekar, B.S. Assistant Professor of Co-operation, Maharaja's College, University of Mysore, Mysore, Karnataka.

Channabasavaiah H.M. Assistant Professor, Department of Economics, P.G. Centre, Smt. Saraladevi Sathischandra Aggarwal Government First -Grade College, Bellary, Karnataka.

Chethana.B. DoS in Economics and Co-operation, University of Mysore, Mysore, Karnataka.

Chikkasidde Gowda. M.Phil. student, Department of Economics, Sir M.V. Post-graduation Centre, University of Mysore, Mandya, Karnataka.

Damodaran K. Assistant Professor, Department of Economics, Annamalai University, Annamalai Nagar, Chidambaram, Tamil Nadu.

Debasis Mondal. Research Scholar, Centre for Journalism and Mass Communication, Visva-Bharati University, Santiniketan, West Bengal.

Deepu B., Director, Jeevajala Organisation, Mysore, Karnataka.

Devidas G. Maley., Assistant Professor of Law, Department of Post-graduate Studies and Research in Law, Gulbarga University, Gulbarga, Karnataka.

Dileep Kumar M., Research Scholar, DoS in Communication and Journalism, University of Mysore, Karnataka.

Dinesha P.T., Assistant Professor-cum-Assistant Director, Centre for Study of Social Exclusion and Inclusive Policy, University of Mysore, Mysore, Karnataka.

Divya B.S., Asstistant Professor of Economics, Government First-Grade College for Women, Mandya, Karnataka.

Divya Pradeep., Assistant Professor, Christ University, Bangalore, Karnataka.

Gagan K., Research Scholar, Department of Studies in Law, University of Mysore, Karnataka.

Gayathri N.K., Rtd. Associate Professor, DoS in Economics and Co-operation, University of Mysore, Manasagangothri, Mysore, Karnataka.

Gayathri, A., Assistant Professor, Economics Wing, DDE, Annamalai University, Annamalai Nagar, Chidambaram, Tamil Nadu.

Geetha M. C., KSOU, Manasagangothri, Mysore, Karnataka.

Geetha M. L., Associate Professor, Government First-Grade College, Mangalore, Karnataka.

Harish D. N., Associate Professor, Department of M.B.A. Visvesvaraiya Technological University, Regional Centre, Gulbarga - 585105, Karnataka, India

Harish S. N., Research Scholar, Deptartment of Business Administration, KSOU, Manasagangothri, Karnataka.

Huchhe Gowda., Assistant Professor, Department of Studies in Economics, Rani Channamma University, Vidyasangama, Belagavi, Karnataka.

Jayadev K. A., Business Analyst, TARGET Corporation, Bangalore, Karnataka.

Jayaraj M., Department of Economics and Applied Economics, Sri Krishnadevaraya University, Ananthapuram, Andhra Pradesh.

Kiran Kumar P., Assistant Professor, Department of Economics, Rani Channamma University, S.R. Kanthi P.G . Centre, Bagalkot, Karnataka.

Kumara J.N., Research Scholar, Dos in Economics and Co operation, University of Mysore, Manasagangotri, Mysore, Karnataka.

Lakshmikantha A., Department of Political Science, Mangalore University, Mangalagangothri, Karnataka.

Lavanya V.L ., Research Scholar, Department of Economics, Avinashilingam Institute for Home Science and Higher Education for Women, Coimbatore, Tamil Nadu.

Likitha S. Anuradha., Lecturer, Post-Graduate Satellite Centre, Chamarajnagar, Mysore University, Karnataka.

Lokesha M. N., Assistant Professor, Government First-Grade College, Channarayapatna, Karnataka.

Lokeshnath B., Assistant Professor, Government First Grade College, Uppinangady, Dakshina Kannada, Karnataka, India.

Mahesh chandra Guru B.P., Professor, Department of Studies in Communication and Journalism, University of Mysore, Manasagangotri, Karnataka.

Mahesha M., Associate Professor, DoS in Economics and Co operation, University of Mysore, Mysore, Karnataka.

Mangala T., Assistant Professor of Economics, Government Women's College, Mandya, Karnataka.

Manish R. Patel., Faculty at Department of Economics, S. P. University, VV Nagar, Anand, Gujarat.

Mariswamy H.K., Associate Professor, Department of Communication, Central College, Bangalore University, Bangalore, Karnataka.

Meghadeepa Chakraborty., Research Scholar, Tata Institute of Social Sciences, Mumbai.

Mohan Das. K., Assistant Professor, Department of Research and Studies in Political Science, Vijayanagara Sri Krishnadevaraya University, Bellary Karnataka.

Mudduraju. N., Assistant Professor in Law, SBRR Mahajana Law College, Mysore, Karnataka.

Muthamma, K.S., Lecturer, Post-Graduate Satellite Centre, , Chamarajnagar, Mysore University, Karnataka.

Naga Jyothi M.J., Assistant Professor of Economics, Govternment First Grade College, Channapatna, Karnataka.

Nagabhushana R., Assistant Professor, Department of Economics, Government First-Grade College, Kuvempunagar, Mysore, Karnataka.

Nanjunda D.C., Associate Professor, Centre for Study of Social Exclusion and Inclusive Policy, University of Mysore, Mysore, Karnataka.

Narasimha Murthy B., Assistant Professor in Economics, Govternment First-Grade College, Varthur, Bangalore, Karnataka.

Nataraj H.K., Faculty Member, Department of Political Science, Mangalore University, Mangalagangothri, Karnataka.

Naveen Chandra, C.B., Research Scholar, Department of Studies in Law, Manasagangotri, University of Mysore, Mysore, Karnataka.

Niranjana Babu Reddy, H.S., Assistant Professor, Government First Grade College, T.N. Pura, Mysore, Karnataka.

Prakruthi, A.R., Assistant Professor in Law, SBRR Mahajana Law College, Mysore, Karnataka.

Ramesh. Director, Centre for Study of Social Exclusion and Inclusive Policy, University of Mysore, Manasagangothri, Mysore, Karnataka.

Ramesha K., Research Scholar, Department of Studies in Law, University of Mysore, Mysore, Karnataka.

Roopa Patavardhan., Junior Research Fellow, DoS in Economics and Co-operation, Manasagangotri Mysore, Karnataka.

Sathyanarayana., Faculty in Economics, Department of Justice School of Studies in Law, University of Mysore, Manasagangothri, Mysore, Karnataka.

Savitha K.P., Assistant Professor, Oxford College of Engineering, Bangalore, Karnataka.

Sharmista., Assistant Professor in Education BGS, B.Ed College Mysore, Karnataka.

Shashi Kumar T.P., Assistant Professor, Department of Post-Graduate Studies and Research in Economics, Karnataka State Open University, Mysore, Karnataka.

Shekhar., Associate Professor, Department of Sociology and Social Work, Govternment First Grade College, Shikaripura, Shimoga District, Karnataka.

Shiv Kumar., Assistant Professor of Economics, A.S. College, Khanna, District Ludhiana, Punjab.

Shivakumara Reddy, K., Ph.D. Research Scholar, DOS in Economics and Co-operation, University of Mysore, Karnataka.

Shivanand Nari., Associate Professor of Economics, Karnataka University, Dharawad, Karnataka.

Shivaraju H.S., Research Scholar, DoS in Communication and Journalism, University of Mysore, Karnataka.

Shri Krishan., Professor of History and Dean, Faculty Member of Social Sciences, Indira Gandhi University, Meerpur, Rewari, Haryana.

Shridevi J. Darabare., Research Scholar, P.G. Department of Studies in Law, Karnataka University, Dharwad, Karnataka.

Siddaraju V.G ., Associate Professor, Centre for Study of Social Excusion and Inclusive Policy, University of Mysore, Mysore, Karnataka.

Sobha Rani. Bt., Assistant professor Department of Economics, S.S.A. GFGC, Bellary, Karnataka.

Somashekaraiah N.T., Assistant Professor, Department of Post-graduate Studies in Economics, Maharani Arts and Commerce College for Women, Mysore, Karnataka.

Sowmya N., DoS in History, Maharani PG College, Mysore, Karnataka.

Sreedhara T.N., Professor, Department of Business Administration, Mangalore University, Mangalore, Karnataka.

Srinivasa, D., Project Fellow, UGC-UPE Focus Area–II, University of Mysore, Mysore, Karnataka.

Subhaschandra D. Rathod., Research Scholar, P.G. Department of Studies in Law, Karnataka University, Dharwad, Karnataka.

Swetha, S., Junior Research Fellow, SBM chair, DoS in Economics and Co operation, Manasagangothri, Mysore, Karnataka.

Uma, H.R., Professor of Economics, Deptartment of Economics, Sir M.V. Post-graduation Centre, University of Mysore, Mandya, Karnataka.

Usha Rani, K., Assistant Professor, Mahajana Tourism Development Institute, Pooja Bhagavat Mahajana P.G. Centre Campus, K.R.S. Road, Metagalli, Mysore, Karnataka.

Vibhudi Venkateshwarlu., Research Scholar, Department of Law, Osmania University, Hyderabad, Andhra Pradesh, India.

Vijay S. Jariwala., Faculty Member, Department of Economics, M K Bhavnagar University, Bhavnagar, Gujarat.

Yuvaraja P., Programmer (Teaching), Department of Economics, Annamalai University, Annamalai Nagar, Chidambaram, Tamil Nadu.

1

The Role of Micro and Small Scale Industries in Inclusive Rural Development in India

B Chethana and M. Mahesha

Introduction

Micro, Small and Medium Enterprises (MSME) sector has been recognised as an engine of growth all over the world. This MSME sector has acquired a prominent place in the growth of the rural economy of India. The role of MSME in the economic and social development of the country is well established. Lending to the MSME sector has acquired significance with the enactment of Micro, Small and Medium Enterprises Development Act in the year 2006 [MSMED Act, 2006] by the Government of India to have a focussed and balanced growth of Micro, Small and Medium Enterprises. The MSME sector has a great role in the creation of employment, development of rural economy, growth of an economy and distribution of wealth. Through giving the opportunity of work to the unemployed people, it helps to lead a good life of the people, who are living below poverty line. Presently, it provides employment to over 100 million of people in India. It contributes to an economy not only in terms of employment generation but also in terms of share in total exports. Currently, it contributes to nearly 40 per cent of exports out of total exports of India. It is producing 8,000 of different products.

The MSMEs sector is characterised by low investment requirement, operational flexibility, location-wise mobility, and import substitution. In India, the Micro, Small and Medium Enterprises Development (MSMED) Act, 2006 is the first single comprehensive legislation covering all the three segments. In accordance with the Act, these enterprises are classified into two:

(i) Manufacturing enterprises engaged in the manufacture or production of goods pertaining to any industry specified in the first schedule to the Industries (Development and regulation) Act, 1951. These are defined in terms of investment in plant and machinery;

(ii) Service enterprises engaged in providing or rendering of services and are defined in terms of investment in equipment. The significance of MSMEs in terms of fostering new entrepreneurship is well-recognised. This is because, most entrepreneurs start their business from a small unit which provide them an opportunity to harness their skills and talents, to experiment, to innovate and transform their ideas into goods and services and finally nurture it into a larger unit. Over the years, the small scale sector in India has progressed from the production of simple consumer goods to the manufacture of many sophisticated and precision products like electronics control systems, micro-wave components, electro-medical equipments, etc. The process of economic liberalisation and market reforms has further exposed these enterprises to increasing levels of domestic and global competition.

Objectives

The important objectives of this paper are:

1. To examine the role of MSMEs in the generation of employment in the rural India;
2. To compare generation of employment by MSMEs among gender and social groups.

Hypotheses

1. MSMEs have significant contribution to rural employment generation.
2. There is a significant difference in employment generation among gender and social groups by MSMEs.

Methodology

This study makes use of the secondary data from the report of Fourth All India Census of Micro, Small and Medium Enterprises - 2006-07 and Annual Report of MSMEs - 2012-13. The data collected for the research are analysed with the help of simple statistical techniques such as percentage and graphs to come to meaningful conclusion. Simple Regression analysis, Independent sample T test and ANOVA test has been used to test the hypotheses.

Results and Discussions

Micro, small and medium enterprises (MSMEs), including *khadi* and village as well as rural enterprises, play a pivotal role in the overall rural development of the country. They have been the significant contributors to the national income, with their huge involvement in country's industrial production, exports, etc. They not only help in providing employment opportunities to millions of people across the country, especially to the village artisans and rural people, but also check the problem of economic concentration in the hands of a few. They create a sound entrepreneurial base in the economy by developing and nurturing the talents, skills, etc., of small and medium scale entrepreneurs. The labour intensity in the MSME sector is estimated to be considerably higher than the large enterprises. Thus, this sector has been regarded priority status by both the Central and the State Governments. In this context, an attempt has been made to examine the role of micro and small scale industries in inclusive rural development in India.

Worldwide, the Micro, Small and Medium Enterprises (MSMEs) have been accepted as the engine of economic growth and for promoting equitable development. The MSMEs constitute over 90 per cent of total enterprises in most of the economies and are credited with generating the highest rates of employment growth and account for major share of industrial production and exports. In India, too Tab MSMS too the MSMEs play a pivotal role in the overall industrial economy of the country. It is estimated that in terms of value, the sector accounts for about around 40 per cent of the total export of the country. It produces over 8,000 value-added products further, in recent years the MSME sector has consistently registered higher growth rate compared to the overall industrial sector. The major advantage of the sector is its employment potential at low capital cost. In the year 2009-10, the industrial sector share in the employment was nearly 100 million; within that MSMEs share was 69.5 million. Nearly 70 per cent of the employment generation was contributed to the industrial sector by MSMEs.

Figure 1: Employment Generation by MSMEs in India (*In Lakh*)

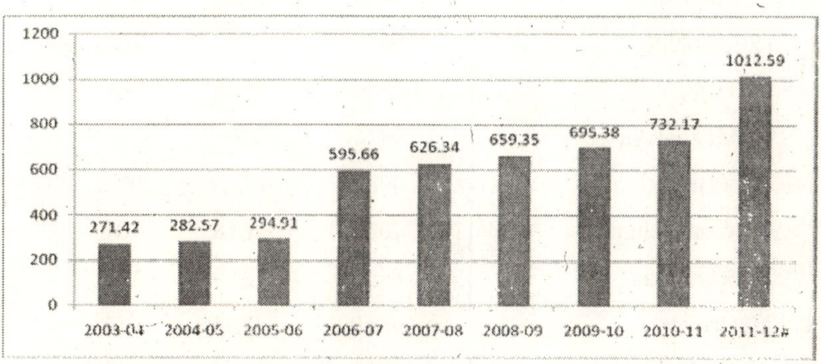

Source: Annual Report of MSMEs- 2012-13.

As the above figure-1 shows that the employment generation by MSMEs was increasing rapidly. After 2005, the rate of increase in the generation of employment was very high, finally it reaches upto 73 million employment. In 2011-12, it has projected to reach 101 million employment.

Table – 1: State-wise Percentage Distribution of Employment by Type of Enterprise in Rural India

State/UT Name	*Micro*	*Small*	*Medium*
1. Jammu and Kashmir	82.55	13.37	4.07
2. Himachal Pradesh	60.88	28.76	10.35
3. Punjab	67.04	30.86	2.10
4. Chandigarh	88.96	11.04	0.00
5. Uttarakhand	70.53	27.23	2.24
6. Haryana	68.34	27.82	3.84
7. Delhi	71.84	13.91	14.25
8. Rajasthan	76.86	19.76	3.39
9. Uttar Pradesh	88.05	10.64	1.32
10. Bihar	95.86	3.70	0.44
11. Sikkim	58.43	41.57	0.00
12. Arunachal Pradesh	35.67	45.53	18.80
13. Nagaland	93.31	6.69	0.00
14. Manipur	99.71	0.29	0.00
15. Mizoram	98.17	1.83	0.00
16. Tripura	72.50	26.45	1.06
17. Meghalaya	94.89	3.59	1.52
18. Assam	47.42	42.36	10.22
19. West Bengal	70.26	26.68	3.06
20. Jharkhand	84.56	12.69	2.75
21. Orissa	78.50	18.34	3.17
22. Chhattisgarh	88.10	11.52	0.39
23. Madhya Pradesh	88.86	8.65	2.49
24. Gujarat	71.52	19.40	9.09
25. Daman and Diu	38.18	51.47	10.35
26. Dadra and Nagar Haveli	89.44	10.56	0.00
27. Maharashtra	60.57	33.29	6.15
28. Andhra Pradesh	72.65	26.10	1.25

29. Karnataka	80.36	16.78	2.86
30. Goa	42.25	52.55	5.20
31. Lakshadweep	100.00	0.00	0.00
32. Kerala	88.88	10.03	1.10
33. Tamil Nadu	67.62	28.57	3.81
34. Puducherry	37.29	53.70	9.01
35. Andaman and Nicobar	98.93	1.07	0.00
All India	**74.32**	**21.94**	**3.74**

Source: 4th All India Census of MSMEs -2006-07.

The Table-1 reveals that state-wise percentage distribution of employment by types of enterprises in rural India. As the table states micro-industries has acquired large share in employment generation compared to other enterprises in rural India. In most of the states, micro-industries generated more than 90 per cent of the employment, followed by small and medium enterprises in the MSME sector. Within the three types of enterprises only in the five states, medium enterprises have generated more than 10 per cent of employment. In only four state, the employment generation by micro-industries was less than 50 per cent. This information tells us how micro-industries are very important to the economy like India.

Table – 2: Ownership of MSMEs by Gender and Social Category in Rural India

Type of Enterprise		*Number of Enterprises Owned by (Numbers in Thousand)*							
		Female	*Male*	*Total*	*SC*	*ST*	*OBC*	*Others*	*Total*
1.	Micro	106.74	580.68	687.42		71.61	28.18	305.45	282.18
2.	Small	1.20	18.06	19.26		0.56	0.22	3.36	15.13
3.	Medium	0.05	0.68	0.72		0.02	0.03	0.11	0.56
	Total	107.99	599.42	707.40		72.19	28.42	308.92	

Source: 4th All India Census of MSMEs -2006-07.

The Table-2 depicts that Ownership of MSMEs by Gender and Social Category in Rural India. In all types of enterprises, male-owned enterprises were significantly very high compare to female-owned enterprises. Around 85 per cent MSMEs were owned by males only. And if we come to ownership of MSMEs by social category, OBC and others have played a major role. Only 14 per cent of MSMEs were owned by SC and STs. This situation was similar even in all types of enterprises.

Table 3: Employment Generation by Types of Enterprises among Types of Gender/ Social Category in Rural India (In Thousands)

Type of Enterprise		*Female*	*Male*	*Total*	*SC*	*ST*	*OBC*	*Others*
1.	Micro	2099.61	636.83		400.24		167.17	
2.	Small	645.78	162.04		106.42	48.73	242.39	410.28
3.	Medium	110.86	26.88		15.85	11.39	34.63	75.87
	Total	2856.25	825.75	3682.00	522.51		227.30	

Source: 4th All India Census of MSMEs -2006-07.

The Table-3 reveals that Employment generation by types of Enterprised among Gender and Social Category in Rural India. Among three types of enterprises, micro enterprises have occupied major role *i.e.,* it contributed around 75 per cent of employment generation in rural India, followed by small and medium enterprises. Within the three types of enterprises, the numbers of female employ were very large. And if we come to employment generation by enterprises among social categories, OBC and others were more benefitted, *i.e.,* around 80 per cent of employment was occupied by these two categories only, SC and STs were seldom benefited.

Table - 4: Results of 'T' Test to Show Differences in Employment Between the Males and Females in Rural India.

Independent Samples Test										
		Levene's Test for Equality of Variances		t-test for Equality of Means						
		F	Sig.	t	df	Sig. (2-tailed)	Mean Difference	Std. Error Difference	95 per cent Confidence Interval of the Difference Lower	Upper
Employment	Equal variances assumed	.000	1.000	-23.29	68	.000	-63.57543	2.72869	-69.02045	-58.13041
	Equal variances not assumed			-23.29	68.000	.000	-63.57543	2.72869	-69.02045	-58.13041

Table-4 shows independent sample 'T' test results. This test has been used to test the significant difference in employment generation by MSMEs between males and females in Rural India. Since, the probability value is 0.000, the result is statistically significant at one percent level of significance. It means that there are significant differences in employment generation by MSMEs between males and females in Rural India.

Table 5: Results of 'ANOVA' Test to Show Differences in Employment among Social Categories in Rural India

Source of Variation	df	Sum of Sq.	Mean Sq.	Value	Probability
Between	1	273316.1	273316.1		
Within	46	1694852.	36844.60	7.418078	0.0091
Total	47	1968168.	41875.91		

Table – 6: Regression Results

Variable	Coefficient	Std. Error	t-Statistic	Prob.	R square
Employment	-0.000173	8.46E-05	-2.048375	0.0500	0.3589
C	14.55296	26.82783	0.542458	0.5918	

Source: Dependent Variable: Poverty

Since unemployment and poverty are highly related and the level of employment effect on poverty, this paper estimates the impact of employment generation by MSMEs on poverty among Indian states for the year 2006-07 by using simple regression analysis. The results of the model are reported Table-6.

There is a negative relationship between the employment generation and poverty level. It means that, if one person gets employment in the MSMEs sector it leads to 0.000173 lakh reduction in poverty. The result is also significant at five per cent level of significance. As the R square value tells us that 35 per cent of the variation in the poverty is explained by employment generation by MSMEs.

Conclusion and Policy Suggestions

The overall conclusion emerging from the analysis of the role of Micro and Small scale industries in inclusive rural development in India is that, it brings to light development MSMEs which plays vital role in contributing significantly to social and economic development objectives such as labour absorption, income distribution, rural development, poverty eradication and promotion of entrepreneurship. For the healthy growth of the Indian economy MSMEs shouldn't be viewed from the angle of competitiveness but that of complementariness. So, when government is going to make policies related to employment generation, it should have to give more importance to MSMEs in Rural India to achieve more inclusive growth. And government should also have the attention towards the employment of marginalised sections, because even though MSMEs playing very big role in the employment generation in Rural India, most of the beneficiaries are upper class people. So to achieve the more rural inclusiveness in India, employment generation is not enough within the share of marginalised sections should has to increase.

References

Abdul Naser. V, (2013), "*A Critical Evaluation of the Contributions Made by the Micro, Small and Medium Enterprises in Indian Economy*", International Journal of Marketing, Financial Services and Management Research, Vol. 2, No. 7, pp 151-8.

Angela W. Browne (1982), " *Rural Development in Botswana – the Role of Small-Scale Industries*", Geographical Association, Vol. 67, No. 3, pp. 255-8.

Annual Report 2012-13, Ministry of Micro, Small and Medium Enterprises, Government of India.

Dattam and Sundaram, (2007), *Indian Economy*, S. Chand and Company Ltd, New Delhi.

Fourth All India Census of Micro, Small and Medium Enterprises (2006-07), Government of India.

Mishra S.K., "*Recent Trend of Village and Small Enterprise Sector Exploring and Exploiting its Opportunities in the North Eastern Region of India touching upon its Profile and Barriers*", Electronic copy available at: http://ssrn.com/abstract=997310.

Nirankar Srivastav and Rickey Syngkon (2008), *"Emergence of Small Scale Industries and Entrepreneurship in the Rural Areas of North-Eastern States of India: An analytical approach"*, the ICFAI University Journal of Entrepreneurship Development, Vol. V, No.2.

Syed Vazith Hussain (2004), "*Performance of Small Scale Industries in India and the Challenges Ahead*", Indian Journal of Industrial Relations, Vol. 39, No. 3, pp. 391-401.

Venkata ramanaiah. M, "The performance of Small Scale Industries (SSI) in India: An Overview", Electronic copy available at: http://ssrn.com/abstract=1737836.

www.dcmsme.gov.in .

www.msme.gov.in .

www.nsic.co.in.

2

Strengthening of Rural Infrastructure - A Golden Key to Inclusive Growth

B.S. Divya

Introduction

Infrastructural bottleneck is the ugliest face of rural area. Welfare of ruralites and inclusive growth go in the same direction and they are positively correlated. The provision of the best infrastructural facilities accelerates the production as well as the productivity of the rural economy and pushes the country up to realise the cherished long destination, *i.e.,* inclusive growth. Today's buzz word 'Inclusive growth' aims at tapping all the available resources to include the excluded group of all sectors of the economy of both urban and rural area. It also ensures decent life, healthy environment and economic justice to rural platform. As indeed, development starts at the grassroot level. So inclusive growth concept has become a powerful instrument to bring anticipated social standards and economic freedom. India's soul lies in villages. According to 2011 census, there are 6,40,867 villages in this country. The 68.84 per cent of Indian population has found its shelter on rural landscape. A major portion of this group is illiterate, poor and seasonally unemployed. No doubt that those rural parts of India have become islands of inequality. Therefore, the strong implementation of developmental strategies in rural areas undoubtedly pumps the pulse-rate of rural economy and brings satisfaction to millions of households. If India wants to see stainless progress, villages need to be filled with proper and essential infrastructural facilities. Rural infrastructure is an umbrella concept. It comprises different sectors such as banking, irrigation, transportation, housing, telecommunications, drinking water supply, electrification and toilet facilities.

Need For the Study

According to the reports of Consumer Electronics And Appliances Manufacturers Association, 2013; during the year 2012-13, 16.4 million TV sets were sold in rural India and out of them 5.6 million were LCD sets. Rural India has 35 per cent of automobile industry sales and has 351 million of mobile phone users, but the paradox of rural India is that ruralites today are buying more mobile phones, But there is no proper network coverage, purchasing bikes and cars but no smooth roads, having TV sets but no adequate power supply, consuming more soft drinks at stall, but no pure drinking water availability. In this background, the present paper focusses on the following four important aspects:

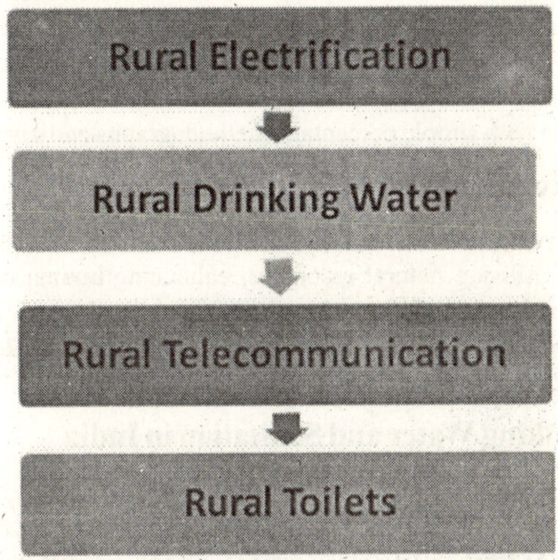

Even today households in rural parts hardly get two or four hours of power supply and as on 31.03.2014, all over India 21,318 villages are unelectrified. Around 60 per cent of households do not have proper toilet facilities and to get one bucket of drinking water they have to walk miles together and 200 million people do not get hygienic water. It is the irony of our country that rural India has more mobile phones than toilets, more Pepsi and Coca Cola than pure and hygienic water.

Objectives

The present study is based on the following objectives:

1. To study the status of infrastructural bottlenecks in rural India in general and Mandya district in particular;
2. To know the role of rural Infrastructure in the process of Inclusive growth.

Hypothesis

H-1: Strengthening rural infrastructure assures inclusive growth in India;

H-2: Rural Parts of India are still facing infrastructural bottlenecks.

Methodology

The study is based on both primary and secondary data. Primary data is collected from 120 households of six villages *viz.,* Gaamana Halli, Niluvaagilu, Kurahatti, Phalli, Kothathi, Annooru of Mandya district of Karnataka state. To collect primary, data random sampling method was followed. For primary data purpose's personal interview and observation methods were used to collect information. For secondary data, census of India 2011, Indian infrastructure report, journals, working papers and Internet were reviewed. Collected data were analysed with simple percentage method, graphs and diagrams are used.

Status of Rural Infrastructure in India

Rural development is a multi-dimensional and multi-faceted concept. It is a process of utilising natural resources, enhancing human capabilities and choices, upgrading technological tools, organising economic institution and empowering quality life of rural mass. Infrastructure facility is like nectar to the rural development process.

Rural Drinking Water and Sanitation in India

Water is one of the most essential basic needs of our life; without proper food it is possible to live for some days, but without water we cannot run even a single day. At least getting clean water for drinking purpose in our life is a human right.

In India 44 million people are drinking water, which is polluted with excess of arsenic, nitrate and fluoride metals. Only 18.7 per cent of villages are provided clean water by taps, others depend on village tanks, wells etc., but 32 per cent of villages do not have water supply at all. In India rural parts are facing hygienic-related illness. Poor sanitation and irregular water supply have become a great menace to the process of rural development. On the other hand, lack of toilets and manual scavenging are the bad features of rural India. This disgraceful situation, in these parts not only shows economic backwardness but also questions the dignity of labour. Even after 65 years of independence nearly three lakh people are involved in this inhuman work, *i.e.,* manual scavenging. Suppose all the households afford toilet facility at their houses the target of safe and healthy sanitation and dignity of labour is achieved with a great success at national level. It is really a shocking feature of rural India's only 30.7 households in this area have toilet facility.

Table 1: Households having Toilet in India (2011)

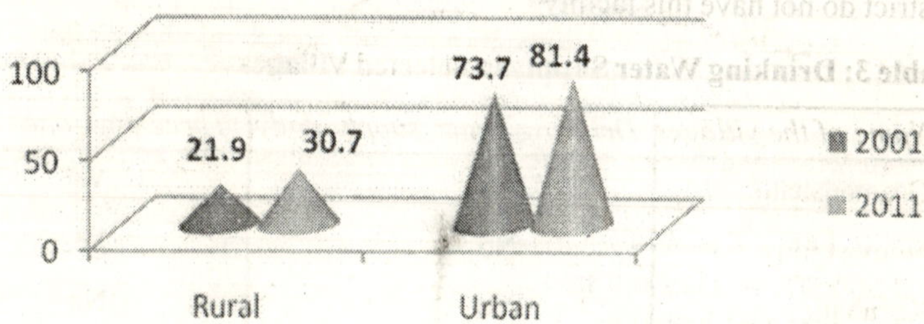

Year	*Households with Toilet*	
	Rural	*Urban*
2001	21.9	73.7
2011	30.7	81.4

Source: Census 2011, Government of India

The Table-1 shows that in the year 2001, only 21.9 per cent rural households had toilet facilities. In urban area, it was 73.7 per cent. Only 36.4 per cent households in India have hygien toilets. The 2011 Census figure reveals a little bit increase in the graph but the increase is not showing such a big difference. In rural area, there is only 8.8 per cent increase in toilet facility.

Table 2: Households Having Toilet Facility in Selected Villages of Mandya District

Sl. No	Response	Respondents (in number)	Percentage
1.	Toilet facility available	57	47.5
2.	Toilet facility unavailable	63	52.5
3.	Total	120	100

Source: Primary data

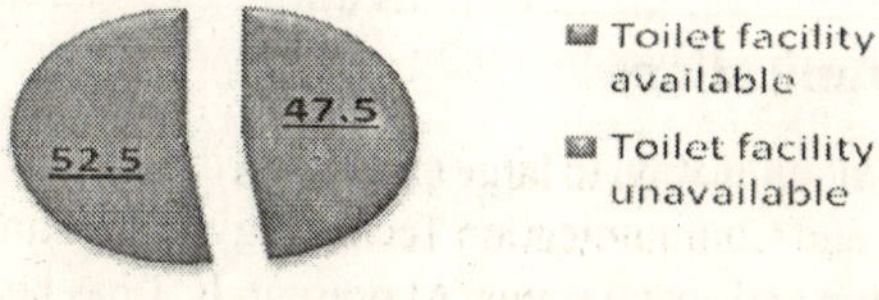

The Table-2 shows that only 47.5 per cent of respondents have toilet facility in their houses but 52.5 per cent households of six villages of Mandya district do not have this facility.

Table 3: Drinking Water Supply in Selected Villages

Name of the villages	*Drinking water supply daily*	*Three days once*
Gaamanahalli	No	Yes
Niluvaagilu	No	Yes
Kurahatti	Yes	No
P Halli	No	Yes
Kothathi	No	Yes
Annooru	Yes	No

Source: Primary data.

The Table-3 shows only two villages namely, Kurahatti and Annooru are facilitated the supply of drinking water on daily basis; other villages have drinking water facility for three days once, especially during summer, village dwellers suffer hard to get water for domestic purposes .

Table 4: Households Having Bathroom Facility in India (2011) (In percentage)

Area	*Bathroom*	*Bathroom without roof*	*Don't have bathrooms*
Rural	25.4	19.7	55.0
Urban	77.5	9.5	13.0
Total	42.0	16.4	41.6

Source: Census 2011, Government of India.

The provision of bathrooms in rural area also gets serious attention especially with great concern to women group. According to 2011 Census 55 per cent of rural households do not access to bathrooms and 19.7 per cent households have bathrooms without roof; only 25.4 per cent households have secured and safe bathrooms to some extent. Keeping in the view of the safety of women, providing toilet and bathroom facilities in these areas needs a great concern.

Telecommunications

Telecommunication to large extent is bringing new change in rural India. Information and Communication Technology is updating ruralites to increase their economic and social status. At present, ICT has become omnipotent and omniscient. Rural sector is no exception for this. It is gradually sinking into the life style of rural people. Especially, mobile phones and Internet users in rural parts are increasing. Apart from other infrastructural facilities, telecommunication infrastructure in rural India has been successful.

Table 5: Telecommunications in Rural India as on January 31st, 2014

Telecommunication Services	Subscribers (rural parts) in (million)
Internet users	46
Landline phones	6.1
Mobile phones	364.1

Source: Telecom Regulatory Authority of India (2014).

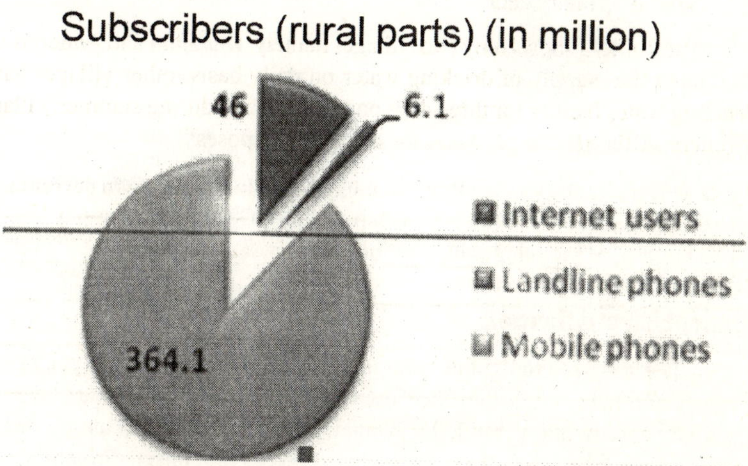

In the Table-4 and diagram, it is shown that there are about 46 million internet users in rural area in this country. Wire line connections were 6.1 million in January 2014. People are not interested to have landline phones. There is a considerable demand for wireless or mobile phones in rural area. There are 364.1 million mobile users in these rural parts. Only five per cent of villages in the country do not have mobile phone coverage. Every month, 2.73 million mobile phone users are added to rural parts of this country.

Table-6: Mobile Phone Users in Selected Villages

Sl. No	Response	Households (in number)	Percentage
1.	Mobile phone users	100	83.3
2.	Non users of Mobile phones	20	16.7
3.	Total	120	100

Source: Primary data.

Mobile Phone Users In Selected Villages

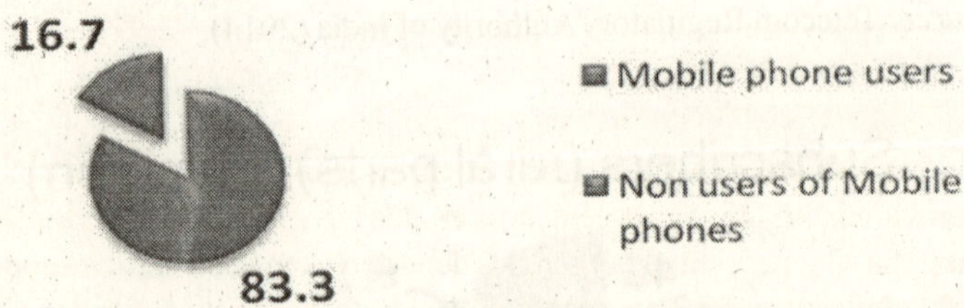

It is really surprising thing that mobile phones in rural parts are in no way luxurious items, they have become part and parcel of their day-to-day life. The 83.3 per cent of households have mobile phones, only 16.7 per cent households cannot afford mobile phones.

Rural Electrification

There is need to light up rural India. Villages do not have regular power supply and many times they face low voltage problem. Night time power-cuts actually pose so many problems. Women in these areas are becoming victims. Even banks, petty shops have to be closed before the sunset. *Shining India* in rural area is in darkness.

Table 7: Sources of Lighting for Households in India

Sources of Lighting	*Rural (percent age)*
Electricity	56
Kerosene	43.2
Solar	0.2
Others	0.3
No lighting	0.3
Total	100

Source: Census 2011, Government of India.

Rural Electrification

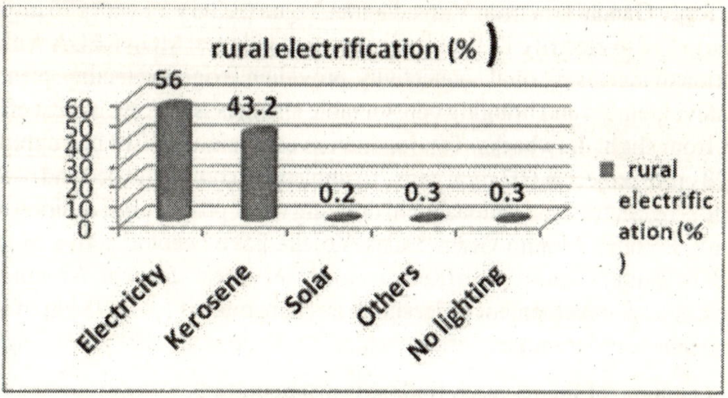

Source :

The Table-6 shows that nearly 56 per cent of households were electrified in rural area, only three per cent households have electrified yet to be. Still in rural India 43.2 per cent of households depend on kerosene for domestic lighting and 0.3 per cent and 0.2 per cent households respectively depend on solar and other sources. The three per cent of households in this twenty-first century in the so called developed and civilised country do not have electricity facility in their houses.

Table 8: Power Cuts in Selected Villages

Name of the villages	Power supply for 24 hours	Power supply for 16 hours
Gaamanahalli	No	Yes
Niluvaagilu	No	Yes
Kurahatti	Yes	No
P Halli	No	Yes
Kothathi	No	Yes
Annooru	No	No

Source :

Except Kurahatti, other selected villages have been provided 16 hours power supply. Kurahatti village has 24 hours power supply except some interception by rain and other natural disturbances.

Conclusion and Findings

Rajiv Gandhi Grameen Vidyudikaran Yojna (RGGVY) with 576 projects had targetted to electrify 1.10 lakh unelectrified villages. MGNREGA with the intention of increasing rural connectivity, providing irrigation facility, planning land development and bringing considerable changes is making honest efforts apart from slight drawbacks. Total sanitation campaign in 2012 had approved 22.022 crore project in 607 rural parts. To implement community led and people-centric programmes and national rural drinking water programme, Indira Awaas Yojana, Pradhan Mantra Gram Sadak Yojana have become active in these areas to ensure quality infrastructural services. *Bharat Nirman* an infrastructural development programme has constructed 1,41,095 km of roas. Despite these programmes, infrastructure in village area is not promising.

Outcome of the research finding is disappointing.

- Out of 120 households, 63 households still do not access to basic facilities, especially access to proper toilets.
- Out of six villages, one village alone has uninterrupted power supply except in summer and rainy seasons.
- Out of six villages, only two *viz.*, Kurahatti and Annooru villages are provided with drinking water daily, remaining villages are supplied three days once.
- Out of 120 households, 100 households have mobile phone facility, only 20 households do not have mobile phones.

Economic independence of rural India is much lauded by eminent economists and it is considered to be the foundation for the concept of self-reliance. Growth process must include rural uplift with better infrastructural facilities. The marathon of growth must include all. There should not be any discrimination. Uplift of exploited and backward classes and well-being of all are the central goals of inclusive growth. Adequate infrastructural facility is crucial for economic growth. Investment on rural sector like education, health, transport, irrigation etc., increases the productivity and production. In India, domestic electrification is not sufficient especially in rural area. So, providing sufficient electrification facility has become a big challenge, though the rural electrification policy of 2006 and Rajiv Gandhi Grameen Vidyutikarana Yojana are introduced in these areas. The hundred per cent rural electrification is still a surprising thing and power-cuts that, too, in summer are common features of Indian villages. India still has its breath in villages. India is experiencing sea changes powered by information and communication technology wave, raising millionaire and billionaires, rapid growth of service sector etc., have made

India's to move to greater heights and have shown wonders to the world economy. People in this country are dreaming big by seeing these marvellous developments one must but, not forget that this is only one part of the story. In reality, development in India is unbalanced and asymmetrical. Metropolitan cities project India as glittering economy, but poor hamlets show the real face of India.

References

Alexander, Ian, and Antonio Estache (1999), *"Infrastructure Restructuring and Regulation Building Base for Sustainable Growth"*, The World Bank.

Das, Aditya Raj (2001), *"Economic Reforms and the Poor"*, Deccan Herald, March, 3rd.

Das, Keshab (2001), *"Rural Drinking Water Supply in India: Issues and Strategies"*, pp. 207-77, in Sebastian Morris (ed.), India Infrastructure Report 2001: Issues in Regulation and Market Structure, Oxford University Press, New Delhi.

Das, Keshab and Leela Visaria (1998), *"Issues in Rural Sanitation: Lessons from Gujarat"*, Working Paper No. 98, Gujarat Institute of Development Research, Ahmedabad.

Dev, S. Mahendra and Ajit Ranade (1999), *"Persisting Poverty and Social Insecurity: A Selective Assessment"*, in Kirit S. Parikh (ed.), India Development Report 1999-2000, Oxford University Press, New Delhi.

Fan, Shenggen, Peter Hazell and S.K. Thorat (2000), *"Impact of Public Expenditure on Gasifier for Village Electrification"*. Current Science 87(7): p. 932.

Planning Commission (2003). *National Mission on Bio-diesel*, The Planning Commission, New Delhi.

"Poverty in Rural India", Economic and Political Weekly, Vol. 35, No. 40, pp.3581-8. Public Finance, NCAER.

Ravindranath, N. H. (2004). *Sustainable Biomass Power for Rural India*: A Case study of Bio-mass.

3

Women Entrepreneurs in Rural Areas: Problems and Remedies

Ashwini H. Bidaralli and Shekhar

Introduction

Women have been successful in breaking their confinement within the limits of their homes by entering into varied kinds of professionals and services, Women entrepreneurs have proved to be on par with their men counterpart in business acumen and are emerging as smart and dynamic entrepreneurs. There are many reasons for women to enter into entrepreneurial ventures in a predominant society. Entrepreneurship among women is an important avenue through which women can overcome their subordination within the family and the society as a whole. Therefore, development of entrepreneurship among women has received special attention of the policy makers. In this direction, a special character in the seventh plan has converted into the integration of women in economic development. The new industrial policy has stressed the need for conducting special Entrepreneurial Development Programme (EDPs) for women. Besides today, a network of institutions exists in the country to promote women entrepreneurship. The commercial banks and the financial institution are an integral part of this network. Many organisations/institutions and association promote and develop women entrepreneurship by providing financial assistance at concessional rates of interest and also organise industrial fairs and exhibitions. Entrepreneurship Development Programme (EDPs) for women creates entrepreneurial awareness among them.

"Women" as Entrepreneurs in India

Women-owned businesses are highly increasing in the economies of almost all countries. The hidden entrepreneurial potentials of women have gradually been changing with the growing sensitivity to the role and economic status in the society. Skill, knowledge and adaptability in business are the main reasons for women to emerge into business ventures. 'Women

Entrepreneur' is a person, who accepts challenging role to meet her personal needs and become economically independent. A strong desire to do something positive is an inbuilt quality of entrepreneurial women, who are capable of contributing values in both family and social life. With the advent of media, women are aware of their own traits, rights and the work situations. The challenges and opportunities provided to the women of digital era are growing rapidly that the job-seekers are turning into job-creators. They are flourishing-as designers, interior decorators, exporters, publishers, garment manufacturers and still exploring new avenues of economic participation. In India, although women constitute the majority of the total population, the entrepreneurial world is still male dominated. Women in advanced nations are recognised and are prominent more in the business world, but the Indian women entrepreneurs are facing some major constraints like :

- Lack of confidence in their strength and competence,
- Socio-cultural barriers,
- Market-oriented risks,
- Motivational factors,
- Knowledge in Business Administration,
- Awareness about the financial assistance,
- Exposed to the training programmes,
- Identifying the available resources.

Objectives of the Study

The present study has been carried out with the following objectives :

1. To study the socio-economic background of women entrepreneurs in Shimoga District;
2. To analyse the motivational factors and other factors that influence women to become entrepreneurs;
3. To analyse the major strength and weakness of women entrepreneurs and the environmental opportunities and threats which promote the entrepreneurship;
4. To offer suggestions to improve the satisfaction of women entrepreneurs and framework for promotion of women entrepreneurship of selected districts in Karnataka.

Scope of the Study

The study focusses on the women entrepreneurs in selected villages in

Shimoga district, Karnataka selected depends on industrial growth has been phenomenal. The selected districts with its good infrastructural facility, offers sound prospects for industrial development. The scope of the study encompasses women entrepreneurs in Shimoga district and the problems faced by women entrepreneurs, who are engaged in starting new enterprise. The study is limited only to the women entrepreneurs of selected groups in Shimoga district.

Sampling Design

Women entrepreneurs who are the main source of primary data are collected from the women entrepreneurs through a well-structured questionnaire. As the area of study is limited in Shimoga district of Karnataka and as the total population of women population is numerable, the researcher has proposed the sampling techniques for the selection of respondents. To identify the right respondents which are also very essential for the collection of primary data the following process has been adopted scientifically. Finally, 90 respondents were selected and included in the study from various taluks of Shimoga district, who have engaged to start an enterprises running successfully.

Tools of Analysis

Personal interview is the major tool of data collection. Interview technique is to be made at women entrepreneurs. The secondary data are also proposed to collect from various departments. All these data are to be arranged in various form of tables and proposed to critically analyse with the help of a number of statistical tools. Percentage Analysis and Chi-Square Test are the various applied statistical tools.

Socio-economic Background

The personnel characteristics of the selected respondents like age, educational status, marital status, family income, business type, size of the business, financial sources and spend expenses are discussed in this section.

Analysis and Interpretation

This study is aimed on the problems and prospects of women entrepreneurs in Shimoga district. For this purpose, the study was conducted for 90 respondents of the women entrepreneurs. An attempt has been made in this section to analyse the data collected with reference to activities of the women entrepreneur, detailed analysis is given below. The Table-1.1 shows problems faced by women entrepreneurs, that the weighted ranking method applied. It inferred that the most of the respondents have given first rank for lack of strong leadership; the respondents have given second rank for financial deficit. The third rank was lack of systematic planned working followed by health problem, non-awareness of government scheme, non- repayment of loan by the members, leader's misusing the group's money, and lack of education.

Table 1 Socio-economic Background of Respondents

Factors	*Category*	*No. of Respondents*	*Percentage (%)*
Age	Below - 30	20	22.22
	30 - 40	32	35.56
	40-50	26	28.89
	50 and above	12	13.33
Marital Status	Unmarried	31	31
Married	69	69	
Educational Qualification	Illiterate	5	5.56
Primary	9	10	
Secondary	16	17.78	
Higher Secondary	42	46.67	
Graduate Level	18	20	
Annual Income	Below Rs. 10,000	15	16.67
	Rs.10,000 - 20,000	32	35.56
	Rs. 20,000 - 30,000	21	23.33
	Rs. 30,000 - 40,000	14	15.56
	Rs. 40,000 and above	8	8.89

Source :

Chi-square Analysis

The opinion of respondents and socio-economic characters relationship is applied for Chi-square test. The selected variables to apply only this model. Table 1 reveals the summary of respondents. The Chi-square analysis reveals that the factors are Age and Education are significant at one per cent level. Marital status, business type and sources of finance are significant at five per cent level. The remaining factors are not significant at five per cent level.

Table 2: The Summary of Opinion of Women Entrepreneurs

S.N.	*Factors*	*Chi-Square Value*	*Degree of Freedom*	*Table Value*	*Result*
1.	Age	17.26	6	16.81	Significant**
2.	Educational Qualification	14.97	4	13.28	Significant**
3.	Marital Status	12.56	2	5.99	Significant*
4.	Family Income	3.65	6	12.59	Not Significant
5.	Business type	11.54	4	9.49	Significant*
6.	Size of the Business	7.23	4	9.49	Not Significant
7.	Sources of Finance	13.68	6	12.59	Significant*
8.	Amount Spend	7.26	4	13.28	Not Significant

Note: * Significant at five per cent Level, ** Significant at one per cent Level.

Source :

Findings

1. The 35.56 per cent of respondents are belonging to 30–40 years age group of entrepreneurs. The 28.89 per cent of respondents are between the ages of 40-50 year. The 22.22 per cent of respondents are below the 30 years age group and rest of the respondents are above 50 years.
2. The 46.67 per cent of respondents are belonging to higher secondary level of entrepreneurs. The 20 per cent of the respondents are graduates and 17.78 per cent of the respondents have secondary level of education. The 10 per cent of the respondents have primary level and rest of the respondents are illiterates.
3. The 35.56 per cent of the respondent belonging to Rs.10,000 to 20,000 income of families. The 23.33 per cent of the respondents are in Rs. 20,000 to 30,000 income group and only eight per cent of the respondents have their family income above Rs. 40,000.
4. The 42.22 per cent of the respondents deal with manufacturing types

of business. 26.67 per cent of the respondents, are engaged in trading type of business. Only 16 per cent of the respondents are doing business for service sectors. The 10 per cent of the respondents have combined all type of business.

5. The 69 per cent of the respondents are married and rest category of the respondents are unmarried. Therefore, marital status is important factor to determine women entrepreneurs.

6. The 46.67 per cent of respondents invested below Rs. one lakh in their business. The 24.44 per cent of respondents are under Rs. one lakh to Rs. five lakhs category.

7. The 35 per cent of the finance sources from spouse income, 30 per cent respondents financed from personal savings and 25.56 per cent have loan from banks as well as eight per cent respondents finance from other sources.

v. Suggestions

1. Most of the women entrepreneurs are of the opinion that because of lack of training, they are not able to survive in the market. Hence, the government should frequent training programmes with regard to new production techniques, sales techniques, etc; this training should be made compulsory for women entrepreneurs.

2. Finance is the first major problem for women entrepreneurs. Hence, the government can provide interest free loans to encourage women entrepreneurs. To attract more women entrepreneurs, the subsidy for loans should be increased.

3. Since the number of entrepreneurs from scheduled caste and most backward communities is very low, awareness is to be created among those women, by special attention.

4. Women entrepreneurs should be encouraged to start their entrepreneurs him as joint stock companies rather than as sole trade and partnership concerns to avail the advantages of large scale operation.

5. Parents of potential unmarried women entrepreneurs should be encouraged in spending money on setting up business rather than giving preference to marriage.

6. Marketing product is one of the main problems for women entrepreneurs. Here, women co operative societies can be started to procure the products from women entrepreneurs. They will help them in selling their products at reasonable price.

7. Improper location and inadequate infrastructure facilities are the hurdles in the way of development of women entrepreneurship. Hence, separate industrial estates may be exclusively set up for women entrepreneurs to reduce the initial investment and to create a special environment.

Conclusion

It is evident from the study that women are ready to face challenges associated with the setting up of business. Society is very much receptive to the concept of women entrepreneur, so is the family. Women are not into business for survival, but to satisfy their inner urge for creativity and to prove their capabilities. Women education is contributing great extent to the social transformation. The future will see more women venturing into areas traditionally dominated by men. The socio-economic background include factors, type and mode of business, training programmes. These are the important problems of women entrepreneurs in Shimoga district.

References

Bhatia Anju (2000)' "*Women Development and NGOs*", Rawat Publication, New Delhi.

Lalita .N (2005)' "*Micro Finance and Rural Development*", Gandhigram Rural Institute, Gandhigram.

Lipi (2009)' "*Women Empowerment: Globalisation and Opportunities*" in Empowerment of Rural Women in India, Kanishka Publishers, New Delhi.

OECD Second conference of Ministers responsible for Small and Medium-sized enterprises promoting entrepreneurship and innovative SMEs in a Global Economy (2004), Organisation for Economic Cooperation and Development, Istanbul, Turkey.

Prabha Singh (2009), "Rural Women and Development of Entrepreneurship with special reference to Punjab" in *Empowerment of Rural Women in India,* Kanishka Publishers, New Delhi.

Ram Naresh Thakur (2009), "Rural Women Empowerment in India" in *Empowerment of Rural Women in India* Kanishka Publishers, New Delhi.

Shobana Nelasco and Junofy Antorozarina (2009), "Rural women empowerment through Self-Help Groups" in *Empowerment of Rural Women in India,* Kanishka Publishers, New Delhi.

4

The Role and Importance of Human Resource Development in Rural Development

K.G.Ashoka

Introduction

The Human Resource Development (HRD) deals with all aspects of human development whether they relate to poverty, gender discrimination, denial of human rights and liberty, impact of globalisation and environmental concerns. Human Resource Development is an organised learning experience aimed at matching the organisational need for human resource with the individual need for growth and development. Leonard Nadler has defined HRD in a broad sense. The term 'human resource development' means, "those learning experiences which are organised for a specified time and designed to bring about the possibility of behavioural change."

The former President of India, Dr. A.P.J. Abdul Kalam, a renowned scientist, projected a vision for India in 2020 as a strong democratic country. He firmly believed that his vision of a strong country will be fulfilled by 'building upon the contributions of each individual citizen. This statement clearly demonstrates the significance of HRD in the development of the country. The present paper focusses on health, education including skill development of people, as aspect of HRD- as it constitutes one of the most significant challenges being faced by rural areas.

Development of People

The UNDP Human Development Report (2001) states that "development must be around people, not people around development... and it should empower individuals and groups rather than disempower them." Human development has two aspects; one is the formulation of human capabilities such as improved health, knowledge and skills, and the other is the use of acquired capabilities for productive purposes and being active in social, political and cultural affairs.

Development must be not only for the people but by the people, too. They must participate fully in the decisions and processes that shape their lives. It is the people, who must first undergo change because it is only the people, who make change in community and contribute to rural development. Village leaders are to be trained and educated for bringing change in a free society. It must always be realised that changes in the minds and hearts of people come first before any changes are made in the actions. That is possible only through continuous training, refreshers, exposure visits, exchange of experiences with peer groups and on-the-job working experience over a number of years in the field.

The number of village leaders is constantly growing due to the policy of reservation of seats for SCs/STs/OBCs/ women in every election since 1994, and moreover, if they are illiterate, the task of building the capacity of such leaders becomes all the more herculean. Any amount of material aid, development of technology, and government attempts will not be able to change society unless people at the grassroots level are empowered through training and education. Rural development is possible when it becomes 'a people's programme with government aid' rather than "a government programme with people's aid.'

There are a range of concepts and perspectives associated with the development of human resources. There are also different focusses of interest; individual; organisational; present needs; future challenges; different functions and occupations; different stakeholder interests. Increasingly, managers are required to facilitate change and innovation through an expanding repertoire of approaches, which include the development of people.

Objectives

The important objectives for selecting and study of this topic are:

1. To understand the need of rural development in developing economy;
2. To know the different areas where the human resources required development in rural areas;
3. To identify the different opportunities available for development of the people and their contribution to the nation;
4. To understand the significance of the human resource development in rural areas for the overall development;
5. To discuss about the simple concepts of rural development with major problems and to get solution to such hurdles.

Methodology

For the study of this topic, secondary sources are used. Books were referred for the better understanding of different theories and concepts on Rural Development and the Human Resource Development. Internet sources are also used for collecting data and some inputs. The important case studies are discussed to support the role of rural areas.

Philosophy of Rural Development

- Man as the end of development which therefore, is to be judged by what it does to him.
- De-alienation of man in the sense that he could feel that he becomes the subject and the object in the process of development.
- Development of collective personality of man in which he finds his richest expression.
- Participation as true form of democracy in rural community development.
- Self-reliance as the expression of man's faith in his own abilities.

The fundamental objectives of rural development imply the standard of living of the rural population. The rural development has the following main objectives:

(1) Providing certain social goods and services in terms of social and economic infrastructure;

(2) Increasing the income of every rural family and to see that those below the poverty line come above that line in coming years;

(3) Creation of additional employment opportunities is rural areas;

(4) It is essentially concerned with the improvement of the living standards of low income population living in rural areas on a self-sustaining basis through socio-spatial structure of transforming in their productive activities;

(5) It implies broad based re-organisation and mobilisation of the rural masses so as to enhance their capacity to cope effectively with the daily tasks of their lives and with consequent changes upon this;

(6) Improvement of services of rural masses in the process;

(7) Improvement of know-how which is to be implemented for the rural people to infuse sense of pragmatism in the process of development.

Human Resource Development and Change through Groups

Teams can be regarded as a defined set of people working within a particular context, sharing common purpose and somehow in touch with each other, either face to face or virtually. Groups represent the heart of resistance to both achieving strategy where they are changeovers, and the powerhouse for change in dynamic organisations. The development of any group must integrate with wider HR policies and practices, and also:

- Make sense strategically;
- Involve an appreciation of the complexities of change;
- Consider how change is facilitated either consciously and deliberately or not;
- Take into that consideration with work force patterns and boundaries changing considerably from traditional forms, the agents of change may be positioned inside or outside the organisation. [The group of people affecting and managing change, conventionally, are regarded as change agents].

In the context of functionaries of the rural development, HRD implies that capacity building of the newly-elected public representatives as well as officials done in such a manner that they are not only equipped with knowledge but are also imparted various practical skills. An attitudinal change is brought about in their behaviour through training and development of various skills to sharpen their capabilities. Their competencies, motivation, dynamism and effectiveness are developed so as to serve the public and discharge their duties and responsibilities as well as exercise their powers in the most effective manner. The HRD is concerned with improving the skills of communication, leadership, teamwork, collaboration conflict resolution, attitudes and behaviour of trainees in organisational settings.

Rural Development through Linkage

In case of rural development, it's not only because of government plans but also influenced by individuals or any groups or any organisations, NGO's etc. "True democracy could not be worked by some men sitting at the top. It had to be worked from below by the people of every village," Believed /Mahatma Gandhi.

Panchayats were formed throughout the country after the Independence. The *gram sabha* is a grassroot organisation consisting of, not representatives of people, but of the people themselves. Besides, promoting direct democracy in the country at the local level, the institution is expected to play an important role in the working of village panchayat.

A meaningful linkage between the two systems:

(1) Representing the formal sector (panchayats);

(2) Representing the informal sector (NGOs/CBOs) will go a long way in facilitating development process at local levels.

Development of participatory culture at the local level is called for a greater awareness on the part of the people and the leadership manning the voluntary organisations. This in turn, will require sustained efforts in respect of capacity-building measures so that there is greater awareness among the people, among the elected representatives, and among the people managing voluntary sector. Unless the capacity-building measures for both formal and informal sectors are initiated, it may not be really possible to achieve the desired results. For this, the time-bound strategy for improving public awareness and general disposition towards the *panchayati raj* system is needed.

Rural Development through Training, Education and Health

Education is for capability and academic excellence, whereas training combines excellence in work with it while coping with problems of day-to-day life. Education deals with knowledge and understanding, and training helps participants to improve their performance, training in personality development, and it improves their confidence, sharpens the ability to make decisions, and solve problems, and leads to sustained self-generating development.

Nadler identifies three types of learning programmes. The first is training, which is related to learning the present job; the second is education, which is the learning related to job for which a person is being prepared; and the third is development, which stands for the learning related to general growth of the individual and to the organisation.

Training is the application of knowledge, the awareness about rules and procedures related to work, and steps taken for change in behaviour. Training attempts to improve the performance on current job or prepare one for the intended job.

Development is an understanding of concepts, sharpening of specific skills of communication, decision-making, problem solving, and other related interpersonal skills for team work, coordination, and conflict resolution. It moulds mental attitudes and prepares person for higher responsibilities. It aims at growth of personality and progress towards maturity.

Whenever proper educational approaches have been made, it has been found possible to change people in the following four broad areas:

(a) Changes in what people know; their knowledge about themselves, of their society and of their physical environment;

(b) Changes in what people can do, their skills-mental and physical;

(c) Changes in what people think and feel; their attitude towards themselves, towards their society and towards their physical environment.

(d) Changes in what people actually do; their actions related to factors determining their own welfare. It is possible only through education, training, people's empowerment and capacity building of village leaders.

Villagers are to be viewed as individual human personalities. They possess many inherited traits, tendencies, and capacities. This human personality should be recognised as one highly capable of independent action as well as group action. They have an extensive mental capacity to learn, think, reason and understand.

As per the *Human Development Report* (HDR), 2011 published by the United Nations Development Programme (UNDP) in terms of three basic capabilities: to live a long and healthy life, to be educated and knowledgeable, and to enjoy a decent economic standard of living). The HDI for India was 0.547 in 2011 with an overall global ranking of 134 (out of 187 countries) compared to 119 (out of 169 countries) in HDR 2010. The growth rate in average annual HDI of India between 2000-2011 is among the highest, a finding corroborated also by the *India Human Development Report (IHDR) 2011*, brought out by the Institute of Applied Manpower Research and the Planning Commission. According to the IHDR, HDI between 1999-00 and 2007-08 has increased by 21 per cent with an improvement of over 28 per cent in education being the main driver.

The Government of India has taken necessary steps for the rural health. It has launched the National Rural Health Mission (2005-2012), through which adopts synergetic approach by relating health to determinants of good health, *viz.*, segments of nutrition, sanitation, hygiene and safe drinking water. The programmes like Accredited Social Health Activist (ASHA) with AYUSH played an important role in developing of rural health.

A comprehensive education system would help into one that has sound ethical base and a strong sense of social responsibility. Culture paves the way for education while education is responsible for flavouring the cultural values in life. So, whenever rural people get education it also boosts the spread of cultural values in and around the rural places. Here is one case study related to an educated, who utilised his profession and talent for the benefit of rural people (Case Study-1). Another is related to one private co operative bank which is developed by giving first preference to rural people (Case Study-2).

Case Study - 1

A Role Model for Success

The future of Human Resource Development will depend on being able to demonstrate some quick wins but also flexibility of approach and real role models of behaviours required for success. Dr Hanumappa Sudarshan Reddy is a social worker and tribal activist. He is well-known for the uplift of the forest dwelling tribes in the Chamarajanagar, district of Karnataka. After graduation, he became medical doctor in the year 1972. His profession made him travel all over India and his experience inspired him work in rural areas instead of cities. He decided to work with tribal communities and in 1980, he started Vivekananda Girijana Kalyana Kendra (VGKK) for the integrated development of tribals in the Chamarajanagar, district of Karnataka. Later, he started 'Karuna Trust,' which is dedicated to the rural development in the states of Karnataka and Arunachal Pradesh. It provides the primary health-care to million people in different states. VGKK is an organisation with mission of sustainable development of tribals through rights-based approach to health, education, livelihood are security and bio-diversity conservation. It runs 450- pupil school for the tribes of BR hills where the students are provided education equivalent to the cities. He headed different positions in his life including member of six working group on Macro-economic and Health organised by WHO, and was steering group member of the planning commission on empowerment of STs, in India's 11th five year plan. In such a way, a doctor inspired many people all over the world by following his own principles and Gandhism.

Case Study - 2

A Bank as a Co-operative Movement

As a result of *Indian Co-operative Societies Act, 1912,* a number of co-operative societies came into existence. One of these is the Puttur Rural Credit Co-operative Society, which was established in June 1912. Due to ups and downs, it can't be in existence with the same financial condition. So, on November, 30, 1913, the south Canara District Central Co-operative was started. It started functioning on January 24th, 1914.

Molahalli Shive Rao, father of the co-operative movement of the district and his team of selfless workers were responsible for the establishment and development of the bank. The veteran co-operators have helped the movement to spread far and wide and served the necessities of the villages in the district resulting in a strong base for the co-operative institution and the co-operative movement.

At present, the bank provides customer service by computerising its branches and by introducing several innovative service activities like single window system at any branch banking, ATM facilities and 12 hours of banking from 8 am to 8 pm through banking on wheels -- a unique introduction of mobile bank to facilitate services to the rural, where there is no banking facilities. A customer can avail banking transactions like depositing, withdrawals and loan facilities. This bank is inter-connected with branches of the bank and one can avail the required facilities through any branch banking. In such a way, a co-operative bank lead rural people for the development.

Significance of Rural Development Programmes

During the past few years, rural development has received greater deal of attention in development literatures, in development plans, on political plat forms and in the international lending programmes of most of the donors. Policy for rural development has become major pre-occupation of the government of poor countries since the successful tackling of rural development problems depend on the pace and tone of development of economies of poor countries. The rural development programmes occupy significant position in India's economic planning, as nearly three-fourth of its population lives in villages. Hence, without uplifting rural masses, we cannot think over accelerating the pivot of overall economic development. It hardly needs to be emphasised that the rural development is a matter of great concern in India's overall economic development. In this context, the programmes of the department, *viz..*, IRDP, NREP, RLEGP, Rural water supply, DPAP, DDP, TRYSEM and DWCRA assume great significance.

Rural development has considerable significance in India, because of the following social, economical and political reasons as mentioned below:

A. Social Significance

1. The rural development programmes provide composite package to solve all sorts of problems regarding finance, agricultural inputs, production and marketing, employment and income of large number of rural farmers.

2. Rural development programmes educate rural poor in such a way to accept the social change and to get the benefit of programmes.

3. Through rural employment and other development schemes, human and natural resources can be utilised best in the interest of nation.

4. These programmes are of integrated nature for basic amenities like roads, primary schools, health centres and drinking facilities.

B. Economic Significance

1. Agriculture is the most important source of national income. The farmers depending on agriculture will contribute maximum food grains and poultry. So, the farmers must get latest equipments and financial help.
2. Directly or indirectly, agriculture has been the source of raw materials to India's leading industries. So, the development of both sectors are important.
3. Internal trade is mostly in agricultural products. The main support for railways and roadways, which transport bulk of agricultural products from farm to mandis and factories, comes from agriculture.
4. Agriculture contributes a very large part of export and leads to the foreign exchange.

C. Political Significance

1. A stable and developing rural economy can help in political stability which is equally important for economic development.

Conclusion

The success of Rural Development programmes depends on how rural people get the benefit from the said programmes. Whatever the plan and policies carried that must depend on the development of people. All efforts must be put in to ensure that villagers, tribal people and aboriginals stay in the rural areas, which will be possible only, if we are able to bring them what they seek from urban areas like, access to proper education, training and development, and employment and income-generation opportunities on par with their urban counterpart. Higher levels of HRD will positively impact the delivery and access of the development programmes being implemented by the Central and State Governments in India for providing greater employment opportunities and increased income in the hands of the masses. Literacy, education and skill development, which help together to raise the level of Human Resource Development, are important for continued progress of a nation. Therefore, endeavours towards further improvement in HRD must continue with full vigour and commitment by stakeholders including international partners. This calls for increased bilateral and multi-lateral co-operation in order to fully exploit the potentials of human resource development.

References

Books

Jennifer Joy-Mathews, David Megginson, Mark Surtees (2004), "*Human Resource Development*", Kogan Page India Pvt. Ltd, New Delhi.

Madan Mohan (2007), "*Rural Development Administration*", Omega Publications, New Delhi.

Misra S.K., Puri V.K. (1991) "*Economic Development of India,*" Himalaya Publishing House, Bombay.

Narwani G.S. (2002); "*Training for Rural Development*", Rawat Publications, Jaipur.

Tanuria B.G. (2012), "*Rural Development*", Ritu Publications, Jaipur.

Thomas William A, Christopher A.J. (2011), "*Rural Development- concepts and Recent Approaches*", Rawat Publications, Jaipur.

Vasant Desai (1991), "*Fundamentals of Rural Development*", Himalaya Publishing House, Bombay.

Web sites

- http://www.mkgandhi.org/articles/role_edu.htm.
- http://www.scdccbank.com/.
- http://www.nextwealth.in/about-us/advisory-board/dr-sudarshan.
- http://en.wikipedia.org/wiki/Hanumappa_Sudarshan.
- www.nird.org.in/brgf/doc/Rural%20HealthMission_Document.pdf.

5

The Role of NGOs in Rural Development through Inclusiveness of Marginalised Groups: A Case of Bellary and Bagalkot Districts

S. Ananth Panth

Introduction

5.1. Profile of Bagalkot and Bellary Districts

Bagalkot is a new district formed in 1997; it consists of six taluks -- Badami, Bagalkot, Bilagi, Hunugunda, Jamakhandi and Mudhol. The geographical area of the district is 6,593 sq. kms. and consists of 163 *gram panchayats*. Historically, Bagalkot is the homeland of the great Chalukya dynasty. Aihole-famous for architecture and Badami-famous for cave carvings in monolithic single stone in the period of Immadi Pulakeshi-I are situated in this district. The other places of archaeological importance are famous temples of Pattadakal, Mahakuteshwar temple in Mahakuta, Shivayog mandir and Banashankari temple in Badami.

Bellary was part of Hyderabad Nizam province and it was made later a part of Karnataka since 1948. It has seven talukas after the re-organisation of the districts in 1997-98. The total population of the district, according to census 2011 is 24.32 lakh; 8.87 lakh among this are SC/ST. The sex ratio is 969/1000 male. Population density is around 238/sq km. about 65 per cent live in the rural and 35 per cent live in the urban areas. There are 1,627 primary schools, 258 higher primary schools. The total literacy rate in the district is 57.40 per cent, male is 69.20 per cent and female is 45.30 per cent.

5.2.Socio-economic Problems of the Region

The rural sector of the region is dominant with communities belonging to scheduled castes, other backward communities and considerable scheduled tribe population. Majority of the people depend on agriculture, agriculture labour, mining, and other unskilled labour such as collection of firewood and minor forest produce. The women and children also work as wage earners. The women experience vulnerability and inequality. They are economically disadvantaged, socially neglected, politically ignored. The women are deprived of good education and health. Lack of skills and knowledge in modern agricultural practices, lack of information on government schemes, lack of alternative income generation source are making the women to battle for survival without having access to various opportunities and benefits.

Due to abject poverty, most of the parents are sending their children to work because the families are highly dependent on the earnings of their children. As a result, the children at an early age are discontinuing their studies, losing their childhood and turn into dropouts. The children are gradually engaging themselves as child labourers in various sectors such as mining, sheep rearing, cattle grazing, brick industry, farm works, siblings care, quarry works etc., and leading unscarred, unnoticed and unprotected life. In this region particularly, education and its importance has not reached the minds of the people and as a result the children are deprived of education. It is therefore essential that the children are allowed to grow which is suitable to meet their social, emotional and educational needs.

In addition, there is food insecurity in the region due to low yield and unemployment. Families do not have proper health care or nutritional food due to economic crunch most of the families are becoming anaemic and malnourished. The maternal and child mortality in the proposed project area is common due to inaccessibe health services. The other major social problems prevalent in this region are the *Devadasi* system and child marriage. Poverty, illiteracy, and lack of women empowerment are the major reasons for the continuation of these social evils.

5.3. Objective of the Paper

The objective of this Paper is to highlight the best practices of non-governmental organisations on comprehensive and integrated approach to rural development and with focus on the problems of child labour and child marriage in the northern districts of Karnataka.

The social development project titled "Mines to Safer Childhood through Schools in Hungund Taluk of Bagalkot District and Sandur, Hospete and Bellary Taluks of Bellary District". The project is carried out in three phases since 2004-05 in 150 villages across Hungund taluk of Bagalkote district; Hospet and Sandur taluks of Bellary district by two NGOs namely, VRDO (VIKASA Rural Development Organisation, Bangalore) and READS (Rural Education and Action Development Society, Bellary). The project is funded by *Terre des Hommes*, Germany. The main objective of the project is to promote and protect the basic rights of children enshrined in Indian Constitution and UNCRC; and empowerment of women. The specific objectives of the project are:

- Prevention, rescue and rehabilitation of children working in the mining and allied industries in the 150 villages, create social responsibility and norms that denounce child labour and encourage children's education;
- To strengthen its village level organisations/committees for retention of children in school, complete ban on child marriage and efforts for child labour free village;
- To protect and promote the Rights of women and children and encourage their increased participation in their overall development;
- Building of the community base leading to sustainable change -- ownership of programmes, processes and resources by the people;
- Ensure food security through increased access and opportunities of government programmes, and integration of local adaptation and coping mechanism in the context of climate change.

A: Intervention Activities: With focus on Issues of Child Labour and Child Marriage, Women Empowerment and Institutional Development

The NGO intervention is with a holistic view to rural development with focus on school drop out, child labour, child marriage and women empowerment. The intervention includes providing informal education to children of migrant workers, working children and school children drop out in the form of camp school, non-formal education centers, and residential bridge schools. The second dimension is through awareness creation among the people on child labour, child marriage and importance of education. The third dimension is the empowerment of women through self-help group concept. The fourth dimension is the capacity-building of other stakeholders at the grassroots level i.e., SDMC members and the *grama panchayat* members.

5.1. Camp School

Camp schools focus on children of migrant mining workers, the school drop out children and working children of local residents. The camp schools operate with twin objectives of taking care of them including preventing them from working, as well as providing them with informal education. The camp schools are operated where there were no *Anganwadi* centres. *Initially* due to high influx of migrant workers in the mining area, on an average there was one camp school per village. Over a period of time, specially after the ban on illegal mining by the Supreme Court of India, the inflow of migrant families has completely stopped. The number of camp schools operating has also reduced. For instance, currently there are only two camp schools in operation. In a couple of other villages where camp schools were operated, the NGOs have facilitated the opening of *Anganwadi* centres by mediating through department of women and child development.

The CDPO had not taken any initiative earlier to start *Anganwadi* centres due to its locational disadvantages. The activities at the camp school included mainly learning through various games and songs. Children were also provided with midday meals. There is one teacher in each camp school, who teaches and inspires the children with good education. The children are later mainstreamed into regular government schools. Two health camps are held each year to take care of the overall health of children as well as against the specific health hazards prevalent in the region. By and large, the children suffered from respiratory problems and skin allergy due to the dust. Few children suffered from blisters in hands due to their working in the fields, especially with stones and heavy objects.

5.2. Residential Bridge School

The Residential Bridge Centre (RBC) supports the school drop-out children and working children to get into regular schooling after a short bridge course. The children, both boys and girls, in the age group of 8-13 years are tutored for six months before enrolling them into formal government schools. During the bridge course period, the children are provided with a place to stay and nutritious food thrice a day. General healthcheck-up is carried out once and referral cases to the local primary healthcare centre in the village as and when required. There are two residential bridge schools, one by each NGO. Each year about 80 to 85 children benefit from the special coaching at the RBC. About 40 to 45 children boys and girls across target villages are enrolled in each batch. The first batch is held from April to September. The second batch is held from October to March.

To make learning a fun, the pedagogy of the course in the RBC includes regular class teaching, games, role play, etc. The children are also trained to speak and express their opinion in the midst of their batch mates and other platforms attended by government officers. In addition to regular activities at the RBC premises, the children are taken out on the learning-cum-recreation exposure visit to Jindal Iron factory, Tungabhadra dam, and Hampi in Bellary district; Bijapur in Bijapur district; Aihole, Pattadakallu, and Badami in Bagalkot district. During the bridge course, meetings with the parents are held once a month to discuss the progress of the children. In addition, the parents also are made aware of child rights, the importance of education, concept of right to education, de-merits of child labour and child marriage etc.

5.3. Non-formal Education Centres

The non-formal education centre (NFE) is mainly to provide informal education to school drop-out children, who also go to work during day time. The NFE functions in the evenings from 05.30 pm to 08.00 pm. However, children who are going to formal schools and who are only the school drop out also attend the classes at NFE. People in this region are ignorant on the importance of education and lack information, time and inclination to send their children to school. Due to poverty, they prefer sending their children for work in return for petty amounts as wages, as a priority rather than schooling. Thus, children are deprived of basic education and would remain illiterate throughout their lives. Taking these factors into consideration, the NGOs have opened NFE centres.

There are 20 NFE centres with 25 to 30 students and one teacher set up in each centre. The NFE teachers with the support of SHG members identify school dropout children and enroll them in NFE centre. The children are allowed to play in the first one hour before beginning the class sessions. The class activity includes all basic subjects and general knowledge. Cultural event is conducted in each NFE centre once a year to exhibit the talent of the children. Some children, when they improve, are sent to RBC before being enrolled into formal school.

5.4. Teacher's Deputation Programme

As a part of the programme, in addition to operating of non-formal education centre, The NGOs support the government schools by providing good teachers in government primary schools where there is shortage of teachers. The teachers are paid an honorarium by the NGOs, though no financial compensation is paid by the education department. The NGOs have provided fourteen teachers across 14 such schools working in interior villages of all working areas. There is an ongoing dialogue with the education department to pay some honorarium to teachers deputed by the READS on par with guest teachers appointed by the education department.

5.5. Crash Course/Summer Camp

Summer camp is conducted in the month of May/June each year during summer vacation for the children in the target villages. The primary objective of the summer camp is to reduce school drop-outs and encourage the children to attend school. About 400 children attend the camp held across the target villages with about 50 children in each camp. The camp is semi-residential and lunch is provided to the children. The duration of the camp is two days, giving awareness about child rights, importance of education, cleanliness, health and hygiene. The activities in the camp are mainly through games, songs and dance, and plays. Thus, children also enjoy and participate in the activities.

5.6. Children's Forum and Federation

The programme promotes children's forum and their federation in the target villages. The children's forum is formed in each government school in the target villages with children studying in fifth to eighth standard. The objective of the children's forum is to create peer pressure groups in each of the target villages to spread the message of promoting literacy among children, eliminating child labour, creating leadership qualities among the children and create awareness about their rights. The forums meet once in fortnight and discuss the problems of children at home as well as in school, provide information on school drop-out children, working children, etc. The children are provided with skill training, carry out street plays in villages on social problems including child marriage.

Federation

There are two federations formed representing the forums together consisting of two members from each forum. The members of the federation are provided with orientation programme on personality development, and leadership qualities. The federation members in turn would disseminate the learning to their respective forum members. Inputs were also given on child rights, education and its importance, cleanliness, child marriage and its implications, to identify child drop-outs and bringing them to school and educating them. The 224 children representing 126 forums were covered in five training programmes conducted by the NGOs for a period of two days each.

The federation members were provided with exposure for two days visit to NGOs – PRERANA and POWER, wherein they have been working on child rights and federation of children forum for over ten years. Children were able to learn about different professions, ideas and opportunities during this visit, and sharing was done outside their own neighbuorhood. This trip for the federation children has awakened the desire in a child to try new things and pursue previously unconsidered dreams.

During this visit, the children organised cultural programmes that gave an opportunity to expose their hidden talent and skills. This programme has helped the children to acquire knowledge and helped them learn through observation and interaction. This visit was aimed at exposing them to different situations contributing to their overall personality development. The outcome of the visit was that the children in the process of sharing the information mentioned new interests and passions. It was a service-oriented trip; there was a new learning of helping others in the community. This trip resulted in greater achievement in all subjects. By seeing real-life application of the lessons that they are learning in school, children were more likely to understand and appreciate the importance and relevance of what they are learning.

5.7. Elimination of Child Marriage and Child Labour

With high levels of poverty, illiteracy, and backwardness, child marriage is major social evil that is still being practised in the rural and interior areas of Bellary and Bagalkot districts. Despite law enforcement, child marriage and child labour are being promoted by the people. In order to educate the people on the consequences and implications of child marriage and child labour, awareness is carried out through social marketing process to tackle these two social practices. There are several channels adopted by the NGOs to tackle the problem including awareness through cultural programmes, cycle rally, pamphlets, banners, street plays and advocacy.

The community members at the village have their age-old tradition and false notion about getting the child marriage done in the name of God. In spite of legal actions by the government departments, the issue of child marriage and child labour persists. There have been incidences of child marriage, *devadasi* system and child labour. The awareness and the implication on children needs to be addressed and this awareness was towards it.

In order to bring in the awareness among the village's at the new villages, the organisation organised awareness programme in 63 villages for one week. The NGO team along with the representatives of the local CBOs (members of the federation, SHGs teachers and youth leaders) went on for a rally distributing pamphlets and announcement was made through the villages and they warned about the legal actions that would be taken by the Departments, if found going for it and also sensitised the ill effects on the children.

Awareness through cultural programmes includes street plays and skits in the villages on aspects such as education and child labour, health, atrocities against women, child rights and child marriage. Video shows were also held on aspects such as environment, health, and child labour. Cycle rally were held by both NGOs in about 50 villages for about a week to create awareness against child labour; school enrollment; and awareness against child marriage. The NGOs also held special school enrollment campaign during the month of June for a period of two weeks in 70 villages through street rally. The awareness would be through mike announcements, and hand bills distribution. Street rallies were also being held in over 40 villages using pamphlets, banners. Calendars were distributed in all the villages with information on child marriage. SHG women, children from RBC, NFE, children's forums and the NGO staff would participate in all the activities including cultural programmes and rallies. The NGOs would meet the taluka officials regularly to update on the progress, problems faced and the support required to accomplish the tasks.

5.8. Special Programmes

i. *Celebration of World Environment Day*: The programme is organised at the government school, with the participation of school children, members of the SHG teachers and members of the *grama panchayat*, SDMC members, school teachers and an officer from the forest and agriculture department, village head, officer of the CRC. Totally 50 members were involved in this programme. The programme started with planting of 50 saplings in each village and the children of the school assured of taking care of these saplings which was provided by the forest department.

ii. *Celebration of World Children's Day*: The NGOs organised a one-day programme to celebrate the "World Day Against Child Labour" on November 22, 2013 in 82 target villages. It was attended totally by 2,375 children. Local leaders, *gram panchayat* members, department officials attended the programme and advised children on the importance of education.

iii. *Red Hand Campaign*: In solidarity with the child victims of conflicts around and in protest against forcibly recruiting children into warfare, civil society organisations concerned with the welfare of children observe one day in February each year as Red Hand Day. The red hand denotes blood-stained hands of innocent children, who do not know why they wield guns and kill other children and adults, very often the same people they grew up in their villages. This year both organisations joined the worldwide efforts of *Terres de Hommes* (TdH) to raise awareness on the issue of child soldiers observed 12th February as the Red Hand Day. By observing the Red Hand Day, the NGOs join the international coalition to stop the Use of Child Soldiers". The youngsters were convinced that using children in areas of conflict by vested interests was not merely wrong but outright immoral and violate the rights of the child. The 405 children and 23 teachers participated in the campaign.

5.9. Skill Training

Skill training is provided to the target group members for capacity building, to enhance and diversify their livelihood practices. It is also to improve the socio-economic conditions of the households of the target groups -- working children (15 + years age group) and SHG women members. The technical skill provided to them is based on the needs, interests and feasibility. The programme had components of imparting vocational and entrepreneurship training to prepare them for self-employment at the village level. The trades include tailoring, vermicompost, *agarbatti*, candle, and four -wheeler driving. The skill training programme is in response to the expectations of this section of the community and to help further in the economic advancement of the community. Advanced training for weavers in Ilkal and its surrounding villages in the taluka, which is famous for saree weaving. VRDO facilitates about 20 women members each year from its target group to provide two weeks advanced training in saree weaving.

5.10. Women Empowerment

Women empowerment has become pivotal to overall development varying from household level to community level. Role of women has in each sphere of development is also important and thus is an essential stakeholder in the process of development. The process of empowerment includes not only access to certain types of resources, but more importantly their role in decision-making process. Women empowerment has normally three dimensions – economic, social and political. The overall empowerment comprises the three dimensions, and gaining access to each of these in the same order. Thus to empower women, they need to have economic empowerment *i.e.,* access to financial resources and participation in decision-making in financial matters. This would lead to social empowerment – having access to social resources and participation at household and community level in decision- making process on social issues. This would give impetus for political empowerment through participation in political process.

The self-help group concept is not restricted to micro-finance and enterprise development issues (economic empowerment) but also to social and political issues. The women collectively decide on social issues, mainly health and education of children, child labour, child marriage at household and village level. However, self-help groups can be made independent and sustainable with some training and creating system, that is the role of promoters *i.e.,* the NGO. However, for the self-help group concept to be functional, the members need to be aware of such leadership, knowing one's roles and responsibilities, maintenance of books and records, etc. Similarly, they also need to be aware of legal aspects, entitlements, etc.

The programme has been working towards the sustainability of these groups and made the following efforts towards strengthening the self-help group members, to motivate the members to become part of the SDMC, motivating the SHGs to become affiliated with the women federation, linkages with other institutions in general and financial institutions in particular, helping the groups to evolve their own norms, rules and regulations, capacity building programmes on various aspects of SHG help the groups to take up local issues.

The intervention in SHG development includes training on SHG concept, capacity building training for federation concept and book keeping, exposure visit for federation members, legal aid training programme, right to work and MGNREGA, health camp for women and children and annual convention of women. The NGOs provide training to the SHG representatives each year on SHG management, book keeping and credit management, and leadership that accounts for about 50 to 60 SHGs, *i.e.*, to about 600 members. Federation of these SHGs is formed covering 250 members and trained in federation concept, village development laws, government scheme, human rights, socio-economic empowerment, self-development, leadership quality, money management, internal loan and external loan. The SHG representatives are taken for exposure visit to MYRADA at Holalkere.

Gender and legal training were organised for the members of selected representatives of the federations, who were able to take up the training as TOT and then train other members. A large number of women got awareness on legal aspects, which was very informative and was a residential programme for two days. This programme was a fight against harassment, awareness and legal rights.

Right to work and MGNREGA has been a continuous process of both the organisations and this has been initiated in new villages. It was basically on availing employment under NREGA in the flood affected areas. Information was shared on how to avail the necessary information about NREGA from the department. The problems identified in the training were that of the job cards and no employment to the families, when people asking job-panchayat people don't giving the job and they call some other time. Participants were very firm to apply for job cards. This programme was basically on availing employment under NREGA and preparing to submit the application for work. Job seekers were trained in availing information relating to NREGA through utilising RTI. Some 356 members were benefitted with job cards and 150 days of employment.

Health awareness camp for the children and women were organised at the project area. The underlying issues such as lack of basic amenities, about their housing, and the struggle of steady income, majority of the community in these areas are being left with little time and inclination to even consider health and their issues as an important area of concern. Some 991 members with children benefitted from the health camp.

One day women's convention is an annual celebration conducted by both the organisations coinciding with the World Women's Day. The objective is to bring out the women's progress through the intervention in addition to the problems faced by them. The women also share their ideas with regard to role of *gram panchayats* and SDMC, etc. For instance, in year 2013-14, the convention focus was on the government's *Women and Child Atrocity Act, 2012.*

5.11. Local Institution Building

The Local Institutional Building includes training programme for School Development and Monitoring Committee (SDMC) members, *gram panchayat* members and *Anganwadi* centre teachers. In both the organisations, emphasis was made towards involving the GP members into the programme, so that they play the key role along with the local community-based organisation in shouldering the responsibility of the organisations. The 194 SDMC members, 198 GP members and 181 government and *Anganwadi* teachers from six *gram panchayats* were provided training.

The focus was made on the roles of the GP members, in school development, about the drop-out children in their respective villages and the mechanism to enrol them. The objective of the workshop was to make the GP members aware of the responsibilities and understand the impact of their intervention on the children.

For the government and *Anganwadi* teachers, the emphasis was laid more towards quality education, consciousness of protection of child rights, working towards reduction in drop out ratio. As these trained *Anganwadi* teachers have been striving towards the children school enrollment and as a few of them are in the SDMC committee, they would also look towards retention of these children. The teachers and the SDMC committee took a close look at the regularity in attendance by children.

5.12. Local Area Networking

At VIKASA and READS working area, networking comprised the NGOs working in and around Bellary and Bagalkot districts. Meetings were also organised under chairmanship of the Deputy Commissioner in the districts. Plans are towards formation of taluk level committees to monitor the taluk level activities. Eradication of the child labour at taluk and village level through mass awareness and collective action will be the main function of taluk level networks. The network plans to meet quarterly and plan for taluk level activities every year. Both organisations are building the capacity of the target group members, *i.e.,* the SHG members to take up the tasks carried out by VIKASA and READS in future.

Topics of discussion and networking at district/regional level include small scale food production, food security, nutrition and right to organic farming, environmental rights, understanding self, society and environment common understanding of mining issues, child rights, child marriage, child traffic, nature, globalisation, illiteracy, and youth cultural rights.

B. Impact of the Intervention

5.1. Camp School

The camp school has helped the children to show interest in studies. The 1,149 children (687 boys and 462 girls) belonging to the migrant families working in the mining areas were provided with informal education. The 506 children, accounting for 44 per cent were mainstreamed into regular government schools. Child drop-out has reduced to a large extent. The children as well as the parents have understood well the importance of education. Parents also do not force the children to work and allow them to attend school. The follow-up of the children enrolled previously shows that incidence of school drop-outs have reduced significantly as a result of the intervention. The children and the parents of the camp schools of previous years give good feedback and recommend other parents to send their children to the camp school.

The children are able to express their hidden talent and are being encouraged/motivated, which gives the children good confidence. Each child has learnt to interact, behave and share the feeling, thought and ideas. The government health department have been regularly visiting the camp schools and the regular health check-up for the children have helped in reducing their health problems such as blisters and other skin problems. There has been involvement from the parents and SHG members. Community has actively participated in the construction of camp school and accommodated the place to put the tent.

5.2. Residential Bridge Centre (RBC)

Firstly, the children receive good and nutritious food thrice a day. They are together all day learning through playing and interesting activities. The teachers are also very affectionate to the children. Hence, the children enjoy the stay at the centre as well as the learning. The children learn new skills and gain more knowledge than the average children of their age group studying in formal government schools. As a result, the confidence levels of the children in RBC are very high and wish to continue their education. Thus, enrolling them into the government formal schools became an easy task.

About 1,000 children have benefitted from the six months bridge course conducted by both the NGOs of which 704 children have been mainstreamed into regular government schools. The parents are also happy and satisfied with their children's progress and are aware of the importance of education and child rights. So, the parents now do not insist on sending children for work and instead encourage them going to school.

The individual growth displayed by the children after the six months training is phenomenal. Without any inhibition the children share their experience and learning at various camps and workshops. The follow-up of previous batch RBC children shows that the children when enrolled in government school are very active with co-curricular activities; provide suggestions to teachers and headmaster to carry out specific activities and programmes in the school. The previous batch students have completed schooling and some of them are into doing industrial training and pre-university course. The alumni from RBC also visit the RBC and share their experience.

The concept of child rights is embedded into the minds of children that the children are very vocal of their rights at home and other places. They even call up 1098 (child helpline) by themselves if necessary. The girls talk against child marriage. The overall impact is that school drop-out has significantly reduced in the target villages. The self-help group members make it a point to discuss children's issues during weekly meetings. This includes health and education – issues of school drop-outs, their educational progress at NFE and RBC. Recommendations are made by SHG members to other members to send their children to RBC for improvement.

RBC Exposure Visit

The inter-personal relationship between the children improved during this exposure visit. Children were able to recollect their memories of the exposure visit later during the class sessions. The exposure visit built up the confidence levels of the children. Children developed social values, knowledge skill and attitude, useful for the purpose of their personality development. Children are encouraged for a holistic development.

RBC Parent is Orientation

The parents were happy to see their children showing interest in studies. The parents are not insisting their children now to go for work. Parents are aware about their responsibilities and encourage their children to go to school / RBC. There has been a good relationship between the children and the parents.

5.3. Functional Literacy Centre (FLC) / Non-formal Education Centre (NFE)

The 2,976 children were provided with non-formal education, of which over 40 per cent were enrolled into government schools. Skills of various forms – reading, writing, and speaking - of the children have improved. Their knowledge and talents in various fields have widened. It has helped to prevent children from working in the mines and to concentrate on education. Children participate in all types of activities confidently. These activities helped the children to develop many positive traits through activities and children are self-disciplined and self-confident. Due to the multi-dimensional teaching approach at the RBC, the children fare better than other children of the same age group. There is a considerable change in the attitude of parents by personally experiencing the change in profile of their children. The incidence of school drop-outs have also reduced substantially. The children from NFE after getting enrolled in formal government schools, their dropout rates have reduced. As the children at NFE get enough encouragement to go to school, absenteeism is also less both at the NFE Centre as well the schools.

FLC Teacher Support

With NGOs deputing teachers to government schools, the contribution has been very handy at the respective schools. Contribution of the deputed teachers at the government schools is significant and purposeful. The loss of teaching hours due to lack of teachers is avoided. This is a good and innovative approach to public-private partnership in the field of education.

5.4. Summer Camp

There was lot of fun and learning made by the children. The children were made aware of their rights, and importance of school education system. Children showed interest to go to school and joined NFE Centre and RBC run by the READS and VRDO.

Child Forum

In all, 300 children's forums were created in the target villages by the NGOs consisting of 5,860 children (3,096 boys and 2,764 girls) across 150 villages. The forum acts as the platform for children to share their problems. It has helped in the enrollment of drop-out children into formal schools. These children help in identifying school dropouts and child workers in the village. They help as peer pressure group in making children to attend school. The children have helped in stopping child marriages in villages by informing NGO staff in advance about the child marriage. The children have participated in street plays on concepts of school drop-out, child workers, illiteracy, alcoholism, and child marriage carried out by NGO staff. In all, they provide a voice for the voiceless and marginalised children, both boys and girls. The children speak up against the problems faced by children to the government authorities. Recently, there was a convention of children at the state level in Bangalore and two children from the forum participated in the programme attended by the chief minister of Karnataka. The children spoke with courage on their problems. The matter was taken seriously and enquiry was also set up based on the problems mentioned by the children in the convention.

The children were taken to two NGOs working in the area of child rights for exposure. This trip resulted in greater achievement in all subjects by seeing real-life application of the lessons that they learn in school. Children were more likely to understand and appreciate the importance and relevance of what they learn. Children are pro-actively involved in initiating programmes in schools on special occasions such as children's day, world environment day, world water day, etc.

5.5. Child Labour and Child Marriage Awareness

Community people are aware of the importance of primary education and are concerned about children's regularity to school. Parents have understood their roles and responsibilities towards their children in terms of providing education and not sending them for work. Enrollment in the primary school has steadily increased. School drop-out children are motivated by the forum as well as RBC children. Parents are voluntarily enrolling their children into school. Mass awareness on the key issues was more effective due to involvement of the local institution (SHGs, children forum) and community members. The awareness programme has provided great opportunity for the members of community to learn about the rights-based issues. The community members have vouched to follow the law and are actively involved in disseminating the message.

Several child marriages have been stopped on the day of marriage. Children have informed READS in advance about arranged marriages. Children have also used 1098 (child helpline) to inform about such marriages. Child labour has also reduced in the region significantly.

5.6. Skill Training

Each year about 30 to 35 youth were trained in vermicompost making, 10 youth were provided four-wheeler driving skills, 30 women were trained in tailoring, 15 to 20 women in making candle and incense sticks. About 30 women were supported for trade diversification into home-based food processed products each year. The NGOs supported the women also in improving their business such as branding and linking the entrepreneurs to wholesalers, etc., most of the women with tailoring skills have started their own tailoring units at home and earn about Rs. 200 to Rs. 300 per day. Youth with four-wheeler skills have obtained employment and earn about Rs. 4,000 to Rs. 6,000 per month. Youth with vermicompost making skills prepare vermicompost in their farm and sell them locally. The NGOs have provided special training in saree weaving to certain groups and they have gained expertise in better weaving techniques.

5.7. Women Empowerment

VIKASA and READS have promoted 861 SHGs with total membership of 12,641 members. Total savings is Rs. 2.51 crore and mobilised more than Rs. 4.88 crore from banks and credit Institutions. The training provides capacity to the groups to evolve their own norms, rules and regulations. Training has improved capacity on various aspects of SHG. It has helped the groups to take up local issues. Training has motivated the members to become part of the SDMC.

There has been regular participation by members of the SHGs for meetings, training programmes, and *Gram Sabha*s at their respective village level. Attempts have been made to discuss with the government officials. There is a cordial support from the bank officials. The books of accounts of SHGs have been maintained in a very systematic manner. The loan repayment is regularised. The women are empowered to take decisions on issues related to them at the village level. The SHG members discuss with GP members on issues related to their village. The SHG members help the organisations in supporting the children's enrollment in camp schools, NFE, RBC as well as in regular schools. The SHG members participate in awareness creation programmes on "Child labour and Child Marriage" issues. The SHG members are discussing directly with GP members related to MNREGA for creation of wage employment and more than 150 days of employment on average has been generated per person during the year. The women are aware of their legal rights.

5.8. Institution Building for SDMC and *Grama Panchayat* Members and *Anganwadi* Teachers

The SDMC members and *gram panchayat* members are more aware of their roles in the society. They are more proactive in the school enrollment-process. The *gram panchayat* members are responsive when the SHG members meet them with certain demands. They have released grants for purchase of tailoring machines for women through government schemes. The teachers came to know more about child rights and a child in particular. They have been very actively involving themselves with the child forum and the activities of VIKASA.

5. Conclusion

READS/VIKASA has implemented four sets of programmes during the current year 2013-14 namely, camp schools, non-formal education centre, Residential Bridge Centre, and Women empowerment. In addition are the children's forum and federation, and CLM activity. All the programmes and activities have been implemented successfully and the objectives are also being met. The literacy levels in the target areas are improving. There is a significant decline in the child labour as well as school drop-outs. Awareness among the parents has improved on the importance of education and the power of child rights. Children have realised their potential, their rôle in the society and understood their rights. The impact has also been positive and significant. The programme has reached a stage, where the target groups do not require hand holding. Some support is needed to make the institutions such as the SHG, children's forum and federations to be independent, sustainable and play their role in the society. Complementarily, VIKAS and READS should increase the stakes of certain other players such as SDMC and *gram panchayat* in the village.

6

Rural Health Infrastructure in India: An Overview

P T Dinesha

Introduction

Economic growth in a country largely depends on the standards of its social infrastructure and among social infrastructures health plays an important role. Health is not only an important input in the development process; it also assumes the role of infrastructure for development of other social indicators. It is understood that there is a positive correlation between the health status of people and the economic development of the country is a well-established fact. Though health has been considered a fundamental human right since the *Alma Atta Declaration (1978)*, yet expenditure on health in India is often lower than expected and the condition of health infrastructure in the country, especially in rural areas has not improved up to a satisfactory level due to numerous reasons. Government of India has started National Rural Health Mission with a goal to provide quality healthcare to isolated rural communities in India; still the condition is not good. Keeping the above facts in view, this paper has the following objectives:

1. To discuss the status of existing health infrastructure in rural areas,
2. To understand the problems faced by rural health infrastructure, and
3. To suggest suitable policy alternatives.

This paper will discuss only three major rural health infrastructures, they are Health Centres, Manpower and Buildings. The paper is based on the secondary information and it was gathered from various publications of government departments, journals and books.

Rural Health Infrastructure: The Status

As per the Census of India, 2011, the total population of India was 1,210.2

million, of this, the rural population stands at 833.1 million and in absolute numbers, the rural population has increased by 90.47 million in the last decade (GoI, 2011). And to this vast population of the rural areas, the primary health care infrastructure has been developed as a three-tier system based on population norms with Sub-Centre, Primary Health Centre (PHC) and Community Health Centre (CHC) being the three pillars of Primary Health-Care System. In a developing country like India, rural environments present unique challenges for health care access. According to the *Rural Health Statistics Report* of 2012 by Ministry of Health and Family Welfare, Government of India during March 2012 , there were 14,366 SCs, 24,049 PHCs and 4,833 community Health centres (CHCs) existing in India. However, they face many problems like shortage of health centres, buildings and shortage of manpower etc.

Present Status of SCs, PHCs, CHCs

The Sub-Centre is the most peripheral and first contact point between the primary healthcare system and the community. During March 2005, there were 1,46,026 sub-centers in the country and it increased to 1,48,366 during 2012 (Table-1). Here, we can see that about 2,340 sub-centers were increased and this increase is mainly concentrated in states like Haryana, Jammu and Kashmir, Karnataka, Chhattisgarh, Maharashtra, Uttarakand, Tamil Nadu, Tripura, Punjab, Rajasthan, and Odisha. Data also reveals that there is an increase of 1.6 per cent in SCs can be seen. Next to SCs, there is PHC's and is the first contact point between village community and the Medical Officer. According to the data, there were 23,236 PHCs functioning in the country during March 2005, whereas, it increased upto 24,049 PHCs during March 2012 and increase of 813 PHCs can be seen and it accounts 3.4 per cent growth (Table-1) (GoI, 2012).

Table-1: Number of Functioning Sub-Centres, PHCs and CHCs

Health Centres	2005	2012
SCs	146,026	148,366
PHCs	23,236	24,049
CHCs	3,346	4,833

Source: Rural Health Statistics in India 2012, GoI.

Community Health Centres serves as a referral centre for four PHCs and provides facilities also for obstetric care and specialist consultation. With respect to community health centres, data reveals that there were only 3,346 CHCs in the country during March 2005 and it reached to 4,833 CHCs during March 2012 (Table-1). A massive increase of 1,487 CHCs can be seen during those seven years. It shows that a 44.4 per cent of increase in CHCs in the country (GoI, 2012). A sudy by Ashok Vikhe Patil found that it is unfortunate that while the incidence of all diseases are twice higher in rural than in urban areas, the rural people are denied access to proper healthcare, as the systems and structures were built up mainly to serve the better off (Ashok Vikhe Patil *et al*, 2002),

Shortfall in SCs, PHCs, CHCs

Though there has been a steady increase in health care infrastructure available over years (Table-2), progress is not satisfactory, as, there is a shortage of health centers and infrastructure to the existing population norm. Data reveals that we have a shortfall of 23 per cent of sub-centres, where as there is 26 per cent shortage of Primary Health centres. However, most pitiable situation is that there is a shortage of 40 per cent in community health centres, which has become a daunting task for the government.

Table-2: Shortfall in Health Infrastructure as per 2011 Population

Health Centres	*Required*	*In Position*	*Shortfall*	*Percentage Shortfall*
SCs	1,89,094	1,48,366	43,776	23
PHCs	30,565	24,049	7,954	26
CHCs	7,631	4,833	3,044	40

Source: Rural Health Statistics in India 2012, GoI.

Building Status of Sub-centres, PHCs and CHCs

Rural health sector also faces the problem of shortage of buildings for health centres. Many primary health centres are functioning in government or rented buildings which have limited available space. Data reveals that there is 63.61 per cent of Sub-centres functioning in government buildings and there is shortage of 36,654 sub-centres. With respect to Primary Health Centres 83.22 per cent are functioning in government buildings and there is a shortage of 1,069 primary health centres in India. However, the status of community health centres is comparatively good and we have shortage of only 58 community health centres in India during March 2012 (GoI, 2012). However, poor up-keep and maintenance and high absenteeism of manpower in rural areas have eroded the credibility of the health delivery system in the public sector.

Table 3: Health Centres Functioning

Building Position For	Functioning In					
	Total Number	Govt. Building	Rented Building	Rent Free Panchayat / Vol. Society Building	Buildings Under Construction	Buildings Required to be constructed
SCs	148366	94380	35936	16231	15543	36654
PHCs	24049	20015	1235	936	1384	1069
CHCs	4833	4688	118	28	401	58

Source: Rural Health Statistics in India, 2012 GoI.

Shortfall in Manpower

The availability of manpower is one of the important prerequisite for the efficient functioning of the rural health services. As on March, 2012, the overall shortfall (which excludes the existing surplus in some of the states) in the posts of Health Worker Female (HW (F) / Auxiliary Nurse Midwife (ANM) was 3.8 per cent of the total requirement as per the norm of one HW (F) / ANM per Sub-centre and PHC and in case of HW (Male), there was a shortfall of 65.2 per cent of the requirement. At the sub-centre level, the extent of existing manpower can be accessed from the fact that 3.8 per cent of the sub-centres were without a Female Health Worker / ANM, 51.6 per cent sub-centres were without a Male Health Worker and 2.7 per cent sub-centres were without both Female Health Worker / ANM as well as Male Health Worker. In case of PHC, for Health Assistant (Female)/ Lady Health Visitor (LHV), the shortfall was 38.2 per cent and that of Health Assistant (Male) was 52.6 per cent . For allopathic doctors at PHC, there was a shortfall of 10.3 per cent of the total requirement. Data also reveals that 7.8 per cent of the sanctioned posts of HW (Female)/ ANM were vacant as compared to 44.4 per cent of the sanctioned posts of Male Health Worker. At PHCs, 37.1 per cent of the sanctioned posts of Female Health Assistant/ LHV, 34.4 per cent of Male Health Assistant and 20.4 per cent of the sanctioned posts of doctors were vacant. As on March 2012, 4.0 per cent of the PHCs were without a doctor, 36.5 per cent were without a lab technician and 23.1 per cent were without a pharmacist (GoI, 2012).

The Community Health Centres provide specialised medical care in the form of facilities of surgeons, obstetricians and gynaecologists, physicians and paediatricians. The current position of specialist, manpower at CHCs reveal that as on March, 2012, out of the sanctioned posts, 51.8 per cent of surgeons, 40.7 per cent of obstetricians and gynaecologists, 53.3 per cent of physicians and 43.1 per cent of paediatricians were vacant. Overall 43.7 per cent of the sanctioned posts of specialists at CHCs were vacant. Moreover, as compared to the requirement for existing infrastructure, there was a shortfall of 74.9 per cent of surgeons, 65.1 per cent of obstetricians and gynaecologists, 79.6 per cent of physicians and 79.8 per cent of paediatricians. Overall, there was a shortfall of 69.7 per cent specialists at the CHCs as compared to the requirement for existing CHCs. The shortfall in specialists is significantly high in most of the states. However, along with the specialists, about 9,911 General Duty Medical Officers (GDMOs) are also available at CHCs as in March, 2012.

Concluding Suggestions

After discussing the problems, the urgent need of the hour is that, there is a need to improve the condition of rural health infrastructure for the sustainable health sector development and improving the health condition of the rural people. New infrastructure, SCs, CHCs, PHCs need to be created to make quality services available to a larger population and wider area. Besides creating new infrastructure, existing health infrastructure should be strengthened with appropriate stock of beds, laboratories, ambulances, telephones, medicines etc. It is also suggested that budget allocations to the health sector be increased. There should be a shift from the current emphasis on curative, advanced and urban services to increase funding for preventive services and better services in the rural areas. There is also need to fill up the vacant posts through proper measures. Besides, convenient and standard residential accommodation needs to be provided for the key staff at least as a motivation for them to stay on so, as to ensure the availability of services to the people.

The mismatch between manpower and infrastructure facilities should be done away with so as to enhance efficiency as a whole. Besides of the construction building for hospitals, houses for the staff should be constructed to increase the morale and efficiency of the personnel working. Finally, while opening a new health centre care may be taken in selecting such site which should be easily accessible to largest number of people in the block. India does have a systematic health policy. However, in order to improve the rural health sector, there is a need for its effective implementation, monitoring and evaluation for promoting holistic health and economic welfare of the people. The focus of the current debate should be on the health of the rural population of India. Achieving health standards similar to those living in urban India in the foreseeable future should be the goal. Pragmatism, rather than ideological arguments is called for. Support for better essential health services, rather than the current status quo, of neglect is a fight for social justice and for the human rights of all people.

References

- GoI (2008), *Economic Survey of India*, 2005-06.
- GoI (2012): *Rural Health Statistics in India*, 2012, Ministry of Health and Family Welfare Government of India.
- Srinivasan, Sandhya (2005), '*Public health infrastructure: What we need and what we have*', Info Change India News and Features, June. http://www.infochangeindia.org/HealthIbp.jsp
- GoI: (2011): *Census of India, Provisional Populations Total,* Census of India.
- Ashok Vikhe Patil, K.V. Somasundaram and R. C. Goyal, Current Health Scenario In Rural India, Austrak an Journal for. *J. Rural Health* (2002) *pp. 10*, 129–35.

7

Social Media for Inclusive Rural Development in India

B.P. Mahesh Chandra Guru and M. Dileep Kumar

Preamble

Rural development is the main pillar of national development in a pluralistic society like India. About 65 per cent of the people live in rural India by primarily depending on agriculture, cottage industry and other fields. Media intervention for inclusive rural development is widely acknowledged by the policy makers and scholars. They have argued that social media have cut across all barriers to communication, participation and development in rural India. The role of social media in the inclusive rural development is primarily discussed in this paper.

Inclusive Rural Development: Social Media Perspective

Rural development communication is an interactive process in which information, knowledge and skills, relevant for development are exchanged between farmers, extension/advisory services, information providers and research either personally or through media such as radio, print and more recently the new media of communication. In all rural development support communication approaches, rural people are at the centre of any given development initiative and view planners, development workers, local authorities, farmers and rural people as 'communication equals', equally committed to mutual understanding and concerted action.

The closing decade of twentieth century was the opening of historic information and communication technology intervention for development. This period has witnessed enormous and unprecedented changes in every aspect of communications technologies, policies, infrastructure development and services. Political leaders of India have begun abandoning archaic government control over communication that has lately moved from government to national and international private players.

Finally, air waves and electronic signals have achieved their freedom from centuries-old colonial bondage to reach out and connect people through privately owned and operated communication network and infrastructure.

Ramirez (1998) noted that social media are a fundamental element of any rural development activity. The *World Development Report* of World Bank (1999) observed that there is a renewed impetus to integrate knowledge into countries' development strategies. There is a trickle down communication effect in many areas of development including rural development. UNDP (2001) emphasised the need for technology transfer in the rural areas through proper media intervention packages.

The social media operate on many levels, from families up to the level of nations, and play a critical role in determining the way problems are solved, organisations are run, and the degree to which individuals succeed in achieving their goals. Empirical studies have reported that social networks are also powerful mechanisms for rapidly shifting and transforming social norms throughout the network, through a process of 'social contagion'. The prominent categories of social media include – social news (digg, twitter and slashdot), social networking (facebook, myspace and orkut), social sharing (youtube, flickr and tumbir), social bookmarking (stumble upon, declicious, meneame) and social knowledge (wikipedia, yahoo answers and squidoo). The social networking sites (SNS) have grown commendably across the world during the last decade.

Scholars have asserted that knowledge gap is an important determinant of persistent poverty, combined with the notion that developed countries possess the knowledge already required to assure universally adequate standard of living. They have suggested the need for policies that encourage greater communication and information flows within and between countries. One of the best possible ways to achieve this greater interaction is through the use of social media, which have benefitted the people immensely in this age of digital divide.

Chapman and Slaymaker (2002) state: "Rural areas are often characterised as information-poor and information provision has always been a central component of rural development initiatives. The rural poor typically lack access to information vital to their lives and livelihoods". The social networks have gained the power to sensitise various stakeholders of the integrated rural development.

The social media has the capacity to overcome many of the obstacles to ICT adoption and can empower individuals educationally and economically. They have become an integral part of contemporary economic, political, and social lives, altering the way people purchase goods, the way they bank, and the way the people communicate with one another. In reality, a larger segment of the world population misses the tremendous political, social, economic, educational, and career opportunities created by the new media revolution.

Gilbert *et al* (2009), conducted an empirical study on the impact of social network sites on the rural people in America and reported that the rural users demonstrated very different SNS behaviour than urban users. The study revealed that the rural users clearly signed up much later than urban users and rural users publicly articulated far fewer friends than urban users. The social media holds out a possibility of on-demand access to content anytime, anywhere, on any digital device, as well as interactive user feedback, creative participation and community formation around the media content. What distinguishes new media from traditional media is not the digitising of media content into bits, but the dynamic life of the 'new media' content and its interactive relationship with the media consumer. The social media is also widely known for the 'democratisation' of the creation, publishing, distribution and consumption of media content, which benefit various stakeholders of rural development in India.

Moni (2010) has strongly advocated the digital inclusion for fostering rural prosperity and grassroot development in India. Yamamichi (2011) emphasises the role of new media in rural development thus: "Social media can enhance people's access to information, change flows of information and communication, and provide traditionally disadvantaged groups with communication channels. In the context of social development, their poverty can be alleviated by faster and easier information delivery, information exchange and network creation, efficiency and transparency, transformation of people's lives and decentralisation and empowerment programmes.

Development administrators and other professionals use social media for various purposes in modern society. The social media facilitate rapport development between the rural development administrators and beneficiaries. The social network interactions are also a form of emphatic communication which defines a type of expression that is used for social reasons instead for the purpose of sharing information. The new communication technologies have created world in which the traditional and advanced social media are becoming more personal, participatory and development-oriented. The application of social media has become widespread over a period of time, indicating a shift in the way people use the internet to connect with each other developmentally.

The social media have been used extensively by social movements to educate, organise, share cultural products of movement, communicate, coalition build, and more. Similarly, these media are widely used by the government and non-government agencies to enlist the active participation of people in the process of development. The goals of inclusive development, integrated development and sustainable development are also achieved by the active utilisation of social media, which have emerged, has an alternative media source across the globe. Some scholars even view this advantage over the traditional mass media as an indication of the creation of 'radical, socio-technical paradigm to challenge the dominant, neo-liberal and technologically determinist model of information and communication technologies.'

The information and communication technological revolution is commonly talked about as phenomenon that affects everybody, bringing fundamental changes to the way people work, entertain themselves and interact with each other. Yet, the reality is that for the most part, such changes have bypassed the majority of humankind, the billions of poor people for whom computers and the Internet mean nothing. However, in a growing number of instances, and as part of quieter revolution, variety of local organisations, aid agencies and government bodies are discovering that new media can be used to extend the reach of information revolution to the poorest of people living in the rural, tribal and remote areas in India and other parts of the world. News media have also proved their capacity for inducing social and economic development of the women and weaker sections of society in several aspects. The intervention of social media for rural development has been widely discussed and debated all over the world. Scholars have emphasised that there is a need for field practitioners to take stock of the experience that has so far been accumulated.

Willard (2009) examined the relationship between social networking and governance for sustainable development and observed that communication technology has enabled new approaches to governance in which stakeholders across sectors and jurisdictions are engaged in consensus building and implementation processes. In order to maximise contacts among those interested in sustainable development, many sustainable development-specific SNSs have been created. The best known of these sites have been developed as stand-alone SNSs with customised technology platforms. However, the creation of 'out-of-the-box' SNS platforms and hosted services provide cheaper and easier ways for the sustainable development community to launch a wide variety of new niche communities.

The social media and particularly the Internet provide the potential for democratic post-modern public sphere, in which citizens can participate in well informed, non-hierarchical debate pertaining to their social structures and development endeavours in urban and rural areas. The social media has been dramatically speeding up the execution of various developmental activities in the rural areas. They have increased communication between the implementers and beneficiaries of rural development projects over a period of time. They have enabled various stakeholders of rural development to express themselves through blogs, websites, pictures, and other user-generated media. People have also witnessed the great development such as the 'death of distance' between the project authorities and themselves in the rural, tribal and remote areas.

Social media have allowed numerous views and practices to be more widespread and gain more public attention in the rural areas. Interactivity has become a term for number of new media use options evolving from the rapid dissemination of Internet access point, the digitalisation of the media, and media convergence. The social media with technology convergence shifts the model of mass communication, and radically shapes the ways the people interact and communicate with one another. The development of social media networks and technologies has enabled the policy makers and administrators to share their views, responsibilities and works and interact with the big world consisting of various stakeholders of rural development in a vast sub-continent like India. The interactive social media has become a true benefit to everyone because people can express their views, needs and demands in more than one way with the technological advancements in this age of right to information and participation. The World Bank (2000) has called upon the policy makers to decentralise and democratise the new media networks and operations in order to bridge the digital divide and facilitate the active participation of beneficiaries in the process of rural development.

Conclusion

Reaching out to the beneficiaries of various rural development programmes has become a challenging task for the policy makers and the administrators in present times. The Central and State Governments have launched advertising and publicity campaigns to reach the people and create awareness among them about the rural development activities undertaken by them. The social media has proved resilient in view of has strengths and opportunities from participatory communication and development points of view. There is increasing use of social media for rural development endeavours. Social media are decisively influencing the attitudes and behaviours of people in the rural areas about constitutional safeguards, social responsibility of corporate houses. developmental obligations of elected representatives, accountability of development administrators and so on. It is imperative to formulate a national policy on application of social media for inclusive rural development at this juncture of commercialisation media in India. The challenge facing the policy makers, administrators, developmentalists and others today is how to widen the reach of social media for rural development, how to make them accessible to people everywhere and how to empower the marginalised sections of society in every respect. It is here that the importance of social media application for inclusive rural development needs to be recognised in accordance with the goal of integrated rural development in India.

References

Chapman, Robert and Tom Slaymaker (2002), *ICTs and Rural Development: Review of the Literature, Current Interventions and Opportunities for Action*, Working Paper 192, Overseas Development Institute, London, UK.

Gilbert , Eric, Karrie Karahalios and Christian Sandvig (2009), *The Network in the Garden: Designing Social Media for Rural Life Department* of Computer Science and Communication, University of Illinois at Urbana-Champaign-www.csandvig]@uiuc.edu.

Moni, Madaswamy (2010), *Digital Inclusion for Fostering Rural Prosperity and Grassroots Development,* National Informatics Centre. Department of Information Technology, Ministry of Communications and Information Technology, New Delhi; e-mail: moni@nic.in.

Ramirez, R. (1998), Communication: A Meeting Ground for Sustainable Development' in Richardson, D. and Paisley, L. (1998), *The First Mile of Connectivity. Advancing Telecommunications for Rural Development through a Participatory Communication Approach.* Rome: FAO.

UNDP (2001), Human Development Report 2001. *Making Technologies Work for Human Development.* Washington, D.C.

Willard, Terri (2009), *Social Networking and Governance for Sustainable Development,* International Institute for Sustainable Development, www.iisd.org.

Yamamichi, Masatake (2011), *Mobile-enabled Social Media in Social Development, Technologies Information and Communication,* www.worldbank.org/ICT.

8

Media Intervention for Inclusive Rural Development in India

H.K. Mariswamy and H.S. Shivaraju

Preamble

The champions of development communication have observed that the essence of ideology development communication is the creation of new society on the basis of inclusive development, social justice and collective welfare. Communication indeed is major development resource in the process of inclusive rural development in India. A new upward movement for development has begun with the decentralisation of democratic system in Indian republic. The article provides an overview of the communication support for inclusive rural development in India.

Rural Development Communication in India

Buddha fought against the dominant forces, which ruled the ancient India and liberated mankind from the draconian clutches of traditionalism which was responsible for uneven development of people in India. Basava established *Anubhavamantapa* which is regarded as the foremost democratic forum in Karnataka and created several *Vachanakars,* who served the mankind as torch bearers and path makers. Basava also fought against the dominant forces which hindered equality and progress of the mankind. Mahatma Gandhi used traditional cultural symbolic systems, print media and inter-personal communication tools to propagate new ideas, values and behaviours among the masses. His papers namely- *Indian Opinion, Young India, Harijan and Navajeevan* were great tools of developmental communication since Gandhi provided multi-faceted education to the people of India.

Ambedkar was a great visionary of twentieth century and fought for social justice and economic equity through his life. He also brought out

Mooknayak, Bahishkrit Bharat, Samata, Janata and Prabuddha Bharat which stand as testimonials in the history of Indian journalism as master pieces of developmental communication. He is rightly remembered in the history of Indian media as the founder of 'parallel communication and journalism.

The framers of Indian Constitution have accorded priority to Freedom of Speech and Expression vides Article 19.1 a which is a fundamental right to communication and development. The five year plan was a major instrument for achieving the goals of social change and economic development through public sector investment in industrialisation under the leadership of Pandit Nehru. There was a significant difference of opinion between Nehru and Gandhi with respect to the adoption of development model and achievement of the goals of inclusive rural development. Nehru wanted to industrialise the nation and achieve progress in accordance with the international thinking on modernisation based on dominant paradigm of development. Gandhi argued that India can prosper economically by according priority to agriculture and rural development based on local culture, environment and experience.

The Government of India (1953) emphasised the role of communication in development in the First Five Year Plan document. The five year plan documents reveal the significance of communication in the process of inclusive rural development in India. The establishment of agricultural universities, directorates of development, extension divisions, media units, training organisations and other agencies reveals are the significance of development communication in India. Though communication for development or development support, communication grew out of agriculture and rural development communication, the term comprehensively includes all spheres of development such as education, health, family welfare, social change, environment protection, industrial development, employment, training, personality development and so on. All these spheres of development required planned, deliberate and systematic communication inputs to widen the horizon of development and expedite the process of development.

Narula (1994) identified the approaches to development communication in India, which include – diffusion/extension approach, mass media approach, instructional approach, localised approach and planned approach. The Government of India and state governments have formulated rural development policies and implemented programmes to eradicate poverty, develop community infrastructure, generate gainful employment opportunities and improve the living standard of the people in the country.

The Government of India established the Directorate of Field Publicity and created regional information units with mobile cinema vans that showed films on rural developmental endeavours. The Films Division produced news reels and documentaries on communal harmony, national integration and other subjects related to development projects. Agriculture and family planning were the thrust areas of development communication services offered by the government. The Green Revolution gave a fillip to the practice of development communication in the country.

Agricultural universities established Krishi Vigyan Kendras and spearheaded the campaign for increased agricultural production and productivity in the rural areas. The Department of Health and Family Welfare was also actively involved in the family planning communication programme implemented by the Mass Education and Media Division (MEMD). In 1966, the Mass Education and Media (MEM) organisation was created within the department of Family Planning to promote health and family welfare. In 1970, the campaign for distribution, sale and use of condoms was launched on the basis of knowledge, attitudes and practices (KAP) formula. The extension education approach was adopted to facilitate effective implementation of health and family welfare programme all over the country with the help of a bandwagon of field workers spread across the length and breadth of the country.

Kakar (1987) observed that extension communication services were expanded all over the country to enlist the active support of various stakeholders of rural development. The implementation of Minimum Needs Programme, 20-Point Programme, New 20-Point Programme, Integrated Rural Development Programme, National Rural Employment Programme, Training the Rural Youth for Self-Employment, Jawahar Rojgar Yojana, Prime Minister Rojgar Yojana and other programmes in the post-Independence era called for utilisation of communications media for the purpose of inclusive rural development. The non-government organisations employed certain communication tools and techniques to reach out to the people and disseminate development information to the beneficiaries.

The Satellite Instructional Television Experiment (1975-76) is a landmark in the field of rural development communication in India. Ghosh (2006) noted that SITE amply demonstrated that sophisticated broadcasting systems could be used in the context of rural communication quite effectively and that it was quite possible to organise and manage the maintenance of Direct Reception Sets (DRS) for TV viewing in rural areas. The Indian Space Research Organisation (ISRO) developed satellite communication services to facilitate the goal of integrated rural development in India.

Several institutions started using broadcasting technologies for development communication purposes in the country. Prominent among them include-Chitrabani in Calcutta, Xavier Institute of Communication Arts in Bombay, Centre for Development Communication in Hyderabad, Centre for Development of Instructional Technology in New Delhi, Jabhua Development Communication Project in Jabhua, and so on. These organisations produced slide-tape presentations, films and video programmes that supported the face-to-face communication work of voluntary organisations engaged in social work and rural development activities.

International agencies like UNESCO, WHO, UNICEF and FAO extended necessary educational and financial support in order to promote the active participation of voluntary organisations as facilitators of social change and economic development in the country. Non-profit organisations also used communication tools and technologies to document their nation building activities and enlist support from various sources. Video became very effective tool of development communication since it opened up communication channels within the community and between the community and the outside world. The progressive movements also provided a rational dimension to the practice of development communication in India.

These progressive movements were influenced by the international issues, trends and developments. *Chipko* Movement in Uttar Pradesh, *Narmada Bachav Andolan* in Gujarat, Silent Valley Movement in Kerala, Movement against Bhopal gas tragedy, Movement against Enron Project, Movement against Cogentrics, etc., demonstrated the strength of people and 'bottom up' mode of communication in the country. Effective networking of individuals, agencies and institutions became a possibility of progressive movements, which strengthened the process of grassroots communication in the country. These instances aptly illustrate the innovative means of participatory communication that were adopted by the progressive organisations for reaching out to the people, registering the protest of the people, building public opinion against injustice and pleading for justice-centred progress in the country.

McKee (1992) highlights the importance of social mobilisation in the context of rural development communication thus: "Social mobilisation is defined as the process of bringing and practical inter-sectoral social allies together to raise people's awareness of and demand for a particular rural development programme, to assist in the delivery of resources and services and to strengthen community participation for sustainability and self-reliance" An element of advocacy has been added to the process of inclusive rural development communication in India by the progressive organisations and movements over a period of time.

Conclusion

In the new millennium, mass media, government agencies, non-government organisations and social groups put forth united efforts toward creating awareness among the people about various developmental issues, trends and opportunities. The Twelth Plan (2012), called for review of rural communication and development approaches in the country. The document emphasised that communications media including the social media should be harnessed for purpose of rural development in India. The vision of twenty-first century may remain empty and the progress towards that goal tardy, if the policy makers and implementers of various rural development programmes fail to establish the communications network at various levels and widen the base of informed, skilled and competent people for participatory and balanced development in the countryside. In the absence of planned, systematic and sustainable development communication, inclusive, integrated and sustainable rural development is blocked, poverty is spread and self-reliance becomes a casualty.

References

Ghosh, Avik (2006), *Communication Technology and Human Development: Recent Experiences in the Indian Social Sector*, Sage Publications, New Delhi, p-41.

Government of India (1953), *First Five Year Plan*, The Publications Division, Ministry of Information and Broadcasting, New Delhi.

Government of India (2012), *The Twelth Plan Document*, Planning Commission, New Delhi.

Kakar, V.N. (1987), *Communication in Family Planning:* India's Experience, National Institute of Health and Family Welfare, New Delhi.

McKee, Neill (1992), *Social Mobilisation and Social Marketing in Developing Countries: Lessons from South-bound, Communicators.* Penang.

Narula, Uma (1994), *Development Communication:* Theory and Practice, Har-Anand Publications, New Delhi.

9

The Impact of MNREGA: A Case Study on the Development of Tribal Women of Birbhum District, West Bengal.

Debasis Mondal

Introduction

MNREGA has brought out a positive change especially on the employment sector in rural areas. Tribal women are individually benefitted through this scheme. They independently earn the money in order to the fulfilment of their own needs. They also provide economic contribution for the well-being of their family. Indeed, MNREGA makes out the tribal women self-reliance and self-sufficient. Tribal women are an integral part of rural economy. Most of the tribal women live below poverty line. It basically helps to improve the poor economic condition of rural poor as well as the marginalised sections of the society such as women in general. MNREGA has been enacted by the Central Government of India in August 2005, for securing jobs of hundred days for households in rural areas. It is the most remarkable landmark that was taken by the Ministry of Rural Development after independence. The aims of MNREGA is to enhance securied livelihood of rural households in India by promoting at least hundred days of guaranteed wage employment in every financial year for those, who are ready to do unskilled manual work. The primary objectives of this act is to provide wage employment in rural areas in the country and the auxiliary objective is to strengthen natural resource management through work, which are the major reasons of chronic poverty like drought, deforestation and soil erosion. The main focus of this act is employment, wage of unskilled labourers in rural areas. This act has been set up with clear aim of enhancing jobs to the unemployed rural poor especially those people, who are unskilled and living below poverty line by mentioning special remarks under this act that one third of the beneficiaries' should be women.

Scheduled Tribe women play crucial role in their family decision-making and take part in social, cultural, and economical activities of the society. MNEREGA empowers tribal women to make decision in the social and economic spheres of life. The importance of MNREGA is inevitable in the livelihood of tribal women. Today's so, MNREGA has improved the economic condition of the tribal women but there has to be greater necessity of economic empowerment of tribal women by which they can leave to keep the social barriers aside like inequality, discrimination and exploitation and walk faster in order to achieve their all-round development in the rural society. Even though, the goals can't be achieved without the active participation of tribal women. As per the census data, it has been seen that women are covering almost half of the population. Even they are not aware about their constitutional rights such as quality health-care, economic security, and access to education. For developing the condition of tribal women, MNREGA plays vital role in the rural society. Even as far as tribal society concerns, it has positive impact on changing scenario of rural livelihood of tribal women.

Literature Review

Sanjay (2012) says that women are considered as durable assets in the tribal society. The main target of MNREGA programme is intended to increase outreach to the poor and marginalised sections of the society such as women. MNREGA gives empowerment to tribal women through providing employment opportunities in the rural milieu. Some structural problems like ineffectiveness and improper implementation of scheme, social attitudes, exploitation and corruption have created question mark over the implementation of the scheme. Since the introduction of this scheme, the positive changes has taken place regarding participation of tribal women in the MNREGA, but the challenges are still ahead which creates some barriers in the way of women participation at certain levels of empowerment by providing employment opportunities in the rural areas.

A study on Implementation of MNREGA and social inclusion by Rath Jitendra (2005), stated that MNREGA has come with the objective of providing hundred days of employment to rural labourers, but it should not be seen as government welfare programme as like others. It might have welfaristic approach but more of that gives rights to the people to demand, work and earn wages to live their life. In this context, it becomes important where the most deprived, scheduled caste, scheduled tribe, women and the disabled included in the programme and got maximum benefit out of it. The state governments who are responsible for the purpose of implementing this flagship programme needs to keep it in mind. Although MNREGA is a demand driven programme and the supply of work depends on the demand made by labourers, it shall be the duty of the government to carry out awareness programmes in such a mammer, so that the most deprived gets maximum benefit.

Kumar Bebarta Prabeena (2013) observed that his paper assess the implementation of *Mahatma Gandhi National Rural Employment Guarantee Act (MNREGA)*, and its various impacts in the lives of tribal people in the district of Gajapati. It empowers the marginalised sections of the society through decentralised planning and ensures the livelihood security by creating durable assets. The tribal households in the Gajapati district have been benefitted from MNREGA in many ways as it has increased their income resulting multiple impacts in their social and economic life.

Nayak Smita (2013), observed the involvement of tribal women in the MNREGA programme in the study area was found very marginal as compared to men. Where women are involved in MNREGS, they are more likely to be exploited by their male counterpart. The study finding revealed that various bottlenecks such as lack of tribal women's involvement at the time of planning for NREGS work, lack of awareness, lack of crèche facilities at work sites, lack of women's ownership of job cards and bank accounts, wage discrimination between men and women, harassment at the workplace and lack of appropriate gender- friendly methods of information dissemination etc., have adversely impacted and questioned thus the efficacy of the MGNREGA in enhancing the status of tribal women in the study area.

Puttaraja and Heggade, O. D. (2012) remarked that the tribal women are not empowered economically as well as socially. The socio-economic empowerment of tribal women could be kept as long-term development goal in India. Economic independence and education of tribal women will go a long way in attaining self-reliance. So, development awareness, education, competitiveness, willingness, confidence, self-motivation, mindset, encouragement from family and society are essential for the economic empowerment of tribal women. Tribal women can be empowered through decreasing the poverty and problems of life like education, employment, good health and economic empowerment etc. This paper exploring the fact that lack of education, poor health status and infant mortality rate, low-level of wage work, lack of self employment opportunity, organising capacity and leadership quality are the main reasons in the way of economic empowerment of tribal women.

Poonia Jyoti (2012) noted that her paper is highlighted about the impact and women participation in MNREGA. The paper uses data from various issues of RBI Annual report. The study puts the fact MNREGA has the potential to stimulate local development, if the management and delivery are good; and that women's weak position in the labor market has been greatly helped. The evidence further suggests these benefits are due to strong state apparatus and not to the demand of citizens *per se.* This paper reviews India's approach to social protection since independence and places the MNREGA within the broader social protection discourse.

Objectives of the Study

- To examine the impact of MNREGA on tribal women development.
- To examine the coming challenges before the government for proper implementation of MNREGA.

Research Methodology

A study has been conducted in three less connected Scheduled Tribe villages of Birbhum District, West Bengal. The names of these villages are Donaipur, Jaljalia, Padmabatipur respectively, which come under Kankalitala gram panchayat of Bolpur-Sriniketan Block of Birbhum district, West Bengal. Kankalitala is one of the fifty-one *Shakti Peethas* where the dead body of *Maa Parvati* was cut by the *Lord Shiva* and the waist fell at that place. It is more or less 15 km away from the Bolpur city of Birbhum district West Bengal, where eleven km are metal road and four km that of red soil.

Research Approaches

Qualitative and Quantitative research approaches were both employed for picking up the empirical data from the field. Hence, the secondary data were picked up from various sources like books, journals, articles, conferences, published and unpublished research work etc.

Methods and Techniques

A case study method has been applied by following observation participant and in-depth interview techniques for picking up the empirical data from the field. Structure questionnaire and some open-ended questions had been used as tool of data collection.

Universe and Population

Here, the research universe is scheduled tribes and the populations are two sub-castes of the schedule tribes like Santals, Koras. The present study has been made in Kankalitala gram panchayat of Birbhum district, West Bengal. Three villages have been taken such as Donaipur, Jaljalia, Padmabatipur for the fulfilment of this research study.

Sampling Method and Sample Size

Non-probability sampling like purposive sampling were utilised here as well:

The total sample size is 71, whereas 33 Kora and 38 Santal families are the inhabitants of these villages. Hence, the total scheduled tribe population here are 311, in which 155 are females and 156 are males, respectively.

Results and Discussions

The present data has been collected from the regular field visits of the several tribal villages of Birbhum district, West Bengal. Here, I have tried to draw the real picture of the scheduled tribe in rural areas and showed the educational status of the tribal women in three villages. In fact, I have been distributed the population of three villages in various categories such as age, sex, education etc. Hence, the three tables such as distribution of village-wise population, distribution of age-wise population, distribution of sex-wise population and bar charts have been utilised for the presentation of whole primary data in this favour.

Table – 1: Distribution of Total Scheduled Tribe Households Population of Birbhum District, West Bengal

Villages	*Total House Holds*	*Percent age*	*Female*	*Percentage*	*Male*	*Percent age*	*Total*	*Percent age*
Donaipur	12	16.9	30	9.6	26	8.3	56	18.0
Jalialia	17	23.9	36	11.6	42	13.5	78	25.1
Padmabatipur	42	59.2	89	28.7	88	28.3	177	56.9
Total	71	100	155	49.9	156	50.1	311	100

Source :

In the first Table, it is denoted that the name of three villages of Birbhum district, West Bengal, where the present research study has been conducted. In the above Table, total population have been distributed by indicating clearly the total household number, segregating the different tribes existed separately in the three villages and the distribution of male and female population elaborately decorated on the basis of in-depth field survey.

Table-2: Age and Sex-wise Distribution of Scheduled Tribe Population and Percentage of Birbhum District, West Bengal

Age	Female	Percentage	Male	Percentage	Total Population	Percentage
0 to 4	11	3.50	16	5.10	27	8.6
5 to 9	12	3.90	19	6.10	42	13.1
10 to 14	10	3.20	14	4.50	24	7.6
15 to 19	15	4.80	20	6.40	35	11.5
20 to 24	16	5.20	9	2.90	25	8
25 to 29	18	5.80	17	5.40	35	11.5
30 to 34	6	1.90	14	4.40	20	6.4
35 to 39	10	3.20	7	2.20	17	5.5
40 to 44	8	5.20	9	2.90	17	5.5
45 to 49	16	5.20	9	2.90	25	8
50 to 54	5	1.60	7	2.20	12	3.8
55 to 59	5	1.60	6	1.90	11	3.5
60 to 64	7	2.30	3	0.90	10	3.2
65 to 69	6	1.90	4	1.30	10	3.2
70 to74	0	0	2	0.60	2	0.6
75 to 79	0	0	0	0	0	0
80+	0	0	0	0	0	0
Total	**155**	**49.30**	**156**	**49.70**	**311**	**100**

Source :

In this second Table, age and sex-wise population and percentage have been meticulously distributed in order to show the clear picture of the scheduled tribe villages of Birbhum district, West Bengal.

Chart 1: Age and Sex-wise Distribution of the Schedule Tribe Population of Birbhum District, West Bengal

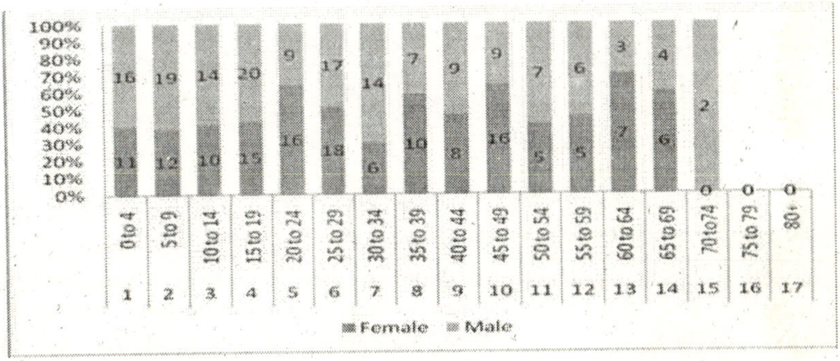

Source :

In this chart, total population has been distributed by age and sex-wise. In the age between zero to four; the total number of females and males are 11 and 16; five to nine; the total numbers of females and males are 12 and 19; 10 to 14 the total numbers of females and males are 10 and 14; 15 to 19; the total numbers of females and males are 15 and 20, 20 to 24; the total numbers of females and males are 16 and 9; 25 to 29; the total numbers of females and males are 18 females and 17 males, 30 to 34; the total numbers of females and males are six and 14, 35 to 39 the total numbers of females and males are 10 and 7 , 40 to 44; the total numbers of females and males are eight and nine, 45 to 49; the total numbers of females and males are 16 and 9;50 to 54; the total numbers of females and males are five and seven , 55 to 59; the total numbers of females and males are five and six, 60 to 64; the total numbers of females and males are seven and three, 65 to 69; the total numbers of females and males are six and four , 70 to 74; the total numbers of females and males are zero and two, 75 to 79; the total numbers of females and males are none are existed respectively.

Chart- 2: Percentage of the Scheduled Tribe Population by Age and Sex-wise of Birbhum District, West Bengal.

	0 to 4	5 to 9	10 to 14	15 to 19	20 to 24	25 to 29	30 to 34	35 to 39	40 to 44	45 to 49	50 to 54	55 to 59	60 to 64	65 to 69	70 to 74	75 to 79	80 +
Female%	3.5	3.9	3.2	4.8	5.2	5.8	1.9	3.2	5.2	5.2	1.6	1.6	2.3	1.9	0%	0%	0%
Male%	5.1	6.1	4.5	6.4	2.9	5.4	4.4	2.2	2.9	2.9	2.2	1.9	0.9	1.3	0.6	0%	0%

In this chart, the total population has been denoted by age and sex. The percentages of each category being segregated from the age between zero to four the percentage of female and male are 3.5 per cent and 5.1 per cent , five to nine, the percentage of female and male are 3.9 per cent and 6.1 per cent , 10 to 14, the percentage of female and male are 3.2 per cent .and 4.5 per cent, 15 to 19, the percentage of female and male are 4.8 per cent and 6.4 per cent , 20 to 24, the percentage of female and male are 5.2 per cent and 2.9 per cent, 25 to

29, the percentage of female and male are 5.8 per cent and 5.4 per cent, 30 to 34, the percentage of female and male are 1.9 per cent and 4.4 per cent, 35 to 39, the percentage of female and male are 3.2 per cent and 2.2 per cent, 40 to 44, the percentage of female and male are 5.2 per cent and 2.9 per cent , 45 to 49, 5.2 per cent and 2.9 per cent, 50 to 54, the percentage of female and male are 1.6 per cent and 2.2 per cent, 55 to 59, the percentage of female and male are 1.6 per cent and 1.9 per cent, 60 to 64, the percentage of female and male are 2.3 per cent and 0.9 per cent, 65 to 69, the percentage of female and male are 1.9 per cent to 1.3 per cent, 70 to 74, the percentage of female and male are zero per cent and 0.6 per cent, 75 to 79, the percentage of female and male are none and 80+ the percentage of female and male are none respectively.

Table-3: Sex-wise Primary Occupational Status Distribution of the Schedule Tribe Population and Percentage of Birbhum District, West Bengal

Category	*Female*	*Percentage*	*Male*	*Percentage*	*Total*	*Percentage*
Agriculture	11	6.2	32	17.8	43	24
Day Labour	31	17.6	44	24.3	75	41.9
100 Days Work	30	17.0	7	3.70	37	20.7
Old Ration Money	12	6.7	2	1.0	14	7.7
Government Service	0	0	1	0.50	1	0.6
Business	1	0.6	0	0	1	0.6
Other Services	3	1.7	5	2.8	8	4.5
Total	88	49.9	91	50.1	179	100

Source :

In this Table, sex-wise primary occupational status of the Schedule Tribes of Donaipur, Jaljalia,Padmabatipur, Birbhum district, West Bengal, have been categorised in percentage as per data concerned.

Chart-3: Distribution of Sex-wise (Population) Primary Occupational Status of Birbhum District, West Bengal

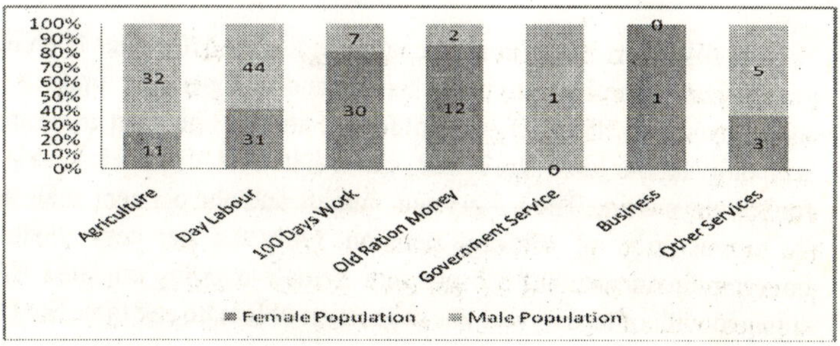

Source :

In this chart, sex-wise primary occupational status of the schedule tribes has been categorically distributed. In agricultural fields, the numbers of female and male population are 11 and 32. In day labour segment, the number of female and male population are 31 and 44. In 100 days work, the number of females and males are 30 and seven. The number of people getting old age pension twelve are females and two are males. Only one male government service holder has been found among three villages. One female doing business. The persons involved with other services are three females, five males respectively.

Chart-4: Distribution of Sex-wise (Percentage) Primary Occupational Status of Birbhum District, West Bengal

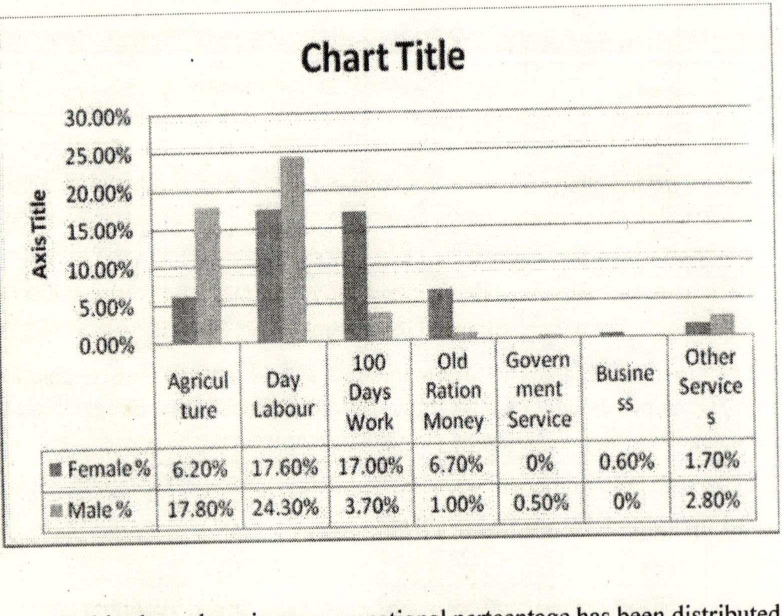

	Agriculture	Day Labour	100 Days Work	Old Ration Money	Government Service	Business	Other Services
Female%	6.20%	17.60%	17.00%	6.70%	0%	0.60%	1.70%
Male %	17.80%	24.30%	3.70%	1.00%	0.50%	0%	2.80%

In this chart, the primary occupational pertcentage has been distributed categorically.The 6.2 per cent of female and 17.8 per cent male are involved with agriculture. The 17.5 per cent female and 24.3 per cent male are engaged with daily labour jobs. The 17 per cent female and 3.7 per cent male are going for 100 days work. The 6.7 per cent female and one per cent male are getting the oppurtunity of old-age pension. Only 0.5 per cent male is doing government service and 0.5 per cent female is doing business. The people engaged with other services, the proportion of female and male are 1.7 per cent and 2.8 respectively.

Chart-5: Distribution of Sex-wise (Total Population) Employment Status of Birbhum District, West Bengal.

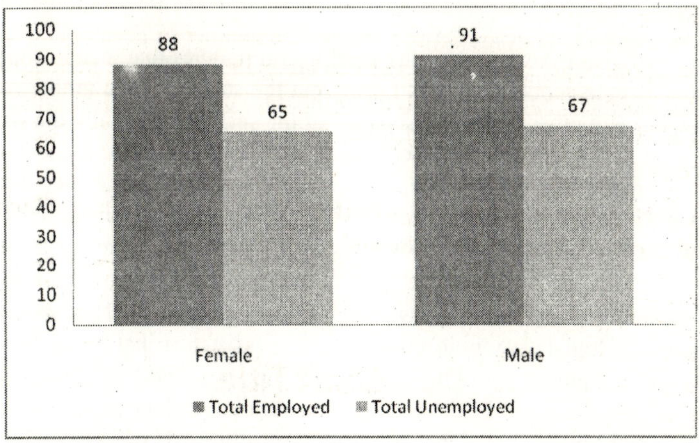

In this chart, sex-wise employment status of the scheduled tribes has been distributed accordingly. Hence, the total 88 females and 91 males are employed and the 65 females and 67 males are unemployed as well.

Chart-6: Distribution of the Employment Status of the Scheduled Tribes (Total Population and Percentage) of Birbhum District, West Bengal

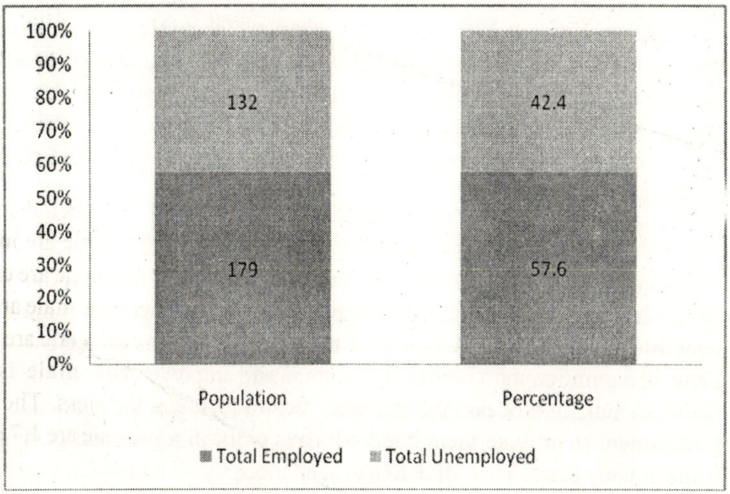

In this chart, it has been indicated that the total number of people are employed and unemployed of these scheduled tribes' villages of Birbhum district, West Bengal. Here, the total 179 means 57.6 per cent people are employed and total 132 means 42.4 per cent people are unemployed per as the chart concerned.

MGNREGA is one of the most useful policies that lead to support the poor people economically and bring out the social change in the life of the weaker and other backward sections of the society, especially the women at the grassroot level. It has provided economic empowerment to the poor tribal women and has a greater impact on rural life. The poor women have been benefitted most with the arrival of this MNREGA. They get themselves secured and self-reliante. Even, they feel very happy to earn money through the MNREGA work. MNREGA empowers the tribal women to make the decision in their family. So, MNREGA has changed the status of the rural poor by providing them hundred days' jobs in a year. In fact, most of the tribal women have taken MNREGA jobs as one of their primary occupation. Tribal women are likely, to work in agricultural fields on daily basis. They spend the money every day in order to bear the cost of the household expenditure. Having visited the fields several times and interacting with the tribal women, they are very much like to work in MNREGA project. Hence, some factors are influencing the tribal women to work in MNREGA. These factors are as (1) the timing of the work is only five to six hours (2) unskilled labour required, (3) standard mode of payment, (4) cultural factor. The last factor is very essential which encourage them to work in MNREGA. Cultural factor means they are very down to the earth. They like to work in natural environment. They are very much nature lovers and the protector of the environment. Any work which is related to the forests, soil, agriculture, they love to do it because the tribal people have their own tradition and culture. Now, women in tribal society are considered as an asset and sending their women to the MNREGA work. MNREGA build positive attitudes among the women in tribal areas. Despite some challenges before the government, the dissatisfaction was seen among the beneficiaries. Qualitatively, interacting with the tribal women, it has been revealed that some problems recurred for the implementation of this act

Firstly, the government has failed to provide 100 days work in a year.

Secondly, they are getting late payment. Indeed, if the government has succeeded to overcome these problems, then the tribal women will be more benefitted. So, MNREGA is one of the most wonderful projects that have given economic support to the tribal women and empower them to take part in decision-making process in their family. Nowadays, it is the challenge of the government to provide them hundred days work in a year and paying their wage in daily basis. That MNREGA is enhanced the livelihood of the tribal as well as the rural poor, weaker and the backward sections of the society. So, the implementation of this policy has to be much emphasised for providing 100 days work in a year and paying the labourers wage in time.

Conclusions

The present study depicted the picture that MNREGA helps the tribal women in the way of economic development. It provides economic empowerment to the tribal women and leads to take the decision to in their family. They spend the money in social and economic spheres of life like education, health and for their own purpose, MNREGA not only provides empowerment to the poor women but also make them capable and self-reliance. Hence, MNREGA itself is a popular scheme for the economic development of rural poor and the backward sections of the society which ensures the hundred days of work and income to the tribal women in order to achieve the sustainable long term livelihood and gender equality in the tribal society. So forth, improving the status of tribal women, the problems of MNREGA implementation should be resolved and removes the barriers keeping aside to increase the women participation at greater level. Indeed, this Government policy has an enormous impact on women employment as well as rural development at this present juncture.

References

Illuru Narendra Kumar and Suneetha Kondeti - 2014, "Impact of MNREGA Programme, in Karnataka" *Review of Research, Vol -3, Issue- 4, Jan. 2014.*

Kar Spandita 2013, "Empowerment of Women through MGNREGS: Issues and Challenges", *Odisha Review; February - March, 2013.*

Khera Reetika and Nayak Nandini – 2009, "Women Workers and Perceptions of the National Rural Employment Guarantee Act," *Economic and Political Weekly, October 24, 2009, Volume- XIV, No - 4349.*

Kumar Bebarta Prabeena- 2013, "Impact of MGNREGA in the Lives of Tribal People" : A Study of Rayagada Block in Gajapati District, *Odisha Review, February - March- 2013.*

Nayak Smita-2013, "Impact of MGNREGA on Status of Tribal Women in Odisha: A Case Study of Rajgangapur Block of Sundergarh District," *Journal of Agriculture and Environmental Sciences, Vol. - 2 No. - 2, December 2013.*

Poonia Jyoti - 2012, "Critical Study of MGNREGA: Impact and Women's

Participation", International Journal of Human Development and Management Sciences" Volume -1. No-1 (January-December, 2012), Mind Reader Publications.

Poorani R, and Jahan Kamar 2013 "Empowerment of Rural Women Through MGNREGS, An Overview", *Indian Stream Research Journal, Volume-3, Issue-10, November, 2013.*

Pradhan Sanjay Kumar, 2012, "The NREGA and Rural Women: Employment Opportunities and Challenges", *International Conference on Inclusive and Sustainable Growth (Role of Industries, Government and Civil Societies', October 4-6, 2012, Organised by IMT and BAIF.*

Prasad K.V.S., 2012, "Performance of Mahatma Gandhi National Rural Employment Guarantee Act (MGNREGA): An Overview" International Journal of Management and Business Studies, (IJMBS), Vol. -2, Issue - 4, October- December 2012.

Puttaraja and Heggade O. D. 2012, "Economic Empowerment of Tribal Women in Karnataka: A Case Study in Mysore and Chamarajanagara Districts", *Study Tribes and Tribals, 10(2): 173-81, Kamla Raj.*

Rout Gurukalyana, 2013, "Women Need More Protection Through MGNREGA: Role of Gram Sabha and PRIs", *Inernational Journal of Social Science Volume, 2 no. 2, December 2013: pp.129-39.*

Saravanan M., 2013, "Impact Assessment of Mahatma Gandhi National Rural Employment Guarantee Scheme On Rural Women Empowerment", Golden Research Thoughts, Volume-3, Issue-2, August, 2013.

Thomas Bigi and Bhatia Ruby, 2012, "Impact of NREGA Scheme: A Study on the overall Quality of life of its Beneficiaries", *Asia Pacific Journal of Social Sciences, Volume 4(2), July–December 2012, pp.213-27.*

10

Resource Use Efficiency of Sugarcane Growers in Karnataka

N. T. Somashekaraiah

Introduction

Cultivation of sugarcane in India dates back to the Vedic period. The earliest mention of sugarcane cultivation is found in Indian writings of the period 1400 to 1000 BC. It is now widely accepted that India is the original home of *Saccharum species. Saccharum barberi* and *Polynesian* group of island especially New Guinea is the centre of origin of *S. officinarum*. It belongs to family *Gramineae (Poaceae)*, class *monocotyledons* and order *glumaceae* sub-family *panicoidae*, tribe *Andripogoneae* and sub-tribe *saccharininea*. The cultivated canes belong to two main groups: (a) thin, hardy north Indian types *S.barberi* and *S.Sinense* and (b) thick, juicy noble canes *Saccharum officinarum*. Highly prized cane is *S. officinarum*.

Sugarcane is an important commercial crop in the country occupying about 4.36 million hectare with an annual production of 281.6 million tonne (2002-03). Sugarcane occupies about three per cent of the total cultivated area and it is one of the most important cash crops, contributing about seven and half per cent of the gross value of agricultural production. About 50 million farmers depend on sugarcane cultivation for livelihood and equal number of agricultural labourers earn their living by working in sugarcane farms. Sugarcane is the primary raw material for major sweeteners produced in the country. It also supports two important cottage industries; *viz., gur* (Jaggery) and *khandsari* industries, which together produce about 10 million tonne of sweeteners (*gur* and *khandsari* sugar) consuming about 28-35 per cent of the cane produced.

As per 2012-13 data, sugarcane occupies an area of 4.25 lakh hectares with production of 357.32 lakh tonnes of cane in Karnataka. The productivity in the state is high (84.40 tha) as compared to the national average (64.6 tha) with more than 50 sugar factories (Anon, 2005). Karnataka sugar industry ranks third in terms of its of contribution sugar to total sugar production and stand fourth in the country in the area of cultivation of sugarcane. The sugar industry in Karnataka has more than 50 sugar factories distributed well across the state. The major benefits of Karnataka sugar industry are it has generated many facilities in the state such as communication, employment and transport. The major sugar factories of Karnataka sugar industry are Godavari Sugar Mills Ltd., Bannari Amman sugar Ltd. and Sri Chamundeswari Sugars Ltd. The total sugar production of Karnataka sugar industry was 17.98 lakh tonnes in 2003-04, in 2004-05 the figure came down to 11.57 lakh tonnes, and in 2005-06 the figure increased marginally to 13 lakh tons (DSO, 2007). The sugar industry in Karnataka contributes around Rs. 36 crore every year to the state exchequer in central excise duty.

National development could be achieved only by the rural development. Rural development means overall development of rural areas to improve the quality of rural people. Quality of life is determined by number of factors like income, employment, education, good health including nutritious food. This rural development is done only by the increasing standard of living of the sugarcane growers. Because, sugarcane cultivation is one of the important key factors of rural development. When the sugarcane growers are economically strong no doubt about there is existence of rural development.

In rural development, resource use efficiency of sugarcane growers occupies an important place. Resource use efficiency means that land, human labour, animal labour, capital, seeds, fertilisers, organic manures, power, pesticides, and credit for sugarcane cultivation are used in an efficient manner. The tube-well irrigation confers number of benefits, both direct and indirect, on the community. It paves the way for adoption of multiple cropping and use of modern inputs including improved varieties of seeds, thereby enhancing sugarcane production. It stabilises crop yield by saving crop from drought situation and increases employment potential in rural areas through changes in cropping pattern. Studies have shown significant change in the resource use efficiency of sugarcane growers.

Objectives

The main objectives of this paper are:

- To analyse the resource use efficiency of sugarcane growers in study area;
- To identify the various findings in resource use efficiency of sugarcane growers and suggestions.

Methodology

To achieve the above objectives, the present study was carried out in Hassan district of Karnataka. A three-stage random sampling technique was adopted to select the taluk, villages and the farmers. Accordingly, out of the total of eight taluks in the district, one taluk *i.e.,* Channarayapatna was selected as first stage unit of sampling representing irrigated taluk on the basis of selected economic indicators. For the selection of sample villages, the second stage unit, the villages are listed out and four villages under selected taluk were selected using random sampling procedures. All the sugarcane growers in the selected villages are listed out. From each sample village, 25 sugarcane growers are selected in probability proportional to the existing number in each category in the selected village. Thus, the study covers 100 sample households, which were selected for the primary survey considering their experience in sugarcane growing, land holding sizes and other relevant characteristics.

The study is based on both the primary and secondary sources of data. The primary sources are the sugarcane growers. Appropriate statistical tools were used in accordance the with needs to analyse various aspects of resource use efficiency in Research work, Stochastic Frontier Production Model, Paired'T' test, and ANOVA test were used.

Estimates of Frontier Production Function and Technical Efficiency

This study has adopted stochastic frontier production function to measure the resource use efficiency of sugarcane growers in study area. The study is carried out in Channarayapatna taluk and covers one crop like sugarcane. The sugarcane crop requires more capital, labour and fertilisers etc., the analysis of factors contributing to the output variables and the result of CD production function of sugarcane crop is presented in the following table.

Table -1: Estimates of Stochastic Frontier Production Function for Sugarcane Cultivators

Variables	*OLS*	*ML (Half Normal)*
Constant	0.2042* (0.0053)	0.3851** (0.0225)
Human Labour	0.1469** (0.0570)	0.2626** (0.0547)
Animal Labour	0.1189 (0.3590)	0.1477 (0.3323)
Capital	0.4201** (0.0410)	0.5399** (0.0435)
Seed	0.1934 (0.2881)	0.1668 (0.8932)
Organic Manure	0.1586 (0.3148)	0.1832 (0.1211)
Fertilizer	0.2514** (0.0276)	0.3290** (0.0294)
Pesticides	0.1289 (0.3813)	0.1025 (0.1488)
σ2	0.5718	0.1457** (0.0201)
Γ	15.2481	21.6917
Log - Likelihood		0.5681 (0.0824)
γ2		23.3376
No of Iteration		31

Source: 1. Figures in parentheses indicates standard errors.

2. * and ** indicates one per cent and five per cent significant level, respectively.

The results of OLS and ML estimates of the parameters for sugarcane crop are reported in column no two and column no three in above Table. OLS estimation results indicate that the estimated co-efficient of all the input variables are positive, but only three of them are found to be statistically significant namely, human labour, capital and fertiliser. Although remaining inputs have positive influence on output their influence is not significant. It is found that the elasticity of capital was higher than the other inputs-elasticity in terms of magnitude and animal labour is less sensitive when compare to other inputs. In study area, Cheni and Pattapatti are the popular local varieties of sugarcane. Cheni or Marakabbu is a thin white cane which takes 12 to 18 months to mature, but give good juice and is largely grown in the study area. Pattapati is not as hard as Cheni, but responds well to manuring and capable of yielding fine jaggery. The improved varieties introduced recently are C.O.419 and I.C 26 which now occupy about 50 to 60 per cent of the total area under sugarcane. The water requirement of the crop depends upon the variety of cane, the nature of the soil and the amount of rainfall. The average yield per acre is nearly about 40 to 50 tonne. Out of the production of sugarcane, 60 to 70 per cent of the cane was used for crushing and the remaining for preparing jaggery, seed and chewing purposes.

The processes involved in raising sugarcane crop involve intensive work by human labour; and this work cannot be done in phased manner, and has to be finished within reasonable period of time. The processes which demand such attention are sowing or planting, weeding and crushing. As the work involved in these processes is heavy and has to be finished at a stretch, family labour alone cannot cope with it. Naturally, therefore, the sugarcane cultivator has to hired labour as supplement to family labour. Besides, it may be noted that the farmer is now more willing to pay for hired labour, because he expects that his crop will yield him reasonably good return. Under sugarcane cultivation, more capital was used for the purpose of purchasing quality seeds, floughing, plantation, weeding, maintaining plants, apply of fertilisers and transportation for crushing etc. Sometimes sugarcane is also affected by some disease. For example, when the plants are about two months old, the stem-borers or top shoot-borers may affect and kill the plant. It encourages the more use of pesticides in sugarcane cultivation. Therefore, in sample villages of sugarcane cultivation, the majority of farmers have used more capital, labour, fertilisers and pesticides for the purpose of grown sugarcane. It indicates that the estimated co-efficient of all the inputs variables are positive but only three of them (as per result) are found to be statistically significant namely human labour, capital and fertiliser.

The results of ML estimates indicate all factor inputs have positive signs and here also human labour, capital and fertilizer are significant in influencing the production of sugarcane. σ^2 and σ terms are positive and statistically significant for this crop also which indicate the observe outputs differ significantly from frontier outputs due to factors within the control of farmers. The likelihood ratio test σ^2 rejected the null hypothesis of $\sigma = 0$. The results shows that estimated value of σ is 0.58, implying that about 58 per cent of the difference between actual and potential outputs is primarily due to technically inefficient performance of cultivators. The assumption of hicks' neutral technical change is supported by the results.

As per analysis, the factors contributing to the output variables and the result of CD production function of sugarcane crop is presented in Table 2, indicate that labour, capital, fertiliser and pesticides are significant and other input variables namely, seed, animal labour and organic manure are not significantly influenced on sugarcane. It is observed that the elasticity of capital and labour was higher than other input elasticity in terms of magnitude and animal labour has less sensitive when compared to other inputs.

Chart No– 2. Technical Efficiency Levels of Sugarcane Cultivators

Frequency distribution of technical efficiencies for sugarcane cultivators is shown in the following Chart No.2. The result (Chart No.2) reveals that 26 per cent of sugarcane farmers have technical efficiency between 80 per cent to 90 per cent followed by 22 per cent between 90 per cent to 100 per cent, 20 per cent between 70 per cent to 80 per cent, 10 per cent between 40 per cent to 50 per cent and six per cent between 50 per cent to 60 per cent. This indicates that technical efficiency of sugarcane is more dispersed, which is revealed by the higher value of SD 17.81.

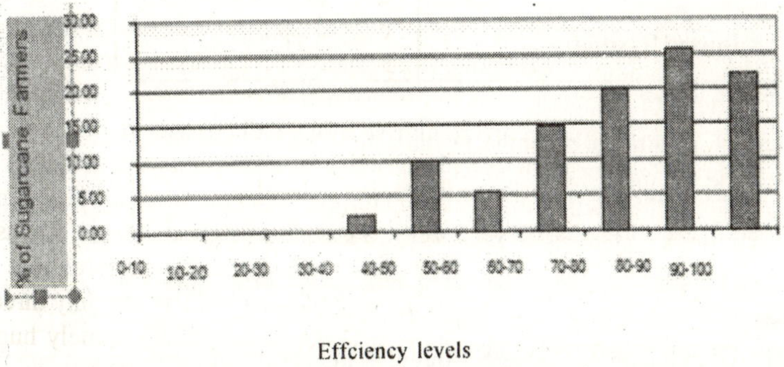

The mean efficiency of sugarcane growers is 76 per cent. Hence, the sugarcane growers have an opportunity to increase nearly about 24 per cent of output with given input. Hence, there is scope for farmer to increase output with existing input and improve their income.

Determinants of Technical Efficiency in Sugarcane

As revealed in the previous section, that is the levels of technical efficiency of cultivators are not similar due to several factors influencing technical efficiency of sugarcane growers.

Table 3: Estimates of Determinants of Technical Efficiency in Sugarcane

Variable	Sugarcane
C	0.078373
	(0.813914)
AGE	-0.023410
	(0. 13890)
EDUCATION	0.363270*
	(0. 03410)
CASTE-2	0.216683
	(0.900813)
CASTE-3	0.101036
	(0.278412)
LAND SIZE-2	0.252320
	(0.289096)
LAND SIZE-3	0.105213
	(0.380508)
Adjusted R- square	0.5728

Note: 1. Figures in parentheses indicates standard errors.

2. * indicates one per cent significant level.

The study has estimated the determinants of technical efficiency by including age, education, and caste and land size as determinants. The results are shown in the above Table No-three, as per results of the determinants of technical efficiency of sugar cane shown in column No 2 of Table 3. It reveals that the education has played a significant role in achieving higher level of technical efficiency. The influence of age on technical efficiency is negative. There were no significant differences in technical efficiency between caste and land sizes.

To measure the resource use efficiency of selected crop the study has employed stochastic frontier production function. The results of frontier analysis indicate human labour, capital, fertilisers and pesticides are more significant influence on production of selected crop like sugarcane. The average mean technical efficiencies of selected crop are 76 per cent. The study indicates that sugar cane growers are less efficient. Further the study, estimated the determinants of technical efficiency of selected crop. The result reveals that only education is found to be significant in enhancing efficiency of sample crop growers.

The analysis revealed that the non-availability of assured irrigation leads to, low level usage of fertilisers and in turn, low yields in some of the regions of the state, and thus there are enough indications about importance of tube-well irrigation in the agricultural production. Further, significant intra-farm variations in the usage of important inputs at the district level, leads to variations in the efficiency levels of farmers in the cultivation of sugarcane. The results also showed that education and rainfall have significantly influenced the technical efficiency levels of sugarcane growers. Thus, public investments in the irrigation and education would go a long way in increasing the agricultural productivity as well as, bridging the gap between the efficiency levels of sugarcane growers, besides achieving the individual efficiencies to the optimum. The existing gap between the realised and potential yield highlights the need for improving farmers' practices through extension services and training programs.

Major Findings

The major findings of this study are as follows.

- Among the inputs used by sample farmers between crops, human labour, capital and fertiliers are found to significantly influence production, whereas other inputs have less influence on production.
- The study found that only certain level of education significantly influence the technical efficiency levels of cultivators in sugarcane studied. Other variables like age, caste and land size are insignificant.
- The result shows that education of farmers has helped in the efficient use of resources in the study area.

Findings, Suggestions and Recommendations

The study of the resource use efficiency of sugarcane growers in sugarcane cultivation has led to the following findings, suggestions and recommendations.

- The present study highlights that the majority of sugarcane growers belong to small and marginal farmers' category. But, the condition of small and marginal farmers in the study area needs an exhaustive re-appraisal. In spite of their receiving proportionately more substantial benefits of irrigation, some positive steps have to be taken to raise their standard of living. A considerable proportion of small and marginal farmers live below the poverty line: a good number of them are even below the critical line. Therefore, it is essential that the Government, in the face of the very low-level of living of these classes of agriculturists, should formulate and implement policies to ameliorate their conditions on permanent basis. Otherwise, the entire exercise of investment in irrigation and other planned programmes of economic development at the district level would be self-defeating. In the ultimate analysis, social benefits and social justice, even if they are congruent, should coincide.

- Water management under tube wells becomes very poor that is why the availability of water for irrigation is negligible even when monsoons are successful. Therefore, the system of water management has to be introduced. The treated water should be available for domestic purposes. Thus, much water can be saved which would be used by many more household families.

- In study area, the location of tube-well point is at present done on the traditional basis, which should be replaced by scientific method and provide proper guidance to the sugarcane growers at the time of digging tube-wells by Irrigation and Agricultural Department. And, there should be a regulatory methodology to see that there is a considerable distance between one tube-well and another.

- In study area, the lack of transport facility is affecting severely on sugarcane crop. Majority of the sugarcane growers have sold their products at low prices to local agents. Therefore, the road transport facilities may be provided to the remote villages, so as to help the farmers bring their products to the market area and avoid the role of middlemen.

- In tube-well irrigation, water supply for irrigation depends on continuous working of electric motors. This is possible if power supply is not interrupted. It has been observed that planned power shutdown is a regular feature. Unpredicted and sudden closing down of power stations is also familiar. This affects the working of pumping house of tube-well irrigation, and water supply for irrigating farms is not available. To encourage production, supply of electric power must be provided to marginal and small farmers regularly.

- As per sugarcane growers opinion, there is was that not sufficient price to their crops. Therefore, the government is requested to increase the procurement price of sugarcane.

- The main problem of sugarcane growers in study area is the lack of availability of credit. The majority of the marginal sugarcane growers have taken loan from money lenders. Some of them are unable to obtain tube-well due to lack of finance even they have more land. It is suggested that the nationalised banks and co-operative banks lend more credit for the digging of tube wells and the conditions of borrowing may be liberalised.

- Some of the sugarcane growers used low quality seeds due to lack of knowledge. Therefore, the government is requested to provide good quality seeds and give proper guidance about various deceases.

- There is inequality of sugarcane production because some farmers produced more per acre but some farmers are produced less per acre even though they have used same materials. For example, Farmer A produced 60 to 80 tonnes of sugarcane per acre but farmer B produced only 40 to 50 tonnes with same materials used by the farmer A. This low yield lead to the high cost of production for A. Therefore, Agricultural and Horticultural Officers must be giving the proper advice to the low yield farmers. If these farmers enhance their production definitely the cost of production is less and they gain more profit and land is also saved, Saved land is use for cultivation of another crop.

- Crushing problem is affected on sugarcane cultivation. Majority of sugarcane growers in the study area are suffering this problem. Sometimes sugarcane burned by farmers due to the delay of crushing. Therefore, the government is requested to give proper guidance to sugar industries to make an arrangement for crushing at right time and providing attractive prices to sugarcane cultivators. Sugar factory is also providing good qualities of seeds to the farmers.

- Marginal sugarcane growers are unable to purchase the farm implements. Therefore, a complete set of farm implements and a pair of bullocks must be provided in kind through loan finance.

- In some sample villages in study area, some sugarcane growers does not have any idea about the check dams and rain harvesting. It is necessary to awaken the farmers to construct check dams and to adopt the rain harvesting for the purpose of maintaining the water table. The government must be constructing some check dams in all villages with the help of sugarcane growers. Otherwise, the water level is become down within short period.

- It was found that under sugarcane cultivation, hired labour was used more in sugarcane crop and family labour was found to be underutilised. Therefore, the hired labour should be decreased and when-ever family labour is available it can be efficiently utilised.
- Majority of sugarcane growers in the study area use maximum quantity of chemical fertilisers in cultivation of sugarcane crop. As a result, the fertility of land is become decrease. It is necessary to develop organic farming for sustainability. Uses of chemical fertilisers may be decreased and encouragement should be given for earthwarm and organic manure.
- In study area, number of sugarcane growers does not have any knowledge about the sprinkler and drip-irrigation system. Maximum gallon of water can be waste. It needs to adopt sprinkler and drip irrigation for sugarcane crop.
- Tractor power not efficiently utilised and products and by products from allied activities were found to be unsold. Therefore, the sugarcane growers must be utilising the tractor power systematically and the government is requested to create marketing facilities to products of allied activities. More concentration of by products has to be thought of and allied agricultural activities should be increased.
- In sample villages, the livestock density was very less. Therefore, the livestock should be increased for better prosperity.

Conclusion

The study shows that, when the government should be providing good transport facilities, crushing facilities, quality seeds, credit facilities, procurement price, irrigation facilities and encouragement to sugarcane growers, the sugarcane growers are able to utilise the available resources in efficient manner. This indicates that, these facilities are enhancing the resource use efficiency of the sugarcane growers. Therefore, the resource use efficiency in sugarcane is always depending upon the available sufficient facilities requiring water management. I hope this study can provide useful information to the planners in pursuit of rural development through increasing resource use efficiency of the sugarcane growers.

Bibliography

Adinarayana, S. (1984), "Impact of Irrigation unemployment Farm Productivity and Income Under Kakatiya Canal of Sri Ram Sagar Project in Andhra Pradesh", *Indian Journal of Agricultural Economics, 39(3), 543.*

Aditi Mukherji (2007), "Implications of Alternative Institutional Arrangements in Ground Water Sharing", Economic and Political Weekly", Mumbai.

Alshi M.R and V.D. Galgalikar (1984), "*Impact of Irrigation on Productivity of Wheat"*, Indian Journal of Agricultural Economics, 39 (3), p. 550.

Coward E. W. (1980), "*Irrigation and Agricultural Development in Asia*", Cornell University Press, Ithaca, London.

Dhawan B. D. (1982), "Development of Tube well Irrigation in India, Agricole, New Delhi.

Dhawan B.D. (1994), Irrigation in India's Agricultural Development. Commonwealth Publishers, New Delhi.

Dr Ne.Thi Somashekar, Karnataka Arthikathe, Chaithra Book House, Bangalore.

Somashekaraiah N.T. and Dr. S. Mahendra Kumar (2008), "Impact of Irrigation on Agricultural Production", Anmol Publication, New Delhi.

11

Livelihood Strategies of Poor Household and its Significance in Rural Development

Meghadeepa Chakraborty

Introduction

Households in the rural areas are heterogeneous in nature, their vulnerability towards shock; their coping mechanism in dealing with situations and their ability to absorb the benefits of different initiatives also vary accordingly. The Poor who experience internal and external (Ellis, 1998) shocks, fight every day to survive under the threat of structural changes, environment degradation, and natural calamities, etc., that often make them vulnerable in terms of having food security, livelihood, and poverty reduction (Tessema, 2005). Under such circumstances, poor people are constantly engaged in formulating strategies at different levels for different situations that are diverse and complex (Chelliah and Sudarshan, 1999). They have their own perspective, judgments, wishes and priorities (Becker, 1997), taking decisions at the household level, considering their available assets and making choices in terms of available options, looking at the feasibility, relative cost and expected return of each option (Mahoney, 2006) to respond to their immediate pressure for their survival.

While talking of livelihood, it becomes important to focus the research on the household level, because it is ultimately household that gets affected by any action taken by the individual family member for their survival. Messer and Townsley (2003:7), rightly said that "household livelihood and the strategies that people use to create them are at the core of development. People may be involved in different social and economic activities as individuals, but it is at the household level the real impacts of those activities are seen most clearly, and that well-being of the household is generally a key objective for most of the people, at least in rural societies."

The basic assumption underlying livelihood research is that rural households aim to secure livelihood and come out of poverty by formulating strategies based on the assets portfolio, both tangible and intangible, and on their capacity to take advantage of the livelihood opportunities. As poverty is the outcome of inadequate livelihood, so under such circumstances, it is important to pay explicit attention to the actions of the people, the choices they make, the decisions they take to respond to different vulnerable situations at the local level to achieve livelihood security.

In the livelihood studies, literature being generated upon people's livelihood in relation to their ecology, natural resources, community, institutions, but there is a dearth of studies focussing on the internal aspects of households, such as their preferences, their aspirations, culture, beliefs etc., in strategy making within household *vis-à-vis* external and overall vulnerability context. Moreover, the literature discuss the strategy in the context of outbreak of physical hazards and put less attention on the everyday risk, stress and shock in people's life and their strategy of dealing and managing their life to reduce the vulnerabilities. Wherever, there is any event, it immediately affects individuals, living in household and as a whole affects the livelihood of the household.

It is important to address the question on household action and reasons for that under different situations. However, there is a dearth of available knowledge about the process and strategies (Ellis, 2000). The importance of understanding the household as an individual unit emerges from the fact that it is the household that absorbs all the shocks and stress at the first place and remains vulnerable to the situation. The process of managing day-to-day stress and managing the crisis for the future is important to understand. With the similar vein, Krishna (2006), suggested that to provide poor with meaningful assistance, it ought to be most important to develop understanding about the household strategies, their understanding about poverty within certain social context which lack in the government policy towards reducing poverty.

To bring effective policy or programmes for the rural poor, it is important to develop detail understanding about rural poor action in different situations as high-income risk, climatic risk, economic fluctuation, etc., and individual specific shock that often makes the household's vulnerability more acute.

Considering the background above discussed, the study comes out with the broad research question such as 'How does rural household manages the livelihood' in the context of livelihood vulnerabilities that is experienced through risks, stress and shock due to internal and external factors at the household level.

The paper set out with the aim to explore the livelihood strategies that rural poor household formulates to deal with different situations to minimise the risk and attain secured and better livelihood.

Identified Scope of Study from the Review Literature

The review of literature gives an impression that there is wide range of literature in livelihood research, both conceptual and empirical. There is much literature on the concept of 'livelihood' and on 'sustainable livelihood' (Mahapatra, 2007). There are studies on livelihood focussing on the holistic approach, people's access to different assets, poor people's vulnerability, and multi-faceted nature of livelihoods (Dorward *et al,* 2003). There is literature on household that reflects on more optimistic households, studies that approach household from livelihood perspective and shows how people are able to survive (DeHann and Zoomers, 2005). Literature on rural livelihood diversification is considered an individual or household level survival strategy (Ellis, 1998), exploration of what is the range of pathways of change over period and what are multiple determinants of these Scoones and Woolmer, (2000). There are studies on household strategies and household livelihood strategies (Emigh, 2001; Carter and Barrett., 2006; Hunter, 2006; Rakodi, 1991; Wallace, 2002; Orr, 2001). Study by Lovenbalk *et al* (2003) aimed to look at the farmers' motivation for decision-making on agricultural intensification, Mahapatra's (2007) study on livelihood pattern of agricultural labour households in rural India, Brycesons (1996) study on reasons for de-diversification, literature related to livelihood and migration (Rafique , 2006; McDowell , 2007). There is literature that discuss household decisions to follow coping strategies for risk management, (Dercon 1999; Kochar 1995, as cited in Dercon, 1999). A study by Devereux (1993) tried to understand decision-making of households among various strategies. Pomeroy *et al.* (2006) tried to understand the root cause of vulnerability of coastal people and communities in South and South East Asia.

The spectrum of literature has limited scope in having focussed studies on household livelihood strategies. Much of the literature on livelihood, and especially sustainable livelihood approach talks about types of strategies that households adopt for making their living; however, there is a lack of focus on the characteristics of strategies, factors other than assets influence the strategy formation, nuances in those strategies. Lots of work has been done on livelihood strategies, bounded under coping and adaptive strategies. However, elaborate discussion on specific strategies by households within that broad categories are less discussed.

It has been observed that though livelihood strategy holds an important position in the framework, it is not discussed much beyond typology of strategies and thus lacks insights into the factors influencing these strategies, the process of formation of the strategy, reasons behind adopting a particular strategies by household, decision-making at household, etc. The review gave an impression that the strategies are studied and discussed in the literature in the context of specific crisis such as drought, flood, changes in the policies or climatic variations; in short, more in terms of external factors, whereas these studies have limited focus on the strategies in course of regular day struggles of life which is vital to understand in order to have effective interventions for rural development.

Methodology

Recognising the objectives of study, prior importance was given to understand subject's own perception for which the non-positivist paradigm was considered; adhered to constructivist epistemological position, following qualitative methodology with ethnographic approach of data collection adopted. In-depth interview with interview guide, group interview, informal conversation, participant and non-participant observation was adopted as methods of data collection to fulfil the research objectives.

Qualitative methodology was adopted for the study as that follows the constructivist approach of the non-positivist epistemological position (Denzin and Lincoln, 2000). The applied methodology helped in understanding the social phenomenon from the natural setting where poor interpreted their situation and constructed meaning of their lived experiences through interaction, development of shared meaning and communication (Neuman, 1997). This was possible with the use of flexible research methods that facilitated inside view through data collection and analysis (Blumer, 1978; Dezin , 1978, cited from Mahatani, 1999). To get into the depth of understanding of how household uses their resources, why they behave in a particular manner in situations, how they set up their choices and priorities while taking decisions and formulate strategies etc., and researcher used unstructured interviews, non-participant observation, and focus group discussions. Many of the cultural aspects, differences between the groups of people within the community, could be understood through non-participant observation as the researcher attended group meetings, cultural events, witnessed individual-level interactions, observed their daily lifestyle in the community without participating in any of the activities, except making observations from a distance.

The next section discusses the different strategies formulated by interviewed households in different situations of their life span.

1. Rural Household Livelihood Strategies: Shades and Complexities

(a) **Reactive Coping Strategies:** Sudden unwanted events experienced by households direct them towards reactive strategies where they look for immediate solution. These strategies are usually taken in response to an event that has already taken place. These strategies do not have any prior planning, or long-term thinking for which all possible sources are explored to manage the situation.Taking a reactive coping strategy is common and active among many households irrespective of place, group and culture. The strategies are common among households with low or limited assets than those, who have the better asset accumulation many a time, the strategies go against the household's welfare, which means some of the strategies do bring solutions but weaken other aspects for long term. For example, disposal of household assets (selling livestock, jewellery, mortgaging property), dis-saving, borrowing, curtailment in consumption items are the examples of reactive strategy. Whenever there is an unexpected event like illness, sudden death, loss of production, loss of productive assets like livestock, natural calamities (drought, flood) etc., households deal with the situation by making use of all the available resources.

(b) **Sacrificing Strategies:** Sacrifice strategies are those where households tend to give up many of their desire, wish and requirement to fulfil the immediate need on the bases of crisis and the necessity of moment. It has been observed that to secure on aspects of their life, households sacrifice other aspects. From the household interview, a pattern as evolved that shows they sacrifice in many ways for reducing their risk and to fulfil their priorities. Within these kinds of strategies, they do those things which make them choose one aspect at the loss of others. Examples of sacrificing strategies are women, non-participation in income earning activities, phenomenon of school drop-out, adjustment with the craving for good food, compromising with the family life, forced migration, withdrawal from taking the treatment.

(c) **Faith-based Strategies:** Faith-based strategies are those strategies that are formulated on the basis of their traditional belief and cultural norms which households observed in their areas. These are completely based on their faith that they develop over certain practices of exorcism. Examples of faith-based strategies are opting-low cost traditional treatment – exorcism, delayed breeding of livelihood, traditional treatment of livestock.

(d) **Compensatory Strategies:** Compensatory strategies means, the strategies that household took up to cover losses that might have affected their livelihood. By taking these strategie households try to compensate the loss or fill up the gap. Examples of compensatory strategies are women's involvement into the labour market, working for long hours to compensate absenteeism.

(e) **Self-securing Strategies:** Self-securing strategies are those strategies which households take with prior planning. It includes their well-thought arrangements for securing the future. There are ranges of action that households do to minimise the risk from any kind of crisis. Examples of self-securing strategies are stocking of food items, stocking of old agricultural seeds, stocking of firewood, saving, maintain loop of creditor, on time repayment strategy.

(f) **Investment Strategy:** Households invest in different ways with the expectation of getting good return. These investments are not bound within monetary dimensions, rather they have wider implications. The data which emerged from the field reflects in different ways. Households make investment as part of their strategically taken decision based on thefuture expectation. The examples of investment strategies are investment towards children's education, investment for accumulation of assets, investment to build social capital.

(g) **Resource Pooling Strategies:** Resource pooling means bringing resources together from all possible ways to accomplish any task. For example share-cropping, sharing of group well, group fishing, group activities.

(h) **Livelihood Diversification:** According to Ellis (2000:232), livelihood diversification refers to the process by which households construct diverse portfolio of activities that ensure social support for survival to improve their standard. It is the strategy that household follow by maintaining portfolios of activities by using increasingly diverse combination of resources and assets (Niehof, 2004). In the studied villages, household diversified their asset and maintained portfolio of activities. The examples are diversifying crop and livestock, pluriactivity as livelihood strategy, diversification from the individual activity to group enterprise.

(i) **Intensification Strategy:** Intensification strategy is defined by Scoones (1998), which demands increase in the input or capital to increase the value of productivity. This is done either by intensifying resources in large quantities or application of technology to get maximum benefit. Though intensification is majorly discussed in agricultural activities it also happens in other activities like livestock rearing etc. The examples are on-time preparation of farm field, construction of *baad* (fencing), shift in the occupation, and involvement of other family members in livestock rearing, revival of traditional breed.

The section gives the understanding on the wide range of strategies the household formulates to secure and protect the livelihood. These strategies can be categorised based on their characteristics and temporal dimension which are discussed in the next section.

2. Strategies Connecting Two Poles of Problems and Solutions

This part of discussion attempts to enquire about the livelihood strategies undertaken by the households in India's rural areas. The emerged data, evolved from people themselves, brought out wide range of livelihood strategies which are not simple but complex. The strategies are influenced by multiple vulnerabilities situations, household's aspiration for better future and their available asset base. The very first understanding developed from the study is that household make strategies when there are naturally driven to shocks like drought, earthquake, flood, and cyclone etc. Majority of research studies have discussed livelihood strategies of household from the context of the natural disaster indicating to multiple coping and adaptation mechanism.

These studies looked into the household livelihood strategies in a very restricted way over a phase of time. Whereas, the present study could identify household livelihood strategies beyond that boundary and could tap strategies that household does not follow only when shocks occur, rather they also look for their future and their current situation. The identified strategies against livelihood vulnerabilities discussed in chapter five can broadly be categorised under three major sections – post-event strategies, concurrent strategies and future-oriented strategies.

a) **Characteristics of the Strategies:** The rational for tagging all the identified strategies under three broad categories are based on the characteristics that emerged from the data. For example, it has been observed that all the strategies taken under the reactive strategies have the characteristics like action taken after the event which are short span in nature, have immediate or instant action, and are not done with too much of the planning or are well-thought of. Similarly, in case of concurrent strategies, action taken is on the basis of present day context, neither past nor future, the problem occurred now, so work towards the solution to deal with the situation in normal life situation. And the third category included the strategies that households take considering the futuristic outcome which has long-term objective, are well-thought and planned for future-oriented strategies. These are not for solving immediate problems rather to develop means that can protect and build up capacity to deal with the situation better in future.

b) **Post-event Strategies:** These are strategies that households have taken up after the event to deal with. Strategies are taken for short period to get instant relief or to solve the immediate problem. In literature, these are called coping strategies. However, in the study, it is considered as reactive coping strategies, defined by Greenglass (2002), who stated that this strategy is used while they experience stress to reduce the adverse consequences. Because within the post event strategy household decide with reaction to the situation and not simply for coping which also has positive connotation in the field of its origin. Reactive coping refers to the strategies that occurs post event either to solve the problem or to deal with the problem with the available resources *(ibid)*.

Household take these strategies when there is shock, so it is not long-term and are taken considering the immediate asset base. The strategies are taken out of reaction to deal with the emergency because of which these strategies are probably not very well thought of or planned. Because of which, these strategies takes the maximum out of a household and they are left with little for the future. The strategies have the possibility to shaken the household's sustainability and increase their vulnerability.

The reactive coping strategy can become pro-active, if households manage to choose their action selectively and in a constructive manner. This may not drive them towards further risk in future and for that more support from formal institutions becomes very important. The argument aligns with the thought put forward by Davies (1993), whose work concluded that those strategies are not pre-planned and taken in emergency bear a high cost because they run down the accumulated assets that further makes their livelihood unstable.

c) **Concurrent Strategies:** In the study, data reveals that households do not formulate strategies or take action only when they encounter risk or for securing their future. But, in between these two broad categories, household do live in current situation. They also act and formulate strategies to deal with their day-to-day living and crisis, keeping in mind their present situation, past experience and future expectation. These are the strategies that do not fall conveniently in the other two broad categories and they have their own space in the understanding of household strategies.

d) **Future-oriented Strategies:** The data reveals that households do not always engage in making strategies to resolve the problems which are immediate. They take initiatives that can provide better results to them in future. Though households are not sure if the out-come of certain action would be positive or not, yet they prefer to adopt future-oriented strategies. The main future-oriented strategies emerged from the field are investment for strengthening asset base, accumulation of physical asset base, stocking of different household items, saving and insurance. These are the strategies that households consciously take up to be secure from future uncertainties and risks. These are the self-securing strategies which are future-oriented.

The discussed strategies have very clear objective to get return which might not be immediate but in the long run. Households tend to follow these strategies with an understanding that the investment will make their future secure.

Conclusion

To conclude, household maintain multiple shades of strategies that are intertwined with each other. This result of the study is similar to the study by the Zoomer (1999), among the rural people of Andes, who mentioned that livelihood strategies are multi-dimensional as no single strategy can serve the wider range of the socio-economic problems. No household maintains strategies for the single phase of life and their strategies are influenced by multiple factors. Strategies are time-bounded and have importance of the temporal component as whenever household formulate them they think of the action in a specific time frame in both the case of internal and external strategies. The findings from the data give an impression that even though strategies are taken to get positive outcome, however the outcome is negative in many occasions.

The reactive or sacrificing strategies may support households in dealing with the situation after the shock or in their day-to-day life challenges, but in the long-term they are performed at the cost of loss to other aspects of life. These strategies have major negative implication for the future that weakens the livelihood security of the household. On the other side, there are strategies that are taken under normal circumstances on normal day-to-day challenges in the life of the people. These strategies are future-oriented, have positive implication on reducing the risk against livelihood vulnerabilities and in maintaining and securing the livelihood in present and future times. This strategy works towards fulfilling the household aspiration and look for long-term goal to achieve secured and protected livelihood outcome.

The study further communicates the message that it is significant to look at the household dynamics and complexities with the microscopic lens as this will provide guidance to capture the real picture of the phenomenon at the grassroots level and guide in the formulation of pro-poor policies. The study findings show that households do not always take the right strategy to deal with particular situation. So, it is important to have policies that enhance and facilitate the positive strategies that households follow and provide them with the all kind of support they require. In addition, it becomes important to check and protect households from taking strategies that has negative implication in the long run and disturb the existing asset base which they may find difficult to regain in future.

References

Becker, G. S. (1997), *Responding to Poverty: The Politics of Cash and Care.* Addison-Wesley Longman, Limited.

Chelliah, R.J., and Sudarshan, R. (Eds.), (1999). *Income-poverty and beyond: Human Development in India.* Anthem Press.

De Haan, L., and Zoomers, A. (2003). "Development geography at the crossroads of livelihood and globalisation". *Tijdschrift voor economische en sociale geografie, 94* (3), pp 350-262.

Denzin, N. K., and Lincoln, Y.S. (Eds), (2000). "Introduction: The discipline and practice of qualitative research", In *The Handbook of qualitative research* (2nd Edition), Thousand Oaks: Sage.

Devereux, S. (1993). "Goats before ploughs: Dilemmas of household response sequencing during food shortages". *IDS Bulletin, 24* (4), pp 52–59. doi:10.1111/j.1759-5436.1993.mp24004006.

Dorward, A., Poole, N., Morrison, J., Kydd, J., and Urey, I. (2003). "Markets, institutions and technology: missing links in livelihoods analysis". *Development policy review, 21*(3), pp 319-332.

Ellis, F. (1998), "Household strategies and rural livelihood diversification". *Journal of Development Studies, 35*(1), pp 1–38. doi:10.1080/00220389808422553.

Ellis, F. (2000) "The determinants of rural livelihood diversification in developing countries" *Journal of Agricultural Economics, 51*(2), pp 289-302.

Hunter, L. M. (2006) "Household strategies in the face of resource scarcity in coastal Ghana: Are the associated with development priorities?" *Population Research and Policy Review, 25*(2), pp 157-74. doi:10.1007/s11113-006-9002-9.

Krishna, A. (2006). "Pathways out and into poverty in 36 villages of Andhra Pradesh, India", *World Bank,* 34 (2), pp. 271-288.

Lovenbalk, J., Hjarne, D., Taoutaou, A.A., Mertz, O., Dirir, M., Dyg, P.M., Lasses, K.M. and Sahested, M. (2003). "Opportunities and contstraints for agricultural intensification in communities adjacent to the Crocker Range National Park Sabah, Malaysia, *ASEAN Review of Bio-diversity and Environmental Conservation (ARBEC).* Retrieved on February 3, 2011 from www.arbec.com.my/pdf/art.

Mahapatra, S. (2007). "Livelihood Pattern of Agricultural Labour Households in Rural India Evidence from Orissa, *South Asia Research*, *27*(1)", pp. 79–103. doi: 10.1177/026272800602700105.

McDowell, C., and De Haan, A. (1997). "Migration and Sustainable Livelihoods: A Critical Review of the Literature". *IDS Working Paper (65).* Retrieved on November 1, 2008 from http://www.ids.ac.uk/download.cfm?file=wp65.pdf.

Messer, N., and Townsley, P. (2003), *Local institutions and livelihoods: Guidelines for analysis*, Food and Agriculture Org. Retrieved on 04/03/2009 from http://www.fao.org/docrep/006/y5084e/y5084e04.htmdoi:10.1080/713650975.

Niehof, A. (2004) "The Significance of Diversification for Rural Livelihood Systems" *Food Policy*, *29*(4), pp. 321–338. doi:10.1016/j.foodpol.2004.07.009.

Pennartz, P., and Niehof, A. (1999) *The domestic domain: chances, choices and strategies of family households.* Aldershot and Vermont, England and USA: Ashgate Publishing Ltd.

Scoones, I., & Wolmer, W. (2000), *Pathways of change in Africa: crops, livestock & livelihoods in Africa. Lessons from Mali, Ehtiopia and Zimbabwe*, James Currey.

Tessema, A. (2005): "Household Livelihood Adaptation in a High Population Density Area in Ethiopia: The Case of Wolaita Zora" A *Ph.D. Proposal in Development Studies*.

Wallace, C. (2002). "Household strategies: their conceptual relevance and analytical scope in social research". *Sociology*, *36*(2), pp 275-292.

Zoomer, A. (1999), *Linking livelihood strategies to development: Experience from the Bolivian Andes,* Netherland: Royal Tropical Institute, Centre for Latin American Research and Documentation (CEDLA).

12

The Role of Third Sector in Empowering Rural Population: Evidence from Disaggregate Level

Roopa Patavardhan and Divya Pradeep

Introduction

Through several interesting strategies for achieving a better society, NGOs have gained wide attention among the researchers and other practitioners of development. On the other hand, there is a current view that NGOs constitute a viable alternative to government as channels of development assistance, particularly in developing countries. Some of the NGOs' functions and advantages, according to Streeten (1997) are:

(1) They are good at reaching and mobilising the poor and remote communities;

(2) They help empower poor people to gain control of their lives and strengthen local institutions;

(3) They carry out projects at lower costs and more efficiently than the government agencies;

(4) They promote sustainable development. Further, by a wide range of participatory developmental schemes they are able to empower rural masses as well as achieve sustainable community development. In this regard, this study attempts to investigate the role of SKDRDP- Sri Kshetra Dharmastala Rural Development Project [a secular NGO in Karnataka, backed by religious shrine], in the process of empowerment by studying the Pragathi Bandhu – marginal farmers, self-help groups under SKDRDP. In this study, two aspects will be identified, first, the relationship between NGO and empowerment, and second the strategy and programmes undertaken by NGOs that contribute to sustainable micro-finance. In other words, the purpose of this study is to

explore the role of SKDRDP in terms of empowerment of members of Pragathi Bandhu (PB) groups.

Before directly venturing into the role of SKDRDP, it is worthwhile to notice how these genres of organisations come into picture in a society. Thus, in the subsequent lines this issue is dealt.

Theories on the Origin of the TSOs

Gratification of human wants with limited available resources is the major concern of economics. In other words, this is communicated popularly as problem of economic efficiency in the situation of scare resources as the disposable. Economists have widely accepted the state of economic efficiency[1] as defined by Vilfred Pareto. But, this is not regarded as complete definition of economic efficiency as it does not necessarily result in socially desirable distribution of resources or the overall well-being of society. But at this juncture, it becomes important to consider the issues that economic efficiency is a situation in which resources are allocated in such a way that common of human wants are satisfied. Human beings have organised themselves to different set of institutional arrangements in order to achieve the state of economic efficiency. Two broadly classified categories of such institutional arrangements are the Market and the State. But when both of the arrangements yield inefficient results in their process of satisfying human wants, it is regarded as Market and State failure, espectively.

Market failures can be viewed as scenarios, where individuals' pursuit of pure self-interest leads to results that are not efficient – that can be improved upon from the societal point-of-view. Market failures are often associated with information asymmetry problems, imperfect market conditions, presence of externalities or in the provision of public goods etc., to mention few. The existence of market failure is often used as justification for government intervention in particular market.

State failure or government failure is the public sector analogy to market failure and occurs when government intervention causes more inefficient allocation of goods and resources that would occur without intervention. Likewise, the government's failure to intervene in market failure that would result in a socially preferable mix of output is referred to as passive government failure (Weimer and Vining, 2004). Just as with market failures, there are many different kinds of government failures that describe corresponding distortions. The idea of government failure is associated with the policy argument that, even if particular markets may not meet the standard conditions of perfect competition required to ensure social optimality, government intervention may make matters worse rather than better.

In an attempt by individuals to overcome this problem of failures of market and state, with the evolution of civilisation there emerged third set of complex institutions often referred to as third sector organisations. These failures are the most popular explanation for the emergence of third sector organisations or the third sector; however economists have different views regarding the origin of the third sector organisations which are also known as non profit distributing or voluntary sector etc. But what is relevant to this context is that this wider sector, which comprises the range of organisations from sports clubs to emergency relief camps, from religious institutions to secular institutions, has a major contribution in the economic development of any nation in the modern world.

The theories of public good model highlight that as market and state fail to supply public goods and hence individuals voluntarily form organisations to increase the supply of public goods. The private good model states that people volunteer in order to enjoy the 'warm-glow' utility gained from volunteering and the Investment model states that the individuals, to gain labour-market experience, skills and contacts; form TSOs, (Ziemek 2002). All these models reflect only a part of the reason that individuals form TSOs, but the origin of TSOs must be understood not only from the view of market failure in the process of economic development but also in the light of self-sufficiency, which aim at reducing high transaction costs and non-profit distribution (Valentinov, 2008). This argument is noteworthy for the reason that since the scholars began to understand the origin of the third sectors, the major of their attention was devoted to the cause that TSOs originate so as to fill in the gap of failures on part of the state and the market. Information asymmetry and high transaction costs which cause the state and market to fail were not the matter of concern for the scholars but only the 'State and Market fail'; not the reasons that caused that failure.

Role of the NGOs in Empowerment: A Review of Literature

NGOs, which are one of the prominent institutional arrangements under the umbrella of TSOs, are playing decisive role in empowering the rural masses through varied activities. Women empowerment has been the major concerns of most of the studies related to NGOs. NGOs have been successful in increasing women's access to resources in Cameroon. Their interventions have improved women's access to health, credit, training, employment, and family decision-making and they provide opportunities for women to exchange ideas. All these satisfy women's immediate needs such as food, health and water, which are required by everybody (Fonjong 2001). The empirical evidence – qualitative and quantitative from Rural Bangladesh states that NGO micro-credit programs targetting women, which are spreading quickly throughout rural Bangladesh, are likely to bring about rapid economic improvement in the situation of women (Amin *et al,* 1998).

NGOs have brought about many regional achievements regarding sustainable development strategies (economically, socially, and environmentally), structural adjustment and economic liberalisation, alternative and appropriate technologies in agriculture, natural resource management, human resource development, political participation, democratisation processes, and social empowerment in Caribbean (Lewis, 1994). The creation of NGOs which are group-based cooperative organisations based on mutual trust, strongly promotes participatory development and the empowerment of its members and also leads to sustainable community development in rural areas. The two NGOs- PROSHIKA and BRAC contribute to the process of social capital formation by infusing in the target group the spirit of cooperation and involving the groups in cooperative activities in order to improve the quality of life of the common people (Hye Mondal, 2000).

In Sri Lanka, the *Sarvodaya* Movement has served thousands of villages through the process of labour sharing, knowledge, community conceived and community-based activities. The religious associations sustain development process through faith (Candland, 2000). The study states that NGOs, rooted in religiously articulate programmer for social reform can particularly be effective in community development and building social capital, especially in political environments in which state does not promote particular civic religion. While comparing this in Indian context as State is secular, the working of religious NGOs can be studied with an aim to check the fact stated by this study. NGOs through hiring, training and empowering process provide performance accomplishments, vicarious learning, verbal persuasion and physical affective status and spirituality can be the social glue bonding the members of an NGO and perhaps an explicitly shared vision and common values may provide the 'spiritual capital' to empower masses and thereby enable sustainable community development in case of secular NGOs (Handy and Kassam, 2004).

All these studies are one side picture, but there exists the other side which highlights the lacunas of NGOs in participatory development and thus achieving sustainable community development. NGOs have had little impact in reversing discrimination against and subordination of women (Fonjong, 2001). NGOs can hinder the growth of social capital and thereby form obstacles in the achievement of sustainable development (Carmona, 2004 and Abon, 2004). They put into words that NGOs work on the basis of traditional interventionist approaches which are limited - which give emphasis on the programme rather than individuals and state that there is need to rethink the strategic role of NGOs. The NGOs promoted by religious institutions appear to rely more on faith and belief as the respondents in organisations repose faith in religion and religious practices than the merit of the programmes. Further in this respect, they appear more as extension of sponsoring religion and charitable institutions than autonomous democratic associations based on the spirit of participation and self-help (Uday Kumar and Sreedhar, 2004).

NGO projects also suffer from the fact that they are not easily replicable. Often they rely on the charismatic qualities of a particular organiser. The movements that empower the poor are normally initiated and led by exceptional visionary leaders with selfless courage who do not come from the poor. These charismatic leaders cannot easily be multiplied, and their successes cannot readily be replicated (Streeten, 1997). Further NGOs have a lot of institutional difficulties in the way they work. Their ability to provide just and equal access to available resources, for the population, depends on status quo social relationship. NGOs always may not succeed because of the neglect of power. The relationships the NGOs are expected to maintain with their donors and the bureaucrats are neglected by NGOs staff because of lack of soft skills and training (BRONIC, 2005).

SHARE, an NGO in Tamil Nadu is not effective in poverty reduction, because there was no difference between the economic status of the comparison group and the member group. Different types of interventions – not entirely based on economic programmes should be initiated, if poverty reduction is to take place (Rajasekhar, 2002).

Objectives and Methodology

The general objective is to highlight how a TSO can look beyond mere credit and thrift activity of micro-finance and the specific objective is to explore the role of SKDRDP in terms of empowerment of members of Pragathi Bandhu (PB) groups. The concept of empowerment has been conceptualised under three heads – Economic empowerment, political empowerment and social empowerment for the study. It is an exploratory study using qualitative data. The main source of data is primary data fundamentally, collected at a point of time during 2011-12. The secondary data is also used. Data was elicited using face-to-face semi-structured interview technique with members of Pragathi Bandhu groups. The method of 'Analytic comparison' is used as the tool of analysing qualitative data collected. This is given by John Stuart Mill, the British philosopher and social thinker. This method involves logical methods for making comparisons. The method of agreement and method of difference form the basis of analytic comparison in qualitative data analysis. The whole of population involves all the Pragathi Bandhu Self-Help Groups of SKDRDP. Pragathi Bandhu group is the unit of analysis and each group becomes a case. The sample size is thirteen Pragathi Bandhu groups, which in total comprises 62 members; four to five members on an average in each group. The data was collected till the newer insights were emerged both in terms for similar and diverse pattern of responses and it was stopped at the number of 62 respondents because nothing new emerged beyond responses from 50th member either in terms of similarity or diversity in opinions.

Findings of the Study

Demographic Profile of Respondents

Majority, *i.e.,* nearly 80 per cent of the respondents' age range between 30 to 55 years and only a few of respondents are aged below 30 years and above 55 years. Only two of the 62 respondents have attended pre-university college and other respondents have basic primary education, say, till third or fourth grade; but most of the respondents have not gone to school at all. But one of the interesting elements among a handful of respondents was that some of those individuals do not remember whether they have gone to school or even if they have gone they do not remember the grade which they last attended. Apart from for three individuals – two Muslims and one Christian, the rest of the respondents belong to Hindu religion. Except for seven respondents, all other respondents are married. The number of dependents on each respondent is three members on an average.

Role of SKDRDP in Empowerment of Pragathi Bandu Group Members

For analysis of qualitative primary data collected from respondents the method of analytical comparison has been adopted and to make the analysis, the 13 groups interviewed are taken as cases and have been assigned a letter from alphabet for easy reference. The details of this procedure are depicted below in Table-1.

Table 1: Details of the Pragathi Bandhu Groups and Letters Assigned for Analysis.

Name of the Pragathi Bandhu group	*Letter assigned to the group for reference during the course of interpretation*	*Number of members*
Gaanialu	A	7
Baremalu	B	4
Kattada Bailu	C	5
Nellikatte A	D	4
Samboliva	E	4
Padavu	F	4
Nellikatte D	G	5
Kulai	H	4
Raktheshwari Padavu A	I	5
Naala B	J	4
Battemaru	K	5
Sri Durga	L	5
Kaje	M	6
	Total number of respondents in total : 62	

Source: Compiled by the authors based on primary data.

The concept of economic empowerment has been reduced to certain features and these features depicting the role of SKDRDP in economic empowerment are represented in statements below; each statement has been assigned with a number for analysis of the data according to analytical comparison method. If the respondents do not agree with the statements, then it has been left blank in the table. This applies to all the tables included in this entire section.

SKDRDP has

- provided the opportunity to save- 1,
- led to increase in income-2,
- led to food security-3,
- improved standard of living-4,
- built the capacity to keep accounts book- financial management training-5,
- fulfilled demand for credit-6,
- created awareness on the working of banks and other financial institutions-7,
- facilitated to practice increased income generating agricultural activities-8,
- provided facility of micro-insurance -9,
- provided easy access to loan-10.

The responses of the members of the Pragathi Bandhu groups on the issue SKDRDP's role in economic empowerment has been presented in the following Table-2.

Table 2: Responses of the Members of the Pragathi Bandhu Groups on the Issue SKDRDP's Role in Economic Empowerment.

A	*B*	*C*	*D*	*E*	*F*	*G*	*H*	*I*	*J*	*K*	*L*	*M*
1	1	1	1	1	1	1	1	1	1	1	1	1
2	2	2	2	2	2	2	2	2	2	2	2	2
3	3	3	3	3	3	3	3	3	3	3	3	3
4	4	4	4	4	4	4	4	4	4	4	4	4
5	5	5	5	5	5	5	5	5	5	5	5	5
6	6	6	6	6	6	6	6	6	6	6	6	6
7	7	7	7	7	7	7	7	7	7	7	7	7
8	8	8	8	8	8	8	8	8	8	8	8	8
9	9	9	9	9	9	9	9	9	9	9	9	9
10	10	10	10	10	10	10	10	10	10	10	10	10

Source: Compiled by the authors based on primary data.

As per the Table-2, SKDRDP has been able to economically empower the Pragathi Bandhu members, according to the above primary data tabulated. All the members shared similar opinion that after joining this group they are able to avail loans readily as well the constant guidance to use these loans helped them utilise the loan amount to venture intoincome generating activities. Also, all the members have agreed to the statements mentioned above.

In terms of SKDRDP's role on social empowerment, according to the responses depicted in Table-3, it can be stated that SKDRDP has been moderately able to empower them because, all dissimilar responses are related to the aspect of 'decision-making' in the community.

Certain features of SKDRDP's role in social empowerment and are represented in statements below; each statement has been assigned with a number for analysis.

Joining SKDRDP has

- Developed self-confidence and confidence of self-expression in public – 11,
- Provided platform for personality development- 12,
- Increased social status-13,
- Increased one's positive self-image and overcoming stigma –14,
- provided ability to make decisions about personal circumstances-15,
- led to involvement in decision making in the community-16,
- Created unique identity in the society-17,
- Led to involvement in community development activities-18,
- Provided ability to exercise assertiveness in collective decision-making–19,
- Provided ability to access information and resources for decision-making-20.

The Table-3 below shows the pattern of responses across Cases or groups on the role of SKDRDP in social empowerment. The letters A to M in the first row of the table stand for thirteen cases and each number [11-20] in the rest of the table stand for corresponding feature, which are represented in statements above.

Table-3: Responses across Cases or Groups on the Role of SKDRDP in Social Empowerment

A	*B*	*C*	*D*	*E*	*F*	*G*	*H*	*I*	*J*	*K*	*L*	*M*
11	11	11	11	11	11	11	11	11	11	11	11	11
12	12	12	12	12	12	12	12	12	12	12	12	12
13	13	13	13	13	13	13	13	13	13	13	13	13
14	14	14	14	14	14	14	14	14	14	14	14	14
15	15	15	15	15	15	15	15	15	15	15	15	15
16	16	16	-	-	16	-	-	-	16	16	16	16
17	17	17	17	17	17	17	-	17	17	17	17	17
18	18	18	18	18	18	18	-	18	18	18	18	18
19	19	19	-	-	19	-	-	-	19	19	19	19
20	20	20	-	-	20	20	-	-	20	20	20	20.

Source: Compiled by the authors based on primary data.

The pattern of response is similar among eight groups [A, B, C, F, J, K, L and M] about the role of SKDRDP in socially empowering the members of Pragathi Bandhu groups considered under the study. But the five cases [D, E, G, H, I] differ with other eight cases in terms of three responses: 16, 19 and 20: led to involvement in decision-making in the community, 19 - provided ability to exercise assertiveness in collective decision-making and 20-provided ability to access information and resources for decision-making. Case eight further differs with the rest of twelve cases on the responses 17- created unique identity in the society, and 18 led to involvement in community development activities. Cases D, E and I are similar in all responses.

The pattern of responses which are similar across cases can be interpreted in the following lines. The statements on which all cases have similar responses are the statements which represent social empowerment at an individual's level or participation in the community development activities but the dissimilar views across the cases arise on statements which stand for the decision-making process at the community level. Cases D, E and I have similar responses which are different from the rest of cases' responses. But, there is no regularity across these cases, which can be pointed out as a cause for similar views which are dissimilar from the rest of the cases nor does there a striking regularity in the eight cases, which have similar responses on the statements. One of the cases - H is not empowered in the sense of decision-making or participating in community development activity. This group consists of family members-siblings and relatives as group members. So, this might be the reason for them not to participate in community as a whole or the decision-making process of the entire community or it can also be interpreted as that the community can be looking down them as a group because it is comprising members from the same family. This can be the only cause, for the reason that this group is similar to other groups in terms other features-may be education, number of dependents, location etc. So, it can be said that SKDRDP has been moderately helpful for the respondents to become socially empowered.

When it comes to the political empowerment of the people, only two statements are common across the cases that is one about increased access to public goods and two about the contacting the officials with confidence that is with no sense of being inferior and weak and then extracting information from them. But other responses are diverse for the reason that when questions about political process or *panchayat* or *Grama Sabha* were asked they clearly exhibited the view that they know it naturally even before the inception of SKDRDP. According to respondents, SKDRDP efforts in this direction are least in the recent years in relation to few years back, when Dr Veerendra Heggade – the head of SKDRDP used to educate the members during elections stating 'vote for the right candidate' and the importance of casting vote for right candidate. So, they disagree with the idea that SKDRDP provides them with the knowledge about politics. In fact, the conversations with most of them threw light on their knowledge about the Karnataka politics and the unethical election practices etc.

Certain features of SKDRDP's role in political empowerment are represented in statements below; each statement has been assigned with a number for simplified analysis.

Joining SKDRDP has:

- Been encouraging to participate in Grama Sabha and its meetings -21,
- Created awareness about panchayat and its works -22,
- Created a sense of freedom from oppression-23,
- Created awareness on political process: importance of voting –24,
- Created ability to influence the local political decisions-25,
- Created ability to increased access to public goods-26,
- Created ability to take individual decision on voting-27,
- Created confidence to participate in local elections as candidates-28,
- Created confidence to interact with government officials and thereby increasing access to information –29,

- Has been able to be elected representative of the local government - 30.

The Table-13 below shows the pattern of responses across cases on the role of SKDRDP in political empowerment. The letters A to M in the first row of the Table stand for thirteen cases and each number [21-30] in the rest of the Table stand for corresponding feature, which are represented in statements above.

Table 4: The Pattern of Responses across Cases on the Role of SKDRDP in Political Empowerment

A	*B*	*C*	*D*	*E*	*F*	*G*	*H*	*I*	*J*	*K*	*L*	*M*
-	-	-	21	-	-	21	-	-	21	-	-	-
-	-	-	22	-	-	22	-	-	22	-	-	-
-	-	-	-	23	-	-	-	-	-	-	-	-
-	-	-	24	-	24	-	24	-	24	-	-	24
25	25	-	-		-	-	-	-	25	-	-	25
26	26	26	26	26	26	26	26	26	26	26	26	26
-	-	27	27	27	-	27	-	-	27	-	27	27
28		-	-	-	28	28	-	-	28	-	28	28
29	29	29	29	29	29	29	29	29	29	29	29	29
30	30	-	-	-	-	-	-	30	-	-	-	-

Source: Compiled by the authors based on primary data.

The pattern of responses is diverse across cases on the role of SKDRDP in the political empowerment of members of Pragathi Bandhu involved in this study. There are only two responses which are similar across all cases they are response 26-created ability to increased access to public goods and 29-created confidence to interact with government officials and thereby increasing access to information. A set of seven cases [A, F, G, J, L and M] have similar response on the statement 28-created confidence to participate in local elections as candidates and another set of seven cases [B,C,D ,E, H, I and K] have similar response on statement 27-created ability to take individual decision on voting, a set of four cases [D,F, H and J] have similar response on statement 24-created awareness on political process: importance of voting and another bunch of four cases [A, B J and M] have similar response on statement 25- created ability to influence the local political decisions. Three cases [D, G and J] have similar response on statements 21- been encouraging to participate in Grama Sabha and its meetings and 22- created awareness about panchayat and its works and another group of three cases [A, B and I] have similar response on statement 30 - has been able to be elected representative of the local government and only a single case has agreed on statement 23- created a sense of freedom from oppression.

As noted the responses on the statements 26- created ability to increased access to public goods and 29- created confidence to interact with government officials and thereby increasing access to information, that are similar across all the cases. By and large these statements may appear to be the features of political empowerment; but it is in fact very interesting to dig a little deeper and thus it can be noted that, these statements have strong economic dimension. This interpretation can be justified with the evidence of similarity in response across cases. Another significant element which has to be considered at this juncture is the objectives of SKDRDP. In the set of statements of objectives, it is given that SKDRDP works in direction of empowering the poorest and in other statements it has declared clearly on socially and economically empowering the poor; further in the specific objectives on Pragathi Bandhu project, it has been stated SKDRDP strives to build the leadership qualities of members. But leadership at what level is not specified. So, it is unclear so as to determine whether this organisation has political empowerment in its agenda, because the use of empowerment is not clearly defined but loosely used.

So, on exploring the role of SKDRDP in empowerment of Pragathi Bandhu farmers; it can be stated in gist that SKDRDP has been able to significantly cause economic empowerment of these thirteen Pragathi Bandhu groups but moderately has led to social empowerment and very meagerly has led to political empowerment. The pattern of responses from respondents was almost similar on their views on the role of SKDRDP in empowering them; though each one's stories were different.

Unique Features of SKDRDP

From the review of the programmes carried out by SKDRDP, certain unique features in the working of this institution has been recognised. These features stand distinct from other approaches to sustainable microfinance and are thus highlighted under following heads.

1. **Loans plus guidance on using loans:** NGOs involving credit facilities or with the programmes of financial inclusion, in most of the cases stop with transferring the money, but SKDRDP differs in this regard because it has been seen that the dedicated and trained officials get into each family's grassroots level problems and provide guidance on how to utilise money to improve the beneficiaries, living conditions. This kind of service will be a transaction cost to the State or the Market, but NGO views this as service towards achieving sustainable micro-finance.

2. **Eradication of alcoholism:** Alcoholism is a major problem among rural down-trodden class. SKDRDP has identified this problem and to eradicate this problem, the institution organises de-addiction camps. Commendable effort of the institution is the follow-up activity they undertake to make sure that the victim of addiction does not start drinking again post the camp. Also invites the beneficiaries to share experiences in the other camps so that it will provide boost the moral decision taken by the individual and enhance his or her status in society.

3. **Member's whole family under nexus of benefits:** Another distinct feature of SKDRDP is involving the family members of the beneficiary while distributing loans. This will help women to keep track of economic activities carried out by their husbands and avoid thereby misuse of loans by male members or the other way round. Also the institution provides educational help to children in family.

4. **Provision of public goods**: Electricity is major constraint in agriculture and domestic activities of the farmers in rural areas. SKDRDP to a certain extent provides methods, materials and training to promote use of alternative sources of energy in areas where there is no provision of electricity. Some of the facilities in this direction are setting up of *Gobar* gas plants and solar energy etc., to mention few.

5. The models of **Pragathi Bandhu** and **Sampoorna Suraksha** have been able to attract international recognition and awards- 'Change makers Award' promoted jointly by the US-based Ashoka Foundation and Citi Bank in the competition 'Banking on social change – seeking financial solutions for all'.[2]

Summary and Conclusions

The objective of the study was to examine the role of SKDRDP in empowerment and thus creating sustainable community development. This was in line with the broader idea of role of third sector organisations in economic development. It was seen that TSOs emerge not just in the wake of state and market failure, but in tune with the urge of self-sufficiency. This self- sufficiency has been identified to lead to sustainable community development. Further literature on the success and failure of NGOs in the before mentioned process was reviewed. Finally, in this third part, the lessons which can be drawn from this kind of approach will be looked into. The interventions and guidance provided by SKDRDP is projected as the major factor for the achievement of hundred per cent repayment of loans. In the wake of micro-finance crisis in Andhra Pradesh, a southern state of India, and scepticism about the model of micro-finance; it can be stated that mere provision of the facility of credit and thrift will not help in materialising the arrangement of micro-finance but efforts must be taken to guide and provide information on the optimal utilisation of loans they avail. At the policy level, the Government must think in lines of holistic approach to empower the marginal section than providing mere credit and thrift facilities, while framing the draft and implementation of the micro-finance facilities to marginalised sections. The marginalised section need a background or foundation stone in the form of guidance on one-to-one basis and this is what is exactly done by the *sev anirathas* and supervisors of SKDRDP.

In a situation where the state as well as the private players encounter obstacles of reaching the poor in terms of guidance and empowerment, NGOs stand better chance, if they follow this holistic approach for achieving sustainable community development. Banks and micro-finance institutions; even with all formal interventions have failed recently because of high repayment arrears at Andhra Pradesh, but in the case of SKDRDP, the procedures of deciding and provision of a micro-loan is relatively not so formal, the repayment capacities are almost cent per cent. This leaves the radical debate on the two contradictory functioning institutional arrangements, where state and market are at one extreme end, SKDRDP on the other extreme. State and Market face institutional hindrances for achieving sustainable community development, because they follow rigid, one-dimensional idea of financial inclusion for empowerment of masses through mere provision of loan but SKDRDP at the other extreme following a quasi- rigid but holistic one-to-one approach for empowerment which will eventually equip people to move towards sustainable development. "India's problem is not too much micro-credit, but too little, too narrowly directed. The MFIs are less abusive and far cheaper than traditional moneylenders. Their troubles in Andhra Pradesh stem from lack of favourable institutional arrangement."[3] This substantiates the above argument.

Another area of contribution of SKDRDP which is evident in the data is that of the direct supply of public goods. This evidence also supports the theories behind the origin of the third sector organisations in order to supply public goods. Where state or market have failed in providing electricity or roads or providing shelter or such basic necessities to the poorest of the poor, SKDRDP has been able to bridge this gap in this geographical area. The transaction cost involved for the institution are observably higher for the reason that most of the respondents reside in the remote interior rural areas where there are no proper facilities to reach, In such the place situation, the institution which has a crew of dedicated staff and supporters has been able to provide certain public goods .This may not have been possible if the state or market were to undertake. This is because state takes longer time for approval of project and implementation and in case of market, higher transactions cost would provide disincentive for the players to venture in these projects. Thus,

SKDRDP has been extremely successful in providing benefits to the marginalised section and improving their empowerment levels. In these situations, the benefit enjoyed by marginalised section and their empowerment levels are to be viewed as the profits for the organisation and the community or the nation as a whole from the policy point of view, so that the dream of sustainable community development is materialised.

End notes

[1] "Given an initial allocation of goods among a set of individuals, a change to a different allocation that makes at least one individual better off without making any other individual worse off is called a Pareto improvement". An allocation is defined as 'Pareto efficient' or 'Pareto optimal' when no further 'Pareto improvements' can be made.

[2] On December 1, 2008, three most popular models comprising the *Pragathibandhu, Sampoorna Suraksha* and a micro- finance model from Argentina were declared the best. Announcing this, the Asia Director of Ashoka Foundation Mrs Kalpana Kaul (Ph: 033-24172587) complemented SKDRDP for their amazing performance in developing unique models for the poor. For more information, visit www.changemakers.net.

[3] "In India, micro-credit faces uncertainty", January 4, 2011 by Micro-finance Africa posted on *Myanmar Times*.

References

Amin *et al.* (1998) "NGO-Promoted Micro-credit Programmes and Women's Empowerment in Rural Bangladesh: Quantitative and Qualitative Evidence"; *The Journal of Developing Areas*, Vol. 32, No. 2, pp. 221-36.

Annual Reports of SKRDP : 2008-09 and 2010-11.

Babu and Sahu, "A case of Sri Kshethra Dharmastala Rural Development Project linking Micro-finance with Livelihood Augmentation" http://www.thelivelihoodschool.in.

Bill Abom (2004) "Social Capital, NGOs, and Development: A Guatemalan Case Study" *Development in Practice*, Vol. 14, No. 3 , pp. 342-53.

Bronic (2005), "The Role of Non-Governmental Non-Profit Organisations in the Provision of Social Services and the Palliation of Poverty," *Financial Theory and Practice* 29 (1), pp. 99-114.

Candland (2000), "Faith as Social Capital: Religion and Community Development in Southern Asia", *Policy Sciences*, Vol. 33, No. 3/4, *Social Capital as a Policy Resource* pp. 355-74.

Carmona (2004), "Development NGOs, Local Learning, and Social Capital: The Experience of CARE Bolivia in Villa Serrano", *Development in Practice*, Vol. 14, No. 3 pp. 354-65.

Fonjong (2001), "Fostering Women's Participation in Development through Non-Governmental Efforts in Cameroon", *The Geographical Journal*, Vol. 167, No. 3, pp. 223-34.

Handy and Kassam (2004), "Women's Empowerment in Rural India", Paper presented as the ISTR conference, Toronto, Canada.

Hye Mondal (2000) "Social capital formation: The Role of NGO Rural Development Programmes in Bangladesh". *Policy Sciences*, Vol. 33, No 3/4, *Social Capital as a Policy Resource*, pp. 459-75.

Kumar and Sreedhar (2004), "From passive participation to effective leadership: A study on the advances in women leadership in Dakshina Kannada, India", *Sixth International Conference of International Society for Third Sector Research (ISTR) Ryerso Universtiy And York University Toronto, Canada* .

Lewis (1994), "Non-governmental Organisations and Caribbean Development". *Annals of the American Academy of Political and Social Science*, Vol. 533, Trends in US-Caribbean Relations, pp. 125-38.

Rajasekhar (2002), "Economic Programmes and Poverty Reduction: NGO Experiences from Tamil Nadu". *Economic and Political Weekly*, Vol. 37, No. 29, pp. 3063-68.

Streeten (1997), "Non-governmental Organisations and Development". *Annals of the American Academy of Political and Social Science*, Vol. 554, The Role of NGOs: Charity and Empowerment, pp. 193-210.

Valentinov (2008), "Non-market Institutions in Economic Development: The Role of Third Sector". *Development and Change* 39(3) pp.477-85.

Vidyavathi and Jayakumar (2010), "SKDRDP's Successful Experiment with Group Entrepreneurship" *SSRN*.

Weimer and Vining (2004), *Policy Analysis and Concepts* 4th ed. p. 206.

Ziemek (2002) "Economic Theories on motivations for volunteering – A Cross-Country Analysis," Revised Draft Paper presented at the *Fifth International Conference of the International Society for Third-Sector Research*, Cape Town, South Africa.

13

Greening Rural Development in India: Strategies and Programmes

V.G. Siddaraju

Introduction

India with an area of 3.28 million sq. km is the seventh largest country in the world. In population, which has already crossed the billion mark, it is next only to China. The democratic set-up combined with its billion population gives the country the unique status of being the largest democracy in the world. "India lives in its villages". Literally and from the social, economic and political perspectives, the statement is valid even today. Around 65 per cent of the State's population is living in rural areas. People in rural areas should have the same quality of life as is enjoyed by people living in suburban and urban areas. Further, there are cascading effects of poverty, unemployment, poor and inadequate infrastructure in rural areas on urban centres causing slums and consequential social and economic tensions manifesting in economic deprivation and urban poverty. Hence, Rural Development which is concerned with economic growth and social justice, improvement in the living standard of the rural people by providing adequate and quality social services and minimum basic needs becomes essential. The present strategy of rural development mainly focusses on poverty alleviation, better livelihood opportunities, provision of basic amenities and infrastructure facilities through innovative programmes of wage and self-employment. The above goals will be achieved by various programme support being implemented creating partnership with communities, non--governmental organisations, community-based organisations, institutions, PRIs and industrial establishments, while the Department of Rural Development will provide logistic support both on technical and administrative side for programme implementation. Other aspects that will ultimately lead to transformation of rural life are also being emphasised simultaneously.

Most of the rural population of India depends on natural resources for their subsistence and livelihood. At the national as well as global levels, there is increasing focus on environmental issues and sustainable development across various economic and social sectors. The major emphasis of greening of development programmes has been on (a) restoring and conserving natural resources and eco-systems (b) developing clean technological solutions and infrastructure, and (c) innovations for reducing carbon emissions and environmental pollution. The greening development can stimulate rural economies, create jobs and help maintain critical eco-system services that are vital to the economy and human health and well-being and, also strengthen resilience to climate-induced change particularly of the rural poor, who are amongst the most vulnerable to the impacts of climate change and natural resources degradation (Musyoki, 2012). Eco-system goods and services are crucial to ensuring viability of agriculture, livestock and non-timber forest based livelihoods. Besides, they are main things to safe drinking water, health-care, shelter and more.

Defining 'Greening'

In its simplest, the term 'green' implies to 'environmental friendly'. Therefore, 'greening development' implies to the environmental-friendly outcomes of development. In this context, it encompasses environmentally-friendly and sustainable provision of sanitation services in a village that enhance the quality of natural resources.

Green Economy

The green economy is defined as an economy that results in reducing environmental risks and ecological scarcities, and that aims for sustainable development without degrading the environment. It is closely related with ecological economics, but has a more politically applied focus.

The Global Green Economy Index (GGEI), measures selected national economies as judged by expert practitioners and third party indicators and datasets. The 2014 GGEI will measure four primary dimensions defining a national green economy as follows:

1. Leadership and the extent to which national leaders are champions for green issues and addressing climate change on the local and international stage.
2. Sectors and domestic policies supporting the greening of buildings, transportation, tourism and energy sectors in home market.
3. Markets and investment and the perceived and actual opportunities for cleantech investment and the climate for innovation and commercialisation of green products and services in each country.

4. Environment and natural capital and the extent to which countries protect their environmental assets and use natural capital efficiently.

The Concept of 'Greening Rural Development'

The concept of 'greening rural development' implies the kind of development that induces the desired improvements in the environment, provides the sustainability of livelihoods and incomes and helps in the mitigation of scarcity. The greening of rural development aims to improve the quality and carrying capacity of ecosystems, strengthen the resilience of ecosystems and, reduce the ecological footprints of development interventions.

In India, the Ministry of Rural Development (MoRD) has been implementing a wide spectrum of programmes which are aimed at poverty alleviation, employment generation, infrastructure development and social security. MoRD programmes have significant potential for green results, both at the local and global levels.

Objectives and Methodology

The present study tries to analyse the strategies and programmes undertaken for the purpose of eco-friendly rural development in India. The study is based on secondary data collected from various government reports.

Rural Development Schemes in India

The Ministry of Rural Development (MoRD) spearheads the country's efforts to reduce poverty in the rural areas. Until recently, its work was divided among three departments: (i) Department of Rural Development (ii) Department of Land Resources (iii) Department of Drinking Water and Sanitation. In July 2011, the Department of Drinking and Sanitation was converted into a separate ministry, the Ministry of Drinking Water and Sanitation. Greening rural development refers to variety of activities that regenerate and conserve the natural resource base, innovate and use clean materials, technologies and processes to create environment-friendly products, livelihoods, enterprises and jobs. The following schemes are mainly focusses on greening rural development in the Indian context.

1. **Mahatma Gandhi National Rural Employment Guarantee Scheme (MGNREGS):** This aims at enhancing the livelihood and security of people in rural areas by guaranteeing hundred days of wage employment in financial year to a rural household whose adult members volunteer to do unskilled manual work. (Budgetary allocation in 2012-13: INR 33,000 billion).

2. **National Rural Livelihoods Mission (NRLM):** The basic objective of the National Rural Livelihood Mission is to create efficient and effective institutional platforms of the rural poor that enable them

increase their household income through sustainable livelihood enhancement and improved access to financial services. It plans to cover 70 million households living below the poverty line (BPL) in rural India. (Budgetary allocation in 2012-13: INR 3,563 billion).

3. **Integrated Watershed Development Programme (IWDP):** The main objectives of the IWDP are to restore ecological balance in watershed by harnessing, conserving and developing degraded natural resources such as soil, water and vegetative cover, and thereby, help provide sustainable livelihoods to the local people. (Budgetary allocation in 2012-13: INR 2,744 billion).

4. **Indira Awaas Yojana (IAY):** This scheme provides financial grants to rural BPL families and the next of-kin of defence personnel killed in action for construction of houses and upgradation of existing unserviceable kutcha houses. (Budgetary allocation in 2012-13: INR 9,966 billion)

5. **National Rural Drinking Water Programme (NRDWP):** The goal of this scheme is to provide adequate safe water for domestic use on sustainable basis. (Budgetary allocation in 2012-13: INR 10,500 billion).

6. **Nirmal Bharat Abhiyan (NBA):** The Total Sanitation Campaign, now renamed as the Nirmal Bharat Abhiyan, assists *Gram Panchayats* to achieve comprehensive sanitation coverage. (Budgetary allocation in 2012-13: INR 3,500 billion).

The major schemes listed above can potentially make significant contribution to sustaining and regenerating natural resources and ecosystem services. Some examples are:

- A vast majority of works under the MGNREGS are linked to water, soil and land. The list of 'permissible' works provide environmental services such as conservation of water, groundwater recharge, reduced soil erosion, increased soil fertility, conservation of bio-diversity, reclamation of degraded crop and grazing lands, enhanced leaf manure, fuel wood and non-wood forest products supply.

- Watershed Development programmes (IWDP) are focussed primarily on ecological restoration by reducing soil erosion, increasing water storage (*in-situ* moisture conservation, surface water bodies and groundwater recharge), improving vegetative cover, particularly on fallow lands and strengthening related livelihoods. IWDP can also encourage sustainable natural resource use, particularly in watershed projects' consolidation phase.

- Under NRLM, the guidelines for non-timber forest produce-based livelihoods under the *Mahila Kisan Sashaktikaran Pariyojana (MKSP)* identify regeneration and sustainable harvesting of NTFP species as key objectives; similarly, increased soil health and fertility to sustain agriculture-based livelihoods is an objective under the sustainable agriculture component of the MKSP.
- The NRDWP guidelines have earmarked 20 per cent of the funds for sustainability of water supply, including long-term source sustainability. If water supply schemes under NRDWP include components to ensure water source sustainability, NRDWP will have a significant green impact. The scheme, with its commitment to safe water quality, is expected to invest in water treatment facilities to address contamination. The scheme could further invest in safe disposal of the sludge from such water treatment to augment green results.
- *Nirmal Bharat Abhiyan*- formerly the Total Sanitation Campaign (TSC) - is by its very nature a green programme. In recent years, its scope has been extended beyond the eradication of open defecation to comprehensive sanitation. Due to this expansion in scope, ten per cent of the project funds is earmarked for solid and liquid waste management. NBA, thereby, can ensure that such waste does not contaminate the water system.

Greening Rural Development uses green indicators and metrics for monitoring and evaluation of rural development projects and schemes. As per MoRD, greening rural development refers to five broad "green outcomes":

i. **Improved resource conservation:** Rural development schemes especially MGNREG's and IWDP focus on regeneration of natural resources. Conserving and regenerating land and water resources enhances their productivity, leading to increased agriculture outputs and improved livelihoods derived from agriculture, forests and pastures. These schemes can assist in reducing run-off and soil losses, recharge groundwater, increase vegetative cover and improve bio-diversity, and thereby, augment the productivity of natural resources and ecosystems.

ii. **Improved resource efficiency:** Rural development schemes can substantially improve the efficiency of natural resource use in rural livelihoods and essential services. Under IWDP, there is opportunity to support farmer groups to adopt practices that improve efficiency of irrigation water. This can be done through appropriate crop choices, farming techniques, drip and sprinkler irrigation systems and improved field irrigation methods. Under NRLM, women's self-help-groups and farmers can be supported on efficient nutrient management by combining chemical inputs with organic inputs. Under MGNREGs, soil erosion can be reduced leading to lower run-off of chemical fertilisers and higher yields per unit of applied chemical fertiliser.

iii. **Reduced negative environmental impact:** Greening Rural Development schemes can potentially reduce the negative environmental fall out of economic development (pollution, waste generation etc.). Solid and liquid waste management in the *Nirmal Bharat Abhiyan* (formerly the Total Sanitation Campaign) improves local sanitation and hygiene and thereby, the well being and health of local residents. In the *Indira Awaas Yojana*, the use of locally-available resources-such as rice husk, ash and flyash reduces diesel required to transport manufactured materials over long distances, and thereby, environmental pollution. Organic farming and sustainable harvesting of NTFPs under NRLM and the use of renewable energy for lifting water in NRDWP are other examples.

iv. **Strengthened climate resilience of communities:** Greening rural development schemes can potentially enhance the resilience of rural population and production systems, and reduce risks arising from climatic variation and extreme events such as droughts, floods and cyclones. Afforestation, plantations, fodder development and vegetation belts in coastal areas under MGNREGs, IWDP or NRLM build livelihood resilience and improve local communities' coping capacity to potential impacts of climate change. They also increase biodiversity and make the local ecosystems more resilient. Flood control measures under MGNREGs and IWDP enhance resilience in flood-prone areas.

v. **Contribution to climate change mitigation:** Large-scale forestry and soil conservation measures can sequester carbon and reduce greenhouse gas emissions. For example, afforestation, plantations and vegetation belts under MGNREGs and IWDP can help sequester carbon and contribute to national and global efforts to address climate change.

Relevance of Green Outcomes for Indian Economy

The rationale for greening rural development emerges from the Twelfth Five-Year Plan (2012-17) strategy of 'faster, sustainable and more inclusive growth' for poverty alleviation and MoRD's mandate to reduce rural poverty and ensure a better quality of life especially for the poor. There are four major ways in which greening rural development schemes can contribute to the Twelth Plan priorities:

1. **Contributions to inclusive growth:** A critical element in meeting the planned target of nine per cent annual GDP growth is to sustain an annual growth rate of four per cent in the agricultural sector. This is important for ensuring that growth as more inclusive. Although agriculture contributes to only 14 per cent of India's GDP, it is the main source of income for 58 per cent of the rural population, particularly small farmers with limited opportunities for migrating to the modern growth sectors. Agriculture also has a strong influence on food security and the prices of food, and therefore, on monetary wages. Further, agriculture has a very strong multiplier effect because of its impact on rural income and demand, and its supply of raw materials to several industrial sectors. While there has been a marked revival in agricultural growth in India since 2004, for the Eleven Five-Year Plan as a whole, the growth rate is 3.6 per cent. This is lower than the target for the Twelf Plan. The year-to-year variability of agricultural growth has been declining, both on irrigated and rainfed land. Yet, the importance of climate-resilient domestic production of food grains has been highlighted by the recent spikes in global food grain prices. The impact of this variability goes further, with one per cent decline in agricultural growth pulling back industrial growth and GDP growth by 0.52 per cent.

2. **Environmental sustainability of economic growth:** RD schemes can contribute significantly to conserving water resources, soil quality and bio-diversity. RD schemes such as Mahatma Gandhi National Rural Employment Guarantee Scheme (MGNREGS), Integrated Watershed Development Programme (IWDP), and the source sustainability component of **National Rural Drinking Water Programme (NRDWP)** can help arrest and even reverse the decline in groundwater levels in critical regions. This is particularly useful for hard-rock regions where groundwater depletion is at its most acute. Soil conservation works are a large part of MGNREGs and IWDP activities. Soil fertility enhancement is a key objective of the ***Mahila Kisan Sashaktikaran Pariyojana*** **(MKSP)** and sustainable agriculture components of **National Rural Livelihood Mission (NRLM). MGNREGS, IWDP** and **NRLM** activities can play major role in conserving India's bio-diversity which is so essential for providing the country with ecological and livelihood security.

3. **Increase climate resilience of production systems, livelihoods and habitats**: RD schemes can help reduce the impact of metereological droughts by conserving soil moisture, slowing down water runoff and increasing water storage in surface reservoirs as well as aquifers. It can also improve vegetative cover in common lands, making more

fodder and fuelwood available during droughts. Resilience in the face of floods can be provided by improving drainage.

4. **Green outcomes will help making public expenditure more effective:** RD schemes can strengthen livelihoods security for the rural poor thereby reducing demand for work under MGNREGs. Investment on source sustainability will result in greater longevity for drinking water supply systems and will reduce the number of 'slipped-back' habitations. MGNREGs and IWDP can help bridge the gap between irrigation potential created and utilised, for small and micro-irrigation projects.

Conclusion

As the UN Secretary General's High Level Panel on Sustainability notes, there exists tremendous opportunity for dramatic improvement in the lives of the rural poor, even while they move towards more sustainable production models. Resource users will need access to assets, technology and markets. Success will depend, in great part, on investment. Success will also depend on institutions and initiatives with capacity to effectively coordinate efforts. The above actions by the Ministry of Rural Development can succeed by directing investment and coordinating institutions and resource users to achieve green outcomes. Thereby, the Ministry will not only help overcome the constraints posed by environmental degradation, but utilise environmental resources as an opportunity to spur growth and reduce poverty.

References

- Greening Rural Development in India, UNDP India 2012. Published in India.
- Musyoki A. (June 2012), 'The Emerging Policy for Green Economy and Social Development in Limpopo, South Africa'. Occasional Paper Eight. Social Dimensions of Green Economy and Sanitation Development. Unitted Nations Research Institute for Social Development.
- National Sample Survey, 2009-10.
- Sastry, D.V.S., *et al.* (2003): "Sectoral linkages and growth prospects: reflections on the Indian economy," Economic and Political Weekly, June 14, 2003.

14

Challenges Faced by MGNREGA in the Eradication of Rural Poverty and Unemployment- A Case Study

Uma H.R. and Chikkasidde Gowda

Introduction

As we know the majority of Indian populations are living in rural area and their main occupation is agriculture, their level of annual income which is derived from agriculture is too small; therefore they are having insufficient income to lead their lives. The main reason for aggravating poverty is unemployment during non-agricultural season and decline in the agricultural productivity. So, this is a challenging task for GoI, in order to overcome from this problem they have undertaken many programmes such as 'Sampoorna Grameen Rozgar Yojana' (SGRY) or Universal Rural Employment Programme and National Food For Work Programme (NFFWP) etc., but unfortunately these programme were not able to reach targetted people. This made them to introduce new programme, i.e., MGNREG *(Mahatma Gandhi National Rural Employment Guarantee Act)* If is a combination of both SGRY and NFFWP also provided short-term unskilled employment to poor, assured food and job security and created durable assets.

The MGNREGA provides legal guarantee for 100 days of employment in every financial year to adult members of any rural household to do public work related unskilled manual work at the statutory minimum wage. Thus, it is a universal programme. This minimum wage varies from state to state, in some states, it is Rs 80 whereas in other, it is Rs. 125 or Rs. 120. In Karnataka, it was Rs.155 in 2012-13 and Rs. 195 in 2014-15. According to the Act, the minimum wage cannot be less than Rs. 60. The 100 days of work figure was estimated because the agricultural season is only supposed to last roughly around 250 days and unskilled workers have no alternative source of income in the remaining parts of the year.

Salient Features of MGNREGA

- All adult members of rural household willing to do unskilled manual work have the right to demand employment.
- Such household will have to apply registration to the *Gram Panchayat.*
- After verification, the *Gram Panchayat* will issue a Job Card with photograph of adult members of the household willing to work under the programme.
- The Job Card must remain in the custody of the householder.
- Job Card holder can apply for work to the *Gram Panchayat,* which will issue him/her a dated receipt of the work application.
- Employment will be provided by the *Gram Panchayat* (local self-governing body) within 15 days of work application, failing which unemployment allowance will be paid.
- Disbursement of wages has to be done conweekly basis and not beyond a fortnight.
- Wages will be paid at the wage rate to the wage earners through their Bank/Post office accounts.
- An annual shelf of works be prepared in advance for each year.
- A ratio of 60:40 for wage and material costs should be maintained at GP level.
- No contractors/and no labour-displacing machinery shall be used in execution of works.
- *Panchayati Raj* Institutions will have principal role in planning, monitoring and implementation.
- At least, one-third of the workers should be women.
- In-built incentive-disincentive structure to the State Government for guaranteeing employment.

As a result of many welfare programmes like MGNREGA from the government, the level of poverty has decreased significantly from 37.2 per cent to 21.9 per cent in 2004-05 to 2011-12, respectively, in which rural poverty in 2004-05, it was 41.8 per cent but in 2011-12, it we is 25.7 per cent (According to recent Suresh Tendulkar Committee report).

However, the unemployment rate is estimated to be 3.8 per cent at All

India level in which rural areas, unemployment rate is 3.4 per cent whereas in urban areas, the same is 5.0 per cent (Ministry of Labour and Employment, Government of India 2011-12). So, the contribution of MGNREGA is significant to reduce unemployment level in rural area. But due to many problems, the MGNREGA has failed to achieve expected goal.

Literature Review

Since the launching of MGNREGA, there have been several studies looking into its implementation aspects, such as wage formation processes in the rural labour markets, its finances, its democratic administration and implementation, and socio-economic impact such as rural poverty alleviation, gender issues, self-esteem, livelihood and food security, and migration. Among them, some of the important studies are reviewed below,

A study which was done by Sankar V and Dr. Sivamurugan, C. (2009), in their article entitled "*Economic Impact of NREGP on Employment Generation*", has analysed that in India unemployment is the main reason for the existence of poverty in rural areas. For that the government has launched various employment generation programmes, mere providing such employment programmes does not improve their economic condition. But with the launching of the NREGP, it has improved the economic condition of the people by giving employment opportunities to the rural poor in the country, with special social safety needs, helping in reduction of poverty and improves the rural infrastructure in many ways.

Another one which was studied by Angel Anila, A. (2010), titled "*Persistence of Poverty in India a critical Assessment of National Rural Employment Guarantee Act*" reveals that GoI introduced various programmes, but unfortunately they have failed to properly implement the programmes. Even in case of MGNREGA programme GoI has failed because of the lack of adequate administrative and technical manpower at the Block and GP (*Gram Panchayat*) levels. This lack of manpower has adversely affected the preparation of plans, inspection, approval, monitoring and measurement of works and maintenance of the stipulated records at the Block and *Gram Panchayath* levels.

Indian Institute of Technology, Madras, (2009), "*Evaluation of National Rural Employment Guarantee Act: In Districts: Cuddalore, Dindugal, Kanchipuram, Nagai, Thiruvallar, State: Tamil Nadu*, study reveals the impact of MNREGA in the state of Tamil Nadu by under taking five districts into account. In each districts, four GPs were chosen.

This study shows many positive aspects of the programme. These are mainly:

- Villagers consider that NREGA is promising to be a boon for improving rural livelihood.
- Provision of job within the village is very much encouraging to villagers.
- NREGA also ensured gender equality in rural Tamil Nadu.
- The programme employed very good proportion of scheduled caste and backward caste people.
- Involvement of SHG members improves people's NREGS awareness and this is very important for future NREGS planning.
- Financial inclusion strategies like bank account opening and rural ATM for NREGS beneficiaries at four villagers of Cuddalore block has resulted in multiplier effects of savings, financial safety etc.
- Registrations are open throughout the year.
- Most of the respondents perceived that payment were received within a week.

The present study is an attempt to describe challenges of MGNREGP faced in the way of eradicating poverty and unemployment.

Objectives of the Study

- To find challenges of MGNREGP in the way of eradicating poverty and unemployment.

Methodology

The present study is based on both primary and secondary data. Primary data have been collected through the questionnaire by the respondents in the study area Tubinakere *Gram Panchayat* of Mandya district, Karnataka. The secondary data have been collected by various related journals, research studies, government publications etc.

Introduction of NREGA in Karnataka State

NREGA was enacted in September, 2005 with an objective of 'enhancement of livelihood, security of rural households by providing at least one hundred days of guaranteed wage employment in every financial year to every household whose adult members volunteer to do unskilled manual work' simply put, the primary objective of the Act is to 'provide 100 days of unskilled manual work in rural areas' NREGA was launched in two hundred most backward districts of India on February 2nd, 2006 in Phase-I, and was extended to 130 more-districts in 2007-08 in Phase-II. It was further extended to the remaining districts from April, 1st 2008 onwards, in Phase-III. In Karnataka, in Phase-I, the programme was initiated in the rural areas of five districts, namely, Bidar, Chitradurga, Davangere, Gulbarga and Raichur. The programme was extended to other six districts, namely, Bellary, Hassan, Chikmagalur, Belgaum, Shimoga and Kodagu, by Phase-II and to the remaining 16 districts by Phase-III. The Government of Karnataka has issued detailed guidelines for implementing NREGA.

Case study

Introduction about Panchayat:

It is on Mandya-Mysore road far away from Mandya only 12 km. The 7,091 population are living under this *Gram Panchayat*. Main occupation is agriculture and small scale industries are surrounded by this *Gram Panchayat*.

MGNREGA programme has been implemented in 2008.

Under this Panchayat, there are five villages:

- Yelechakanahalli and Tubinakere,
- Ragimuddanah alli,
- Nodekoppalu, and
- Uramarakasalagere.

Challenges of MGNREGA

Illiteracy among village people: Under this panchayat, there are 7,091 people in which 3,733 are people male and 3,358 people are female. The literacy level in this *Gram Panchayat* is only 63.8 per cent due to illiteracy they canbe easily cheated by an administrator.

Lack of response from village people: Among 7,091 people, only 1,841 persons have registered their names under this programme in *Gram Panchayat*. And most of them didn't know how their names were registered. At present, only 50 registered members are working, in which only two members were got more than 90 days work. It shows that the village community is not showing interest on MGNREGP. The details can be had from the Table - 1.

Table – 1: *Tubinakere Gram Panchayat Registered Households and Persons*

Villages	*No of Registered*		*SCs*		*STs*		*Others*		*Male*	*Female*
	House Holds	Persons	House Holds	Persons	House Holds	Persons	House Holds	Persons		
Nodekoppalu	76	198	0	0	0	0	76	198	107	91
Ragimuddanahalli	139	307	31	99	0	0	108	208	171	136
Uramarakasalagere	160	495	15	57	2	4	143	434	281	214
Yelechakanahalli andTubinakere	413	841	29	93	0	0	384	748	490	351
Total	**788**	**1841**	**75**	**249**	**2**	**4**	**711**	**1588**	**1049**	**792**

Source: Primary Data.

Low Wage and Working Hours is too Long: Another challenge of this programme is low wage , nearly 90 per cent of the respondents said that the wage which is paid by *Gram Panchayat* by MGNREGP is too low and there is a possiblity to get more wage for same work. And working hours also long, they can get Rs 300 to 350, if they work in another discipline.

Deficiency in Understanding the Importance of NREGA amongst Villagers: *It was witnessed during the survey, that there is lack of awareness among the villagers, especially among the people, who live in the interior villages of the panchayat. An officer at the stature of Panchayat Development Officer should be appointed at every panchayat to not only monitor the planning and implementation but also to arrange workshops regarding awareness of the programme among the villagers. The workshops will provide detailed breakdown about th programme with its ways of implementation and effectiveness. A proper guidance and scrutinising of project selection by the officer will increase the efficiency of the village-level coordinators. Also, the NREGA cell at the gram panchayat should be strengthened by providing more staff.*

Reluctance to Work: The villagers are assured of the minimum payment of Rs 195 per day once they register have in the muster roll, whether they work or not. Therefore, some of them take advantage of this fact and do not perform the required task for the day:

Discrepancies and Favouritism: Some villagers complained about the discrepancies and favouritism for the number of days of employment. Again, few villagers have also alleged that there is a tendency of local influential people of the village to get their names registered in the muster roll, without actually engaging themselves in the assigned projects. This leads to work burden on the other labourers as their work is divided amongst the workers in order to provide wages to them.

Poor Quality of Works: There is no proper execution of works. Hence, it is a matter of concern that throughout the GP, the approved works are not always publicly displayed. It was revealed by the villagers that there was no *gram sabha* meeting regarding the activities of NREGS. Even maximum numbers of people are not aware about *gram sabha* meeting, which reflects non-participation of villagers or community in decision-making. The villagers used to work on any work assigned by the contractor or *gram panchayat*, president PDO. The internal understanding between contractors, *gram panchayat* president, PDO and JE used to confine the work in paper only. Site account registers in respect of receipt and issue of materials to the work and temporary advance register in respect of advance availed for payment of wages had not been maintained, despite their mandated requirement for departmental execution. MGNREGA guidelines permit execution of road projects providing all weather connectivity in rural areas. However, during field work, it was observed that the road remain *kuchha* and incomplete and is not able to provide all weather access.

Fake accounts: In this study, we also found that many fake accounts, which has been created by local political leader in the name of their followers. They have been getting money without working under this programme for the sake of their strong local political leader.

Poor participation of women, non-organisation of workshop, local government corruption, lack of responsibility etc,. are other challenges.

Suggestions

- The success of the programme depends upon its proper implementation. Much of the pitfalls of MGNREGA implementation can be overcome, if proper processes and procedures are put in place. Thus, there should be continuous efforts towards creating adequate awareness on different provisions of MGNREGA amongst the people. Creating awareness is necessary not only to motivate the people to work under the scheme but also to encourage them to participate in its planning and implementation.
- Participation of woman in MGNREGA programme must be increased

through raising awareness as her role in the programme plays vital factor in family's income.

- The MGNREGA Programme is not much popular in the rural area due to lack of awareness. Hence, a special awareness campaign should be conducted for the beneficiaries.
- Under the MGNREGA programme, large number of workers have suffered from the interference of middlemen. *Gram panchayat* officers have not given any proper guidance about the programme and they have not supervised the workers at the work site. The workers' usual contact was only with the *gram panchayat* development officer, and if he has committed fraudulent activities, no one question him. In order to reduce this, specialised supervisory board is necessary.
- In addition to rural employment, this programme should give importance for education of rural poor because majority of them working under this programme are uneducated.
- There should be the ability and willingness of local government and *panchayat* to plan works and run the programmes effectively.
- A proper monitoring mechanism should be developed that can assure correct procedure in job card.
- Social Audit should be carried out in regular interval.

Conclusion

According to 2011 census of India, nearly 83.35 crore people of India are living in rural area. The real development of country lies on development of villages and not with the expansion of industrial hubs in urban area (Mahatma Gandhi). To develop rural area, in terms of alleviating poverty and unemployment there is need to create basic infrastructure and employment opportunity to the rural people. As a result of many welfare programmes like MGNREGA from the government, the level of poverty has decreased significantly from 37.2 to 21.9 in 2004-05, to 2011-12, respectively in which rural poverty in 2004-05, it was 41.8 but in 2011-12 it was 25.7 (According to Suresh Tendulkar Committee recent report). There is a need to give much importance to alleviate poverty in terms of abolishing loopholes of welfare programmes. MGNREGA came in to force for targetting rural uneducated mass to improve their livelihood in terms of providing 100 days of guarantee employment opportunity. If they are not involved in such programme it may cause to complete faifure of the programme. Therefore, if we solve the above stated problems then only the programme can reach targetted goal and *gram panchayat* should stop corruption and make the programme grand success.

References

Dey, S. and Bedi, A. (2010). "The National Rural Employment Guarantee Scheme in Birbhum, *Economic and Political Weekly*, XLV (41).

Indian Institute of Technology, Madras, Chennai (2009). *Evaluation of National Rural Employment Guarantee Act: In Districts: Cuddalore, Dindugal, Kanchipuram, Nagai, Thiruvalallur: State: Tamil Nadu, May.*

Samik Shome, Ramanna Shetty, T.J. Joseph, and Mihir Dash1 (2012), *Impact of Workfare Programmes on Quality of Life: A Case Study of National Rural Employment Guarantee Act in India.*

Soumya Mohanty (2012), *Mahatma Gandhi National Rural Employment Guarantee Act (MGNREGA) and Tribal Livelihoods: A Case Study in Sundargarh District of Odisha.*

15

Bharat Nirman - A Resilient Road Infrastructure in India: Will it be a *Sampark Kranti*?

R Arjun and D Srinivasa

Introduction

India has a road network of about 3.2 million kms of which rural roads account for around 2.7 million kms (85 per cent). According to the Road Development Plan Vision–2001 of the Ministry of Road Transport and Highways, overall village accessibility stood at 54 per cent by 2000.

Better rural infrastructure has primarily two effects – promotion of economic growth and decline in the incidence of poverty. Jocelyn A. Songco (Columbia University and the World Bank, 2002) in a study has pointed out that rural infrastructure investments benefit the rural poor through increased income and improved consumption patterns. Some empirical studies illustrate a strong relationship between infrastructure and economic growth. According to World Bank sources, one per cent increase in infrastructure stock is associated with a proportionate increase in GDP across all countries. A specific sectoral study by Deichman *et al* for Mexico shows that a 10 per cent increase in market access leads to increase in labour productivity by six per cent. Linkages between public investment on rural connectivity, agricultural growth and poverty alleviation in the Indian context were investigated in a research report authored by Shengenn Fan, Peter Hazell and Sukhadeo Thorat (Research Paper No.110, IFPRI, 1999).

Research Objectives

1. To study the Tasks and Achievement of *Bharat Nirman.*
2. To study the role of *Bharat Nirman* Programme in Rural roads.

Research Methodology

On the basis of fundamental objectives of research, our study is a type of Descriptive Research - also known as statistical research. Method of data collection – Secondary Data:- Large amount of secondary data is available in the forms of articles, manuals and previously conducted researches on the similar topic. Also the data gathered will help in identifying key parameters to examine through further exploration and thus will help in defining the Objectives.

Bharat Nirman

A flagship programme of the Government of India conceived as time-bound business plan to provide rural infrastructure during 2005-06 to 2008-09. Six major rural infrastructure namely, rural roads, telephone connection, irrigation, water supply, housing and electrification are identified and over Rs. 1, 74,000 crore was yearmarked for development. The programme was initiated during the year 2005-06, under rural road component, it targetted to provide all weather connectivity to all habitations having population of 1,000 or more (500 or more in hill, tribal and desert areas) by 2009. While the primary objective of PMGSY has been to provide 'last mile connectivity' to all eligible unconnected habitations, it also includes an upgradation component in order to ensure farm to market connectivity.

It is pertinent to mention that the rural road component of the *Bharat Nirman* programme is actually embedded in the PMGSY the target for connectivity to habitations with 1,000 or more population. Thus, the rural road component is concomitant to PMGSY with wider funding base and extended scope. *Bharat Nirman* envisages a massive scaling up of the programme in terms of habitation connectivity coverage, construction targets and financial investment.

Target and Achievement till 10th Five Year Plan

To achieve the targets of *Bharat Nirman*, 1, 46,185 kms of rural road is proposed to be constructed to benefit 66,802 unconnected eligible habitations in the country. It is also proposed to upgrade nearly 1.94 lakh kms of the existing rural roads, which are identified through routes of the core network. The total investment on rural connectivity under *Bharat Nirman* has been estimated at Rs. 48,000 crore during 2005-09. Table-4 provide, the national level habitation connectivity targets set and achievements under PMGSY/ Bharat Niman, and Table-5 provides the national level road length in km for connecting the above-targetted habitations under PMGSY/Bharat Nirman. The year-wise targets for new connectivity are covered under Table-1 and upgradation Table-2.

Table-1: Targets and Achievements of Plans for Road Development.

(In kms.)

Road category	*Nagpur Plan (1943-61)*		*Bombay Plan (1961-81)*		*Lucknow Plan (1981-2001)*	
	Target	*Achievement*	*Target*	*Achievement*	*Target*	*Achievement*
1. National Highways	33,395	22,636	51,500	31,737	66,000	57,700
2. State Highways	86,825	62,052	112,650	95,491	145,000	124,300
3. Major District Roads	80,145	113,483	241,400	153,000	300,000	2,994,000*
4. Rural Roads (Other District Roads and Village Roads	332,335	500,802	651,780	912,684	2,189,000	
Total	**532,700**	**698,973**	**1,057,330**	**1,192,912**	**2,700,000**	**3,176,000**

* Includes 1000000 km of earth tracks, mostly under employment generation programmes.

Note: Figures for targets and achievement relate to the end of the plan period. (*Source*: Road Development Plan-Vision: 2021 (IRC-2001).

Table 2: Bharat Nirman- Targets for New Road Connectivity (Length in km, Habitations in Numbers)

S.No	Name of the State	2005-06		2006-07		2007-08		2008-09		Total	
		Length	Habs	Length	Habs	Length	Habs	Length	Habs	Length	Habs
1.	Andhra Pradesh	0	0	0	0	0	0	0	0	0	0
2.	Arunachal Pradesh	162.5	22	637.5	85	646.875	86	671.875	105	2118.75	298
3.	Assam	605.852	421	2864.063	1988	3889.845	2701	5793.46	4022	13153.22	9132
4.	Bihar	1665.831	896	3928.75	2062	6121.425	3214	7230.306	3784	18946.312	9956
5.	Chhattisgarh	1501.365	478	4367.606	1310	6450.644	2007	8255.181	2514	20574.796	6309
6.	Goa	0	0	0	0	0	0	0	0	0	0
7.	Gujarat	402.955	230	429.723	246	438.675	251	438.675	251	1710.028	978
8.	Haryana	0	0	0	0	0	0	0	0	0	0
9.	Himachal Pradesh	464.583	127	795.833	209	638.542	166	479.167	123	2378.125	625
10.	J&K	169.972	57	1059.49	352	1781.869	593	1405.099	466	4416.43	1468
11.	Jharkhand	1051.779	526	2594.39	1295	1812.298	901	2319.31	1155	7777.777	3877
12.	Karnataka	0	0	0	0	0	0	0	0	0	0
13.	Kerala	0	0	0	0	0	0	0	0	0	0
14.	Madhya Pradesh	2602.139	768	6162.451	1760	8326.848	2399	10470.17	2905	27561.608	7832
15.	Maharashtra	0	0	0	0	0	0	0	0	0	0
16.	Manipur	100	11	460.714	48	464.286	48	719.048	74	1744.048	181
17.	Meghalaya	123.609	35	135.971	39	140.091	40	144.211	41	543.882	155
18.	Mizoram	82.746	12	274.819	39	277.884	39	306.498	43	941.947	133
19.	Nagaland	93.318	9	104.529	10	109.507	10	114.485	11	421.839	40
20.	Orissa	1055.95	493	1985.609	874	2524.021	1087	4427.774	1993	9993.354	4447
21.	Punjab	0	0	0	0	0	0	0	0	0	0
22.	Rajasthan	2153.615	743	3629.519	1252	3554.217	1225	2123.494	732	11460.845	3952
23.	Sikkim	75.031	22	104.042	30	108.043	31	132.053	37	419.169	120
24.	Tamil Nadu	0	0	0	0	0	0	0	0	0	0
25.	Tripura	94.774	66	261.74	183	334.701	248	447.661	313	1138.876	810
26.	Uttar Pradesh	1966.416	1236	2390.632	1504	2059.213	1295	1378.761	867	7794.362	4902
27.	Uttaranchal	380.609	95	422.008	106	1025.641	257	1020.299	255	2848.557	713
28.	West Bengal	739.378	787	2572.767	2738	3265.307	3473	3643.359	3876	10220.811	10874
	Total	**15492.42**	**7034**	**35182.16**	**16130**	**43989.93**	**20071**	**51520.83**	**23567**	**146185.34**	**66802**

Achievement till 10th Plan

The proposals prepared by states based on inputs provided by PRIs were submitted to NRRDA for year-wise implementing of the programme. NRRDA approved the proposals under PMGSY prepared by states after scrutiny of NRRDA and cleared in different phases since 2001. The total road length constructed up to end of phase IV is about 93,000 km. Against the target originally set for the new connectivity, the proposals cleared so far (May, 2006) are expected to provide connectivity to only 56,638 habitations. The works completed so far have provided connectivity to only 27,303 habitations. The status of habitations coverage achieved so far under this scheme has been indicated in Table-2.

The figures show that only 15.80 per cent of habitations have been actually connected so far, it is envisaged that the scheme would miss the 10th Plan target (original target of PMGSY) by a huge margin. Recognising this slippage, the time frame for providing full connectivity to habitations with population above 1,000 (above 500 in hill, desert, and tribal areas) has been reset under *Bharat Nirman.*

Analysis of Performance of States

A glance at the physical and financial performance of the states under PMGSY/ *Bharat Nirman* clearly brings out the fact that those states, which took initiatives in streamlining the institutional arrangements have performed well compared to others. The state-wise statement showing physical and financial progress under PMGSY (Phases I-IV and ADB/WB) is presented in Table-3 of Discussion Paper provided in Appendix - 1. The physical target represents the length of road works and number of road works sanctioned and completed. The financial targets are represented by the total amount released and expenditure made.

Table: 3 Length of Rural Roads- Target and Achievements under PMGSY/ Bharat Nirman Programme (Length in kms).

Length	*Total Target completion upto 10th FYP*	*Expected completion during 07-09*	*Expected completion during 10-12*	*Overall Targets for 11th FYP*	*Balance work for 12th FYP*	*Core Network Estimate*
New Connectivity	95960	95510	69734	165244	104601	365805
Upgradation	83757	128067	64397	192464	96595	372816
Total	**179717**	**223577**	**134131**	**357708**	**201196**	**738621**

Table 4: Bharat Nirman Targets for Upgradation (Length in kms.)

Sl. No.	Name of the State	2005-06 Length	2006-07 length	2007-08 Length	2008-09 Length	Total Length
1.	2	3	4	5	6	7
1.	Andhra Pradesh	1821.494	2258.652	2258.652	2258.652	8597.45
2.	Arunachal Pradesh	0	0	0	0	0
3.	Assam	0	2005.71	2269.808	2219.843	6495.361
4.	Bihar	0	2393.617	3510.638	3390.958	9295.213
5.	Chhattisgarh	0	1986.063	3240.418	3222.996	8449.477
6.	Goa	190.114	190.114	190.114	190.114	760.456
7.	Gujarat	0	1557.971	1557.971	1413.043	4528.985
8.	Haryana	229.358	1146.789	1146.789	1238.532	3761.468
9.	Himachal Pradesh	0	1515.923	1694.268	1503.185	4713.376
10.	Jammu & Kashmir	0	1007.584	920.91	1007.584	2936.078
11.	Jharkhand	0	2108.433	2123.494	1987.952	6219.879
12.	Karnataka	2573.529	2573.529	2573.529	2573.529	10294.116
13.	Kerala	524.109	628.931	524.109	524.109	2201.258
14.	Madhya Pradesh	0	5189.543	6614.379	6823.53	18627.452
15.	Maharashtra	4334.365	4334.365	4334.365	4334.365	17337.46
16.	Manipur	0	0	0	0	0
17.	Meghalaya	0	587.583	587.583	665.189	1840.355
18.	Mizoram	0	257.998	257.998	216.718	732.714
19.	Nagaland	0	246.914	246.914	370.371	864.199
20.	Orissa	0	4438.574	4663.144	5059.445	14161.163
21.	Punjab	423.729	1483.051	1483.051	1680.791	5070.622
22.	Rajasthan	0	4764.543	4653.74	3656.51	13074.793
23.	Sikkim	0	196.85	137.795	98.425	433.07
24.	Tamil Nadu	1297.71	2824.427	2824.427	4167.939	11114.503
25.	Tripura	0	373.737	383.838	414.141	1171.716
26.	Uttar Pradesh	0	7158.962	6956.031	14408.12	28523.113
27.	Uttaranchal	0	889.454	1283.354	1270.648	3443.456
28.	West Bengal	0	2549.942	2878.965	4054.053	9482.96
	Total	11394.408	54669.259	59316.284	68750.742	194130.693

Table 5: Connectivity Status

Population category	*Total No. of villages*	*No. of villages connected*				
		By 1980	*By 1985*	*By 1990*	*By 1995*	*By 2000*
1500 & above	71623	37950 (53%)	49495 (69%)	59722 (83%)	65704 (92%)	70000 (98%)
1000-1500	58229	21970 (38%)	28732 (49%)	35362 (61%)	44120 (76%)	50000 (86%)
Less Than 1000	459465	107324 (23%)	142020 (31%)	166311 (36%)	173837 (38%)	200000 (43%)
Total	**589317**	**167244 (28%)**	**220247 (37%)**	**261395 (44%)**	**283661 (48%)**	**320000 (54%)**

Note: Figures within brackets give the percentage of villages in each population category (1981Census) to the total number of villages in that category.

Source: Planning Commission and North Road Development Plan Vision 2021 (published by IRC in 2001).

It may be seen from Table 5 that under the aforesaid long-term plans emphasis was particularly made on achieving the length targets and no specific targets for providing connectivity to villages/habitations were actually set. *Secondly*, in all these plans, a network approach to rural road planning was noticeably missing. While achieving the length targets, in many states, more than one connection was provided for a village, resulting in redundancy and development of a large network which was difficult to maintain. Furthermore, the issues of regional imbalances were not specifically addressed in these plans.

At this point, some comments on the prevailing system of maintenance of road statistics particularly with reference to rural roads would be in order. The existing system of planning and management of various categories of roads involves a lot of judgement and empiricism due to lack of systematic and adequate database on the status of roads, traffic volumes etc. Even in respect of national highways, the database is reported to be inadequate with regard to road and bridge inventories. The position with regard to accuracy and reliability of statistics with regard to rural roads is far more unsatisfactory. There are multiplicities of agencies involved in construction and maintenance of rural roads and a nodal agency coordinating projects being undertaken by these agencies is absent. The need, therefore, is for creation of a dynamic database for all categories of roads, including rural roads, for which a coordinating agency needs to be identified with defined responsibilities and precise methodology for data collection and validation. It is hoped that this issue would be given due consideration during the 11th Five Year Plan.

While the primary objective of PMGSY has been to provide 'last most connectivity' to all eligible unconnected habitations, in order to ensure full farm to market connectivity *Bharat Nirman* also includes an upgradation component. It is estimated that under *Bharat Nirman* 66,802 habitations would be provided new connectivity with a road length of 1,46,185 kms. Besides, 1.94 lakh km of existing through routes of the core network would be upgraded/ renewed. The total investment on rural connectivity under *Bharat Nirman* has been estimated at Rs. 48,000 crore over 2005-09. The year-wise targets for new connectivity and upgradation have been detailed at Table-5 and Table-1.

Bharat Nirman envisages a massive scaling up of the programme in terms of habitations coverage, construction targets and financial investment. While around 19,000 habitations were provided connectivity during 2000-05, coverage is targetted to register more than three-fold increase over 2005-09. While average annual spending during 2000-05 was around Rs. 2,500 crore, it is targetted to increase by four to five times under *Bharat Nirman*. While this is a bold initiative to address the infrastructure deficit in the rural areas, the quantum increase envisaged in the programme size call for commensurate efforts in augmenting the programme implementation capacity, contracting capacity, materials planning, construction management systems and work processes.

Targets for the Coverage by the End of 11th Five Year Plan

PMGSY envisages providing connectivity to all habitations of 500 and above in all states and 250 and above in hill states, tribal and desert areas. Based on the projects already approved under PMGSY, a further 2,39,000 km of new link roads will have to be built to provide connectivity to the remaining eligible habitations under PMGSY. It is expected that about 56,600 habitations will get connected, with new link roads of 1,26,670 kms by the end of 10th Five Year Plan. It may not be possible to complete the new connectivity target during the 11th Five Year Plan at the current pace. Even on the premise that absorption capacities of states will increase with time and make it possible to set higher targets, it appears that the total target is beyond the reach of getting completed during the 11th Five Year Plan. Therefore, it may be necessary to set a workable target for achievement during 11th Five Year Plan. The expert group preparing the Rural Roads Development Plan–Vision: 2025 have recommended completion of 1,20,000 kms of roads for new connectivity and 50,000 km of upgradation during the 11th Five Year Plan. This would require investment of Rs. 34,000 crore at current prices.

The issues for consideration are setting feasible physical targets, both in terms of road length and habitation coverage, for the 11th Five Year Plan.

While setting physical targets the working group may also consider the absorption capacity of the states and constraints on the contracting capacity and the measures that may be required to address these constraints.

Conclusion

In order to develop a strategy for rural road development for the 11th Five Year Plan, the key issues are to be taken note for deliberation and focus on the possible measures. The spectrum of the issues covers different facets of Rural Roads Development including achievable targets, implementation strategy. Institutional development for enhancing absorption capacities, technologies for cost effectiveness, management of assets created, quality assurance and possible synergies with other programmes meant for rural development.

- For integrated development of rural connectivity, upgradation is required to be included in addition to new connectivity links, as envisaged in *Bharat Nirman.*
- Rural roads development targets (based on 2001 census and to modify after next census) will require continuance of the programme even beyond 11th Plan period.
- The structure and systems of delivery developed so far should be strengthened and continued.

Maintenance of Road Assets: Rural roads created as assets deteriorate over a period of time. Hence, it must be maintained to a minimum level of acceptable serviceability. If proper attention is lacking, for whatever reason, it is bound to accelerate the process of deterioration, which in turn results in:

- Loss of time,
- Loss of agriculture output,
- Heavy rehabilitation cost,
- Increase in the vehicle operating costs,
- Loss of Access,
- Acceleration of Isolation, and
- Loss of asset itself.

Differed maintenance entails rehabilitation of the road many more times of resources required to be spent on the maintenance. Because of the neglect in the maintenance in the past, the same roads in effect are being constructed over and over at a high social and economic cost. Such situation has to be avoided, therefore, even on the principals of economics the key to prevent this and other ill-effects are to adopt an assured and sustainable maintenance strategy for the rural roads. Regular maintenance of rural roads is a critical pre-condition for sustaining the positive impacts that roads bring to rural communities. Minor maintenance is often neglected not only because of lack of funds, but also because there is a little political capital, or mileage in maintaining roads regularly as the outcome is not highly visible.

An important point to note here is that maintenance of any asset depends upon the care with which it is planned, designed, constructed. A meticulously planned, scientifically designed, and properly constructed with merciless quality control results in minimum maintenance intervention.

The expert group of Rural Roads Development Plan–Vision: 2025 recommended the following strategies for putting maintenance of rural roads on sound footing:

- Introduction of Rural Road Maintenance Act with clearly defined functions and powers;
- Estimation of realistic norms;
- Providing dedicated funds with streamlined management;
- Making the roads maintainable by removing backlogs;
- Bringing *Panchayati Raj Institutions* with necessary capacity building;
- Planning of maintenance works on the principles of asset management;
- Review of gang labour system;
- Documentation and introduction of incentives;

While the PMGSY guidelines envisage that state governments transfer the responsibility of maintenance of rural roads to the *Panchayati Raj Institutions* (PRIs), hardly any worthwhile effort has been made during the 10th Five Year Plan to enable the state governments to move forward in this direction. This issue should, therefore, merit consideration on priority in the 11th Five Year Plan. Specifically, the working group may deliberate on a model of decentralisation laying down which tier of the PRI should take up which segment of the maintenance responsibility, mobilisation of finances for enabling the PRIs to meet the maintenance needs, provision of technical and administrative support at each level of the PRIs to discharge the maintenance responsibilities entrusted to them.

Market Committee Fund strategy should be extending levying of market fee and rural development cess on agricultural produce which has been successfully tried in states like Punjab, Haryana etc. Part of these funds should be earmarked for rural road maintenance. There have been suggestions for laying stamp duty on land transactions, since land values close to roads tend to increase, the beneficiaries may pay additional stamp duty on sale of such lands. Vehicle Fee in addition to taxes on fuel additional funds may be generated to special purchase tax on passenger vehicles and agricultural tractors using a part of this for the maintenance of rural roads. User charges scope in rural roads, which unlike the highways are meant to provide basic access, is rather limited. At best, this may be a potential source only in selected roads with very high commercial traffic volumes (*e.g.,* mining areas). However, even in those cases, user charges may cover the maintenance requirements and not the rehabilitation/upgradation requirements. Public private Partnership (PPP) - while there is little experience of PPP in the context of rural infrastructure in India, it would be a worthy exercise to explore partnership that might work taking in to the complexity of the rural context, creating space for private financing, the economic, social and political nature of the service sought to be provided and the end users. In this context, it may be mentioned that there has been some success in Latin America for rehabilitation and maintenance of roads through service contracts by forming community based micro enterprises. The possibility of replication of this model may be considered. Research and Development is an integral part of any development. Although rural roads were built for last 70-80 years in this country, its construction as engineering structure has just began. Therefore, huge amount of research is required for these low volume roads, which must attempt for low cost construction while ensuring quality. Generally R and D is starved of funds in most cases; and it will be disastrous if R and D is not given prominence in the context of rural roads, as we have just began to accept rural roads construction as scientific work. Most significant areas to be researched are the means of cost cutting by choice of materials and design, and also evolving the innovative financing mechanisms for such roads. It is proposed that the state executing agencies of rural roads shall make it possible to take at least five per cent of the road works under R and D using cost-effective new materials, adoption of new technology and/ or new process, which are likely to ensure R and D culture to the field engineers.

References

Economic Survey, 2011-12.

Gupta Sumit and Mukta Gupta (1998), *Water and Sanitation in Five Year Plans in Natural India.*

Kurukshetra Vol. 60, No.12, October 2012.

Kurukshetra–A journal on Rural Development. Vol. 61, No.02, December 2012.

Pratiyogita Darpan, General Studies, Indian Economy 2012.

Resource Management, Sarup & Sons, New Delhi, p. 160.

The Indian Economics Journal, Special Issue, December 2011, pp. 223-5.

The Indian Express, March 15, 2012, p. 03.

16

The Contributions of Indian Financial System Towards Rural Development – With Special Reference to Coconut Farmers in the Tumkur District

S N Harish and M C Geetha

Introduction

The Indian financial system is the well-designed structure, helps for economic transformation. The nationalisation of banks, Five Year Plan of Central Government, establishment of regional rural banks, division of sector into priority and non-priority measures are forced banks to operate in rural India. This created breathy environment to the rural people to access the banking services. During post-Independence, the rural development is the passionate word debating among the government officials. More than 70 per cent of Indian population is situated in the villages. Majority of village population still have no adequate access to financial services, therefore, this is the needed area of the development. The government adopts many policies to develop the rural people. Out of which, changing the financial practices in the nation is also important move, this helps to generalise the financial services to marginalised sections. The accessibility to the functions of financial system plays the key role in the development. Mainly, the Indian government undertakes reforms in the financial system to enhance the accessibility of financial services to rural people. Specifically, nationalisation of banks, credit co-operatives, NABARD activities and *grameen* banks bring major institutional change in the financial system. Accordingly, new innovations in banking services like micro-finance, Kisan credit cards, subsidies for the agricultural equipments motivate the rural people to access the financial services. The objectives of these activities are to improve the usage of financial system by the rural people and to achieve the economic development. According to Census 2009-10 more than 50.19 per cent population depends on the agriculture sector. In Karnataka also agricultural sector contribution towards employment is very high. The agricultural sector is developing by innovations, adopting new technology and foreign collaborations. Meantime, Indian farmers are categorised as poor an organised. Thus, financial assistance to the farmers is needed. The accessibility of financial services to the farmers mainly depends on the financial system flexibility and strength. In this study, we try to analyse the farmers' experience, and involvement of financial system in rural development. We empirically assess the farmers' opinion on Indian financial system by using questionaire method. We selected coconut farmers for the reason that coconuts are main crop in Tumkur District and the coconut crop is long-term crop which needs several years of maintenance and care. Therefore, it requires huge amount, it creates the farmers to depend on the financial assistance from different sources. In this study, we analysed the accessibility and usage of financial services by rural people for their development by the organised financial sources. Our study covers the sample of 85 coconut farmers located across the Tumkur District and five nationalised bank branch managers. We have used well-designed questionnaire to collect the information from farmer families. Our empirical study shows that, the awareness and usages of financial services are increasing in the coconut farmers. The banks crop loan helps farmers to undertake developmental activities in the farm. The government programme like, less interest in agricultural loan and a few repayment incentives to prompt customers, motivates rural people to correct repayment of loans. The discussion with bank managers revealed the agriculture as the priority sector and this helps coconut farmers access loan. These measures are helping economic condition of the farmers.

The paper is organised as follows. The next section describes the review of related literature; Section-3 points the objectives of the study. Section-4 discusses the sample, data and methodology used. Section-5 presents and discuss the empirical results. Section-6 concludes the paper.

Review of Literature

The financial system plays key role in the economic system by transferring excess fund from investors to needed group for economic activities. This also speed up the growth of economy and the nation by providing financial assistance (Goldsmith, 1969). Bank fragmentation helps to achieve economic growth of banks and portfolio of credit allocation and minimise the risk. Subsequently, satisfy the needs of farmers can be achieved. Schultz (1964), and Hayami and Ruttan (1971) stated that development in the agriculture was possible with the rapid adoption of innovation and technology and this contribute to the overall growth ofnation. Millor (1998), argued that there was a positive relationship with agricultural and other related sector growth of the country. Mellor (1976), found the agricultural employment and other sectors' employment linkages have the relationship and impacts on the growth of rural areas. Thirtle *et al*. (2003) and Christiaensen and Demeny (2007) demonstrated that agricultural growth significantly reduce the poverty of rural households. Dasgupta (2001) based on the review of three reports suggests that banker needs to understand the logic and spirituality of rural banks and banks needs to follow certain steps to uplift weaker sections of rural areas. He remarked that banks accountability is needed to increase the credit facilities to the farmers, meantime, there was a necessity to assess genuine requirements and also direct farmers to right path. Addition to this, he pointed that supply of credit to the agricultural sector increased the development activities.

The above studies related to contribution of banking sector towards agriculture and rural development reveal that the rural development is needed to country, economic development. The studies also exhibit that there is a positive association between the agricultural development and rural development. These factors motivate us to assess the contributions of banking sector to the agriculture development which significantly leads to rural development.

Objectives of the Study

1. To examine the awareness of the agricultural loans in the rural farmers.
2. To assess the purpose of agricultural loan as used by the farmers.
3. To evaluate the impact of standard Agri-loan features on selection of agricultural loan by the farmers.
4. To assess the bankers (Branch-Managers) opinion about agricultural loan.

Null Hypothesis

1. The purpose of farmers loan do not influence on selection of agricultural loan.
2. There is no difference between the purpose of agricultural loan.
3. The loan features like less interest, easy availability, government subsidy does not influence on loan selection process of coconut farmers.
4. There is no difference between loan features like less interest, easy availability and government subsidies.

Methodology

This study covers Tumkur District coconut farmers, sample of 85 farmers selected, those who availed loan from organised banking regime. We use simple averages, charts and Anova to analyse the data obtained from the sample. Based on the objectives three and four, we developed our hypothesis motivation factors.

Empirical Results

In this section, we present the empirical results obtained by tests.

Table - Presence of the Farmers the of Awareness Level About Agri-Loans

Sl. No.	Awareness Agri-about Loan by the Farmers	Yes	No	Yes p.c.	No p.c.
1.	Agricultural Term Loans,	39	46	45.88	54.11
2.	Land Purchase Scheme	5	80	5.88	94.11
3.	Equipment Loan	16	69	18.82	81.17
4.	Agri-land Development Loan	15	70	17.64	82.35
5.	Agri-gold Loan	25	60	29.41	70.58

The Table shows that minority of the coconut farmers are aware of agricultural term-loans, and Agri-Gold loans, meantime farmers are less aware of land purchase scheme and land development loan scheme. The equipment loan involves the tractors, cultivating machines, harvesting and other innovative machines, which are subsidised by the government. The awareness about equipment's loan and development loans are good sign. Anti-poverty programmes of the World Bank show that more spending on the irrigation and land development activities helps to increase the productivity of agriculture and it leads to development.

Chart 1. Presents the Farmers preference of Banks for Agri-Loans(No. of Respondents)

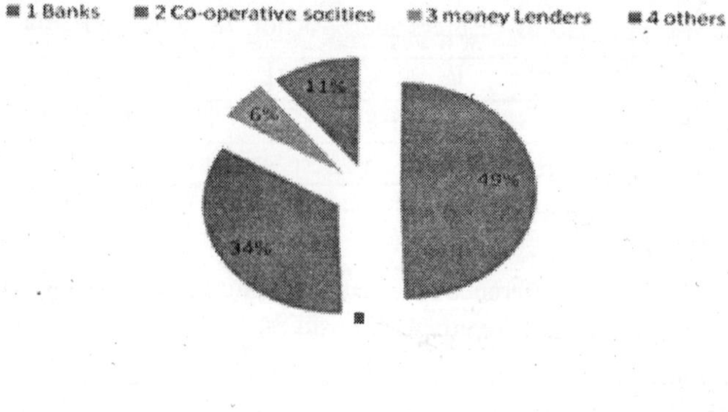

The chart 1 reports the farmer preference of institutions' selection while taking loans. Nearly, 50 per cent of the farmers use to take loans from the nationalised commercial banks. The co-operative banks and societies

participation is 34 per cent this shows that the majority of farmers prefers organised financial institutions. This also signs that farmers are comfort to have relationship with the banks compare to other types of institutions. The RBI directions like collateral, simplicity, and security towards agricultural loan helps farmers to avail the loan from banks. This has achieved by increasing number of participation in the banking sector.

Table – 2: The Farmers Purposes for Taking Agri-Loans

Sl. No	Purpose for the loan	strongly agree	agree	no decision	Disagree	strongly disagree	F test	
1.	To form	24	41	2	10	8	F statistic	P Values
2.	For development	23	48	2	8	4	=0.34050	=0.84664
3.	For irrigation	21	39	0	17	8		
4.	To pay old loans	22	34	6	12	11		
5.	For other purposes	19	36	0	21	9		
Ftest	F statistic = 138.5169							
	P Value = 337E-12							

The Hypothesis one and two are tested by the above Table.The calculated P value (3.37E-12= 0.00) is in accepted region at one per cent level, therefore, null hypothesis one is rejected. Hence, we conclude that the purpose of loan significantly influence on the selection of agricultural loan by the farmers. The P value (0.84664) belongs to acceptable region at five per cent level, therefore we accept the null hypothesis. Hence, we conclude that there is no significant difference between the purposes of farmers while selecting Agri-loans.

Table – 3: The Farmer's Response on Standard Loan Features

Sl. No	Standard features of loan	Strongly Agree	Agree	Undecided	Disagree	Strongly Disagree	F test	
1	Less interest	47	16	6	14	2		
2	Easy availability	25	31	0	22	7		
3	Government subsidy	19	33	15	23	2	F statistic =0.06078	P Values = 0.94145
Ftest	F statistic=6.39260 P Values =0.01305							

The P-values (0.01305) for the column is in rejection region at five per cent level. Therefore, we reject the null hypothesis three and point out that loan features like, less interest, easy availability, Government subsidy significantly influence on loan selection process of coconut farmers. Therefore, government can monitor the agricultural loans by differentiating these factors. The P-value (0.94145) is insignificant for row items in the above. This leads acceptance of null hypothesis and evidence to conclude that there is no difference between features of loan like, less interest, easy availability and government subsidies.

Further, we had discussion with five different managers of nationalised banks. They pointed out that agriculture is the priority sector; this directs banks to sanction enough loans to agricultural sector. The farmers expect more loan than their credit worthiness and repayment of agricultural loan. Farmers are less compared to other sectors. And farmers do not visit banks frequently. Therefore, communication also one barrier found to the branch managers.

Conclusion

In India, the RBI and government of India have taken several measures. to extend fanatical services to rural people. The accessibility of financial services enhances the confidence among people and creates infrastructure for growth. Therefore, we study the accessibility and usage of the credit facilities by the coconut farmers of Tumkur district. Our study covers 85 coconut farmers as sample and five branch managers. We use simple average and ANOVA-tests to analyse the data. Based on the results, we find that Agricultural Term Loans and Agri-Gold loans are more familiar to the rural farmers. More than 83 per cent of the farmers prefer take loan from the organised financial sector. This gives guidance to extend banking services to rural area. The less interest rate, easy availability and government subsidy factors significantly influence the farmers in selection of Agri-loans. Further, the discussion with the branch manages reveals that priority sectors preference of the Central Government and banks policy help farmers to avail the loans. Overall, we observed that the organised financial banking sector pays significant role in the rural agricultural development.

References

Christiaensen, Luc, and Lionel, Demery (2007), *Down to Earth: Agriculture and Poverty Reduction in Africa, Directions in Development.* Washington, DC: The World Bank.

Dasgupta, R. (2001), "Rural Banking and Credit: Tale of Many Committees", *Economic and Political Weekly*, Vol. 36, No. 9, pp. 733-737.

Goldsmith, R. W., (1969), "*Financial Structure and Development. New Haven*", CT: Yale University Press.

Hayami, Y., and V. Ruttan. (1971), *Agricultural Development: An International Perspective.* Baltimore, Maryland: John Hopkins University Press.

Liberman, S., and D. Ahluwalia. (1990), Review of GoI Agricuiltural Product

Market Interventtions, World Bank, New Delhi (mimeo).

Mellor, J.W. (1976), *The New Economics of Growth* Ithaca, NY: Cornell University Press.

Mellor, John 1998. Agriculture on the Road to Industrialisation. In Carl Eicher and John Staatz, eds., *International Agricultural Development*. Baltimore: John Hopkins University Press.

Schultz, T.W. (1964), *Transforming Traditional Agriculture:* New Haven, Yale University Press.

Shah,Tushaar. (1993), Agriculture and Rural Development in 1990s and Beyond" *Economic and Political Weekly*, Vol. 28, No. 39, pp. A 74-A85.

Thirtle, C., L. Lin, and J. Piesse. (2003) "The Impact of Research-led Agriculture Productivity Growth on Poverty Reduction in Africa, Asia, and Latin America," *World Development*, Vol. 31(12), pp. 1959-75.

17

ICT Enablement of Rural Development in India: A Study

N Mudduraju and C.B. Naveenchandra

Introduction

How can information technology (IT) contribute to rural development? What are the channels through which impacts can be realised, and what are the practical means for realising potential benefits? This paper examines several on-going projects that aim to provide IT-based services to rural population in India. These projects are distinguished by the goal of commercial sustainability, which supports *scalability* and, therefore, more widespread benefits. The analysis highlights the common building blocks required for successful implementation, and the relative strengths and weaknesses of different approaches. India is a country of villages and about 50 per cent of the villages have very poor socio-economic conditions. Since the dawn of independence constant efforts have been made to emancipate the living standard of rural masses. The five-year plans of the Central Government also largely aim at rural development. The Ministry of Rural Development in India is the apex body for formulating policies, regulations and acts pertaining to the development of rural sector. Agriculture, handicrafts, fisheries, poultry, and dairy are the primary contributors to the rural business and economy. Rural development is concerned with economic growth and social justice, improvement in the living standard of the rural people by providing adequate and quality social services. The present strategy of rural development mainly focusses on poverty alleviation, better livelihood opportunities, provision of basic amenities and infrastructure facilities through innovative programmes of wage and self-employment. ICT is the new tool for rural development. Information and Communication Technology, if used properly can be of great advantage for the development at grassroot levels. At the same time, the challenge remains with the administration to capture the minds of rural masses, mostly illiterate, to make them *adapt* the new technology which is completely alien to them. There are various rural development schemes run by the government of India and organisations are also present to look after the implementation of these programmes.

Information and communication technology (ICT) is often used as an extended synonym for information technology (IT), but is a more specific term that stresses the role of unified communication and the integration of telecommunications (telephone lines and wireless signals), computers as well as necessary enterprise software, middleware storage, and audio-visual systems, which enable users to access, store, transmit, and manipulate information. The phrase ICT had been used by academic researchers since the 1980s, but it became popular after it was used in a report to the UK government by Dennis Stevenson in 1997, and in the revised National Curriculum for England, Wales and Northern Ireland in 2000. As of September 2013, the term 'ICT' in the UK National Curriculum has been replaced by the broader term 'computing'. The term ICT is also used now to refer to the convergence of audio-visual and telephone networks with computer networks through single cabling or link system. There are large economic incentives (huge cost savings due to elimination of the telephone network) to merge the telephone network with the computer network system using a single unified system of cabling, signal distribution and management. The term 'Info' communication is sometimes used interchangeably with ICT. In fact Info communication is the expansion of telecommunication with information processing and content handling functions on a common digital technology base.

Rural Development

Rural development generally refers to the process of improving the quality of life and economic well-being of people living in relatively isolated and sparsely populated areas through ICT enablement. Rural development has traditionally centre on the exploitation of land-intensive natural resources such as agriculture and forestry. However, changes in global production networks and increased urbanisation have changed the character of rural areas. Increasingly, tourism niche manufacturers, and recreation have replaced resource extraction and agriculture as dominant economic drivers. The need for rural communities to approach development from wider perspective has created more focus on broad range of development goals rather than merely creating incentive for agricultural or resource-based businesses. Education, entrepreneurship, physical infrastructure, and social infrastructure play an important role in developing rural regions. Rural development is also characterised by its emphasis on locally produced economic development strategies. In contrast to urban regions, which have many similarities, rural areas are highly distinctive from one another. For this reason, there is a large variety of rural development approaches used globally.

Benefits of ICT

Information Technology (IT), as defined by the Information Technology Association of America (ITAA), is 'the study, design, development, implementation, support or management of computer-based information systems, particularly software applications and computer hardware.' IT deals with the use of electronic computers and computer software to convert, store, protect, process, transmit, and securely retrieve information. Recently, it has become popular to broaden the term to explicitly include the field of electronic communication so that people tend to use the abbreviation ICT (Information and Communications Technology). Basically, IT is a valuable set of tools because it benefits you immediately and directly. Knowledge of IT is important because:

1. IT is everywhere,
2. IT can help you to be more productive,
3. IT will enhance your career, and
4. IT will give you a world of opportunity.

Today, the term information has ballooned to encompass many aspects of computing and technology, and the term has become very recognisable. IT professionals perform variety of duties that range from installing applications to designing complex computer networks and information databases. A few of the duties that IT professionals perform may include data management, networking, engineering computer hardware, database and software design, as well as the management and administration of entire systems. When computer and communications technologies are combined, the result is information technology, or 'Info-Tech'. Information technology is a general term that describes any technology that helps to produce, manipulate, store, communicate, and/or disseminate information. Presumably, when speaking of Information Technology (IT) as a whole, it is noted that the use of computers and information are associated.

ICT as a key for Rural Development

Through uses of technology farmers or people get aware about things and productivity increases. If the productivity increases then the economic growth is increased at high rate. All the people in the rural areas know about the instruments, materials and price of the product by the use of technology. If people are aware about the technology they get maximum profit by using them, so that the growth of rural development increases rapidly. Technology helps in manufacturing new goods and with the use of new and latest technologies, one can make good and attractive infrastructure. Now-a-days technology changes day-by-day and its use plays an important role to improve the living and mental status.

ICT and e-Governance

Information and communication technology and e-governance are very helpful for development of our country. Without the help of government, we cannot implement technologies in rural areas. Government provides the authority to the organisations for implementing the technology in rural areas and also provides various services to citizens for rural and urban area through internet or other media like markets, health, and education. Furthermore, ICT can empower the poorer by expanding the use of government services, and reduce the risks by widening access to micro-finance (Cecchini and Scott, 2003). Application of ICT processes in governance is divided into two categories, *i.e.,* improving government process and bounding interaction within civil society. ICT is applicable to the rural areas since 1990's. Applying information and communication in public domain by the government is known as e-governance. Further, e-governance help in providing information to citizens and it also generate innovative ideas for wealth generation for rural citizen. A study by Wilson (2000), concludes that in a developing economy like India, ICT has developed in education, governance, health, human rights promotion, communication, economic growth and other areas. By applying supply chain management in selling agriculture products, the transaction costs have substantially reduced.

Present Scenario on ICT

The twenty-first century was the opening of historic information and communication technology interventions for rural development. This period has witnessed enormous and unprecedented changes in every aspect of communication technologies, policies, infrastructure development and services. Political leaders of India have begun abandoning archaic government control over communication that has lately moved from government to national and international private players. Finally, airwaves and electronic signals have achieved freedom from century's old colonial bondage to reach out and connect people through privately owned and operated communication network and infrastructure in rural area. Both international and national private players have taken a dominant role in redefining, reshaping and providing telecommunication, broadcasting and information services for rural development. It has initiated an era of partnership of public and private entrepreneurial skills and abilities to bring about unlimited connectivity. It has already started reshaping the life of number of elites in India. But, what about the rest? Little is known, though there is a trickle down communication effect in many areas of development including rural development. The role of communication technology for development must be viewed in this changed environment. How these ICT global and regional changes have influenced the access and use of ICT for development remains an issue of discussion and analysis.

ICT Facilities in Rural Development

1. Efficient services for health care and education,
2. Access to vast education in content for improving literacy,
3. Help to farmers with value-based information to improve productivity and provide timely information to traders, artisans etc.
4. Entertainment through broadcasting and multi-media services at doorsteps in rural areas and
5. Relevant news at one's door-step.

Governance and Policy Reforms

ICTs have a dual role to play in the case of governance and administrative reforms.

First, the use of ICTs for improving internal government processes is important, through its potential to increase the efficiency of these processes. For example, the costs can be lowered, and accuracy improved of data entry for tasks, such as the preparation of electoral rolls and lists of welfare eligibility.

Second, and perhaps more importantly (because it can hasten the first change), transparency, accountability and responsiveness can be enhanced by using ICTs to alter the citizen-government interface. This second avenue is particularly relevant in rural areas, where government is both extremely important and also stretched very thin: effective access to government services can be difficult and costly for the average rural citizen.

In traditional situations, rural citizens have to expend high levels of time and money to gather information or to submit to government agencies. They can be subject to predatory activities of touts when they travel to towns where government offices are located. Urban citizens may face similar problems, but benefit from greater proximity, more effective social networks, and lower social distance (*i.e.,* in class, education, etc.). Rural ICT kiosks have the potential to bypass severe problems faced by rural citizens, by making information exchange possible without physical proximity. The costs for citizens can be as low as 10 to 20 per cent of traditional means of interaction. Here, using ICTs to 'computerise' back-end government processes is a necessary complement to the use of ICTs to improve the exchange of information between government and the rural masses, and ultimately to improve the responsiveness of government to rural citizens. In this respect, rural ICT kiosks have a potentially important role to play in increasing the capacity of nascent rural local governments to the point where they, enhance rural decentralisation, can be truly effective.

Conclusion

ICT enablement systems in rural area have been traditionally focussed on supplying information to the rural poor about rural areas to policy makers, but it is now recognised that past systems have been largely ineffective in addressing the needs of the rural poor. The extension of agricultural information in particular is evolving beyond merely transmitting messages (although this is still important). It is becoming more open, more participatory and more demand driven, involving interactivity, negotiation and two-way information exchanges. There is a new emphasis on the acquisition of information and enabling the rural poor to request information specific to their particular livelihood needs. Communication specialists increasingly recognise the enormous potential of ICTs to support and enhance these changes.

References

Agranoff, R. and Radin, B.A. (1991). "The comparative case study approach in public administration" *Research in Public Administration,* Vol. 1 pp. 203-231.

Ahrens, J. (1997) "Prospects of institutional and policy reform in India' *Asian Development Review,* Vol. 15, No. 1, pp. 111-146.

Baark, E. and Heeks, R. (1999). *Donor Funded Information Technology transfer projects in Information Technology for Development,* 8, 4, pp. 185-197.

Bihari, G. and Jokay, C. (1999). *Telecottages in Hungary: The Experience and the* Castells, M. (1996). *The Information Age: Economy, Society and Culture. Vol. I: The Rise of the Networked Society*, Blackwell, Oxford.

Courtright, C. (2004). 'Which lessons are learned? Best practices and World Bank rural telecommunications policy, *The Information Society* Vol. 20, pp. 345–356.

DfID (2000) *Making e-Government work for poor people: Governments and Electronic Information & Communication Technologies (EICTs) in Development,* DfID Target Strategy Paper Executive Summary Report.

Garnham, N. (1992) "The media and the public sphere" in *Habermas and the Public Sphere,* ed. Craig Calhoun Cambridge, MA: MIT Press.

Gasco, M. (2003), "New Technologies and Institutional Change in Public Administration", *Social Science Computer Review, Vol.* 21, No. 1, pp. 6-14.

Harris, R. (1999) "Evaluating Telecentres within National Policies for ICTs in Developing Countries" in *Telecentre Evaluation: A global perspective (Report of an international meeting on telecentre evaluation)*, eds. Gomez, R. and Hunt, P., Far Hills Inn, Quebec, Canada, September 28-30, 1999.

Indian Institute of Information Technology, (2005), *Drishtee Soochana Kendras, Sirsa, Haryana,* Last accessed: 18/03/05 : Address.

Kjaer, A. M. (2004), *Governance,* Polity Press, Cambridge.

Kooiman, J. (2003). *Governing as Governance,* Sage, London.

Kraemer, K. and J. Dedrick (2001), *The productivity paradox: Is there a new one? What does it all mean for managers?* Irvive, CA: Centre for Research on Information Technology and Organisations, University of California.

Madon, S. (1991), *The Impact of Computer-based Information Systems on Rural Development: A Case Study in India.*

Negroponte, N. (1998), *Being Digital*, Vintage Books, New York.

Norris, P. (2001). *Digital Divide: Civic engagement, information poverty, and the Internet worldwide* ,Cambridge: Cambridge University Press.

Opportunities, Hungarian Telecottage Association, Available at: *www.telehaz.hu.*

Petiteville, F. (1998), "Three Mythical Representations of the State in Development Theory", *International Journal of Social Science,* Vol. 155. pp. 115-124.

Rhodes, R. A. W. (1997), *Understanding Governance: Policy Networks, Governance, Reflexivity and Accountability,* Open University Press, Maidenhead.

Roman, R. and Colle, R.D. (2001), *Themes and Issues in Telecentre Sustainability*, Development Informatics Working Paper Series, Paper No. 10, IDPM, University of Manchester.

Sen, A. (1999), *Development as Freedom,* Oxford: Oxford University Press.

Stoker, G. (1998) 'Governance as theory: Five propositions' *International Journal of Social Science,* Vol. 155, pp. 17 - 28.

Taylor, J.A. (1998) 'Governance and electronic innovation: Whither the information polity' *Information, Communication and* Society, Vol. 1, No. 2, pp. 144-162.

Thomas, A. (2000) Meanings and views of development in *Poverty and Development: Into the 21st century,* eds. T. Allen and A. Thomas, Open University and Oxford University Press, Chapter-2.

18

E-Governance and Rural Development - A Study on E-Bhoomi Project in Chamarajnagar

Muthamma K.S. and Likhita S. Anuradha

Introduction

To the population of our country increasing day by day, providing public services has become a challenging task for the government. The exposure to happening around the country has increased public expectation from government departments. A growing number of government agencies are reforming and re-engineering their structures and processes from the inside. The goals of these government organisations are the same; greater efficiency, cost effectiveness, flexibility, improved responsiveness to the public, and a greater focus on services.

The ministry of revenue is finding an important place in the public administration. This department is maintaining records pertaining to land, mutation, purchase and sale of land, land holding size, nature of soil towards land owners. Earlier this process was maintained an traditional basis by entry in the big registration book and it was completely manual. The advancement of computer and information technology finds revolutionary changes in the field of administration with the concept of e-governance.

The burning issues in governments the world over that need to be addressed through an effective e-governance policy include transparency in government functioning, increased public sector-private sector partnership, privatisation and deregulation, output-oriented government both at Central and State levels, lean form of government, etc. In order to cope with such challenges, governments have been adopting the new philosophy of ART, *i.e.*, Accountability, Responsiveness and Transparency, at the point of delivery of public services and utilities. The minister of Information Technology, Government of India, had declared the year 2001 as the year of e-governance.

Electronic governance is all about managing knowledge that exists and continues to be generated every day within the government departments. In the government department, the delegation of responsibility should be clearly defined to enable services providers to deal with the queries and problems of the citizens electronically. Thus, through e-governance, the distance between government and citizens will be reduced in terms of interaction, feedback and redress, which will lead to avoidance of intermediaries thus encouraging transparency. The greatest advantage for citizens will be the availability of government services in required places.

The land records are the most important testimony of rights to land-owners in the huge agro-economy of India. The crucial document which records various parameters and information pertaining to land-holding is the Record of Rights Tenancy and Cultivation (RTC). In Karnataka, data entry work started in 1995, but up to 1999, there were few concrete benefits. In 1999-2000, modifications were made in the software and all the databases were updated when the bhoomi project was launched. Chamarajanagara is considering as a district in the year of 1997. The Bhoomi project is practicing in the year of 2001 in Chamarajanagara.

Need for the Study

The emergence of Information and Communication Technology (ICT) has provided means for faster and better communication, efficient storage, retrieval and processing of data and exchange and utilisation of information to its users like, individuals, groups, businesses, organisations or governments. ITC has led to 'business process re-engineering' So far as governments are concerned, the coming together of computerisation and Internet connectivity/ web-enablement in association with process re-engineering, promises faster and better processing of information leading to speedier and qualitatively better decision-making, greater reach and accountability, better utilisation of resources and overall good governance. In the case of citizens, it holds the promise of enhanced access to information and government agencies, efficient service delivery and transparency in dealing and interaction with government.

E-government aims to enhance access to and delivery of government services to benefit citizens. More important, it aims to help strengthen government's drive toward effective governance and increased transparency to better manage a country's social and economic resources for development.

Objectives of the study

1. To analyse the awareness of 'e- governance' project.
2. To evaluate the 'e-Bhoomi' project services provided in Chamarajanagar.

3. To know how the 'e-Bhoomi' project reduce the work burden of the land record officers.
4. To conduct the beneficiary survey about 'e-Bhoomi' project.
5. To find the problems in e-Governance and suggest the ways for improvement.

Research methodology

The study is based on both primary data and secondary data. An effort is made to collect the actual data about "e-Governance project –A study on e-Bhoomi project" for this purpose structured questionnaire administered and interaction made to sample respondents. A respondent includes farmers, village accountants, and field officer of the selected revenue office in Chamarajanagar.

The sample size is 70 in toto, 50 are farmers, 18 village accountants and two are field officers and NIC officer in Chamarajanagar. Cluster random sampling method is used to select respondents.

The collected data and observed responses are analysed with the help of percentage method. This method is based in making comparison between two or more series of data. Percentages are used to describe relationship.

Definition of 'e-Governance' According to the World Bank

"E-Government refers to the use by government agencies of information technologies (such as Wide Area Networks, the Internet, and mobile computing) that have the ability to transform relations with citizens, businesses, and other arms of government. These technologies can serve variety of different ends: better delivery of government services to citizens, improved interaction with business and industry, citizen empowerment through access to information, or more efficient government management. The resulting benefits can be less corruption, increased transparency, greater convenience, revenue growth, and/or cost reduction."

Scope of e-Governance

E-Government services focus on four main customers: citizens, the business community, government employees, and government agencies. E-Government aims to make interaction with citizens, businesses, government employees, government agencies and other governments more convenient, friendly, transparent, inexpensive and effective.

A. Government to Citizen (G2C),

B. Citizen to Government (C2G),

C. Government to Government (G2G), and

D. Government to Business (G2B).

This chart showing the Scope and the Objectives of e-Governance

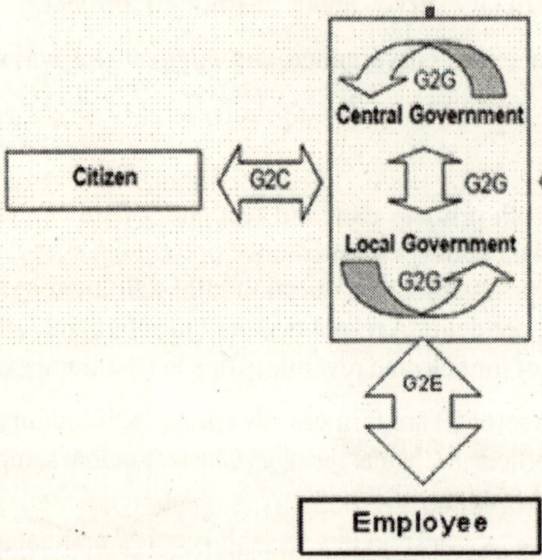

1. To build an informed society,
2. To increase government and citizen interaction,
3. To encourage citizen participation,
4. To bring transparency in the governing process,
5. To make the government accountable,
6. To reduce the cost of governance, and
7. To reduce the reaction time of the government.

The object of e-Governance is to provide a SMART government. The Acronym SMARRT refers to Simple, Moral, Accountable, Responsive, Responsible and Transparent government.

e-Governance Challenges Specific to India

- Lack of integrated services,
- Lack of key persons,
- Population, and
- Different languages.

e - Governance Initiative in Karnataka about Bhoomi project

'E-Bhoomi' the land records management systems is the first e-Governance project that has been successfully implemented for the benefit of common man.Under this project, Land Records kiosk has been setup in each taluk of the state to issue:

- Land records documents to public on demand,
- Finger-print (Bio-metric) authentication to ensure fool proof system,
- Easy and quick access to land record documents and status of mutation, using Touch Screen kiosk.
- Mutation requests processed on First-in-First-out Basis, and
- Workflow based online system to carry out mutation on land records data.

Introduction about e-bhoomi project

Bhoomi (land) is the project of on-line delivery and management of land records in Karnataka. It provides transparency in land records management with better citizen services and takes discretion away from civil servants at operating levels. The revenue department in Karnataka with the technical assistance from National Informatics Centre (NIC), Bangalore, has built and operating the Bhoomi system throughout the state. Bhoomi has computerised 20 million records of land ownership of 6.7 million farmers in the state. Bhoomi has reduced the discretion of public officials by introducing provisions for recording a mutation request online. Farmers can now access the data base and are empowered to follow up. In the Bhoomi project, a printed copy of the RTC can be obtained online by providing the name of the owner or plot number at computerised land record kiosk in 177 taluk office, for a fee of Rs. 15. A second computer screen faces the clients to enable them see the transaction being performed. A farmer can check the status of a mutation within 45 days; a farmer can now approach a senior officer with grievance. Operators of the computerised system are made accountable for their decisions and actions by using a bio-log in system that authenticates every login through a thumbprint. A log is maintained of all transactions in a session. The new system has brought about a sea change in the way land records are maintained and administered in the state. The system has not only simplified the process of record keeping, but has also provided many collateral benefits. This governance model has financially proven to be self-sustainable. It has become a trendsetter for e-governance projects in the state as well as other parts of the country.

In the next phase of *Bhoomi*, the 'LAND RECORDS ON WEB' has been established where in all the taluk database are getting uploaded to web-enabled central database so as to allow the private agencies set up the village-level kiosk to download land records documents at the village and issue to the farmers. In this Private Public Participation (PPP) model, all the stakeholders will be benefitted in land records delivery. *Under this prestigious Bhoomi e-Governance project of the government all 20 million land records of 6.7 million land owners in 176 taluks of Karnataka have been computerised. This system works with the software called "Bhoomi" designed fully in – house by National Informatics Center, Bangalore.* While the project is largely funded by Government of India; some critical components of this project are funded by State Government.

Objectives and goals

- To facilitate easy maintenance and prompt updating of land records.
- To make land records tamper-proof.
- To provide farmers easy access to their land records.
- To create and a construct database of land revenue, cropping pattern, land use, etc.
- To utilise the data for planning and formulating development programmes.
- To enable usage of this database by courts, banks, private organisations and Internet Service Providers (ISPs).

Important Features of *Bhoomi* Project

This software provides printing of land records as and when required.

- It incorporates process of online updating to ensure RTCs provided to farmers are in sync with the time.
- All the mutation to land records database is done on computer itself to ensure that data on computer remain current with time.
- It incorporates the state of the art bio-log on metrics system from Compaq, which authenticates various users on the Bhoomi software on the basis of finger prints. This ensures that nobody can hack the system by imitating other users.
- This software has the provision of scanning original mutation orders of the revenue inspector (who is the authorised person to pass orders in the mutation in the field) and notices served on interested parties. Both documents are scanned to ensure that not only responsibility can be fixed on officials by showing the original documents signed by them but also to ensure that the interested parties do not claim in the court that they were not served with the notice before effecting mutation.

- The software enables the administrators to generate various reports based on type of soil, land holding size, type of crops grown etc. This information would enable administrators to take informed policy decision.

Committees

Government has constituted the following two committees for implementation for computerisation of land records in the state.

Bhoomi Advisory Committee: This committee will look into improvement required in the *Bhoomi* software.

State Level Committee: This committee will review the progress of the project in Karnataka and decide about its expansion and broad banding.

Components of Bhoomi Project: There are three main components in Bhoomi system.-

- The computer centre where mutation and updation are done in online fashion. It includes finger print authentication and scanning of important documents to ensure robust and secured system. Most of the components of the Computer Centre are being funded under the Central scheme.
- Land Records kiosk from where the farmers can collect the copy of their record by paying Rs. 10. They can also lodge request for mutation to their land records. The kiosk is fully funded by the State Government.
- Touch Screen Kiosk, where farmers can see their land related information without anybody's intervention or help.

Benefits of Bhoomi Project

Farmers

1. Farmers can quickly get their land records from kiosks and are protected from harassment and extortion,
2. Reduction in processing time for mutation,
3. On-line tracking of mutation status,
4. Easy access to farm credit, and
5. Ease in case of legal matters.

Administrators

1. Ease of maintenance and updating of land records documents,

2. Quick and easy access to land records for analysis purpose, and
3. Ease of monitoring Government lands.

Others

1. Financial Institutions, on-line farm credit related activities..
2. Information availability for private sector.

Types of e-Bhoomi Transactions

The e-Governance project, *e-Bhoomi* offers following types of transactions to be carried out on a piece of land in *e-Bhoomi* software:

1. Khata Change,
2. Slip Transaction,
3. Pledge and release,
4. Court Order,
5. Crop Change, and
6. Cultivator Change.

Findings

- An informed society is an empowered society. Only informed people can make a government responsible. Due to e-Governance people can easily get the required information.
- E-Governance aims at build a feedback framework, to get feedback from the people and to make the government aware of people's problems.
- E-governance carries an objective to make the governing process transparent by making all the government data and information available to the people for access. *E-Bhoomi* project increased transparency of land related transactions.
- *Bhoomi* project is introduced for the benefit of rural people. *E-Bhoomi* project is used for getting land records, transfer of ownership, purchase and sale of land, to avail the loan facility, documenting crop loan and crop grown,this is also used for pledge and release the land.
- *Bhoomi* project services are available in the taluk office, *Nemmadi Kendra*, district office. Rural people are facing technical, electricity and staff problems while getting records.
- Technology and innovations are developed in order to reduce time

taken to complete the work. *E-Bhoomi* project has reduced the time for getting land records.

- Technology is introduced to reduce the human effort, error in manual work, work burden; time consumption etc. *Bhoomi* project is helps to reduce the work burden of the staffs.
- Proper maintenance of land records reduces illegal activities by influential persons and corruption it will lead to rural development. In time getting, RTC enables the formers to avail crop insurance. It is really a boon to farmers.

Suggestions

Land-owners are facing some problems while getting land records in *Nemmadi Kendra* due to lack of expertise in staff. Government should take measures in this direction by arranging training programmes.

- Any project will get success only if it is cost effective that is both to the government and to the beneficiaries. Government should take initiative to reduce the cost.
- The *Bhoomi* project work is simple, easy to access information, but not updated land record regularly. If it is updated regularly it increases the effectiveness of the project and reduces the work burden to the staff members, unless updated regulosly.
- Timely training programmes are to be conducted by the government for the employees to avoid the inconveniences to the land owners.

Conclusion

In the information era, e-Governance is of recent origin. It is going to replace all the manual work which is in practice from a long way. E-Governance projects are reflecting the general public in a large manner. E-Governance resulting benefits can be less corruption, increased transparency greater convenience, revenue growth and or cost reduction it is maintaining all the land records, where one can access frequently, effectively and accurately. With the help of e-Governance even farmers access the information very much easily.

Bhoomi is the first e-Governance project in Karnataka state to reach the rural people in providing land records and its related documents on demand to rural farmers at taluk office. The *Bhoomi* project increases the efficiency of taluk revenue department and ensures transparency in its transaction. reduction in illegal activities and corruption, increase in transparency all are the results of e-Governance. Definitely, we can say that e-Governance is supportive to the rural development.

References

Good Governance-Stimuli and Strategies: - Rajiv Sharma and Ramesh Arora.

Electronic Governance: A key Issue in 21st Century:- Bubhiraju, R.

http://egov.mit,gov.in.

http://www.bhoomi.karnataka.in.

http://cause.list.kar.nic.in.

19

Issues and Challenges of Rural Financial System of India: A Case Study in I.D. Hally Village at Madhugiri Taluk

B. Narasimha Murthy

Introduction

Rural finance comprises credit, savings and insurance (or insurance substitutes) in rural areas, whether provided through formal or informal mechanism. The word 'credit' tends to be associated with enterprise development, whereas rural finance includes savings and insurance mechanisms used by the poor to protect and stabilise their families and livelihoods (not just their businesses).

An understanding of rural finance helps explain the livelihood strategies and priorities of the rural poor. Rural finance is important to the poor. The poorest groups spend the highest proportion of their income on food – typically more than 60 per cent and sometimes as much as 90 per cent. Under these circumstances, any drop in earning, or any additional expenditure (health or funeral costs, for instance) has immediate consequences for family welfare – unless savings or loans can be accessed. Financial transactions are therefore an integral part of the livelihood system of the poor.

Rural finance consists of informal and formal sectors. Examples of formal sources of credit include: banks, projects and contract farmer schemes. Reference is often made to micro-credit. *Micro* underlines the small loan size normally associated with the borrowing requirements of poor rural population, and micro-credit schemes use specially developed pro-poor lending methodologies. Rural population, however, are much more dependent on informal sources of finance (including loans from family and friends, the local moneylender, and rotating or accumulating savings and credit associations).

Rural finance is a set of financial services that are not limited to credit only. Financial services in rural finance include: loans, savings, investment, guarantee funds, remittance services, inventory credit, trader finance and insurance.

Rural Finance

Financial services offered and used in rural areas by farm and non-farm population of all income levels through a variety of formal, informal and semi formal institutional arrangements and diverse type of products and services, such as loans, deposits, insurance, and remittances. Rural finance includes agriculture finance and micro-finance and is a sub-sector of the larger financial sector.

Financial services for the rural poor are represented by the shaded overlap of micro-finance with rural and agricultural finance. It includes financial services for all purposes and from diverse sources tailored to the needs of poor people in rural areas. Providers include both financial institutions, such as banks, credit unions and non-financial mechanisms. State-owned banks include agricultural development banks, regional development banks, savings banks, and postal banks. Often they have extensive rural networks of branches or outlets. Privatised state banks may also have significant rural outreach, although in many cases the privatisation process has reduced rural branch coverage.

Definitions

'The Consultative Group to Assist the Poor (CGAP)' defines 'rural finance' as 'financial services offered and used in rural areas by people of all income levels' and 'agricultural finance' as 'a sub-set of rural finance dedicated to financing agriculture-related activities, such as input, supply, production, distribution and wholesaling, and marketing' (Pearce, 2003).

'Schmidt and Kropp (1987)' rural finance as treated in this paper as encompassing all the savings, lending, financing and risk minimising opportunities (formal and informal) and related norms and institutions in rural areas.

Rural Finance Comes in Three Major Forms

1. Informal financial institutions which are not regulated by banking sector such as rotating and savings groups, church groups or similar groupings of people.
2. Semi-formal institutions which are not regulated by banking sector but are usually licensed and supervised by another government agency, such as self-help groups, NGOs involved in provision of financial services and micro-finance organisations (in some instances).

3. Formal institutions are subject to banking regulations and supervision, such as micro-finance institutions, banks. In order to enhance the quality of rural livelihoods, a more holistic approach to development is needed. Governments need to design and implement agriculture-friendly policies that will encourage the development of financial sector and market-oriented enterprises. Governments and donors need to invest into human and institutional development in rural areas.

Challenges of Rural Finance

Despite the success of micro-finance services in many countries, access to financial services in remote rural areas remains a challenge. The three main challenges that contribute to rural poverty are:

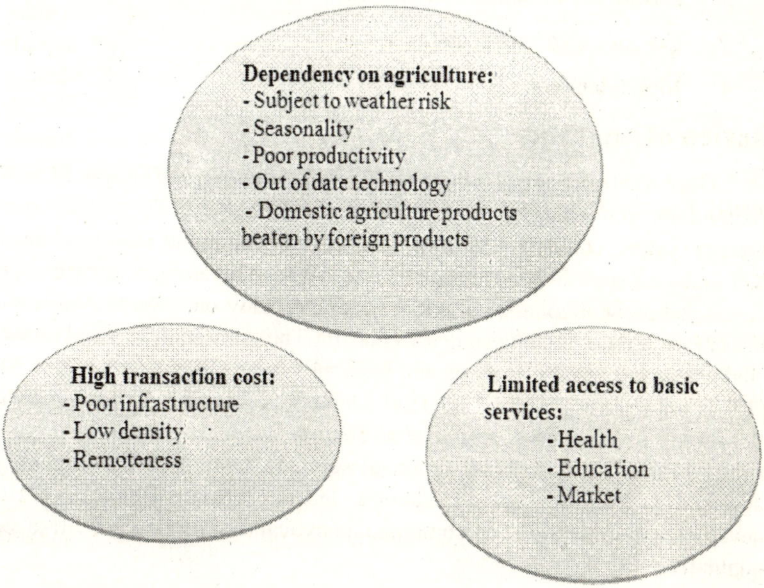

Small size average farm size, low population density, higher loan servicing costs due to limited lending volume and high information costs.

1. No branches or a limited branch network in rural areas.
2. Lack of collateral or adequate security among rural people.
3. Lack of technical knowledge at the bank level to evaluate and analyse the creditworthiness of rural customers.

4. Risk correlation when lending to farmers: All borrowers are affected by the same risk, such as low market prices and reduced yields due to the weather.
5. Underdeveloped communication and transportation infrastructure.

The major challenge, the country's financial system faces today, is to bring informal loans into the formal financial system. That would not only provide huge business opportunity but also serve social purpose by significantly reducing the interest rate the poor have to pay. That calls for genuineness of intent, flexibility and hard work.

Rural Financial Institutions

1. Public sector banks,
2. Private sector banks/ financial institutions,
3. Co-operative banks, and
4. Moneylenders.

Review of Literature

Gaamaa Hishigsuren (2006) a study on "*Information and Communication Technology and Micro-finance: Options for Mongolia*" They study rural finance system, challenges in rural finance, rural credit and savings analysis ICT analysis, mobile banking model and ATM's advantages, a case study conducted on Mongolia. N. Kavitha (2007), A study on, "*Rural Finance in World Perspective (A Contempary Scenario)*". The study analyses rural finance challenges and SWOT analysis and banking systems. Faustine Karrani Bee (2007) on a study, "*Rural Financial Markets in Tanzania: An Analysis of Access to Financial Services in Babati District, Manyara Region*" The study analysed constrains to rural financial services, examined the impact on households livelihood and recommended appropriate financial sector development strategies. The combined analytical tool used quantitative and qualitative.

Statement of the Problem

Dispersed demand- due to low levels of economic activity and population density; on the other hand paralleled by larger family sizes and higher population growth rates; high information and transaction costs - linked to poor infrastructure (roads, institutional, telecommunications) and lack of client information (no personal identification or functioning asset registries); weak institutional capacity-related to the limited availability of educated and well-trained people in smaller rural communities.

Objectives of the Study

1. To investigate the issues and challenges for rural financial system in India.
2. To study the challenges of rural financial system in study area.

Research Questions of the Study

1. Rural financial system to impact on rural development in India/study area?
2. Rural financial system to improve the economic status for rural people.

Methodology

The study has used both primary and secondary data. Primary data collected from samples of rural people in study area. Secondary data collected were from journals, books, reports, and website sources. To select the samples in randomly, the researcher has selected 60 samples (Male 35 and 25 Females) from the study area. The researcher used for self-structured questionnaire in area of rural financial system. The questionnaire includes 20 Yes or No questions. The researcher collected the primary data from study area through. Questionnaire to directly meet the people to collect information. The present study was used percentage analysis to interpret the data.

Data Analysis and Interpretation

Table-1: Demographical Profile

Sl.No.	*Group*	*Samples*	*Percentage*	
1.	Gender	Male	35	58.33 pc
		Female	25	41.66 pc
2.	Education Level	Uneducated	10	16.66 pc
		1 to 10th Std	25	41.66 pc
		PUC to BA	18	30 pc
		Post-graduation and above	7	11.66 pc
3.	Occupation	Agriculture	20	33.33 pc
		Business	25	41.66 pc
		Employees	5	8.33 pc
		Students	10	16.66 pc
4.	Age group	20-30	20	33.33 pc
		30-40	30	50 pc
		40-50 and Above	10	16.66 pc

The Table-1 shows the demographic details from the study. The first category in Gender to have two components, male 58.33 per cent and female 41.66 per cent . The second category has four components from the Table. The first component uneducated 16.66 per cent, second component 1 to 10th std 41.66 per cent, the third component PUC to BA of 30 per cent and Post-graduation and above 11.66 per cent from the table. The third category has four components from the table. The first component agriculture 33.33 per cent, second component business 41.66 per cent, the third component employees of 8.33 per cent and students 11.66 per cent from the Table. The fourth category age group has three components from the Table. The first component 20-30 years 33.33 per cent, second component 30-40 years 50 per cent, the third component 40-50 above of 30 per cent and Post-graduation and above 16.66 per cent from the Table.

Percentage Analysis

The researcher discussed about only for main questions from the questionnaire they are.

Sl. No.	*Statements*	*Yes*	*Percentage of Yes*	*No*	*Per cent of No*
1.	Rural finance to improve rural development (Education, Health, Transport etc.)	50	83.33 pc	10	16.66 pc
2.	Rural finance institutions easily provide the finance for rural people.	20	33.33 pc	40	66.66 pc
3.	Rural finance to reduce the poverty, illiteracy rate etc.	35	58.33 pc	25	41.66 pc

Results of the Study

1. The 58.33 per cent of respondents need rural finance to improve rural development.
2. The 66.66 per cent of respondents view rural finance institutions cannot easily extend financial facilities.
3. The 58.33 per cent of respondents need rural finance to reduce poverty and illiteracy rate.

Suggestions of the Study

1. Government and NGO's to share to improve the rural financial system.
2. Government to conduct the awareness programmes to rural finance system and daily provide finances for rural people.

References

Kavitha N. (2007), *Rural Finance in World Perspective (A Contempary Scenario).*

http://www.ruralfinance.org.

http://ww.worldbank.org.

www.ifad.org/ruralfinance.

www.fao.org/ag/ags/subjects/en/ruralfinance/index.html.

20

Rural Housing Schemes: A Strategy for Rural Development and Eradicating Rural Poverty

Sathyanarayana and S Swetha

Introduction

Rural development is the process of improving the quality of life and economic well-being of people living in relatively isolated and sparsely populated areas (Malcolm J. Moseley, 2003). In this regard, the provision of housing and eradicating of poverty are pre-requisite condition for rural development. The United Nations and its agencies including the World Health Organisation, United Nations Human Settlements Programme (UN-Habitat), United Nations Human Rights Commission and International Labour Organisation consider access to adequate housing to be integral to the fulfillment of other basic human rights (United Nations, 2009). It is not only a basic need but also a production activity that stimulates employment and generation of savings (NHP, 1988). Ownership of a house provides significant economic security and social status for a citizen in the society. The identity and social recognition associated with ownership of a house provides an individual with immense confidence to get involved into many social activities. Stable, affordable and accessible housing is directly and indirectly linked to human well-being (social, physical and psychological). Good housing and its surroundings indicate the standard of living of the family; it provides facilities for education, recreation and many other facets of life. A person deprived of this basic need faces all odds of life and remains discriminated and marginalised in the society. Poor housing conditions, including over crowding and unhygienic infrastructure leads to ill-health, increase in sickness and lack of productivity at work.

Indian economy has been growing at an impressive pace for last one decade but it remains predominantly rural. About 70 per cent of population is residing still in the rural areas (Census of India, 2011) and nearly 25 per cent of the rural people in that are living in poverty (Planning Commission, 2011-12).

As we know, 'poverty' is the deprivation of common necessities, such as food, clothing, housing and clean drinking water, which determine the quality of life. Among the basic requirements, housing deprivation is the common problem in rural India.

This paper-divided into seven parts. Part-I is introductory in nature. Part II highlighted on the research gap and the objectives of study. Part-III mentioned the methodology and the data sources forstudy. Part-IV assesses the rural housing shortage in India. Part-V focus on the rural poverty in Karnataka. Part-VI briefly examines two rural housing schemes and last part is on conclusion.

Research Gap and Objectives of the Study

Since housing deprivation is the common problem for rural development in India, the agenda of rural housing has attracted mainline attention amongst the policy makers and various stakeholders in the last few years. But, rural housing has been one of the neglected sectors in rural development and most of the literature reveals that till date less study has been conducted so far on rural housing except by the government institutions. In this direction, the present study has been formulated on the following objectives to fulfill the above said research gap;

1. To highlight on the assessment of rural housing shortage in India and
2. To examine the performance of rural housing schemes such as Indira Awaas Yojana (IAY), Bharat Nirman Programme (BNP).

Methodology and Data Sources

This paper relies upon the secondary sources of data for fulfilment of the above objectives. It is collected from the census documents of India, Ministry of Rural Development, Government of India, Planning Commission documents of India, National Housing Bank, Awaassoft, Knowledge network and related research articles, etc. The simple descriptive statistics such as percentage, forecasting, correlation has been used to analysis the data.

Assessment of Rural Housing Shortage

It has been understood by all that growth in the rural areas is a major catalyst for fuelling the overall economic growth of the nation. But shortage of housing is becoming a major impediment in the growth process. Moreover, it is emerging as a critical and unique challenge considering the varied dimensions of the rural landscape and lifestyle. To understand the magnitude of the challenge posed by the shortage of rural housing and formulate appropriate interventions, it is important to understand the extent of shortage as accurately as possible. Shortage can be drawn from the data on growth of households and housing stock in a country.

Table-1: Number of Households and the Housing Stock in India – 1991-2011

Census year	Households (in crores)	Housing Stock (in crores)	Housing Shortage (in crores)
1991	15.1	14.7	0.4
2001	19.2	18.7	0.5
2011	24.7	24.5	0.2

Source: Census of India.

Table-1 indicates that the gap between households and housing stock is narrowing. As per the Census 2011, the number of households increased from 19.2 crore (2001) to 24.7 crore (2011). There has been considerable increase in the housing stock from 18.7 crore (2001) to 24.5 crore (2011). Census 2011 also indicated the gap between the households and housing stock has been contracting at India level.

Table 2: Estimation of Rural Housing Shortage for 11th Plan Period (in million)

Year	Households	Housing stock	Housing Shortage (No. of Households not having houses)
2006	153.41	149.84	3.57
2007	156.63	152.97	3.66
2008	159.92	156.16	3.76
2009	163.28	159.43	3.85
2010	166.7	162.76	3.94
2011	170.21	166.16	4.05
2012	173.78	169.63	4.15
2013	177.43	173.18	4.25
2014	181.16	176.8	4.36
2015	184.96	180.49	4.47
2016	188.84	184.27	4.57
2017	192.81	188.12	4.69

Source: Working Group on Rural Housing for 11th Five Year Plan.

Table-2 shows that there is increasing trends in growth of households, housing stock and housing shortage from 2006 to 2017 (projected year) according to working group on rural housing for 11th Five Year Plan. The housing shortage obtained by the deduction of total housing stock from total number of households. The increasing trend of housing shortage shows that the existing rural housing schemes are inefficient in providing the proper shelter facility to the poor.

Table 3: Overall Estimation of Rural Housing Shortage for 12th Plan Period *(in million)*

Sl. No.	Factors taken into account for assessing housing shortage	Calculation	No. (million)
1.	Shortage in 11th plan Working Group of 11th FY Plan	Assessment of Data from MoRD	47.43
2.	IAY houses constructed		10.97
3.	Houses constructed by states under their own housing schemes	Estimated using data from some of the states	3.00
4.	Houses constructed in rural areas by families themselves using their own resources	As per NSSO, over a 365-day period, 12 per cent of rural households undertook construction, 14 per cent of which were new constructions. The 66 per cent of construction was undertaken using own funds	8.96
5.	Balance of houses left during XIth Five Year Plan	S. No. 1 – (S No. 2+3+4)	24.50
6.	Additional Housing Shortage due to Obsolescence and congestion	Obsolescence[1] @ 3 per cent, Congestion[2] @6.5 per cent	16.57
7.	Increase in number of households during the XIIth Plan Period	No. of households in 2017 – No of households projected for 2012 (based on calculations of the WG for 11th Plan)	7.75
8.	Total Housing Shortage for 12th Plan period	S No. (5+6+7)	48.81
	Assuming 90 per cent of total Rural Housing Shortage for BPL families 2012-17		43.93

Source: Derived from the Calculations of the Working Group on Rural Housing Under the 11th Plan.

Table-3 clearly shows the total housing shortage for 12th plan period is 48.81 million. It also assumed that the total housing shortage in rural areas is estimated at 43.93 million units. Of these, 39.30 million units (90 per cent of the rural housing shortage) pertain to the Below Poverty Line Population (BPL). It means that the housing problem in rural India is one of the important factors in determining the rural poverty.

Rural Poverty

In rural areas, poor are the landless labourers, small and marginal farmers, and rural artisans including fishermen, and backward classes and backward tribes. Moreover, the problem of poverty in India is found in most of the weaker sections of the society. The Working Group on Rural Housing (XIIth plan) estimate 90 per cent of total Rural Housing shortage of BPL families 2012-2017. The present paper with this background tries to estimate the correlation between total rural families and BPL families in Karnataka. It is explain in the below table.

Table- 4. Below Poverty Line (BPL) List in Rural Karnataka

Sl.No.	*District*	*Total Rural Families*	*BPL Families*
1.	Bagalkot	1,89,347	56,457
2.	Bangalore (R)	1,20,297	23,983
3.	Bangalore (U)	1,88,409	41,444
4.	Belgaum	6,35,049	1,56,811
5.	Bellary	2,54,413	61,799
6.	Bidar	1,80,259	30,992
7.	Bijapur	2,26,992	56,278
8.	Chamarajanagara	1,86,274	72,381
9.	Chikkaballapura	1,70,916	50,331
10.	Chikkamagalore	1,64,942	80,312
11.	Chitradurga	2,46,913	47,102
12.	Dakshina Kannada	2,33,095	41,578
13.	Davanagere	2,46,722	51,620
14.	Dharwad	1,32,178	21,341
15.	Gadag	1,10,637	21,157

16.	Gulbarga	3,97,408	1,94,238
17.	Hassan	2,91,845	89,570
18.	Haveri	2,20,433	84,743
19.	Kodagu	98,580	25,320
20.	Kolar	1,78,736	56,865
21.	Koppal	1,85,539	61,498
22.	Mandya	3,09,218	55,076
23.	Mysore	3,68,865	1,22,511
24.	Raichur	2,40,431	1,28,261
25.	Ramanagaram	1,71,041	42,943
26.	Shimoga	2,14,307	36,498
27.	Tumkur	4,01,485	86,897
28.	Udupi	1,66,962	40,297
29.	Uttara Kannada	2,00,220	80,712
	Total	**67,31,513**	**19,19,015**

Karl Pearson Correlation Co-efficient value is 0.77

Source: Economic Survey of Karnataka 2010-11.

Table-4 shows that the northern districts of Gulbarga and Belgaum have the maximum number of BPL families, revealing that poverty is more acute in these regions. The Pearson correlation coefficient value is 0.77 which is a highly positive correlation. It means that greater the number of total rural families larger is the number of BPL families and *vice versa*. Since, there is positive relationship between rural families and BPL families and the northern district have maximum number of BPL families, it is clearly observed that housing is the common problem in those regions.

Rural Housing Schemes

Empirical evidences shows that better rural housing always has a positive relationship with creation of wealth, raises productivity and reduces poverty in the rural areas. In this regard, fulfilling the need for rural housing and tackling housing shortage particularly for the poorest is an important task to be undertaken as part of the poverty alleviation efforts of the government (Planning Commission, 2013). Increasing the shortage of rural housing is forced to dump the people into poverty. Most of the studies evince that there is direct relationship between shortage of rural housing and rural poverty. Eradicating of poverty through provision of basic needs, such as housing, food, cloth, basic education, health, etc., is always a fundamental duty of a welfare state. As part of the efforts to meet the housing needs thereby eradicating poverty of the rural poor, both Central and State Governments in India have undertaken various schemes, such as Indira Awaas Yojana (IAY), Homestead, Provision of Urban Amenities in Rural Areas (PURA), Bharat Nirman, as also schemes of the Banking sector, viz. NHB – Rural Housing Fund (RHF), IAY Top-up Loan Scheme and Golden Jubilee Rural Housing Finance Scheme (GJRHFS), NABARD's – Schemes for non-farm sector (NFS) etc. But the present paper tries to examine the performance of IAY and Bharat xNirman over a period.

Indira Awaas Yojana (IAY)

The Indira Awaas Yojana (IAY) is a flagship scheme of the Ministry of Rural Development to provide houses to Below Poverty Line (BPL) families in the rural areas. The target groups for houses under the IAY are below poverty line households living in the rural areas belonging to Scheduled Castes/ Scheduled Tribes, Freed Bonded Labourers and non-SC/ST BPL rural households, widows and next of kin to defence personnel/paramilitary forces killed in action residing in rural areas (irrespective of their income criteria), ex-servicemen and retired members of paramilitary forces fulfilling other conditions. The funding of IAY is shared between the Centre and States in the ratio of 75:25. In the case of UTs, entire funds of IAY are provided by the Centre. However, in the case of North Eastern States, the funding pattern has been revised and at present is in the ratio of 90:10.

The criterion for allocation of IAY funds to the States and UTs involves assigning 75 per cent weightage to housing shortage and 25 per cent to poverty ratio. The allocation amongst districts is based on 75 per cent weightage age to housing shortage and 25 per cent weightage to SC/ST component. The financial assistance provided for new construction in the form of full grant is Rs 70,000 per unit for plain areas and Rs 75,000 for hilly/ difficult areas. Further, an IAY beneficiary can avail top-up loan up to Rs 20,000 under the Differential Rate of Interest (DRI Scheme) from any Nationalised Bank at an interest rate of four per cent per annum. The assistant for upgradation of unserviceable *kachha* house to pucca/semi-*pucca* houses is Rs 15,000. Upto 20 per cent of the total funds can be utilised for upgradation of existing *kachha* house and towards subsidy for construction of houses under credit-cum-subsidy scheme.

Table- 5 Performance of Indira Awaas Yojana (Rs in Lakh)

Year	*Central Release*	*Target (No. of Houses)*	*Houses Constructed/ Completed*	*Performance level (Houses constructed - Target)**
2002-03	162853	13.14	15.49	2.35
2003-04	187108	14.84	13.61	-1.23
2004-05	288310	15.62	15.21	-0.41
2005-06	273823	14.41	15.52	1.11
2006-07	290753	15.33	14.98	-0.35
2007-08	388237	21.27	19.92	-1.35
2008-09	879579	21.27	21.34	0.07
2009-10	863574	40.52	33.86	-6.66
2010-11	1013945	29.08	27.15	-1.93
2011-12	986478	27.26	24.71	-2.55

Source: Annual Report 2012-13 (page 70), Ministry of Rural Development. Authors' calculation.

Table-5 shows that the amount released from Central Government is varied during 2002-12. The target to construct houses is fluctuating in nature. It was 13.14 lakh in 2002-03 but it increased to 40.52 lakh in 2009-10, which is highest than 2011-12 year target (27.26 lakh). Even though the housing shortage is increasing over a period, the target to construct houses under IAY has been decreasing. It is found that during 10 years, IAY achieved its target in 2002-03, 2005-06 and 2008-09 but failed in remaining seven years. This shows that IAY is not performed very well in order to achieve its estimated target providing housing facilities.

Bharat Nirman Programme

Bharat Nirman Programme launched by the Government of India in 2005 represents a vision for rural infrastructure development on a national scale. Provision of rural housing is one of the six components of Bharat Nirman Programme. Other provisions under this programmes are water, sanitation, sewage, local roads and connectivity etc. This programme is implemented in two phases, the first phase and second phase implemented in 2005-09 and 2009-14, respectively.

Table-6 Physical Achievements under Bharat Nirman (Phase-I, 2005-06 to 2008-09)

Year	*Target in lakh*	*Houses Constructed (in lakh)*	*Performance level (Houses constructed - Target)**	*Expenditure (in Crore)*
2005-06	14.41	15.52	1.11	3654.09
2006-07	15.33	14.98	-0.35	4253.42
2007-08	21.27	19.92	-1.35	5464.64
2008-09	21.27	21.34	0.07	8348.34
Total	**72.28**	**71.76**	**-0.52**	**21720.4**

Source: Annual Report, 2012-13 (page 72), Ministry of Rural Development, GoI. 'Authors' calculation.

Table-6 shows the performance of houses constructed and expenditure under Bharat Nirman Programme (Phase–I). About 72.28 lakh houses were envisaged to be constructed all over the country during the four years, i.e., from 2005-06 to 2008-09. Against this target, 71.76 lakh houses were constructed with an expenditure of $ 21,720.39 crore. It is observed that in the year of 2005-06 and 2008-09, the programme achieved its target, but it failed in 2006-07, 2007-08 and overall in Phase-I.

Table: 7. Physical Achievements under Bharat Nirman (Phase-II, 2009-10 to 2011-12)

Year	*Target in lakh*	*Houses Constructed (in lakh)*	*Performance level (Houses constructed - Target)**	*Expenditure (in Crore)*
2009-	40.52	33.86	-6.66	13292.46
2010-	29.09	27.15	-1.94	13406.51
2011-	27.27	24.71	-2.56	12926.33
Total	**96.88**	**85.72**	**-11.16**	**39625.3**

Source: Annual Report 2012-13 (page 72), Ministry of Rural Development, GoI. *Authors' calculation.

Table-7 shows the performance of houses constructed and expenditure under Bharat Nirman Programme (Phase – II). The target under Phase-II of

Bharat Nirman Programme is for construction of 120 lakh houses over a period of five years starting from 2009-10 to 2013-14. During the first three years, approximate 85.72 lakh houses have been constructed. But in the performance level indicator the Phase-II is working poor than Phase-I of the programme, even though the expenditure has been increasing over a period. Because, the Phase-II of the programme has not achieved its target houses in the beginning of three years.

Conclusion

It is found that there is increasing trend of rural housing shortage in India, which shows the existing rural housing schemes are inefficient in providing the proper shelter facility to poor. Nearly 90 per cent of the rural housing shortage for BPL population in India shows that housing deprivation is the common factor in determining rural poverty. Further, it is found that the number of total rural families is the number of BPL families and *vice - versa.* The target to construct and complete houses under IAY and Bharat Nirman programme is fluctuating in nature. It shows that programmes are not performed very well in order to achieve estimated target.

Unequal distribution of land and other assets, corruption at administrative level, lack of public-private partnerships, financial resources, lack of convergence of various programmes of village infrastructure run by various departments and ministries, non-poor getting the benefits of poverty alleviation programmes especially of rural housing schemes, borrowing from informal sources continues to be the major source of finance for the rural population which at times are exploitative, especially for the poor, formal finance options, on the other hand, are still few and remain mostly inaccessible to the rural population, non-participation of local level institutions, lack of active involvement of the poor and unawareness of the people etc., are the common reasons for failure of make rural housing schemes such as IAY and Bharat Nirman programme. So, in order to rural development through provision of rural housing and eradicating rural poverty, the above mentioned impediments should be minimised. Moreover, the rural local bodies should identify dedicated rural areas for development of affordable housing in the area's master plans and should develop them within a planned schedule. Even though housing is one of the determinante factor of rural poverty and low rural development in India, it has been given low priority by government. So, it should be given main priority. Despite various rural housing schemes, housing shortage is continuing in many parts of the country. In this direction, the emphasis of rural housing should be more on inclusiveness and quality improvement.

References

Government of Karnataka (2010-11), *Economic Survey of Karnataka.*

Malcolm J. Moseley (2003), '*Rural Development: Principles and Practices*'. London: SAGE Publication. P.5. ISBN 0-7619-4766-3. Online available at: http://books.google.co.in/books?id=EGxdWANxzt8C &pg=PR3&source=gbs_selected_pages&cad=2#v= onepage&q &f = false.

Ministry of Rural Development (2011, Sept). '*Working Group on Rural Housing for XIIth FiveYear Plan*'. Government of India, New Delhi. Online available at: http://planningcommission.gov.in/aboutus/committee/wrkgrp12/rd/wgrep_iay.pdf.

Ministry of Rural Development (2012-13). *Annual Report – 2012-13*, Government of India, New Delhi. Online available at: http://rural.nic.in/sites/downloads/annual-report/ MoRD English_AR2012_ 13.pdf.

National Housing Bank (2012). '*Report on Trend and Progress of Housing in India*', Online available at: http://nhb.org.in/Publications/Report-Trend-and-Progress-of-Housing-in-India-2012.pdf.

Planning Commission (2013), *Evaluation Study of Indira Awas Yojana*, Government of India. New Delhi. Online available at: http://planningcommission.nic.in/reports/peoreport/peo/rep_iay2202.pdf.

Planning Commission Documents, Government of India.

Population Census Documents, Government of India.

Sathya Narayana and Navitha Thimmaiah (2013). *'Trends of Poverty in India and Karnataka'*. *Asian Journal of Development Matters.* 7(2), pp. 25-40. ISSN (print): 0973-9629. ISSN (online): 0976 4674. Onlineavailableat:http://www.indianjournals.com/ijor.aspx?target=ijor:ajdm&volume=7&issue=2&article=002.

Singh, S. Swaminathan, M. Ramachandran, V.K. *'Housing Shortages in Rural India'*.

UnitedNations. (2009), 'The Right to Adequate Housing Fact Sheet No. 21/Rev.1'. Office of the United Nations High Commissioner for Human Rights and UN--Habitat, Geneva. Online available at: http://www.ohchr.org/Documents/Publications/FS21_rev_1_Housing_en.pdf.

21

Tracing Corporate Social Responsibility (CSR) in Rural Development: Evidences from India

D C Nanjunda and Appaji Gowda

Introduction

It is found that Corporate Social Responsibility (CSR) has much bigger implications for rural development of the any country. It reduces dependency on the government for social expenditure and helps for speedy rural growth. The scale of CSR emerged significantly in the last decade in India pertaining to the rural sector. Since business houses required doing business in the society only; it would be an obligation to share small portion of their profit for betterment of the disadvantaged section of the society. To relate fundamental business philosophy, to make CSR sharper, smarter, and focussed is what really matters is the chore for ahead. However, critiques are emerging on the recent government bill on CSR which makes mandatory on the part of the companies to spend small portion of their profit for social causes. Many companies have invested noted share profits in various rural development sectors. Also there is research evidence to show that CSR work of the companies reach where government could not reach so far like remote part of the country. Although various Indian corporate involve in rural development activities; it is not enough when contrast to their actual financial strength. This paper gives solid background on initiatives of various companies' for speedy rural development in the country.

What is CSR?

The world business council for sustainable development in its publication defines, 'CSR means Making Good Business Sense', Next, Holme and Richard Watts used the following definition "Corporate Social Responsibility is the continuing commitment by business to behave ethically and contribute to economic development while improving the quality of life of the workforce and their families as well as of the local community and society at large. CSR activities in India today's may be classified under two headings:

1. CSR activities normally taken by the corporate giants, and
2. CSR activities taken by the small and medium scale enterprises.

This classification will be based on commitment and transparency is maintained inside the companies. Recently, Central Government has issued a notification to spend two to five per cent of the company's net profits on CSR activities to all big corporate giants. This had mixed reaction from many corporate people across the country. Some of them have welcomed the decision while others have criticised the move. They opined government should not make CSR as mandatory. Even through government intention is good, before finalising the Bill, government would require to consult the business people to seek their opinion. There should be no hurry to bring such Bill in the country. Also small and medium scale industry should be a part of the CSR.

What is Corporate Philanthropy?

"Corporate Philanthropy (CP) refers to the practice of companies of all sizes and sectors making charitable contributions to address variety of social, economic and other issues as part of their overall corporate citizenship strategy. Companies make philanthropic donations either through company-sponsored foundations or directly giving programmes. These are different in their relationship to the company and it is important to understand the difference" (the Voluntary Foundation). Further World Business Council for Sustainable Development (WCSD) defines "...CSR is the continuing commitment by business to behave ethically and contribute to economic development while improving the quality of life of the work force and their families, as well as of the local community and society at large".

The present scenario in India has many companies (over 90 per cent), which have put in their own individual and collective efforts in promoting Corporate Social Responsibility activities in rural part of the country. The foremost areas in which corporates are involved in Corporate Social Responsibility activities include livelihood promotion, education, health, environment and women empowerment. The Tata Group has been promoting inclusive growth since long. ITC, one of the major companies in India, presently has been focussing on empowering farmers and has made this initiative vital part of its business strategy. HUL has initiated '*Shakti Amma*' using micro-enterprises to strategically uplift the rural entrepreneur and in turn generate demand for consumer (FMCG) products in rural markets. Software giants Wipro and TCS have developed software that assists in better knowledge dissemination at the primary and secondary school level. Banks have been promoting micro-credits through very accommodating and supportive schemes to assist migrant labourers and street vendors take up entrepreneurship in the form of auto loans (light vehicles for taxi, auto, goods carrier etc.,) and also for setting up small business outlets for street vendors.

As Warhust (2001) points out the three major elements of CSR are product use which focusses on contribution of industrial products which help in well-being and quality of life of the rural society, business practice which focusses on good corporate governance and gives high impetus for the environmental well-being and equity, which tries for distribution of profits equitably across different societies. Thus, CSR exhorts firms to diverge from their sole aim of maximising profits and to lay more importance on improving the economic and social standards of the community in their countries of operation (Sandeep and Rakesh, 2002).Thus, the focus is more on ethical practices expected of a business house. Whereas "Inclusive" growth refers to the ability of the system to bring together opportunities and capabilities which would help sustained growth. It points out improvement in the governance model. But inclusive growth cannot be achieved by government alone. Bhujbal and Sharma (2011) write "The government being only one of the three pillars of the Governance Model requires support of other two actors as well for a Sustained Inclusive Growth. It requires an optimal blend of three sets of actors and their respective responsibilities. These are Government Social Responsibilities (GSR), Corporate Social Responsibilities (CSR) and Public Social Responsibility (PSR). Apart from Government Responsibilities (GR), which include law and order, defence, foreign relations etc., the government should also pay special attention to GSR, Government Social Responsibility for Inclusive Growth."

The trend of evaluating the contribution of a corporate towards Corporate Social Responsibility is slowly becoming a conventional activity being included by business houses to ensure transparency and promote more such activities. In fact, the Companies Bill which called for a two per cent compulsory Corporate Social Responsibility spending proposal, led to intense debate with majority of the Corporate favouring voluntary corporates Social Responsibility spending. However, the million dollar question whether Corporate Social Responsibility activities fulfill their objectives of social responsibility can only be ascertained when the outcome of such measures can be measured against its effect on society.

Presently, the trend seen in the corporate scenario is the formation of foundations which are run by the respective corporate houses which are totally dedicated towards corporates Social Responsibility activities. These foundations work as an NGO in promoting Corporate Social Responsibility activities and have become a supportive stem in the subsistence of the business house. The Tata Group, ITC, Reliance Industries, SAIL, Wipro, L & T, Procter and Gamble, Bennett and Colemann, to mention a few, have accomplished several initiatives through respective foundations for the inclusive rural development in many northern parts of the country. Some of the big Indian corporate like Infosys, WIPRO, TATA, have become role model in CSR activities focussing rural India. Some of them have really done wonders in the selected rural social sectors. Further, some companies' social involvement helps for rural inclusive growth and eradicates social exclusion in the country. Companies' rural presence will help the company in increasing stronger financial performance, social accountability, reputation and branding etc. Also some reputed companies are spending more than 15-20 per cent of their profit for rural development. Although various Indian corporate sector involved in CSR activities; it is not enough when compare to their actual financial capacity. In addition, the companies have institutional and other problems in having CSR policies.

Table 1 : CSR Initiatives of Some of Indian Companies Focussing Rural Development

Sl No.	*Name of the Companies*	*Area of Working*	*Specific Rural Initiatives*
1.	Coca-Cola India Inc	Health and Education	• Education for children through "The Schools into Smiles Project" • Environment • Sustainable water management • Construction of check dams, • schools
2.	NTPC	Community Development	• Repaire and maintenance of bore wells, schools, community centres • Education, vocational training
3.	Ambuja Cement Ltd	Health and Education	• HIV/AIDS awareness • Environment • Water management and conservation
4.	Asian Paints	Infrastructure	• Developmental programmes • Improving infrastructure

5.	Bharat Petroleum	Health and Education	• Construction of schools • Health camps, HIV/AIDS care and prevention • Primary education,
6.	Indian Oil Corporation	Income generation	• Income generation • livelihood activities • Environmental protection
7.	Tata Steel	Entrepreneurship	• Enterprise promotion • Fellowship, coaching programmes
8.	Care India	Finical inclusion	• SHG • Micro-finance

Sources: Sanjay Pradhan and Akhilesh Ranjan, 2010.

CSR initiative in India beyond 1990s have become an average for most of the corporates to contribute to rural Indian society through various inclusive growth activities.

E-choupals of ITC group that leverages the authority of internet to authorise small farmers within the order of best opportune, relevant weather information, and practice, clear disclosure of prices and a great deal more. Likewise Jaipur Rugs have been rising into weaving skills among people of distant villages so that they can make constant living for themselves. These initiatives have showed in the uplift of disadvantaged sections and allocation of wealth focussing rural people. TCS is creating software business that aid an illiterate start reading and writing by 40 days. Infosys has been serving rural student to get computer educated by scheming course circular for them. Aviva, a life insurance firm have started to fund rural schools to teach the under opportunity students.

Experts have found, four areas identified require concentration for effective linking among sustainable rural development and CSR:

1. Institutional mechanisms,
2. Stakeholder engagement,
3. Knowledge management,
4. Capacity building.

Public sector-government and community engagements-public sector have to be more efficient. Institutional mechanism has to be developed to see whether CSR projects are delivering and effective. Prominently, executives at all levels require an improved concer of CSR through inclusive development. While most of the projects running in rural areas, the consideration of urgent rural issues and sustainability is extremely significant. Lastly, such a big scale work out in CSR should have an information management instrument to learn from the achievement and mistakes of the early time.

Conclusion

Business houses are playing an important role in the overall social development process. This is due to the policy adopted themselves by the companies. Many Indian companies have grown in size and capabilities conducting development policy and innovative programmes in the field of health, livelihood, education, micro-financing, and income generation programmers focussing rural development. These programmes have made important contribution in the effort to eradicate various rural problems as these are closely intertwined with the rapid inclusive growth of rural society. There are some reports showing rapid rural growth possible with the more participation of the private sectors. However, unless big companies make significant improvement and constructive changes in promoting philanthropic behaviours their best efforts may not prove sufficient for ending severe problems being faced by larger section of the rural society.

Acknowledgment: Author is highly grateful to ICSSR, New Delhi for funding the project.

References

Chaudhary. N.K. (2009), Facilitators and Bottlenecks of Corporate Social Responsibility" *The Indian Journal of Industrial Relations*, Vol. 44, No. 3.

Friedman. M. (1970), The Social Responsibility of Business is to Increase its Profits", *New York Times Magazine Supplement*, September 13.

Gugler. P. and Shi. J.Y.J. (2009), Corporate Social Responsibility for Developing Country Multinational Corporations: Lost War in Pertaining Global Competitiveness?" *Journal of Business Ethics,* Vol. 87, pp. 3-24.

Gupta, A.D. (2005), "Corporate Social Responsibility in India: Promoting Human Development Towards a Sacro-Civic Society", *Social Responsibility Journal*, Vol.-1 Issue: 3. pp.- 6.

Gupta. S. and Sharma (2009), CSR A Business Opportunity" *The Indian Journal of Industrial Relations,* Vol. 44, No. 3, pp. 396-401.

Jayashri Shetty, (2010), "Corporate Social Responsibility: A means for Inclusive Growth" *International Journal in Multi-disciplinary and Academic Research,* Vol. 1, No. 4, pp-34.

Joseph. A.V. (2009), "Successful Examples of Corporate Social Responsibility" *The Indian Journal of Industrial Relations*, Vol. 44, No. 3, pp. 347-54.

Nilesh R. Berad (2011), *Corporate Social Responsibility – Issues and Challenges in India,* International Conference on Technology and Business Management, March 28-30.

Peter Utting, (2003), *"Promoting Development through Corporate Social* Responsibility - Does it Work?" Source: Global Future, *Third Quarter.*

Prabhash Dalei and Pravesh Dalei (2011), *"Corporate social responsibility in India, international conference on Humanities, Geography and Economics* (ICHGE '2011) Pattaya December 2011.

Ramakrishnan and Reshma K.P. (2010), "Corporate Social Responsibility Initiatives of Companies in Karnataka, Prabandhan", *Indian Journal of Management*, 3(7), pp. 23-28.

Sanjeev Verma and Rohit Chauhan (2007) *Role of Corporate Social Responsibility in Developing Economies,* International Marketing Conference on Marketing and Society, *April 8-10, 2007, IIM.K.*

Sarika Tomar and Rakesh Gupta (2007), *Development of Corporate Social Responsibility in Indian Family Business: A case of TATA Iron and Steel Company* (website article).

Shefali Bhujbal and Aasha Sharma, *A Study on Innovations in Corporate Social Responsibility: Moving from Philanthropy to Inclusive Growth,* ICOQM-10 June 28-30, 2011.

Sumeet Gupta and Debashish Bagga (2011) *Corporate Social Responsibility of Indian Corporate and its Contribution to India's Inclusive Growth,* Conference on Inclusive and Sustainable Growth Role of Industry, Government and Society Conference Proceedings (UK).

Sweta Singh (2010) *Philanthropy to Corporate Social Responsibility: An Indian Perspective, Review of International Comparative Management,* Volume 11, Issue-5.

Vandana Lamba (2012), *The future of corporate social responsibility: Challenges and Opportunities in India, Gianjyoti e-journal*, Volume 2, Issue 3 (July-Sept 2012).

Warhust, A. (2001). "Corporate Citizenship and Corporate Social Investment: Drivers of Tri-sector Partnerships", *Journal of Corporate Citizenship*, Spring, pp. 57-73.

Wartick, S. and Cochran, P. (1985) "The Evolution of the Corporation Social Performance Model, *Academy of Management Review,* vol. 4, pp. 758-69.

22

Role of e-Governance and Information Technology in Progressive Growth of Rural India

Vibhudi Venkateshwarlu

Introduction

The roots of the Internet and the current revolution in individual access to information goes back to many decades, even centuries, but the Internet as widespread social phenomenon is just concluding its first decade. At the present time, even the definition of e-Governance is unclear. We have entered a period of history when technological change is extremely rapid and unpredictable. e-Governance is the application of information and communication technology (ICT) for delivering government services, exchange of information, communication transactions, integration of various stand-alone systems and services between government to customer (G2C), government-to-business (G2B), government-to-government (G2G) as well as back office processes and interaction within the entire government framework. The word 'electronic' in the term e-Governance implies technology driven governance. It is accepted that the governance is exercised by private sector, civil society as well as the state. The World Bank has developed six indicators of governance encompassing Voice and Accountability, Political Stability, Non-violence, Government Effectiveness, Regulatory Quality, Rule of Law and Control of Corruption. Through e-Governance, government services will be made available to citizens in a convenient, efficient and transparent manner.

There are 638,387 villages in India that represent more than 72 per cent of the total population living in rural India. This rural India does not know the technology especially information technology. Indian literacy rate is approximately 74 per cent, male coming having 82.2 per cent and female 65.5 per cent[5]. Education is provided by the public sector as well as the private sector, with control and funding from three levels: Central, State, and Local;

96.5 per cent of rural children between the ages of 6-14 were enrolled out of which 83 per cent from rural 15-16 years old were enrolled in school[6]. The per capita income of Indian villagers is not more than Rs. 12,000-18,000 (USD 240-360) per annum, as compared to the average national income of Rs. 25,000 (USD 500). Even after 66 years of independence, the monthly highest income of 39 per cent of Indian population is less then Rs. 1,000, living below poverty line. With this meagre earning, the information technology is a distant, non-existent dream for them. Few among them have seen or heard of a computer. Software licensing model is unaffordable; electrical power, air-cooled office spaces, and phone connections are no way near ubiquitous. These facts are showing that education at rural India is not high and there is no quality in education.. The point is very less people there know the computer knowledge, may be one per cent of the population is able to operate computers; those are mostly forward communities or upper castes naturally because they are financially strong. Remaining more than 85 to 90 per cent is financially, politically and socially very weak; practically, they are innocent people leading their life like animals.

Television sets were installed in 2,334 remote villages for creating awareness among the rural population and India's daily transmission time of four hours was divided into 90 minute morning programme for primary school children and a 150 minute evening programme of national news, public affairs, health and nutrition, and the dissemination of indigenous culture. Computers came to India in 1959, but were slow to catch on because of the resistance from workers fearing loss of jobs. In the course of time, the advantages became apparent. National Informatics Centre (NIC) was set up under the Electronics Commission. The NIC has brought e-Governance to India through networking and computer applications in various organs of the Government at Central, State and Local levels. Even after 20 years (since its inception in 1985 with the establishment of NIC, National Informatics Centre) of careful exercises, only one per cent of Indian Administration can be computerised or we can say only one per cent of government can be converted to e-Government.

The rural population needs to be convinced that IT solutions would help them in improving their income and livelihood with concrete experiments. The transformation of work in the information age and on the quantity of jobs that are alleged to have resulted from the use of IT, even though there is general agreement that IT has contributed both to productivity in the workplace and profitability for businesses, many social theorists have raised concerns with respect to the impact of IT on the quality of work life. This is well exemplified in the case of dairy co-operatives of Anand in Gujarat, where automatic milk collection system (AMCS) allows them reading of quality and quantity of fat content, and maintains daily record of milk societies at village level. In Dhar district of Madhya Pradesh, a programme of administration known as *Gyandoot,* meaning 'ambassador of knowledge', that was launched in January 2000, was awarded Stockholm Challenge Award for public service and democracy. In five blocks of this district, 26 major centers are connected through an intranet network. With each center connecting about 15 *gram panchayats* and 25-30 villages, the benefits are supposed to be reaching to over half a million people in more than 600 villages. This model seems to be under replication in 44 other districts in Madhya Pradesh. It is, however, known that the original *Gyandoot* project has been closed, which brings into question the issue of sustainability of ICT projects in rural areas.

The National Institute of Agricultural Extension Management (MANAGE), Hyderabad has taken up a number of what are called 'Cyber Extension' initiatives in the country. It has established Internet connectivity in 24 districts in seven states namely, Andhra Pradesh, Bihar, Himachal Pradesh, Jharkhand, Maharashtra, Orissa and Punjab under National Agricultural Technology Project (NATP). Ten villages in Ranga Reddy district of Andhra Pradesh were selected to test the efficacy of the experiments. These villages had successful Mutually Aided Co-operative Thrift and Credit Societies (MACTCS). Multi-media CDs are distributed to these groups on several aspects of agriculture, rural development, health and education, etc., (the Interactive Self-Learning Package on Watershed Management, the *Vyavasaya Panchangam* encyclopedia of agricultural practices, cultivation of paddy, cotton, mango and coconut, etc.). The experiences of these groups have shown that they have been using the Internet regularly for browsing web sites for government programmes and schemes, weather forecasts, market prices, job opportunities, news etc. It seems that they have started charging nominal amounts for some of services selectively. MAN-AGE is planning to connect over 350 Blocks in 28 districts on Internet in the near future (www.manage.gov.in). There is a need to assess the impact of intervention on the quality of life in those villages. The other notable experiments in applying IT to rural livelihoods are being carried out by the Chennai-based (Tamil Nadu) M.S. Swaminathan Research Foundation in about eight villages around Pondicherry in which information on fisheries, agriculture, buses, healthcare, jobs, etc., is received by coastal people through the network that is all driven by solar power.

Objectives of This Work

This paper exposes real difficulties in rural India and tries to understand the reality in rural India, for whose purpose, the policies are made. It studies how the benefits of policies are reaching the rural masses and how those are implemented on ground. It studies the reasons on why proper training is not given to people by identifying issues. This article seeks to aid the transition to e-Governance by providing realistic overview of the types of implementation challenges that lie ahead for local governments. This should be helpful to public officials contemplating information technology options as well as academics, who have an interest in the implementation literature. The explosion of new information technologies is a landmark event in the history of local government management. It will surely 'test' our knowledge of local government environment as well as our understanding of how these governments function.

Methodology

This doctrinal work follows critical methodology-based on available literature that is books, articles, published and non-published work and reports of various agencies. This work gives a note of caution that this finding is based on the survey of existing literature and no field work was undertaken to test its validity on the ground. Keeping this in view, this work followed a critical evaluation of the schemes and projects involving public expenditure during the last few years taken up by research institutions. For this work, I have visited ICSSR library in Hyderabad, Osmania University library, and have downloaded books from Internet source and articles of EPW from EFL University e-Library. This work mainly followed critical approach for improvement of rural efficiency, quality of information technology for individual, institutional and economic development in rural India.

Education and Languages

The Task Force submitted three reports (June 1998, August 1998 and March 1999). These reports sought to orient policies towards creation of appropriate investment climate. It observed that in the systems previously implemented, the existing rules and procedures of the government were simply automated into computerised information system which served bureaucratic interest and not people's interest. Another side argument is even though India has achieved more than 96 per cent rate of school admission at government primary school level 40 per cent per cent of drop out rate at the elementary level shows majority of the population in rural India are not having access to quality public primary education and primary health care at affordable rate. There is no proper training for communication skills in public primary schools as most of the children study in their vernacular language due to which computer operation and communication skills are not improving in rural level. It is somewhat better in private schools. One seemingly negligible but very significant reason for this digital divide is incompetence of major portion of population in English language; English language keyboard keeps out of use for many. Moreover most of the information available is also in English.

India's overall literacy rate increased from around 17 per cent in 1951 to 65 per cent in 2001. Literacy in rural areas increased from 36 per cent in 1981 to 59 per cent in 2001. During the same time, literacy in urban areas increased from 67 per cent to 80 per cent. The rural-urban gap has declined from 31 to 21 percentage points in the last two decades. Female literacy increased over time but still around 53 per cent of rural females were illiterate in 2001. Also, 30 to 33 per cent of rural girls in the age group 6-14 were not attending school in 1999-00. Similarly, among SCs and STs 40 to 45 per cent of girls were not attending school. There are significant interstate disparities in literacy and education. For example, rural female literacy in Kerala was 87 per cent while in Bihar it was 30 per cent in 2001. Similarly, the school attendance ratios for Kerala girls (6-13 years) were 97 per cent, but in Bihar they were 35 per cent in 1995-96. There are also significant interstate variations regarding school facilities like access to schools, teacher-pupil ratios, classrooms, etc.

Political Responsibility

e-Governance has to be viewed as a part of political process, dealing with reform of governance towards good governance. Thus, the will of the actors, who control, guide and affect the political process, is a determining factor in ensuring good governance through e-Governance. Where political will exists, electronic governance can significantly catalyse the reform process towards good governance. In absence of political will, the impact of electronic governance models will be weak and may not lead to qualitative change in governance processes. While discussing the administrative constraints, it has been clearly demonstrated that administrative reforms are an essential prerequisite for the success of e-Governance and obviously administrative reform is a slow process, requiring engaging with political institutions and bringing about both attitudinal and constitutional changes. All has accepted the significance of the role of political leadership in bringing about these changes. "The need of the hour is to change the present governance to e-Governance by the political leadership at the top.

For e-Governance to succeed, a strong political will and commitment are necessary. The success stories of two southern states of India, *viz.,* Andhra Pradesh and Karnataka, during the last couple of years to guide in e-Governance, advocating diverse use and application of ICT for improving the quality of life of their citizen, undoubtedly, owe their success to their IT sawy chief ministers. Thus, the lack of political will can be described as the biggest barrier in realising the e-Governance. Unfortunately, in most parts of India, we still lack the political awareness and political will needed to initiate the process of e-Governance.

Infrastructure and Budget

A multitude of factors such as limited local participation, lack of availability of local resources, fractured relationship with the state agencies, limited integration with local CSOs and the exogenous social and economic environment are identified as some of the factors for the inability of ICT projects to deliver their full range of output in rural areas. These factors are often overlooked while projecting the promises of the projects. Indian industry and scientists would have to come together to provide the resources and drive to design and deploy low cost technology that best caters to Indian conditions. The Logue Communications, set up by the IIT, Chennai-based TeNet Group, realised that it is not just the connectivity but the availability of relevant content for rural people in the Internet is the key to success. Further, efforts are needed to incorporate local language and local content in Internet in a massive way. Having the need to use key board by everyone may limit the use of Internet. There is a need to develop voice-enabled Internet service (with Indian languages) soon. Ultimately, to be successful in India, Internet requires Indian applications that emerge from the Indian way of life.

The lack of infrastructure like electricity is one of the major factors responsible for the failure in sustaining the e-government in rural India. Likewise, lack of adequate funding for e-Governance has restrained its reach to the masses. In the present 'crucial decade' of this millennium, a high rate of investment in IT and a supportive environment are expected to achieve 'digital society'. Some key imperatives for the government, identified by the study include ensuring, three per cent of the budget committed towards e-Governance and the amount should be spent in the ratio of 40:30:30 on hardware, software and services respectively. It is obvious that to re-engineer the whole administrative machinery, to provide adequate infrastructure as well as to increase share in national and state budget the existence of a strong political leadership is must. But unfortunately though IT and e-Governance are the new shibboleths for most of the Indian politicians, soon after coming to power, chief ministers of almost all state governments promptly begin working on an IT policy and push for public services going online, but they never mind the crippling lack of infrastructure like power, roads, buildings, etc., extremely poor bandwidth and the administrative reforms become the matter of discussion by commissions and committees only.

Caste and Gender Issues

Caste has been a part of Indian society. It is very authoritarian in rural India since the last 2,000 years. It was institutionalised into government organisations by Mughal, British colonies. The removal of the boundaries between 'civil society' and 'political society' meant that caste played a huge role in the political arena, and also influenced other government-run institutions such as police, revenue, medical and judiciary etc. Though caste seemed to dictate one's access to such institutions, the location of that caste also played a pivotal role. If a lower caste is concentrated enough in one area, it could then translate that pocket of concentration of its caste members into political power and then challenge the hegemony of locally dominant upper caste. Gender also plays a significant role in the power dynamic of caste in politics. Women's representation within the political system seems to be tied to their caste. Lower, more conservative castes have less female participation in politics than upper, more socially liberal castes. This has caused a disproportionately large number of upper-caste women to occupy political office, when compared to their lower caste counterparts.

Education spread to the lower castes after India gained Independence. The younger generations of all castes have had access to educational resources since the 1980s. The number of the Scheduled and Backward Caste people receiving education increased at faster rate than that of the upper caste groups. The spread of education to all castes generated democratising effects. Some representatives of the SC and ST groups obtained access to political power due to their higher education levels. They are less likely to respond to the upper-caste patrons, but are sensitive to the needs and interests of the lower caste vote bank as these people participation is increasing every election to election in favour of their own person or caste or party.

The information technology will remove the caste barriers in political life of rural India, because it creates confidence among the people and they can get the information without support or assistance of upper caste, so that caste influence may be eradicated by the technology, quality of education and information technology. The caste system has traditionally had significant influence over people's access to power. The privileged upper caste groups benefit more by gaining substantially more economic and political power, while the lower caste groups have limited access to those powers. The caste system distributes to different castes of different economic strength. The upper caste groups can then manipulate the economic and political system to transfer economic strength into political power. Governments are intentionally avoiding to give quality training or education to rural people and children, because they have threat from the lower castes people that upper caste people lose their political, financial and social powers in rural India. Agricultural schemes and peripheral rural development often reveal more about political control than about the economics of agricultural development.

Today, government is introducing online applications for getting benefits of various schemes and introducing e-payments for students in their education at the time of entrance, admission, examination result etc., but more than 70 per cent of rural students are not able to operate computer systems and complete the online process of work, for which they are depending or getting assistance from their friends, internet centers, and other sources, who know the operating of computers, not only village students in town, cities colleges and university students are not able to complete online work of applications e-payments etc. Online networking and e-mails, Facebook etc., are bringing network around the globe by which people are creating their thoughts and changing their opinions by comments, debates, discussions and chatting on online networks. Smart phones creating huge influence network among the people and the information is available a every corner of the society because of these changes political leaders are having great threat for their vote bank. All this experiences taught lessons to ruling class not to allow rural people access to quality education by introducing computers, computer education, quality of training etc., due to which rural students are not able to access and operate computer network for their work.

Suggestions

An important priority is to increase public investment in rural infrastructure. Infrastructure includes irrigation, electricity, agricultural research, roads and communications and new technology. Investment in rural infrastructure is more important for agricultural growth and rural development than trade liberalisation *per se.* Although, the share of agriculture in GDP has declined to 22 per cent, the share of employment in agriculture is still 60 per cent. Therefore, increase in agricultural growth is important for rural development.

Institutional reforms are important, particularly in the domain of public systems and e-Governance, for sustained technical progress and output growth in agriculture. Three aspects of improving basic education in rural areas are:

Firstly, more resources have to be allocated to education, particularly to primary education, from the budget. The international norm is six per cent of GDP. India has been spending less than four per cent of GDP on education. In rural areas, infrastructure is poor and there is a need for greater spending. The ninety-third amendment of the Constitution is in the right direction, but funds are needed to realise universalisation of elementary education.

Secondly, the quality of education in terms of curriculum, better infrastructure and teaching has to be improved.

Thirdly, retaining children in the schools is more difficult than enrolling them. While the demand factors are important in influencing the extent of literacy and drop out rates, access or supply or quality factors influence enrollment rates. Specific policies are required to address gender and social disparities. Non-Governmental Organisations and Non-Profit Organisations should take initiatives for e-Governance at rural level, take steps for implementation of such policies and pressurise the existing governments for implementation.

Conclusions

There is little doubt that public demand for e-Governance will increase in the coming years. As more and more business is transacted online, lagging performance in the public sector will not be tolerated. This is true, because the growth of technology will make using the Internet easier and better and because the general public will become increasingly familiar with the online world. Eventually, we will have a generation that does not even remember a time when the Internet and related communication technologies did not exist.

The IT industry in rural India has several advantages for growth with large pool of scientific manpower and proactive government. The software exports have grown impressively in the last decade. The IT enabled services may play significant role in creation of employment opportunities in the coming period. There is need to move away from concepts of electronic development that places ICTs on center stage. Instead, the approach must be information centered, integral to its environment, integrated with development objectives, intermediated, interconnected, and indigenised. Above all, it must be intelligent. Our development priority for the future will depend on electronic approach in every field and every act. As the knowledge- based economy has tendency to reverse the sources of equality, the basic challenges lie in improving the social sectors like education, health, poverty, etc., and develop infrastructure. If these problems are not tackled on priority basis, the fast growing IT sector will leave majority of the population behind that may lead to more inequalities in polarised society. Giving effective training to rural students in IT, improved communication skills to rural areas, conducting seminars, debates, discussions in institutes, colleges and Universities are useful to rural people.

On the basis of discussion above, it is obvious that e-Governance cannot turn bad governance into good, what it can do is that it can make governance better. But even to achieve this, the constraints, explained above are to be removed. In the coming years, we will see e-governance flourish. Some governments will move ahead quickly, and others will fall behind. Hopefully, this article helps local government officials, managers and other administrators to assess the situation and develop solid plan of action.

End Notes

1. Schwabach, Aaron. (2005), *Internet and the Law: Technology, society, and compromises.* ABC-CLIO, Inc, Santa Barbara, California, p. IX.
2. Anupama Saxena (2005), e-Governance and Good Governance: the Indian Context. *The Indian Journal of Political Science, Vol. 66, No. 2. 328.* The Indian Political Science Association. Accessed: 23/05/2014. p. 313.
3. R. P. Sinha, review by K.L. Rawal (2007). e-Governance in India: Initiatives and Issues, *Indian Journal of Industrial Relations,"* Vol. 42, No. 4. Trade Unions and Civil Society: Papers Submitted for IIRA Asian Regional Congress, Shri Ram Centre for Industrial Relations and Human Resources. Accessed: 23/05/2014.

4. *Census Report 2011*, Government of India.
5. UNICEF Retrieved Report, October 10th , 2013.
6. Annual Status of Education Report (ASER), 2012.
7. Rajesh Jain's weblog, Monday, March 10, 2003, *Emerging Technologies, Enterprises and Markets Tech Talk: Transforming Rural India*, http://www.emerg.
8. William J. Stover (1983), *Information Technology in the Third World: Can IT Lead to Humane National Development*. Boulder, Co. Westview Press, p. 81.
9. Reid, op. cit.1.
10. Herman T. Tavani (1999), *Social and Ethical Aspects of Information Technology* John Wiley and Sons Inc, Online Article. Accessed on 27-12-1999. p.416.
11. Reid, op. cit. 2.
12. Reid, op. cit.1.
13. S. Mahendra Dev (2004), *"How to Make Rural India Shine,"* Economic and Political Weekly, Vol. 39, No. 40 (Oct. 2-8, 2004), pp. 4417. *Economic and Political Weekly*. Accessed: 17/05/2014 07:57.
14. Guy Berger (1992), *Social Structure and Rural Development in the Third World*, Cambridge University Press, New York. P. 130.

References

Annual Status of Education Report (ASER) 2012.

Anupama Saxena (2005). E-governance and Good Governance: the Indian context. *The Indian Journal of Political Science*, Vol. 66, No. 2. p. 328 The Indian Political Science Association. Accessed: 23/05/2014.

Guy Berger (1992), *Social structure and rural development in the Third World*. Cambridge University Press, New York.

Herman T. Tavani (1999), *Social and Ethical Aspects of Information Technology*. John Wiley and Sons Inc, Online Article. Accessed on 27-12-1999. p.416.

R. P. Sinha review by K. L. Rawal (2007). E-governance in India: Initiatives and Issues. *The Indian Journal of Industrial Relations*, Vol. 42, No. 4, Trade Unions and Civil Society: Papers submitted for IIRA Asian Regional Congress. Published by Shri Ram Centre for Industrial Relations and Human Resources. Accessed: 23/05/2014.

Rajesh Jain's weblog (2003) *Emerging Technologies, Enterprises and Markets TECH TALK: Transforming Rural India*, http://www.emerg. March 10, 2003.

S. Mahendra Dev (2004) How to Make Rural India Shine, *Economic and Political Weekly*, Vol. 39, No. 40 (Oct. 2-8, 2004), pp. 4415-22. *The Economic and Political Weekly*. Accessed: 17/05/2014 07:57.

Schwabach, Aaron (2005), *Internet and the Law: Technology, society, and compromises*, ABC-CLIO, Inc, Santa Barbara, California.

Census Report 2011, Government of India, 2011.

Shirin Madon (2009), *e-governance for Development: A Focus on Rural India*, Palgrave Macmillan: London.

UNICEF Retrieved Report, October 10th, 2013.

William J. Stover (1983), *Information Technology in the Third World: Can IT Lead to Humane National Development*, Boulder, Co. Westview Press.

23

Rural Development through Entrepreneurship Education

Sharmista

Introduction

Entrepreneurship and entrepreneurial education is a panacea to guarantee amiable rural development. Rural development is more than ever before linked to entrepreneurship. Institutions and individuals promoting rural development now see entrepreneurship as a strategic development intervention that could accelerate the rural development process. Furthermore, institutions and individuals seem to agree on the urgent need to promote rural enterprises: development agencies see rural entrepreneurship as an enormous employment potential; farmers see it as an instrument for improving farm earning; and women see it as an employment possibility near homes which provides autonomy, independence and a reduced need for social support. To all these groups, however, entrepreneurship stands as vehicle to improve the quality of life for individuals, families and communities and to sustain healthy economy and environment.The entrepreneurial orientation to rural development accepts entrepreneurship as the central force of economic growth and development, without it other factors of development will be wasted or frittered away. However, the acceptance of entrepreneurship as central development force by itself will not lead to rural development and the advancement of rural enterprises. What is needed in addition is an environment enabling entrepreneurship in rural areas. The existence of such environment largely depends on policies promoting rural entrepreneurship. The effectiveness of such policies in turn depends on a conceptual framework about entrepreneurship, *i.e.,* what it is and where it comes from.

The Concept of Entrepreneurship Education

The need for entrepreneurship education started emerging in the mid-1980s. This is because before this period, unemployment and poverty were not a national concern as it is currently. It has been observed that tertiary education has not been able to include philosophy of self-reliance, such as creating new cultural and productive environment that will promote pride in primitive work and self-discipline, encouraging people to take part actively and freely in discussions and decisions affecting their general welfare, promoting new sets of attitudes and culture for the attainment of future challenges. Nwangwu (2007) opines that the failure of tertiary education to inculcate the above philosophy in students has led to wastages in terms of both human and natural resources. This is because the youth and graduate from tertiary institutions are not equipped with the skills needed to exploit the natural resources. All these factors have rendered the pursuit of self-reliance among our graduates difficult to retain. Ayodele (2006) identified inadequate capital to be one of the principal factors hindering entrepreneurship in the country. Other problems identified by Ayodele include irrelevant education that is bookish, theoretic and 'white-collar job' oriented, another problem is the fear of failure by the people to take risk on entrepreneurial activities. Entrepreneurship, according to Omolayo (2006), is the act of starting a company, arranging business deals and taking risks in order to make profit through the acquired education skills. Another view of entrepreneurship education is the term given to someone, who has innovative ideas and transforms them to profitable activities. Nwangwu (2007) opines that entrepreneurship is a process of bringing together the factors of production, which include land, labour and capital so as to provide a product or service for public consumption.

However, the operational definition of entrepreneurship is the willingness and ability of person or persons to acquire educational skills to explore and exploit investment opportunities, establish and manage successful business enterprise. Emeraton (2008), describes entrepreneurship education as that which deals with those attitudes and skills that are necessary for the individual to respond to its environment in the process of conserving, starting and managing business enterprise. Some basic attitudes and skills are essential for an individual to respond positively to his environment and explore its potentials. This implies that entrepreneurship education prepares the individual to be properly equipped to acquire saleable skills which could be used to manage his own business or that of other persons (Oduwaiye, 2005). Entrepreneurship education is therefore that education which assists students to develop positive attitudes, innovation and skills for self-reliance, rather than depending on the government for employment. This will inturn produce graduates with self-confidence and capacities for independent thought to discover new information leading to economic development.

Who is an Entrepreneur?

Entrepreneurship is the act of being an entrepreneur. The word 'entrepreneur' which is a French word means "one who undertakes innovations, finance and business acumen in an effort to transform innovations in economic goods". Entrepreneur can be defined as an innovating individual, who has developed an ongoing business activity where none existed before. Meredith (1983), defined an entrepreneur as a person, who possesses the ability to recognise and evaluate business opportunities, assemble the necessary resources to take advantage of them and take appropriate action to ensure success. Entrepreneurs are people, who constantly discover new markets and try to figure out how to supply those markets efficiently and make profit. He is a person that searches for change, responds to change, and exploits change by converting change into business opportunity. In today's world, anybody, industry or business leader with innovative and creative business abilities is described as an entrepreneur or someone, who engages in entrepreneurship.

Objectives of Entrepreneurship Education

The objectives of entrepreneurship education are:

- To offer functional education for the youth that will enable them self-employed and self-reliant.
- Provide the youth graduates with adequate training that will enable them to be creative and innovative in identifying novel business opportunities.
- To serve as catalyst for economic growth and development.
- Offer tertiary institution graduates with adequate training in risk management, to make certain bearing feasible.
- To reduce high-level of poverty.
- Create employment generation.
- Reduction in rural-urban migration.
- Provide the young graduates with enough training and support that will enable them establish career in small and medium sized businesses.
- To inculcate the spirit of perseverance in the youths and adults which will enable them persist in any business venture they embark on.

Entrepreneurship Education and Rural Development

Entrepreneurship is seen as a force that mobilises other resources to meet unmet market demand, it is the ability to create and build something from practically nothing, it is the process of creating value by pulling together unique package of resources to exploit an opportunity. Entrepreneurial, orientation to rural development, contrary to development-based on bringing in human capital and investment from outside, is based on stimulating local entrepreneurial talent and subsequent growth of individuals.

Most of the rural population depends, directly and indirectly, on small-scale food crop agriculture, fishery, pastoral animal husbandry or rural wage labour associated with plantations and ranches, and ancillary activities linked to rural townships. Many rural families need to diversify their sources of income and employment in view of increasingly smaller parcels of land, low agricultural productivity, volatile weather conditions and soil erosion. The rural non-farm economy plays an important role for wealth creation and well-being across countries. This in turn would create jobs and add economic value to a region and community and at the same time keep scarce resources within the community. To accelerate economic development in rural areas, it is necessary to increase the supply of entrepreneurs, thus building up the critical mass of first generation entrepreneurs (Petrin, 1992), who will take risks and engage in the uncertainties of new venture creation, create something from practically nothing and create values by pulling together a unique package of resources to exploit an opportunity. By their example, they will stimulate an autonomous entrepreneurial process, as well as a dynamic entrepreneurship, thereby ensuring continuous rural development. It is important to stress that rural entrepreneurship in its substance does not differ from entrepreneurship in urban areas.

Entrepreneurship in rural areas is finding unique blend of resources, either inside or outside of agriculture. This can be achieved by widening the base of farm business to include all the non-agricultural uses that available resources can be put to or through any major changes in land use or level of production other than those related solely to agriculture. Thus, a rural entrepreneur is someone, who is prepared to stay in the rural area and contribute to the creation of local wealth. To some degree, however, the economic goals of an entrepreneur and the social goals of rural development are more strongly interlinked than in urban areas. For this reason, entrepreneurship in rural areas is usually community-based, has strong extended family linkages and a relatively large impact on a rural community. Many individuals from rural areas have difficulties in translating their business ideas to realities and creating new business ventures because of lack of necessary information and skills needed to achieve their targets. To him, the university curriculum was in the past-oriented towards making graduates suitable only for white-collar jobs. This underscores why millions of our youth and lot of university graduates roam about the streets of major cities and towns in search of white-collar jobs. It is necessary and possible to position universities to stimulate economic growth through deliberate agenda of production of entrepreneurial graduates.

In many countries, including US, high schools offer entrepreneurship education for life-long trade. And many of them offer courses that enable students to meet their general academic requirement while learning a trade. However, because of the recent challenges in world economy many schools have shifted emphasis to training in computers, information technology, and related fields. Public schools work closely with willing industries to establish curriculum and programmes to meet their skill demand. While career education has continued to thrive in many societies, it is unfortunately an area that is neglected (Ajao, 2004). The neglect of entrepreneurship education is rubbing nation of the contribution their rural graduate would make on the economy; the graduates could establish. It is, therefore socially injurious to neglect this important area. Given these facts, it is a disservice to the society to neglect entrepreneurship education. Hence, there is a need for effective strategies for entrepreneurship education.

Strategies for Effective Entrepreneurship Education

In order to achieve viable entrepreneurship education that will enhance rural development the following strategies, according to Ayodele (2006), will help to alleviate the problem of entrepreneurship education in the country:

- There should be some form of genuine school work-based learning incorporated in some studies as part of the national economic development strategies. The development of apprenticeship scheme would give new graduates some work skills and experience.
- Pool local public and private funds to create a small venture capital fund.
- School-based enterprises where students identify potential business, plan, create and operate small business using the school as mini-incubators.
- Provide small business schools where interested students and community members can participate.
- Develop entrepreneur internship programmes matching students with locally successful entrepreneurs with clearly established education programmes.
- Establishing an enterprise college aimed at fostering the specific skill sets required for entrepreneurship to serve as skill-acquisition centers for the youths.
- Creating an economic-friendly political environment.
- Improving on the government taxation on small scale businesses.

Conclusion

Entrepreneurship education promotes rural development. The problems facing the country are many ranging from high rate of poverty, youth and graduate unemployment, over-dependence on foreign goods and technology to low economic growth and development; among others. Entrepreneurship education will equip the students with the skills to be self-reliant. Government and other education stakeholders should make sure that educational programme at all levels of education are made relevant to provide the rural youths and graduates the needed entrepreneurial skills. It is also recommended that the government should give adequate attention to entrepreneurial development in the country through the provision of good economic environment.

References

Ajao, W. (2004), "Neglect of Technical, Vocational Education Increase Youth Unemployment-DON;" *The Vanguard*, Dec 23, 2004.

Ayodele, J.B. (2006), "Obstacles to Entrepreneurship Development in Nigeria", In F. Omotosho, T.K.O. Aluko, O.I. Wale-awe and G. Adaramola (Eds), *Introduction to entrepreneurship development in Nigeria*. Ado-Ekiti, UNAD Press L.

Fernando, L. (2012), Promoting Sustainable Development: The Role of Entrepreneurship Education, Sage Publications, Los Angeles, London.

Meredith, O. (1983), *The Practice of Entrepreneurship*. Geneva: International Labour Office.

Nwangwu, I. (2007), *Higher Education for Self-Reliance: An Imperative for the Nigerian Economy*. NEAP Publication, pp. 1-8.

Oduwaiye, R.O., (2005), *Entrepreneurship Education in Nigerian Universities: Implementation and Way Forward*. Retrieved June 20th, 2010.

Omolayo B. (2006), *Entrepreneurship in Theory and Practice*. In F. Omotosho, T.K.O. Aluko, O.I. Wale-awe and G. Adaramola (eds). *Introduction to Entrepreneurship Development in Nigeria*. Ado-Ekiti; UNAD Press.

Petrin, T. (1992), "Partnership and Institution Building as a Factor in Rural Development", the paper presented at the Sixth Session of the FAO/ ECA *Working Party on Women and the Agricultural Family in Rural Development*, Innsbruck, Austria, October 13-16.

Smith, C. (1998), *Economic Development,* Second edition. Basingstoke: Macmillan. ISBN 0-333-72228-0.

24

Problems Faced by Rural Women Entrepreneurs in India: A Case Study of Mysore District

Niranjana Babu Reddy H. S. and B. Deepu

Introduction

Entrepreneurship is the key answer for many economic problems in any developing country. It creates numerous employment opportunities by setting up new enterprises. As per Frank young, entrepreneurs are agents, who effect changes in their enterprises and act as catalyst of economic development by perceiving opportunities and putting them into practice. Entrepreneurs are people, who have the ability to see and evaluate business opportunities, together with the necessary resources to take advantages and to initiate appropriate action to ensure success (ILO).

India is a country having more than six lakh villages. So, real spirit of India lives in rural areas. Now-a-days, more and more young people are migrating more from rural areas to urban in search of job opportunities. Industries are concentrated more in urban areas. This has created further pressure on government to provide additional infrastructure facilities for growing population in cities, which is not possible in short pressure. The solution for all these problems is 'Rural Entrepreneurship'.

Rural entrepreneurship implies establishing more and more business enterprises in rural areas, giving more importance for setting up of agro-based and food processing industries. This results in creation of more employment opportunities in rural areas and thus rural development becomes possible.

Importance of Women Entrepreneurship in Rural Areas

Six out of ten of the world's poorest people are women who must, as the primary family caretakers and producers of food, shoulder the burden of tilling land, grinding grain, carrying water and cooking. Yet, some 75 per cent of the world's women cannot get bank loans, because they have unpaid or insecure jobs and are not entitled to property ownership. This is one reason why women comprise more than 50 per cent of the world's population, but own only one per cent of the world's wealth.

Equality between men and women is more than a matter of social justice - it's a fundamental human right. But, gender equality also makes good economic sense. When women have equal access to education, and go on to participate fully in business and economic decision-making, they are a key driving force against poverty. Women with equal rights are better educated, healthier, and have greater access to land, jobs and financial resources. Their increased earning power in turn raises household income. By enhancing women's control over decision-making in the household, gender equality also translates into better prospects and greater well-being of children, reducing poverty of future generation (United Nations Development Goals, 2014).

Gender Equality

To achieve economic progress, both men and women must be included in the development process. Women constitute half of the world population. But due to socio-cultural barriers and attitude of the male domination in the society, it has not permitted her to participate equally in areas of development. So, women's potentialities are untapped to that extent. If given a chance, women can play major role in every aspect of building economy and society.

Empowerment of Women through Entrepreneurship

Empowerment of women is the "creation of such environment where women can make independent decisions on their personal development to claim equality in the society. If a woman gets empowered economically, she spends all her income for the betterment of her family members, especially children. When opportunities are created for women to make an income, accumulate assets and increase their economic security, they improve industrial capacity and spur economic growth by creating new jobs, as well as expanding the pool of human resources and talents available in a country" (UNO, Women 2012). Women entrepreneurs are defined as a 'woman or group of women who initiate, organise and run a business enterprise.'

Businesses and individuals have been affected by a wide range of changes in the universal community. The emergence of a universal market caused the development of excessive competition. At the same time, many factors have contributed to the existence of significant potentials of action on a local level, such as the ever-rising percentage of unemployment, the demographic trends (ageing), and the changes in the daily lifestyle, the rising urbanisation, the citizens, interest for sustainable development and their pursuit of active participation in politics. One of the most basic factors for the achievement of local and regional development is the local human resources. Specifically, it could be argued that the role of women is fundamental and their participation is necessary for local economies.

During the past few years, female entrepreneurship has been developed into a dynamically upcoming phenomenon on global level. The variety of enterprises that women develop contributes to the stability and sturdiness of local economies and designates a new role for them in the rapidly changing economic circumstances. On a local level, and particularly in agricultural areas, entrepreneurship has been considered to be the medium through which women can access labour-market and achieve full integration in the process of an accomplished local development.

Review of Literature

Anitha D.Pharm and Dr. R.Sritharan (2013) performed a study which aimed at undertaking the entrepreneurial development among women highlights their motivational forces and relationship between socio-economic background of women entrepreneurs, motivational factors and their existing entrepreneurial traits. The study suggests for providing subsidised loan in its concluding remarks facilities to women entrepreneurs, to start women co-operative societies to help in marketing area, to set up separate women industrial estates.

Veena M. Dr. N. Nagaraja, (2014) made a study and objective of this study was to study problems, faced by women entrepreneurs in Mysore district. This study found that women entrepreneurs mainly have financial constraint, inadequate institutional support, problems in marketing, Social attitude, and non-availability of good workers/employees as the five major problems/ constraints faced by women entrepreneurs in Mysore district to carry out their entrepreneurial activity in efficient and effective manner. They suggested for the financial institutions should take steps to facilitate easy availability of credit to encourage the women entrepreneurs and government should also think over to solve the problems faced by women entrepreneurs.

Tambunan (2009) made a study on recent developments of women entrepreneurs in Asian developing countries. The study focussed mainly on women entrepreneurs in small and medium enterprises-based on data analysis and review of recent key literature. This study found that in Asian developing countries SMEs are gaining overwhelming importance; more than 95 per cent of all firms in all sectors on average per country. The study also depicted the fact that representation of women entrepreneurs in this region is relatively low due to factors like low- level of education, lack of capital and cultural or religious constraints. However, the study revealed that most of the women entrepreneurs in SMEs are from the category of forced entrepreneurs seeking for better family income.

Das (2000) performed a study on women entrepreneurs of SMEs in two states of India, *viz.,* Tamil Nadu and Kerala. The initial problems faced by women entrepreneurs are quite similar to those faced by women in western countries. However, Indian women entrepreneurs faced lower level of work-family conflict and are also found to differ from their counterpart in western countries on the basis of reasons for starting and succeeding in business. Similar trends are found in other Asian countries such as Indonesia and Singapore. Again the statistics showed that the proportion of business set up and operated by women is much lower than the figures found in western countries.

Singh (2008), identifies the reasons and influencing factors behind entry of women in entrepreneurship. He explained the characteristics of their businesses in Indian context and also obstacles and challenges. He mentioned the obstacles in the growth of women entrepreneurship are mainly lack of interaction with successful entrepreneurs, social un-acceptance as women entrepreneurs, family responsibility, gender discrimination, missing network, low priority given by bankers to provide loan to women entrepreneurs. He suggested the remedial measures like promoting micro-enterprises, unlocking institutional framework, projecting and pulling to grow and support the winners etc. The study advocates for ensuring synergy among women related ministry, economic ministry and social and welfare development ministry of the Government of India.

Lall and Sahai (2008) conduct a comparative assessment of multi-dimensional issues and challenges of women entrepreneurship, and family business. The study identified psychographic variables like, degree of commitment, entrepreneurial challenges and future plan for expansion, based on demographic variables. Through stratified random sampling and convenience sampling the data collected from women entrepreneurs working in urban area of Lucknow, the study identified business owner's characteristics as self-perception, self- esteem, entrepreneurial intensity and operational problem for future plans of growth and expansion. The study suggested that though there has been considerable growth in number of women opting to work in family owned business they still have lower status and face more operational challenges in running business.

Need of the Study

Female-run enterprises are steadily growing all over the world, contributing to household income and growth of national economies. However, women face time, human, physical, and social constraints that limit their ability to grow their businesses.

The Female Entrepreneurship Resource Point responds to increasing demands for best practices and tools to integrate gender in private sector development and entrepreneurship promotion programs, and address the needs and constraints faced by female entrepreneurs. It is designed to have two functions—provide practical guidance and recommendations, and serve as a clearing house of programmes, emerging research and data on the topic.

Female entrepreneurs make significant contributions to economic growth and to poverty reduction around the world. In the United States, for example, women-owned firms are growing at more than double the rate of other firms, contribute nearly $3 trillion to the economy and are directly responsible for 23 million jobs. In developing countries, female entrepreneurship is increasing—there are about eight also to 10 million formal small and medium enterprises (SMEs) with at least one female owner. These women-owned companies create much-needed jobs, boost household income, and contribute to overall economic prosperity.

So, there is a need for the study about issues related to women entrepreneurship and its development in the society.

Objectives of the Study

- To study the socio-economic background of rural women entrepreneurs in Mysore district,
- To find out the problems faced by rural women entrepreneurs, and
- To offer suggestions to improve the status of rural women entrepreneurs.

Scope of the Study

The present study mainly focusses on rural women entrepreneurs in Mysore district, Karnataka. The scope of the study is confined to problem being faced by them to start new enterprise and running it successfully. To achieve this, 110 women entrepreneurs were selected from various taluks of Mysore district.

Techniques of Data Analysis

For the purpose of easy understanding, percentage statistical tool is used for analysing respondents' responses. Wherever necessary, unprompted percentage is used.

Method of Data Collection

Primary as well as secondary data are collected for the present study. Primary data were collected through questionnaire. Personal interviews with the help of scheduled questionnaire were conducted and gathered the data. Secondary data include articles in journals, and subject related books.

Limitations of the Study

This present study is done based on the responses provided by limited number of women entrepreneurs in Mysore district.

Analysis and Interpretation

Here is the detailed analysis of the data collected in the survey.

Table – 1: Age Group of the Respondents

Age group	Frequency	Percentage
20-30	22	20.00
30-40	45	40.90
40-50	32	29.09
Above 50 years	11	10.00
Total	110	100 per cent

Source :

As per the above Table-1 40.09 per cent respondents are belonging to 30-40 age groups. 29.09 per cent belongs to 40-50 age groups. The 20 per cent of them belong to 20-30 age groups.

Table 2: Education Level of the Respondents

Education Level	Frequency	Percentage
Illiterates	15	13.63
Primary level	56	50.90
Secondary level	20	18.18
Higher secondary	16	14.54
Graduates	3	2.72
Total	110	100 per cent

The above table shows 50.90 per cent of the respondents belong to primary level of education, 18.18 per cent have got secondary education, and 14.54 per cent got higher secondary education, and 13.63 per cent were found illiterates and only 2.72 per cent were graduates.

Table – 3: Income Level of the Respondents

Income level (In Rupee)	*Frequency*	*Percentage*
10,000-20,000	54	49.09

20,000-30,000	32	29.09
30,000-40,000	16	14.54
40,000-50,000	6	5.45
50,000 and above	2	1.81
Total	110	100

Source ;

The above Table-3 exhibits that 49.09 per cent of respondents belong to income level of Rs. 10,000-20,000. The 29.29 per cent to Rs. 20,000-30,000 group, 14.54 per cent to Rs. 30,000-40,000 groups, rest above Rs. 40,000 income level.

Table -4: Area Involved of the Respondents

Area involved	*Frequency*	*Percentage*
Manufacturing	28	25.45
Trading	42	38.18
Service	33	30.00
All types	7	6.36
Total	110	100

Source :

This Table-4 reveals data related to area of enterprising activities that respondents are involved. The 38.18 per cent involved in trading, 30 per cent in service sector, 25.45 per cent are in manufacturing field, and 6.36 are in all types of activities.

Table - 5: Marital Status of the Respondents

Marital status	*Frequency*	*Percentage*
Married	76	69.09
Unmarried	34	30.91
Total	110	100

As per the above Table, 69.09 per cent of the respondents are married and only 30.91 are unmarried.

Table - 6: Level of Investment Made by the Respondents

Level of investment (In Rupee)	*Frequency*	*Percentage*
Below 50,000	58	52.72

50,000-1 lakh	34	30.09
1,00,000 above	18	17.19
Total	110	100 per cent

From the above Table, it is revealed that 52.72 per cent of the respondents have made below 50,000 rupees investment, 30.09 per cent from 50,000-1,00,000 rupee investment and 17.19 per cent have made above one lakh Rupee investment.

Table - 7: Problems Faced by Women Entrepreneurs

Problems faced by women entrepreneurs	*No. of respondent sunprompted percentage*
A lack of self-confidence	78 per cent,
B social barriers	96 per cent,
C male dominated society	85 per cent,
D lack of training	92 per cent,
E lack of adequate finance	82 per cent,
F motivational problem	88 per cent,
G socio-cultural problems	92 per cent ,
H lack of marketing knowledge	77 per cent,
I lack of managerial ability	79 per cent,
K high cost of production	75 per cent
	For 100 per cent

The above Table shows the problems being faced by the women entrepreneurs in rural areas to start and run their own small enterprise. Unprompted percentage results show that, due to lack of confidence 78 per cent respondents cannot run their units successfully. The 96 per cent of them told that social barriers are the main hindrance to step into the world of entrepreneurship. The 85 per cent say problem of male-dominated society doesn't allow women to do business, lack of training option up to 92 per cent, 92 per cent of them told that finance is the main problem, 88 per cent are with motivational problem to start their own enterprise. The 92 per cent says that there is socio-cultural problem for women, 77 per cent express they lack marketing skills, 79 per cent say the lack of managerial ability is the main problem, 75 per cent of the respondents have expressed that high cost of production is also important problem.

Suggestions

1. The rural women must be given an opportunity to study entrepreneurship basics at the primary level of education, because for many social problems girls will discontinue their studies after primary education. This will boost their self-confidence.
2. In this male dominated society, social barriers must be removed through proper awareness among social leaders about the importance of entrepreneurship in the economic development and especially involvement of women.
3. Rural women entrepreneurship development cells must be set up by the government to give them adequate training in marketing, production, and in running their small business enterprise.
4. Rural women credit societies or rural special women banks must be set up to provide adequate financial support.
5. Managerial skills must be imported through short-term training programmes in rural circumstances itself.
6. Family members and society together must motivate women to enter entrepreneurship world, so that better economic development can be achieved.

Conclusion

All over the world development is a big issue. To achieve this objective woman should be included in the development process through encouraging her in entrepreneurship field. Every rupee earned by women goes directly for the betterment of her family members and her children. So, government, society and organisations must work together to motivate her, train her, to help her to make her economially independent and in turn to achieve more development in the economy.

References

First Development Conference in Karditsa, February 8-10 http://www.1169.syzefxis.gov.gr/syn/6/Gidarakou.doc 4.

Gidarakou, J., 2008, *Women Entrepreneurship and Local Development*, Presentation International Finance Corporation, Strengthening Access to Finance for Women-owned SMEs in Developing Countries October 2011, p. 3.

Ioannidou, A., Nazou, D., 2006, *Between Tourism, Olives and Household: the Entrepreneurship of Women in Petra and Molyvos of Lesvos,* Presentation at the Ninth National Congress of Rural Economy Theme section: The gender dimension in rural development, Athens, pp. 1.135 154.

Mari E., 2007, *Mentoring and Women Entrepreneurship*, Presentation at the conference titled "Business -Kainotomein"/ Harokopio University, Athens, November 22. http://kallithea.hua.gr/epixeirein/hmerida6/Mari.pdf.

World Bank, 2013, *Female Entrepreneurship Resource Point — Introduction and Module-1: Why Gender Matters.*

Dhameja S. K. (2002), *Women Entrepreneurs: Opportunities, Performance, Problems*, Deep Publications (p) Ltd, New Delhi, p-11.

Rajendran N (2003), "Problems and Prospects of Women Entrepreneurs" *SEDME*, Vol. 30 No.4, December.

Zaridis, A., Rontogianni A., 2006, T*he role of women in rural development countryside*. The case of City Kalpaki Ioannina, Presentation at the ninth National Conference of Agricultural Economics, Topic: Gender in rural development, Athens, pp. 101-16.

25

Yeshasvini Healthcare Scheme: Health Security for the Rural Poor

R Nagabhushana

Introduction and Need for the Study

Right to good health is a fundamental right. However, it is rather unfortunate that 'Health for all' is still a distant and elusive goal in most of the developing countries, and India is no exception. About 1.3 billion people all over the world do not have access to effective and affordable healthcare. As per the findings of the WHO, developing countries bear the burden of 93 per cent of the world's diseases. The people in these countries, on their own, are unable to pay for the high cost of healthcare. It is estimated that the poor households tend to spend nearly one fifth of their income on treatment. Such high spending on health has catastrophic effect on the poor households. Unequal access to healthcare is a major cause for impoverishment in many countries. Ill-health in the household is one of the most common sources of impoverishment, as earnings are lost and medical expenses are incurred. Public spending in many of the developing countries, including India has been abysmally low. Financing healthcare has become a highly daunting task for these countries. It is desirable that everyone should be entitled to the same quality of healthcare. Several countries have attempted to provide and finance universal health coverage. Public health services are, by and large, not efficient, generally resulting in healthcare system in which poor people receive inferior quality services. Health services targetted to the poor generally remain underfunded. Governments have sought to reduce private out-of-pocket spending, increase pooled health finance and improve the reach and quality of health services.Though India has made great strides in healthcare since Independence, the overall access and quality of healthcare for vast majority of Indians remain below par.

Most national governments in developing countries in recent years have been trying to promote Community Health Insurance (CHI) programmes as part of their health policy. CHI has gained popularity as one of the modes of accessing healthcare. CHI schemes allow many people's resources to be pooled to cover the costs of unpredictable health related events. They protect individuals and households from the risk of catastrophic medical expenses in exchange for regular payments of premiums. Several CHI schemes have been gaining popularity in India in recent years.

Yeshasvini Co-operative Farmers' Healthcare Scheme (Yeshasvini Scheme) is one such CHI scheme. It was launched by the government of Karnataka to provide quality healthcare to cooperative farmers all over the state at affordable premium. The scheme is considered to be one of the largest self-funded healthcare schemes in the country covering more than 800 surgical procedures to the farmer's cooperatives and their family members. It's a contributory scheme, wherein the beneficiaries contribute a small amount of money every year to avail any possible surgery during the period. The beneficiaries are offered cashless quality healthcare facilities in about 500 Network Hospitals across Karnataka. All the members of rural cooperative societies and their family can become members of the scheme and avail the benefits. From June 2014, the scheme was being extended to members of the urban co-operatives.

Need for the Study

The scheme has been lauded as very novel and one of the largest such schemes. From the study of limited available literature, it seems that this unique scheme is not without drawbacks. The scheme, having completed decade of existence needs a look into its working and effectiveness. This paper attempts to look at the working of the scheme and concerns thereof.

Objective of the Study

The main objectives of the study are:

- To analyse the working of the scheme,
- To find out the shortcomings if any,
- To highlight the challenges faced by the scheme, and
- To look at the recent concerns.

Methodology

The paper is based mostly on the secondary data collected from various sources and interaction of the author with the stakeholders.

The Scheme

Yeshavini Co-operative Farmers' Healthcare Scheme' is governed by

Yeshasvini Trust. The scheme became operational in June 2003. The Trust and its insurance scheme are based on the initiative of Dr Devi Shetty, a renowned cardiologist and chairman of the Narayana Hridayalaya Hospital in Bangalore. Mr A Ramaswamy, then Principal Secretary in Department of Cooperation, Government of Karnataka, gave concrete shape to Shetty's idea.

Yeshasvini's goal is to provide quality healthcare to co-operative farmers and other cooperatives all over the state of Karnataka at affordable premium. The target group mainly consists of the poor farmers organised in co-operative societies. The Department of Co-operation, Government of Karnataka has been entrusted with the responsibility of enrolling the members through its wide network of co-operative societies. The members pay a small annual premium that allows them access to high quality treatment including critical surgeries numbering more than 800 of the stomach, gall bladder, bones, eyes, uterus, brain and heart in about 500 empanelled hospitals all over Karnataka. MD India Healthcare Network Pvt Ltd is the Third Party Administrator (TPA). The TPA takes care of empanelling hospitals, issuing preauthorisation for the surgeries and processing the claims by the empanelled hospitals.

The Journey So Far

Yeshasvini scheme has just completed a decade of its successful existence. The scheme drew the attention of many when in the very first year of inception, it enrolled about 1.6 million members and carried out more than 9,000 surgeries. In 2012-13, there were more than three million members and performed 80,000 surgeries. The target for 2014-15 is to enroll at least half a crore members.

Achievement Since Inception of the Scheme

The Government of Karnataka provides financial assistance in the form of grants to cover the deficit of resources every year. The table below gives an overview of the scheme since its beginning.

Table-1: Overview of Yeshasvini Scheme

Year	*Members Enrolled (in lakh)*	*Members Contribution (in crore)*	*Government Contribution (in crore)*	*No of free OPD availed*	*Noof Surgeries availed*	*Surgery Amount Reimbursed to Hospital (in crore)*
2003-04	16.01	9.49	4.50	35,814	9,047	10.65
2004-05	21.05	12.87	3.57	50,174	15,236	18.47
2005-06	14.73	16.94	11.00	52,892	19,677	26.16
2006-07	18.54	21.56	19.85	2,06,977	39,602	38.51
2007-08	23.18	27.75	25.00	1,55,572	60,668	54.09
2008-09	30.47	36.10	30.00	1,91,109	75,053	61.03

2009-10	30.69	41.36	30.00	1,34,534	66,796	55.08
2010-11	30.47	41.68	30.00	1,57,480	73,963	57.23
2011-12	30.70	45.08	30.00	1,16,690	77,619	60.09
2012-13	30.36	58.88	35.00	1,10,842	80,401	74.12

Source: www.yeshasvini.kar.nic.in

An Analysis of the Scheme

Yeshasvini is a major community health insurance programme aimed at making expensive surgical treatments affordable at low subscription to the disadvantaged population in rural areas. The scheme is innovative as it is embedded in a tripartite paradigm involving three sectors: public, private and cooperative. The programme has increased healthcare use among insured households. Yeshasvini covers surgical treatment which involves catastrophic expenditures; offers, unlike most CBHI programmes large pay-offs through cashless transactions; and has a vast network of hospitals spread throughout the state to ensure accessibility. Financial sustainability, however, remains an issue because membership is voluntary and the premium is very low. While membership has grown steadily since inception with three million members currently enrolled throughout the state, it forms only 15 per cent of the target population.

Yeshasvini's product provides cashless in-patient surgical benefits for 805 different surgeries, including procedures for gastrointestinal, orthopaedic and cardiovascular conditions. The coverage limit is Rs. 2,00,000 and includes free outpatient consultation as well as 25 per cent discount on clinical investigations. The premium is Rs. 250 (Rs. 50 in case of members belonging to SC/ST) per person per year. Families receive a 15 per cent discount when five or more members enrol. From 2014-15, the scheme has been made available to the urban cooperatives (to be called '*Nagara Yeshasvini*') at a premium of Rs 710 (Rs. 510 in case of members belonging to SC/ST) per person per year.

There are apprehensions that this programme may face some challenges to long-term sustainability, notably:

- Its reliance on state government subsidy makes it vulnerable to political changes, and funding may be cut for reasons beyond the control of the non-government stakeholders.
- In addition to state subsidy, the trust also relies on cooperative remittances.
- The program has reached only 25 per cent of target market. Growth has been limited in recent years, and there does not appear to be significant incentive for any of stakeholders to push for growth.

Further growth may require additional investment in marketing and outreach.

- The claims-ratio statistics of the scheme clearly shows the growing graph of claims ratio every passing year, from 109 per cent in its first year of operation in 2003-04, to 150 per cent in 2004-05 and stands at 125 per cent in 2012-13. While much of the costs of the premium are subsidised by the scheme, it remains to be seen if in future such trend will continue.

- The risk pool of the scheme mostly comprises the Below Poverty Line (BPL) population with least ability to pay leading to segmentation of the society. If the same schemes are extended to other population of the society, the pools will become bigger and more financially unsustainable unless the beneficiary contribution is increased as in the case of rich subsidising poor in typical health insurance.

Recent Challenges

Private hospitals form more than 90 per cent of the empanelled hospitals and hold key to the successful implementation of the scheme. Of late, these hospitals have come together and formed a forum called Karnataka Private Hospitals Forum (KPHF). These hospitals are not happy with the way the scheme is being run. KPHF has come out with some concerns and grievances. A few of them are:

1. Patients with prior surgeries outside this scheme, presenting with complications.
2. Inclusion of OPD, investigations and medications in the scheme.
3. Non-qualified decision makers.
4. Non-subject experts make decisions on pre-authorisation.
5. Unscientific decisions forced on Hospitals.
6. Time lag in approving emergency pre-authorisation.
7. Delay in approval / reimbursement.
8. Disrespectful interaction by TPA / co-ordinator.
9. Ever changing TPAs, software platforms.
10. Concerns on impact of '*Nagara Yeshasvini*' and extending the scheme to APL families.

Impact as Perceived by the Empanelled Hospitals

The empanelled hospitals have the following apprehensions about the scheme:

1. Entire Healthcare industry may get affected,
2. Existing hospitals will close down due to financial losses,
3. Disincentive for new 'state-of-the-art' Hospitals,
4. Quality of care will drop drastically,
5. Larger impact on doctors and hospitals in tier-two cities and smaller towns.

In order to overcome the treat these hospitals are facing, the KPHF has been demanding the following:

- Urgent revision of procedural charges and services under the existing health schemes immediately and scientifically. These should then be reviewed annually and revised.
- Government's payment should be treated as the subsidy for network Hospitals and reimbursement for others, and the extra cost if any, for the treatment availed will be paid by the patient directly to the Hospital. Scheme subsidy should be paid as follows- 70 per cent of the procedural charges before discharge, the rest within 15 days of submission of claims and with interest for any further delay.
- To release all pending payment to the Hospitals under all schemes immediately.
- To subject all the schemes to Insurance Regulatory and Development Authority (IRDA) norms. There should be both a cashless and reimbursement options.

Suggestions and Conclusion

The managers of the Yeshasvini programme have been trying to maintain low operational costs and a fixed surgery price schedule. The rules for reimbursement are also stringent. However, these steps have created dissatisfaction among service providers. There is a general feeling that the prices fixed for most of the procedures are inadequate and irrational. Hospitals cannot cover even the cost. The introduction of a sliding contribution scale rather than a single flat rate contribution, and family packages may improve membership and collection of resources. Further, strategies may be adopted to widen the membership base through initiatives that enhance trust and caring. Interaction with the co-operative members revealed that lack of information presents a major obstacle to enrollment, in particular, in far-flung areas. Campaigns for information dissemination, training of co-operative societies' representatives, free health checks on regular basis, and incorporation of a formal complaint mechanism within the programme may prove to be important trust building measures. Besides, efforts need to be made to augment the resources with other means of financing including government subsidies, donations, and sponsorships of information campaigns. Finally, managers should seriously consider compulsory membership for co-operative members as a viable option. The co-operative network provides a platform where the informal sector workers in rural areas are organised in an institutional framework. This institution can be used to take a leap forward in the direction of implementing social insurance. This would also help create a large pool of resources and offer a better package of services. Thus, there is need to carry the programme to the next level.

References

Aggarwal, Aradhna (2010), "*Achieving Equity in Health through Community-based Health Insurance: India's Experience with a large CBHI Programme*", Discussion paper, Research Institute for Economics and Business, Kobe University, Kobe, Japan.

Joris Michielsen *et. al* (2011), "Can Health Insurance Improve Access To Quality Care For The Indian Poor?" *International Journal for Quality in Health Care* 2011; pp. 1–16.

Public Health Foundation of India (2011), *A Critical Assessment of the Existing Health Insurance Models in India*, A Research Study.

Rajasekhar , D and R Manjula (2012), *A Comparative Study of The Health Insurance Schemes in Karnataka*, Submitted to Planning Department, Government of Karnataka.

Venkitasubramanian, Akshay (2010). *A Study of PPP Models for Social Healthcare Insurance*, Centre for Public Policy Research, Kochi, Kerala.

www.kphforum.org.

www.sahakara.kar.gov.in.

www.yeshasvini.kar.nic.in.

26

Determinants of Willingness to Pay for Health Insurance among Rural Households in Coimbatore

Lavanya V.L.

Introduction

In recent times, there has been a growing concern with the increasing cost of health services and the existing mechanisms for financing health care costs. Like other developing countries, in India, the Ministry of Finance seems to undervalue health development particularly for the rural and tribal population because modern health facilities are getting concentrated in the urban areas. In many developing countries, governments are facing increasing pressure to improve the efficiency and financial viability of health care services delivery system to improve the living conditions of poor people (World Bank, 1993). The household expenditure on health accounts for a major share of about 70-80 per cent of the total health expenditure in India. Majority of the poor households, especially the rural ones, reside in remote regions where neither government facilities nor private medical practitioners are available. They have to depend on poor quality services provided by local, often unqualified, practitioners and faith healers. Moreover, rural people have relatively higher burden of indirect costs (such as expenses on transport, food/stay, tips given to secure access to any person or facility, opportunity cost of lost wages of the sick as well as the accompanying person, etc.) associated with an illness episode (Sodani, 1997). Rural households in India bear the maximum burden as they account for about 85 per cent of the total household expenditure on health (Sanyal, 1996). The lack of appropriate and consistent information on out-of-pocket expenditure is found to be the prime reason for the exclusion of this important category from the health policy planning in India (Selvaraju, 2000).

Most studies of health care spending have found that out-of-pocket spending in India is actually progressive, or equity neutral; as a proportion of non-food expenditure. Richer Indians spend marginally more than poorer Indians on health care. However, because the poor lack the resources to pay for health care, they are far more likely to avoid going for care, or to become indebted or impoverished trying to pay for it. To tie over this situation, we have health financing scheme. Health financing systems through general taxation or through the development of social health insurance are generally recognised to be powerful methods to achieve universal coverage with adequate financial protection for all against healthcare costs. These systems intend to respond to the goal of fairness in financing, beneficiaries in that are asked to pay according to their income meanwhile guaranteeing them the right to health services according to need. Health insurance has emerged as one of the financing options to overcome some of the problems of our system. Health Insurance (HI) has emerged as part of the reform drive in many countries, both as a way of augmenting financial resources available for care, and as a means of better linking health demand to the provision of services (Dror and Preker, 2001).

Health insurance is becoming a major policy pre-occupation, as it can provide risk management that respects the complexity of risks and is one of the best financial tools to prevent a situation whereby people with income above the poverty line would fall under. Health insurance is an emerging social security instrument for the rural poor, for whom a multitude of health problems and inaccessibility to an affordable health care system, constitute major threat to their income earning capacity. The share of GDP on health expenditure is only 0.9 per cent compared to other developed countries. In the light of the fiscal crisis facing the government at both the Central and State levels, the shrinking public health budgets, the escalating healthcare costs coupled with the demand for healthcare services and lack of easy access of people from the low income group to quality healthcare, health insurance is emerging as an alternative mechanism for financing of healthcare. The policy concern in developing countries including India is not only to reach the entire population with adequate healthcare services; but also to secure an acceptable level of health for all the people through the application of primary healthcare programmes and also to make them part of the health financing coverage through insurance. Against this background, the current study focussed on determinants of willingness to pay for health insurance among rural households in Coimbatore.

Review of the Literature

The review of literature of this study is related to awareness and willingness to pay for health insurance. Very few studies exist in India that has looked at willingness to participate in health insurance programmes in the rural sectors. Mathiyazhagan (1998) examined the willingness to pay for a viable rural health insurance scheme through community participation in India. The socio-economic factors and physical accessibility to quality health services appeared to be significant determinants of willingness to join and pay for such scheme. Health care expenditure has also been found to influence the decision to participate in a given health insurance (Kronick and Gilmer, 1999). The relationship between healthcare expenditure and health insurance purchase decision is premised on the fact that families with higher probability of requiring hospitalisation will purchase health insurance. Obinna Onwujekwe *et. al* (2010) found that less than 40 per cent of the respondents were willing to pay for CBHI membership for themselves or other household members. Sumninder *et.al* (2011) investigated the awareness and willingness to pay for health insurance in Punjab; moreover, there are significant associations that exist between the gender, age, education, occupation and income of respondents with their willingness to pay for health insurance.

Objectives of the Study

Based on the background, an attempt has been made to undertake study with following objectives:

- To examine the socio-economic conditions of the sample respondents.
- To determine the willingness of households to pay for health insurance.
- To identify the problems behind the respondents to join the health insurance scheme.

Data Sources and Methodology

Growth of population, increase in the number of illness coupled with escalating medical cost has led many people to make use of the Primary Health Centre (PHCs). The city of Coimbatore stands second to Chennai in the map of Tamil Nadu for highly affordable and quality healthcare services. There are quite a number of private hospitals which cater to the multi-faceted needs of the people. The health centres started and operated by the government is a hub to many poor people epecially those in the village area. The primary data forms the basis for the study. The present study was done in a village called Kaliveerampalayam is at Thondamuthur block in Coimbatore district. The Primary Health Centre (PHC) at Kaliveerampalayam provides 24x7 services to the people residing in and around the area. This PHC takes lead in providing healthcare services and involved in giving health awareness to the rural people. Many of the government programmes are taken by this PHC and caters to their health needs. The primary data forms the basis for the study. Based on the 200 households residing near the PHC and availing services from the particular PHC, are taken as sample for the current study. Data for the study was collected with help of pre-tested questionnaire covering the socio-economic profile, willingness to pay for health insurance and identify the obstacles to join the health insurance. The study was done during the period of January-February 2012. Though questionnaire were administered to 200 samples, seven were not found fit and 'therefore' the sample size is 193.

Findings of the Study

The general notion is that the social environment is a combination of factors such as religion, caste, family structure, marital status, size of family and age, while economic environment is made up factors such as education, occupation, income and expenditure which reflected the standard of living of a person. Table-1 depicts the socio-economic characteristics of the sample respondents.

Table 1: Socio-economic Conditions of the Sample Respondents

Socio-economic Characteristics		Frequency	Percentage
Gender	Male	87	45.1
	Female	106	54.9
Age (in years)	Less than 30	49	25.4
	30-45	83	43.0
	Above 45	61	31.6
Marital status	Married	84	43.5
	Unmarried	53	27.5
	Widowed	37	19.2
	Separated	19	9.8
Education	Illiterate	38	19.7
	Primary	57	29.5
	Secondary	43	22.3
	Higher Secondary	31	16.1
	Degree/diploma	24	12.4
Occupation	Agriculture activity	63	32.6
	Trade/business	51	26.4
	Job in organised sector	35	18.1
	Other activity	44	22.8
Monthly Income	Below Rs. 5,000	63	32.6
	Rs. 5,000-10,000	71	36.8

	Above Rs. 10,000	59	30.6
Total	**193**	**100.0**	

Source: Field Survey, 2012.

In the above Table, a significant proportion of the sample was female members. Majority of the respondents belonged to the age group of 30-45 years and were married. Maximum respondents had completed primary education followed by secondary. The study found that only 12 per cent had done their degree course. It was observed that a majority (33 per cent) of the sample respondents were involved in agricultural activity and 18.1 per cent of them were employed in organised sector. A major percentage of the respondents (37 per cent) were earning income between Rs 5,000-10,000 and 31 per cent of the respondents were earning above Rs10,000 per month and there was no one who belonged to professionals or employed in any concern.

Willingness to Pay for Health Insurance Scheme

The demand or willingness to pay for health insurance by the rural people for protection against the financial risk associated with ill-health is rising mainly because of out-of-pocket expenditure. At present, people who are working in the informal sectors like agriculture workers, labourers and self-employed are not covered under any risk-sharing scheme in the country. On the other hand, awareness of health has increased during the past few years and people like to have a better quality health care service. In this section, an attempt was made to examine what distinguish the households willingness to pay for health insurance by fitting a binary logie model, where the dependent variable takes a value 'one' if the household is *yes* and 'zero'; otherwise. The probability of the household's willingness to pay for health insurance scheme or not is hypothesized to be an association of age, household size, education, occupation and monthly income. The estimated result is shown in Table-2.

Table 2: Estimated Logitc Model

Variable	*Coefficient*	*Standard Error*	*Odd Ratio*
Age	0.482*	.110	1.031
Household size	1.216**	.167	0.832
Education	0.578*	.094	1.056
Occupation	0.386*	.114	1.194
Monthly Income	0.514*	.072	1.037
Constant	5.519	.570	.262

Nagelkerke R square	0.619
Hosmer and Lemeshow test (χ^2)	30.998*
Number of Observation	193
Classification Percentage	58.1

Source: Estimation-based on Field Survey, 2012

* Significant at one per cent level,

** Significant at five per cent level.

The estimated Logic model gives a good fit to the data from the statistical perspective the value was significant at one per cent level. Nagelkerke R^2-value signifies nearly 62 per cent of the variations accounted by logistic model. Similarly, the percentage of correctly predicted cases was also high (nearly 62 per cent).The estimated model shows that the sign of all the co-efficients were more or less according to expectations. The probability of willingness to pay for health insurance increases due to age, education, occupation and monthly income. The household size decreases the willingness to pay for health insurance. The evaluation of the coefficient for statistical significance revealed that all variables emerged as significant factor-based on Wald statistics. The income and education of the households has statistically significant role in willingness to pay for health insurance. It means that higher income and educational qualification of the households has positive impact on the willingness to pay for health insurance. Thus, the willingness to pay for health insurance increases due to education, income, while household size it decreases.

Problems to Join Health Insurance among the Sample Respondents

Health Insurance is an effective social security mechanism for low-income families, especially in the rural population as they remain at very nascent stage in India. Health insurance has not been able to make inroads in the rural areas because high cost of delivery and low awareness among the rural population. Health insurance suffers from problems like adverse selection, moral hazard, cream-skimming and high administrative costs. In the meanwhile there are many constraints faced by the insurance holders in claiming the insurance. In this study, an effort was made to identify various problems encountered by policy holder in claiming the benefit of health insurance. The respondents were asked questions, relating to problems of health insurance on five point scale ranging from - 2 (strongly disagree) to +2 (strongly agree).

Factor analysis was used in the present study to identify the underlying pattern of relationship between various problems for not having health insurance and whether these problems can be grouped in terms of composite variable. The Cronbach's alpha to test the reliability or internal consistency of the scale, gave a value of 0.953 greater than the norm of 0.70 indicating good scale reliability. To determine the appropriateness of applying factor analysis, the KMO and Bartlett's test measure were computed and the results are presented in Table 3.

Table-3 : KMO and Bartlett's Test Measures

Variable	*Coefficient*	*Standard Error*	*Odd Ratio*
Age	0.482*	.110	1.031
Household size	1.216**	.167	0.832
Education	0.578*	.094	1.056
Occupation	0.386*	.114	1.194
Monthly Income	0.514*	.072	1.037
Constant	5.519	.570	.262
Nagelkerke R square	0.619		
Hosmer and Lemeshow test	30.998*		
Number of Observation	193		
Classification Percentage	58.1		
KMO and Bartlett's Test			
Kaiser-Meyer-Olkin Measure of Sampling Adequacy.	.924		
Bartlett's Test of Sphericity Approx. Chi-square	2.273E3		
Degrees of freedom	45		
Significance level	.000		

Source: Estimation-based on Field Survey, 2012.

KMO statistics is 0.924 which is signifying higher than acceptable adequacy of sampling. The Bartlett's test of Sphercity was also found to be significant at one per cent level providing evidence of the presence of relationship between variables to apply factor analysis. All the variables had value greater than 0.50 signifying substantial portions of the variance accounted by the factors. The communalities for each variable were assessed to determine the amount of variance accounted by the variable to be included in the factor rotations.

Table-3.1 enlists the Eigen values, their relative explanatory powers and factor loadings for 12 linear components identified within the data set.

Table 3.1: Rotated Component Matrix

Reasons	**Component**	
	1	**2**
Low salary/non availability of funds		0.840
Saving in some other areas to meet healthcare needs	0.877	
Lack of knowledge about the health insurance schemes	0.826	
Difficulty to approach insurance agents	0.767	
Lack of Availability and Accessibility of Services	0.841	
Lack of comprehensive coverage		
Lack of reliability and flexibility		0.757
Lack of diseases/illness	0.792	
Difficulty in availing services in hospitals		
Poor co-ordination between companies and hospitals		0.848
Conditions are very narrow to buy health insurance schemes	0.789	
Eigen value	7.046	1.032
Percentage of variance	70.460	10.325
Cumulative percentage	70.460	80.784

Source: Estimation-based on Field Survey, 2012.

Extraction method: Principal component analysis. Rotation method: Varimax with Kaiser Normalisation, rotation converged in three iterations.

The Kaiser rotated component matrix presented in Table reveals that factor one had significant loadings on five dimensions namely 'saving in some other areas to meet health care needs' 'lack of knowledge about the health insurance schemes', 'difficulty to approach insurance agents' 'conditions are very narrow to buy health insurance schemes' 'lack of availability and accessibility of services' and 'lack of diseases/illness'. Factor one was very powerful because it explains 70 per cent of the variance. Factor-two had significant loadings on three dimensions namely 'low salary/non availability of funds' 'lack of reliability and flexibility' and 'poor co-ordination between companies and hospitals' and explains only 10 per cent of the variance. These are various factors acting as main problems to join the health insurance.

Conclusion

Majority of the rural households are facing lots of destitution due to healthcare expenditure and households therefore are willing to join and pay for health insurance which helps them to meet their out-of-pocket expenditure towards unforeseen medical care. The study found that age, education and occupation were found to have significant association with awareness regarding health insurance. This implies that high levels of awareness of health insurance were found among the respondents with better education and occupation. The demand or willingness to pay for health insurance depends not only, on the premium and benefit package, but also on socio-economic characteristics of households. Meanwhile, the respondents underwent many problems in encountering of joining the health insurance. Nowadays, the government introduce the health insurance scheme for all poor people without any obstacle.

Suggestions

- There is an urgent need to focus on health insurance as distinct from other insurance, and constitute a body that can go into the planning as well as implementation of health insurance, taking into account the objectives of equity and efficiency in healthcare.
- The government of India must take immediate attention in health insurance by focussing on public spending on primary and healthcare services and reformation of Employee State Insurance Scheme and Central Government Health Scheme.
- Withdrawal of public services on 'ability to pay basis' and restructuring of premiums will increase visibility and awareness on health insurance.

References

Mathiyazhagan, K (1998), "Willingness to Pay for Rural Health Insurance through Community Participation in India", *International Journal of Health Planning and Management,* 13, pp. 47-67.

Obinna Onwujekwe, Ekechi Okereke, Chima Onoka, Benjamin Uzochukwu, Joses Kirigia and Amos Petu (2010), "Willingness to Pay for Community-based Health Insurance in Nigeria: Do Economic Status and Place of Residence Matter", *Health Policy and Planning,* Vol.; 25 pp.155–61.

Sanyal K.S. (1996), "Household Financing of Healthcare", *The Economic and Political Weekly,* Vol. 31, No. 20, pp. 1216-222.

Selvaraju, V. (2000), "Role of ESIS in the Emerging Health Insurance Market" Report on Conference of Health Insurance, IIM, Ahmedabad, April.

Sodani, P. R. (1997), "Determinants of Demand for Healthcare in Surveyed Tribal Households of Selected Three Districts of Rajasthan", *The Demography India*, Vol. 28, No 2.

Sumninder Kaur Bawa and Ruchita (2011), "Awareness and Willingness to Pay for Health Insurance: An Empirical Study with Reference to Punjab India" *The International Journal of Humanities and Social Science* Vol. 1, No. 7, pp.100-08, June.

World Bank (1993), *World Development Report; Investing in Health,* New York: Oxford University Press.

27

Co-operatives and Rural Development in India

B.S. Chandrashekar

Introduction

Since time immemorial, India has been, still continues to be and will remain in the foreseeable future, a land of village communities. With more than 742 million people living in rural areas and with rural sector contributing about 29 per cent of its gross domestic product at factor cost at the 2001 prices (GoI 2009-10S5), no strategy of socio-economic development of India that neglects the rural people and the rural areas can be successful. Rural development is, therefore, a *sine qua non* of overall development in India. The term, rural development, is a sub-set of the broader term development, which is subjective and value-loaded concept and hence difficult to define. Howsoever we define it's development is a universally cherished goal of individuals, families, communities and nations all over the world. The term, rural development', connotes overall development of rural areas as revealed in improved quality of life of rural people. In this sense, it is a comprehensive and multi-dimensional process and phenomenon. It encompasses the development of agriculture and allied activities, village and cottage industries and crafts, socio-economic infrastructure, community services and facilities, and, above all, the human resources in rural areas. Generally speaking, development can be conceptualised as non-decreasing set of desirable societal objectives such as increase in real per capita income, improvement in income distribution (equity), political and economic freedom, and equitable access to resources, education, health-care, employment opportunities, and justice.

Rural development is influenced by multitude of factors such as natural resources, human resources (labour), capital, technology, public policies, and institutions and organisations. Although, the old school of institutionalises led by Thorsten Veblen, John R. Commons, and Karl Marx emphasised the role of institutions in economic development, the neo-classical economists did not assign any place to institutions in their theories. However, of late, as a result of failure of neo-classical economics to explain international and Intra-national differences in economic development, it is now widely recognised that institutions and organisations are an important aid to development. The economic life of a community takes place in a milieu of institutions and organisations; the former embodying the rules of the game and the latter denoting formal or informal structures comprising groups of individuals having common interests. They together largely determine the economic structure of the community and set the rules in which the economic game is played. Organisations affect rural development in many different ways including provision of production inputs and services, reduction of transaction costs, enhancement of bargaining power of rural producers *vis-à-vis* those to whom they sell their produce and from whom they buy production inputs and services, facilitating investments and savings and bringing the two together, and so on. Vaidyanathan (1996:2451-58) examines in detail the institutional imperatives of agricultural development in India. He highlights the crucial importance of institutional reforms, particularly in the domain of public systems for sustained agricultural development. There are many forms of organisations such as public (government) agencies, sole proprietorships, partnerships, companies, co-operatives and charitable trusts that can and are, in fact, serving the needs of rural people in India. Government intervention in the rural sector in India can be traced to the last quarter of the 19th century. Since then, the government has expended thousands of crore of rupee on agricultural and rural development programmes and is, by all accounts, the biggest agent of rural development. Co-operatives also have played an important rôle in promoting agricultural and rural development in India, particularly in the field of credit, processing, and marketing. The dairy co-operatives of Gujarat and sugar co-operatives of Maharashtra are good examples of co-operatives that can promote and sustain rural development.

Gandhiji saw a great virtue in co-operation as an instrument of rural development. He assigned specific roles to co-operatives in the field of agriculture commending the promotion of co-operative farming and thereby preventing further fragmentation of land holdings. He also advocated the establishment of other types of co-operatives such as credit co-operatives, weavers' and spinners' co-operatives and dairy co-operatives. Pt. Jawahar Lal Nehru, the first Prime Minister of India, had a strong faith in the co-operatives. He wanted India to be convulsed with the co-operative movement. Sardar Vallabhbhai Patel, the first Deputy Prime Minister and Home Minister of India, had grate faith in co-operation as a means of promoting farmers well-being. He was the prime source of guidance and assistance for the Kheda District Co-operative Milk Producers' Union Limited, popularly known as AMUL, which later became model of co-operative dairy development in India.

Objectives and Methodology

The present study tries to examine the role of co-operatives in rural development in India and to study the role of co-operatives in economic development. The present study is based on the secondary data published by office of the commissioner of co-operative and Registrar of Co-operative societies. The required data for the study purpose were collected from the number of reference books, magazines, journals, Internet and daily newspapers.

The Genesis and Evolution of Co-operatives

A co-operative is a form of organisation that is widely prevalent in developing countries including India. It has great potential as an instrument of rural development. Co-operation as an ethical norm has been eulogised all over the world since time immemorial. As a mode of social behaviour, it is manifest in countless activities of people performed for the purpose of achieving common goal. From the philosophical perspective, co-operation and its opposite, competition are two basic tendencies of human behaviour and both co-exits in every individual. Co-operation can emerge under highly diverse situations and accordingly there are several theories/propositions that seek to explain why people do and do not co-operate (Singh, 1996). The origin of formal co-operation in the form of a co-operative organisation is traced to Europe, particularly, England, France and Germany, in the mid-nineteenth century. Robert Owen of England, Charles Fourier of France, and Herr F.W. Raiffeisen and Herr Franz Schulze of Germany are considered as the founding fathers of the modern co-operation (Craig, 1980:38; Madan, 1994:25-27).

In 1844, a group of people in Rochdale, England, formed the Rochdale Society of Equitable Pioneers to obtain higher wages from their employers and to set up a co-operative store. The Rochdale Society became the model for similar stores and related enterprises throughout the world. Around the same time, Fourier established phalanxes in France and Raiffeisen and Schulze pioneered and implemented the idea of co-operative banks in Germany. Subsequently, in other European countries also, co-operatives emerged primarily as people‘s response to their exploitation by moneylenders and traders. With the emergence of co-operative movement in Europe, the International Co-operative Alliance (ICA) was established in 1895. Its main responsibility was to co-ordinate with the activities of affiliated co-operative federations in various parts of the world. Establishment of communism in USSR and subsequently in other countries was instrumental in promoting government directed or parastatal co-operatives. Some co-operatives failed and some others succeeded. Despite their failures and weaknesses, co-operatives have survived over time and now control significant shares of markets in many developed and developing countries including market-oriented economies. For example, in USA, co-operatives command 70 per cent of the fluid milk market, 80 per cent of the fresh fruits market, 35 per cent of agricultural credit of all types, and 30 per cent of the grains and oilseeds market (Dwivedi, 1996:723). In most developing countries including India, co-operatives were promoted by their governments as instruments of rural development.

In India, thanks to the British legacy, the co-operative form of organisation was born in 1904 consequent upon the enactment of the *Co-operative Credit Societies Act*. Subsequently, a more comprehensive act, the *Co-operative Societies Act*, was enacted in 1912. This Act provided, *inter alia*, for the creation of the post of Registrar of Co-operative Societies, registration of co-operative societies for various purposes, and audit. Under the Montague-Chelmsford Reforms affected in 1919, co-operation became a Provincial Subject and the provinces were authorised to make their own co-operative laws. Under the *Government of India Act* 1935, co-operative societies were treated as a State Subject. In order to facilitate the establishment of co-operatives having membership from more than one Province, the Government of India enacted the *Multi-Unit Cooperative Societies Act, 1942*. Later a more comprehensive Central legislation, the *Multi-State Co-operative Societies Act, 1984*, was enacted by Parliament with a view to consolidate different laws governing the same types of co-operative societies.

After India attained Independence in August 1947, co-operatives assumed greater significance as an instrument of socio-economic development and became an integral part of India's Five Year Plan. The All India Rural Credit Survey Committee Report, 1954 recommended an integrated approach to co-operative credit and emphasised the need for viable credit co-operative societies by enlarging their area of operation, encouraging rural savings, and diversifying their business. The Committee also recommended that the government should contribute to the share capital of the co-operatives. In 1958, the National Development Council (NDC), adopted a Resolution on National Policy on Co-operatives. Subsequently, in January 1959, the Working Group on Co-operative Policy set up by the Ministry of Food and Agriculture, Government of India, recommended a blueprint for implementing the NDC's Resolution. The Government of India has since provided massive financial, technical and administrative support to co-operatives both directly and indirectly through State governments (Dwivedi, 1996:13-14).

Table: 1: Employment Generation through Co-operative in India (2009-10)

	(No. in million)
Total Working population as per population census	1,21,01,93,422
Total Employment in public sectors	17.862
Private sectors	10.846
Total employment generated in co-operative sector	17.80

Credit co-operative	0.416
Non-credit	0.799
Self-employment	16.58

Source: NCUI (2013) Indian Co-operative Movement, A Profile, NCUI, New Delhi.

A Profile of Co-operatives in India and their Achievements

India can rightly claim to have the largest network of co-operatives in the world. As of March 31, 2010, there were nearly 6.10 lakh rural co-operatives of 24 different types having the total membership of some 249 million and the total working capital of Rs. 72.95.765.7 million (Tables 2, 3 and 4). They occupy an important place in India's rural economy in terms of their coverage of rural population and their share in the total supply of agricultural inputs including credit. For example, co-operatives now cover approximately 100 per cent of India's villages, 67 per cent of the total rural population and account for 17 per cent share in the rural credit flow for agriculture, 31 per cent in rural deposits, and 36 per cent of the total quantity of fertilisers distributed in the country. The two giant co-operative fertiliser plants the Indian Farmers Fertiliser Co-operative (IFFCO) and the Krishak Bharati Co-operative (KRIBHCO) - manufacture about 28 per cent of the fertilisers produced in the country.

The co-operatives account for over 60 per cent of the total sugar output in the country and about 50 per cent of the edible oil marketed under brand names. They are responsible for 27 per cent of the total wheat procurement and 21 per cent of the total jute procurement in the country. They also own 26 per cent of the total rural fair price shops. Since their birth in 1904, Co-operatives in India have treaded a long and arduous path. They have performed well in some places and badly in many other places. But, the fact remains that most of them have survived, albeit with a rather heavy dose of oxygen, for over 110 years and there is no reason for anyone to believe that they will all die in the near future. So, it is worth our time and energy to examine their performance, and the factors affecting it. So far as the determinants of performance of co-operatives are concerned, there are three distinct schools of thought. One, which may be called structuralist believes that it is primarily the strategy, and the organisation structure/design of a co-operative that determine to a large extent its performance – success or failure. Shah (1996), who is an ardent proponent of this school, studied a large number of cases of successes and failures in the co-operative sector and identified three critical determinants of success of co-operative, namely, Swayambhu (creation by members themselves), complete autonomy, and member loyalty and allegiance. He asserts that these attributes are an outcome of design and not of exceptionally good leaders and managers (Shah, 1996:285-86).

The second school of thought, who may be called conceptualist, emphasises the importance of the context socio-economic, political, legal, and policy—as a major factor affecting the performance of co-operatives (Baviskar 1980, and Attwood and Baviskar 1987). The third school, which is management-oriented, argues that it is the quality of management and leadership which matters most in determining the success and failure of co-operatives Singh (1996 and 2000). We believe that it is all the three sets of factors, *i.e.*, structural, contextual, and management, that together determine the performance of a co-operative, or for that matter any other organisation and that, to some extent, they could be substituted for one another.

Table 2: A Profile of Co-operatives in India, 2009-10 (Value Rs. in Million)

1. Credit Co-operatives

Type of Co-operative	*Number*	*Membership (million)*	*Share capital*	*Govt. share (in per cent)*	*Working capital*
State Co-operative Banks	31	3,30,808	16,295.8	21.17	12,20,573.3
District Central Co-operative Banks (1996-97)	372	3.975660	77,765.3	31.11	20,69,184.4
Primary Agriculture Co-operative Societies including LAMP and FSS	94,647	126.42	71,484.2	9.18	14,42,219.0
State Co-op Agriculture and Rural Dev. Banks	19	4.02	8210	-	-
Primary Co-op Land Agriculture and Rural Development Banks	728	9.90	15280	-	-
Urban Banks (000)	1674	17,204	37,351.7	0.09	13,10,664.9

Source: NCUI (2013) Indian Co-operative Movement, A Profile, NCUI, New Delhi.

Type of Co-operative	*Number*	*Membership (000)*	*Share Capital*	*Government Share (In per cent)*	*Working Capital* (In Rupee)
Non-agriculture Credit Co-operatives (Primary)	50,942	27.6268	68,564.69	0.38	505,0309
Marketing Co-operatives	7,202	6.105898	3,403.16	45.64	19,681.3
Consumers' Co-operatives include students' co-operatives.	21,014	8,622	2126.5	30.72	6940.8
Sugar Co-operatives (factories)	324	5.927	81641	40.59	-
Co-op Spinning Mills	172	0.283543	-	-	-
Dairy Co-operatives	140,766	14.1903	3869.9	25.30	21266.4
Fishery Co-operatives	15,526	2.091219	1009.43	45.07	2894.24

Source: NCUI (2013) Indian Co-operative Movement, A Profile NCUI, New Delhi.

4. Other Co-operatives (Primary)

Type of Co-operative	*Number*	*Membership (000)*	*Share capital*	*Share capital (In pc)*	*Working capital* (In Rupee)
Labour Construction Co-operatives	39,857	2.572	477.44	12.62	4515.21
Forest Labour Co-operatives	2,789	0.423	36.69	-	2854.48
Weavers Co-operatives	47,426	2.02	1190.6	30.5	4353.4
Women's Co-operatives	11,615	1,028,934	261.9	18.71	1734.88
Co-operative Farming Societies	6902	362,283	80.06	36.27	742.06
Irrigation Co-operatives	17066	11,32,519	1354123	-	1,073,286
Housing Co-operatives	1,00,000	7.0	6,349.41	-	1,25,348.1
Electricity Co-operatives	59	9,56,520	-	-	4946.39

Source: NCUI (2013) Indian Cooperative Movement, A Profile, NCUI, New Delhi.

Co-operatives and National Economy

The following Table-5, present brief profiles of important types of co-operatives in India and examine their performance by mainly drawing upon some of the published research studies.

Table 5: Share of Co-operatives in National Economy at a Glance (In percentage)

Rural Network (Villages covered)	100.00
Agricultural Credit Disbursed by Co-operatives	16.9
Fertiliser Disbursed (6.103 Million Tonnes)	36.60
Fertiliser produced (For Nitrogen N)	14.80
Fertilizer produced (For phosphorous-p)	28.50
Sugar produced (million tonnes)	39.7
Capacity utilisation of sugar mills	44.70
Wheat procurement	24.80
Jute procurement	21.50
Retail fair price shops	28.00
Milk procurement to total production	7.85
Milk procurement to marketable surplus	45.00
Oil marketed / Procurement	49.00
Spindle adge in Co-operative (3,1313 million)	10.00
Cotton marketed/ procurement	67.50
Cotton yarn/ fabrics production	22.00
Handloom in co-operatives	55.00
Fishermen in co-operative (active)	23.00
Storage facility (Village level PASS)	62.50
Soyabeen production	7.50
Self- employment Generated for person (min)	17.50
Salt manufacture	7.40

Source: NCUI (2013) Indian Co-operative Movement, A Profile NCUI, New Delhi.

Conclusion

Rural development is affected by a multitude of factors including institutions and organisations. Co-operatives as a form of organisation are widely prevalent in both developed and developing countries of the world. They are considered an important instrument of rural development in developing countries including India. Since their birth in 1904, co-operatives in India have treaded a long and arduous path. Now, they occupy an important place in India's rural economy in terms of membership, business turnover, and contribution to the socio-economic welfare of their members, and hence rural development. They have performed well in some sectors in some places and badly in many other places. But the fact remains that most of them have survived, *albeit* with rather heavy dose of oxygen in many cases, for over 90 years and there is no reason for anyone to believe that they will die in the near future. Despite their overwhelming importance in India's rural economy, most of the co-operatives are, however, not financially viable due to variety of reasons and suffer from many other internal and external constraints. The major constraints include lack of professionalism in management; lack of good leadership; archaic co-operative law and excessive government control; small size of business and hence inability to afford the services of professional managers; and internal work culture and environment not congenial to professionalisation of management. Co-operatives could have bright future in India in the new era, if they are transformed into member-owned autonomous organisations governed by the elected representatives of their members, managed professionally and liberated from unnecessary government controls.

References

Attwood, D.W. and B.S. Baviskar (1987), 'Why Do Some Co-operatives Work but not Others? A Comparative Analysis of Sugar Co-operatives in India' *The Economic and Political Weekly,* 22(6), June 27, A-38-56.

Attwood, D.W. and B.S. Baviskar (1988), *Who Shares: Co-operative and Rural Development* New Delhi: Oxford University Press.

Chadha, G.K. and H.R. Sharma (1996), "Co-operatives Succeed in Mountains Too: The Case of Bhutti Weavers Society, Kullu." *The Indian Journal of Agricultural Economics*, 51(4).

Craig, J.G. (1980), *Managing Co-operative Organisations, Co-operative Future Directions Project*, Working Paper No. 4, The Co-operative College of Aanada, Saskatoon, Saskatchewan, Canada.

Craig, J.G. (1992), "Indian Co-operatives in the 21st Century: Breaking the Bureaucratic Noose", In *Governance and Management of Rural Co-operatives: Six Distinguished Lectures*, Lectures delivered at the Symposium on Management of Rural Co-operatives, December 7-11, 1992, The Institute of Rural Management, Anand.

Department of Agriculture and Co-operation, Ministry of Agriculture, New Delhi.

Dwivedi, R.C. (1996), Role of Co-operatives in Rural Economy, *The Indian Journal of Agricultural Economics*, 51(4), pp. 712-27.

Dwivedi, R.C. (2005), *Hundred Years of Co-operative Movement in India*, The Centre for Promoting Co-operatives.

Government of India (1995), *Co-operative Movement in India -- A Statistical Profile.*

Government of India (2012), *Report of the Task Force on Revival of Cco-operative Credit Institutions*, Ministry of Finance.

Khodaskar, R.D. (1996), *Rural Development Through Co-operatives: A Case Study.*

Madan, G.R. (1994), *Co-operative Movement in India*. New Delhi: Mittal Publications.

Mukherji, R. (1996), *Co-operatives in India's Rural Economy, Indian Journal of Agricultural Economics,* 51(4).

NCUI (2013), *Indian Co-operative Movement, A Profile NCUI*, New Delhi.

RBI (1954), *Report of the All India Rural Credit Survey Committee.*

28

Corporate Social Responsibility in Rural Development of India

B Lokeshnath and T. N. Sreedhara

Introduction

Corporate Social Responsibility (CSR) has recently gained lot of momentum and has become buzzword. So far, CSR activities are carried voluntarily by the business enterprises but may have to be compulsorily carried out by them due to the amendment made in the *Companies Act* in India. As per the new companies Act, business enterprises are required to spend two per cent of their profits on CSR activities. Historically, in India business enterprises was carrying CSR activities voluntarily. The tradition of giving in India can be traced from its early civilisation. All the religious philosophies always advocated the need for giving to the needy. Even if we look back, our successful business enterprises always pioneered and championed in the welfare of the society. In this respect, the Tata group can be taken as role model in India. Azim Premji of Wipro group transferred $ 2.2 billion (Rs. 12,300 crore) worth of shares to the Azim Premji Foundation engaged in the educational activities. He also previously donated to the same foundation the shares worth of $ 125 million in 2001 and $ 2 billion in 2010. Recently, the Government of India brought new companies Act, and thereby making companies net worth of Rs. 500 crore or more, or a turnover of Rs 1,000 crore or more, or a net profit of Rs.5 crore or more, shall spend mandatorily at least two per cent of their net profits on welfare of society by way of CSR. But already the Indian companies are spending substantial amount as part of CSR on the welfare of the society. In India, CSR activities are carried by almost by all the enterprises. It is usually carried by business enterprises by way of donating to charitable institutions, religious institutions, hospitals, educational institutions, orphanage institutions, old-age institutions and the promotion of recreational activities. Many of the business enterprises are also actively involved in awareness campaign for the eradication of diseases like HIV/AIDS etc. They also involved in the beautification of cities and planting trees. Some of the business enterprises have established separate foundation or trust to carry out CSR activities and many others have separate wing in their business to carry CSR activities. Few of the business enterprises tied with NGOs in discharging CSR. But tall claims of CSR by business enterprise are not visible on the ground. In reality, CSR has become mere marketing promotion tool. The fruits of the developmental activities carried by the business have not reached vast sections of the society. Many stakeholders in the developmental process are left out especially marginalised groups like SC/ST, women and children. Even the people living in the rural areas are also the victims of lopsided development agenda of the business sector.

India is country of rural masses, which is evident from the various census data. As per the 2011 census, out of the total population of 1,210.2 million, the size of the rural population is 833.1 million which accounts 68.84 per cent of the total population. But the development of rural not gained momentum as seen in urban counterpart. The urban places in India in the recent past have grown tremendously living behind wide gap between rural and urban places. The government of India have made lot of efforts towards the development of rural areas and in this respect, it has created a separate department namely, Ministry of Rural Development. But government alone cannot do all the work in rural areas. Therefore, it is also the responsibility of the business to carry out rural development as part of their CSR.

The corporate sector has a very important role to play in this direction and it should ensure flow development activities towards the remote and rural areas of our country. The marginalised groups in rural areas are completely left out of the developmental activities so far and it is the responsibility of the business to undertake all round human development of these marginalised groups in rural areas.

With the introduction of new companies act, the companies are required to spend two per cent of the profit towards the welfare of the society. Similarly, rapid globalisation and environmental concerns have made the business spend some profits back to the society. Some business houses are already spending more than the mandatory ceiling, but big problem is the wrong priorities of business in spending the amount. Nevertheless, this kind of activities termed 'Corporate Social Responsibility' (CSR) has become buzzword among the business enterprises.

Generally, CSR is understood as "the commitment of business to contribute to human development by working with employees, their families, the local community and society at large to improve their quality of life, in ways that are good for business and good for development." The World Business Council for Sustainable Development (1999) defines CSR as "CSR is the continuing commitment by business to behave ethically and contribute to economic development while improving the quality of life of the work force and their families as well as of the local community and society at large" CSR involves ethical behaviour of the business towards the internal and external stakeholders. CSR also focus on the role of the business towards the society in which it operates. CSR is the medium through which business gives back to the society in which it operates. It also involves providing feasible solution to the challenges faced regarding the environment and social issues. But real challenge is the identification of the right priorities and area of business intervention in the promotion of the human development in rural areas.

In this context, there is a need to study and understand how corporate enterprises are using CSR initiatives in rural development. I am also essential to know impact created by CSR activities in the promotion of the rural development. The present paper is studied under four sections. The first section deals with the literature review of CSR activities. The second section deals with objectives, methodology and limitations of the study. The third section deals with the results and last section covers the conclusion of the study.

Corporate Social Responsibility

Bowen Howard is thought as father of CSR movement defines the CSR as "the obligations of businessmen to pursue those policies, to make those decisions or follow those lines of action which are desirable in terms of the objectives and values of society"(Bowen, 1953). His focus is on considering the broader societal interest in managerial decision-making and not just the internal factors. CSR is usually studied from four different dimensions namely economic, legal, ethical and philanthropic (Carol, 1979). CSR focussed much on ethical practices of business and business ethics, environmental concerns and challenges of buiness and philanthropic activities of business evolved into distinct subject of deliberation (Balderjahn, 1998). Later, CSR and environmental concerns were merged to make a holistic understanding of CSR that included environmental concerns, corporate ethics and corporate philanthropy (Schlengemilch, 1994). CSR reflects today the social consequences of the success of business and concerns for wider societal well-being. The understanding of CSR changes from one country to another, from one region to another and one economy to another. It is difficult to find the universally accepted definition of CSR. But it will be interesting to look into different definitions of CSR.

The CSR is essentially a concept wherein the focus is on quality of life of the people and these will be the utmost priority while taking business decision. The World Council for sustainable development aptly states, "CSR is the continuing commitment by business to behave ethically and contribute to economic development while improving the quality of life of the work force and their families as well as of the local community and society at large" Assumption of CSR by the business will be in the interest of the business itself in the long run. CSR is also defined as "the commitment of businesses to contribute to sustainable economic development by working with employees, their families, the local community and society at large to improve their lives in ways that are good for business and for development" (International Finance Corporation, 2008). The main trust of the CSR should be that CSR is voluntary and it should come within the organisations. The legal impositions will not be of much help. In this connection, CSR can be termed as "a concept whereby companies integrate social and environmental concerns in their interaction with their stakeholders on a voluntary basis." (Euopean Commission 2001).

Literature Review

There are lot of studies carried out at international and national levels on the subject of CSR and rural development. The studies are focussing mostly on the strategic nature of CSR activities. Many of the studies advocate the strategic CSR and competitive advantage CSR offers to the company. Some view CSR as 'avoiding bad' which believes that the business cannot be considered responsible for citizen, if it is unable to prevent corporate social irresponsibility. So, they argue that CSR is the combination of responsible and irresponsible behaviour of the business (Nick Lin-Hi and Karsten Muller, 2013). Some studies focus on the consumption patterns and seek co-operation of other actors in sustainable development. The business requires the active participation and co-operation of governments, civil society and citizens in order to set sustainable consumption as a common goal (Gyorgy Malovics, 2008). Some argue CSR is still at its infant stage. Despite good awareness and intentions, the CSR approach of the many companies is unprofessional and unclear. Many of these companies have not developed the clear targets, and are not keeping due diligence in their pursuit of CSR (Dima Jamali, 2007). Khan and Atkinson (1987) conducted a comparative study on the managerial attitudes to social responsibility in India and Britain. The study shows that most of the Indian executives agreed CSR as relevant to business and felt that business has responsibilities not only to the shareholders and employees but also to customers, suppliers, society and to the state. Indian Industries and Price Water House Coopers have also highlighted the emerging Indian participations in the CSR process. The findings of these surveys emphasised companies across India reveal that philanthropy is the most significant driver of CSR, followed by image building, employee morale and ethics respectively. Centre for Social Markets (2003) conducted a study in which it was found that social responsibility is seen to be an important business issue within the sample firm, irrespective of firm size, age, sector, location, primary purpose or legal status. Arora and Puranik (2004) reviewed contemporary CSR trends in India concluding that the corporate sector in India benefitted immensely from liberalisation and privatisation process, its transition from philanthropic mind-sets to CSR has been lagging behind its impressive financial growth.

There were number of studies carried in the area of Human Development. The most notable work was carried by United Nations Development Programme (UNDP) under the aegis of United Nations (UN). Every year UNDP publishes Human Development Report (HDR). Beginning in 1990, these Reports have drawn attention to critical issues of inequality, human deprivations, gender, and social in justice that affects the lives of human being across the world. They also offer practical approachs to reduce poverty and enhance human security. UNDP works in four main areas such as:

(i) Poverty reduction and achieving the Millennium Development Goals (MDGs), (ii) Democratic governance, (iii) Crisis prevention and recovery, and (iv) Environment and sustainable development. UNDP set target to achieve MDGs by the year 2015. The eight MDGs are:

(1) Eradicate extreme poverty and hunger,

(2) Achieve universal primary education,

(3) Promote gender equality and women empower,

(4) Reduce child mortality,

(5) Improve maternal health,

(6) Combat HIV/AIDS, malaria and other diseases,

(7) Ensure environmental sustainability, and

(8) Develop a global partnership for development.

The HDR for the year 2011 with a theme of "Sustainability and Equity: A Better Future for All" lays emphasis on environmental sustainability and reduction of deep inequalities among nations. It argues that environmental sustainability can be achieved by addressing health, education, income and gender disparities together with the need for global action on energy production and ecosystem protection. These reports are very useful in the promotion of human development, because it not only highlights the problem but also suggest remedial measures to further human development.

Many a time people ascribe wrongly to mean only economic development, the development includes not only economic development but also development of capabilities of human beings. It is development of the masses and not just the development of elite sections of the society. The basic purpose of development is to enlarge people's choices. (Mahbub-ul-Haq, UNDP-2009).

The most critical choices that people should have include a long and healthy life, access to knowledge and income, assets and employment for a decent standard of living... (HDR of India, 1999). People often feel happy in achievements that do greater access to knowledge, better nutrition and health services, more secure livelihoods, security against crime and physical violence, satisfying leisure hours, political and cultural freedoms and a sense of participation in community activities. The human development has come to be accepted expansion of human capabilities, enhancement of freedoms, and a fulfillment of human rights. It also concerns the use of these capabilities. The objective of development is to create an enabling environment for people to enjoy long, healthy and creative lives. (Mahbub-ul-Haq, UNDP-2009). Rising incomes and expanding outputs in the human development are seen as the means and not the ends of development. Indeed, defining people's well-being as the end of development and treating economic growth as the means of development. (Sakiko Fukuda-Parr, 2005).

The focus on Human Development must be included from the beginning of any economic reform programme. Economic growth itself will not be sustained unless preceded or accompanied by improvements in Human Development (Gustav Ranis - 2000). It is seen that many of the countries which have high economic growth fairs poorly in terms of human development, which will, in turn, hinder the economic progress in the long run. On the contrary, there are country like though it is poor countries doing very well in terms of human development, (Sudhir Anand, 1993). We can also find that some countries are successful in both economic development and human development. However, these countries will need to change their policies as development proceeds in order to sustain their success. The priority should be given to primary education and some comprehensive health interventions, both from the perspective of improving human development and that of increasing economic growth. At a later stage, the roles of science and technology institutions and higher education become more important for strengthening Chain B (from human development to economic growth), while, along Chain A (from economic growth to human development), hospitals assume greater role than before, (Gustav Ranis 2000).

The human development approach tend to attach a higher weight to supplying public services relative to expanding private incomes--as instruments of public action, (Sudhir Anand, 1993). The cross-country evidence suggests that, at least for basic health, average affluence matters to the extent that it delivers lower income poverty and better public services. Indeed, the commonly observed positive correlation across countries between life expectancy and affluence vanishes, once one controls for incidence of poverty and public spending on health. Though, both these variables matter, it is notable that the quantitative significance of public health spending appears to be sizeable. Recently, human development started to give much focus on climate change and its impact on human beings. There should be a proper balancing of the climate challenge and development challenge; otherwise the very foundation of development will collapse, (HDR, 1999).

The above findings of different scholars at different points of time require that they have rightly observed and underscored the CSR practices and performance of companies in India. But little attention has been paid to the marginalised and poor people as stakeholders. Most of the studies focus CSR from the business perspective. These studies highlight the importance of strategic adoption CSR by the business enterprises. However, it is found that some business undertaking is promoting the human development. It will be interesting to know what impact CSR activities will have on human development. But there are very few studies on the area of impact of CSR activities of the business in promoting human development. Therefore, the present study fills this gap by finding out in what impact CSR practices will have on the business promotion of human development.

The Study

In an effort to understand the answers to the above questions, the present study was undertaken in ten public and private companies registered in the state of Karnataka.

Objectives of the Study

The main objectives of the study were:

1. To study and understand the CSR initiatives being taken by selected public and private companies for rural development;
2. To examine the corporates' approach to work and their mode of action for implementation for CSR initiatives;
3. To assess the impacts of CSR actions on the rural development of people in the state of Karnataka.

Methodology

To study the above objectives, ten public and private companies/firms registered in the state of Karnataka have been selected. While selecting these companies, efforts were being made to select them from a variety sectors to get comprehensive picture. Thus, the selected companies were from different industrial sectors like pharmaceuticals (Biocon, Bangalore), metals (KIOCL), financial institution (Corporation Bank, Mangalore, Canara Bank, Bangalore), Chemicals and Fertilisers (MCF Ltd., Mangalore), InfoTech (Infosys, Bangalore, Wipro Bangalore), Beverages (UB Group, Bangalore), Oil and Petroleum (MRPL, Mangalore), Manufacturing company (BEML). The methodology of the present study relied on the web-based research, review of print literature to understand CSR practice within the context of rural development in India. For the purpose of analysis, CSR initiatives for rural development were classified under five areas: livelihood, health, education, environment and infrastructure.

Limitations

The main limitation of this paper is that this study has only focussed on a small sample of companies situated in Karnataka. *Secondly*, information collected from print literature, websites of these companies and no primary data were collected directly from the stakeholders through interviews or surveys.

Results and Discussion

The CSR Policies and Initiatives: The study shows that all surveyed companies present themselves as having CSR policies and practices. A substantial number of companies reflect their CSR philosophy or social, environmental and ethical objectives, in mission statements, vision documents, organisational policy and plans. However, even though surveyed companies have CSR policies and objectives but no link was observed between policy of CSR and rural development. Table-1 shows number of companies taking CSR initiatives for human development in India.

It is interesting to note from the Table-1 that health and infrastructure takes the top priority of the companies surveyed, followed by environment. About 50 per cent of surveyed companies take CSR initiatives in the area of education and 40 per cent in livelihood. Though companies are working towards the promotion of rural development, the real progress is not penetrating into the remote and inaccessible areas of our society.

The Corporate' Approach to Work and Modes of Action: So far as CSR approach adopted by the companies is concerned, it is observed that most of the companies have adopted CSR approach into their overall business strategy. Therefore, they have been successful in achieving the objectives of businesses. But, it seems that they failed in terms of human development in rural areas. Their approach to work is mainly relief, welfare and service delivery, but it is human development, which have long-term benefits to the society. Wipro and Infosys believe in promoting human and social sustainable development through poverty alleviation by building capacity of poor people.

The study shows that out of ten companies surveyed, two companies implemented their CSR initiatives directly through dedicated CSR divisions which are responsible for planning and implementation of such activities. For other two companies, CSR initiatives are implemented through local management of manufacturing unit and Human Resource Department (HRD). Many companies like Infosys have set up dedicated foundations for implementation of CSR initiatives for rural development. Most of these foundations encourage participation of local communities while planning and implementation of their CSR activities. It is also interesting to note that such foundations implement their programmes in partnership with government departments, a good example of Private-Public Partnership (PPP). For example, Biocon foundation is working in partnership with the rural development department of the Government of India (GoI). The study also reveals that four companies, who have or do not have their foundations but partner with third sector organisations for effective implementation of CSR initiatives. In such an arrangement, the company provides finance, infrastructure, whereas the third sector provides grassroots level support for implementation of CSR activities.

The Impact of CSR Programmes on Rural Development

The impact of CSR programmes reflected by a sample of ten prominent companies in the state of Karnataka were classified under five areas: livelihood, health, education, environment and infrastructure.

Livelihood

MRPL under the name of 'SAMRAKSHAN' is promoting a holistic and sustainable manner, development of under-privileged communities afflected by poverty, illiteracy, illness and physical disabilities. It is focussing on the promotion of livelihood for economically weaker section of people by organising computerised stitch craft, JCB and crane-operating training programme. Wipro initiated Communication Skills Enhancement Programme (CSEP) at Manjakkudi to upskill the students/existing employees to a Voice and Accent (VA) entry level of communication skills. Phase-I was held in September 2012 and Phase-II was held in February 2013, both were attended by 73 participants. The Corporation Bank Self-Employment Training Institute, established on 22.03.1996 in Chikmagalur, is an institute sponsored by the Bank to cater to the training needs of the rural unemployed youth hailing from the districts of Chikmagalur and Kodagu, where the Bank has the Lead Bank responsibility. The training is imparted free of cost with free boarding and lodging to the trainees. The trained youths are also assisted in getting credit facilities from banks to set up self-employment ventures.

The 23,719 candidates have been trained in the institute since inception. The 9,323 candidates were trained under regular EDPs, of which 6,233 have settled indicating a success rate of 67 per cent. The bank has incurred an expenditure of Rs. 17.01 lakh during the year of which Rs. 13.40 lakh has been reimbursed by NABARD/Govt./ZPs etc. The bank has established one more COBSETI at Kodagu which has started functioning from the Bank's Lead Bank Office at Madikeri. The Bank has approved a financial grant of Rs1.07 crore for construction of the building and providing amenities to the Kodagu unit. The institute is managed by governing body at apex level and local advisory committee at local level. COBSETI, Chikmagalur has been graded as A+ Training Institute by the Ministry of Rural Development, Government of India for the year 2012. BEML has provided vocational training to 52 persons of the employees' dependants and the local population in areas such as para medical, tailoring, computer application, typing, shorthand, music/dance courses etc., for gainful employment.

Health

MRPL along with ONGC has extended its commitment by putting up separate block to the 162-year-old Lady Goschen Hospital at an estimated cost of Rs. 21 crore. It has constructed toilets and bath rooms for students' hostel and running free primary health centre. Wipro has supported a population of 51,000 covering 40 villages across Karnataka, Maharashtra and Andhra Pradesh with OPD and RCH facilities. It is carrying five Primary Health Care Projects: Project *Sanjeevani,* around Waluj WCCL Plant, Tumkur Health Care Project, around Tumkur WCCL Plant, Hindupur Healthcare Project, around WIN Hindupur Plant, Mysore Healthcare Project and Amalner Healthcare Project. The ambitious project of Wipro '*Sanjeevani*' in a span of three years reached out to more than 45,000 patients through mobile health clinic and the Reproductive Child Health (RCH) clinic-aided more than 6,000 pregnant women, with regards to their health requirements. Malnutrition in the ten project villages in the age group of 0-6 years saw significant drop from 51.2 per cent to 17.63 per cent. MCF during the year 2012-13 under the scheme "Project Eye Care", five free eye camps and cataract surgery camps were conducted in the neighbouring villages like, Permude, Gunduri, Manjeshwara, Sacharipete and Belvai. Free spectacles were distributed for the needy. Free Medical and Dental check-up camp was conducted at Marakada near MCF township. KIOCL has provided one Ambulance and Oxygen Concentrators to Chikkanaykanahalli Government Hospital and provided financial assistance to Shankar Eye Hospital for setting up of Ocularistry Clinic. Biocon is engaged in comprehensive healthcare efforts span preventive, primary, secondary and tertiary healthcare programs. They have micro-health Insurance programme, *Arogya Raksha,* which serves nearly 2,00,000 people across nine primary health centres in rural Karnataka. They also focus on chronic illnesses through tobacco cessation and oral cancer screening programmes. They have launched innovative programme for the early detection of oral cancer through screening and education. This is a collaborative programme with the State Government and ASHA (Accredited Social Health Activist) workers. Oral cancer screening was conducted in high risk groups in three pilot villages this year. This screening relied on mobile phone technology which used specially developed software. Over 5,000 people were screened, of which over 300 individuals were detected with positive lesions; they were taken to the nearest diagnostic center for biopsy. This has led to early intervention and potential cancer cure. This programme also aims to drive the cessation of tobacco products usage, which is the root cause of oral cancers.

Education

MRPL has the major programme of mid-day meal to support continuing education, setting up of computer lab, add on facility to government schools, providing scholarship and financial assistance to girl and SC/ST students for the Academic year 2012-13, construction of classrooms, *anganwadi,* toilets and bathrooms for students' hostel and running free primary health centre. Wipro has supported the education of more than 71,500 children in five cities and one village through six projects. MCF during the year 2012-13 under the scheme "*Mangala Akshara Mitra*" programme, the basic infrastructures that are required, but are lacking in identified schools in remote locations provided by the company. Those include desks, tables, chairs, green boards, racks, cupboards, school bags, lunch plates, water glasses and computers. The 28 government primary and higher primary schools located in the districts of Belguam, Hassan, Kolar, Kurnool, Chickballapur, Uttara Karnataka, Bagalkot, Bijapur, Davanagere, Bellary and Chickmagalore and about 5,000 poor students were the beneficiaries under this project during the year. The KIOCL Company is providing infrastructural facilities to various *Anganawadis* and schools and paid school fees to poor students, Bus facilities are provided to the students of Kudremukh and surrounding villages to pursue their studies at nearby town Kalasa,.Wrist watches were provided to poor students. Biocon have focussed on improving the quality of primary education delivery in rural schools. They distributed special work books on mathematics (*Chinnara Ganitha*) to a large number of government schools, has generated data that indicates that children have significantly benefitted from these books. Their computational skills are way above those, who have not had access to these books.

Environment

For sustainable management and development of natural resources, many companies have been working for tree plantation, watershed management, waste management, wind firm etc. Wipro in its Phase-II of the social forestry project has supported the planting of another 25,000 saplings by 22 farmers in Tiruvannamalai district, Tamil Nadu. KIOCL Company provided saplings to school children to spread the awareness regarding environment and ecology. BEML has planted /distributed around 15,000 saplings in and around all its divisions/complexes. Artificial tanks have been constructed in manufacturing complexes to harvest rain water, restrict soil erosion and to raise ground water level. Storage yard facility for hazardous waste at salvage stores at division is constructed as per ISO 14,001 requirements.

Infrastructure

Out of ten companies surveyed eight companies are providing different infrastructural facilities like construction or development of roads, electricity, water facility, sanitation, school, health centre, community centre, etc. Biocon Foundation empowers villages by providing proper infrastructure for schools, sanitation and water supply. In 2009, several hundred villages in North Karnataka suffered from floods. The widespread devastation affected crops, livestock, and houses and inundated villages. Biocon Foundation has been involved in the reconstruction of the Mangalgudda village and has handed over the houses to the government. Apart from this, the foundation is ensuring that the village is self-sufficient by leveraging solar energy to power the village. Over 400 new houses built in Mangalgudda village in North Karnataka have been occupied by the families rendered homeless by floods in 2009. Each house in Biocon Nagara is equipped with solar lights and toilets. KIOCL has constructed community hall at Jamble and laid the roads, culverts, electricity, bus shelter and other facilities at Kunya.

Conclusion and Recommendations

The CSR is becoming prominent in the annual reports of the company. Since Ministry of Company Affairs requires top 100 listed companies in terms of market capitalisation to publish Business Responsibility Report, the companies are eagerly practising CSR in companies. Some of the companies like TATA group have pioneered the CSR activities in India. The other companies are starting to realise need of CSR practices in the present complex business environment. With the activism of civil society and third sector business has realised the need to build good rapport with the local communities. The local communities are becoming vigil against the exploitation by big corporate houses. The study found that all the companies in this sample is practising CSR. But study found that most of the companies carry CSR activities within their plants, township or nearby places but very often they ignore rural places. They mainly focus on the strategic CSR activities. A wide range of CSR initiatives ranging from income generation activities for livelihood, health check-up camps, mobile health services, education, adult literacy, agricultural development, provision of drinking water, management and development of natural resources, infrastructure facilities being carried out by these companies. Their approach is the use of their product as a tool of CSR activities. It is also noted that many companies promote and implement CSR initiatives through Human Resource Departmnet, foundation or in partnership with third sector, but do not have full-fledged CSR department. But the real problem of these CSR activities is that they are not reaching the marginalised and poor sections of our society especially in rural areas. The developmental activities carried by the business are most of the time looks like cosmetic up keep because vast sections of the society in rural areas are not able to enjoy the fruits of development carried by the business. Therefore, business should focus on all round human development of the society in rural areas and it should incorporate promotion of human development as its core agenda. The companies should partner third sector organisations for the effective implementation of human development activities in rural areas. They should focus on the skill development of the local masses in order to increase their competency. The companies should carry social audit through external agency to find the impact of social performance. The government should make mandatory for all the companies to publish Business Responsibility Report as part of Annual Report.

Table-1: Number of Companies Taking CSR Initiatives on Human Development

CSR initiatives	*Number of Companies*	*Percentage of Companies Taking CSR Initiatives*
Livelihood	04	40
Health	08	80
Education	05	50
Environment	07	70
Infrastructure	08	80

Source: Company website.

Table-2: Stakeholders Identified by the Company

Name of the Company	**Stakeholders**
Wipro	Customers, Investors, Employees, Suppliers, Government, Education partners, Community Partners and Future Generations
MRPL	Employees, Suppliers, Customers, Investors and Shareholders, Trade Union, Local community, Government regulatory authorities
MCF	Employees, Health, Education, Environment
KIOCL	Health, Education, Community Development, Sports
Corporation Bank	Charitable Institution, Health, Edcation, Skill Development
Canara Bank	Education, Health, Charities, Social Welfare and Relief, Energy Conservation, Women

	Welfare, Skill Development
Biocon	Education, Health, Infrastructure
BEML	Education, Health, Environment
Infosys	Clients, Employees, Investor, Alliance Partner, Government, Acdemia, Vendors, Local Communities
UB Group	Charitable Institution, Health, Education, Skill Development

Source: Company website.

References

Acosta, Pablo, Business and human development in the base of the pyramid: Exploring challenges and opportunities with market heat maps," *The Journal of World Business (2011).*

Daniels, Mark Gordon and Donna R. "Bridging the Divide: Principles for Healthy Corporate Social Responsibility Partnerships," *The Journal of Social Change (2009).*

Dayna Simpson, Kathryn Lefroy and Yelena Tsarenko, "Together and Apart: Exploring Structure of the Corporate–NPO Relationship." *The Journal of Business Ethics (2011).*

Deene, Kundhan Basavaraj and Shivakumar, "Corporate Philanthropy in India: A New Business Model of ITC Ltd." *The Journal of Indian Management Studies (2011).*

Desai, Sonalde B. and *et al, Human Development In India.* New Delhi: Oxford University Press, 2010.

Dholakia, Ravindra H, "Regional Disparity in Economic and Human Development in India." *The Economic and Political Weekly (2003).*

Diana Mitlin, Sam Hickey and Anthony Bebbington. "Reclaiming Development? NGOs and the Challenge of Alternatives." *World Development (2007).*

Frynas, Peter Newell and Jedrzej George. "Beyond CSR? Business, Poverty and Social Beyond CSR? Justice: an introductionl." *Third World Quarterly* 28:4 (2007): pp. 669-81.

Fulton, Gabriel Kasper and Katherine. *The Future of Corporate Philanthropy: A Framework Understanding Your Options*. New York, USA: Monitor Institute, 2008.

Gustav Rains, Frances Stwert and Alejandro Ramirez, "Economic Growth and Human Development." *World Development* (2000).

Hamann, Ralph, "Can business make decisive contributions to development? Towards a research agenda on corporate citizenship and beyond" *Development Southern Africa 23.2 (2006).*

Hasan, Samiul, "Third Sector Growth and Governance: Contexts, and Traditions in Asia" Onyx, S. Hasan and J, *Comparative Third Sector Governance in Asia.* Springer, 2008.

Marx, Jerry D. (1999) *"Corporate Philanthropy: What Is the Strategy?" Non-profit and Voluntary Sector Quarterly,* Vol. 28,. No. 2.

Nelson, Shannon Murphy and Jane, *Business Partnerships for Development: The Case of the National Beverage Company in the West Bank and Gaza,* Cambridge, USA: CSR Initiative at the Harvard Kennedy School, 2010.

Parker, John W. Selsky and Barbara, "Cross-Sector Partnerships to Address Social Issues: Challenges to Theory and Practice." *The Journal of Management* (2005).

Pednekar, Achut, "CSR : Is it philanthropy or a lip service." *The Journal of Commerce and Management Thought* (2008).

Pei Bin., *Building Strategic Philanthropy in China. CiYaun,* China: China Partnership Development, BSR and CiYuan Initiative, 2010.

Ravallion, Sudhir Anand and Martin. "Human Development in Poor Countries: On the Role of Private Incomes and Public Service." *The Journal of Economic Perspectives (1993).*

Reed, Ananya Mukherjee Reed and Darryl, *Corporate Social Responsibility and Human Development: Towards a New Agenda and Beyond,* Toronto: York University, 2004.

"Partnerships for Development: Four Models of Business Involvement," *The Journal of Business Ethics* (2009): 90:3–37.

Reed, Ananya Mukherjee Reed and Darryl, 'Business and Development.' *Indian Institute of Management Bangalore, Management Review (2010).*

Singh, Sweta, "Philanthropy to Corporate Social Responsibility: An Indian Perspective," *Review of International Comparative Management* Vol. 11. No 5 (2010).

Srivastava, D.K., *"Perspectives on Corporate Social Responsibility (CSR): A Case Study of the Tata Group of Companies,"* Sage Publications India Pvt Ltd (2010).

UNDP, *Business Solutions for Human Development,* Egypt: Ministry of Investment, Egypt, 2007.

29

Role of NGO's in Uplifment of Tribals — A Study on Vivekananda Girijana Kalyana Kendra (VGKK) B.R. Hills

Balraj M and Sowmya N

Introduction

Today non-governmental organisation as the third sector is playing major role in respect of eradication the social evils and they are also working together with government in many projects like, improving backward areas and major social problems as well as child labour, tribal development, basic education, employment opportunity etc.

India is a democratic country. The Constitution has provided some provisions in development of all communities. In Part 9, Articles 244 and 244-A of Indian Constitution it clearly mentions the topic of tribal development..

The tribal development is the most important issue in the present situation of India. Tribal community nearly consists of 8.5 per cent of total population in India.Primitive tribe as well as ancient tribes, who live in the three southern region states namely, Karnataka, Tamil Nadu and Kerala. In Karnataka, the *betta kuruba* and *jennu kuruba* lives in Nagarahole and Bandipura national reserve forest and also *Soligas* lives in MM Hills and BR Hills. These groups remain backward particularly in health, education and socio-economic aspects, poverty and poor drinking water. When two sectors fail to uplift this tribal people in the nation, the third sector NGO is working towards the upliftment to bring sustainability in their lives.

NGOs which are called as third sector played a very important role in the twenty-first century. They have a greater role and responsibility in the development of tribal and upliftment of other backward communities.

VGKK is also one of the NGO situated in BR Hills by founder Dr. Sudharshan; it was established in the year of 1981 with objectives of development of tribal health and education. Dr Sudershan was awarded Magsaysay award by his services through VGKK, Rs.75 lakh cash award.

Review of Literature

The tribal population is identified as the aboriginal inhabitants of our country. They are seen in almost every state of India. For centuries, they have been living simple life based on the natural environment and have developed cultural patterns congenial to their physical and social environment. References of such tribal groups are found even in the literature in the ancient period, right from the *Ramayana* and the *Mahabharata* periods.

Meaning of Tribe

As the name implies, tribals are *adivasi* or original dwellers, living in the sub-continent from unrecorded time and possibly driven into the forests by more aggressive settlers - Aryans being the earliest one to socially subjugate them. In order to resist complete domination, tribals evolved their distinct identity through endogamy, their cropping pattern, hunting and food gathering. Above all, in their intensely personal relationship with the forest around them, they formed perfectly balanced rhythms which can best be described as symbiotic.

According to L.P. Vidarthi: the tribe is a social group with definite territory, common name, common district, common culture, behaviour of an endogamous group, common taboos, existence of distinctive social and political system, full faith in leaders and self-sufficiency in their distinct economy.

P.G. Krishnan defines: "Tribe is a social group of simple and kind, the members of which speak a common dialect, have a single government act together for common purposes and have a common name, a contiguous territory, a relatively uniform culture or way of life and traditions of common descent."

A. B. Bardhan defines the Tribe as "course of socio-cultural entity at a definite historical stage of development, it is a single, endogamous community with a cultural and psychological make-up".

According to D.N. Majumadar, the Tribe is " a collection of families or common group bearing common name, the members of which occupy the same territory, speak the same language and observe certain taboos, regarding marriage, professions and have developed a well-assured system of reciprocity and mutuality of obligations".

Concept of Development

The term development has been used in a wider sense. The purpose of development is to provide increasing opportunities to all people for a better life. It is essential to bring about more equitable distribution of income and wealth for promoting social justice and efficiency of production, to provide a greater variety of facilities like education, health services, nutrition, housing etc.

According to ILO, development involves 'humans' as distinct from material product. It is defined as a process which involves improvement of the masses in the process of decision- making in the economic, social, political and cultural life of a society.

Schumpeter defines, Development as only such changes in economic life that are not forced upon it from without, but arise by its own initiative from within.

Concept of Tribal Development: Meaning and Scope

The goal of tribal development in India was best summarised in Nehru's foreword to Verrier Elwin's book on NEFA. It is otherwise known as 'tribal panchsheel'. The Nehru's Panchsheel (five points) are:

1. People should develop along the lines of their own genius, and we should avoid imposing anything on them. We should try to encourage in every way their own traditional arts and culture;
2. Tribal rights in land and forests should be respected;
3. We should try to train and build up a team of their own people to do work of administration and development. Some technical personnel from outside will, no doubt, are needed, especially in the beginning. But we should avoid introducing too many outsiders into tribal territory;
4. We should not over-administer these areas or overwhelm them with multiplicity of schemes. We should rather work through, and not in rivalry to, their own social and cultural institutions;
5. We should judge results, not by statistics or the amount of money spent, but by the quality of human character that is evolved.

Statement of the Problem

The tribal's communities in Karnataka consist of eight per cent of total population. Tribals are live majority in the following district, namely in Raiachur, Bellary, Chitradurga, followed by Chamrajanagara. Chamarajanagara is the backward district and consists nearly of eleven per cent of tribals among the total population.

Majority of the tribals are living in remote forest area, remain untouched by the civilisation. They are largely unaffected by the development processes going on the rest of states. Therefore, they are backward particularly in health, education and socio-economic aspects. After the launching of Project Tiger, the tribals are forced to take valuable touch with a civilised society.

The government of India had implemented Project Tiger in Chamarajanagara, especially in BR hills to protect the predator. In this regard, the protection of tribals is very important for the Central and the State Governments and also VGKK has taken some steps in development of tribals in Chamarajanagara district.

Need for the Study

Tribals practise indigenous system of heritage, culture, and evil things that is child marriage and have own traditions and values. In Chamarajanagara district, the *Soligas* are dominating tribals. The government of Karnataka launched the entry of third sector in movement of the upliftment of Soligas.

It is a difficult task for government to develop the tribals in this regard the VGKK mainly focus on development of tribals through impart education, creating awareness about health and hygiene and vocational training for self-employment.

This primitive tribe as well as ancient tribes, live in three southern states namely Karnataka, Kerala and Tamil Nadu. There are discernible differences in the levels of socio-economic and educational development achieved by four tribes during the last 60 years of planning.

Soligas live in MM Hills and BR Hills (Karnataka) and Nilgiri Hills (Tamil Nadu) and Yarava tribes in Karnataka and Tamil Nadu, this is this geographical distribution of these four tribes.

Objectives of the Study

1. To study the uplift tribal community in Karnataka.
2. To study the problems faced by the tribal community in Chamarajanagara.
3. To study the values, cultures and tradition of tribals.
4. To study the factors influencing development of tribals.
5. To analyse the role of VGKK in uplift of tribals.

Research Methodology

The research paper was carried out on the basis of both primary and secondary data. Primary data collected through interaction with tribals, government agencies, forest department and welfare department and questionnaire issued to educated people. Secondary data collected through the text books, articles, magazine journal project reports. The research contains 100 respondents. The respondents are chosen using stratified sampling method, that's 80 respondents from tribals and 20 respondents from VGKK employees. The collected data are analysed with tables, frequencies and percentage.

Data Analysis and Discussion

A) Responses from the Tribal People

Table 1: Are you satisfied with your living condition?

Particulars	*Respondents*	*Percentage*
Excellent	12	15 per cent
Good	16	20 per cent
Satisfactory	12	15 per cent
Not satisfactory	40	50 per cent
Total	80	100 per cent

Source: Field Survey.

The Table-1 shows that majority of the respondents (50 per cent) are not Satisfied with their living condition. So, government and NGO's have taken certain measures creating good living environment to tribal peoples.

Table 2: Are you aware about the programmes of NGO's (VGKK)?

Particulars	*Respondents*	*Percentage*
Yes	52	65 per cent
No	28	35 per cent
Total	80	100 per cent

Source: Field Survey.

The Table-2 shows that 65 per cent of respondents are aware about the NGO's programmes and also getting the benefit from programmes.

Table 3: Who are all Assisting for Your Upliftment?

Particulars	*Respondents*	*Percentage*
Government	20	25 per cent
NGO's	52	65 per cent
Co-operative Society	04	05 per cent
Other members	04	05 per cent
Total	80	100 per cent

Source: Field Survey.

Table-3 interpret that government, NGOs, and co-operative societies are involved in development of tribals but the majority of assistance is given by the NGOs. Therefore, government will come forward to give more assistance to tribal people development.

Table - 4: What are the problems you have been Facing in this hadi?

Particulars	*Respondents*	*Percentage*
Basic needs	40	50 per cent
Forest animals	20	25 per cent
Tiger project implementation	08	10 per cent
Other problem	12	15 per cent
Total	80	100 per cent

Source: Field Survey.

The Table-4 shows that tribal community suffers from several problems. Majority of the respondents facing the basic needs for their lives, therefore government will provide the basic needs to tribals as much as possible.

B) Responses from the VGKK Employees

Table 5: What are the factors Influence in development of Tribals?

Particulars	*Respondents*	*Percentage*
Basic education	08	40 per cent
Child marriage	04	20 per cent
Lack of culture	02	10 per cent
All of the above	06	30 per cent
Total	20	100 per cent

Source: Field Survey.

The Table-5 shows that the basic needs and child marriage are main factor influencing tribal development. Therefore, the government will provide the basic education to tribal pupils and have taken certain steps to reduce child marriage.

Table 6: Are you Protecting the Value, Culture of the Tribal's?

Particulars	*Respondents*	*Percentage*
Yes	20	100 per cent
No	00	000 per cent
Total	20	100 per cent

Source: Field Survey.

Table 6 says that the VGKK play major role in protecting value, culture of the tribals.

Table-7: What are the programmes conducted for development of Tribals?

Particulars	*Respondents*	*Percentage*
Vocational training	02	10 per cent
Self-employment training	02	10 per cent
Healthcare unit	02	10 per cent
All of the Above	14	70 per cent
Total	20	100 per cent

Source: Field Survey.

The Table-7 shows that VGKK provides the vocation training, self-employment training, healthcare unit, basic education. These are the progrmmes conducted by the VGKK to uplift the tribals.

Findings

1. Majority of tribal people are living from the last 15 years.
2. Tribal people are not satisfied with their living condition.
3. Majority of the tribal people are aware about non-governmental organisation.
4. For the uplift of tribals, there are many government departments, NGOs and other co-operative societies.
5. Majority of the tribal people are suffering from basic needs.
6. More number of tribals is aware about VGKK.
7. The majority of the tribal people practise child marriage.
8. The tribals follow the tradition-culture and they are not civilised in well-manner.
9. In the area of BR Hills, the VGKK is working for the last 20 years for the uplift of tribals.
10. VGKK provides vocational training, self-employment training, healthcare unit, basic education for tribal development.

Suggestions

1. The government and NGOs have taken some of projects the concerning basic needs of tribals.

2. The government has to implement many more development programmes to uplift tribals.
3. There is need to provide an awareness programme through the government and NGOs on health and hygienie.
4. The government gives special provisions and facilities to tribals people.
5. The government and other NGOs must take initiative to create awareness about proper agriculture activity for their sustainable development.
6. The government takes certain measures to control child marriage practice and give them proper guidelines for living as civilised people.

Conclusion

The tribal people of India also called *adivasi* live from past many centuries in India with specific geographical region, with common language culture and values, co-operation and feelings. They form seven per cent of the total population of India. Tribal people are leading their lives depending on their practised occupation like hunting, traditional agriculture, sale of domestic animals collection and selling of honey and so on. The educational status, social status, are economical status, cultural status and political status, very low while compared, to other urban and rural communities .

VGKK is also one of the NGO, situated in BR Hills, founded by Dr Sudharshan. It was established in the year of 1981 with objectives of development of tribals health and education. Dr Sudershan was awarded Magsaysay Rs.75 lakh cash award worth his services through VGKK .

References

Government of India website, www.ministryofruraldevelopment.gov.in.

Indu Bhaskar and Geethakutty (2001). "Role of Non-governmental Organisations in Rural Development: A Case Study" *The Journal of Tropical Agriculture*, 39, pp. 52-54.

P. D. Kulkarni- *NGO's and Social Welfare.*

Ravichandran (2007). *'The NGO's in India'.*

Sachcideva DR - *Social Welfare Administration in India.*

Stephen Clark - *Community Organisation Practice.*

30

PMGSY and Sustainable Rural Road Infrastructure in India

M. N. Lokesha

Introduction

The agricultural sector has been one of the most important components of Indian economy. Agriculture continues to be a mainstay of life for majority of the population. It contributes around 17 per cent (Karnataka economic survey, 2010-11) of the GDP; about 67 per cent people are living in rural areas and are still dependent on agriculture. About 43 per cent of India's geographical area is used for agricultural activity and employs 53 per cent of the work force in the country. Since, the responsibility of providing infrastructure is with the state which aims at rapid growth of agricultural production for attaining other kinds of developmental goals, such as poverty alleviation, relieving unemployment, attaining food security and promote industrial development etc. The agricultural sector in our country has flourished over the years due to government's constant thrust on increasing agricultural production. Still, the benefits are not percolating down to the farming community. Indian agriculture is characterised by lack of proper infrastructure facilities. As far as nature of infrastructure is concerned, there are different kinds of infrastructure such as economic infrastructure, social infrastructure, financial infrastructure, technological infrastructure, agricultural infrastructure, etc., defined in broader terms. Among all kinds of infrastructure mentioned above, agricultural infrastructure plays an important role especially in a developing country context, where larger percentage of poorer section of the society depends on this sector for subsistence. The agriculture sector continues to be the single largest occupation as it still provides livelihood to 53 per cent (Economic Survey, 2010-11) of the population. The enhancing infrastructure warrants closer relationship between the levels of agricultural development. This assumes importance because, the agricultural sector plays dominant role in alleviating poverty and the overall growth of agricultural sector and its components, such as growth of agricultural employment, income, output, etc., depend largely on the level of investment made in infrastructure. In other words, level of infrastructure in agricultural sector is one of the major factors that could explain the agricultural growth. This being our major aim here is to analyse the role of infrastructure in promoting agriculture.

Among agricultural infrastructures road infrastructure plays a very significant role in accelerating agricultural production. Rural Roads Connectivity is one of the key components for rural development, as it promotes access to economic and social services, generating increased agricultural income and productive employment. About 600 million people of India live in nearly six lakh villages scattered all over the country. Access roads provide the means to bring the rural population on to the mainstream. A good road network accelerates efficient delivery of farm inputs, reduce transport cost and enhance special agricultural production and distribution. A good network of roads will expand the distribution of agricultural goods as well as open up additional opportunities for agricultural trade (Inoni, 2009). Improved infrastructure leads to expansion of markets, economies of scale and improvement in factor market operations. It also opens up the rural economy to greater competition from outside. This may take the form of cheaper products from lower-cost sources of supply or new or improved products that may displace some locally produced items. The majority of studies recognise that infrastructure investment has strong impact on rural income and especially on small land holders. There was a direct relationship between increase in acreage of export crop cultivation and the standard of roads and distance from the main commercial centers. There is enhanced entrepreneurship activity, sharp decline in freight and passenger charges and improved services as a result of investment in rural roads (Bonney, 1964). Roads are always recognised as an infrastructure and arteries of the nation. Rural infrastructure assumes great importance in India because of the country's predominantly rural nature.

Rural roads were not only providing connectivity to rural area, but also affecting change in cropping pattern due to access to markets, increasing productivity by facilitating availability of inputs like fertiliser, seeds and pesticides, realisation of better prices to the farmers for agriculture and allied products like, milk, improving attendance in schools and above all opening new employment opportunities in non-farm and service sectors (Sangwan S. S., 2010).

The rural road in India forms a substantial portion of the Indian road network. These roads are in poor shape, affecting the rural population's quality of life and Indian farmer's ability to transfer produce to market post-harvest. Over 30 per cent of Indian farmer's harvest spoils post-harvest because of the poor infrastructure. Many rural roads are of poor quality, potholed, and unable to withstand the loads of heavy farm equipment. These roads are also far from all seasos, the total length of rural road is of the order of 2.7 million kilometers in 2001, and which is 3.1 million kilometers in 2011. Of which 1.2 million kilometers are paved, not maintained rural roads and 1.9 million kilometers of unpaved rural roads.

The condition of Karnataka is not different from the rest of India. Total road length in Karnataka comprises national highways, state highways, important district roads, other districts roads, Z- P roads and village roads. The total length of road at present is 2,31,997 kilometers in 2010-11. Of which 4,490 kilometer national highways 20,770 kilometers are state highways, 49,959 kilometers are major district roads, 8,366 kilometers are municipal roads and 1,48,412 kilometers is village roads (public works, ports and inland water department, 2012). On an average, about 80 kilometers of road exists per every 100 sq km. of geographical area. However, the distribution of the roads between the districts and within the districts is not at all balanced. The national standard envisages a road network of *about 100 km per 100 sq. km. of area.* Thus, the state as a whole is lagging behind in the suggested norms.

In pursuance of the nationally significant cause of providing complete rural road connectivity through all weather roads, to set villages free from the handicap of isolation and deprivation of accessibility, Government of India set up the National Rural Roads Development Committee (NRRDC) in January, 2000 chaired by Nitin Gadkari. This committee after dwelling on the effects of deprivation of rural accessibility and keeping in view of expected benefits from rural connectivity recommended a special intervention, the *Pradhan Mantri Gram Sadak Yojana* (PMGSY) which was launched on December,25th 2000 as 100 per cent centrally-assisted scheme. The focus of the programme is to construct good quality all-weather roads for new connectivity and upgradation of existing roads. For the first time, the focus is directly on the rural connectivity under dedicated road fund, and the 50 per cent of the cess amount collected on high speed diesel has been allocated for this programme. In earlier programmes, the village with defined population was the target for providing connectivity, while the PMGSY envisages 'habitation' as the unit, to reach out to more settlements and more people with accessibility. Upgradation of selected rural roads to provide farm to market connectivity is the secondary objective of PMGSY Programme. In earlier programmes, the village with a defined population was the target for providing connectivity, while PMGSY envisage the habitation as the unit, to reach out to more settlements and more people with rural accessibility.

Research Objectives

1. To study the tasks and achievement of PMGSY.
2. To study the role of *Bharat Nirman* programme in rural roads and agriculture development.

Methodology

Research Design: On the basis of fundamental objectives of research, our study is a type of Descriptive Research: also known as statistical research method of data collection. Secondary Data:- Large amount of secondary data is available in the forms of articles, manuals and previously conducted researchers on the similar topic. Also, the data gathered will help in identifying key parameters to examine through further exploration and thus will help in defining the objectives.

Role of *Bharat Nirman* Programme in Rural Roads

Rural connectivity is the key component of rural development and poverty alleviation in India. Rural roads provide accessibility for the rural habitations to market and other facility centres. In order to give boost to rural connectivity rural roads programme, *Pradhan Mantri Gram Sadak Yojana* (PMGSY) was launched as 100 per cent centrally sponsored scheme in December 2000. *Bharat Nirman* envisages massive scaling up of the programme in terms of habitation connectivity coverage, construction targets and financial investment. To achieve the targets of *Bharat Nirman*, 1,46,185 kms of rural roads are proposed to be constructed to benefit 66,802 unconnected eligible habitation in the country. It is also proposed to upgrade nearly 1,94,132 kms of the existing rural roads, which are identified through routes of the core network. *Bharat Nirman* envisaged providing connectivity to all habitation of 1,000 and above (500 and above in the case of Hill states including North East, Tribal and Desert Areas) by 2009. Upto March 2010, around 34,000 villages were provided all weather road connectivity through construction of 96,000 km of roads. Systematic District Rural roads plans were prepared listing out the complete network of all roads in the district village roads, major district-roads, state roads and national highways and construction and allocation of resources were prioritised. To ensure quality control measures were followed, backed by independent quality checks and measurements. The inbuilt clause of five years maintenance within the construction contract has helped in maintenance of the newly-created assets. Upto June 2011, as many as 40,712 habitations were provided connectivity under this programme. The achievement in case of new connectivity and upgradation of roads infrastructure were 68.5 and 90.7 per cent respectively, as in June 2011.

Table-1: Habitations Connected and Length Completed under PMGSY

Sl.No.	*States*	*Habitations Connected Up to March, 2012*	*Length Completed Up to March,2012 (km)*
1.	Andra Pradesh	1,354	20,107.71

2.	Arunachal Pradesh	295	3,345.15
3.	Assam	6,613	12,238.69
4.	Bihar	7,443	19,776.17
5.	Chhattisgarh	6139	19,462.21
6.	Goa	2	158.70
7.	Gujarat	2,462	7,587.84
8.	Haryana	1	4,484.39
9.	Himachal Pradesh	1,872	10,025.46
10.	Jammu and Kashmir	984	2,883.77
11.	Jharkhand	3,150	7,285.28
12.	Karnataka	269	15,540.79
13.	Kerala	362	1,487.94
14.	Madhya Pradesh	10,901	49,444.85
15.	Maharashtra	1,120	21,347.89
16.	Manipur	237	2,963.55
17.	Meghalaya	147	1,009.43
18.	Mizoram	131	2,103.08
19.	Nagaland	90	2,665
20.	Odisha	6,650	23,080.65
21.	Punjab	406	4,434.36
22.	Rajasthan	10,438	48,617.36
23.	Sikkim	166	2,401.46
24.	Tamil Nadu	1,934	9,909.76
25.	Tripura	1,425	2,337.67
26.	Uttar Pradesh	11,129	39,836.79
27.	Uttrakhand	649	4,051.59
28.	West Bengal	8,045	11,845.54
	Grand Total	*84,414*	*3,50,501*

Source :

Role of Road and Road Transport in Agricultural Development

One of the major obstacles to progressive agriculture in India has been the lack of all-weather village to market roads. A large number of villages still lack road links with market towns and with one another. Road improvement would contribute to decline in both average and marginal costs of production by encouraging the use of more productive inputs and farming techniques as well as by reducing the costs of holding inventory of inputs and of procuring inputs from the market. Improved communication and inability provided by all weather roads would expose farmers to modern agricultural practices. All-weather motorable roads would also reduce the input costs to the farmers by permitting them to substitute low-cost motor truck transport for high-cost bullock cart transport in the procurement of farm inputs from the market. In the marketing of farm products when it is recognised that the "rural road improvements would contribute to cost reductions by lowering the costs of transporting them to market and by reducing their spoilage while in transit" as in the haulage of farm inputs, improved roads would permit a shift to truck transport in the marketing of farm products and would thus reduce the marketing costs. Some research studies showed that while the cost reductions permitted by improved rural transport would create incentives for expanding production for the market, there is no likelihood of sharp decline in prices of farm products to completely offset these incentives. The studies also found that the market demand for agricultural commodities in India is potentially very high due to population growth, increasing urbanisation, progress in industrialisation and rising income. As such, in spite of large expansion in agricultural output, the agricultural price level would tend to remain relatively stable.

Economic Importance of Roads

As indicated earlier, the development of roads affects agriculture directly by enlarging the areas under cultivation. There is a two-fold relation between road development and increased agricultural products. Easy transport of manures, good seeds and better agricultural equipment, pesticides are made possible in time due to easy road transport. Better roads neutralise locational disadvantages in farming. Road development also prompts a change in the pattern of agricultural production by diversion of cultivation from food crops to commercial crops. Paucity of good roads in rural area compels the cultivator to dispose of his produce to the village moneylender at cheap prices. Good roads would open up the urban markets to the cultivator, which would facilitate marketing of his product at higher prices. Moreover, bad roads are responsible for higher cost by transportation, which increases the cost of marketing. A good road system also aids agriculture indirectly by breaking up the isolation of villages, spreading education and creating a general sense of awakening.

The rural industries like dairy farming. bee-keeping, poultry-farming, sericulture I.c., can be developed as subsidiary industries to supplement their income in their spare time. Development of small scale and cottage industries becomes possible in rural areas due to the close road contact with their urban markets and the availability of raw materials at cheap prices. The important role played by the roads is very much felt during the days of famines. It has been observed regarding some of the Indian famines that the food scarcity in an area was not due to total deficiency, but owing to the isolation from the surplus area. Further, road development would facilitate flow of food from surplus to deficit areas and also equalise the prices in different markets. For relieving unemployment and promoting economic activity, road construction is an important item of the state governments to be taken up, as 56 to 70 per cent of the cost of road construction is spent as wages.

Rural Roads and Change in Agricultural Production

All-weather roads would promote the production of agricultural commodities. Its impact is likely to be relatively greater in the production of soft and highly perishable farm products such as milk, eggs, poultry, fresh fruits, fresh vegetables, etc. Those would lend themselves to year-round production and, therefore, require almost daily use of the road for their marketing. These products are also easily susceptible to spoilage on account of rough and slow haulage. Because of these characteristics, lack of all weather village-to-market roads act as great deterrent to the expansion of their production for the market. Rural road network and transport bring about desirable communication related to agriculture and farm practices and breaks isolation of villages by evoking awakening in the rural farmers. Rural goods transport services which could facilitate the free flow of the natural produce to consumer centers and agricultural inputs to rural areas are warranted to facilitate proper distribution of available food and to speed up the rural development in India. It helps the farmers and other rural artisans alike in supplementing their slender earnings and in protecting from the ill-favoured and squeezing brokers and middlemen.

Conclusion

It is well-known that the roads are playing an important role in upliftment of the social, economic and cultural life of the people; access to better road network to rural areas substantially enhances the socio-economic status and improves the living condition of rural population. There is an inter-related relationship between roads and agricultural production, and also, the impact of such enhanced agricultural production on income, living standard, attitudes and other activities of the rural people. For this reason, government of India gave importance to rural road construction by launching *Pradhana Manthri*

Gram Sadak Yojana (PMGSY) in 2000. This programme provides improved infrastructure to rural farm sector and improving agriculture and socio-economic upliftment of rural poor.

References

Annual Report of National Rural Roads Development Agency (NRRDA), Ministry of Rural Development, Government of India, 2010-11.

Basic Road Statistics of India, Government of India, Ministry of Road Transport, and Highways Transport Research Wing, New Delhi, August 2012.

Fan, Shenggen, Peter Hazell and S.K. Thorat (1999), *"Linkages between Government Spending, Growth and Poverty in Rural India"*, International Food Policy Research Institute, Washington, DC, USA.

Inoni O.E. Omotur D.G . *Effect of Road Infrastructure on Agricultural output and income of Rural Households in Delta State*, Agricultural tropica, sub-tropica, *et al* Vol. 42(2) 2009.

Karnataka Development Report (2005), the Planning Commission, Government of India.

Karnataka Economic Survey (2012), Government of Karnataka.

Sangwan S.S. (2010), Occasional Paper – 53 *Infrastructure for Agriculture Development National Bank for Agriculture and Rural Development*, Mumbai.

31

Rural Sanitation in Hyderabad-Karnataka Region: Practice vis-a-vis Policy Perspectives

Devidas G Maley

Introduction

The Indian economy has been growing rapidly. The paradox is that while India is now in the front ranks of fast-growing emerging economies, it is also one of the countries wherein a lot of efforts are still required to eliminate many ill-practices among which is the open defecation (OD). In rural areas, though reduced in scale, it continues to be a socially and culturally accepted traditional behaviour at large. Lack of priority to safe confinement and disposal of human excreta poses significant health risks manifest in the sanitation challenge facing the nation today.[1]

Till the day, the problem of supplying pure drinking water is not met by the governments of the world especially in poor countries like India and Pakistan. According to UNICEF and WHO, the world is still on track for reaching the MDG drinking water target, but the trend appears to be deteriorating. On current trends, the world will miss the sanitation target by more than half a billion people[2]. Department of Drinking Water and Sanitation, Ministry of Rural Development, Government of India, Draft 2.1, 18 December, 2010, towards Nirmal Bharat: rural sanitation and Hygiene Strategy, 2010–22. The purpose of the strategy is to provide a framework to realise the vision of *Nirmal Bharat*, an environment that is clean, healthy and contributes to the economic and social well-being of all rural citizens.

Diseases linked to poor sanitation and hygiene lead to substantial loss of life and potential. It is estimated that one in every ten deaths in India is linked to poor sanitation and hygiene. Diarrohea, a preventable disease, is the largest killer and accounts for every twentieth death. Around 4,50,000 deaths were linked to diarrohea alone in 2006, of which 88 per cent were deaths of children below five.[3] Prevalence of 47 per cent[4] of child under-nutrition in India is among the highest in the world and nearly doubles that of sub-Saharan Africa.

Studies[5] have shown the impact of diseases caused by poor sanitation among children to their cognitive development. Due to the decreasing immunity suffered by the children in their early years as a result of sanitation linked diseases, the development of cognition is found to be significantly hampered, resulting in a life-long impact on their development.

Studies[6] have also shown that the education of children, especially the girl child, is also significantly impacted by poor sanitation. Frequent bouts of illness among children leads to their missing school for significant number of days. Elder children have to stay at home to take care of their sick siblings, again leading to loss of attendance. Girls are often forced to miss school or even drop out of education due to lack of sanitation facilities in their schools.

Other implications of poor sanitation and the resultant illness is the loss of productivity of the family members. The adult members of households have to either forego going for productive labour, or become weak to fully realise their productive potential or have to stay home away from work to take care of sick members of the household. This leads to loss of wages, which leads them to getting trapped in the vicious cycle of poverty.

It is also known that lack of adequate sanitation leads to significant losses for the country. As per recent study, carried out by Water and Sanitation Programme (WSP), if the economic losses linked to poor sanitation are monetised, the results are staggering. The adverse economic impact of inadequate sanitation in India could be of the order of Rs. 2.4 lakh crore (US$ 53.8billion), or Rs. 2,180 (US $ 48) per person based on published details like sanitation coverage, child mortality etc., as of the year 2006. This is the equivalent of 6.4 per cent of Gross Domestic Product (GDP).[7] While the country has come a long way since then and all these indices stands improved to great extent, the linkage between inadequate sanitation coverage and economic loss is of extreme significance.

Within the economic losses suffered by the people due to poor sanitation, the poorest bear disproportionate share of the burden as the sanitation coverage requires more improvement among poor. Examining the impact of economic losses by wealth quintiles, it is found that impacts are more heavily borne by those in the rural areas, and among this, the largest sufferers are those in the first wealth quintile in the rural areas. This quintile includes the poorest in rural areas.

Objectives of the Paper

The aims and objectives of the paper are as follows:

1. oEvaluate the implementation of the policies and programmes which are meant for achieving total sanitation in India and in Karnataka especially in Hyderabad-Karnataka Region.
2. oTexamine the real situations of the sanitary practices in India generally and in Hyderabad-Karnataka particularly.
3. oTanalyse the policies, programmes and practices of sanitation in India and in Karnataka especially in Hyderabad-Karnataka region.
4. oSuggest the measures which are to be taken for achieving the total sanitation in India generally in Karnataka especially in Hyderabad-Karnataka region particularly.

Methodolgy

The methodology adopted for this study is one of the doctrinal and content analysis methods of research. This paper analyses the laws, policies, programmes and schemes on the rural sanitation system more specifically in the Hyderabad-Karnataka region of the Karnataka state. Sanitation today comprehensively includes a whole range of issues like liquid and solid waste disposal, food hygiene, and personal, domestic as well as environmental hygiene. However, the paper touches upon the sanitation with respect to toilet system and Open Defecation (OD) only.

Policy Framework on Rural Sanitation

There are numbers of the legal and policy frameworks on the subject of sanitation in India which are meant for observing the sanitation practices. In India, we are having these policy frameworks: the Constitution of India, the Minimum Wages Act, 1948, the Untouchability Offences Act, 1955 later it has been renamed as Protection of Civil Rights Act, 1955 in the year 1976, Bonded Labour Abolition Act, 1976, the Prohibition of Child Labour Act, 1986, the Scheduled Castes and Scheduled Tribes (Prevention of Atrocities) Act, 1989, The Protection of Human Rights Act, 1993, The Employment of Manual Scavengers and Construction of Dry Latrines (Prohibition) Act, 1993, and the Bhopal Declaration, 2002 and recently enacted the Prohibition of Employment as Manual Scavengers and their Rehabilitation Act, 2013. Among these, it is pertinent to focus on two important instruments which have been enacted directly to deal with the sanitation.

(1) The Employment of Manual Scavengers and Construction of Dry Latrines (Prohibition) Act, 1993

This law is a landmark in the history of sanitation which is meant for achieving sanitation and eradication of manual scavenging in India. It is pertinent to aims, objectives and some provisions of this Act. This Act is a concrete step in the direction of abolishing the age-old and hereditary occupation, but the respective governments have taken rains in ratifying and implementing Act indicates the Union as well as the State Governments negligence and reluctance towards this voiceless, oppressed and unorganised community, involved in manual scavenging. The Act was passed by the Parliament in 1993, and delayed three and half years for its application. Though the Act was passed in 1993, but came into practice from January 26, 1997. The Act was passed on the initiative of five State Legislatures, *i.e.,* Goa , Karnataka, Maharashtra, Tripura and West Bengal. Later some States have adopted the Act. The Act applicable States are Andhra Pradesh, Goa, Karnataka, Maharashtra, Tripura, West Bengal, Orissa, Punjab, Assam, Haryana, Bihar and Gujarat.[8] State of Delhi ratified as late as in 2010. Some states have been requested to frame the rules for effective enforcement. The main objective of the Act is seeking permanent solution to total eradication of the manual scavenging.

Section-2 defines various terms used in the Act among which some important ones have been reproduced hereunder:

1. "Dry latrine" means a latrine other than a water-seal latrine;[9]
2. "Latrine" means a place set apart for defecation together with the structure comprising such place, the receptacle therein for collection of human excreta and the fittings and apparatus, if any, connected therewith;[10]
3. "Manual scavenger" means a person engaged in or employed for manually carrying human excreta and the expression "manual scavenging" shall be construed accordingly;[11]
4. Water-seal latrine" means a pour-flush latrine, water flush latrine or a sanitary latrine with minimum water-seal of 20 millimetres diameter in which human excreta is pushed in or flushed by water.[12]

Section-3 of the Act prohibits,

- Employing or engaging manual scavengers,
- The construction or maintenance of dry latrines.

If any one, who violates the provisions of the Act, can be treated as cognizable offender, he shall be punished with imprisonment to the extent of one year or with fine to the extent of Rs. 2,000 or with both.

The Act also provides for –

- Formulating various schemes to convert dry latrines into water-sealed latrines.
- Constructing new water-sealed latrines.
- Rendering technical and financial assistance for new or alternative low cost sanitation to local bodies and other agencies.
- Construction and maintenance of community latrines and regulation of their use on a pay-and-use basis.
- Constructing and maintaining shared latrines in slum areas for the benefit of citizens, who are socially and economically backward.
- Registering manual scavengers and rehabilitating them.
- Financing by the Housing and Urban Development Corporation Limited (HUDCO) or other agencies to construct water-sealed latrines or to convert dry latrines into water-sealed latrines.[13]

(2) The Prohibition of Employment as Manual Scavengers and their Rehabilitation Act, 2013

The Supreme Court of India has strictly directed the Government of India to completely ban the manual scavenging in India. The Government of India enacted an Act called *"The Prohibition of Employment as Manual Scavengers and their Rehabilitation Act, 2013"* for abolition of evil of manual scavenging and for the welfare of manual scavengers. The Act received the assent of the President on 18.09.2013.[14] The objectives of the Act are stated as follows:

1. AAct to provide for the prohibition of employment as manual scavengers, rehabilitation of manual scavengers and their families;
2. oTpromote among the citizens fraternity assuring the dignity of the individual is enshrined as one of the goals in the Preamble to the Constitution;
3. oTuphold the right to live with dignity which is implicit in the Fundamental Rights guaranteed in Part -III of the Constitution;
4. oTimplement Article 46 of the Constitution, *inter alia,* provides that the State shall protect the weaker sections, and, particularly, the Scheduled Castes and the Scheduled Tribes from social injustice and all forms of exploitation;

5. oEnd the dehumanising practice of manual scavenging arising from the continuing existence of insanitary latrines and highly iniquitous caste system, still in various parts of the country, and the existing laws have not proved adequate in eliminating the twin evils of insanitary latrines and manual scavenging;

6. oCorrect the historical injustice and indignity suffered by the manual scavengers, and to rehabilitate them to a life of dignity.

The Act provides for various aspects such as discontinuation of manual scavenging, survey and rehabilitation of manual scavengers and of the insanitary latrines which are critically analysed as follows:

1. Section 2(1)(d) of theAct defines "hazardous cleaning." This definition of "hazardous cleaning" in the Act will increase the incidents of entering the drainage/manhole to clean and consequently deaths of manhole workers as the Act allows manhole workers to enter manhole by providing protective gears. It is also a matter of serious concern that what type of protective gear and other cleaning devices will be listed when rules are framed. Instead, manhole workers should be allowed to enter when it is required with full safety equipments like oxygen cylinder, torch, constant observance of manhole worker from computer etc. They must be provided professional training by training institute like fire brigade and only certified manhole worker will be allowed to enter, when it is required with full precautions and safety devices.

2. Section 2(1)(e) of theAct defines -"insanitary latrine" means a latrine which requires human excreta to be cleaned or otherwise handled manually, either *in situ*, or in an open drain or pit into which the excreta is discharged or flushed out, before the excreta fully decomposes in such manner as may be prescribed: Provided that a water flush latrine in a railway passenger coach, when cleaned by an employee with the help of such devices and using such protective gear, as the Central Government may notify in this behalf, shall not be deemed to be an insanitary latrine.[15] Indian railway is one of the major promoters of manual scavenging, and by this Act, it is exempted from the definition of insanitary latrines. So, Indian railway will continue to practice manual scavenging. Water flush latrine in a railway passenger coach at railway stations will make someone to clean manually human excreta and practice will continue as prevalent at present.

3. Section 2(1)(g) of theAct defines "manual scavenger." "Manual scavenger" means a person engaged or employed, at the commencement of this Act or at any time thereafter, by an individual or a local authority or an agency or a contractor, for manually cleaning, carrying, disposing of, or otherwise handling in any manner, human excreta in an insanitary latrine or in

an open drain or pit into which the human excreta from the insanitary latrines is disposed of, or on a railway track or in such other spaces or premises, as the Central Government or a State Government may notify, before the excreta fully decomposes in such manner as may be prescribed, and the expression "manual scavenging" shall be construed accordingly.

Explanation.—For the purpose of this clause,—

(*a*) "Engaged or employed" means being engaged or employed on a regular or contract basis;

(*b*) A person engaged or employed to clean excreta with the help of such devices and using such protective gear, as the Central Government may notify in this behalf, shall not be deemed to be a 'manual scavenger.'[16] The Act has addressed only an insanitary latrine or open drain or pit. Due to growth of population and lack of sufficient public toilets and individual toilets, insanitary toilets and open defecation is wide spread and consequently lead to manual scavenging. Besides, the explanation in the Act 2 (1)(b) has killed the soul of the Act, and it has legitimised manual scavenging by stating that it can be done by using protective gears and other devices.

4. Section 4(1) of the Act empowers the local authority to conduct survey of insanitary latrines and publish the list. Here, the Act talks about the identification of insanitary latrines only. But, the Act does not mention of identification of spots where open defecation is done and consequently someone has to clean manually human excreta from the open spaces. Local authority has not willingness, time as well as expertise to conduct survey to identify insanitary latrines. There is also possibility that local authority will not identify actual numbers of insanitary latrines when insanitary latrines are constructed and maintained by the local authority itself. The survey may be on paper by local authority. Instead, the task to conduct survey may be given to some professional designated agency. Also, period of two months is insufficient for carrying out survey of insanitary latrines.

5. Section 4(2) of the Act provides for constructing adequate number of sanitary latrines within three years from the date of commencement of this Act, so that open defecation can be eliminated. So, the practice of manual scavenging and open defecation will continue for three years from the date of commencement of this Act.

6. Section 39 (1) of the Act provides for exemption of the areas, buildings class of persons from the applicability of provisions of this Act for a period of not exceeding six months period at a time. This is a major gap in the Act, as it empowers the Government to exempt the provisions of the Act. And consequently, manual scavenging will continue to prevail. It is very shocking

that the most inhumane practice will be allowed to continue for six months in particular cases if government intends to continue.

It can be said that, the provisions of the Act are not intended to achieve total sanitation by eradication of manual scavenging. The Act talks more on insanitary latrines, open drain and pit while widespread prevalence of manual scavenging and open defecation due to lack of sufficient sanitation, it does not address effectively. Manual scavenging practised in Indian Railways and especially coaches in train will continue. The Act has given sword to the Government that they provide devices and safety equipments to manual scavengers.[17]

Programmes and Schemes on Rural Sanitation

The concept of sanitation has grown in understanding and perception across the country from being addressed as a simple latrine programme to a much wider program addressing issues related to improvement in the quality of life and is now one of the basic determinants of human development index. The importance of sanitation as a contributory factor for the wealth and well-being of a nation was recognised and addressed by the government of India way back in the pre-independence period by the *Bhore* Committee and soon after Independence by the Environmental Hygiene Committee (1948-49). Sanitation today comprehensively includes a whole range of issues like liquid and solid waste disposal, food hygiene, and personal, domestic as well as environmental hygiene.[18]

The Government of India launched the Central Rural Sanitation Programme (CRSP) in 1986 primarily with the objective of improving the quality of life of the rural people and also to provide privacy and dignity to women. The Total Sanitation Campaign (TSC) emphasises more on Information, Education and Communication (IEC), Human Resource Development and Capacity Building Activities to increase awareness among the rural people and generation of demand for sanitary facility. It also aims at enhancing people's capacity to choose appropriate option through alternate delivery mechanisms as per their economic condition. Encouraged by the success of *Nirmal Gram Puraskar*, TSC has been renamed as "*Nirmal Bharat Abhiyan*" (NBA).

The responsibility for provision of sanitation facilities in India is decentralised and primarily rests with local government bodies – *Gram Panchayat* in rural areas and municipalities or corporations in urban areas. The State and the Central Governments have a facilitating role that takes the form of framing and enabling policies/guidelines, providing financial and capacity-building support and monitoring progress. In the Central Government, the Planning Commission, through Five Year Plan, guides investment in the sector by allocating funding for strategic priorities.

1. Pre-1986: Ad hoc Investments through Five Year Plan

Rural sanitation did not feature on the investment horizon during the first five plan periods as reflected in its negligible funding share. However, it received prominence from the Sixth Plan (1980-85), onwards amid the launch of the International Drinking Water Supply and Sanitation Decade in 1980. In addition, responsibility for rural sanitation at the central level was also shifted from the Central Public Health and Environmental Engineering Organisation to the Rural Development Department.

2. Central Rural Sanitation Programme (1986-99)

In 1986, the Rural Development Department initiated India's first national programme on rural sanitation, the Central Rural Sanitation Programme (CRSP). The CRSP interpreted sanitation as construction of household toilets, and focussed on the promotion of a single technology model (double pit, pour-flush toilets) through hardware subsidies to generate demand. The key issue of motivating behaviour change to end open defecation and use toilets was not addressed, contributing to the programme's failure. Although more than Rs 660 crore was invested and over 90 lakh latrines constructed, rural sanitation grew at just one per cent annually throughout the 1990s and the Census of 2001 found that only 22 per cent of rural households had access to toilets.

3. Total Sanitation Campaign (1999-2012)

In light of the relatively poor performance of the CRSP, the Government of India restructured the programme, leading to the launch of the TSC in 1999. A key learning that informed TSC design was that toilet construction does not automatically translate into toilet usage, and people must be motivated to end open defecation if rural sanitation outcomes are to be achieved. A second key learning was the recognition of the "public good" dimensions of safe sanitation and the realisation that health outcomes will not be achieved unless the entire community adopts safe sanitation. Accordingly, the TSC introduced the concept of a "demand-driven, community-led approach to total sanitation" (DDWS 1999). This was further strengthened with the introduction of the NGP in 2003, which incentivised the achievement of collective outcomes in terms of 100 per cent achievement of total sanitation by a Panchayati Raj Institution (PRI).

Key Features of the TSC Include

(1) A community-led approach with focus on collective achievement of total sanitation;

(2) Focus on Information, Education and Communication (IEC) to mobilise and motivate communities towards safe sanitation;

(3) Minimum capital incentives only for Below Poverty Line (BPL) households, disbursed post construction and usage;

(4) Flexible menu of technology options;

(5) Development of a supply chain to meet the demand stimulated at the community level;

(6) Priority to School Sanitation and Hygiene Education (SSHE), and

(7) Fiscal incentive in the form of a cash prize –NGP

4. Nirmal Gram Puraskar (NGP)

The Nirmal Gram Puraskar of the Government of India, introduced in 2003, is an innovative programme that offers fiscal incentives in the form of a cash prize to local governments that achieve 100 per cent sanitation, that is, they are 100 per cent Open Defecation Free (ODF) and have tackled issues of solid and liquid waste management (SLWM).

5. Nirmal Gram Yojana

Karnataka State commenced an exclusive rural sanitation project under Nirmal Gram Yojana in 1995. The programme concentrated on promoting construction of house-hold latrines (HHL) in rural areas through providing subsidy of Rs. 2,000 for BPL families and Rs. 1,200 for APL families. Till 2004-05, more than 10.30 lakh HHLs have been constructed in the state. Since FY 2005-06, the allocation for the project has become an integral part of the state's contribution to Total Sanitation Campaign.[19]

6. Panchsutra

This is a comprehensive rural habitation improvement project in 1,300 villages under a scheme called *Panchsutra*. The programme is being funded through a HUDCO loan of 80 per cent, 10 per cent contribution from community and 10 per cent by the state government. Under the project, community contribution can be partly in cash and partly in kind. The project is a comprehensive sanitation programme of a village with five components, *viz.*, covering paved roads, sullage and storm water drains, individual household latrines, community compost yards and smokeless *chullahs* for every household. Each village gets an allocation of around Rs 20 lakh.[20]

Practice and Performance of Rural Sanitation Programmes

1. National Level Sanitation Performance

After sluggish progress throughout the eighties and nineties, rural sanitation coverage received a fillip with the implementation of the TSC. As can be seen from Figure 1 below, individual household latrine coverage has nearly tripled from just 21.9 per cent at national level as reported by the Census in 2001 to around 65 per cent in 2010, according to the latest self-reported data by districts to the Department of Drinking Water and Sanitation on line monitoring system. This translates to 35 crore of rural people gaining access to sanitation in the last decade.

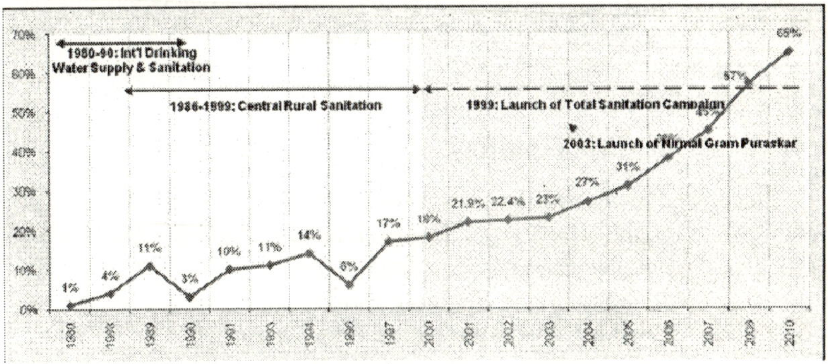

Fig. 1: Rural Sanitation Coverage in India

Source: Government of India, Department of Drinking Water and Sanitation. http://ddws.nic.in. Accessed in March, 2010.

Since its launch, the NGP has been successful as a fiscal incentive to motivate scaling up of rural sanitation. The number of winners has gone up from approximately 40 in 2005 to 22,569 in 2009, as can be seen from Figure-2. The number of people, who are living in normal communities, is well above 14 crore (18 per cent of the total rural population).

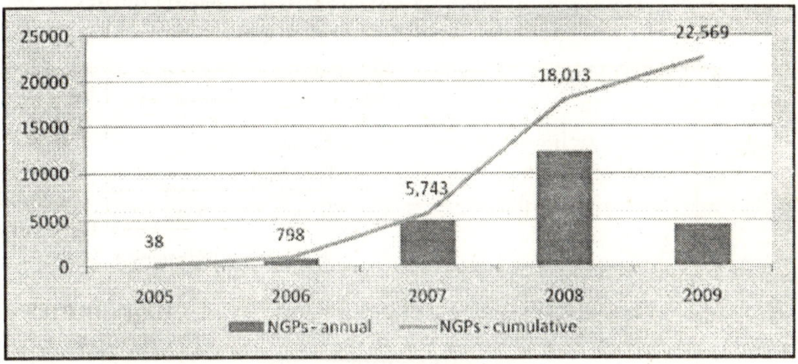

Fig. 2: NGP Winners (2005-09)

Source: Government of India, Department of Drinking Water and Sanitation. http://ddws.nic.in. accessed in March, 2010.

2. State Level Sanitation Performance

Despite the undeniable upward trend at the national level, these aggregated performance figures do not reflect disparities between and within states in terms of coverage on IHHL. The national level TSC monitoring system, which is based on the self-reported data by the districts, demonstrates this wide disparity. In terms of Individual Household Latrines (IHHL) coverage, whereas some states have achieved full coverage, some others have barely managed to reach about 30 per cent. On the achievement of NGP GPs, while some states have managed to make about 97 per cent of their GPs Nirmal, others have had none of their GPs winning NGPs.

3. Hyderabad-Karnataka Region

Hyderabad-Karnataka Region consists of revenue Districts of Gulbarga, Bidar, Yadgir, Raichur, Bellary and Koppal. This region is highly backward in terms of economic conditions of the people, peoples, access to educational and employment opportunities. For these reasons, the region has been given special status under the Constitution by inserting new Article 371J in 2013.

Hyderabad-Karnataka region is suffers with open defecation wherein the sanitation programme is not fully successful. In Hyderabad-Karnataka region Bidar District 56 per cent, Bellary 54 per cent, Koppal 63 per cent, Gulbarga 38 per cent, Yadgir 26 per cent and Raichur 22 per cent toilets has been built.[21] It means the poor and middle class people used to go open defecation and some handy people of rich people used to build sanitary latrine and rest of the people used to build insanitary latrines which necessarily demand the services of manual scavengers.

Table-1: Individual Household Latrines (IHHL) Coverage in H-K Region (Except Bellary and Koppal)

Districts	*No. Of Households*			*Per Cent of Households having IHHL*			*Per Cent of Households having Community Toilets*	*Per cent of Households not using Toilets*
	Total	*BPL*	*APL*	*Total*	*BPL*	*APL*		
Gulbarga	4362	3020	1342	9.90	11.42	6.48	0.46	89.64
Bidar	6581	4508	2073	13.99	11.76	18.86	0.23	85.78
Yadgir	5409	3352	2057	9.13	9.93	7.83	0.55	90.31
Raichur	14761	9486	5275	17.13	15.05	20.87	29.69	53.18

Source: NLM Regular Monitoring by NLMs 2013-14, Phase–I, (Karnataka), Ministry of Rural Development, Government of India.

Table-2: Individual Household Latrines (IHHL) Coverage in H-K Region (Except Bellary and Koppal)

Districts	*No. Of Villages Visited by the NLMs*	*No. Of Villages Visited NGP Awarded*	*Per cent of Households in the Village having access to Toilet Facility*					*Evidence/Reporting of Open Defecation Observed*
			Upto 25	*26-50*	*51-75*	*76-99*	*100*	
Gulbarga	10	1	0.00	100.00	0.00	0.00	0.00	100.00
Bidar	10	0	0.00	0.00	0.00	0.00	0.00	0.00
Yadgir	10	0	0.00	0.00	0.00	0.00	0.00	0.00
Raichur	10	0	0.00	0.00	0.00	0.00	0.00	0.00

Source: NLM Regular Monitoring by NLMs 2013-14, Phase–I, (Karnataka), Ministry of Rural Development, Government of India.

Table-3: Institutional Coverage under TSC in H-K Region (Except Bellary and Koppal)

Districts	*No. Of Villages Visited by the NLMs*	*No. of Total Schools*	*Per cent of Schools having toilet facility*	*Per cent of Up. Primary*	*Per cent of Schools found defunct/not use/locked*	*No. of Total Anganwadis*	*Per cent of Anganwadis having toilet facility*	*Per cent of Anganwadis having baby friendly toilet*	*Per cent of Anganwadis toilet found defunct/not in use/locked*
Gulbarga	10	15	100.00	84.62	33.33	24	16.67	0.00	8.33
Bidar	10	30	99.67	62.50	10.00	41	14.63	0.00	9.76
Yadgir	10	15	93.33	88.89	6.67	22	50.00	0.00	18.18
Raichur	10	244	25.00	4.00	0.00	107	30.84	14.02	0.00

Source: NLM Regular Monitoring by NLMs 2013-14, Phase–I, (Karnataka), Ministry of Rural Development, Government of India.

The facts and figures of the individual districts of the Hyderabad-Karnataka region are highlighted in the following manner:

(1) Gulbarga District

Gulbarga district in Karnataka state is one of the most backward districts in the State and occupies a lowest position in economic as well as human development. The district is a drought- prone area which further adds to the vulnerability of the poor and the minorities living in the district.

The houses in rural areas generally lack sanitation facilities. In Gulbarga district, in rural areas only 10 per cent of households have proper sanitation facilities. The availability of toilets and drainage facility at the household level is presented in the following table.

Table-4: Community-wise Availability of Toilets and Drainage in Gulbarga District (Per cent)

Community	*Toilet*		*Drainage*
	In-house	*Outside*	
Hindu	3.40	96.60	12.14
Muslim	1.22	98.78	11.04
Total	**3.03**	**96.97**	**11.95**

Source: A Baseline Survey of Minority Concentration District of India – Gulbarga – Karnataka, for Institute of Human Development, New Delhi, sponsored by the Ministry of Minority Affairs, Government of India, 2008.

The facilities providing sanitation and drainage are highly inadequate and need urgent attention. Only 3.4 per cent of the Hindu households and 1.22 per cent of the Muslim households have toilet facilities. About 96 per cent of the households do not have any toilet facilities and practice open field defecation. This situation prevails despite of the total sanitation campaign being implemented in the district. Lack of toilet facilities puts the women folk into difficulty. About 12 per cent of Hindu households and 11 per cent of Muslim households have drainage facilities. In case of remaining households, the water used by the households is left flowing on the road which causes many health problems in the District.[22]

The survey conducted by Arghyam in 2008-09, reveal as seven per cent of the population of the Gulbarga District having access to toilets and most of them use pour-flush toilets and 23 per cent of the population is having facility of drainage outside the home.[23]

(2) Bidar District

Bidar District in Karnataka is one of the most backward districts in the state and occupies a lower position in economic as well as human development. The position of the district in Human development is 21st among 27 districts in the state.[24] Bidar district is consists of five taluks namely Bidar, Humnabad, Basavakalyan, Bhalki and Aurad. Bidar District is primarily a rural district. As per 2001 Census 77 per cent of the total population lives in rural areas.[25]

The District is 100 per cent dependent of ground for their domestic needs. The sanitation in Bidar District is weak as the toilet facilities are seriously lacking in rural households in the district. Only 9.4 per cent of the households in rural areas have this facility. Others practice open defecation. There is no significant difference across the Hindu and Muslim households, which indicates poor level of sanitation in rural areas. Sanitation is an important requirement of better health conditions of the people. This situation prevails in the district despite of the implementation of Total Sanitation Campaign programme which aims at universalisation of sanitation facilities by 2009; the district is nowhere near the target. The gap between the district and the nation is 29.8 per cent. Drainage facilities are also not available in rural areas. The multi-sectoral plan should bridge this basic development gap in the district.[26]

Table- 5: Percentage of Households with Water Close Set Latrines

Bidar District in 2008	All India in 2005	Development Gaps Between All India and District	Development Priority of the District
9.4	39.2	-29.84	1

Source: Baseline Survey, 2008.

In the year 2010 under the Total Sanitation Campaign (TCS), a Centrally sponsored programme, 58,384 toilets for Below Poverty Line (BPL) and 1,09,155 toilets for households of Above Poverty Line (APL) families have been built. The best success rate has been with school toilets. All the 1,024 toilets in schools across the district have been built. The success rate in building toilets in *Anganwadis* has also been 100 per cent.[27]

The survey conducted by Arghyam in 2008-09, four per cent of the population of the Bidar District having access to toilets and most of them use pour flush toilets and 23 per cent of the population is having facility of drainage outside the home.[28]

(3) Yadgir District

Yadgir District population according to Census 2011 is 1,172,985 of which male and female were 591,104 and 581,881 respectively. The average literacy rate of Yadgir District according to 2011 is 52.36 per cent compared to 39.90 per cent of 2001 Census. If things are looked out at gender-wise, male and female literacy was 63.33 and 41.31 respectively.[29]

Government of India has been implementing various schemes and programmes since 1986 to ensure total sanitation in rural India. Yet, open defecation has remained a problem that perplexes policy-makers and civil society alike. So, Yadgir District is no exception. This can be known from this Table.

Table-6: Individual Household Latrines (IHHL) Coverage in the District

No. of Households			*Per cent of Households having IHHL*			*Per cent of Households having Community Toilets*	*% of Households not using Toilets*
Total	*BPL*	*APL*	*Total*	*BPL*	*APL*		
5409	3352	2057	9.13	9.93	7.83	0.55	90.31

Source: NLM Regular Monitoring by NLMs 2013-14 Phase – I, (Karnataka), Ministry of Rural Development, Government of India.

(4) Raichur District

The Raichur District is one of the districts of the Hyderabad-Karnataka region comparatively less in development when it is compared with the other districts of the region. Raichur District consists of five talukas with population of 16,69,762 having literacy rate of 62 per cent .

As far as sanitation is concerned as per the survey conducted by Arghyam in 2008-09, 2 per cent of the population of the Raichur District having access to toilets and most of them use pour flush toilets and 38 per cent of the population is having facility of drainage outside the home.[30]

(5) Bellary District

The Bellary District is one of the districts of the Hyderabad-Karnataka region comparatively superior in developmental aspect when it is compared with the other districts of the region. As per 2001 census, the population of the district stood at 20.27 lakhs. The rural population constitute 65 per cent. The density of population is 240 per sq. km. which is slightly higher than the state average of 235 per sq. km.[31]

As far as sanitation is concerned as per the survey conducted by Arghyam in 2008-09, 13 per cent of the population of the Bellary District having access to toilets and most of them use pour flush toilets and 32 per cent of the population having facility of drainage outside the home.[32]

(6) Koppal District

The Koppal District consists of four taluks having 134 *Gram Panchayats* with population of 11,96,089 having literacy rate of 62.39 per cent .Tthe district receives average rainfall of 572 mm. The district is basically depending upon ground water which has been over exploited; the water contains high fluoride and nitrate in some areas.

As far as sanitation is concerned as per the survey conducted by *Arghyam* in 2008-09, four per cent of the population of the Koppal District having access to toilets and most of them use pour flush toilets and 14 per cent of the population is having facility of drainage outside the home.[33]

Conclusion

Sanitation is one of the glaring problems of the human society especially in Hyderabad-Karnataka region as the people of this region is highly poor, illiterate, unaware about the importance of sanitation and hygiene. Many kinds of the survey indicated that the region is still having the poor sanitation leading towards open defecation (OD) resulting in various kinds of health problems which requires urgent attention so as to address the problem of the sanitation. The role of Parishudhan NGO of Infosys collaborated with Kottala Bsaveshwara Education Society, Sedam can be appreciated here for doing yeoman service to bring awareness about the sanitation and construction of toilets in the region. It is all depend upon both the people and the government to observe and implement the instruments and policies and take the advantages and benefits of the schemes and programmes pertaining to the sanitation for achieving total sanitation in India and in Karnataka especially the Hyderabad-Karnataka region.

End Notes

1. Department of Drinking Water and Sanitation Ministry of Rural Development, Government of India, Draft 2.1, December, 18th 2010.

Towards Nirmal Bharat: Rural Sanitation and Hygiene Strategy, 2010 –2022, p. 5.

2. See http://www.indiasanitationportal.org/397.
3. Water and Sanitation Programme (WSP) Economics of Sanitation Initiative 2010.
4. National Family Health Survey- III, 2005-06.
5. UNICEF, 2009; Dillingham and Guerrant, 2004.
6. IRC 2009a; UN Water 2008; Wash in Schools, undated.
7. Water and Sanitation Programme (WSP), Economics of Sanitation Initiative, 2010.
8. Press Information Bureau, Government of India, www.pib.nic.in.
9. Section 2(c) of the *Employment of Manual Scavengers and Construction of Dry Latrines (Prohibition) Act, 1993.*
10. Section 2(i) of the *Employment of Manual Scavengers and Construction of Dry Latrines (Prohibition) Act, 1993.*
11. Section 2(j) of the *Employment of Manual Scavengers and Construction of Dry Latrines (Prohibition) Act, 1993.*
12. Section 2(n) of the *Employment of Manual Scavengers and Construction of Dry Latrines (Prohibition) Act, 1993.*
13. Know Your Rights Series, *Manual Scavenging*, Published by the NHRC, New Delhi, p. 1.
14. *The Gazette of India Extraordinary* [Part-II, Section-1], New Delhi, the 19th September, 2013.
15. Section 2(1)(e) of *The Prohibition of Employment as Manual Scavengers and their Rehabilitation Act, 2013.*
16. Section 2(1)(g) of the *Prohibition of Employment as Manual Scavengers and their Rehabilitation Act, 2013.*
17. Jitendra Rathod, *Critical Analysis of the Prohibition of Employment as Manual Scavengers and Their Rehabilitation Act, 2013, Beyond Headlines*, see http://beyondheadlines.in/2013/09/critical-analysis-of-the-prohibition-of-employment-as-manual-scavengers-and-their-rehabilitation-act-2013/ visited on 9.10.2013.
18. *Sector Status Study of Rural Water Supply and Sanitation in Karnataka* (Draft Final Report, Sector Status Study Team, Bangalore, February, 2006), p. 70.

19. *Ibid.* p. 37.

20. *Ibid.*

21. *Vijaya Karnataka,* Kannada Daily, December 15, 2012, p. 5.

22. Chaya Deogankar, *A Baseline Survey of Minority Concentration District of India – Gulbarga – Karnataka,* for Institute of Human Development, New Delhi, sponsored by the Ministry of Minority Affairs, Government of India, 2008, p. 35.

23. *Report of ASHWAS (A Survey of House-hold Water and Sanitation) Karnataka – 2008-09,* conducted by Arghyam See http://www.ashwas. indiawaterportal.org/downloads/state/report.pdf.

24. *Baseline Survey of Minority Concentration District (Executive Summary of Bidar District (Karnataka))* of the Ministry of Minority Affairs, Government of India, 2008 see. http://www.icssr.org/Bidar.pdf.

25. *Census Report, 2001.*

26. *Baseline Survey of Minority Concentration District (Executive Summary of Bidar District (Karnataka))* of the Ministry of Minority Affairs, Government of India, 2008 see. http://www.icssr.org/Bidar.pdf.

27. http://hindu.com/thehindu/thscrip/print.pl?file=20100910583803OO.htm&date=2010/09/10/&prd=th&.

28. Report of ASHWAS (A Survey of House-hold Water and Sanitation) Karnataka – 2008-09 conducted by Arghyam See http://www.ashwas.indiawaterportal.org/downloads/state/report.pdf.

29. http://en.wikipedia.org/wiki/Yadgir.

30. Report of ASHWAS (A Survey of House-hold Water and Sanitation) Karnataka – 2008-09 conducted by Arghyam See http://www.ashwas.indiawaterportal.org/downloads/state/report.pdf.

31. District Profile, Bellary District Disaster Management Plan.

32. Report of ASHWAS (A Survey of House-hold Water and Sanitation) Karnataka – 2008-09 conducted by Arghyam See http://www.ashwas.indiawaterportal.org/downloads/state/report.pdf.

33. Report of ASHWAS (A Survey of House-hold Water and Sanitation) Karnataka – 2008-09 conducted by Arghyam See http://www.ashwas.indiawaterportal.org/downloads/state/report.pdf.

32

Evalution of SAARC Agriculture Perspective on Agricultural and Rural Development

Huchhe Gowda

Introduction

Region-wide agriculture is facing several challenges, threatening its growth and sustainability. The physical and economic environment in which agricultural activities are undertaken is changing rapidly and getting complex. This necessitates preparedness to face upcoming challenges and unfolding new reality. Many changes affecting agriculture transcends geography and are trans-boundary in nature: climate change, trans-boundary animal and plant diseases pose formidable challenges which require strong regional co-operation to face. 'SAARC Agriculture Vision- 2020' would help maximise benefits from available options; enhance ability to face threats and new challenges and to harness the opportunities forthcoming. Develop science-based strategy for collective response to threat, challenges and opportunities and global shocks, based on ground realities of SAARC countries.

Objectives of the Study

The main objective is to evalute the SAARC Agriculture Perspective on Agricultural and Rural Development. The specific objectives of the study include:

1. To study the challenges and opportunities of agricultural and rural development in SAARC countries.
2. To access the vast agricultural development policies and current issues of agriculture.

3. To evaluate the farmers with value-based information to improve their productivity and provide timely information.

Methodology

This study is largely-based on secondary data, along with some amount of primary data. The secondary data were collected from National Council for Applied Economic Research (NCEAR), Census of India, National Sample Survey Organisation (NSSO), Central Statistical Organisation (CSO), District Rural Development Authority (DRDA), and District Statistical Handbook, etc.

SAARC Region : Ground Reality

The region is home to 1.567 billion people (23.7 per cent of global population). The share of the region in terms of global land and water resources is, however, much lower than the population share, e.g., region's geographic coverage is mere 3.95 per cent of the global land mass. Because of high population pressure on land, percentage of arable land to total area is much higher than the global average, e.g., the share of the region in global arable land is 14 per cent . The region also has very high incidence of poverty and hunger. Based on the country-wise data (Asian Development Bank), it is estimated that 451 million people in the region live below poverty line; and proportion of these hardcore people in the total population is 28.83 per cent. The principal reason for high incidence of poverty in the region is low per capita income and inequitable distribution of income; with 23.7 per cent share in global population, the region has only 2.62 per cent share in global income.

Low Income, High Poverty, Under-nutrition

Per capita Gross National Income (GNI) in the eight member states ranges from $345 to $3,277- lowest per capita income is in Afghanistan while the highest is in Maldives. Per capita GNI in India and Pakistan is around US$ 1,000. Low level of income is one of the primary reasons for wide prevalence of poverty and severe under-nutrition. Poverty in the region varies between 21 per cent – 53 per cent while 17 per cent – 30 per cent of population in different countries does not consume minimum level of globally recommended dietary energy.

Predominance of Agriculture

Majority population in South Asia lives in rural areas, depending on agricultural activities as their principal source of income and employment. Share of rural population in total population varies between 66 per cent in Pakistan to 86 per cent in Nepal. Except for Maldives, share of agriculture in total GDP varies between 16.5 per cent – 40 per cent (approx.). In Maldives, less than three per cent of total GDP is contributed by agriculture. Due to low productivity of agriculture, per worker income in agriculture is low and, as a consequence, the proportion of population living under poverty is quite high. Agriculture farming in South Asia is dominated by small holdings, *i.e.,* average size of holding is below 0.5 hectare in Bangladesh, below 1.0 hectare in Sri Lanka and Nepal. In India, average farm size is 1.41 hectare. Pakistan is much better endowed with land resources (average farm size is 3.0 hectare). Except Pakistan, holdings below one hectare account for more than 60 per cent of total farm holdings. Small size of holding is reflected in very low land to labour ratio. Except Pakistan and Afghanistan, one hectare of arable land supports more than one agriculture worker. Close to five workers draw their livelihood from one hectare of arable land in Bangladesh and Nepal. Another disquiet aspect of agriculture is increasing dependence on land for livelihood in all the countries, as manifested by rising ranks of workers per hectare of land.

Another serious disadvantage faced by the farmers in the region is heavy dependence on rain-fed agriculture. Area under irrigation as per cent of arable land is around 33 per cent in India, 39 per cent in Sri Lanka, 47 per cent in Nepal and 56 per cent in Bangladesh. In Pakistan, however, 90 per cent of agriculture is under irrigation. Livelihood security, eradication of poverty, reduction in hunger, and sustainable and inclusive growth of economy of each country thus critically hinge on the future of agriculture.

Agricultural Productivity

Cereal and pulses are the main staple region-wide. Per hectare yield of main staples in all the countries is however lower than world average. Growth rate in productivity is also low. Agricultural output growth has slowed down in most of the countries and, in other countries where growth is still at reasonably high level, it is becoming increasingly difficult to maintain that. Despite the high potential, agricultural productivity is getting stuck at low level and increase in productivity requires increased use of inputs. This is lowering efficiency of production and diminishing profit margins.

Major Challenges of Regional Agriculture

Increase and Sustaining Agricultural Growth

Growth rate of agriculture in SAARC region is low and unstable. Whereas total GDP in most member states has shown high growth in the recent past, except for Nepal and Sri Lanka, total GDP of other SAARC countries increased by more than five per cent per annum over the first six years of the present decade. Gap between growth rate of agriculture and non-agriculture sector is rising in all the countries.

Disparities between Agriculture and Non-agriculture Sectors

Labour force in agriculture is not shifting to non-agriculture sector despite high growth of the latter. As a result, per capita income in non-agriculture sector and urban areas is rising at a much faster rate compared to agriculture sector and rural areas. This raises concern over equity; and is adversely affecting the interest and investments in farm sector. Such inequality could be addressed in two ways: (i) by shifting work force from agriculture to non-agriculture sectors; and (ii) by raising overall growth in agriculture sector. Both the options are important for reducing income inequality and poverty in the region.

Poverty, Hunger, Under-nutrition

Reduction in poverty and under-nutrition is slow in most of the countries. Concerted efforts need to be put to meet the MDGs and SDGs – to which all SAARC countries have committed. Agriculture growth is necessary condition for access and affordability to ensure food and nutrition security.

Natural Resource Degradation

Natural resources *i.e.,* land, water and ecosystem are showing symptoms of degradation and fatigue and causing adverse effect on sustainability and prospects of future growth.

Climate Change

Climate change is now an accepted reality and, in some cases, is predicted to cause heavy damage to the region. South Asia is among the most vulnerable regions in the world to natural disasters related to climate change. Two main dimensions of climate change that would impact agriculture are increased temperature and changes in precipitation pattern. These changes taking place on a global scale would impact local agriculture and therefore affect the local and global food supply. It's difficult to precisely estimate how farming might be affected in different regions, as the impact on the agrarian economy in a given region/country will depend upon the interplay of the dynamic factors specific to each area.

Energy Scenario

In the context of deepening energy demand-supply imbalance, diversion of crops for use as feedstock for bio-fuel, especially in developed countries, is a growing concern. As future of all economic activities would be shaped by energy demand-supply, production choices, methods of production and product movement may become unpredictable. Energy solution in one part of the globe is causing more serious problem elsewhere, *e.g.,* rising energy prices are directly impacting food prices in several ways through increase in prices of agriculture inputs namely, fertiliser, pesticides, insecticides, increase in cost of operation of farm power and machinery, increase in transport cost. While agriculture is seen to have potential to provide an alternative to rising energy crisis, future course of agricultural production also considerably depends on global crude oil prices. Agriculture production would be required to move towards less energy-intensive production system in the future.

Bio-safety, Bio-security

Vulnerability and susceptibility of agriculture production are rising and resilience is declining. Plant and animal species are getting vulnerable to pest and diseases, sometimes turning into epidemic proportion causing large-scale destruction. Many of such occurrences are not confined to a particular location or to limited geography but are of trans-boundary in nature. Mechanisms to deal with these threats are either missing or weak.

Opportunities

New opportunities are arising on account of choice of technology, change in demand patterns, surge in value chains and supermarkets, revolution in Information and Communication Technology, institutional innovations and globalisation. Trade-based on comparative advantage is also offering many opportunities. Agriculture research is getting increasingly capital intensive. These necessitate sharing of technology and resource in research, extension and infrastructure. Opportunities are also unfolding in green energy and bio-fertiliser. If physical, ecological and socio-economic environment in which agriculture production takes place is not managed judiciously, it could lead to serious consequences in terms of production, food and nutrition security, vulnerability, economic stability, well-being and even survival of the majority population. The governments need to reflect upon the emerging scenario in and around agriculture; and prepare a medium and long-term perspective of agriculture in the region to adjust to emerging challenges and opportunities being faced by the agriculture sector.

Producers and Production Base

No productive activity can be sustained in the long-run by overlooking the health of the production base and the producers. The region thus needs to focus on farmers and natural resource system or, agriculture production base, *i.e.*, land, water, vegetation. Policies focussed on farming ignoring their implications on the farmers are not sustainable. Growth and development of farming therefore must improve welfare of farmers.

Output Growth Acceleration

Agriculture growth not only helps address poverty within the sector, but also promotes employment in non-farm rural activities and facilitates migration to non-agricultural avenues without causing distress. Growth in agriculture and overall rural development are thus essential for reducing poverty - not only by raising income of the poor, but also by checking escalation in food prices and keeping price of wage-goods low. This recognition calls for a shift in emphasis from 'growth' *per se* to 'inclusive growth.' Empirical evidence suggests its agriculture growth which has greater impact on reducing poverty than non-agriculture growth. Growth in output and farm income depends upon a numerous factors, *viz.,* prices of output and inputs, non-price factors. Raising growth requires remunerative pricing environment for output, access to improved technology, application of quality inputs and machinery. Further, growth has to be achieved from a shrinking natural resource base, *i.e.,* growth would come largely from increase in productivity. Much scope exists in raising farm output and income by diversification towards horticulture (fruits, vegetables, tuber crops, spices and medicinal and aromatic plants), livestock and fisheries.

Technology

Technology is the prime mover for growth. Considering the costs and constraints of resources, *e.g.,* water, nutrients and energy, genetic enhancement of productivity should be coupled with 'input use efficiency'. This can be made possible only by utilising full potential of the existing improved technologies; and by developing newer technologies. Large gaps exist between what can be attained at farmers' fields with adoption of improved technology and what is obtained with the existing practices followed by farmers. Potential for raising output through effective dissemination of technology is considerable. One primary reason is lack in marketing of technologies. As public extension system is proving increasingly inadequate for dissemination of technology, there is a need to involve private sector in marketing and dissemination of technology. This would require increased public-private sector participation through appropriate returns and incentives for the innovators and disseminators.

Several MNCs in developed countries are investing heavily in bio-technology; and are expected to come out with new seeds, inputs of high commercial value. There should be appropriate mechanism to access these frontier technologies and to ensure that costs of such technologies are affordable by the farmers.

Seed and Other Inputs

Quality seed is another primary determinant of productivity. Harnessing benefit of technology requires well-developed system for sales and distribution of seeds and plant propagation material. In almost all SAARC countries, supply of seed and plant propagation material is highly inadequate to meet the emerging and growing demand. The advantage of this is being taken by unscrupulous private trade. Development of a competitive and regulated seed industry, by involving private sector in seed production and distribution, is a critical imperative. The existing production farms are not able to cater to rising demand for fertilisers, agro-chemicals and other inputs. The region may consider more FDI inflow in these areas as domestic corporate sector is also found to take interest in these new ventures when there is challenge from outside.

Food Requirements

Long-term trend in consumption pattern at household-level demonstrates that per capita direct consumption of foodgrains has been on decline; and that of livestock and horticulture products has been on rise in most of the SAARC countries. Despite shift in dietary pattern, foodgrains are considered to be important for household food and nutrition security on four considerations: cereals and pulses are staple foods and there is no perfect substitution between staple foods and other foods; owing to inadequate level of intake of almost all foods, increased consumption of other foods, in most cases, fill dietary deficiency; foodgrains are the major and cheapest source of energy and protein as compared to other foods, and are thus vital for food and nutrition security of low income masses; increased production and consumption of livestock products resulting from rising per capita income require high growth in use of grain as feed for livestock. Foodgrains/cereals thus continue to be central to ensuring food security in South Asia. Any disruption in production leads to deep price shock and adverse impact on common people.

Demand projections for South Asia for low-income and high-income scenarios demonstrate that demand for cereals in the region would grow at one per cent and pulses by 1.7 per cent per annum; demand for edible oil is projected to grow by more than 1.6 per cent ; demand for fruits, vegetables and livestock to rise by approximately three per cent or more under high income scenario.

Sustainable Use/Management of Natural Resources

Agriculture is the main user of natural resources and it affects land, water, forests, soil conservation, genetic diversity of crop and livestock and other eco-system services. However, land and water resources need special attention for their sustainable use as they show increasing signs of stress/ degradation in all countries. Improving natural resource management requires right price signals to farmers, strengthening property rights and strengthening of natural resource-based institutional arrangements, *i.e.,* devolution of control to local organisations for community natural resource management. Better technologies and efficient ways of managing water and modern farm inputs are now available to make farming more sustainable. But, their widespread adoption is hindered by inappropriate pricing policies, insufficient training of farmers and a failure to manage negative externalities. Many opportunities exist to harness agriculture's potential as a provider of environmental services. The emergence of new markets and programmes like 'carbon credit' for payments for environmental services and 'green energy' manifests high promise; and should be pursued by local and national governments across the region.

Resource-conserving technologies are now available for various ecological regions. These can be very helpful to save water and energy, reduce cost and increase farmers' income. Adequate emphasis and investments are required to harvest and conserve rain water and optimally use available water. As water is emerging as the main constraining factor, particular attention needs to be given to check its wastage. Rain water going waste needs to be harvested and conserved. Major emphasis is needed on water conservation and recharging schemes, including restoration and renovation of traditional water bodies, as an integral part of watershed development with the involvement of local communities and NGOs. A paradigm shift is needed in promoting agricultural productivity – not only per unit of area, but also per unit of water and time. Water being a Common Pool Resource serving a large number of users, it's impossible to monitor the behaviour of individuals to ensure that its use is efficient, equitable and sustainable (from social view point). Strong governance is essential but not sufficient. Therefore, institutional changes to improve overall water governance need to be reinforced by creating strong incentives for individual users to make prudent and economical use of water. Increasing effective cost of water for individual users and aligning the relative costs for different uses to serve social priorities is essential.

Farm Structure

Small-sized farms in South Asia face serious constraints in adopting modern technology and in marketing their produce. To some extent, the size disadvantage can be obviated through contract and co-operative farming. In most cases, the size of farm would remain unviable and insufficient to provide enough income for the farmers and their families. One way to raise size of operational holdings is to create suitable jobs in non-agriculture sector to attract or pull out unviable marginal and small farmers from agriculture sector.

Experience of Developing Asia shows that Thailand and Vietnam achieved substantial reduction in poverty by shifting large work force out of agriculture. During 1990-2005, share of work force in agriculture in the two countries declined by about 20 per cent, *i.e.*, a shift of more than one per cent work force from agriculture to non-agriculture each year. Unlike the experience of South-East Asia and the developed economies, high growth in SAARC countries is not leading to large shifts in work force from agriculture to non-agriculture sector. The reasons for this seem to be: strong attachments of people in Asia with own land, native place and the society; and inhospitable and harsh conditions for migrants in the urban areas, particularly for unskilled low-wage labour. These can be overcome through industrialisation in rural areas and by generating employment opportunities in non-agriculture sector in and around the rural growth centres.

Bio-technology

Some countries in the region have effectively applied bio-technology tools to raise yield, reduce cost of production and improve quality of some edible oilseeds. These have imparted them significant advantage: the new bio-tech crops have drought-tolerant varieties, consume less inputs and water. The immediate benefit of success of transgenics is reduction in cost of production. However, these technologies involve environment and health risk due to which caution/safeguards are needed while adopting those. It's claimed, transgenic crops and genetically modified foods can play a crucial role in raising quantity and quality to address the future demand and food security; while others question suitability of such technologies for the Region. Its observed, traditional germplasm and conventional methods of breeding are much superior to GM approach to improve nutrition quality and to enhance productivity of various crops. Furthermore, GM technology is expensive and has much concomitant hazards which cannot be checked through weak regulatory mechanisms prevailing in developing countries. In order to take advantage of future bio-tech crops, the region need to observe and learn from experience of other countries which have successfully used bio-technology.

Adaptation to Climate Change

A wide variety of adaptive actions may be taken to face adverse effects of climate change on agriculture. Before that, each country/region need to know, with some degree of confidence, what kind of changes in temperature, rainfall and other climatic factors its likely to face. This should be followed by necessary adaptation and coping-up mechanisms. On-farm adjustments to climate change would require crop varieties suitable for late/early sowing, new cropping sequences, supply of seed and inputs on demand, water conservation, diversified production. All these call for investments. Climate change is a global challenge. The regional countries need to collaborate to promote strategies to mitigate the risks associated with climate change. Agricultural adaptations to climatic variation, *i.e.,* from cereal crops to fruits and vegetable production require new types of market, credit arrangements and input supply chain. Similarly, greater demand on water and land - in response to climate change – would require different set of protective and regulatory policies and agricultural institutions. Success in adapting to possible future climate change will depend on a better definition of what changes will occur where, and on prudent investments and policies.

Energy Prices

Increase in price of crude oil, gas and such energy sources impact directly on food prices in several ways; through increase in prices of fertiliser and agriculture chemicals used as inputs in agriculture, increase in cost of operation of farm power and machinery, and increase in transport cost [During 2004 – 2007, crude oil prices increased by 89 per cent and prices of urea (*FoB Ukraine*) increased by 77 per cent]. While agriculture is seen having potential to provide an alternative to rising energy crisis, future course of agricultural production also depends considerably on prices of crude oil prices. There is incremental pressure to move towards less energy-intensive production system. Escalating prices of crude oils and compulsions to develop alternative energy sources lead to increasing use of food and agricultural crops for production of bio-energy in the form of ethanol and bio-diesel. Bio-energy is also seen as a cleaner fuel as it emits much less green house gases compared to hydro-carbons. The immediate impact of diversion of food crop and diversion of area from food crops to energy crops is felt in terms of food shortage and increase in food prices, which poses new food security risks and challenges for majority of small/marginal farmers.

Conversely, bio-energy production is believed to having potential to benefit small/marginal farmers and rural poor by creating employment and new market opportunities, provided appropriate technologies are used to make use of degraded or marginal lands for bio-fuel production. SAARC countries depend heavily on import to meet demand for crude oil and would be hit by increase in crude prices. These countries need to develop strategies to harness potential of bio-energy crops and tree species and develop technologies for use of agricultural waste and surplus for generating energy.

Food Prices – Challenges, Opportunities

High global food prices offer opportunity to increase food and agriculture production in South Asia. This could provide the best opportunity to improve income of small/marginal farmers and harness potential of agriculture in developing countries. At present, agriculture in developing countries is caught in a vicious cycle of low income – low investment – low technology – low productivity – low income. The reason being that agriculture prices in real terms have been declining since the beginning of the twentieth century notwithstanding their occasional increase. While keeping food prices low is helpful for poor, it should not end up affecting incentives to produce. High food and agriculture prices can convert vicious cycle in agriculture to a virtuous cycle, if high prices reach farmers and improve their income translating into high investment – improved technology – high productivity.

If increase in food prices does not percolate to rural poor and their incomes do not improve consequently, they would need strong Safety Net-either in the form of direct income transfers or, provision of subsidised food. Food security of such vulnerable segments should not become a binding force to maintain food prices at low level, if it stifles production. High food prices resulting from increase in bio-fuel production or, other factors would help in raising food and agriculture production in several areas which have high potential for raising food production and where this potential is blocked due to low prices. This calls for ensuring efficient functioning of market – so that benefits of higher prices reach producers and vulnerable segments.

Food Safety and Food Standards

Consumer preferences for quality, variety and safety are rising rapidly. Modern trade and retail asks for conformity to specified standards and their enforcement, as these help in segregating product distribution to suit requirement of suppliers and consumers; and help ensure public food-safety. SAARC countries would need to upgrade and enforce standard(s) in line with changing consumer and trade demand. This would eventually help in better Sanitary and Phyto Sanitary (SPS) compliance and export promotion.

Infrastructure, Research and Development (R&D)

While agriculture infrastructure remains weak in all the SAARC countries, priority accorded to public investments in agriculture receded considerably during the last two decades. Countries are also spending very small fraction of Agricultural GDP on R&D. Conversely, research in advanced Agricultural Science is getting increasingly expensive.

However, in order to tap advantage of emerging market opportunities and technological breakthrough, SAARC countries ought to invest heavily in rural infrastructure (roads/ transportation, electrification, markets, water, land, R & D,.

Technology Delivery System

Agriculture is fast becoming more knowledge-intensive, market-oriented and demand- driven. Extension is thus required in a systemic perspective- from production to consumption in a value chain mode. Conventional systems of technology-transfer are inadequate in the fast evolving agriculture. Diversified nature of farming demands, against economic liberalisation and globalisation, is radically changing the spectrum of service providers to farmers. Indeed, the private sector, farmers' organisations, co-operatives, self-help groups, para-professionals, non-governmental organisations, input suppliers and small agri-businesses are increasingly engaged in providing information and services. Increased reliance on private sector extension, however, does not imply a complete withdrawal of the public sector – which must continue to finance public goods' extension and information services and co-ordinate extension activities. There is a need to have a re-look at the basic extension strategy considering the strengths of both public and private sector. The extension system has to capitalise on the complementarities and harness coherent synergies between public and private sector. Further, 'Research–Education–Extension–Marketing' needs to be in a continuum.

Rapid development of Information and Communication Technology (ICT) and Telecommunication Network have paved way for creation of information network, knowledge pool and services on new agricultural technology, products and marketing of produce. These need to be used intensively. It's necessary to develop farmer-friendly information network/ tools to provide whole range of information leading to delivery of knowledge of new agricultural technology, products, procedures and related services – to enable them to take control of their farming environment in near future. Rapid spread of ICTs in semi-urban and rural areas, especially the mobile telephony in recent times, coupled with continuing cost reduction in real terms, provides an unprecedented opportunity to utilise ICTs in serving farming community. In future, SAARC countries should focus on new ICT-mediated engagements in Research-Education-Extension continuum that promote greater ease of technology exchange among relevant entities and with farmers while improving farmers' opportunities for improved income and livelihood security.

Capacity Building

Development of institutional capacities for facing agricultural challenges and harnessing opportunities differ across SAARC countries. Some countries do not have sufficient trained manpower and institutional capacity to implement required programmes for achieving the objectives of the Regional Agriculture Vision. Thus, mechanisms should be put in place for these countries in capacity development for manpower and institutions.

Regional Complementaries and Collaborations

Some evolved challenges, *e.g.,* spread of plant and animal pests and diseases, climate change require co-operation – both at regional and global levels. While there already exists intra-regional co-operation in core areas of agriculture and livestock in training, sharing of best practices and capacity building, there is a need to strengthen and harmonise the existing SAARC institutional mechanisms. Regional and sub-regional projects promoting intra-regional co-operation and collaboration, both in short and long-term, need to be identified: in areas of food production, food security, food safety, conservation of soil and water resources, bio-fertiliser, linking farmers to markets, strengthening of delivery mechanisms, intensification of farming systems, tackling animal and plant diseases. In such endeavours, focus and priority should be given to tapping local talent and local resources. This vision relates to the SAARC region as a whole. Its certain aspects are general in nature. Realisation of this vision would require actions at local, national and regional level; and specific strategies. Within the broad framework, each country would be required to follow area-specific strategies. This would involve clear understanding of area-specific linkages between new driving forces and operating environment and characteristics of agriculture. Each country, and the Region as a whole, should estimate linkages. Similarly, optimal combination of policies to achieve growth, sustainability, food security and poverty reduction have to be developed along with risk assessment involved in different types of options. Upon finding answers to the questions, SAARC countries would have to identify policy interventions that help in achieving optimal results. These policies would relate *inter alia* to investments, credit, incentive structure, trade, marketing, risk and insurance, technology and institutions.

Conclusion

Global community is witnessing strong surge of regionalism. As a consequence, countries in the neighbourhood are contemplating different ways of co-operation to maximise benefit from available options; and ways to face new challenges and harness the opportunities arising. Thus, the number of regional groupings is rising; and regional co-operation is deepening. Growing interdependence among countries is putting further catalysing such co-operation. Regional co-operation in agriculture should be the core strategy for implementing SAARC Agriculture Vision-2020; and this should focus around the identified challenges and opportunities. The major challenges for agriculture in the region are to raise and sustain agriculture growth; ensure food and nutrition security; to face the challenge of climate change; adjust to changes in energy scenario; maintain bio-safety and bio-security; make sustainable use of natural resources; and protect bio-diversity. The new opportunities lie in trade, marketing, bio-technology, shifting demand preferences in domestic and global market, technology sharing, resource-sharing and investments in research, extension and infrastructure. SAARC countries need to develop science-based strategy for collective response to challenges and opportunities and global shocks.

To that end, on a priority basis, a consensus is to be arrived at on identified areas for co-operation in agriculture; and then form partnership and institutional mechanisms to operationalise regional co-operation. Concrete areas for co-operation and action in Agriculture Sector and Rural Development within the existing SAARC arrangements should be put in place with focussed strategy.

References

Aggarwal, A. 2008, *Regional Economic Integration and FDI in South Asia: Prospects and Problems*, *ICRIER Working Paper*-218.

Asian Development Bank (ADB), and ADB Institute (ADBI), (2009), *Infrastructure for a Seamless Asia*, Manila and Tokyo: ADB and ADBI.

Dee, P., ed. (2012), *Economic Reform Processes in South Asia: Toward Policy Efficiency*, Abingdon: Routledge.

Michael, Arndt (2013). *India's Foreign Policy and Regional Multi-lateralism* (Palgrave Macmillan), pp. 57–112.

Weerakoon, D. (2010), "SAFTA: Current Status and Prospects". In S. Ahmed, S. Kelegama, and E. Ghani, eds. *Promoting Economic Co-operation in South Asia Beyond SAFTA*, New Delhi: Sage.

33

A Study of Green Entrepreneurship: To Promote Sustainable Development in Karnataka

K.P. Savitha

Introduction

Globalisation has often pushed aside the notion that business owners can use their businesses to create household income, influence community behaviours and values, and impact natural resource management. Here, we identify patterns of social awareness described by green entrepreneurs and how they may be drawn into the natural resource management process. A few themes emerged from in-depth interviews with a sample of green entrepreneurs, including: low levels of interest in economic success; high degrees of awareness about the business environmental impact; and high levels of concern for social justice. In addition, several constructs emerged, which included personal motivation and mission, locality, and a forward-thinking orientation about sustainability.

This paper concentrates mainly on 'green' businesses – that is, businesses that are founded on the principle of sustainability (Isaak, 1998) – our scope encompasses all possible forms of green business. Isaak uses the expression 'ecopreneur' to mean individuals, who found/set-up green-green businesses. He suggests that ecopreneurs pursue social and ecological goals by means of profit-orientated businesses. In the context of the need to move towards rural development and truly sustainable society, we support Isaak's view that ecopreneurs are increasingly being seen as vital change managers, or experts, driving the sustainability transformation process.

Green Entrepreneurship can be considered as 'green to the power of action'. Green Entrepreneurship being a vital and innovative way encompasses the four Ps:

- Planet (resources),
- Personal, (individual),
- People (social), and
- Profit (commercial).

Defining green entrepreneurship is a difficult task. The concept itself is relatively new and has been receiving growing attention since the 1990s. The interest in green entrepreneurship is not only reflected in the growing literature on the topic, but also in the proliferation of terms used to identify the concept itself. Among the terms available to describe green entrepreneurship, the following are the most commonly used: eco-entrepreneurship, eco-preneurship, environmental entrepreneurship, sustainable entrepreneurship, ecological entrepreneurship, environ-preneurship or sustaino-preneurship.

Beginning of twenty-first century took a greater momentum towards sustainability. We believe that the challenges of our world today require us to examine the above said four P's (Planet, Personal, People, Profit), – Is this sustainable? – To all that we do in our lives at home and at work.

Review of Literature

A small, but growing, literature has argued that individuals seeking to combine environmental awareness with entrepreneurial action represent the paradigm of ecological modernisation in action. Thus, we are seeing the development of new business forms where a new generation of sustainable entrepreneurs or 'eco-preneurs' are seeking to combine environmental awareness with business success and conventional entrepreneurial activity (Anderson, 1998). 'Eco-preneurs are social activists, who aspire to restructure the corporate culture and social relations of their business sectors through proactive, ecologically-oriented business strategies' (Isaak 1998: 88). Ecopreneurship has developed as a new field of research, mainly within management and business studies, and places emphasis on the key role of individuals and organisations in engendering a shift towards more sustainable practices. The argument is that, far from being antithetical to environmentalism, entrepreneurial activity may be increasingly central to market success. In many ways, this goes back to the roots of work on entrepreneurialism and Schumpeter's (1934) vision of entrepreneurial activity as 'a process of creative destruction', whereby entrepreneurs create new products, processes and working methods that challenge and overturn conventional methods.

Entrepreneurs are seen as agents of change, with entrepreneurship being about the process of change (Audretsch 2002). The study of ecopreneurship is therefore an attempt to understand the impact of innovative individuals and organisations can have on the environment within which they act: how they attempt to force their vision upon other factors. It aims to enhance our understanding of the character of such actors and how they interface with and transform their surroundings (Beveridge and Guy, 2005: 668).

The drivers for change that encourage ecopreneurship can take several forms. Post and Altman (1994) identify three main drivers that are:

Compliance-based with environmental improvement emerging as an outcome of government regulation and legislation; Market-driven, with environmentally beneficial behaviour coming through positive incentives; Value-driven with environmental change coming in response to consumer demands as they act on their environmental values.

Such drivers are not mutually exclusive and ecopreneurs may respond to all three drivers (Walley and Taylor, 2002). Eco-preneurs may face additional challenges that conventional entrepreneurs do not. While the challenge of market creation or the limited extent of the market for products and processes is true for all entrepreneurs, it has been argued that... market creation is even more difficult for environmental business ideas than it is for non-environmental business ideas, because the financial community may not yet be mature enough to finance environmental innovations, and the role of ethical reasoning creates confusion within the mainstream business community (Linnanen, 2002: 79-80).

This may impose additional financial barriers, not just through an absolute lack of finance such as 'green' venture capital funds, but also a shortage of investors with knowledge about the ecopreneurial market, as well as a lack of awareness about financial matters by ecopreneurs themselves (Randjelovic *et al.* 2003; O'Rourke, 2005).

As Parrish (2007: 850) states, "to understand the contribution an enterprise can make to sustainable development, attention must be directed to the interaction between the enterprise and other components of the social–ecological system". The transition management literature offers a rich source from which to theorise sustainable entrepreneurship in more detail than has so far been undertaken. In particular, we need research work which takes cognisance of the power relations at work in particular sectors and how these help to promote or inhibit ecopreneurial activities. Thus, ecological modernisation requires not just changes at the level of the firm (as is the major focus in the ecopreneurial literature), but also broader sectoral and institutional shifts (Gibbs, 2000). In this manner, we might see the rise of ecopreneurial activity as involving a struggle for 'discursive hegemony' (Hajer, 1995) over the future form of economic development. While it overstates the case to suggest that this can offer a way out of the kind of legitimisation crisis for capital imposed by environmental constraints (Angel 2000), it may provide the basis of a temporary 'sustainability fix' that involves 'relative (but significant) changes to more environmentally sound directions' (Mol, 2002: 97).

What does Sustainability Mean to Us?

The natural environment is probably at the top of the list, for it encompasses the 'resources' on which we all depend and it brings all the joy by fulfilling the needs and wants of the people. Undisturbed nature also helps to bring the balance and the sense of belonging that is at the core of our human well-being. In simple terms, sustainable development means, "Development that meets the needs of the present without compromising the ability of future generations to meet their own needs."

A sustainable business is any organisation that participates in environmentall friendly or green activities to ensure that all processes, products, and manufacturing activities adequately address current environmental concerns while maintaining a profit. In other words, it is a business that "meets the needs of the present world without compromising the ability of the future generations to meet their own needs." It is the process of assessing how to design products that will take advantage of the current environmental situation and how well a company's products perform with renewable resources. In nutshell, it is about giving justice to our future generations by protecting environment and natural resources.

A New Definition of Entrepreneurship

Green Entrepreneurship is not primarily about starting business but about taking responsibility for your life choices. Once you feel responsible for your environment who you are and what you do, you might discover an opportunity or an opening in a market or you might just find more sustainable process at work. It is this attitude of positive action that defines entrepreneurship to us.

If we extend this new sense of personal responsibility and consider what that might mean in a business sense, we need to not only remember the sustainability test but also consider the long-term perspective.

Sustainability and Long-term Perspective in Business

In today's world, a successful business has typically been judged by its 'bottom line' – *i.e.*, profit in total disconnect of the broader environmental and social cost of production and consumption. For our new sustainable and long-term enterprise, we need to expand this bottom line to include the four Ps. The bottom line for sustainable entrepreneurship is not only profit but also environmental, social and rural development. Personal sustainability and long-term performance will be the by-products of expansion of business bottom line with four Ps.

Rationale of the Study

In simple terms, we intend the scope for our framework of investigation into green entrepreneurs should be a 'broad church' and include most people's common sense understanding of what constitutes a significantly green business. The rationale for this study is that all types of green entrepreneurs – whether ethically-driven, opportunistically-driven or whatever – contribute to the move towards a sustainable society.

Objectives of the Study

- To find out the factors influencing green entrepreneurship.
- To find out the relationship between green entrepreneurship and sustainable society.
- To find out shift in the practices of green entrepreneurs to promote sustainability.

Scope of the Study

The following points describe the scope of the present study.

- Scope is limited to green entrepreneurs. It is remarketed by the definition of green entrepreneurs and it applies to green entrepreneurs where green entrepreneurs are the one, who are responsible to protect our environment.
- It does not cover all the entrepreneurs.
- Scope is limited to finding out factors that affect green entrepreneurship.
- The methodology adopted in the study covers only qualitative approach as the study is purely-based on conceptual research, which by their very nature does not provide a more holistic picture about the patterns in the actual reality.

Green Procurement Programme

Many organisations worldwide are making an effort to purchase products and services that are less harmful to local and global environments. Both public and private sector organisations are implementing purchasing practices that include environmental (and social) considerations—green procurement. These activities are part of a broader movement toward more sustainable forms of production and consumption. Many ecopreneurs are adapting Green Manufacturing Process, which also includes Green Procurement Programme.

The Typical Green Procurement Programme elements are:

- Recycled content products;
- Energy efficient products and energy efficient standby power devices;
- Alternative fuel vehicles, alternative fuels, and fuel efficient vehicles;
- Bio-based products;
- Non-ozone depleting substances;
- Alternative fuels and fuel efficient vehicles;
- Environmental Protection Priority Chemicals.

The Tangible Benefits of Green Manufacturing Process and Green Procurement Programme Include:

- Cost avoidance—lower waste management fees, lower hazardous material management fees, less time and costs for reporting;
- Savings from conserving energy, water, fuel and other resources;
- Easier compliance with environmental regulations;
- Demonstration of due diligence;
- Reduced risk of accidents, reduced liability and lower health and safety costs;
- Support of environmental/sustainability strategy and vision;
- Improved image, brand and goodwill;
- Improved employee and community health through cleaner air and water, less demand for landfill and less demand for resources; and
- Increased shareholder value.

While there are a number of other quantifiable benefits measured from green procurement, cost savings and risk reduction are perhaps the most universal across all types of industries and organisations. Qualitative benefits such as improved image, brand or ability to meet policy commitments is another key benefit and is of note in a business and public sector climate that is increasingly influenced by the public, non-governmental organisations and employees that are well-informed and educated around the environmental and social issues related to products and services. How both public and private sector organisations measure these benefits varies. They often quantify direct costs savings, environmental benefits, money spent or estimate hidden or indirect savings.

Green Entrepreneurship Opportunities

Green entrepreneurship provides entrepreneurs with the opportunity to pursue potentially viable and successful business ventures while protecting the environment. Green entrepreneurship can:

- Create jobs and offer entrepreneurship opportunities.
- Increase energy efficiency, thus conserving natural resources and saving money.
- Decrease harm to workers' health.
- Enable businesses to tap into new sources of local, state, and federal funding.
- Take advantage of consumer preference for environmentally friendly goods. For example, consumer demand for organic food rose 20 per cent or more annually throughout the 1990s and that pace have continued.
- Preserve limited natural assets on which businesses and communities depend for business and quality of life.

Road Map of Green Entrepreneurs in Karnataka

The movement toward environmentally responsible enterprises is growing worldwide. Driven by a desire to integrate corporate responsibility and sustainability principles into their businesses, many entrepreneurs are finding that green enterprises are sound business propositions because they can tap into new as well as existing markets. Across India, entrepreneurs are investing talent, technology and loads of cash to kick-start green businesses. Wind turbines hum in mad whirls in Kanyakumari, Tamil Nadu. Jatropha farms have sprung up on barren land to provide raw organic matter for ethanol in Rajasthan. A business of Rs. 1,000 crore in annual revenues has arisen from machinery that converts sugarcane to fuel in Pune, Maharashtra. Eco-tourism that recycles waste and measures your ecological impact is proving a big draw in Kerala. Indian-Chinese collaboration is betting big on solar power in Hyderabad, Andhra Pradesh. A firm is investing Rs. 1,500 crore on the latest solar technologies in Noida, near Delhi in Uttar Pradesh. And you can plug your electric car as if it's a cell phone for a recharge just off busy Brigade Road in Bangalore, Karnataka.

Karnataka has achieved 122 per cent of its target and was fourth among the seven states that achieved its RPO target. In all, of the 29 states, 22 failed to meet their RPO (Renewable Purchase Obligation) targets, which lead to a loss of over 25 per cent electricity that was expected to be generated from renewable energy sources in 2012. The state had an energy deficit of 893 million units in 2012.

Some of the Studies on Green Entrepreneurship with Special Reference to Karnataka are:

TIDE, a Karnataka-based NGO, disseminates smokeless stoves among rural women in the state using a gender sensitive market driven approach. In 2002, Technology Informatics Design Endeavour (TIDE), launched the smokeless stove dissemination programme in Tumkur district of Karnataka to address the concerns of livelihood and environment preservation. After the initial needs assessment, TIDE identified Sarla stove, designed by the Centre of Science and Technology to be the most effective as it was easy to build, use and maintain. Moreover, it required only agro-waste as fuel, which is very accessible to the rural community. Furthermore, TIDE has made available effective smokeless stoves to reduce the drudgery that rural women face while using traditional stoves, and also contributes in protecting the rural environment. Till date, the stove entrepreneurs have collectively built about 20,000 - 22,000 Sarala stoves in villages of Karnataka, enabling rural households to lead safer and healthier lives.

CHARGED UP WITHOUT PETROL

Chetan Maini of Bangalore is a man in a hurry, though he doesn't always look it. At his automobile manufacturing plant located just outside polluted and congested Bangalore, he is busy talking to engineers at the assembly line. Listen carefully, and you detect more than a hint of pride in this manner. His electric-powered car Reva has already won awards at motorcar shows around the world. Now, he is concentrating on the real thing—market share. "Reva is not just a good idea," says Maini, "with the worldwide concern for global warming, it is a real alternative." With crude oil given to price spikes of the kind seen last year in the international market, "It is also economic sense". Oil price levels may have cooled significantly since their 11th July 2008 peak of $147 per barrel, but the volatility is enough to give Maini confidence in his project. The company is set to expand production capacity from 300 to 30,000 units a year. For this, he has secured $25 million in investment from Draper, a venture fund reputed to stay ahead of the curve (it made rich pickings off *Rediff* during the dotcom boom). Clearly, he knows what he's doing.

Reva is a genuine wonder. At 40 paise to one km, it is the world's most cost-effective motor vehicle. What's more, the firm has already got ten key patents. The only hitch is the life of its battery. The car's range is 80 km, much too less for a metropolis with traffic jams as part of the motoring routine. What if you get stuck midway? Maini's solution: "We are putting in 200 plug points in Delhi and an equal number in Bangalore. A rollout for other cities is also planned over the next three months. Our research teams are working with technology firms and the one-point agenda is to increase the life of the battery. We believe that technology will solve this issue sooner rather than later."

Meanwhile, Reva is working on technology for a lithimine battery option that promises more speed, enhanced battery life and quicker charging. The firm soon expects to launch a new car with a new battery. Other car companies are watching. Of that, you can be sure.

Wipro Ltd., the global giant in the world of software industry tops green peace global ranking is another company which has set benchmark in the state of Karnataka which is otherwise called as 'Knowledge hub of Asia'.

Findings of the Study

- Ecological modernisation requires not just changes at the level of the firm (as it is the major focus in the ecopreneurial literature), but also broader sectoral and institutional shifts (Gibbs, 2000).
- Indeed, 'the degree of change that entrepreneurs bring about depends on the levels of legitimating afforded to entrepreneurship in that particular society'. The policy makers need to consider this factor for the interest of the environment conservation.
- Many of those working in the transition management field are agreed that intervention in the pursuit of sustainability 'is possible and potentially effective' (Walker and Shove, 2007: 219).
- Finally, as the transition management literature suggests, 'there can be niche elements which can be appropriated by the mainstream relatively easily and which may form a first step towards mildly more sustainable reforms' (Smith, 2006: 455).
- Green entrepreneurs make for environmental progress through green procurement and green manufacturing process.
- 'A widespread sustainability orientation in start-ups could speed up the overall process of sustainable restructuring of industry and commerce' (Schick *et al.*, 2002: 60). It is recognised that this may extend beyond purely economic impacts to both social and environmental concerns.

Challenges of Green Entrepreneurs

In addition, green entrepreneurs suffer from a lack of access to the capital and business services that exist for mainstream entrepreneurs and prospective entrepreneurs. In addition, green entrepreneurs often fail to receive information about green enterprise options because most training and/or financing programmes are not aware these market opportunities exist. It can protect natural resources, lower operating costs through reduced waste and pollution, and contribute to more sustainable community economic development, while giving entrepreneurs new and different edge to succeed in the market.

Conclusion

As we look deeper into the global information age, it may well be understood that the emergence of green businesses reflects new social structure. In traditional agrarian society, it was difficult to integrate family, community, personal values, and economy with larger social issues or movements. In our analysis of these emerging business structures, we find that the business owners have clearly integrated personal values of environmental integrity, social justice, fair trade, living wages, and the development of high-quality products and services that are hoped to last generations. The study also proves that ecopreneurs destroy existing conventional production methods, products, market structures and consumption patterns and replace them with superior environmental products and services. They have created the market dynamics of environmental progress all over the world and specifically in Karnataka.

The potential type of product and process innovation is significant when sustainability principles are applied to business. With so many commercial products and industrial processes at odds with sustainability goals, this arena represents an open frontier for innovation. Sustainable development within a business can create value for customers, investors, and the environment.

Thus ecopreneurship is claimed to have the potential to be 'a major force in the overall transition towards a more sustainable business paradigm'. Ecopreneurs being the change agent seek to achieve the social and ethical transformation of their particular business sectors. The transition management literature offers a rich source from which to theorise sustainable entrepreneurship in more detail than has so far been undertaken. Indeed, 'the degree of change that entrepreneurs bring about depends on the levels of legitimation afforded to entrepreneurship in that particular society'. Karnataka state government has taken many initiatives to encourage and promote green entrepreneurship. With proper supports in place, entrepreneurs can benefit from the green enterprise markets and heightened consumer environmental consciousness. Communities benefit because environmentally responsible businesses put less of a burden on local infrastructure, protect the environment, and offer jobs that do not detract from the quality of life. In particular, we need research work which takes cognisance of the power relations at work in particular sectors and how these help to promote or inhibit ecopreneurial activities. Thus, ecological modernisation requires not just changes at the level of the firm (as is the major focus in the ecopreneurial literature, but also broader sectoral and institutional shift is essential to develop sustainability.

References

Article published in *Green Library Tools* on February 24, 2011.

Anderson, D.R. (2006), *'The critical importance of sustainability risk management.' Risk Management,* Vol. 53, No. 4.

Rennie, E. (2008), *"Growing Green, Boosting the bottom line with sustainable business practices." APICS Magazine,* Vol. 18, No. 2.

Lacroix, R., 2008, *Energy and Eco-development in France*, (for NTUA), published on www.brainet.gr – January 2008 (54 pages).

Lacroix, R., Stamatiou, E. 2007, *Green Architecture and Sustainable Development: Applications and Perspectives,* 3rd IASME/WSEAS Int. Conf. on Energy, Environment, Ecosystems and Sustainable Development (EEESD'07), Agios Nikolaos, Crete Island, Greece, July 24-26, 2007, ISSN 1790-5095, ISBN 978-960-8457-88-1, pp. 602-05.

Lacroix, R., Stamatiou, E. 2006, *"The French Experience with Habitat, Sustainability and Quality of Life",* WSEAS International Conf., Vouliagmeni, Greece, 11-13 July 2006, *Journal WSEAS Transactions on Energy, Environment, Ecosystems and Sustainable Development*, issue-5, Vol. 2, May 2006 (ISSN 1790-5079), pp. 584-90.

Lacroix, R., Stamatiou, E. 2006, "Green Roofs – A 21st Century Solution to the Urban Challenges of Green Space, Air Pollution, Flooding and Energy Conservation" *WSEAS International Conference* Vouliagmeni, Greece, 11-13 July 2006, *Journal WSEAS.*

http://www.openthemagazine.com/article/business/green-entrepreneurs.

34

Performance of Mahatma Gandhi National Rural Employment Guarantee Act (MGNREGA) in Karnataka: A Strategic View

T. P. Shashi Kumar and Ananad Gowda

Introduction

The *National Rural Employment Guarantee Act* (NREGA), enacted on 25th August, 2005 and renamed the *Mahatma Gandhi National Rural Employment Guarantee Act* (MGNREGA) on October 2nd, 2009, includes activities under nine different heads to provide employment to village communities and improve their livelihoods. The Act was notified in 200 districts in the first phase with effect from February 2nd, 2006, and then extended to an additional 130 districts in the financial year 2007-08 (113 districts were notified with effect from April 1st, 2007, and 17 districts in UP were notified with effect from May 15th, 2007). The remaining districts have been notified under Mahatma Gandhi NREGA with effect from April 1, 2008.

Thus, the Mahatma Gandhi NREGA covers the entire country with the exception of districts that have hundred per cent urban population. The development of rural India is an imperative for inclusive and equitable growth and to unlock the huge potential of population that is presently trapped in poverty with associated deprivations. MGNREGA is a flagship programme of Government of India which forms the second strand for development of rural areas, the first being the *Bharat Nirman* Programmes have been important programme interventions in India and elsewhere in developing countries since long.

These programmes typically provide unskilled workers with short-term employment on public works. They provide income transfers to poor households during periods when they suffer on account of absence of opportunities of employment. In areas with high unemployment rates and under employment, transfer benefits from workfare programmes can prevent poverty from worsening, especially during lean periods. Durable assets that these programmes create have the potential to generate second-round employment benefits as requisite infrastructure is developed. Based on the experience of these programmes the *National Rural Employment Guarantee Act* (NREGA) was enacted in 2005 to reinforce the commitment towards livelihood security in rural areas. The thrust of the Eleventh Five Year Plan (2007-12) is social inclusion coupled with provision of improved livelihood opportunities. NREGA is conceived as a holistic approach to make the growth more inclusive.

Mandate and Objectives of (MGNREGA)

The mandate of the Act is to provide 100 days of guaranteed wage employment in a financial year (FY) to every rural household whose adult members volunteer to do unskilled manual work.

The objectives of the programme include:

- Ensuring social protection for the most vulnerable people living in rural India through providing employment opportunities,
- Ensuring livelihood security for the poor through creation of durable assets, improved water security, soil conservation and higher land productivity,
- Strengthening drought-proofing and flood management in rural India,
- Aiding in the empowerment of the marginalised communities, especially women, Scheduled Castes (SCs) and Scheduled Tribes (STs), through the processes of rights-based legislation,
- Strengthening decentralised, participatory planning through convergence of various anti-poverty and livelihoods initiatives,
- Deepening democracy at the grassroots by strengthening the Panchayati Raj Institutions (PRIs),
- Effecting greater transparency and accountability in governance.

The *Mahatma Gandhi National Rural Employment Guarantee Act* (MGNREGA) is a landmark legislation aimed at strengthening livelihood security for the rural poor by guaranteeing hundred days of wage employment in a financial year, to a rural household whose adult members volunteer to do unskilled manual work. It has generated more employment for the rural poor than any other programme in the history of independent India. It has the potential to transform the lives of the rural poor not just by guaranteeing wage employment through creation of productive assets, but also by empowering the rural poor through improved governance in rural areas and enhanced capacity and responsiveness of the Panchayati Raj Institutions. Despite achievements, it is plagued by several ills. MGNREGA has become a powerful instrument for inclusive growth in rural India through its impact on social protection, livelihood security and democratic governance.

Salient Features of the Act

Salient features of the Act are summarised below:

- Adult members of a rural household may apply for employment if they are willing to do unskilled manual work.
- Such household will have to apply for registration to the local *Gram Panchayat*, in writing, or orally.
- The *Gram Panchayat* after due verification will issue Job Card to the household as a whole. The Job Card will bear the photograph of adult members of the household willing to work under NREGA. The Job Card with photograph is free of cost.
- A Job Card holding household may submit written application for employment to the *Gram Panchayat*, stating the time and duration for which work is sought. The minimum days of employment have to be fifteen.
- The *Gram Panchayat* will issue dated receipt of the written application for employment, against which the guarantee of providing employment within 15 days operates.
- Employment will be given within 15 days of application for work by an employment seeker.
- If employment is not provided within 15 days, daily unemployment allowance, in cash has to be paid. Liability of payment of unemployment allowance is of the states.
- At least one-third of persons to whom work is allotted work have to be women.

- Wages are to be paid according to minimum wages prescribed under the *Minimum Wages Act*, 1948 for agricultural labourers in the State, unless the Centre notifies wage rate which will not be less than Rs 60 per day.
- Disbursement of wages has to be done on weekly basis and not beyond a fortnight.
- *Panchayat Raj* Institutions [PRIs] have principal role in planning and implementation.

Major Objective and Methodology of the Study

To gain insights into the functioning of MGNREGA, the present study was carried out with the objective of assessing the performance of the *Mahatma Gandhi National Rural Employment Guarantee Act* in Karnataka. In this direction, the secondary data has been collected from various reports, *viz.*, Ministry of Rural Development Government of India and RBI bulletin. The literature has been gathered from published articles, books and other government reports. The data analysis is carried out by using simple statistical methods like percentage and average as these will help us understand the development situation at the grassroots level.

Performance of the MNREGA Act -- An Overview

The MNREGA of 2005 covered 200 districts is the Phase- I district and in 2006-07, this was extended to cover 130 additional districts known as the Phase- II districts. During 2006-07, against the total available fund of Rs. 12,073.56 crore, Rs. 8,823.36 crore was utilised. The average Fund utilisation per district was Rs. 44.12 crore. In 2006-07 out of this Rs. 8,303.82 crore have been released up to November 14th, 2007, out of this Rs. 5,365.99 crore have been released to the Phase-I districts and Rs. 2,937.92 crore has been released to the Phase-II covering 131 districts.

During 2006-07, 2.12 crore households has demand for employment out of which 2.10 crore households were provided employment. During the year 90.51 crore mandays of employment was provided under the programme. Average of 45.2 lakh mandays of employment per-districts has been generated out of total 90.51 crore man days of given employment.

The share of Scheduled Castes was 22.95 crore mandays (25.36) and Scheduled Tribes was 32.99 (36.45) constituting a total of 55.94 crore mandays for SC/STs, which comes out for 62 per cent as per the MNREGA Programme. The share of women person-days should be 1/3rd and the same has 36.79 crore person-days which is about 41 per cent. During 2007-08, 1.97 crore households have demanded employment and 1.88 crore households were provided with employment. A total 56.14 crore mandays of employment has been generated under MNERGA programme. Out of this, share of the Scheduled Castes was 14.70 crore mandays (26.18 per cent) and Scheduled Tribes was 18.44 crore mandays, (32.84 per cent) constituting 33.14 crore mandays, which total about 59.03 per cent. The share of women is 26.61 crore person days which is allowanced for 47.40 percent.

During the year 2008-09, 4.50 crore households have been provided employment. A total mandays 214.56 crore employment has been generated under the programme. Out of this share of Scheduled Castes is 62.88 crore (29 per cent) and Scheduled Tribes is 54.51 crore mandays (25 per cent), the share of women is 102.73 crore man days which consisting 48 per cent. During the year 2009-10, *i,e.,* up to August 2009, 73.05 crore households have been provided employment and the total 21.27 crore man days employment has been generated under the programme. Out of this share of Scheduled Castes is 21.27 crore person-days (28.94 per cent) and Scheduled Tribes is 17.63 crore person days (23.99 per cent) the share of women is 38.22 crore person-days allowanced for 52.01 per cent .

Performance of the MGNREGA in Karnataka

The State of Karnataka has witnessed considerable achievement during the implementation of *National Rural Employment Guarantee Act* (NREGA). These achievements are linked with Ministry of Rural Development's advice to all states for ensuring wage payment to NREGA workers through Bank and Post office accounts. So far, 1.6 crore accounts have been nerated across the country. In Karnataka considerable achievement has been made in the financial inclusion of NREGA workers. Total number of households registered under NREGA in Karnataka are 15, 65,679, the total number of Job Cards issued are 14,79,744. The number of bank accounts opened are 11,36,844, the total number of Post office accounts opened are 2, 11,952.

Table-1: Progress of MGNREGS Across the District (2006-07 to 2010-11) in Karnataka State (Rs in lakh)

Districts	*Total available funds*	*Per cent Share of Funds*	*Expenditure.*	*No. of lakh Man days*	*Employment provided to No. of HHs*	*Per cent Share of Employment*	*Under progress*
Bagalkot	6018.28	3.32	2726.00	16.39	44318	6.00	8822
Bangalore (R)	3501.12	1.93	2124.22	6.18	14980	2.00	3710
Bangalore (U)	2025.52	1.12	532.61	0.98	2894	0.00	3230
Belgaum	16014.44	8.82	9056.69	39.99	95968	13.00	27124
Bellary	9229.67	5.09	6254.11	27.53	50927	7.00	22314
Bidar	6203.79	3.42	3496.69	10.27	37087	5.00	17203
Bijapur	5655.93	3.12	2431.14	2.21	6876	1.00	28054
C.R. Nagar	2817.60	1.55	999.47	1.52	7267	1.00	6097
Chikkaballapur	4407.57	2.43	2190.70	4.30	8858	1.00	6063
Chickmagalur	4336.70	2.39	1506.97	8.27	21821	3.00	9393
Chitradurga	9140.94	5.04	6050.79	13.38	40434	5.00	7067
D.Kannada	3123.90	1.72	305.18	1.68	5661	1.00	29200
Davanagere	10672.49	5.88	7407.82	32.43	78779	10.00	11393
Dharwad	4460.33	2.46	2216.85	11.32	36484	5.00	10490
Gadag	2899.97	1.60	1267.49	2.23	9391	1.00	4020
Gulbarga	14986.16	8.26	4605.61	3.50	8921	1.00	16851

(Contt...)

Hassan	5309.24	2.93	1533.97	7.03	26604	3.00	8924
Haveri	6638.54	3.66	4861.86	13.60	33984	4.00	6757
Kodagu	2264.59	1.25	1067.95	5.47	13305	2.00	5838
Kolar	4223.18	2.33	2393.60	2.25	11299	1.00	53972
Koppal	6423.15	3.54	3891.84	4.61	13419	2.00	19688
Mandya	3824.59	2.11	1136.50	2.02	8671	1.00	16620
Mysore	5531.03	3.05	1484.81	5.97	18030	2.00	17837
Raichur	8525.10	4.70	6343.37	17.06	37168	5.00	23852
Ramanagar	3984.68	2.20	1976.31	1.06	4456	1.00	7957
Shimoga	7338.00	4.04	4505.99	20.35	72637	10.00	19207
Tumkur	12305.66	6.78	3313.66	1.81	4716	1.00	21045
Udupi	1840.35	1.01	92.30	0.70	3242	0.00	3655
U. Kannada	4440.04	2.45	1939.95	10.01	32138	4.00	16812
Yadgir	3330.00	1.83	1686.38	3.41	13037	2.00	12397
Total	**181472.56**	**100.00**	**89400.83**	**277.53**	**763372**	**100**	**445592**

Sources: Ministry of Rural Development and Various Annual Reports.

Table - 1, clearly explained that the district-wise progress of MGNREGA from 2006-07 to 2010-11. The total available funds constitutes of 1,81,472.56 lakh; Belgaum is top on list of it accounts 8.8 per cent, followed by Gulbarga 8.2 per cent. In addition to this Belgaum has the highest share is about 13 per cent, then Davangere and Shivamoga equally shared by 10 per cent in terms of total per cent share of employment in MGNREGA programme.

Table-2: Progress of the Financial and Fisical under MGNREGA in Karnataka

	2010-11		*2011-12*	
	*Allocation**	*Release*	*Allocation*	*Release*
Total Central Share	4781.33 cr.	1573.05 cr	2412.76 cr	662.57 cr
	2010-11			
	Target **	Achievement	Target **	Achievement
No. of Person days Generated (lakhs)	3015.79	1097.84	1155.34	699.57

Source:

Table - 2, illustrated the financial and physical progress for 2010-11 and 2011-12 in Karnataka. During 2010-11, the total central share is around Rs. 4,781.33 crore, on the other hand, the target number of person-days generated is about 3,015.75 lakh, but the actual achievement is of 1,097.84 lakh. In 2011-12, the allocation was Rs. 24,12.76 crore and the target was 1,155.34 of the number person's-days generated, but the achievement was not satisfactory, because it is just around 699.57.

The Major Challenges Faced by MGNREGA

- MGNREGA provides a legal entitlement to manual work. If work cannot be provided on demand, there is provision for unemployment allowance. This demand driven legal entitlement is not functional.
- MGNREGS has been unable to substantially reduce distressmigration from rural areas because workers do not have timely assurance that work will be made available in the periods when required.
- There are significant delays in payment to workers.
- The number of days of work provided under MGNREGS may not adequately meet demand.
- The quality of assets created under MGNREGA and their relevance to livelihood of the poor is inadequate.

- MGNREGS is unable to assure payments of wages at the stipulated rate (minimum wages).
- The works executed under MGNREGS are not based on strong participatory grassroot planning process.
- There are limitations to the current system of flow of funds, which constrain the effectiveness of MGNREGS.
- Grievance redressal mechanism provided are weak. The Working Group on MGNREGA constituted by the Planning Commission has reviewed the planning and implementation of the scheme and made recommendations to address limitations and ensure effective execution in the 12th Plan. The recommendations of Working Group can be discussed under three broad categories; Institutional Architecture under MGNREGS, Operational Processes and Plan Allocations required for the scheme during 12th Five Year Plan.
- An increase in the number of days of employment per job card in response to potential demand for work.
- Reduction in distress migration from the 2,000 most backward Blocks.
- Improvement in the quality of the productive assets created under MGNREGS and their relevance for livelihood security of the rural poor.
- Strengthened capacities of *Gram Panchayats*, enabling them to function effectively as institutions of local self-governance.
- Mobilisation and empowerment of poor and vulnerable communities particularly in remote regions of rural India.

Conclusion

MGNREGA is the only Act, which gives rural people such right and that 'too' in the post-reform period in India. It serves as an effective safety net for the unemployed, especially during famine and drought. It has enabled them with sufficient purchasing power and they are able to at least to support their basic necessity, *i.e.,* food. The Act has confined the rural poor to their areas and stopped migration to cities. It is not only giving rural livelihood but also involving them in other non-agricultural work. This has helped in handling disguised workers. Employment in other non-agricultural work will also improve the rural infrastructure, *i.e.,* rural asset building. It will ultimately lead to overall development of the poor workers.

References

Brenkert, Antoinette L and Elizabeth L Malone (2005), "Modelling Vulnerability and Resilience to Climate Change: A Case Study of India and Indian States", *Climatic Change*, 72, pp. 57-102.

Chandrasekar C.P. and Jayati Ghose, (2004), "How Feasible is a Rural Employment Guarantee", *Social Scientist;* Vol. 32: pp.52-57.

Dutt and Sundaram, 2011. Indian Economy, pp. 380 – 93.

Ganesh Kumar, A. and Manoj Panda, 2004."Employment Guarentee for Rural India", *Economic Political Weekly*. 39(51): 5359-61.

MGNREGA (2012). *Operational Guidelines 2012*", Government of India, Ministry of Rural Development, Department of Rural Development (MGNREGA-I Division), Krishi Bhavan, New Delhi, September 29th , 2012.

MGNREGA (2012), Report to the people", Ministry of Rural Development, Department of Rural Development, Government of India, New Delhi, February 2nd, 2012.

MNREGA Official Website – www.nrega.nic.in.

National Rural Employment Guarantee Act (2005): Government of India, New Delhi.

Ravindranath, NH and Rakesh Tiwari *et al* (2009). "Environmental Services and Vulnerability Reduction through NREGA; Findings of the Rapid Assessment in Chitradurga District of Karnataka", Technical Report, Centre for Sustainable Technologies, Indian Institute of Science, Bangalore.

Shah, M (2007): "Employment Guarantee, Civil Society and Indian Democracy," *Economic and Political Weekly*, 43 (45-46), pp. 43-51.

The National Rural Employment Guarantee Act, 2005: Operational Guidelines 2008, 3rd Edition Ministry of Rural Development.

Vaidyanthan, (2005). "Employment Guarantee and Decentralisation" *Economic Political Weekly*, 40 (16), pp. 1582-87.

35

A Conceptual Study on Rural Tourism in India and its Impacts on Rural Community

Usha Rani K.

Introduction

Tourism is a popular and universal activity and is emerging as leading sector in the world. Prospects for employment generation and economic benefits of this sector are well- recognised world over. This growth potential of tourism can be harnessed as strategy for rural development. The concept of rural tourism is useful for developing country like India, where almost 74 per cent of population resides in seven million villages. Their source of livelihood is agriculture. Rural tourism provides an alternative source of income in the non- agricultural sector for the rural community. There are several factors which favour rural tourism like increasing levels of awareness, growing interest in heritage and culture and improved accessibility and environmental consciousness.

Furthermore, all over the world the trends of industrialisation and development have led to urban-centric approach and the stresses of urban lifestyle have led to counter-urbanisation syndrome. All these factors have led to growing interest in rural areas. This interest has resulted in new style of tourism in which tourist visit villages to experience and live relaxed and healthy lifestyle. This concept is popularly called as rural tourism. ILO (2011) in its report on rural policy states that hotel, catering and tourism sector is the fastest growing sector. It is highly labour-intensive and valuable source of employment and income in rural areas, especially for those with limited access to labour market such as women, youth and migrants. Therefore, sustainable rural tourism based on local economic development and decent work can significantly support socio-economic development and poverty reduction.

Objectives

To understand the concept of rural tourism in India and its significance.

- To know the impacts of tourism on rural community.
- To know the status of rural tourism in Karnataka and its future potential.

Rural Tourism

Rural tourism can be defined as any form of tourism that showcases the rural life, art, culture and heritage at rural locations, benefitting thereby the local community economically and socially as well as enabling interaction between the tourist and the locals for enriching tourism experience can be termed as rural tourism. Rural tourism is multi-faceted and may entail farm/agricultural tourism, cultural tourism, nature tourism, adventure tourism, and eco-tourism. As against conventional tourism, rural tourism has certain typical characteristics like, it is experience-oriented, the locations are sparsely populated, it is predominantly in natural environment, it meshes with seasonality and local events and is based on preservation of culture, heritage and traditions. According to another worker, rural tourism is visiting an area dominated by the natural environment where specific natural, economic and socio-cultural features are harmoniously integrated so as to create unique tourism product.

Rural Tourism in India

India's heart lies in villages. Every rural community in India has own folklore, indigenous art and crafts, cultural and natural heritage. Thus, rural area of India has lot to offer to the tourist and provides an opportunity to know the real spirit of India. The 10th Five Year Plan has identified tourism as one of the major sources of generating sustainable livelihood and employment in India. Government of India has given priority to tourism in the 10th plan as it has great potential particularly in rural areas, to create jobs and ensure sustainable livelihood. The ministry of tourism, government of India has launched the scheme for rural tourism in 10th Five Year Plan period to promote rural tourism as primary tourism product, thereby to spread tourism and its socio-economic benefits in various geographical regions all over the country. The primary beneficiaries are rural communities especially women and youth, *panchayat raj* institution representatives, tourists etc., Under the rural tourism scheme of ministry of tourism, Government of India, the States/Union Territory governments submit proposals for promotion of rural tourism in their respective states. After shortlisting the proposals, the State/Union Territory governments will be requested to draw up a detailed action plan. The selected projects are given substantial funds. At the selected sites to facilitate rural tourism and for improving or creating infrastructure various activities like improvement of the surroundings of the village including landscaping, development of parks, fencing, compound wall etc., improvement of roads within panchayat limits, proper illumination in the village, solid waste management and sewerage management, procuring some equipments directly related to tourism like water sports, adventure sports, eco-friendly modes of transport for moving within the tourism zone, refurbishments of the monuments, signages, reception centers, tourist accommodation and other work/activities related to tourism have been undertaken. The rural tourism project has been taken up with United Nations Development Programme (UNDP) support under the tourism ministry's Endogenous Tourism Project with the local involvement of grassroots workers and village panchayats in 2004. The UNDP has committed $2.5 million for the project. According to project plan, the UNDP will help in areas of capacity building, involvement of NGOs, local communities and artisans. This forges strong community-private and public partnership. The government's role is mainly to develop necessary infrastructure for facilitating rural tourism (*Financial Express*, 2004).

IMPACTS OF RURAL TOURISM ON LOCAL COMMUNITY

Socio-economic Impacts

Rural areas can be transformed through rural tourism, as it allows an inflow of resources and liquidity into host communities through the expenditure of tourist and the creation of new small businesses and employment. This helps in building necessary infrastructure, conservation of rural environment, cultural heritage and identities of each rural tourist destination. Thus, rural tourism brings in social advancement as well as environmental and cultural conservation. This social advancement can be used to change the mind-set of people to such an extent that they start believing in their region as potential source of employment and livelihood.

Role in Poverty Alleviation

Rural population in developing countries account for 75 per cent of worlds' poor. Many a times the concept of poverty alleviation is linked to rural community. In many developing countries, where there is a high level of poverty, receipts from tourism form can considerable proportion of GDP and export earning. Thus, tourism receipts can be used for poverty alleviation through rural development programmes. A shift from one source of employment to multiple sources is necessary, if rural people are to emerge from the poverty trap. In this regard, rural tourism has the potential to contribute positively to job opportunities, entrepreneurial skill development and increased income generation in the host communities. Rural tourism also contributes to pluriactivity.

Improved Standard of Living

Rural tourism significantly contributes to the improvement of living standards among rural community. Social changes associated social benefits, improvement of lives, alleviation of poverty, minimisation of rural depopulation and strengthening of rural identity results from rural tourism due to employment generation and additional family income.

Cultural Impacts

Several studies on rural tourism have shown the positive impacts of rural tourism on local culture. Rural tourism can be a mechanism for preserving the culture of the area. Arts, crafts, rituals, fairs, festivals, cuisine, folklore etc., can be showcased to tourist. This can provide a glimpse of rustic life and enrich tourist experience. At the same time, the locals take pride of their intangible and tangible heritage and become motivated to preserve them. The rural arts and crafts can be rejuvenated and rural artisans can be identified and encouraged to sell their crafts to the tourist. Regular fairs can be organised where rural arts, crafts and home made products can be showcased. At the village level, art and craft centers can be established in order to help the rural artisans find an easy access to the market. This leads to revival of cultural heritage.

Impacts on Human Capital

Developing tourism in rural areas need varied workforce like housekeeping personnel, tourist guides, catering assistants, receptionists etc. Therefore, there is a need to develop human capital in the rural community, skill development and training which can contribute to human capital development. This creates more employable work force leading to very positive economic and social spin offs for the rural community. This factor makes rural tourism a real tool for poverty alleviation and improving standard of living among rural population.

Impacts on Natural Environment

Natural environment can be conserved and protected from rural tourism by means of creating environmental awareness and instilling environmental ethics among the local population. Once, the rural community realises that their natural resources are contributing to rural economy they become motivated to conserve them. Thus rural community begins to exercise environmental stewardship. Then the rural community begins to use those resources judiciously and prolong their availability as part of their livelihood. Thus, the concept of sustainability will be brought in this concept of sustainable tourism help create more sustainable jobs for the benefit of local community.

At the same time, it should be remembered that if rural tourism concept is not planned and managed well, then it can create negative impacts rather than the anticipated positive impacts. The attitude of rural community towards tourism may be different. Interaction between visitors and locals can create social problems, dissipation of community atmosphere, demonstration effect. Unmanaged rural tourism can also put pressure on the natural environment and reduce the access of locals to natural resources.

Rural Tourism in Karnataka and its Future Propsects

Anegundi

Anegundi is a small village in Koppal district of Karnataka. It is located close to world heritage site Hampi. It is a historic site and was once part of erstwhile Vijayanagara Empire. The rural tourism scheme has been implemented here. Deputy Commissioner and District Magistrate of Koppal was involved in the implementation of the project along with NGO, Kishkinda Trust. As part of rural tourism scheme, the following works have been carried out at the site:

- modification of entry gate,
- setting up of village centers,
- sculpture gardens,
- information centres and cafes,
- four main streets have been constructed,
- construction of crafts and souvenir shop (locally made),
- signage have been put up,
- riverside landscaping and restoration of ghats,
- disposal of waste, and
- provision of eco-friendly transport.

Apart from the above infrastructural facilities, the implementing agency has done community mobilisation, created awareness, capacity building and marketing. According to the ministry of tourism, the rural tourism scheme at Anegundi is a success and as a result of rural tourism the locals and artisans are able to increase their socio-economic condition.

Attiveri

Attiveri bird sanctuary is located near Mundgod of Uttara Kannada district. It is home to about 79 species of birds. It attracts tourist and provides experimential product. To facilitate rural tourism at this site, the following infrastructural facilities are provided:

- modern information centre, cafeteria, toilet complex;
- storm water chain, mesh fencing has been constructed;
- watch tower and solar lamps have been provided;
- the existing building has been improved to form dormitories in order to provide accommodation to tourists.

But at this site, not much work has been done to involve and create awareness among local population.

Banavasi

Banavasi is a temple town in Uttara Kannada district. It was the capital of Kadambas and houses 2,000 years old Madhukeshwara temple, dedicated to Lord Shiva. This site was selected for rural tourism project. The project is implemented by BIAF institute of rural development, District Commissioner and Secretary, Tourism.

To facilitate rural tourism, following steps have been taken up:

- Establishing tourist clubs for information, improvement of transport system, solid waste management;
- Improvement of roads, illumination of the village;
- Setting up of accommodation for tourists with rural theme, construction of hotel and cafeteria.

In order to tune up the rural community to receive tourist, the following steps have been initiated. Group formation and management, awareness on environment and cleanliness, health, sanitation, standardisation of services, training and skill development of rural community and establishing market linkages, entrepreneurship development programme. According to ministry of tourism, this project is a success and has improved the socio-economic condition of the locals so that they involve the project in actively. Many Self-Help Groups are also involved actively in this project.

Coorg

Coorg is a popular hill station of Karnataka. It is attracting large number of tourist, because of its picture perfect, enchanting natural beauty. It can provide unforgettable experience to the tourist. Implementing agency is secretary/commissioner/director of tourism, government of Karnataka, Bangalore. The following infrastructure has been created to facilitate rural tourism; ten furnished deluxe type tents with sliding doors as dormitory and kitchen at Naluknad palace and Bettangala have been made, equipments for bird watching, GPS instruments, portable toilets, have been purchased. Efforts to create awareness and train local people have not been done. As a result, this project at this site has not found much success.

Kokkare Bellur

Kokkare Bellur in Mandya district is a renowned bird sanctuary. Rural tourism scheme at this destination has been implemented by Secretary/Director, Tourism, Government of Karnataka. To facilitate rural tourism, the following infrastructure has been created. Interior roads, drains and plantation of seedlings, interpretation center, drinking water facility. Efforts to train locals and create awareness have not been done. Since, there is lack of software component, the project has not found much success.

Future Prospects of Rural Tourism in Karnataka

Through the studies conducted by ministry of tourism, Government of India, it has been found that in the projects where both hardware and software components have been taken care, it has met with success. This suggests furure prospects for rural tourism in the state, which can contribute to improve socio-economic condition of the rural community. Rural tourism projects can be implemented in the state in varied geographical regions like, coastal belt, Malenadu, plains etc., while planning for new rural tourism projects the following aspects need attention:

- Potentiality of attractions,
- Creation of infrastructure and basic amenities,
- Accessibility of the destination,
- Carrying capacity of the destination,
- Environmental issues,
- Sustainability, and
- Active participation of the local community.

Conclusion

Majority of the world's poor live in rural areas. Hence, rural tourism can be used as a tool to help the rural poor to reduce the impact of poverty through creation of jobs, increased income generation and entrepreneurial skill development. Rural tourism development can shift the rural communities from one source of employment to multiple sources of employment (multi-activity) and create population stability. Rural tourism also helps in building on and preserving agricultural practices, cultural and natural heritage of the area. Thus, tourism can become a tool for poverty alleviation, conservation and sustainability. Rural tourism increases participation of the poor in the developmental process and thus brings wider benefits to rural community.

References

Jack Randall, (2011). *Agriculture Tourism*, Discovery Publishing House, New Delhi.

Oppermann, M.,(1996). "*Rural Tourism in Southern Germany", Annals of Tourism Research*, Vol. 23, No.1, Pergamon Press, USA.

Pruthi R.K., (2006), "*Rural Tourism – Challenges and Paradox*, Rajat Publications, New Delhi.

"Rural tourism: It's a niche that India can offer," August 2004, *The Financial Times*, India.

Sonali Kulkarni, (2011). Village Tourism, Viking Books, Jaipur.

Stimulating rural growth, jobs and income through tourism, Rural Policy Briefs, ILO, 2011.

www.tourism. gov.in (accessed on May 16th, 2014).

www.unwto.org (accessed on May16th, 2014).

36

Branchless Banking in Rural India—Some Challenges and Progress–A Case Study of Tarapur Taluka of Anand District in Gujarat

Vijay S. Jariwala and Manish R. Patel

Introduction

Broad-based delivery of banking and other financial services at affordable cost to the poorest sections of society has been the priority of governments across the world. Government of India plans related to financial inclusion emphasises inclusion of maximum number of people under formal financial systems. In the year 2011, out of six lakh villages in India, only about seven per cent had bank branches. There were 296 under-banked districts in the 18 under-banked States and Union Territories in the country. With the Financial Inclusion Plan under implementation, around 73,000 villages, having population of 2,000 and above, would be provided facilities for banking services by March 2012.[1] As of June 2011, banks have opened banking outlets in 1.07 lakh villages. This is 5.4 per cent more than March 2010. Out of these, 22,870 villages have been covered through brick and mortar branches, 84,274 through business correspondents' outlets and 460 through other modes like mobile vans, etc[2]. The business or banking correspondents and the new bank branches being opened in these villages would also provide services in the adjoining areas. Through increased banking, penetration policy makers in India are focussing on financial inclusion of Indian rural and semi-rural areas for three most important needs and they are:

(a) Providing a platform for inculcating the habit to save money for the lower income category people. They are living under the constant shadow of financial duress mainly because of the absence of savings.

(b) Providing formal credit avenues for the unbanked population, which was vulnerably dependent on informal channels of credit like family, friends and moneylenders. Availability of transparent and adequate credit will enhance the entrepreneurial spirit leading to a rise in output and prosperity.

(c) Efficient and affordable banking system that can reach out to all shall enable direct cash transfers to beneficiaries through their bank accounts rather than subsidising products and making cash payments. This will reduce government's subsidy bill and provide relief only to the real beneficiaries.

No frill account are the ones which have either 'nil' or very minimum balances as well as charges that would make such accounts accessible to vast sections of the population. It provides basic facilities of deposit and withdrawal to account holders. It makes banking affordable by cutting down on extra frills that are of no use for the lower section of the society. These accounts are expected to provide low-cost mode to access bank accounts. Banking systems have started to adopt the business correspondent mechanism to facilitate banking services in those areas where banks are unable to open brick and mortar branches for cost consideration. Business correspondents provide affordability and easy accessibility for this unbanked population. Equipped with suitable technology, the business correspondents help in taking the banks to the doorsteps of rural households[3].

Review of Literature

One of the benefits of mechanisation is branchless banking. The initiative of government of India towards financial inclusion of rural population is a noble effort towards the development and inclusive growth. However, without participation of the public sector banks (PSBs), the objective cannot be achieved. PSBs have already started implementing the policy at large scale. Several studies such as Binswanger and Khandker (1995), Pande and Burgess (2003) reveal that Indian rural branch expansion programmes have significantly lowered rural poverty, and increased non-agricultural employment. Eastwood and Kohli (1999), used firm level data and found that the branch expansion and direct lending programmes have enhanced small-scale industrial output. The indirect impact of accessibility of credit for rural development is confirmed through these studies. Access to finance is a critical factor in enabling people to transform their production and employment activities and to exit poverty (Aghion and Bolton 1997, Banerjee; 2001, Banerjee and Newman, 1993; Pande and Burgess, 2003, Yunus ;1999). The access to finance in the unbanked areas is provided through the branchless banking of which business correspondent is one of the modes.

Objectives of the Study

In the light of reviewed literature, present study focusses on the following objectives:

1. To study the business correspondent model of branchless banking and its acceptance in villages.
2. To study the impact of a business correspondent model of banking in rural India.

Research Methodology, Data and Scope of the Study

For the purpose of the study, the researchers have selected Business Correspondent (BC) model implemented by Corporation Bank in Tarapur Taluka of Anand District of Gujarat. Tarapur Taluka has 42 villages. There are several PSBs such as State Bank of India, Bank of Baroda, Central Bank and Corporation Bank. Of these, Corporation Bank has been able to penetrate in a large number of villages through business correspondents in Tarapur Taluka. Moraj village of Tarapur Taluka is one of the model villages for financial inclusion. The service branch of this village is Corporation Bank, Tarapur. The study was based on the secondary data collected from the report of Corporation Bank, Tarapur branch. Primary data have been collected from various households of five villages of Tarapur Taluka of Anand district. A selection of these villages has been based on the BC model of banking. Besides, the study has focussed on some cases without no frills account credit to female borrowers, which has affected the household income and welfare. Data for the study has been collected through structured questionnaire from business correspondents of five surveyed villages and sample of 55 beneficiaries have been considered from these villages together.

Findings and Discussion

Moraj, Indranaj, Issarwada and Tol are surveyed villages and are located in Tarapur Taluka of Anand district. Total number of households residing in these villages are 959, total population is 5,114 among them 2,648 are males and 2,466 are females as per Census 2011.

Out of the total population together in these villages, 52 per cent is male population and female population is 48 per cent. The villages have facilities such as post office, hospital, school and a co-operative milk society. Nearest town is Tarapur and nearest banks are located in Tarapur. Banking facility is available to these villages through business correspondents. Demographic profile of five villages is shown in figure 1. Moraj is the largest village in terms of households with 639 and Isanpur, with 68 households is the smallest village. In total population of surveyed villages, 36 per cent are farmers, 24 per cent are agricultural labourers. More than 50 per cent of the population is dependent on agriculture-

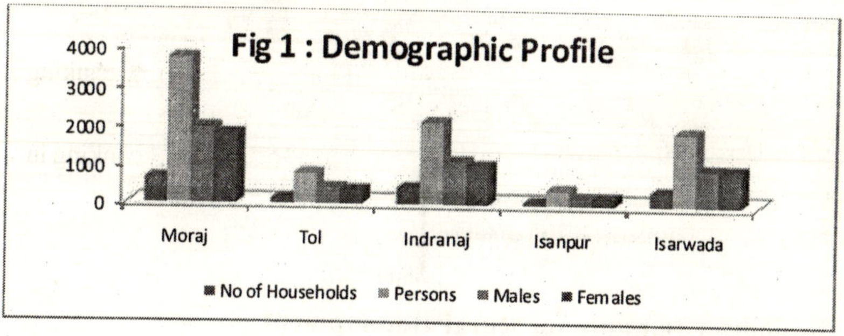

Source :

Major crops grown in these villages are rice, wheat, bajra, sorghum and cotton. Figure-2 provides the nature of economic activity of the surveyed villages. The proximity of these villages to nearest town has given rise to non-agricultural occupations such as transportation and construction. A very good number of population have been engaged in such activities.

The business correspondent model has been successfully implemented in these villages for the last two years. Each of these villages have young and enthusiastic men working as business correspondents commonly called BCs. IT infrastructure costs approximately Rs 60,000 for setting up BC- ICT service in the bank. In 2010, Moraj was selected by Reserve Bank of India as a model village for the implementation of financial inclusion. Tarapur Branch of Corporation Bank is the service branch for Moraj and the surrounding villages.

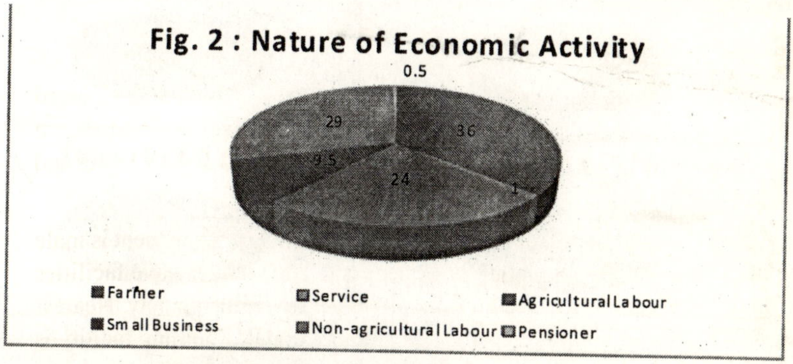

Source :

The banking facilities are not only provided to Moraj but also to the surrounding villages using the similar model. Figure-3 shows the coverage of

Fig. 3 : Finanicial indusion through BC-ICT Model

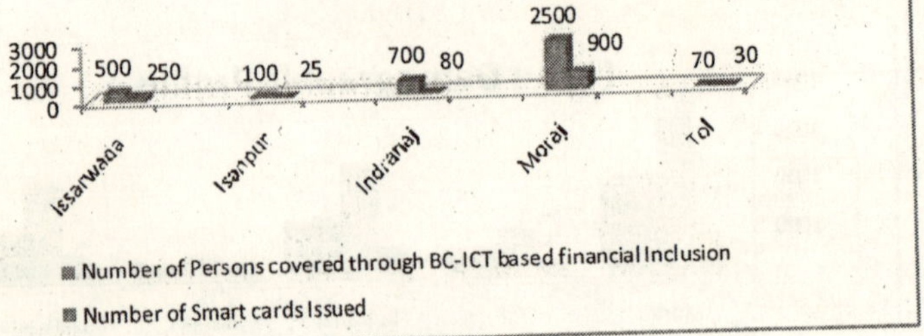

Source:

Impact of Banking on Rural Development

No frill accounts or zero balance accounts are open to include the unbanked into the banking network. The data in Table-1 and following figures 4 to 8 provide the information that small villages like, Issarwada and Tol have nearly 65 per cent females account holders.The figures 4 to 8 represent the share of male and female in no-frill accounts in the respective villages.

Table-1: Village-wise Details of Account and Advance under No-frill Accounts

Village\ Particular	Issarwada	Issanpur	Indranaj	Moraj	Tol
No-frill Accounts	400	100	600	2500	60
Advances (Amount Rs In Lakhs)	2.25	2.5	8.5	NA	1.5
Overdraft in No-frill Accounts (Amount Rs in Lakh)	NA	NA	NA	28	NA

Source: Calculated from the reports of Corporation Bank 2011-12. Note: NA - Data not available.

Fig 4: Issarwada

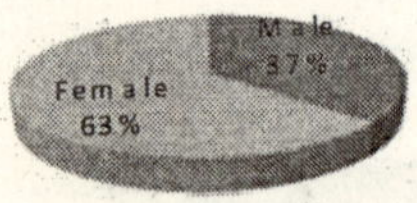

Fig. 5: Isanpur

Fig. 7 Moraj

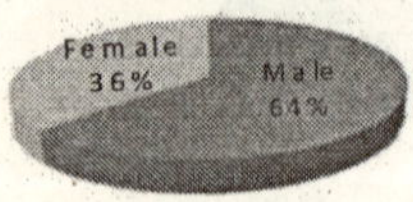

Fig. 6 Indranaj

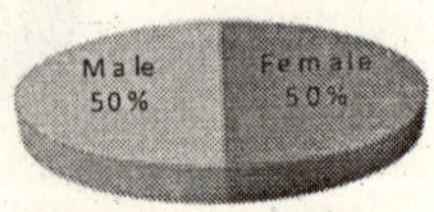

Fig. 8 Tol

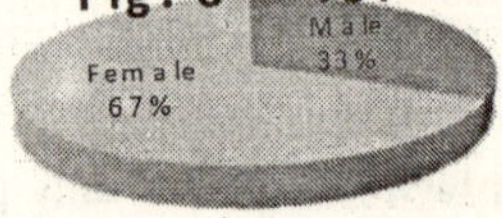

Source:

Table-2 presents the advances and deposits to the surveyed villages in last two years. It is observed that agricultural credit and advances have predominance over the other because of the nature of economic activities in these villages.

Table-2: Deposits and Advances as on June 2013

Village/ Particular	*Issarwada*	*Isanpur*	*Indranaj*	*Moraj*	*Tol*
Deposits (Rs in Lakhs)	07	0.01	10	2500	01
Total Advances (Rs in Lakhs) of which	59	0.07	45	250	11
Agriculture	51	NA	38	175	08
SME	06	NA	05	NA	02
Retail	02	0.07	02	20	01

Source: Calculated from the Reports of Corporation Bank, Tarapur Branch, Anand.

Surveyed villages also avail credit for small and medium industries as well as for retail business. The flow of credit to agriculture is more pronounced than non-agriculture sector. However, there is a spurt in the demand for credit by SMEs and for retail business.

Advances provided through Kisan Credit Cards (KCC) are for farming activities, whereas General Credit Cards (GCC) is for the non-farm purposes. As compared to the farming loans, the non-farming loans are greater for all the surveyed villages. Figure-9 makes it apparent the number GCC account greater than KCC accounts and other categories, which includes education loan, vehicle loan etc.

In Isanpur, there is only one entrepreneurial account, whereas in Moraj the number is 385 in total. Figure-10 depicts the per capita entrepreneurial credit granted during the last two years through the BC Model of operation.

Per capita availability of loans under KCC is highest in the villages except Moraj. Moraj being the model village has highest per capita availability of total credit. It has been observed that large number of account holders under no frill account are borrowing for agricultural purposes and others such as vehicles and education loans etc. Those borrowers, who are disciplined with the repayment, such as, Bismillaben of Moraj is prospering. She has borrowed Rs. 3,000 for buying a rickshaw for her family. Out of the income received, she saved Rs 100 per day in the bank. The bank has happily provided her with one more loan of Rs 15,000. On the other hand, Ramilaben, who is a farm labourer borrowed Rs 5,000 for starting, small leather business but used the money for personal consumption. She has not been able to repay the money for last two years. Cases of success as well as failure are observed. Out of the total no frill account holders in five villages, a random sample of 55 beneficiaries is selected to find the impact of availability of credit and banking facilities through BC model on poverty reduction.

Fig. 9: Entreperneurial credit (No. of Accounts)

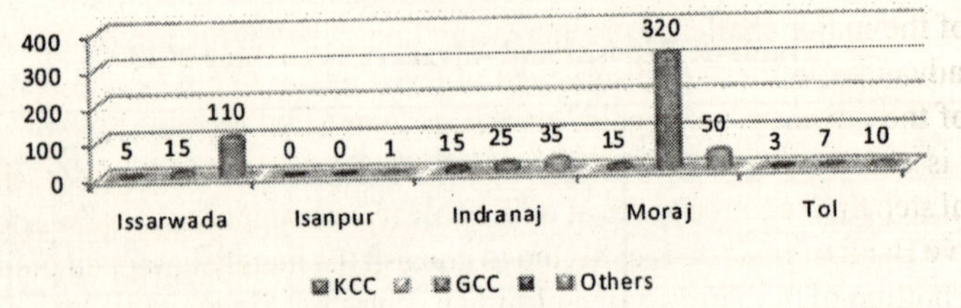

Source:

Fig. 10 : Per Capita Entrepreneurial Credit (Amount in Lakh Rs.)

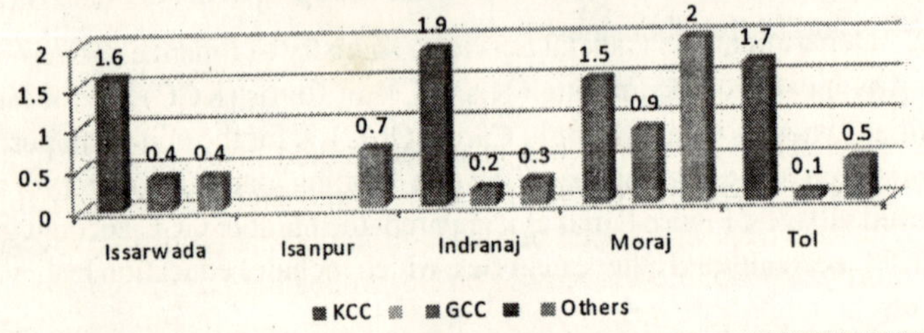

Source:

All the beneficiaries selected are women. The 50 per cent of them felt that the availability of credit has increased their income, confidence level and helped in reduction of poverty. Only 33 per cent of the respondents strongly agree that there is an increase in consumption level, improvement in social status, recognition in the family, increased decision-making power and increased exposure to the outside world.

Corporation bank is facing a challenge of increasing number of non-performing assets in the surveyed villages. Nearly 90 per cent of the borrowers are defaulters. The bank has held two camps in these villages for providing 50 per cent loan waiver for credit provided upto Rs 10,000 under no-frill account. The bank has planned this in order to recover the advances provided during 2010-11. However, very few came forward to take the advantage of this scheme. The ones who did not pay at that time are waiting for another such opportunity and not coming forward to repay the advances provided by the bank. One needs to explore the causes of such behaviour of borrowers.

Conclusions

Financial inclusion activities of the bank are executed as per the directives of Reserve Bank of India. There are several challenges faced by the banks. One of the major challenges is increasing non-performing assets. Out of the total advances in these five surveyed villages in last two years, only 10 per cent of the advances are repaid. NPA is as high as 90 per cent. Recovery of loans is challenging task. Financial inclusion of the unbanked masses is a critical step that requires political will, bureaucratic support and persuasion by Reserve Bank of India. It is expected to unleash the hugely untapped potential of the bottom of pyramid section of Indian economy. Financial inclusion may trigger the next revolution of growth, prosperity and sustainability. Availability of small amount of credit to the needy household helps them in their efforts for growth and instills the banking habits amongst the people.

End Notes

1. Department of Financial Services, Ministry of Finance, Government of India, October 2011.
2. "Banks to open branches in under-banked districts by 2012" *The Hindu*, November 7, 2011, http://www.thehindu.com/business/Industry/banks-to-open-branches-in-underbanked-districtsby-2012/article2606536.ece, accessed on November 2013.
3. Arihant B, *Financial Inclusion - Role of Indian Banks in Reaching Out to the Unbanked*, accessed on http://www.allbankingsolutions.com/Articles/Articles-AB-Financial-Inclusion.htm on December 1, 2013.

References

Aghion, Philippe and Bolton, Patrick (1997), "A Theory of Trickle-Down Growth and Development", *The Review of Economic Studies*, Vol. 64, No. 2, pp. 151-72.

Arihant B (2013), "Financial Inclusion - Role of Indian Banks in Reaching Out to the Unbanked", accessed athttp://www.allbankingsolutions.com/Articles?Articles-AB-Financial-Inclusion.htm on December, 1 2013.

Banerjee, Abhijit V. and Newman, Andrew F. (1993), "Occupational Choice and the Process of Development", *The Journal of Political Economy*, Vol. 101, No. 2, pp. 274-98.

Beck, Thorsten, Demirguc - Kunt, Asli and Peria, Maria Soledad Martinez (2005), "Reaching Out: Access to and Use of Banking Services across Countries", *World Bank Policy Research*, Working Paper- 3754.

Burgess, Robin and Pande, Rohini (2003), "Do Rural Banks Matter? Evidence From The Indian Social Banking Experiment", *London School of Economics and Political Science*, London, Discussion Paper No. DEDPS/40.

Chandan, Kumar and Srijit Mishra (2011), "Banking Outreach and Household Level Access: Analysing Financial Inclusion in India", Paper No. WP-2011-015, IGIDR, Mumbai.

Govt. of India, (2011), Department of Financial Services, Ministry of Finance, October 2011.

The Hindu (2011), "Banks to open branches in under-banked districts by 2012", November 7, 2011.

World Bank (2008), "Finance for All? Policies and Pitfalls in Expanding Access", *World Bank Policy Research Paper*, Washington DC.

World Bank (2009), "Banking the Poor: Measuring Banking Accessing 54 Economies", *World Bank*, Washington DC.

Yunus, Muhammad (1998), "Banker to the Poor: Micro-lending and the Battle against World Poverty", *Public Affairs*, New York.

37

Role of Panchayat Raj Institutions (PRIs) in Rural Development

K. Shivakumara Reddy and M.J. Nagajyothi

Introduction

India lives in villages and unless village life revitalised, the nation as a whole can hardly come alive. When India became independent in the year 1947, perhaps one-third of the villages of India had traditional *panchayats* and many of them were far from flourishing conditions. It is widely accepted that self-governing institutions at the local level are essential for national growth and for effective people's participation and that they are an integral and indispensable part of the democratic process. It also offers unique opportunity to participate in public affairs, including development work.

Mahatma Gandhi favoured *village swaraj* or self-rule and strengthening the village Panchayat to the fullest extent. His idea of *village swaraj* was that the village would be a complete-republic independent of neighbours for vital wants and inter-dependent yet for many others in which dependence is a necessity. These will have the required authority and jurisdiction.

Rural development actions are mainly and mostly to development, which aim for the social and economic development of the rural areas. Its objective is to find the ways to improve the rural lives with participation of the rural people themselves so as to meet the required need of the rural area. Education, entrepreneurship, physical infrastructure, and social infrastructure all play an important role in developing rural regions. If we observe the history of India, overall development of the country is the priority of the government since Independence. At the beginning, the main thrust for development was laid on

Agriculture, Rural infrastructure, Education, Health and Allied sectors, but soon it was realised that the all-round development of the country is possible only through the development of rural India. To achieve the said goals, the *Panchayat Raj* Institutions have been introduced under the 73rd Amendment Act of the Constitution of India. Rural Development includes measures to strengthen democratic structure of society through the *Panchayat Raj* Institutions (PRIs). It also includes measures to improve the rural infrastructure, improve income of rural households and delivery systems pertaining to education, health and safety mechanisms.

Government of India has taken many steps to develop rural areas, for this Department of Rural Development has been set up under the control of Ministry of Rural Development. The department through PRIs has launched various development schemes, such as *Sampoorna Swachchta Abhiyan, Gram Vikas Yojna*, farmer market and livestock market, and underground drainage system construction scheme and so on. Through these schemes, the Government of India seems to accomplish its dream of rural India's development. In spite of all these efforts still the achievement is not out of shortcoming. Without overcoming these drawbacks, Government of India won't be able to foster the growth of rural India. Rural Development implies both the economic betterment of people as well as greater social transformation.

A Brief Evolution of Panchayat Raj Institutions in Karnataka

During the early years as colonisers, they were primarily interested in consolidating their territorial gains. However, during the latter half of the 19th century, for administrative convenience, the concept of self-governance was revived by the imperial government through attempts made by Lord Mayo, Lord Ripeon and the subsequent Montague-Chelmsford Constitutional reforms of 1919 which closely followed the 1875 report on the Decentralisation Commission. All these measures evolved during the pre- and post-independence era, had their impact on the new legislation, the *Mysore Village Panchayats and Local Boards Act, 1959*.

In 1978 to begin with, at the district level, two development planning committees were created, that is District Planning Committee (DPC) and District Development Councils (DDC). Deputy Commissioner of the district is the chairman of the Council. In 1983, more control and devolution of funds and schemes were brought according to the well wish's of state level heads and planning machinery. In this period major change, instead of releasing lump-sum allocation for all sectors for the district, minor-head-wise outlays under each sector were provided.

During 1986-93, the District Planning in Karnataka starts with the implementation of the Act of 1985. The Act was implemented on April 1st 1987. When the Act of 1985 was implemented, there were 19 ZPs, 2,525 *Mandal Panchayats* and 27,024 *Grama Sabhas* covering population of 264 lakh by which 71 per cent of the rural population of the State came under the purview of the Act. This Act gives institutional arrangements for decision-making with people's participation, administrative arrangements for delegation of power and financial arrangements for devolution of funds and schemes to the lower levels from the state for decentralised planning in Karnataka.

The set-up for the district planning was changed altogether along with the change in *Panchayat Raj* system. In the Karnataka *Zilla Panchayats, Taluk Panchayats, Mandal Panchayats*, the *Nyaya Panchayats Act*, 1983 was brought into operation from April 1st, 1987. It was modelled on the Ashok Mehta Committee. Elections to these bodies were held in January 1987 establishing 2,489 *Mandal Panchayats* for a cluster of villages having population between 8,000 and 12,000. A body of village elected and called the '*Grama Sabha*' was intended to be a body to oversee the functioning of *Mandal Panchayats* was also legally established as novel feature.

One of the major responsibilities of the Department is in the realm of implementing the provisions of the *Karnataka Panchayati Raj Act, 1993* to achieve democratic decentralisation in the governance of the rural areas. Karnataka has the distinction of enacting a comprehensive Panchayati Raj Act which incorporates all the essential features of the 73rd Constitutional Amendment. The Act came into force from May 10th, 1993. The *Karnataka Panchayati Raj Act, 1993* provided for an elected three-tier system at the village (*Grama Panchayat*—group of villages), Taluk (*Taluk Panchayat-taluk* level) and District (*Zilla Panchayat*-distrct level) levels (KPR Act 1993). Karnataka has 5,659 gram panchayats, 175 *taluk panchayats* and 30 district *panchayats*. Elections to these bodies have been successfully held twice since 1993. Every 400 people elect one member to the gram panchayat, 10,000 people elect a member to the taluk panchayat and 40,000 people elect a member to the district panchayat. This ensures equitable representation to all sections of society and also social justice by way of a progressive pattern of reservation. The Government gives a statutory development grant of Rs 3.5 lakh to every gram panchayat and intends to progressively increase this amount and the flow of untied resources to encourage and enable local planning in keeping with national and local priorities of the total plan and non-plan budget of the state, Rs. 4,589 crore are devolved to the three-tier *Panchayat Raj* Institutions - Rs. 1,697 crore for plan and Rs. 2,892 crore for non-plan. The idea is that plan and Non-Plan schemes being implemented at the three levels should be supervised by the elected panchayat bodies to ensure better implementation, public participation and accountability. The powers and functions have been devolved to elected bodies at each level and not to any individual.

Objectives of the Study

1. To review the status of PRIs in Karnataka.
2. To examine the sector-wise fund allocation in Karnataka.
3. To find out the issues and challenges of PRIs in Karnataka.

Methodology of the Study

This study is based only on the secondary data. The secondary data were sourced out from the link documents of Rural Development and *Panchayat Raj* (RDPR) government of Karnataka, and other official websites of the concerned department of *Panchayat Raj* institutions. The information was also collected from reviewing various existing theoretical and empirical studies on the topic, official document and periodicals. Internet sources were also browsed and downloaded for necessary information. Appropriate statistical techniques like ANOVA test has been used to analyse the data.

Need of PRIs

The dawn of twenty-first century is marked by decentralised governance both as a strategy and a philosophy to bring about reforms and changes in democracies. This change is expected to lead the transparency, responsiveness and accountability and ensure good governance. Today, PRIs playing an important role in local governments and are the most significant level in the development discourse. In the present context of rapid social change and development activities, PRIs have been found to be much more appropriate to deal with contemporary trends in rural development. An important feature of decentralised governance is interactive policy-making which Rural Local Governance in Karnataka leads to decentralised decision-making. Interactive policy is a process where government and non-governmental sectors such private sector, non-governmental organisations, communities, grassroots organisations, pressure groups participate in decision-making so as to influence issues and suggest alternatives. Therefore, local governance is an alternative strategy of development, which is people-centered, participatory and bottom-up development mechanism. The functions of PRI clearly exhibit the ultimate target, *i.e.,* rural development. Because for any welfare state, the purposeful endeavours of the government is aimed at the social, economic and political uplift of the people in the rural areas.

PRIs and Rural Development

The term rural development is of focal interest and is widely acclaimed in both the developed and the developing countries of the world. There is however no universally acceptable definition of rural development and the term is used in different ways and in vastly divergent contexts. As a concept, it connotes over all development of rural areas with a view to improve the quality of life of rural people. Rural development aims at improving the rural lives with the participation of the rural masses. The concept of rural development targets the social and economic development of the rural areas. It is concerned with the economic growth, social justice and improvement in the living standards of the rural people by deploying an efficient delivery mechanism to provide adequate quality services and essential minimum needs.

Development of rural areas has been at the core of planning process in the country. Rural Development is a broad, inclusive term which takes in its consideration socio-economic and political development of the rural areas. It includes measures to strengthen the democratic structure of society through the *Panchayati Raj* Institutions as well as measures to improve the rural infrastructure, improve income of rural households and delivery systems pertaining to education, health and safety mechanisms. Poverty alleviation is a key component of rural development. Along with these measures, the PRIs also perform certain major functions such as:

- **Core Functions:** Drinking water, roads, culverts, bridges, ferries, waterways, and other means of communication, rural electrification, Health and sanitation, Maintenance of community assets, etc.
- **Welfare Functions:** Rural housing, non-conventional energy sources, technical training and vocational education, adult and informal education, libraries and cultural activities, Family welfare, woman and child development, social welfare, public distribution system, etc.
- **Agriculture and Allied Functions:** Agriculture, minor irrigation, Ffsheries, social forestry and farm forestry, fuel and fodder, markets and fairs, small-scale industries, including food processing industries, etc.

Hence, the critical question for working of PRIs is mainly determined by their financial status, which is allocated by both the Central and the State governments. The efficiency of these Institutions is measured in terms of the amount of funds received by them from both the governments. The study is undertaken by using the data of three years (2010-2013). The data are related to area development and other rural development programmes, energy programmes, employment programmes, water supply, grants to panchayat raj institutions, medical and public health services — rural health, etc.

Table - 1: Sector-wise Fund Allocation of Total Panchayats (ZP+TP+GP, Centre and State - 2010?2013) Rs in lakh

Description	*Total for the Sector - 2010-11*		*Total for the Sector - 2011-12*		*Total for the Sector - 2012-13*	
	Total	*pc*	*Total*	*pc*	*Total*	*pc*
Primary and Secondary Education-2202 General Education	86499.58	17.8	99783.31	16.5	175392.27	22.5
Mass Education - 2202 General Education-04	220.70	0.0	254.22	0.0	260.63	0.0
Medical and Public Health Services- Rural Health-2210	9940.70	2.0	11990.43	2.0	13649.49	1.7
AYUSH- 2210	481.98	0.1	552.96	0.1	604.71	0.1
Rural Water Supply-2215	5809.47	1.2	12924.95	2.1	22938.76	2.9
Welfare of Women and Children-2235	45250.62	9.3	55690.58	9.2	77225.72	9.9
Agriculture-2401	6573.92	1.3	6970.32	1.2	4089.65	0.5
Horticulture-2401	1991.22	0.4	2011.73	0.3	2241.50	0.3
Animal Husbandry-2403	8102.63	1.7	10406.35	1.7	11760.80	1.5
Area Development and other Rural Development Programmes	13274.84	2.7	15797.87	2.6	7182.52	0.9
Rural Energy Programmes	1463.08	0.3	1933.20	0.3	1925.20	0.2
Rural Employment Programmes	84098.75	17.3	126727.10	21.0	151279.81	19.4
Grants to Panchayat Raj Institutions	40790.63	8.4	81642.80	13.5	90291.71	11.6
Minor Irrigation-2702	84.52	0.0	75.89	0.0	74.39	0.0
Village and Small Scale Industries-2851	460.47	0.1	500.70	0.1	315.79	0.0
Sericulture-2851	431.80	0.1	456.36	0.1	465.68	0.1
Employment and Training	50.91	0.0	117.22	0.0	117.73	0.0
Agricultural Marketing	96.30	0.0	102.00	0.0	155.00	0.0
Grand Total (Including All other Sectors)	**487011.11**		**604165.63**		**780893.00**	

Source: Link Document, GOK. (Note: F-observed value is 0.186; F-critical value is 3.168, @ five per cent level)

Hypothesis of the Study:

$$H_0 : \mu_1 = \mu_2 = \mu_n \quad H_0 : \mu_1 = \mu_2 = \mu_n$$

$$H_1 : \mu_1 \neq \mu_2 \neq \mu_n \quad H_1 : \mu_1 \neq \mu_2 \neq \mu_n$$

(H_0 = Null Hypothesis), (H_1 = Alternative Hypothesis)

H_0 = The percentage of Sector-wise Fund allocation of the Government is increasing the level of Rural Development.

H_1 = The percentage of Sector-wise Fund allocation of the Government is critical to increase the level of Rural Development.

ANOVA: Single Factor

Summary				
Groups	*Count*	*Sum*	*Average*	*Variance*
Total for the Sector-2010-11	19	792,633.23	41717.54	12,37,799,1,509.65
Total for the Sector-2011-12	19	1032103.62	54321.24	19192240532.87
Total for the Sector-2012-13	19	1340864.36	70571.81	32436652143.60

ANOVA						
Source of Variation	*SS*	*df*	*MS*	*F*	*P-value*	*F crit*
Between Groups	7951519897	2	3975759949	0.186	0.831	3.168
Within Groups	1152123915350.27	54	21335628062			
Total	**1160075435247.70**	**56**				

Source:

As mentioned above, the data is analysed by using ANOVA technique and the result has proved that the F- observed value of 0.186 is lesser than the F-Critical Value of 3.168, P-value is 0.831 at 0.05 (5 per cent) level. As per the rule, the study has accepted the Null Hypothesis (H_0) and rejected the Alternative Hypothesis (H_1). *It implies that to build the capacity of the PRIs in order to promote the rural development they must financially be strengthened by both the Central and the State governments.* Crucially, the PRIs should efficiently make use of local resources in order to generate their

Table-2: Sector-wise Fund Allocation of Gram Panchayats (Plan - Centre and State - 2010-2013) Rs in lakhs

Description	Gram Panchayat - 2010-11		Gram Panchayat - 2011-12		Gram Panchayat - 2012-13	
	Total	Per cent	Total	Per cent	Total	Per cent
Primary and Secondary Education-2202 General Education	0.00	0.0	0.00	0.0	0.00	0.0
Mass Education - 2202 General Education-04	0.00	0.0	0.00	0.0	0.00	0.0
Medical and Public Health Services-Rural Health-2210	0.00	0.0	0.00	0.0	0.00	0.0
AYUSH- 2210	0.00	0.0	0.00	0.0	0.00	0.0
Rural Water Supply-2215	5809.47	5.4	5424.95	4.8	15438.76	10.9
Welfare of Women and Children-2235	0.00	0.0	0.00	0.0	0.00	0.0
Agriculture-2401	0.00	0.0	0.00	0.0	0.00	0.0
Horticulture-2401	0.00	0.0	0.00	0.0	0.00	0.0
Animal Husbandry-2403	0.00	0.0	0.00	0.0	0.00	0.0
Area Development and Other Rural Development Programmes	10178.36	9.4	12340.55	10.8	3343.00	2.4
Rural Energy Programmes	1463.08	1.4	430.00	0.4	430.00	0.3
Rural Employment Programmes	0.00	0.0	0.00	0.0	0.00	0.0
Grants to Panchayat Raj Institutions	33774.00	31.3	45436.00	39.9	46716.00	33.1
Minor Irrigation-2702	71.05	0.1	75.89	0.1	74.39	0.1
Viliage and Small Scale Industries-2851	0.00	0.0	0.00	0.0	0.00	0.0
Sericulture-2851	0.00	0.0	0.00	0.0	0.00	0.0
Employment and Training	0.00	0.0	68.00	0.1	68.00	0.0
Agricultural Marketing	0.00	0.0	0.00	0.0	0.00	0.0
Grand Total (Including All other Sectors)	**108044.19**		**113846.23**		**141183.12**	

Source: Link Document, GOK.

own sources of income. In this way, the institutions must not highly depend on the governments instead they must self-reliant. Governments have to increase the percentage level of fund allocation of all three tiers (PRIs), because presently the responsibilities and functions of PRIs are increasing.

The study also considered the sector-wise fund allocation of *grama panchayats* for three years period. The data below representing the amount for medical and public health service, rural water supply, animal husbandry, area development and other rural development programmes, etc.

The Table represents sector-wise fund allocation of *gram panchayats* (Plan - Centre and State - 2010-13). As it is shown the total allocation for the three years are in increasing trend. In 2010-11 the amount was Rs. 1,08,044.19, and it has been increased to Rs. 1,41,183.12 in 2012-13. In case of area development and other rural development programmes, we can see highly fluctuating trends. i.e., in the year 2010-11, the percentage of allocation was 9.4 per cent, which increased to 10.8 per cent in the next year. However, in the year 2012-13, it has drastically comedown to 2.4 per cent of the total allocation. It depicts that there is lack of financial support to promote more rural development activities by the PRIs.

Findings and Conclusion of the Study

Karnataka government has undoubtedly taken up number of steps to grant greater responsibilities, powers and financial resources to the PRIs. Thus, the needs of decentralised governance in the state have now begun to evolve. But the present pattern and process of governance in the state is still at crossroads and has a long way to go before it attains maturity. On the basis of the present analysis, the study makes out certain findings:

- It is well-recognised that the success of PRIs depends on adequate power devolution, sufficient financial resource devolution, efficient administrative capacity of the decentralised institutions and effective accountability mechanisms.
- The PRIs are having the tendency of power holders not to give up power and authority to lower level institutions. The PRIs in Karnataka suffer from certain colonial hangovers. For example, the ZPs have been given only administrative roles. The hangover thus continues even today.
- There is lack of financial support to promote more rural development activities by the PRIs.
- The institutions must not highly depend on the governments instead they must be self-reliant.

- The PRIs should efficiently make use of local resources in order to generate their own sources of income.

References

Aziz Abdul, (1994), *Decentralisation : Mandal Panchayat System in Karnataka*, National Institute of Rural Development (NIRD), Rajendra Nagar, Hyderabad.

Devendra Babu M, (2004), '*Finance of Panchayats in Karnataka: A Policy Paper*', working paper No. 143, Institute for Social and Economic Change, Bangalore.

Devendra, Babu, M (2009), '*Fiscal Empowerment of Panchayats in India: Real or Rhetoric*?' Working Paper No. 229, ISEC, Bangalore.

Govinda Rao M., Vasanth Rao UA, (2008), "Expanding the Resource Base of Panchayats: Augmenting Own Revenues", *Economic and Political Weekly* January 26, pp. 54-61.

Mishra A.K., Naved Akhtar, Sakshi Tarika, (June 2011, Article_05). "Role of the Panchayati Raj Institutions in Rural Development, (An Analytical Study of Uttar Pradesh)', *SMS Varanasi*, Vol. VII, No. 1.

Rajasekhar, D.M. Devendra Babu, R Manjula, (March 2011). 'Elite and programme capture in grama panchayats of Karnataka', *Project Report*, CDD, ISEC, Bangalore.

Rao, D.V. Raghava, (1980). "*Panchayats and Rural Development*", Ashish Publishing House, New Delhi.

Sivanna N, (1990), "*Panchayat Raj Reforms and Rural Development*", Chugh Publications.

Subrahmanyam, Siva, K. (February 2003), '*Devolution of Functions and Finances on Panchayats in Andhra Pradesh*', National Institute of Rural Development, Hyderabad.

The Karnataka Panchayat Raj Act, 1993, Karnataka Act No.14 of 1993, Government of Karnataka, Bangalore.

The Karnataka Village Panchayats and Local Boards Act, 1959, Department of Law and Parlimetary Affairs, Government of Karnataka, Bangalore.

The Karnataka Zilla Parishads, Taluk Panchayat Samitis, Mandal Panchayats and Nyaya Panchayats Act, 1985, Government of Karnataka, Bangalore.

38

Crop Insurance and Agricultural Development in Relationship with Rural Development

A.R. Prakruthi and K. Ramesha

Introduction

With over maximum of the world's poor living in rural areas, moreover, up to 90 per cent of the population in many developing countries depends on agriculture and farming for their living, as these provide income, employment and food, as well as raw materials for industry and exports. According to 2011 Census, the country's rural population is almost 83.25 cr (68.8 per cent of total population) those people are depending upon agriculture is main occupation. There has been wide consensus that the rural development should be inclusive and sustainable in order to alleviate the poverty. Although, agriculture now accounts for only 14 per cent of Gross Domestic Product (GDP), it is still the main source of livelihood for the majority of the rural population. As such rapid growth of agriculture is critical for inclusiveness, important structural changes are taking place within the sector and there are definite signs of improved performance.

The agricultural development and rural development are inextricably interwoven, each reinforcing or decelerating their growth because rural India is the agricultural India. Agricultural growth has given more contribution to rural development. Agriculture in India is often attributed as gambling with monsoons because of its almost exclusive dependency on precipitation from monsoons. The failure of these monsoons can lead to series of droughts, lack of better prices, and exploitation of farmers by middlemen, all of which have led to a series of suicides committed by farmers across India; for this dimension the crop insurance spreads the crop losses over space and time, provides social security to the farmers, helps in maintaining their dignity, offers self-help, encourages large investmernts in agriculture for improving crop yield and increasing agricultural production it result agricultural development can take place finally it can turn into rural development.

Objectives of the Study

The Present study tries to interpret the concept of rural development in relation with crop insurance for this analysis the present study consists of following objectives:

1. To study the risk management in Agriculture sectors,
2. To study the crop Insurance and its schemes in India,
3. To analysis the various issues involved in crop insurance in the agricultural development,
4. To critically examine the implementation of Crop Insurance Schemes, and
5. To offer some policy perception.

Methodology

The study is based on secondary data. Secondary source of data were gathered from available literature in books, journals, research reports, Internet, newspapers and other published materials related to the crop insurance and agricultural insurance.

Risks in Agriculture Sector

Agricultural production is an outcome of biological activity, which is highly sensitive to changes in weather. Important weather variables such as temperature, humidity, rainfall, wind etc., influence the biological process directly or indirectly. For instance, low soil moisture due to poor precipitation in the pre-sowing period adversely affects seed germination resulting in reduced plant population. The poor precipitation during growth period results in stunted plant growth. Heavy rainfall during early growth period causes submersion of plants. Similarly, hailstorms, wind and cyclones damage the standing crops by lodging and uprooting especially the perennials (trees and shrubs). High humidity may cause outbreak of pests and diseases. All these result in partial loss in yield and sometimes complete crop failure and hence reduced income to farmers. In other words, deviations in the weather variables from the normal adversely affect the crop yields and hence production and income on individual farms. As variations in weather are more a regular phenomenon, crop yields are not stable. As if all this is not enough, the sword of uncertain agricultural prices always hangs on the farmers' fate. As a consequence, farm incomes fluctuate violently from year to year. These variations in income are referred to as risk. The variations in income due to changes in yield are production risk and due to changes in price marketing risk. There are a lot of risks that effect agricultural production and agricultural producer's income. Nevertheless, the major risks which are of concern to the agricultural sector are:

- Price risk caused by volatility in prices,
- Production risk resulting from uncertainty about the levels of production that primary producers can achieve from their current activities, and
- Uncertainty of rain, irrigation problems.

In order to avoid risk, agricultural producers may transfer all or part of the risks to third party through a crop insurance contract.

Crop Diversification

Crop diversification is the most common and effective risk management strategy that is employed by the farmers. The farmer spreads risk across multiple crops and even if one crop fails, it is compensated by another crop. However, crop diversification leads to spreading of limited resources across crops and the price paid for diversification is income foregone or sacrificed by not growing the most remunerative crop. The same argument holds true in the case of intercropping.

Intercropping

Intercropping lowers yield risks because of lower incidence of insect/ pest damage as well as disease. Intercropping has greater potential for yield compensation. It provides opportunity to grow short duration crops along with long duration crops thus minimising competition for soil nutrients and maximising the use of soil moisture, sunlight, etc. Even though intercropping is not found effective in reducing production risk as shown by positive covariance between the yields of inter crops, it certainly helps in avoiding complete crop failure.

Tenancy or Share-cropping

Tenancy or share-cropping helps to minimise risk in production. Share-cropping is more beneficial particularly when the tenant is a small farmer and averse to risk, as the tenant has to share a fraction of output to the land owner and he is insulated against the fluctuations in output. On the contrary, ease or fixed tenancy shifts the entire risk of production to the tenant farmer. The risk-reducing strategy stabilises farm income but at the same time the farmer has to forego income from other alternative activity, which would have fetched higher income. Similarly, diversification is usually less profitable on average than crop specialisation.

Risk Management in Agricultural Sector

The Risk management implies minimisation of income loss either by reducing variations in output or ensuring certain minimum price or guaranteeing certain level of income to the farmer. It is a process of appraising and reducing risk. The ways devised to do so are referred to as risk management alternatives. These are discussed under the following heads.

(a) Avoiding Risk: Some of the production risks can simply be avoided. For instance, eliminating more risky enterprises would minimise risk but at the cost of decreased total production (returns). Laggards always try to avoid risk. They opt for assured return through low income enterprises.

(b) Preventing Risk: Many a time some risks could be prevented by taking advance action. For instance, risk of loss in crop yield due to pest attack could be prevented by following preventive pest control. The cost of this risk management alternative is the cost of preventive pest control.

(c) Sharing Risk: This alternative of risk management is quite common in India. Important example of risk sharing is the share lease of land to tenants. The production risks are shared between the landlord and the tenant in the ratio they share some inputs and the output. The cost of this alternative to the landowner would be equal to the difference between the net income tenant earns less the cash rent he would have paid for rental lease.

(d) Transferring Risk: Risk may be transferred from one entity to another. For instance, marketing risk could be transferred to buyers by way of forward contract. It guarantees to pay an agreed price for the produce to be realised in future. The cost of this alternative is the difference in value of output at post harvest/market price less the value realised at the agreed price. Crop insurance is another example of transferring production risk to another entity *i.e.*, insurance company. In case, the crop prospects are reduced below certain minimum, proportionate indemnity is paid for the expenditure incurred. The cost of this alternative is the premium paid by the farmer.

(e) Spreading Risk: Risk may be spread over a number of enterprises with varying degree of risk and of course with varying level of net income. This is known as diversification. Diversification could be in terms of mixed farming, diversified farming or even mixed cropping. The idea is not to put all eggs in one basket. It would ensure some income realisation from enterprises/

crops even in the event of adverse weather conditions etc. As net returns from combination of different enterprises/crops would be less than the net returns from the most paying crop (pure), the difference between the two could be the cost of this alternative.

(f) Taking Risk: Taking risk could be one of the alternatives to manage risk where the management cost is nil because no attempt is made to reduce risk. The idea is to plan for maximum returns even at high risk. Innovators and early adopters are the two categories of people, who always are willing to take risk. They go for high return enterprises exposing themselves to high risk.

Need for Crop Insurance

The farmers have to suffer huge loss during natural disasters such as flood, drought or earthquake. Therefore, crop insurance is one of the best ways to protect the farmers from such damages. The India government and private companies are provided offers yield-based and weather-based crop insurance programs in almost 500 districts of India. It covers almost 20 million farmers, making it the biggest crop insurer in the world in number of farmers served. Agriculture Insurance Company of India Limited is a limited company headquartered at New Delhi, India. As AIC aims are follows:

- To provide insurance coverage and financial support to farmers in the failure of any of the notified crop as a result of natural calamities, pests and diseases to restore their creditworthiness for the ensuing season; to encourage fanners adopt progressive farming practices, high value inputs and higher technology;
- To help stabilise farm income, particularly in disaster years. The plan provides comprehensive risk insurance for yield losses due to natural fire and lightning, storms, hailstorms, cyclone, typhoon, tempest, hurricane, tornado flood, inundation, landslide, drought, dry spells, pests/diseases, etc.

Obstacles in Crop Insurance

The principal obstacles are lack of high quality information, inadequate regulatory, frameworks weak, supervision, lack of acturial expertise, lack of professional expertise in designing and monitoring crop insurance products. A mass of income dispersed clients, who may not be willing or able to pay actuarially sounds premiums for multiple peril products, and tendency of government undermine market development through inappropriate use of subsidies and disaster relief funds. For the sustanance of the rural people and development financial assistance will be extended.

Policy and Scheme to Crop Insurance in India

The types and severity of the risks confronting farmers vary with the farming system and with the climatologically, policy, and institutional setting, therefore, the government of India, it is may be state government or Central Government introducing various schemes or policies for farmers due to loss of agriculture before harvesting time and provides or fulfils the financial loss to farmers and their crops. In this way, the government indirectly helps the rural people through the crops insurance to farmers. Some of the important schemes are below discussed.

Pilot Crop Insurance Scheme – PCIS (1979-1984): PCIS was introduced on the basis of report of late Prof V.M. Dandekar and was based on the 'Homogeneous Area' approach. The scheme covered food crops, oilseeds, cotton, and potato; and was confined to loanee farmers on a voluntary basis. The scheme was implemented in 13 states and covered 6.27 lakh farmers, for a premium of Rs. 196.95 lakh and paid claims of Rs. 157.05 lakh.

Comprehensive Crop Insurance Scheme – CCIS (1985-1999): The scheme was an expansion of PCIS, and was made compulsory for loanee farmers. Premium rates were two per cent of the sum insured for cereals and millets and one per cent for pulses and oilseeds, with premium and claims, shared between the Centre and States, in 2:1 ratio. The scheme was implemented in 16 states and two two Union Terrirories and covered 7.63 crore farmers for a premium of Rs. 403.56 crore and paid claims of Rs 2,319 crore.

National Agricultural Insurance Scheme (NAIS): National Agricultural Insurance Scheme (NAIS) is a Central Sector Scheme, being implemented in the country since *Rabi* 1999-2000, as a part of risk management in agriculture with the intention of providing financial support to farmers in the event of failure of crops as a result of natural calamities, pests and diseases. The scheme is available to all the farmers – loanee and non-loanee — irrespective of their size of holding. Loanee farmers are covered on compulsory basis in a notified area for notified crops, whereas for non-loanee farmers, the scheme is voluntary. The Scheme envisages coverage of all the food crops (cereals, millets and pulses), oilseeds and annual commercial/horticultural crops, in respect of which past yield data is available for adequate number of years. Crops covered by the implementing States/UTs during *Kharif* and *Rabi* seasons. In 2010-11, previous national agriculture insurance scheme (NAIS) had modified and then the scheme was implemented modified agricultural insurance scheme (MNAIS). The modified NAIS has been formulated, incorporating the necessary changes/ modifications in consultation with States to remove the deficiencies and make it farmer-friendly and more comprehensive. The scheme will be implemented as a Central Sector Scheme on a pilot basis in 50 districts in last two years of 11th

Five Year Plan starting from the *Rabi* season of 2010-11. Approval has also been accorded for making budgetary provisions of Rs. 358 crore for the Modified NAIS for the years 2010-11 and 2011-12. With the introduction of the modified scheme, it is expected that an increased number of farmers will be able to manage risk in agriculture production in a better way and will succeed in stabilising farm income particularly at the times of crop failure on account of natural calamities. Keeping in view the various risks involved in agriculture production, the Ministry of Agriculture has been implementing the National Agricultural Insurance Scheme (NAIS) as a Central Sector Scheme since *Rabi* season 1999-00 to insure the farming community against these risks. It was reviewed based on the experience gained from its implementation, in which many deficiencies in the scheme were identified. The financial progress of the aforesaid schemes (from 11th Plan) is given as under:

Table-1: National Agricultural Insurance Scheme (NAIS)

Year	*B.E.*	*R.E.*	*Actual Expenditure*
2007-08	500.00	718.88	718.88
2008-09	644.00	694.00	694.00
2009-10	644.00	1,419.00	1,419.00
2010-11	950.00	2,662.00	2,660.00
2011-12	550.00	330.00	360.00
Total XIth Plan	3,288.00	6,324.00	5,851.00
2012-13	400.00	700.00	700.00
2013-14	1,200.00		

Source: The financial progress of the aforesaid schemes (from 11th Plan),

Scope of the Scheme

(a) Area Coverage: The scheme was available to all states and union territories on optional basis. However, the states opting for the scheme were required to take up all the crops identified for coverage in a given year and shall have to continue for a minimum period of three years before it may quit. For *Rabi* 1999, only eight states (Assam, Goa, Gujarat, Himachal Pradesh, Kerala, Madhya Pradesh, Maharashtra and Orissa) and the Union Territory of Pondicherry, opted for the scheme. This number was increased to 17 in *Kharif* 2000 and to 21 in *Kharif* 2002. Currently, the scheme has been implemented in 23 states and two Union Territories. Punjab, Manipur, Nagaland, and Arunachal Pradesh among states and Chandigarh, Daman and Diu, Dadra and Nagar Haveli and Lakshadeep among the Union Territories have not yet opted for the scheme.

(b) Farmers Covered: All farmers including share-croppers and tenant farmers growing notified crops in notified areas are eligible for coverage under

the scheme. However, it is compulsory for loanee farmers availing crop loans from financial institutions (PACS, RRBs, and commercial banks). While all loanee farmers would automatically get compulsorily coverage under NAIS through PACS/ bank branches extending crop loan for insured crops, all non-loanee farmers desirous of availing insurance coverage should contact the nearest bank branch before the stipulated time frame with a proposal for insurance. They must have a bank account and pay the requisite premium to get insurance coverage.

(c) Risks Covered: The scheme provides comprehensive risk insurance against yield losses due to non-preventable risks, *i.e.*, (a) natural fire and lightening, (b) storm, hailstorm, cyclone, typhoon, tempest, hurricane, tornado etc., (c) flood, inundation and landslide, (d) drought, dry spells, and (e) pests/ diseases etc. However losses arising out of war and nuclear risks, malicious damage and other preventable risks shall be excluded.

(d) Crops Covered: The scheme besides food and oilseed crops also covered annual commercial and horticultural crops. The crops in respect of which the past yield data based on Crop Cutting Experiments (CCEs) are available for past 10 years and the state government agreed to conduct requisite number of CCEs for estimating the average yield during the proposed season are covered. The crops to be covered next year will have to be spelt before the close of preceding year. At present, 35 different *Kharif* and 30 different *Rabi* season crops are being insured under NAIS in the country. The crops covered in various states fall under the following groups.

(a) Food Crops (Cereals, Millets and Pulses): Wheat, paddy, jowar, bajra, maize, ragi, korra, kodokutki, green gram, black gram, red gram, horse gram, moth etc.

(b) Oilseeds: Groundnut, sunflower, soya bean, safflower, sesame, niger, castor etc.

(c) Annual Commercial/Horticultural Crops: Sugarcane, cotton, potato, onion, chilly, turmeric, ginger, coriander, cumin, fennel, fenugreek, isabgol, jute, tapioca, banana, pineapple, etc. However mangoes, apples, grapes and oranges are not yet covered.

Pilot Project on Farm Income Insurance Scheme: The scheme is strictly applied to 'crop' income insurance and not 'farm' income insurance as it is designed to protect the income from a particular crop. Under the FITS, the indemnity calculation is modified to account for income shortfall, not just yield shortfall. In this case, the farmer will be paid the difference between the guaranteed income and the actual income per hectare. The guaranteed income is obtained by multiplying the threshold yield by the minimum support price.

The actual income is the actual yield multiplied by the current market price. The market price used for calculation of actual income is subject to a maximum of 120 per cent and a minimum of 80 per cent of the MSP.

Wheat Insurance Policy: Wheat insurance policy is unique technology-based insurance product combining crop vigour/biomass (Normalised Difference Vegetative Index-NDVI) and weather (temperature /rainfall) parameters. The NDVI component of cover measured at peak vigour stage provides effective risk management aid to those wheat growers, who are likely to be impacted by poor growth of the crop arising out of non-preventable natural factors. It is insurance against the likelihood of diminished wheat yield resulting from lower NDVI within the specified taluka preferably during February and/or high temperature consecutively for specified number of days above specified levels in 1st and /or second fortnight of March as measured at RWS. The insurance is linked to biomass triggers. Trigger events could be measured using high technology standards based in satellite imagery from remote sensing technology which could be independently verified and measured, and accurate and allows for speedy settlement of indemnities even before the crop is ready for harvesting. When the current NDVI falls short of the specified trigger level, the benefits payable to the insured will be the sum specified corresponding to trigger level and or the maximum temperature of specified number of days as recorded at RWS is higher than the specified trigger level during first and / or second fortnight of March, the benefit payable to insured shall be the sum specified corresponding to trigger level. The premium chargeable is statistically / actuarially calculated based on the geographical area, the triggers specified and biomass and temperature patterns of the specified area in the historical periods.

Pilot Coconut Palm Insurance Scheme (CPIS): The Coconut Palm Insurance Scheme (CPIS) has also been approved for implementation on pilot basis from year 2009-10 in the selected areas of Andhra Pradesh, Goa, Karnataka, Kerala, Maharashtra, Orissa and Tamil Nadu. The Sum Insured (SI) is based on the average input cost of the plantation and the age of the specific plant which varies from Rs. 600 per palm (in the age group of 4-15 years) to Rs. 1,150 per palm (in the age group of 16-60 years). The premium rate per palm ranges from Rs. 4.25 (in the age group of 4 to 15 years) to Rs. 5.75 (in the age group of 16 to 60 years). Fifty per cent of premium is contributed by GOI; 25 per cent by the concerned state government and the remaining 25 per cent by the farmer. The Insurance Company, *i.e.*, Agriculture Insurance Company (AIC) of India Ltd., is the implementing agency of the scheme and responsible for making payment of claims within a specified period. The CPIS is being administered by the Coconut Development Board (CDB). Since inception of the Pilot in 2009-10, 27.66 lakh farmers have been covered over an area of 0.25 lakh hectare insuring a sum amounting to Rs. 269.53 crore. The claims amounting to about Rs. 1.53 crore have become payable against the premium of about Rs. 1.46 crore benefiting about 3,385 growers.

Table-2: Pilot Coconut Palm Insurance Scheme (CPIS)

Year	*B.E*	*R.E*	*Actual Expenditure*
2009-10	Nil	1.00	0.10
2010-11	1.00	1.00	0.80
2011-12	1.00	1.00	1.00
Total 11th Plan	2.00	2.10	1.95
2012-13	1.00	0.50	0.50
2013-14	1.00		

Source: The financial progress of the aforesaid schemes (from 11th Plan).

Weather-Based Crop Insurance Scheme (WBCIS): Weather-Based Crop Insurance Scheme (WBCIS) aims to mitigate the hardship of insured farmers against the likelihood of loss on account of anticipated crop loss resulting from incidence of adverse conditions of weather parameters like, rainfall, temperature, frost, humidity etc. While crop insurance specifically indemnifies the cultivator against shortfall in crop yield, WBCIS is built upon the fact that weather conditions affect crop production even when a cultivator has taken care to ensure good harvest. Historical correlation studies of crop yield with weather parameters helps in developing weather thresholds (triggers) beyond which crop starts getting affected adversely. Payout structures are developed to compensate cultivators to the extent of losses deemed to have been suffered by them using the weather triggers. In other words, WBCIS uses weather parameters as 'proxy' for crop yield in compensating the cultivators for deemed crop losses. Pursuant to the budget proposals, AICIL introduced a Pilot Weather-Based Crop Insurance Scheme (WBCIS) in Karnataka during *Kharif* 2007 season covering 70 Hoblis (hamlets) in respect of eight rain-fed crops.

Table 2: Pilot Weather Based Crop Insurance Scheme (WBCIS)

Year	*B.E*	*R.E*	*Actual Expenditure*
2007-08	Nil	69.19	69.88
2008-09	50.00	100.00	100.00
2009-10	50.00	120.00	120.00
2010-11	100.00	450.00	450.00
2011-12	450.00	631.00	631.00
Total 11th Plan	650.00	1,300.00	1,370.00
2012-13	655.00	655.00	655.00
2013-14	700.00		

Source: The financial progress of the aforesaid schemes (from 11th Plan).

Coffee Insurance: Coffee insurance was launched in Hassan, Chikmagalur and Coorg districts, of Karnataka. The policy compensates the insured against the likelihood of diminished coffee output/yield, resulting from shortfall in actual rainfall index, within a specific geographical location and specified time period and yield losses, due to other non-preventable natural losses. Maximum sum insured per hectare for the Robusta and Arabica varieties, is Rs. 25,000 and Rs. 35,000 respectively, and insurance is available from 1st March to 30th June.

Role of the Private and Public Sectors for the Purpose of Implementation of Crop Insurance Schemes

Role of the Private Sector

The first license for the private sector was issued in October 2000. As of today, there are ten private sector insurers in the general insurance business: Reliance, Tata - AIG , Royal Sundaram, IFFCO-Toko, Bajaj-Allianze, ICICI-Lombard, HDFC – Chubb, Cholamandalam, ECGC and Star Health. The latter two, are limited to only a few lines of general insurance. The fact remains that these insurers have not yet undertaken agricultural insurance to a significant extent. Only two companies in the private sector have initiated crop insurance, albeit on a small scale. ICICI-Lombard was the first company to experiment with rainfall insurance in 2003. The concept is further extended to weather insurance since 2004. IFFCO-Toko General Insurance (ITGI), the second company in private sector, started piloting rainfall insurance, since 2004.

Role of the Insurance Regulatory and Development Authority (IRDA) has stipulated that every new insurer undertaking general insurance business, has to underwrite business in the rural sector to the extent of at least two per cent of the gross premium during the first financial year, which is to be increased to five per cent during the third financial year of its operation. Crop insurance is included in the rural sector insurance for this purpose. The business targets stipulated in rural insurance apparently are very small. Those, who do not meet even these small targets are getting away by paying penalties of nominal amount. If private insurers are to be spurred to enter the rural insurance market in a significant manner, the business targets have to be raised substantially by IRDA.

The experience of government supported and subsidised crop insurance and the recent entry of private insurers, raise questions about the co-existence of government and private agriculture insurance. One view is that the private sector will be unable to compete with government insurance, given the subsidies and access to the administrative machinery for delivering insurance. An alternative view is that given only 15 per cent coverage by government insurance, the private sector can carve out a reasonable market for itself based on improved efficiency, better design and superior services. Here one can even think of public-private partnership in providing agriculture insurance as against public-private competition. However, it is possible only when crop insurance can be run in a more professional manner with clear objectives.

Role of Public-Private Participatory

Three different models of private partnership could be visualised:

1. First is Implementing Agency (IA) model, where IA bears no risk, earns no return and is reimbursed merely administrative expenses. Such model provides poor incentives for extending coverage and monitoring and controlling moral hazard and adverse selection.
2. Second is a model, where the private insurer bears the risk. Given the significant component of systemic risk in agriculture, such model will require international reinsurance to be sustainable. The premium for such insurance is likely to be high, requiring subsidy from the government. Under this model, the government through technical body works out commercial premium rates and offers up-front subsidy in premium to all insurers, who would be required to write policies. The farmer pays premium less the subsidy. There is a level playing field for all insurers. Another modification in this model could be allocating territories to insurers, who would be exclusively writing policies in specified territories.
3. Third is in between two models discussed above with the possibility of public-private sharing of risks. In this case, the government is likely to be at informational disadvantage, *vis-à-vis* the insurance companies which write the policies. Hence, the risk sharing agreement will have to be appropriately designed to reduce problems of moral hazard and adverse selection. The agreement will have to provide adequate measures to counteract the natural incentive of private insurers, to target larger farmers and pay less attention to small and marginal farmers.

Role of Department of Agriculture and Co-operation (DAC), Ministry of Agriculture: During 2004, invited general insurance companies, both public and private, requesting them submit proposals on rural insurance, particularly agricultural insurance. A few companies submitted proposals and when asked to make presentation, only two companies turned up with proposals for rainfall, farmer's package, and livestock insurance.

Conclusion

Some of the Crop Insurance schemes are a good step forward to insure risk of millions of farmers, whose livelihood depends on the pattern and distribution of monsoon rain in India. However, it suffers from some of the major problems inherent in crop insurance programmes throughout the world. It exclusively insures farmer's yields against the average yield of the area. However, most of the agricultural labourer, rural off-farm and non-farm workers are not covered under the scheme, even though they are equally, if not more affected by the failure of agricultural crops. The existing scheme is wholly government scheme with no incentives to private finance players, which hinders competitiveness of the scheme. The average yield of a region/locality is not many times accurately measurable, which is the basis for calculation of indemnities.

References

Abdul, Rahman Ibrahim (2012) "Agricultural Insurance Schemes for the Development of Rural Economy", The Third International Symposium, "*Agrarian Economy and Rural Development—Realities and Perspectives for Romania*", Bucharest, Romania, October 11-13, 2013.

Agricultural Livelihoods and Crop Insurance in India Study Project: Risk Reduction through Rural Insurance Services Situation Analysis and Assessment Study New Delhi, January, 2013.

Dr Avtar Singh (2002): *Principles of Insurance Law (Life-Fire-Marine-Motor and Accident)*. 7th Edition, – Wadhwa and Co., Nagpur.

KSN Murthy and Dr. KVS Sarma (2002): "*Modern Law of Insurance*" 4th Edition, Lexis Nexis, Butter Worths, New Delhi 2002, p. 3.

M.N. Mishra (2005): '*Insurance Principles and Practice*' S. Chand and Co., Ltd., pp. 3-8.

Mahul, O.,N. Verma, and D.J. Clarke (2011). *Improving Famers, Access to Agricultural Insurance in India,*" World Bank.

Ministry of Agriculture, (2010): *"Pilot Weather-Based Crop Insurance Scheme (WBCIS)"*, Government of India.

Mishra, P.K. 1995. "Is Rainfall Insurance a New Idea? Pioneering Work Revisited," *Economic and Political Weekly*, pp. 84–88.

Rao, K.N., S. Gadgil, P.R. Seshagiri Rao, and K. Savithri, (2000): "Tailoring strategies to rainfall variability – The choice of the sowing window," *Current Science*, 78(10), pp.1216–30.

Report of the Working Group on *Risk Management in Agriculture for the Eleventh Five Year Plan (2007-12)*, Government of India, Planning Commission, New Delhi.

Syroka, J. (2007). "Index-based Weather Insurance for Indian Farmers: Recommendations for Ratemaking", Washington DC, World Bank.

39

Role of RUDSETI and Youth Empowerment in Bangalore Rural District

T. Mangala and Shivanand Nari

Introduction

In its essence, empowerment speaks of self-determined change. It involves fusion of supply and demand, the two sides of development. Development in the strict sense of the term is possible only when change in the environment within which rural youth lives enable them to develop and capitalise on their aptitude or ability or both. Empowerment is a sort of umbrella word, which includes issues ranging from health to governance and economic policy. It is the key to enhancement of their quality of life.

What ails the youth of today? Prime youth is the critical stage in the life of an individual. This is the stage in his or her life when enthusiasm rules the situation. Evidently, they look beyond time-honoured solutions, if offered, by the society to problems. Involving young people in developing villages is, therefore, a critical step towards achieving development at all levels. When the youth embark upon the challenging task of developing village community, in the process, they become familiar with the nature of challenges facing them as well as their neighbouring villages. In addition, they try to provide affordable and viable solution to some of these challenges. But, this is possible only when the youth receive proper training.

Today, the class of youth comprises the largest cohort ever, accounting for 40 per cent of India's total population. As in other developing countries, the youth face various challenges that affect their personal as well as career development. It is generally agreed upon that besides the efforts of government, there is an urgent need to initiate additional efforts by voluntary organisations to impart relevant training which ought to enable the youth employ themselves meaningfully. And in this direction, Non-Government Organisations can be an effective force educated rural youth is inclined or forced? To migrate to cities, as the rural areas are primarily agrarian and do not offer them to many job opportunities.

Unfortunately, they are often at a disadvantage, as they are more diffident than their urban counterparts. They are suffering from confidence crisis. These factors prompted Veerendra Heggade to come up with an innovative solution that would help the youth remain close to their home and still solve their problem of unemployment.

Need for the Study

In any developing economy, the role of youth in various sectors started to influence the social and political structure of the economy. It is felt that only through decent employment opportunities, young people can get the chance to work themselves out of poverty. Focussing on young population is a must for any country and its government. In this context, the effort of NGOs has created lot of impression in the group of youth as a tool for employment generation and to reduce income inequality. Acting on the need of the hour, the voluntary organisation, *i.e.,* RUDSETI is not only working in the rural areas of Bangalore district but also got engaged in innovations to develop methods and models for delivery of services to the marginalised. It has also become the extended arm of the government in the form of implementation of various programmes. Henceforth, this area received lot of encouragement by government. Therefore, it is high time to make an analysis of the impact of RUDSETI on youth empowerment.

Rural Development and Self-employment Training Institute – RUDSETI

RUDSETI is an NGO which is recognised for its role in developing new initiatives, new programmes or components of programmes, new approaches, new mechanisms, etc., to address the problems and issues of rural youth. Undoubtedly, it has been in the forefront of many innovations that have provided ideas and models which have been applied in collaboration with government and banks. RUDSETI identifies opportunities, trains participants in developing the desired skills and assists them in their entrepreneurial activity. This training being highly a valuable tool, caters to the needs of youth without gender bias. There are now twenty six RUDSET institutes spread across sixteen states. Over 2.91 lakh rural youth have been trained in these institutes. Over 70 per cent of them have set up successful entrepreneurial ventures. One such institute is functioning at Nelamangala, Bangalore Rural District since 1996.

Objectives

1. To explore the competence of youth. Against this backdrop, the available training and skill development programmes require to be assessed in terms of relevance.
2. To analyse the changes in the standard of living of the beneficiaries, as a result of training programmes and subsequent efforts by the beneficiaries.
3. To examine the contribution of RUDSETI to the empowerment of youth.

Research Design and Sample

Since this is an empirical study, its analysis and conclusions are based upon primary data collected from the beneficiaries of RUDSETI. The field work and subsequent investigation were carried out and fifty beneficiaries were selected within the geographical boundary of Bangalore Rural district and the target group is in the age group of 18-35 for this investigation. The respondents were selected on the basis of purposive random sampling method. The empirical findings of the study have been supplemented by secondary data. They were sourced out from libraries by reviewing existing theoretical and empirical studies on the topic, official document and periodicals. Internet sources were browsed and downloaded for necessary information. The present study has taken the data for the period of one year (2012-13) for its analysis.

Why RUDSETI?

Unemployment is the major challenge India has been facing in the process of development. Millions of youth are entering the job market every year after completing formal education. The rise in the use of automation and mechanisation in all spheres of commerce and administration has further accentuated the problem. On the rural side, the employment potential in agrarian economy appears to have reached saturation level leading to large-scale migration of manpower from rural to urban areas adding to woes and pressure experienced by over-strained civic infrastructure of cities. Millions of unemployed youth particularly from rural background, who could not access higher or professional education but oriented towards white-collar jobs are driven to despair for not finding job. Of late, these distressed youth are rapidly becoming anti-social elements. This collossal waste of human resources and mismatch of potentiality with profession rural youth have to select has baffled the planners and administrators.

All these clearly indicate the need for promoting self-employment entrepreneurial ventures among the unemployed youth particular in rural India. It is under these circumstances that Rural Development and Self-employment Training Institute (RUDSETI), a unique initiative in mitigating the problem of unemployment came into play its vital role. And this institution got the support of two leading nationalised banks, *i.e.,* Canara Bank and Syndicate Bank.

The following services are provided in an innovative, effective and cost-effective manner, with a spirit of service:

- Creating awareness on self- employment.
- Developing motivation and positive attitude.
- Training to acquire hard skills and soft skills.
- Handholding for establishment and successful running of enterprise and
- Linkages with Banks for financial assistance.

Intense planning and research is undertaken to identify employment opportunities for the youth having some hands-on experience. Facts revealed by market surveys form the basis of this programme. The participants are not only trained in the chosen field, but are put through various exercises to instil immense self-confidence in them. After training them, RUDSETI guided and assisted them to start their enterprise. Once the youngsters are settled, RUDSETI continues their association with successful participants in order to instil in them the sense of confidence that they are not alone and that an organisation is behind them. RUDSETI is imparting all sorts of necessary skills to the participants through the above said programmes, which are required for starting their own business ventures. After training the participants in all respects, RUDSETI guides the enterprising youth in setting up their ventures As a first step, RUDSETI helps them to complete the initial formalities including bank loans. Even after the enterprise is established, RUDSETI continues to be in constant touch with the young entrepreneurs. If the business faces problems and puts the young entrepreneur through severe strain, then RUDSETI supports him for two-three years to help him overcome the problem.

RUDSETI is providing wide variety of training programmes to participants, selected on an objective assessment of their abilities. Below are some of the training programmes conducted by the RUDSETI.

Table-1: Different forms of RUDSETI Training Programmes

Category	*Forms of training*
Agriculture and Horticulture	Dairy Farming, Poultry, Bee Keeping, Plant Nursery, etc.
Product dress	Design for women/men, Making Agarbathis and Soft Toys, Food Processing and Bakery Products, Embroidery and Fabric Painting etc.
Process	Electric Motor Rewinding and Pump Set Maintenance, Beauty Parlour Management, Basic Photography and Videography, Multi Phone Servicing, Repair of Domestic Electrical Appliances, Two Wheeler Servicing, Computer DTP, Refrigeration and Air Conditioning, Computer Tally, Computer Basics etc.
General	Rural Entrepreneurship Development Programme, EDP for Women etc.

Source: Documents of RUDSETI.

During 2012-13, 3,513 candidates were trained here and 1,896 persons have started their own enterprises which mean that 54 per cent of the youths started their own enterprise after receiving loan to the tune of Rs 48.4 million from the banks. RUDSETI is boosting job skills, training them to utilise locally available resources, guiding to start small industries. Many have become financially self-sufficient after being trained in this Institute. A few female respondents have started beauty parlours at home after getting loan from women and child welfare department and according to them the training in RUDSETI has helped them a lot and their life is much happier. Some male respondents said that they are capable of managing mobile service centers and found a way of self-employment and this could happen only because of training programme initiated by RUDSETI, without which owning an enterprise would be a distant dream.

The standard of living of the respondents is analysed with respect to their occupation and changes in their income level before and after participating in the training programmes of RUDSETI. Among the 50 respondents, 35 are male and 15 female, who belong to different occupational background. The table below represent the economic status of respondents.

Table-2: Economic Status of Youth (Gender-based)

Economic Status	Male Per cent age	Female Per cent age	Total per ce
Unemployed	9 (26)	2 (13)	11 (22
Rural occupation	12 (34)	5 (33)	17 (34
Home maker	0 (0)	3 (20)	3 (6
Part-time employee	8 (23)	2 (13)	10 (20
Self- employed	6 (17)	3 (20)	9 (18

Source: Field Survey.

The Table reveals that out of 50 respondents 22 per cent of them are unemployed, out of which nine are male and two are female. Fairly a good number of respondents are engaged in rural occupation, *i.e.,* agriculture and its allied activities. They form 34 per cent of the respondents of which twelve are male and five are female respondents. Six male and three female respondents are self-employed who form 18 per cent of the sample. Interestingly, there are three home makers who form six per cent of the respondents. It shows that sample include diversified respondents.

Table-3: Change in Income Before and After Training

Category	*Income Before Training (Rs)*	*Income After Training (Rs)*
Unemployed	00	5500
Rural occupation	2000	6750
Home-maker	00	3500
Part-time employee	5000	9000
Self-employed	7000	12250

Source: Field survey.

Change in Income Before and After Training

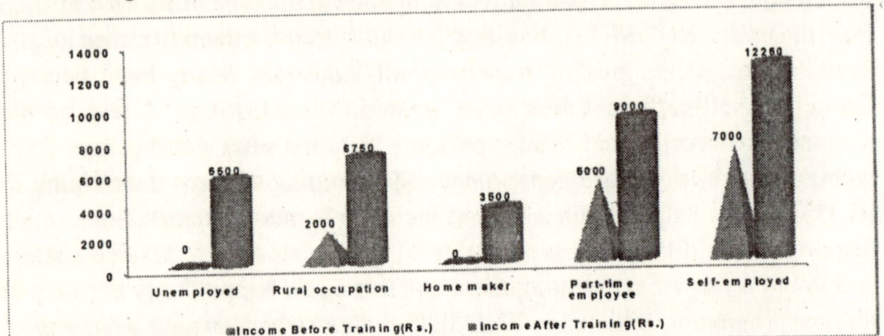

Source:

The field survey data show that there is increase in income of the respondents after attending training programme conducted by RUDSETI. The data reveal that there is 75 per cent increase in the income of the self-employed after they discovered their new source of income. RUDSETI has become a ray of hope for the home makers since it has provided an opportunity to generate their own income by utilising their leisure time. Of course, it has become a boon for the unemployed youths, who were, otherwise, unemployed.

Findings

- RUDSETI is an institution which is providing training for the improvement of the living standard of the needy people.

- In the year 2012-13, it has trained 3,513 candidates on various programmes.
- Fifty four per cent of the youth have started their enterprises, after being facilitated by training in RUDSETI.
- The institute conducts wider variety of training programmes to convert the unemployed youth into self-employed.
- On the way of its operation, RUDSETI is recognised by many organisations. Canara Bank and Syndicate Banks have collaborated with the institute.
- It is promoting rural entrepreneurship, generating self-employment in rural areas, creating awareness, building confidence among youth.
- The institute is promoting service sector in the study area.

The involvement of NGOs in alleviating poverty has changed the life of poor in rural area. By designing and implementing innovative programmes they have enhanced quality of the life of poor. The case of RUDSETI, Nelamangala explained in this paper indicates that at the local level it has intensively engaged in youth empowerment. The conditions of the youth have improved, sometimes quite significantly, as the result of the RUDSETI intervention. Given their valuable experiences and the development of their organisational capacity, it is most likely that its contribution to youth empowerment will increase in future.

References

Clark, J. (1991), *Democratising Development: The Role of Voluntary Organisation*, London: Earthscan.

D.S. and Hansra, B.S. Dhillon, '1995' *Role of Voluntary Organisations in Rural Development. Kurukshetra* 18(5) pp. 10-13.

Fisher, Julie. (1993), *"The Road from Rio: Sustainable Development and the Non-Governmental Movement in the Third World'*, USA: Praeger Publications.

Jimmy Dabhi, (2005), *"NGOs 'Response to Violence against the Marginalised and Discriminated Communities", Social Action*, January-March 2005, Volume 55.

www.karnatakaindustry.gov.in|..|Nelamangala.

www.rudseti_rayof_hop_unemployed_youth.html.

www.rudsetiacademy.org|Annual_Report_Inside.

www.rudsetiacademy.org|objectives.html.

www.rudsetitraining.org|pdf|bt.

40

Role of Social Capital in the Provision of Credit: A Micro Level Analysis of Households in Rural Punjab

Shiv Kumar

Introduction

In industrial economies, households generally obtain credit, against individual guarantees, from commercial sources, that reach loan decisions on the basis of readily available information on borrowers' credit risk. In most developing economies, however, poor households usually do not have access to guarantee mechanisms. This situation combined with the overall lack of information about potential borrowers' credit worthiness, contributes to virtual exclusion of this group of borrowers from formal credit markets. However, several classes of institutional arrangements offer to these borrowers' valid substitutes for individual collateral, and to the lenders low-cost alternatives to imperfect credit worthiness information. An increasing number of finance institutions provide credit to the poor on the basis of 'social collateral', through which borrowers' reputation, or the social networks to which they belong, take the place of traditional fiscal or financial collateral. Since these arrangements build, to various degrees, on the extent and strength of personal relationship, they provide fertile ground for the analysis of the role of social capital in the provision of credit (Bastelaer, 2000). Coleman (1988) described social capital as "an important social structural 'resource' or capital asset for the individual which is productive making the achievement of certain ends possible that would not be attainable in its absence." According to Portes (1998), "social capital stands for ability of people to secure benefits by virtue of their membership in social networks or other social structures." Thus, the main objective of this paper is to analyse the impact of social capital on credit access by households in rural areas of three districts of Punjab: Jalandhar, Ludhiana and Muktsar. The paper is divided into five sections. Following introduction, second section explains the data sources and methodology. Third section highlights various credit arrangements available for rural households. The effect of social capital on amount of credit received by households is explained in section four and the final section.

DATASOURCES AND METHODOLOGY

The present paper is based on both primary as well as secondary data. Primary data are collected through well-organised questionnaire by multi-stage sampling method. In the first stage, three districts of Punjab are selected, namely, Jalandhar, Ludhiana and Muktsar with low, medium and high per cent of rural poor respectively (Chaudhury and Gupta, 2009). In the second stage, within each district, three blocks are selected on the basis of high, medium and low-level of development (Ghuman *et al,* 2007). In the third stage, within each block, three villages are selected based on low, medium and high per cent of BPL families in the village provided the village has at least 10 BPL families. In the final stage, within each of the 27 villages, 20 households (10 poor and 10 non-poor) are selected randomly to participate in the household survey for a total sample of 540 households. However, for the present paper, only those 245 households are studied, which obtained credit from at least one of the credit sources. The collected are analysed in SPSS software by using OLS regression, split sample approach, and Chow statistic in addition to mean, T-test, and F statistic.

TYPES OF CREDIT ARRANGEMENTS FOR THE RURAL HOUSEHOLDS

There are basically five types of credit arrangements targetted at the rural people.

(a) Rotating Savings and Credit Associations: The concept of Rotating Savings and Credit Associations (ROSCAs) is also known as *'committee'* in India. ROSCA is a group of individuals who agree to meet for a defined period in order to save and borrow together. Every transaction is seen by every member during the meetings. This reduces the size of the loss, should someone take funds early and not pay back. The collective trust that enables this system to function can be present at the beginning of the first rotation (if the members are chosen on the basis of pre-existent levels of trust among themselves) (Bastelaer, 2000). But, as Rutherford (2000) pointed out, the system can also create the levels of trust that makes operations possible, even if members didn't know each other at the beginning of the cycle. In sample villages of

Punjab, out of 344 households, which are members of at least one group in the village, 126 (36.6 per cent) households are members of 197 committees (ROSCAs) and in year 2010-11 Rs. 29,78,050 are mobilised through these committees. The importance of these committees for poor households is proved on the basis of the fact that out of 126 households, which are members of these committees, 57.1 per cent households in sample villages are poor. In sample villages of Punjab, 72 poor households are found to be members of 101 committees.

(b) Friends and Relatives: Loans from friends and relatives are the most common form of informal finance. These arrangements are characterised by uncollateralised loans that carry no or little interest, feature open-ended repayment arrangements, and have a strong focus on reciprocity. But for this type of credit, the deep friendship and kinship ties matter a lot. This social capital of networks and reciprocity provides a big relief, both financially as well as psychologically, in case of an income shock. In sample villages of Punjab, overall, 12.1 per cent credit is received by households from friends and relatives (Table 1). However, when it is disaggregated for poor and non-poor households, it is found that poor households received 28.3 per cent credit from friends and relatives, whereas for non-poor households the figure is very small (4.2 per cent). It clearly shows that poor households are significantly more dependent on friendship and kinship ties for credit than for the non-poor households. The social capital of poor households makes these transactions possible and reliable without any formal paper work.

(c) Co-operative Societies: The agricultural co-operative credit structure in the Punjab State is broadly divided into two sectors, one dealing with the short-term and medium-term finance and the other with the long-term credit. In the State, the short-term and medium-term credit structure is based on a three-tier system, *i.e.*, the Apex Co-operative Bank at the state level, the Central Co-operative Bank at the district/tehsil level and the Primary Agricultural Co-operative Societies at the village level. Among the sample households in Punjab co-operative society is the major source of credit. Thirty six per cent credits are received by households from these societies (Table-1). It is also observed that these co-operative societies play a major role for non-poor households than poor households for their credit requirements. As the data in Table-1 show, 45.4 per cent credit is received from co-operative societies by non-poor households whereas poor households received credit from the co-operative societies to the tune of 17 per cent. Local social capital plays a key role to access credit from these societies. The officials working in these societies, virtually, are recruited from the local village, thus make it convenient to the people to access credit from this source. The local networks of officials with villagers are useful to decide the creditworthiness of the borrowers.

(d) Commercial Banks: Poor households in rural areas are not familiar

with formal credit, which deliver funds through formal financial institutions, such as commercial banks. Formal credit institutions need mediation. Narayan and Pritchett (1999) argued that social capital could do better flow of information between creditors and borrowers and hence less adverse selection and moral hazard in the market for credit. The guarantee of groups and pressure by social networks are important techniques to improve credit performance (Brata, 2005). It is found in the villages of Punjab that many of the managers of commercial banks send their agents to meet people in the village and build a network and issue credit after getting appropriate information, both economic and social. about the people. Here, the role of social capital is attributed because in addition to economic condition, the personal reputation of a person and mutual relations among people in the village become the determinant factor in accessing formal credit. The survey results show that commercial banks are the second main source of credit for rural households in Punjab (Table-1). Even for poor households accessing formal credit is common. Table-1 shows that 29.2 per cent credit is received by poor households from commercial banks.

(e) Moneylenders and Commission Agents: Moneylenders and commission agents, typically landowners and traders, are other sources of credit available to the rural people. Their loans are extended quickly and for short periods, and at interest levels that are high in comparison with other sources of lending. Because of their long-term presence in the village and markets and their networks of influence over many aspects of the community life, moneylenders and commission agents have a good knowledge of the creditworthiness of the borrowers, and can design personalised interest rate structures accordingly. As Stiglitz (1990) noted, "The local moneylenders have one important advantage over the formal [lending] institutions: they have more detailed knowledge of the borrowers. They, therefore, can separate out high-risk and low-risk borrowers and charge them appropriate interest rates". In sample villages of Punjab ten to eleven per cent credit is received by households, both poor and non-poor, from this source (Table-1).

Table-1: Percentage of Credit Received from Different Sources by Poor and Non-Poor Households

Source of Credit	*Poor*	*Non-Poor*	*All*
Friends and Relatives	28.3	4.2	12.1
Primary Co-operative Societies	17.0	45.4	36.0
Commercial Banks	29.2	36.6	34.2
Moneylenders and Commission Agents	11.3	10.6	10.9
Other	14.2	3.2	6.8
Total	**100.0**	**100.0**	**100.0**

Source :

Social Capital and Amount of Credit

Social Capital and Credit Model

Now, after discussing the sources for credit for rural households in an environment of social cohesion, the role of social capital can be tested in providing the *amount* of loans. To analyse this, the basic model in equation (1) is used by taking amount of loan received by households as the dependent variable.

$$A_i = a + b_1SC_i + b_2HC_i + b_3PC_i + b_4SZ_i + b_5SX_i + b_6AG_i + u_i \quad \text{.................. (1)}$$

Where, A_i = Amount of Credit Received by Household I; SC_i = Household Endowment of Social Capital; HC_i = Household Endowment of Human Capital; PC_i = Household Endowment of Physical Capital; SZ_i = Household Size; SX_i = Gender of Head of Household; AG_i = Age of Head of Household; and u_i = Error Term.

The key feature of this model is the assumption that social capital is truly 'capital' *i.e.,* a stock, which generates a measurable return (flow of credit) to the household. Social capital has many 'capital' features: it requires resources (especially time) to be produced and it is subject to accumulation and destruction. Much social capital is built during interactions which occur for social, religious, or cultural reasons. The key assumption is that the networks built through these interactions have measurable benefits to the participating individuals, and lead, directly or indirectly, to a higher level of well-being. There is an impact assumption that social capital is embodied in the members of the household. This conforms to the position advocated by Portes (1998), which highlights that, although the source of social capital is the relationship among group of individuals, the capital itself is an individual asset. Hence, social capital is viewed as an individual household asset.

Variable Definitions

(a) *Amount of Credit*: The present total amount of loan taken by the household is measured in rupees.

(b) *Social Capital*: For measuring social capital at household level in rural Punjab a locally relevant indicator relying on six basic dimensions, as suggested by Grootaért *et al.* (2004) –(a) groups and networks; (b) trust and solidarity; (c) collective action and co-operation; (d)information and communication; (e) social cohesion and inclusion; and (f) empowerment and political action – is devised in the study. Responses from 245 sample households for the fifteen basic survey questions, grouped into these six dimensions of social capital, are added after multiplying with the appropriate weight and then the resultant score is rescaled from zero to 100 to construct social capital index where zero represents lowest score and 100 represents highest score on this index.

(c) *Human Capital*: The human capital variable is measured by the total number of years of formal education of the head of the household.

(d) *Physical Capital:* The physical capital owned by the household is measured on the basis of the ownership of three types of assets: land, agricultural tools, and animals. The average value in rupees of each of these three assets is added to get the value of the physical capital.

(e) *Household Size:* Size of household means the number of people living in the house.

(f) *Gender of Head of Household:* A dummy variable is used for the gender of head of household (D=1 if male, D=0 if otherwise).

(g) *Age of head of household:* Age of head of household is measured in years.

Results and Discussion

In Table 2, the OLS regression result shows that F- statistic is 13.375 and is significant with R^2 0.378. This indicates that the model has a good fit to the data. The results show that social capital, human capital, physical capital and age of head of household are the key determinants of amount of credit received by households in rural Punjab. More specifically, social capital and human capital have the coefficients of 0.116 and 0.118 respectively which implies that as social capital and human capital is increased by one unit, the amount of credit received by households' increases by more than 11 per cent. The fiscal capital coefficient is 0.019, *i.e.*, the effect is smaller than the effect of social capital and human capital.

Table 2: Effect of Social Capital on Amount of Credit Received by Households

	Coefficients	*t-values*
Intercept	*–668943.307***	–2.343
Social Capital	0.116***	1.571
Human Capital	0.118***	1.514
Physical Capital	0.019*	3.123
Household Size	–0.034	–0.516
Sex of Head of Household	0.014	0.224
Age of Head of Household	*0.202**	3.119
Number of Observations	245	
R^2	0.378	
Adjusted R^2	0.355	
F-Statistics	13.375*	

*significant at one per cent , **significant at five per cent and ***significant at 10 per cent.
The dependent variable is the amount of credit received by the household.

Source: Computed from field survey data.

Table 3: Effect of Social Capital on Amount of Credit Received by Poor and Non-Poor Households

	Poor	*Non-Poor*
	Coefficients (t-values)	*Coefficients (t-values)*
Intercept	*–93973.887 (–1.268)*	*–14525.546* (–1.236)
Social Capital	0.170** (1.927)	0.082 (0.950)
Human Capital	–0.036 (–0.431)	0.158*** (1.507)
Physical Capital	0.001 (0.002)	0.494* (4.910)
Household Size	0.187*** (1.529)	–0.062 (–0.726)
Sex of Head of Household	–0.025 (–0.291)	0.005 (0.056)
Age of Head of Household	*0.039 (0.437)*	0.247* (2.957)
Number of Observations	92	153
R^2	0.431	0.380
Adjusted R^2	0.391	0.342
F-Statistics	10.730*	12.184*
Chow-Statistics = 30.021*		

Figures in parentheses are *t*-values. *significant at one per cent, **significant at five per cent and ***significant at 10 per cent.

The dependent variable is the amount of credit received by the household.

$$\text{Chow Statistic} = \frac{[Sc - (S1 + S2)]/k}{(S1 + S2)/N1 + N2 - 2k}$$

The Chow test statistic follows the F-distribution with k and *N1+N2–2k* degrees of freedom, where,

Sc = sum of squared residuals from the combined data.
S1 = sum of squared residuals from the first group.
S2 = sum of squared residuals from the second group.
N1 = number of observations in the first group.
N2 = number of observations in the second group.
k = total number of parameters.

Source: Computed from field survey data.

However, in split-sample model for poor and non-poor households in Table-3, it is found that, for poor households, among the three forms of capital only social capital has the significant co-efficient, *i.e.*, 0.170, whereas for non-poor households, both human capital and fiscal capital have the significant co-efficients. This underscores the importance of social capital contribution for the bottom half of the distribution. Also, the age of head of household has a positive significant co-efficient 0.247 for non-poor households which imply that as the age of the household increases in years, the amount of credit received is increased. This is due to the fact that as the age of household increases the good reputation and past repayment records of the person become the strong support to assess the creditworthiness of non-poor households and thus accessing formal credit becomes facile. On the other hand, for poor households, size of the household is found to be significant contributor among household characteristics which reveals that more members in a family increases the chances of memberships in local groups and associations and also in ROSCAs making informal credit sources easily accessible.

Conclusion

The research findings bring to light that social capital among households in rural areas of Punjab, India, is truly capital and it positively affects the amount of credit received by households. The study examined the various credit arrangements available for rural people and the effect of social capital on credit is studied. It is found in the analysis that social capital, human capital, physical capital, and size and age of households drive the amount of credit received by households positively. Thus, the investment in social capital through its relevant dimension should be encouraged in the development policies to make the growth and development more inclusive.

References

Bastelaer, T. (2000). "Does Social Capital Facilitate the Poor's Access to Credit?" A Review of the Micro-economic Literature". *Social Capital Initiative Working Paper No. 8*, Social Development Department, the World Bank, Washington D.C.

Brata, A.G. (2005). "Accessing Formal Credit: Social Capital versus 'Social Position' (Lessons from a Javanese Village)" Paper prepared for the *7th IRSA International Conference,* Jakarta, August 3-4, Session- II C.

Chaudhuri, S. and Gupta, N. (2009). "Levels of Living and Poverty Patterns: A District-wise Analysis for India". *Economic and Political Weekly,* 44(9), pp 94-110.

Coleman, J.S. (1988) "Social Capital in the Creation of Human Capital", *American Journal of Sociology*, 94 (Supplement), pp. S95-S120.

Ghuman, R.S., Singh, I. and Singh, L. (2007)., *Status of Local Agricultural Labour in Punjab.* The Punjab State Farmers, Commission, Government of Punjab.

Grootaert, C., Narayan, D., Jones, V.N. and Woolcock, M. (2004). "Measuring Social Capital: An Integrated Questionnaire" *World Bank Working Paper No. 18.* Washington D.C.

Narayan, D. and Pritchett, L. (1999) "Cents and Sociability: Household Income and Social Capital in Rural Tanzania," *Economic Development and Cultural Change,* 47(4), pp. 871-97.

Portes, A. (1998). "Social Capital: Its Origins and Applications in Modern Sociology", *Annual Review of Sociology*, 24,pp. 1-24.

Rutherford, S. (2000), *The Poor and Their Money*, New Delhi: Oxford University Press.

Stiglitz, J.E. (1990). "Peer Monitoring and Credit Markets", *World Bank Economic Review*, 4(3), pp. 351-66.

41

Foreign Direct Investment (FDI) in Multi-brand Retail and its Effect on Farmers

K. Gagan and Ramesh

Introduction

There are two types of investments, namely – Domestic Direct Investment (DDI), and Foreign Direct Investment (FDI). Foreign Direct Investment is "the acquisition by the residents of a country of real assets abroad. This may be done by remitting money abroad to be spent on acquiring land, constructing buildings, mines or machinery, or buying existing foreign businesses" (*A Dictionary of Economics*, 2012). Retail is the business of "selling goods to the public in shops or by post" (*Oxford English Dictionary*, 2006). Recently, the Government of India allowed 51 per cent FDI in multi-brand retail trade (MBRT). This has come under sharp criticism from the farmers and retail traders. Part-II of the paper provides an overview of retail sector in India; Part-III of the paper gives an account of the law relating to Foreign Direct Investment; Part-IV examines whether FDI in multi-brand retail trade is beneficial to farmers or not.

FDI IN RETAIL SECTOR IN INDIA

Retail Sector in India

Most of the retail sector is unorganised. The size of India's retail market was estimated at US$ 435 billion in 2010. Of this, US$ 414 billion (95 per cent of the market) was traditional/ unorganised retail and US$ 21 billion (five per cent of the market) was organised retail. The Indian retail sector accounts for 22 per cent of the country's Gross Domestic Product (GDP) and employs 44 million people, *i.e.*, eight per cent of the total employment (FICCI, 2014). Food retail trade accounts for 63 per cent of total retail sales. Hence, FDI in multi-brand retail affects the farmers directly. The organised retail sector can be further divided into single brand retail trading and multi-brand retail trading. In a single brand retail trading, only the products of one particular brand are sold. In multi-brand retail trading, products of several brands are sold.

Law Governing FDI in India

FDI in India is regulated by the *Foreign Exchange Management Act, 1999* (FEMA), which was passed with the objective of "facilitating external trade and payments and for promoting orderly development and maintenance of foreign exchange market in India." Section 3 of the Act generally prohibits all types of foreign exchange except under the provisions of FEMA or with the permission of Reserve Bank of India (RBI).

A foreign company planning to set up business operations in India may:

1. Incorporate a company under the *Companies Act, 1956*, as a joint venture or a wholly owned or subsidiary, or
2. Set up a Liaison Office / Representative Office or a Project Office or a Branch Office of the foreign company which can undertake activities permitted under the *Foreign Exchange Management (Establishment in India of Branch Office or Other Place of Business) Regulations, 2000.* (Reserve Bank of India, 2014).

An Indian company can receive FDI under two routes, namely – automatic route and government route. FDI through automatic route requires no prior approval of the government or RBI. FDI through government route requires prior approval of the government, which is considered by the Foreign Investment Promotion Board (FIPB), Department of Economic Affairs, and Ministry of Finance. Sector-wise business operations are listed under different categories in the consolidated FDI policy, issued by the Government of India from time to time. FDI in certain sectors is allowed under automatic route, certain other sectors under the government route. FDI in certain other sectors like, Atomic Energy, Lottery Business and Gambling is totally prohibited. FDI caps are also fixed sector-wise.

FDI Norms for Retail Sector

At present, FDI in 'cash and carry wholesale trading' is allowed up to 100 per cent under automatic route. FDI in single brand retail trade is allowed up to 100 per cent with prior government approval.

On September 20, 2012, Government of India notified 51 per cent FDI in multi-brand retail trade. This came with a pre-condition that the investors shall source 30 per cent of goods from small scale industries, which have total investment in plant and machinery not exceeding $1 million. Due to the opposition to FDI in MBRT from various states, the government made it clear that this is an enabling policy and the respective state governments are free to take their own decisions to implement the policy ('Press Note No. 5, 2012, 2012 Series).

The pre-condition of sourcing 30 per cent goods locally was seen as an unfavourable condition by the foreign investors. The US retail giant Walmart and multi-national retail chains of UK and France expressed their inability to meet the 30 per cent mandatory sourcing norm (Mehdudia, 2013).

Evaluating the Effect of FDI in MBRT on Farmers

Political parties are divided over the decision of allowing FDI in MBRT. Even the public opinion is divided on the benefits ushered by FDI in MBRT (FDI and retail sector, 2012). Even among the economists, some of them feel that this move will tackle inflation, while others feel it will be of no use (Seth, 2011). Nobel laureate economist James Mirrlees has said that FDI in MBRT is likely to perk up the India's financial system (Global Jurix, 2013).

Supreme Court on FDI in MBRT

The decision to allow FDI in MBRT was challenged before the Supreme Court and the court held that the decision didn't suffer from any unconstitutionality, illegality, arbitrariness or irrationality. A three-judge bench of Justices RM Lodha, Madan B. Lokur and Kurian Joseph opined that the policy allowing FDI in MBRT having been based on the philosophy of 'consumer is king' would benefit the consumer by "enlarging the choice of purchase at more affordable prices and by eradicating the traditional trade intermediaries/middlemen to facilitate better access to the market [ultimate retailer] for the producer of goods." The Bench also said that the new policy aims to throw out middlemen, "who are a curse to Indian economy and who are sucking it." The Court stated that the farmers will benefit significantly from the option of direct sales to organised retailers (*Manohar Lal Sharmas. Union of India and Another*, 2013).

Examining the Benefits of FDI in MBRT

It is argued that FDI in MBRT creates 10 million jobs, helps the farmers, benefits the consumers, eliminates the middlemen and boosts investments. Each of these arguments is examined below.

1. *Creation of jobs:* A study has found that a Walmart store opening reduces county-level retail employment by about 150 workers, implying that each Walmart worker replaces approximately 1.4 retail workers (Neumark, Zhang,

and Ciccarella, 2008). P. Sainath (2011) opines that the job forecast "comes from a school of economics that has gifted the world, jobless growth for three decades now".

2. *Benefits to consumers:* Giant retailers would surely be able to sell the goods at lower prices. The retail chains are able to achieve this by supplying farm products that are preserved by way of freezing. This means that the consumer will be deprived of getting 'fresh' farm produce. The damage made by FDI in MBRT on the farmers will eventually affect consumers in the long run.

3. *Elimination of middlmen* – The middlemen, who will be eliminated are those cart vendors who do not have the economic power to squeeze the prices. "The more exploitative middlemen in the chain will be co-opted by giant retail, which needs collectors and contractors, though not so many" (Sainath, 2011).

Harms Caused by FDI in MBRT on Farmers and Rural Communities

FDI in MBRT will create few buyers for the large population of farmers. This will naturally reduce the bargaining power of farmers. In India, the condition of farmers is already bad. According to the National Crime Records Bureau (NCRB), at least 270,940 farmers have committed suicide since 1995 (Sainath, 2013).

In USA, giant retailers are operating for more than three decades. An overview of the situation of farmers in the USA will help us assess the effects of giant retailers on the farmers. In 1950s, the number of people employed in farm sector was over 25 million. This number fell down to 2.24 million in 2002 and to 2.11 million in 2012 ("Employment by major industry sector," 2013). Large corporations have curtailed the independence of farmers by way of production contracts and other forms of vertical integration (Guru and Horne, n.d.). Studies in the State of Iowa have shown that some towns below 5,000 populations have lost nearly half their retail trade in the last 13 years (1997). When this is the effect these large retailers had on the farmers in USA, will it be different in India? One may argue that the Indian government may impose certain 'safety valves' to protect the interest of farmers. It has to be noted that 7.5 million people abandoned agriculture ever since the opening of Indian markets (2011). The effect of FDI in MBRT will be even worse on the farmers of India.

Reforms in Indian Agricultural Markets

One may be tempted to ask, "What else needs to be done to end the exploitation of farmers by the middlemen and benefit the customer" The answer is – reforms in agricultural markets. "Every agricultural market was once a farmer's market. Over time, farmers have lost control over such markets to traders and moneylenders" says journalist P. Sainath (Sainath, 2011). The government has to take steps to free the agricultural markets from the clutches of traders and moneylenders and ensure their operation in transparent manner. If the agricultural markets function in transparent manner, the farmers will naturally get fair price for their produce. Due to widespread corruption, the various schemes for the benefit of farmers have not reached the farmers. Reforms in governance and accountability initiatives would ensure that these benefits reach the farmers.

Conclusion

This study has found out large retailers in USA have caused harm to the farm sector and small retailers. The number of people employed in farm sector which was 25 million in 1950s fell to 2.11 million in 2012. This decline happened over a period of time, when large retailers proliferated across USA. If these large retailers were beneficial for farmers, the number of people in farm sector wouldn't have reduced so drastically. It is submitted that FDI in MBRT will have long-term damaging effects on the agricultural economy of India. Hence, it is recommended that FDI in MBRT is rolled back by the government and reforms in agricultural markets are implemented.

References

Basker, Emek, "Job Creation or Destruction? Labor Market Effects of Wal-Mart Expansion." *Review of Economics and Statistics,* 87.1 (2005), pp.174–83.

Bhargava, Anupam, "FDI in Retail? Say a Big NO.," *The Hindu,* Dec 2, 2012. *The Hindu*, Web, May13, 2014.

"Centre Walks the Talk, Clears Entry of MNCs into Multi-brand Retail." *The Hindu* 21 Sept. 2012. *The Hindu.* Web. 13 May 2014.

Chowdhary, Suvrata. "FDI in Retail: What It Entails?" *The Hindu,* 2 Feb, 2013. *The Hindu*, Web, 13 May, 2014.

"Employment by Major Industry Sector." *Bureau of Labour, Statistics*. N.P., Dec. 2013. Web. May13, 2014.

"FDI & Retail Sector." *The Hindu* Sept 19 2012. *The Hindu.* Web. May 14, 2014.

Retail Sector Profile. FICCI, 2014.

Global Jurix, "FDI In Retail Will Boost Indian Economy, Says Nobel Laureate.", *Mondaq*, N.P., Jan.9, 2013. Web., May14, 2014.

Goetz, Stephan J., and Hema Swaminathan, "Wal-Mart and County-Wide Poverty*" *Social Science Quarterly*, 87.2 (2006), pp.211–26.

Guru, Manjula, and James Horne, *U.S. Farm Crisis*, Oklahoma: The Kerr Centre for Sustainable Agriculture.

Manohar Lal Sharma Vs. Union of India and Another. N.P., 2013. Web. May14 2014.

Mehdudia, Sujay, "30 % Local Sourcing Norm Can't Be Met: Walmart." *The Hindu*, July23, 2013. *The Hindu*, Web, May13, 2014.

"Government to Dilute FDI Retail Norms," *The Hindu*, Aug1, 2013. *The Hindu*. Web. May13, 2014.

Mehra, Puja, "Delhi Government Cannot De-notify FDI in Retail, Says Industry Ministry." *The Hindu* Jan 21. 2014. *The Hindu*. Web. May 13, 2014.

Neumark, David, Junfu Zhang, and Stephen Ciccarella. "The Effects of Wal-Mart on Local Labor Market," *Journal of Urban Economics*, 63.2 (2008): 405–30.

"Number of US Farms Declines, Farmers Getting Older." *The Big Story*. N.P., N.D. Web. May13, 2014.

Parsai, Gargi. "Farmers' Representatives Oppose FDI in Multi-brand Retail Sector." *The Hindu* 15 Jan. 2012. *The Hindu*. Web. 12 May 2014.

Peterson, Mark, and Jeffrey E. McGee. "Survivors of 'W-day': An Assessment of the Impact of Wal-Mart's Invasion of Small Town Retailing Communities," *International Journal of Retail and Distribution Management*, 28.4/5 (2000): 170–80.

Pinstrup-Andersen, Per, and Peter Sande. *Ethics, Hunger and Globalization*. First Edition, New York: Springer, 2007. *Google Scholar*, Web. May15, 2014.

"Press Note No.5 (2012 Series)," Sept.20, 2012. Web. May14, 2014.

Rahman, A. Faizur, "It May End up as Foreign Direct Interference!" *The Hindu* Dec 11, 2011. *The Hindu*. Web. May 12, 2014.

Reserve Bank of India. "Foreign Investments in India." *Reserve Bank of India*. N.p., 7 Mar. 2014. Web. 13 May 2014.

Sainath, P. "Farmers' Suicide Rates Soar Above the Rest." *The Hindu*, May 18 2013. *The Hindu*. Web. May 14 2014.

—. "FDI in Retail — UPA 'retired Hurt'." *The Hindu*, Dec.12 2011. *The Hindu*, Web. May 13, 2014.

Seth, Dilasha, "FDI in Retail No Remedy to Inflation, Say Economists." *Business Standard India,* Nov.26, 2011. *Business Standard,* Web. May 14, 2014.

Sharma, Devinder. "Made in the United States." *The Hindu,* Sept. 15, 2012. *The Hindu,* Web. May 12, 2014.

Stone, Kenneth E. "Impact of the Wal-Mart Phenomenon on Rural Communities," *Increasing Understanding of Public Problems and Policies - 1997,* Vol. 1997. Chicago: Farm Foundation, 1997, pp.1–22. *Google Scholar.* Web. May13, 2014.

U.S. Farms and Farmers, United States Department of Agriculture, 2014. Web, May 13, 2014. Census of Agriculture.

Venkatesan, J, "FDI in Retail Is a Boon: Supreme Court." *The Hindu,* May 2, 2013. *The Hindu,* Web. May13, 2014.

42

Sustaining Rural Women and Floriculture: Constraints and Suggestions

P. Kiran Kumar

Introduction

Agriculture continues to be the mainstay of Indian economy, as it is a major source of livelihood for more than two-third of population. Agriculture provides the bulk of wage goods required by the non-agricultural sector as well as the raw materials for the industrial sector (Kiran *et al,* 2009: 106). Although more than six decades have passed since India's Independence and agriculture production in the country has increased several folds largely due to the green revolution technologies, certain features the Indian agriculture have hampered balanced growth and development. It still exhibits feudal relations of production, mainly because of the land reforms have not been properly enforced (Kiran *et al,* 2008: 29). This similar condition also applies to the field of floriculture.

In recent years, a few large business houses have entered into floriculture for the production of flowers for home consumption as also for export. However, production and trade of floriculture for traditional and industrial purpose is mainly in the hands of small family enterprises, where women folk is prominent worker, the poorer the family, the more it depends on economic productivity of its women. They have invisible hands, 90 per cent of rural women are unskilled and 88 per cent are illiterate which makes them vulnerable to exploits and economically dependent on men. No serious efforts have been made to improve the condition of women in our country. It is possible through empowerment of women. Hence, there is a need to train women for the floriculture-oriented entrepreneurship through which women of rural areas can easily earn money in short run by this occupation and improve their economic condition. However, no training has been given on floriculture till now even to men folk then what will be place of women. If women would be trained for the job related to flower cultivation, future prospect of floriculture would be brighter and so will be national development.

Rural Women in Farm Activities: Review of Empirical Evidences

Review of earlier studies on women participation in agriculture will help to resolve the problem encountered in the earlier studies and to concentrate on the aspects which need more systematic examination. Hence, an attempt is made to synthesise the conclusions of the earlier studies on women role in agriculture. Emphasis will be on access to and control of productive resources and benefits from agricultural production and relevant services.

Gandhi (2005) emphasised that owing to the continuous increase in demand for flowers in recent years both in the domestic and international market, floriculture has emerged as leading industry in terms of trade. Kiran *et al* (2008) emphasised that with the global boom in floriculture trade, hi-tech floriculture, especially cut flower segment, has been identified by the government as a thrust area for exports. At present, about 150 hectare of land is under hi-tech floriculture. Sharma and Singh (1970) found that important agricultural operations were identified in which women actively participated includes, seed storage, winnowing, care of animals, harvesting, weeding, soak pit, sowing, applying manure in the field, using implements, respectively. Study by Joshi and Alshi (1985) revealed that per hectare female labour used on High Yielding Variety (HYV) Cotton and Jowar farms was more as compared to the local variety farm. Pandey and Pareek (1988) indicated that in fruit, vegetable and flower gardens women helped to a great extent in operations like weeding, hoeing, application of manures and fertilisers, harvesting and processing of the produce. Further, noted that farm women should be trained in modern production techniques of fruits, vegetables and flowers. Uberoy (1995) reported that, in India, among 70 per cent of the total working population, 84 per cent of economically active women are involved in agriculture. However, women are facing so many problems in agriculture like mechanisation has affected women by reducing the demand for employment in peak season. Allendorf (2007) noted that, access to and control over land continues to be a major setback for women farmers, which limit their ability to effectively practice sustainable agricultural development. Singh *et al* (2005) revealed that the wage disparity was found to be higher among men and women in agriculture where men enjoyed with higher wages than women while in case of on farm activities. Bala (2000) reported that in Moga district of Punjab, participation of farm women was higher in uprooting of seedlings, transplantation as regards pre-harvest agricultural activities. An opportunity to improve women's access to inputs is through provision of credit to women. Credit gives women the ability to expand their life choices, especially where control over it is exercised hence empowering (Mehira, 1997). Saraswathi Raju Iyer (2004), studied that women in rural areas are depending on agriculture which is the major unorganised sector in India. Women face lot of problems in agriculture like women labour displaced by technology, physical strenuous labour, illiteracy etc. Latha and Brindha (1997) revealed that women were consulted at each and every step of seed production. They decide which company to work with. They also choose the seeds to be produced and allocate the land area for seed production.

Above literature indicate that studies have been conducted on importance of floriculture, its economics and constraints related to adoption and one or other aspects of acceptability of flower cultivation technology in fragmented manner. Whereas acceptability of any technology comprised various stages like exposure, knowledge gain, attitude change, decision-making for adoption, implementation on small scale and confirmation. No study measure the potentiality of floriculture in terms of physical compatibility, cultural compatibility, profitability as an agri-business, so this study is forward step in this direction. A perusal of literature unfolds the fact that none of the study has given any attention to the acceptability of flower cultivation technology as a whole. The present study had made an attempt to incorporate these parameters combined in the broader framework of acceptability along with constraints and factors affecting adoption and non-adoption by farm women. Therefore, in the present study these components have been kept at appropriate place for exploration.

Against this background, the present study is designed with a set of objectives.

Objective of the Study

1. To explore the technical knowledge of rural women on flower cultivation;
2. To study the level of acceptability of flower cultivation enterprised by rural farm women;
3. To understand the constraints faced by the rural women in flower cultivation and suggesting geographically compatible policy suggestions.

Methodology

The study was carried out in Dakshina Kannada and Udupi districts of Karnataka State, because both the districts are climatically best suited for flower cultivation and also most of the farm women population is engaged in flower cultivation enterprise. Secondary sources like District Horticulture office, flower markets of both the districts were visited and collected the informations regarding the existing flower cultivating technology. From the selected districts, two Blocks and one village from each Block was selected by simple random sampling procedure technique. A list of total self- help-groups (SHGs) formed by women in the selected villages was procured from the District Project Manager. Out of the list provided, two SHGs per village (ten women in each group) were randomly selected, so as to have a sample of 80 rural farm women in eight SHGs. The qualitative data were quantified according to the standards laid down and tabulated to draw inferences. Statistical tool, like simple percentage was model used wherever appropriate. On the basis of the statistical test, interpretations of results was done, inferences and conclusions were drawn.

Results and Discussions

Women are a critical component of agriculture in developing countries, ensuring food security and nutrition. They are farmers, unpaid workers on family farms, paid or unpaid agricultural labourers on other farms and agricultural enterprises, food processors and vendors, home gardeners, cooks, and careers for children and the elderly. Moreover, due to specific roles in food production, many women are the repositories of knowledge about cultivation, processing, and preservation of nutritious and locally adapted crop varieties. Given the right possibilities, such knowledge can allow women to be innovation leaders in sustainable agriculture. Social norms can impose even more restrictions on women's mobility, decision-making power and control over family income, limiting their ability to develop small businesses.

Pattern of Flower Cultivation Technology in the Study Area

The information about the existing pattern of flower cultivation technology was collected from the secondary sources, like District Horticulture Office, State Horticulture Database, National Horticulture Database, progressive farmers and from other relevant literature.

Table-1: Area under Flower Cultivation (Area in Hectare)

	Districts		*Villages*			
	Dakshina Kannada	*Udupi*	*Konaje*	*Kotekar*	*Shankarpura*	*Shirva*
Area under floriculture	110	453	19	22	71	83
Jasmine	71	326	12	13	65	80
Chrysanthemum	4	72	1	1	10	9
Marigold	Nil	6	Nil	Nil	1	Nil
Crossandra	11	16	3	1	2	5

Source: Field study.

The flower cultivating area was higher in Udupi district as compared to Dakshina Kannada district. The Jasmine cultivation area was higher covering 376 and 71 ha followed by chrysanthemum cultivation with 72 and four ha both in Udupi and Dakshina Kannada districts, respectively. Cultivation of Crossandra flower with 16 and 11 ha in the district. There is no record for the cultivation of Marigold in Dakshina Kannada and six ha of area covered in Udupi district. Regarding villages, in Shirva and Shankarpura of Udupi district, Jasmine was grown on 83 ha in Shirva and 71 ha in Shankarpura village followed by Chrysanthemum with 10 and nine ha respectively. In Konaje and Kotekar villages of Dakshina Kannada, there was no area under Marigold cultivation recorded. The District Horticulture office provided technical guidance from time to time. The farm women got the knowledge from the progressive farmers regarding the flower cultivation.

Table-2: Profile of the Respondents in the Study Area

Variables	*Districts*				*Total*
	Dakshina Kannada		*Udupi*		
	Konaje n=20	*Kotekar n=20*	*Shankarapura n=20*	*Shirva n=20*	*N=80*
Age					
18-29	8(40)	7(35)	6(30)	5(25)	26(32.5)
30-39	8(40)	11(55)	10(50)	12(60)	41(51.25)
40-49	4(20)	1(5)	3(15)	3(15)	11(13.75)
50 above	0(0)	1(5)	1(5)	0(0)	2(2.5)
Caste					
Low	2(10)	4(20)	1(5)	2(10)	9(11.25)
Middle	6(30)	8(40)	15(75)	14(70)	43(53.75)
High	12(60)	8(40)	4(20)	4(20)	28(35)
Family Size					
Small (upto 4)	7(35)	5(25)	5(25)	6(30)	23(28.75)
Medium (5-8)	11(55)	8(40)	11(55)	14(70)	44(55)
Large (above 8)	2(10)	7(35)	4(20)	0(0)	13(16.25)
Land Holdings					
Upto 1 acres	12(60)	13(65)	8(40)	9(45)	42(52.5)
2-4 acres	5(25)	7(35)	10(50)	6(30)	28(35)
Above 4 acres	3(15)	0(0)	2(10)	5(25)	10(12.5)
Occupation					
Agriculture	12(60)	13(65)	7(35)	14(70)	46(57.5)
Business	2(10)	0(0)	3(15)	4(20)	9(11.25)
Wage Labour	0(0)	1(5)	2(10)	0(0)	3(3.75)
Service	0(0)	1(5)	1(5)	0(0)	2(2.5)
Farming/Labour	6(30)	5(25)	7(35)	2(10)	20(25)

(Contt...)

Education					
Illiterate	7(35)	13(65)	6(30)	5(25)	31((38.75)
Primary	6(30)	5(25)	4(20)	3(15)	18(22.5)
Middle	0(0)	0(0)	1(5)	7(35)	8(10)
High School	7(35)	1(5)	8(40)	5(25)	21(26.25)
Graduate and above	0(0)	1(5)	1(5)	0(0)	2(2.5)
Income					
Low (Up to 2000)	1(5)	9(45)	12(60)	10(50)	32(40)
Middle (2001-5000)	13(65)	5(25)	5(25)	6(30)	29(36.25)
High (above 5001)	6(30)	6(30)	3(15)	4(20)	19(23.75)
Material Possession					
Low	12(60)	14(70)	14(70)	5(25)	45(56.25)
Medium	5(25)	6(30)	3(15)	11(55)	25(31.25)
High	3(15)	0(0)	3(15)	4(20)	10(12.5)
Socio-economic Status					
Low	1(5)	3(15)	6(30)	8(40)	18(22.5)
Medium	15(75)	14(70)	11(55)	10(50)	50(62.5)
High	4(20)	3(15)	3(15)	2(10)	12(15)

Note: Figures in parentheses indicate percentages.

Source: Primary survey.

The Table-2 depicted that majority (51.25 per cent) of the rural women were in middle age group of 30-39 years, which is followed by group of young women folk with 32.5 per cent, there were also women with age group of above 50 years but they were found only 2.5 per cent . Caste-wise distribution of the respondents shows that 54 per cent rural women belonged to middle caste as the population of Christian community dominant in flower cultivation in the study area which is followed by high caste (35 per cent) and low caste with 11.25 per cent. Data related to size of the family found that majority of the women had the medium family (55 per cent), followed by small family with 28.75 per cent and large family recorded was only with 16.25 per cent. Agriculture was the main occupation of respondents which is followed by business and labour. Majority of the women farmers had the land holding upto one acre with 52.5 per cent, two to four acre with 35 per cent and above four acre with as low as 12.5 per cent. As far as education is concerned majority of the farmers are illiterates in the area of study (38.75 per cent), which is followed by high school with 26.25 per cent as the Christian women folks in the study do have some education. There were also the women farmers, who had the education of graduation and above but only with 2.5 per cent. It is found that 40 per cent of respondents belonged to low income group followed by middle (36.25 per cent) and high income with 23.75 per cent recorded in the study area. Data on socio-economic condition revealed that 62.5 per cent respondents had medium socio-economic status, which is followed by low and high socio-economic status.

Table 3: Level of Knowledge Gained by the Respondents about the Flower Cultivation in the Study Area

Categories	*Village wise respondents*				*Total*
	Dakshina Kannada		*Udupi*		*N = 80*
	Konaje n = 20	*Kotekar n = 20*	*Shankarapura n = 20*	*Shirva n = 20*	
Concept and Importance					
Low	2(10)	6(30)	0(0)	2(10)	10(12.5)
Medium	9(45)	10(50)	14(70)	12(60)	45(56.25)
High	9(45)	4(20)	6(30)	6(30)	25(31.25)
Knowledge of Flower Varieties					
Low	5(25)	2(10)	3(15)	0(0)	10(12.5)
Medium	7(35)	8(40)	10(50)	8(40)	33(41.25)
High	8(40)	10(50)	7(35)	12(60)	37(46.25)
Field Preparation, Sowing and Planting					
Low	4(20)	7(35)	12(60)	6(30)	29(36.25)
Medium	8(40)	10(50)	5(25)	12(60)	35(43.75)
High	8(40)	3(15)	3(15)	2(10)	16(20)
Transplantation					
Low	13(65)	18(90)	10(50)	12(60)	53(66.25)
High	7(35)	2(10)	10(50)	8(40)	27(33.75)
Plant Protection					
Low	15(75)	12(60)	11(55)	7(35)	45(56.25)
High	5(25)	8(40)	9(45)	13(65)	35(43.75)
Sowing and Application of Fertilisers					
Low	7(35)	10(50)	6(30)	7(35)	30(37.5)
High	13(65)	10(50)	14(70)	13(65)	50(62.5)
Harvesting					
Low	8(40)	6(30)	18(90)	5(25)	37(46.25)
High	12(60)	14(70)	2(10)	15(75)	43(53.75)
Packing and Marketing					
Low	5(25)	4(20)	3(15)	6(30)	18(22.5)
Medium	12(60)	16(80)	14(70)	8(40)	50(62.5)
High	3(15)	0(0)	3(15)	6(30)	12(15)
Availing of Loan					
Low	12(60)	6(30)	5(25)	8(40)	31(38.75)
Medium	7(35)	14(70)	12(60)	8(40)	41(51.25)
High	1(5)	0(0)	3(15)	4(20)	8(10)

Figures in parentheses indicate percentages. *Source:* Primary survey.

The Table-3 clearly shows that high knowledge gain in the categories, like aware of varieties of the flower (46.25 per cent), sowing season and application of the fertiliser is also high with 62.5 per cent which is followed by harvesting with 53.75 per cent. Medium knowledge gain in concept and importance of floriculture is about 56.25 per cent and knowledge about the preparation of the field and planting time with 43.75 per cent, which is followed by both knowledge of packing and marketing (62.5 per cent) and knowledge of availing of the loan with 51.25 per cent. In the categories like transplantation (66.25 per cent), plant protection (56.25 per cent), the low knowledge gain was recorded. It can be found that training on flower cultivation technology has helped the respondents to gain different knowledge.

Acceptability of Flower Cultivation Technology

Acceptability of flower cultivation technology is depended on decision. Decision relates to the mental readiness of the respondents to go for floriculture cultivation. Decision to adopt the technology may vary from village to village. The analysis had been done statement-wise separately in selected villages.

Table-4: Statement Showing the Willingness to Accept the Floriculture Activity

Statements	*Konaje n=20*	*Kotekar n=20*	*Shankarapura n=20*	*Shirva n=20*	*Total N=80*
I received the knowledge of flower cultivation. So, I am cultivating flower.	6(30)	15(75)	18(90)	12(60)	51(63.75)
To improve the economic condition of the family.	15(75)	12(60)	16(80)	12(60)	55(68.75)
I am more confident for flower cultivation, after getting the training.	17(85)	14(70)	16(80)	11(55)	58(72.5)
It is easy to harvest, pack and marketing of flowers.	10(50)	7(35)	12(60)	9(45)	38(47.5)
In spite of social restrictions, I will go for flower cultivation.	5(25)	10(50)	0(0)	6(30)	21(26.25)
I am fully convinced about the flower cultivation.	6(30)	14(70)	13(65)	15(75)	48(60)
I will implement floriculture when all the trainees have implemented it.	15(75)	7(35)	12(60)	11(55)	45(56.25)

I need good quality seed/ stem to cultivate floriculture.	16(80)	15(75)	7(35)	11(55)	49(61.25)
I am not ready to implement floriculture.	8(40)	5(25)	2(10)	5(25)	20(25)
It is very difficult to avail loan so I quit floriculture.	0(0)	2(10)	4(20)	0(0)	6(7.5)
Cultivation of flowers will have more problems than benefits, so I am not cultivating.	6(30)	2(10)	1(5)	0(0)	9(11.25)

Figures in parentheses indicate percentages.

Source: Primary survey.

The Table-4 clearly shows that more than half of the respondents were of the positive opinion about the flower cultivation. More than 70 per cent of the respondents were more confident in accepting floriculture activity due to knowledge received through training, many of the respondents (68.75 per cent) had adopted this flower cultivation activity to improve their economic condition. Data also reveal that 60 per cent of the respondents were fully convinced about the importance of floriculture and 61.25 per cent of the respondents expected cultivating floriculture, if they got good quality seed or planting material. It was easy to harvest and pack and also to market for about 48 per cent of the respondents. The 25 per cent of the respondents were not ready to take floriculture activity, as it was difficult to avail the loan for seven per cent and again 11.25 per cent have the opinion that floriculture business has more problem than benefit.

Constraints Faced by the Respondents in Implementing the Floriculture Technology

An effort has been made to explore the problems of women cultivators from the study areas. There are several constraints such as social, economic and technical reported in these study areas, besides lack of awareness about the new diseases due to climate change, loss of agriculture products while assembling and marketing, lower price and the like.

Table-5: Distribution of the Women Farmers with Social, Economic and Technical Constraints

Constraints	*Respondents N=80*
Social Constraints	
Male dominance	15(18.75)

Social Customs and Taboos	10(12.5)
Availability of Time	36(45)
Family norms	18(22.5)
Other	5(6.25)
Economic Constraints	
Mobility	44(55)
Access to credit	38(47.5)
Loss of Agriculture Products	21(26.25)
Lower Price	42(52.5)
Technical Constraints	
Literacy	12(15)
Technical Skills	7(8.75)
Lack of Inputs	16(20)
Lack of Awareness	4(5)
Lack of female farm extension workers	25(31.25)
Low Quality of Planting Materials	13(16.25)

Figures in parentheses indicate percentages.

Source: Primary survey.

Table-5 provides the data related to problems, faced by women farmers. It has been observed that, cultural norms, male dominance, less availability of time and resistance from family members were the constraints, being faced by rural women. After cultural norms, our society is male dominated, and women are not allowed to go freely for participating in agricultural activities. Majority of women respondents (55 per cent) indicated the lack of mobility as the major constraints in approaching agricultural services. There may be less availability of vehicles, especially for rural women to access these agricultural services. Moreover, a large majority, 47.5 per cent of the respondents indicated lack of access to credit as the core constraint in approaching agricultural services for rural women. Loss of agricultural products while assembling, packing, or transporting which accounts for 26.25 per cent was also another economic constraint. Low price was another economic constraint in the study area which accounts for 52.5 per cent.

The data show that a great majority of women farmers have reported the lack of women farm extension workers which accounts for 31.25 per cent, the proportion of famers facing the problem of availability of good quality of plants was estimated to be at 16.25 per cent, followed by literacy with 15 per cent. The lack of awareness relating to the new practice of cultivation, new diseases, insecticides, pesticides, harvesting, and packaging is also major problem faced by most of the rural women farmers cultivating in the area of the study. Kundu *et al* (1997) reported that India's poor performance in global market is, because of inadequate infrastructure, lack of appropriate planting materials, production technology, basic inputs like standard containers, quality packing materials etc., and are critical bottlenecks. Suitable market surveys and pricing information were not available (Sundaram, 2003 and Chattopadyay, 2000). Absence of control mechanism and co-ordination between government and firms, absence of cold chains and domestic market was unorganised and there was no established marketing channel.

Conclusion and Recomendations

Women play an indispensable role in farming and in improving the quality of life in rural areas. However, their contributions often remain concealed due to some social barriers and gender bias. Often Government programmes fail to focus on women in agriculture. In spite of social, political and economic constraints, women farmers have proved extremely resourceful and hardworking in their attempt to ensure household food security. Social constraints place barriers around their access to scientific and technological information. Agricultural extension services and other infrastructural support for women farmers should be made available to women farmers. Policies should be designed to ensure women's control over complementary resources including irrigation, credit, water, forest, fuel, fodder, information and training. Technologies must be used that are safe for workers, *i.e.*, reduced use of pesticides ensure that occupational safety and health measures are in place. Measures should be taken to remove middlemen in the sale of non-timber forest products and women's co-operatives should be formed for directly marketing these products. The contribution of women to agricultural and rural development should be maximised by implementing solution to the specific problem they face as economic, social and technical aspects. Credit facilities and input should be made available through farmers' co-operative societies. The existing women's group in the village should be organised and strengthened to increase women's access to extension services, credit facilities, agricultural inputs and even marketing services. More female extension workers should be trained and sent to help female farmers. It is necessary to particularly identify women as an integral part of the agriculture.

References

Allendorf, K. (2007), "Do Women's Land Rights Promote Empowerment and Child Health in Nepal?" *World Development 35* (11), pp.1975-1988.

Bala, R. (2000), "Farm Women Participation in Selected Agricultural and Subsidiary Occupational Activities in Moga District of Punjab", *Ph.D. thesis*, PAU Ludhiana.

Chattopadhyay, T.K. (2000), "Present Status of Floriculture in West Bengal," *Financing Agriculture*, Vol. 32(2), pp. 10-15.

Gandhi, G.P. (2005), "Opportunities Galore for Floricultural Exports," *Facts for You*, Vol. 25(8), pp.11-15.

Joshi, C.K. and Alshi, M.R. (1985), "Impact on High Yielding Varieties on Employment Potential of Female Labour in Akola District of Maharastra," *Indian Journal of Agricultural Economics*, Vol. 40(2), pp. 230-35.

Kiran Kumar P, V.B. Hans and Jayasheela (2009), "Indian Agriculture: Crisis and Challenges under Globalisation," *Social Action*, Vol 59(1), Jan-March 2009. ISSN-0037-7627.

Kiran, P., Jayasheela and Hans (2008), "Indian Agriculture in the Post-economic Reform Period," *Journal of Development Research*, Vol. 1(1), pp. 29-42.

Kundu, K.K., Singh, J., Singh, V.K. and Suhag, K.S. (1997), "India's Floriculture Export-Growth, Status, Constraints and Export Strategies: An Analysis", *Indian Journal of Agricultural Marketing*, Vol. 11 (1 and 2), pp. 14-20.

Latha, B. and Brindha, N. (1997), "Participation of Women in Seed Industry", *Indian Farmer Times*, Vol.12 (5), pp. 17-26.

Mehira, R. (1997). "The Role of Non-Governmental Organisations: Charity and Empowerment." *Annals of the American Academy of Political and Social Science, p.554.*

Pandey, R.M. and Pareek, O.P. (1988), "Appropriate Horticulture Production Technologies for Farm Women", *International Conference of Farm Women*, Indian Council of Agricultural Research, New Delhi.

Sarawathi Raju Iyer (2004), "Women and Rural Economy," *Social Welfare*, March, pp. 4-7.

Sharma and Singh, T. (1970), "Participation of Rural Women in Decision-making Process Related to Farm Business," *Indian Journal of Extension Education*, Section 6, pp. 43-50.

Singh S.N., Anil Kumar B., Singh S.R. (2005), "Labour Wages Discrimination in Agriculture: Gender Bias and Policy Implications", *Agricultural Situation in India*, Vol. LXI, No. 12, March pp. 869-874.

Sundaram Satya, I. (2003), "Floriculture: Fluctuating Fortunes" *Facts for You*, Vol. 23(11), pp. 9-11.

Uberoy, A. (1995), "New Technologies for Women in Agriculture" *Yojana*, Vol. 39(11), pp. 17-20.

43

Problems and Prospects of Cocoon Markets in Karnataka: A Case Study on Chickballapura District

J.N. Kumara and N.K. Gayathri

Introduction

Agriculture is directly linked with many facets of sustainable development, including poverty eradication, sustainable consumption and production, health and education. Agriculture is an integral part of the rural development system, serving the system as a whole. The largest and the most important industry in Indian 75 per cent of the people depend on it directly and cultivation of the living. Agriculture contains not only production of crops by cultivation of the soil, but also the rearing of livestock, thus milk, meat, wool, and silk are agricultural products as wheat, rice and cotton. Besides, handloom weaving, rice milling, oil crushing, sericulture and other small and cottage industries depend on agriculture. Sericulture is one of the agro-based cottage industry, provides employment opportunities to about 62 lakh rural people. The handloom sector which is next to agriculture in terms of employment intensity provides employment to 124 lakh persons (M. Suresh, 2013).

Sericulture and Rural Development

Sericulture is one of the small scale and cottage industries, plays on important role in generating gainful employment opportunities to the rural people. It is not only labour intensive but also a sections income levelling industry. It plays vital role in transferring wealth from richer section of the society to poorer section. This is also labour intensive creative employment and income generating that it is rightly called the *Kalpavriksha* or the *Kamadthenu* of the poor and downtrodden. Women-friendly sericulture industry is highly profitable and less investment activity, hence, the participation of women in sericulture industry is more. For a developing country like India, sericulture plays vital role in the improvement of rural economy through limited availability of land, limited cash return and agriculture being confined to one or two seasons in the year have made villages took for supporting rural industries such as sericulture. Nearly 5.8 million people are employed in various fields of sericulture. It is eco-friendly activity provide sample work for women folk in the rural areas in rearing si!k worms, while the male members work in the fields (M. Suresh, 2013).

Table 1: Cocoon Production and Employment Generation in India

S. No.	*Year*	*Production (MT)*	*Employment Generation(lakh persons)*
1.	2007-08	18,320	61.20
2.	2008-09	18,370	63.10
3.	2009-10	19,690	68.17
4.	2010-11	20,410	72.50
5.	2011-12	23,063	75.60
6.	2012-13	23,679	76.28

Source: www.csb.gov.in.

India is the second largest producer of mulberry raw silk in the world next only to China. One hectare of mulberry plantation can create direct employment to 12 to 13 persons through the year. Apart from labour intensive nature sericulture is the most suitable rural industry for the underprivileged and landless labourers. That is the reason in above Table, employment generation is gradually increasing, from 61.20 lakh persons during 2007-08 to 76.28 lakh persons in 2012-13 (Table-1). Chickaballapura district is the second largest district in Karnataka state with the average cocoon production of 722 kg p/ ha which is higher than the state average of 601 kg/ha. Nearly 16.361 ha of mulberry is cultivated by 25.531 families and also well-established reeling units and support systems are present in the district.

Table-2: Employment Generation through Sericulture in Chickaballapura District

S. No.	*Year*	*Male*	*Female*	*Total*
1.	2008-09	22,715	1,324	24,039
2.	2009-10	18,935	808	19,743
3.	2010-11	13,551	762	14,313
4.	2011-12	14,286	663	14,949
5.	2012-13	14,852	718	15,570

Source: MS Building, Sericulture Office.

Table-2 shows male and female participation in sericulture industry in Chickaballapura district. There is a decreasing trend of employment opportunities, that is, 24,039 persons in 2008-09 have been decreasing to 15,570 in 2012-13. Sericulture activities are decreasing because of agriculture lands are converted into non-agriculture lands and natural calamities like lake of rain, lake of water, lake of labour forces are influencing the reduction of sericulture activities in the study area.

Chickaballapura district is the second largest district in Karnataka in the production of cocoon and cultivation of mulberry plants district has four cocoon markets namely, Shidlaghatta cocoon market, Chintamani cocoon market, Chickaballapura cocoon market and Gowribidanuru cocoon market.

Shidlaghatta cocoon market is one of the second largest class-1 reeling cocoon market in Karnataka providing more employment opportunities and suitable prices for cocoons for improving participation of small and marginal farmers, who engage in mulberry cultivation and silk worm rearing in rural economy.

Problems of Cocoon Markets in India

Cocoon markets are facing lot of problems in India, though government providing facilities to markets, but these facilities not reaching are the farmers. The major problems are explained in detail.

1. *Lack of Organisation:* The striking feature of agricultural marketing is the lack of any kind of collective organisation among the producers. The buyers of cocoon usually operate in an unorganised manner, under this circumstances, it is common to find that the producers of cocoon are being exploited by the purchasers.

2. *Forced Sales:* The farmers in general sell this produce at an unfavourable place at an unfavourable time and usually get unfavourable terms. Especially, when there is glut in the market immediately after harvest, these prices offered are generally low. The nearest place where the farmer disposes of his produce is his village.

3. *Superfluous Middleman:* Majority of farmers dispose of their produce in the village itself. The result is the intervention of host of middlemen between the producers and the final buyers. That in turns creates long chain of middlemen in the marketing channels which results in higher prices for the consumers, while the producer share in consumer's rupee also decrease substantially.

4. *Multiplicity of Market Charges:* The marketing charges payable by producers are numerous and varied in unregulated markets and they tend to

reuse considerably the returns to the producer from the sale of his produce. For instance, the farmer has to pay entry toll, carrying charges, weighing charges, commission charges etc., he also depends on the broker/*dalal* to get into contact with the commission agent/buyer and pays carting, unloading the cocoons cart etc.

5. *Malpractices of Markets:* In unorganised markets, malpractices tend to be common.

(a) Sales and Weights: Sales and weights are manipulated against the seller, non-standardised weights are often used due to absence of regular inspection by concerned authorities.

(b) Arbitrary Deductions: There are all kinds of arbitrary deductions and the seller has to apply effective means of protest against such practices.

(c) Sample: Large quantities are taken away from the produce as sample and the cultivators are not paid for them even when no sale is affected.

(d) Bargain between the Agents: Between sellers and buyers bargaining activity takes place through agents. Agents act as one, who negotiate on behalf of buyers. Sometimes, the bargains are made secretly such that the seller remains ignorant of what actually takes place, and brokers are always in favour of purchasers.

6. *Adulteration:* Adulteration is often resorted to, while marketing crops and one of the most important reasons are the high amount of refraction allowed. In most of the wholesale markets a fixed deduction is made for impurities.

7. *Lack of Information Regarding Prices:* Absence of market intelligence as to prices is another defect that contributes to farmers being unable to take timely and effective market-oriented decisions like to decide whether or not to store, to grow produce out of season, whether or not to grow different products etc.

8. *Distress Sales:* The farmer on many occations has to resort to distress sales, epecially when there is a glut in the market or whenever the market prices are depressed. Due to lack of storage facilities, the farmer generally has to either carry back his produces or sell even at uneconomic prices.

9. *Inadequate Storage Facilities in the Village Level*: The common problem faced by farmers is the absence of adequate scientific storage facilities at farmer, level. The indigenous methods of storage developed by the farmer do not adequately protect the produce from dampness, insect, pest, secondary infestation resulting in very high-level of post-harvest losses (Department of Agriculture, 2011; M. Suresh, 2013).

10. *Lack of Transport Facilities*: There are no proper transport Facilities to cocoon markets. Many markets are not connected by rail transport, *Kacha* (wet) roads become unserviceable during monsoon and the interior villages get isolated.

11. *Lack of Media and Communication Facilities:* Appropriate communication system to rural market may cause reducing the participation of people in the sericulture activities.

12. *Inadequate Infrastructure:* Cocoon markets are facing lack of infrastructure facilities like drinking water, toilet facilities, cleaning. Hence, farmers are not able to stay even for a single night in cocoon markets.

13. *Price Fluctuation:* Price fluctuation is one of the severe problems of cocoon markets. Based on climatic conditions and arrivals of stock of cocoon in market, prices always vary (Department of Agriculture, M. Suresh, 2013, Sunday O.E. Ewah, 2009, V.V. Devi Prasad Kotni).

Brief Review of Literature and Issues

Sunday O.E. Ewah (2009) discussed about problems and prospects of marketing in developing economies; the Nigerian experience. L. Baiteetl (2009) discussed about problems and prospects of agro-based cottage industries in north-east. R.Barathi(2009) discussed about a study on the integration of Ramanagaram and Shidlaghatta markets and forecasting of the prices and arrivals. M. Suresh (2013) in his article presented production and marketing of cocoon study with special reference to Salem district. There is no such study discussed about problems and prospects of cocoon markets in Chickaballapura district. Rural agro-based cocoon industry in sericulture, cocoon rearing is the important practice in developing economy. There are two stages in sericulture activities namely, pre-cocoon and post-cocoon harvesting. In both stages, farmers are facing lot of problems in rearing as well as market level. Cocoon rearing basically depends on mulberry cultivation. There are different varieties of mulberry plants, and it requires scientific methods of cultivation. At market level, farmers are facing lot of problems including entry toll, carrying charges, weighing charges, commission charges etc., hence present research work helps to know impact of sericulture in rural development and problems and prospects of cocoon markets. In this background, the following objectives are set for present study.

Objectives of the Study

1. To know the problems and prospects of cocoon markets in Karnataka as well as in the study area.
2. To know the impact of sericulture on rural development.

Hypotheses of the Study

1. There is no relationship between sericulture and rural development.
2. There are no problems in cocoon markets of Chickaballapura district.

Methodology

The research paper used personal interview method and descriptive research for collection and analysis of data. We used descriptive research design and random sampling method for selection of 100 respondents, who are coming to cocoon markets. The well-structured questionnaire was framed and simple percentage analysis and Chi-square analysis were used to analyse the data. The primary data were collected through observation and questionnaire method.

The secondary data is collected through various books, journals, articles, and websites. The research work was done and the respondents were enquired from the month of January to June in the year 2013-14.

Data Analysis and Discussion

Results and findings of the study we discussed in three phases, *i.e.*, demographic profile, sericulture cultivation, and cocoon markets.

Demographic Profile of Respondents

Demographic profile is the statistical study of human population. It includes the study of size, structure and distribution of different populations. It also includes the analysis of relationship between economic, social, cultural and biological process influencing population. The foundation of research work to build questionnaire and design research.

Table 3: Demographic Profile of Respondents

Sl. No	*Variables*	*Components*	*Number of frequencies*	*Percentage*
1.	Gender	Male	90	90.0
		Female	10	10.0
2.	Educational qualification	School education	60	60.0
		Under education	30	30.0
		Higher education	10	10.0
3.	Age	20-30	20	20.0
		30-40 above	80	80.0
4.	Region	Rural	80	80.0
		Urban	20	20.0
5.	Marital status	Married	60	60.0
		Unmarried	40	40.0

Source: Primary data.

From the Table-3, first component shows Gender, maximum 90 per cent of the respondents belong to male category, only 10 per cent of respondents belong to female category. The second component shows Educational qualification, 40 per cent of respondents studied school education, 30 per cent respondents studied under-graduation and 20 per cent of respondents studied higher education. The third component shows Age, 20 per cent of respondents belong to 20-30 age group, 60 per cent respondents belong to 30-40 and above age category. The fourth component shows Region, 80 per cent of respondents belong to rural area and 20 per cent of respondents belong to urban area. The fifth component shows Marital status, 60 per cent of respondents are married and 40 per cent of respondents are unmarried.

Sericulture Cultivation

Sericulture cultivation refers to all the process of sericulture sector from the chawki rearing activities (egg hatched) to diapause egg from pupa and raw silk production. It contains how farmers are engaging in sericulture activities in an economy, it also includes production of cocoon and cultivation of mulberry plants.

Table 4: Opinion of Respondents Regarding Sericulture Cultivation

Sl. No.	*Variables*	*Components*	*Number of frequencies*	*Percentage*
1.	Occupation	Sericulture	60	60
		Agriculture and Sericulture	40	40
2.	Experience in sericulture activity	5-10 years	40	40
		10-20 years	50	50
		Above 20 years	10	10
3.	Mulberry land	Have Own land	90	90
		Depend on other land	10	10
4.	Problems in sericulture	There is a problems	60	60
		No problems is sericulture	40	40

Source: Primary data.

In the above Table, first component is Occupation, 60 per cent of respondents are purely doing sericulture activity and 40 per cent of respondents are doing both agriculture and sericulture activities. The second component is Experience in sericulture activity, 40 per cent of respondents have 5-10 years, 50 per cent of respondents have 10-20 years and 10 per cent of respondents having above 20 years experience in sericulture activities. The third component is Mulberry land, 90 per cent of respondents are having own land and 10 per cent of respondents are depending on other's land. The fourth component is

Problems in sericulture, 60 per cent respondents are facing problems and 40 per cent of respondents are not facing problems in sericulture activities.

Cocoon Markets

The cocoon markets are established by department of sericulture for facilitating both Rearers and Reealers to get competitive and fair price to their cocoons. Cocoon markets are a place where Rearers (farmers) and Reelers (buyers) go to meet for the transaction of cocoon at regulated transaction system with suitable regulated prices.

Table-5: Opinion of Respondents Regarding Sericulture Cultivation and Cocoon Market

Sl. No	*Variables*	*Components*	*Number of Frequencies*	*Percentage*
1.	Sericulture and Rural development	Sericulture improve RD	62	62
		It is not improve RD	38	38
2.	Problems in cocoon markets	There is problem	81	81
		There is no problem	19	19
3.	Annual income earning by sericulture	Rs.1 lakh to 5 lakh	50	50
		Rs.1 lakh to 2 lakh	30	30
		Below Rs.1 lakh	20	20
4.	Govt providing market facilities	Govt providing good market facilities	40	40
		There is no market facility	60	60

Source: Primary data.

From the above table, first component is sericulture and rural development, 62 per cent of respondents said sericulture activities improve rural development and 38 per cent of respondents said sericulture activities are not improving the rural economy. The second component is problems in cocoon markets, 81 per cent of respondents said there was problem in cocoon markets, 19 per cent of respondents said exist no problems in cocoon markets of Chickaballapura district. The third component is Annual income by sericulture activities, 50 per cent of respondents are earning Rs. 5,48,000 income from the sericulture per year, 30 per cent of respondents are earning Rs 1,62,000 income from the sericulture per year and 20 per cent of respondents are earning below Rs 10,000 per year. The fourth component is Government providing market facilities, 40 per cent of respondents said government providing good market facilities and 60 per cent of respondents said there was no proper market facilities in Chickaballapura district.

Relationship between Sericulture and Rural Development

In the present study to know the relationship between sericulture and rural development and to test the impact of sericulture on rural development, we use Chi-square test. The results are given below. With this background the first null hypothesis is:

Table-6: There is no Relationship between Sericulture and Rural Development

	Observed N	*Expected N*	*Chi-square*	*Asump. Sig*
Yes	62	50.0	5.760	0.016
No	38	50.0		
Total	**100**			

Table-6 shows the Chi-square for one at five per cent level of significance is 3.841. The calculated value of Chi-square is 5.760 which is greater than the Table value (3.841). Hence, null hypothesis is rejected, that means there is significant relationship between sericulture and rural development, because 62 per cent of respondents gave positive opinion and 38 per cent of respondents given negative opinion for sericulture impact on rural development. Hence, there is significant impact of sericulture on rural development.

In the present study to know the problems and prospects of cocoon markets, we use the Chi-square test. The results are given below. With this background the second null hypothesis is:

Table-7: There is no Problems in Cocoon Markets of Chickaballapura District

	Observed N	*Expected N*	*Chi-square*	*Asymp. Sig*
Yes	81	50.0	38.440	.000
No	91	50.0		
Total	**100**			

Table-7 shows the Chi-square for one at one per cent level of significance as 6.635. The calculated value of Chi-square is 38.440, which is greater than the Table value (6.635) Hence, null hypothesis is rejected, there is a problem in cocoon markets of Chickaballapura district because 81 per cent of respondents said about problem in cocoon markets of Chickaballapura district and 19 per cent respondents said there was no problem there.

Suggestions

1. Sericulture department necessary to establish adequate number of cocoon markets to provide marketing facilities to the sericulturists at rural economy.

2. Central silk board should provide training programmes to remove problems in pre- cocoon harvesting or silk worm rearing.
3. The department of sericulture should take necessary steps to conduct training for the sericulturists at regular intervals.
4. The sericulture department should start or establish proper storage facilities for preserving cocoons against the deterioration.
5. The government should take necessary steps to evolve control measures for stabilising cocoon prices in all the markets. Fixing the standard price for all markets could solve the problems.
6. Market information centers should be established in order to provide sericulturists with the day-to-day information about the happening and trends prevailing in the marketing not only within the state but also outside the state.
7. The government cocoon markets should take the initiative to collect marketing information regarding price; demand and supply of cocoon and make it known to the farmers.

Conclusion

Sericulture is playing major role in the development of rural economy. It is found that there is increasing trend of employment opportunities in the sericulture industry. There is significant relationship between sericulture and rural development. It provides year-long employment opportunities to poor people in the rural economy. Hence, there is significant impact of sericulture on rural development to improve the socio-economic status of rural peoples. Central Silk Board should take measures to provide good marketing facilities to sericulturisits through the department of sericulture in all the stages of rural economy.

References

Central Silk Board, Bangalore, WWW.Csb.gov.co.in.

Department of Agriculture, (2011). "Agricultural Marketing in Meghalaya, Problems and Prospects" Shillong, Meghalaya.

Department of Sericulture, MS Building, Bangalore.

M. Suresh, (2013), "Production and Marketing of cocoons--A Study with Special Reference to Salem district", *Aayvagam,* an international journal of multi-disciplinary research, Vol. 1, June 2013, Salem-11.

R. Barathi *et al* (2009), "A study on market integration of Ramanagaram and Siddlaghatta markets and forecasting of their prices and arrivals,"

Department of Agricultural Statistics, University of Agricultural Sciences, Dharwad.

L. Baite (2009), "Problems and Prospects of agro-based cottage industries in North-east" Marketing Co-ordinator, Shillong.

Sunday O.E. Ewah *et al* (2009), "Problems and prospects of marketing in developing economies: the Nigerian Experience," International Journal, Vol. 4, Sept 2009.

V.V. Devi Prasad Kotni (2012), "Prospects and problems of Indian rural markets", International journal, Vol.2, March 2012, ISSN 22498826.

44

How much Gandhian is MGNREGA? An Evaluation of the Mahatma Gandhi National Rural Employment Guarantee Act (2005)

Shri Krishan

Relevance of the Study

Contrary to general belief that globalisation and neo-liberal policies are growth- oriented, the seamy side leading to displacement, misappropriation of common pool of resources by corporate houses are becoming evident. The homelessness has become a global problem and many urban poor are mainly people displaced from rural homes by the processes of development and globalisation of economy and resultant agrarian crisis superimposed on agriculture of small cultivators. This sort of exclusion and invisibility of the urban poor and street children is not unique to any less developed country. Whether it is Sao Paulo in Brazil or Mumbai in India, despite economic growth, the underdeveloped mega-cities absorb only tiny fraction of labour so that unemployment and underemployment remain persistent problem. A sizeable chunk of labour including those of street children find employed in informal sector. Globalisation, however, has had a very uneven impact on various regions and social groups around the world. It is associated with growing economic inequality and social polarisation. In many places, income inequality has multiplied dramatically, increasing economic and spatial segmentation. The signs of absolute economic poverty and deprivations are quite pronounced in cities of South Asia. Gandhi's thinking on socio-economic issues was greatly influenced by the American writer, Henry David Thoreau and the Russian thinker Tolstoy, and John Ruskin. Gandhi's vision regarding full employment, use of technology and the kind of decentralised and participatory development he advocated can still be relevant in our contemporary times. It has been proclaimed that the *Mahatma Gandhi National Rural Employment Guarantee* Act (MGNREGA) notified in September 7, 2005 was mainly to give concrete shape to the Gandhian notion of rural development.

Objective of the Study

The Mahatma Gandhi National Rural Employment Guarantee Act (hereinafter MGNREGA) is a law whereby any adult, who applies for employment in rural areas has to be given work on local public works within 15 days. If employment is not given, an unemployment allowance has to be paid. The employment guarantee subject has to be a limit of 100 days per household per year. It has to be noted that MGNREGA is a law and not just a scheme. The main objective of NREGA was to protect rural household from poverty and hunger. MGNREGA, it was visualised, will also serve other objectives: generating productive assets, protecting the environment, empowering women, reducing rural-urban migration and fostering social equity among others. Thus, MGNREGA was not just an employment scheme: it was designed as a tool of economic and social change in rural areas. This paper will try to analyse and evaluate this law under the lenses of Gandhian model of rural development, his idea as bread earner and food security. Our objective here is to evaluate whether MGNREGA scheme fits and correlates with Gandhian ideals and ideas or not.

Salient Features of MGNREGA

Some of the unique provisions of the NREGA were as outlined below:

(i) Every household in the rural areas of India shall have a right to get at least 100 days of guaranteed employment every year for at least one adult member, for doing casual manual labour;

(ii) Only productive works shall be taken up under the Programme. The State Council shall prepare a list of permissible works as well as 'preferred works'. The identification of preferred works shall be based on the economic, social and environmental benefits of different types of works, their contribution to social equity, and their ability to create permanent assets;

(iii) The Programme may also provide, as far as possible, the training and up-gradation of the skills of unskilled labourers;

(iv) Wages may be paid in cash or in kind or both, taking into account the guidelines and recommendations of the State Council on this matter as far as possible;

(v) Employment shall be provided within a radius of five kilometre of the village, where the applicant resides at the time of applying. In cases, where employment is provided outside such radius, it must be provided within the Block, and transport allowances and daily living allowances shall be paid in accordance with Programme Rules;

(vi) In cases, where at least twenty women are employed on a worksite, provision shall be made for one of them to be deputed to look after any children under the age of six, who may be brought to the worksite, if the need arises. The person deputed for child-minding shall be paid the statutory minimum wage;

(vii) A proportion of the wages, not exceeding five per cent, may be deducted as contribution to welfare schemes organised for the benefit of labourers employed under the Programme, such as health insurance, accident insurance, survivor benefits, maternity benefits and social security schemes.

(viii) The NREGA scheme also comes with important riders:

(a) Public works programmes should not compete with agricultural labour-hiring decisions, and

(b) Public works programmes should generate productive asset that directly impacts agricultural productivity.

However, with most of Indian agriculture characterised by seasonality - a lean season when agricultural labour demand is low and a harvest season when labour demand is high - it was reasonably assumed that the public employment, guaranteed for at least 100 days, will be instituted during the lean season when the rural labour force is most vulnerable. There are eight specific types of works listed in the NREGA:

(i) Drought proofing including afforestation;

(ii) Irrigation canals;

(iii) Provision of irrigation facility to land-owned by SC and ST, land of beneficiaries of land reforms and of Indira Awaas Yojana (IAY) (rural housing for poor);

(iv) Renovation of traditional water bodies;

(v) Land development;

(vi) Flood control works;

(vii) Rural connectivity to provide all weather access; and

(viii) Any other work, which may be notified by Central government in consultation with State government[3].

Gandhian Ideology of Rural Gandhi's Notion of Development, Full Employment, Self-sufficiency:

Gandhi emphasised on the creation of employment. The full employment of human resources, according to him, was the primary need of country. By full employment, Gandhi meant the employment of each and every individual. Gandhi, as you may know, believed that full employment cannot be obtained through the development of large scale industries. In his views, these industries generally use capital intensive and labour saving technologies, and do not provide sufficient opportunities. Moreover, in unindustrialised country like India, most unemployed people live in rural areas. The cause of rural underemployment is the seasonal nature of agriculture. The agricultural workers work on land for six months and for other six months remain idle. It will be disadvantageous for the mechanised industries to employ such underemployed casual labour. Again, rural labour was attached to rural way of life due to religious, cultural and social reasons, and, therefore, cannot be expected to leave homes easily to seek employment in the urban industries. Thus, Gandhi argued that large scale mechanisation and mass production provides no solution to the problem of unemployment in the agriculture-based, over-populated economies like India.

Gandhi said, "Mechanisation is good when the hands are too few for the work intended to be accomplished. It is an evil when there are more hands than required for the work, as is the case in India." The problem of unemployment, in Gandhi's perception, can be tackled only by developing village and cottage industries." 'These industries are capital-saving and labour-using. They take employment opportunities to the doors of the unemployed and are ideal for the rural environment of India."

Gandhi advocated production by masses and the use of appropriate small scale technology. He preferred the decentralisation of small units of production and vehemently criticised the concentration of large scale industries in a urban centres. Gandhi wanted the production occur in the homes of masses, particularly in villages. One advantage of the village and cottage industries is that they increase employment. Another advantage is related to the consideration of efficiency. There are many additional advantages of small scale village industries because,

(1) no separate establishment charges are required;

(2) integration of cottage industries with agriculture;

(3) very few tools are needed;

(4) no problems of storage;

(5) negligible cost of transporting goods to consumer;

(6) no waste - duplication - due to competition, and

(7) no problem of over-Production.

All these factors make the production by small units economical. This is the logic behind the Gandhian scheme of decentralisation of village and cottage industries.

It is wrong to think that Gandhi was against modern technology. According to him, the essence of science was acquiring knowledge through experimentation. He had no objection to the use of machinery to increase production and to lessen the burden of grind on the workers. But he did not approve of machinery that, in his view, produced goods along with starvation. He was against the indiscriminate multiplication of machinery. Gandhi said that he was not opposed to industrialisation as such but the manner in which it took place. In this context, Gandhi remarked:

> "I do visualise electricity, ship-building, iron-works, machine-making and the like existing side by side with village handicrafts. But the order of dependence would be reserved. Hitherto, the industrialisation has been so planned as to destroy the villages and village crafts. In the state of the future, it will subserve the villages and their crafts. I do not share the socialist belief that the centralisation of necessities of life will be conducive to the common welfare when the centralised industries are planned and owned by the state.[4]

Gandhi said, "What I object to is the craze for machinery, not machinery as such. The craze is for what they call labour saving machinery. Men go on 'saving labour' till thousands are without work, and thrown on the open streets to die of starvation." For Gandhi, human consideration was supreme, and that of science and technology was secondary. The goal of Gandhian model of development was to build self-sufficient rural society. Each community should be self-reliant. It should be able to produce for food and other daily requirements. Gandhi regarded an area covered by a radius of five miles as the basic unit of self-containment. The production of each basic unit should be linked with the natural consumption requirements of those living there in. The natural consumption requirements of a basic unit depend on:

(a) The geological situation of the unit;

(b) The physiological and temperamental condition of people;

(c) The traditions and customs of the community; and

(d) The occupational pattern and cultural attainments of people.

As physical, psychological, and temperamental conditions in regions vary, the consumption requirements also differ from region to region, and the production plans of each region must take into account these differences. The production plan should not only be linked with the consumption requirements of the people, but also be matched with the availability of natural resources, and available, human skills combined with climatic conditions. Gandhi's thinking on socio-economic issues was greatly influenced by the American writer, Henry David Thoreau and the Russian thinker Tolstoy. Throughout his life, Gandhi sought to develop ways to fight India's extreme poverty, backwardness and socio-economic challenges, as a part of his wider involvement in the Indian Independence movement. Gandhi's championing of *swadeshi* and non-cooperation was centred on the principles of economic self-sufficiency. Gandhi sought to target European-made clothing and other foreign products, as not only a symbol of British colonialism, but as the source of mass unemployment and poverty in India. The import of European commodities had left many millions of India's workers, craftsmen and women without means of livelihood. By championing homespun *khadi* and clothing and Indian-made goods, Gandhi sought to incorporate peaceful civil resistance as a means of promoting national self-sufficiency. It also provided villagers an additional source of income in their lean season. He wanted to end the system of oppressive taxation, and asked the farmers and workers to defend their economic rights. A major part of this rebellion was a commitment from the farmers to end caste discrimination and oppressive social practices against women. With that objective in mind, he launched a co-operative effort to promote education, healthcare, and self-sufficiency by producing clothes and food that were made locally.

It is also significant that Gandhi's vision of rural society was based on his idea of basic education and imparting of craft education, which would just not offer sop to people but make them permanently self-employed. He said, "Basic education is meant to transform village children into model villagers. It is principally designed for them. The inspiration for it came from the village."

According to Gandhi, there are four components of basic education. These are craft, art, health and education. Instead of regarding craft and industry as different from education, he regarded the former as the medium for the later. Gandhi emphasised on the need for educating the child through manual work, not as side activity, but as the prime means of intellectual training.' Giving importance to manual work Gandhi said- "Useful manual labour, intelligently performed is the means par excellence for developing the intellect. . . . A balanced intellect presupposes harmonious growth of body, mind and soul.... An intellect that is developed through the medium of socially useful labour will be an instrument for service and not easily be led astray or fall into devious paths." The Gandhian concept of human dignity is centred not on false assumptions on manual labour but on penetrating into the very depth of human life from whatever avenues available. He quotes Ruskin's saying "A life of labour, the life of the tiller of the soil and handicraftsman, is the life worth living." Economically Gandian notion of education was designed to create productive labour since the emphasis is on job-oriented education. It can also become an instrument for rapid improvement in the standard of living of the people through increased production of goods and service. Analysing Gandhi's educational discourse, Krishna Kumar feels that Gandhi located the problem of education in the dialectic of man versus machine in which the man represented the universal man, the machine represented the industrialised West.

The concept of food security has emerged as key factor in emerging notions of human-security in recent times. But, Gandhi's notion of rural development envisaged this idea. An international consensus emerged after a process of international consultation leading to the World Food Summit in November 1996. In 1970s, the world had faced severe food crisis. There arose grave concern about the problem of food supply, of ensuring the availability and price stability of basic food items, both at the national and international levels. The issues of famine, hunger and food crisis were examined. This led to re-examination of definition of food security. It was recognised that the affected people were vulnerable despite the availability of food supply in the markets because they did not have enough money to buy food at prevailing prices. It also became evident that the technical success of the Green Revolution did not automatically ensured rapid and dramatic reductions in poverty and hunger. In the light of this evidence, World Food Summit (1974), defined food security as the availability at all times of adequate world food supplies of basic stuffs to sustain steady expansion of food consumption and to offset fluctuations in production and prices. In 1983, Food and Agricultural Organisation (FAO) expanded its concept to include securing access by vulnerable people to available supplies ensuring people at all times have both the physical and economic access to the basic food they need. Thus, both demand and supply side of food production and its supply were taken into account in this new redefinition. The World Bank Report, *Poverty and Hunger* (1986) focussed on the time dimension of food insecurity. It made clear-cut distinction between chronic hunger related to problems of structural poverty and low income and temporary hunger or food insecurity, which resulted from natural disaster, economic collapse or situations of violent conflict. The concept of food security was broadened to mean 'access of all people at all times to enough food for an active, healthy life.' While discussing food security, attention was generally focussed on protein-calorie deficiencies or intake of less than specified quantum of such food items. By 1990s, it was recognised that food preferences and tastes could be culturally determined. So, World Food Summit (1996) adopted a more complex definition. It was stated that Food security, at individual, national, regional and global levels is achieved when all people, at all times, have physical and economic access to sufficient, safe and nutritious food to meet their dietary needs and food preferences for an active and healthy life. Food security, thus, has many facets. We have immortalised our Bapu, we have erected huge statues so that he may be commemorated and his preaching be remembered, but pay lip service to his ideas.

Gandhi laid stress that one could earn his living only if he did physical labour. While he did not disregard the intellectual professions, he felt that all men must engage in some physical labour and service, so that they can rightfully earn their daily bread. By this, he had sought to bring about dignity of labour. Gandhi made it mandatory for physical labour to be undertaken by his pupils at the Tolstoy Farm and later his *Ashrams* in India. The doctrine of bread labour asserts the moral imperative that one must earn one's bread by the sweat of one's brow: "He has no right to eat who does not bend his body and work;" Bodily labour is a duty imposed by nature on human beings. And one who eats but does not do any manual work in effect steals food. Bread labour was not work done under economic compulsions for others to eke out a miserable livelihood. By this 'Gandhi believed the caste distinctions will be erased. The intra- family allocation of labour will be more in favour of women and hedonistic glorification of leisure will cease and local communities will achieve self-sufficiency in food supply, too.

Another facet of Gandhian idea was his notion of decentralisation. Elaborating on the structure of decentralised rural republics, Gandhi said:

> "In this structure composed of innumerable villages, there will be ever-widening, never ascending circles. Life will not be a pyramid with the apex sustained by the bottom. But, it will be an oceanic circle whose centre will be the individual, always ready to perish for the village, the latter ready to perish for the circle of villages, till at last the whole becomes one's life composed of individuals never aggressive in their arrogance but ever humble, sharing the majesty of the oceanic circle of which they are integral units....therefore, the outermost circumference will not wield power to crush the inner circle but give strength to all within and derive its own from the centre."

Conclusions

We have briefly discussed notion of employment generation under the state-sponsored MGNREGA. The colonial context in which Gandhi's idea took root and the contemporary context of neo-liberal economic policies are entirely different. Gandhi's notion of rural development was holistically framed and involved imparting skills to rural people through basic education, engage their creative potential in production, making them independent and self-sufficient in food production and entitlement. Gandhi envisioned the villages of India providing the ideal setting for maintaining traditional values and practices as well as defusing power. It was his local site for a just, equitable, stable community-based on full employment and contentment, if not affluence of the scale which industrialism could furnish. Such an ideal economically insular village perhaps never existed in history; it existed only in Gandhi's imagination. Despite that Gandhi's scheme of rural development provided some human agency to the rural poor. MGNREGA is at best a state-sponsored project which is trying to fight ill-effects of neo-liberal economics and mitigate the diminishing wages of rural poor. The broad ideological trappings of Gandhi are a missing link in the MGNREGA.

Notes and References

1. For the changes in the demographic profile of population and the impact of globalisation on the world economies at the peripheries see the following works: Dorothy Stein, *People Who Count: Population and Politics, Women and Children*, Earth Scan Publications, London, 1995; UN Centre for Human Settlements, *Cities in a Globalising World*, Earth Scan Publications, London, 2001; Barney Cohen, "Urban Growth in Developing Countries: A Review of Current Trends and a caution regarding existing forecasts", *World Development*, Vol. 32, No. 11, 2004, pp. 23-51; and
2. P. Panwalkar, "Upgradation of Slums: A World Bank Programme" in S.Patel and A. Thorner, eds., "*Bombay: Metaphor for Modern India*" OUP, Bombay, 1996, pp. 121-142 and also see T.P.R. Calderia , *City of Walls: Crime, Segregation and Citizenship in Sao Paulo*, University of California, Berkeley, 2000 for the impact of globalisation on the life of urban poor in a Latin American city, a life-experience which can be generalised to other displaced and dislocated people.
3. For understanding the core of economic ideas of Gandhi the following works are important: Ajit K. Dasgupta (2002), *Gandhi's Economic Thought*, Routledge; Ghosh, B.N. (2007), *Gandhian Political Economy*, Asgate Pub, Hampshire; Narayan, S. (1970), *Relevance of Gandhian Economics*, Navajivan Pub, Ahmedabad.

4. House, Pani, N. (2002), *Inclusive Economics: Gandhian Method and Contemporary Policy*, Sage Publication, Delhi and Sharma, R. (1997), *Gandhian Economics,* Deep and Deep Publications Pvt. Ltd., New Delhi.
5. See Ministry of Rural Development, *Mahatma Gandhi National Rural Employment Guarantee Act, 2005, Mahatma Gandhi, Operational Guidelines*, Government of India, New Delhi for details of the scheme.
6. Harijan, January 27, 1939.
7. This reading of Gandhi is based on Parel, Anthony ed. (1997): *Gandhi: Hind Swaraj and Other Writings* (New Delhi: Foundation Books) and Terchek, Ronald (1998): *Gandhi: Struggling for Autonomy*, London: Rowman and Littlefield).
8. See Kumar, Krishna, "Mohandas Karamchand Gandhi (1869-1948)", in Prospects: *The Quarterly Review of Education*, Vol. 23, No. 3/4, 1993, International Bureau of Education, UNESCO, pp. 507-517, regarding Gandhi's educational ideals and also see Kumar, Krishna (2005): *Political Agenda of Education: A Study of Colonialistand Nationalist Ideas*, Sage Publications, New Delhi.
9. Khoshoo, T.N. and John S. Moolakkattu (2009), *Mahatma Gandhi and Environment*, TERI, New Delhi, p. 111.

45

Critical Analysis of Human Resource Development and Rural Development

D. N. Harish

Introduction

Awareness while experiencing something leads to an understanding while consolidation of the same into wisdom has been the distinctive hallmark of the *Homosapiens* in view of their unique capacity to formulate and consciously transmit knowledge from one generation and location to another. *Knowledge society*, of late, has gained prominence – as is evident from its usage in the National Knowledge Commission report – due to technological advances and related applications. The knowledge revolution marks fundamental shift in human development from being limited to material processes to the infinite and creative potential of human processes. Thus, knowledge societies have to address issues about how information and ideas are to be created and, thereafter, adopted at an accelerating pace. Applying new knowledge continuously results in continuous innovation which yields social dividends for the civil society through, *inter alia,* greater levels of education, empowerment of women and improved health, which together result in improved Human Resource Development (HRD).

Human Resource Development and Rural Development

The overriding objective of a country's policy and planning is to raise the standard of living and enhance the productive capabilities of its people. With 1.25 billion populace (of which 72 per cent lives in villages and majority of it depends on agriculture and allied activities for livelihood), this challenge is particularly daunting for developing country like India – an agrarian country, whose economic development should come through rural prosperity.

Hence, human resource development via rural development is a *sine qua non* with the national development and has been a matter of abiding concern in Indian planning. Rural India is different from the urban segment of the country. The Indian village plays very significant role in the progress of the whole nation; it is a source of art, culture, literature, religion, human values, philosophy, economic wealth, and agricultural produce. It is also a storehouse of abundant human resource (HR), though the majority of this resource is underdeveloped, undeveloped, unused, underused, and overused, as well as inefficient and poor in quality. Nevertheless, there are limits to the extent to which unskilled or poorly trained labour could be absorbed productively in the non-agriculture sector.

All the same, an abundant supply of skilled and well-trained labour is likely to encourage the establishment and expansion of labour-using activities, generating both wage employment and self-employment possibilities. Since rural India is characterised by illiteracy, ignorance, unemployment, poverty, and many such stubborn problems of HRD, we cannot realise its full economic potentials without fully harnessing the HR which constitutes the ultimate basis for the wealth of nations with capital and natural resources being the passive factors of production while human beings are the active agents carrying forward national development.

HRD plays an important role in planning and implementation of rural development programmes in the developing countries. Often, it has been realised that shortage of skilled manpower constrains developing countries to implement their development programmes effectively. Therefore, HRD is one of the major contributors in accelerating economic growth. There is an obvious need to emphasise universal HRD, which calls for major commitment of public resources. The balance between resources allocated to education through the traditional academic stream and resources allocated to vocational and technical training streams may also need to be altered in favour of the latter. Despite the pronounced and pious objective of reduction in regional disparity, the area of planned development presents a picture of uneven growth in India. Poverty eradication programmes, in terms of wage employment and self-employment schemes hitherto launched, were ill-conceived and clumsily implemented. However, despite the efforts made by the government to promote various development programmes, over 50 per cent of the rural people in India are still living in poverty.

Concept of People-centred Development

UNDP defines people-centred development as "development of the people, by the people and for the people". Whatever the definition, the precise implications are always that people should be involved in their own development. In effect, according to Cox (1998), people-centred development could be said to rest on five pillars of foundation namely:

1. *Awareness Rising*: People need to be aware of the realities of their situation and their environment as necessary pre-requisite condition for their complete participation in development.

2. *Social Mobilisation:* People need to form into groups and local organisations as necessary condition for utilising benefit on available local resources and for insisting on the right to participate in their own economic development.

3. *Participation:* Development will reflect the realities and needs of people only when the development process is an exclusively participatory one.

4. *Self-reliance*: If the people are to have maximum control over their own development, it is important that development rests, as much as possible, on the resources available within the local community; to maximise self-reliance is to maximise the people-centred nature of development.

5. *Sustainability*: If development has to continue to provide for people's need, it must be sustainable.

Success or failure of any programme will depend on people's participation on developmental activities and empower them to self-sustenance. Literacy leads to sustainable empowerment of people. In illiteracy environment, there is meagre scope for development. Hence, human development is the main stress for providing quality of life to people; the basic prerequisites for this are literacy, people participation, obtaining complete benefits out of welfare programmes, and the role of information and communication.

Development *vis-à-vis* Education

Literacy/education, health, and social well-being are crucial to human productivity, while social safety nets offer vital support mechanisms to cope with crises. The role of rural governance in providing these services remains important, particularly to rural communities that are both physically and economically isolated. Lack of formal and informal education restricts the capacity of rural people to take advantage of alternative job opportunities. The incidence of chronic ill-health due to poor accessibility and affordability to health services and its effect on reducing rural labour productivity has been grossly underestimated. In other words, it is even more important that rural governance goes beyond mundane public administration of civil services, and should be a seamless extension of planning and management of the entire rural space.

Secondly, education facilitates social and occupational mobility among the members of a society. Educational achievements, to a large extent, determine the nature and type of job opportunities that become available to rural people. Functional literacy programmes and rural entrepreneurship programmes bear out the significance of the utility of specific target-oriented education.

In an era of globalisation and economic reforms being observed in the country, the phenomenon of social and economic development has been undergoing through a process resulting in new paradigms of development. Social scientists, being sensitised towards the new developments, have been closely observing the development initiatives in the changed social, economical, and physical atmosphere. As a result, several of new conceptual and strategy-oriented aspects are emerging. In order to ensure sustainable development, especially in rural areas, where incidence of poverty is on higher side, what assumes greater importance in formulating the development programmes are conceptual clarity as well as sound strategy.

Human Resource Development and Education Perspective

"Education is the manifestation of the perfection already in [hu]man," said Swami Vivekananda. Education could be broadly categorised into elementary, secondary, higher, technical, vocational, and adult education. But the one which is very relevant to the rural India for their uplift is skill development. Literacy has both direct and indirect impact on the successful implementation of rural development programmes. Moreover, people's participation in each and every stage of implementation of welfare programmes in a literate environment yields positive results. Further, the programmes either literacy or welfare must be designed with people-centred development approach.

The social demand for education is completely on the rise. People are striving for the higher level than their own level of socio-economic strata. Parents want their children to have higher degree of education than they themselves had. In the current scenario, the media plays big role in influencing the parents to make them aware of the new situations of the society. So, the pressure of education is on at all levels and in all its forms.

Basic Need of Rural Education in India

The education system evolved for this country had an excellent vision of ensuring the whole nation literate, when it was launched way back in 1936, though the purpose was of different kind. The pious downward filtration theory did not work in this country and hence left the majority of the population illiterate. Moreover, the dropout rate is very high comparatively to the urban sector. The present system of education created an artificial, yet psychologically a very potent gap among the people of India.

The system of education is not geared to the objectives of socio-economic development both in respect of its contents, in structure, and in methods of teaching. The system of education is thus, torn between two horns of the dilemma of quality and quantity with an added rider of the financial constraint. Added to this, the system of education in our country has many diverse and numerable problems to face, in addition to the financial problems, which are cultural in nature. The issue of rural education is totally forgotten and as a result, nothing has been done to develop a philosophy of rural education upon which a superstructure of a whole system suitable to our country could be built.

Concept of Development in India

The development of rural areas in India is a multi-dimensional problem, which has been so far viewed by the policy makers and academicians mainly from the economic aspect only. In India rural development is not only an economic problem but also more of a social-psychological-cultural problem. Michael P. Todaro views rural development as the most suitable, in Indian context, in the following manner:

1. Improvement in the level of living standard including employment, formal education, eradication of illiteracy, health, nutrition, housing, and a variety of other connected social services;
2. Decrease in inequality, in distribution of rural incomes, and in the rural-urban imbalances in incomes and economic opportunities; and
3. To sustain the capacity of rural sector.

Concept of Rural Development

"Just as the whole universe is contained in the self, so is India contained in the villages."

—***Mahatma Gandhi*** (1869-1948)

Visionary, Architect of India's Rural Development Programmes.

The villages epitomise the soul of India. With more than seventy per cent of the Indian population living in rural areas, rural India reflects the very essence of Indian culture and tradition. No wonder then that a holistic development of India as a nation rests on sustained and holistic development of rural India.

The term 'rural development' is a sub-set of the broader term 'development'. Development is a subjective and value-based term; this is as difficult to arrive at consensus as to its meaning. At the best, development in the context of society could be conceptualised as a set of desirable societal objectives that country seeks to achieve. Rural development connotes overall development of rural areas with a view to improve the quality of life of rural people. It is a comprehensive and multi-dimensional concept and encompasses the development of agriculture and allied activities, village and cottage industries, crafts, socio-economic infrastructure, community services and facilities, and, above all, the human resources (development) in rural areas in general.

As a phenomenon, rural development is the end result of interactions among various physical, technological, economic, socio-cultural, and institutional factors. As a strategy, it is designed to improve the economic and social well-being of a specific group of people in the rural poor. As a discipline, it is multi-disciplinary in nature, representing an intersection of agricultural, social, behavioural, engineering, and management sciences.

Prof Robert Chambers, who pioneered participatory approaches in rural development with emphasis on Participatory Rural Appraisal techniques, summarised the concept of rural development as a strategy to enable a specific group of people, to gain for themselves and their children more of what they want and need. It involves helping the poorest among those, who seek a livelihood in the rural areas to demand and control more of the benefits of rural development. The group includes small-scale farmers, tenants, and the landless.

Chambers and Conway (1992) define the concept of sustainable livelihood, in the context of rural development, as "a livelihood comprises the capabilities, assets (stores, resources, claims and access) and activities required for a means of living: a livelihood is sustainable which can cope with and recover from stress and shocks, maintain or enhance its capabilities and assets, and provide sustainable livelihood opportunities for the next generation; and which contributes net benefits to their livelihoods at the local and global levels and in the short-term and long-term."

The predominantly rural nature of India emphasises the need to bring about sustainable development of the rural areas and its people, if India is to attain any level of significant global eminence. However, despite best efforts, rural India has not kept pace with urban counterpart. The reasons for this are many and include, besides others, historical as well as geographical marginalisation. Recognising the importance of correcting these developmental imbalances and the need to accord due priority to development in rural areas, efforts were on, ever since independence, to address the problems of rural development in systematic way.

Approaches to Rural Development

For the development of the rural population, the government has made several efforts. These efforts and strategies could be summarised as:

- The Multi-purpose Approach;
- The Minimum Package Approach;
- The Target Group Approach;
- The Area Development Approach; and
- People's Participation Approach

Basic Objectives of Rural Development

India, since independence, has given varying degrees of attention and priority to rural development. The motivations and objectives of public policies have varied over time due to complex combination of political, economic, and social factors as well as opportunities for development provided by foreign assistance and global economic trends. The objectives of rural development followed and implemented by various governments have also been influenced by the overall plans for development and the performance of the economy in global setting during this period. In particular, the international economic environment, especially for foreign assistance, has conditioned them. However, the multiplicity of objectives which rural development was expected to achieve often deviated from the central focus and contributed to its failure though the results achieved were yet emphatic and significant.

- To increase the availability and widen the distribution of basic pre-requisites like food, clothes, shelter, healthcare, and security.
- To raise standards of living, in addition to higher purchasing power, the provision of more jobs, better education, and greater attention to cultural and humanistic values.
- To expand the range of economic and social choice to individuals by freeing them from servitude and dependence.

Indicators of Rural Development

Uphoff and Esman identify seven dimensions of rural development, in their study of eighteen country cases aimed at establishing relationships between local organisations/community-based organisations and rural development.

- Agricultural productivity measured in terms of average cereal yields per hectare and per capita total agricultural production;
- Technology measured in terms of use of fertilisers per hectare, irrigated area as percentage of cultivated area, and adoption of high yielding varieties of cereals – rice and wheat;
- Rural welfare measured in terms of levels of nutrition, health, education, and eradication of Illiteracy;
- Security measured in terms of protection from natural disaster, protection against violence, and access to justice;
- Distribution measured in terms of the ratio of income accruing to the top 20 per cent of households *vis-à-vis* that accruing to the bottom 20 per cent;
- Rate of population growth and level of employment; and
- Political-administrative participation measured in terms of electoral participation, control of bureaucratic influence on rural development policy, and allocation of public services and resources.

Key Issues of Rural Development

These relate to judicious use and management of the resource base on which the rural people depend for their livelihood to ensure that while present economic activities draw dividends from the natural resource base, they do not draw down the natural capital *(i.e.*, the ecosystem) and the future generations will continue to depend on. Consequently, rural governance has vital role to ensure this.

The rural poor will remain poor unless they are able to produce surplus and sell it under the most favourable market conditions, or to divert their surplus labour to economic activities that are not primary resource-based. Good rural governance should be able to provide services such as timely market information for producers to benefit from market fluctuations, as well open up opportunities for broad based rural economy to diversify livelihood strategies.

Nonetheless, in the realm of rural development, there has always been close nexus among the executive (in specific Rural Development Functionaries), the targetted population (in specific poor and deserved communities in rural areas) as well as the mechanism/strategy of implementation of the programme concerned. In other words, the external and internal (including personal and psychological) issues do play vital role among the rural development functionaries, while understanding and implementing the programmes concerned. Among the targetted population, it was also of importance that capacity of individuals or group concerned matters most in vying the options available for development as well as accessing the appropriate programmes and getting benefit thereof. It is not the mere right-minded RD functionaries or enlightened targetted population that matters, but also the way the programmes are being implemented and strategies adopted. Hence, for effective implementation of programmes three major issues do overlap among each other and correct understanding of the factors results in achieving the desired outcomes.

Conclusion

It seems, in the Indian context, rural development is a more sociological problem rather than an economic problem. With the process of economic development and growing awareness, the social system in the country is becoming more complicated and resulting in unequal economic conditions. The caste system continues to be a strong moral phenomenon of social structure in India, which undoubtedly is an influential system in marriage, education, basis of communal participation, a social control agency, and a political instrument affecting the rural development process adversely. So, the policies of rural development may so be designed to crack down the prevalent social structure in the country.

The experiences of development initiatives in rural areas, especially in the last decade or so, have indeed metamorphosed the priorities and pattern of rural development trends: the strong emergence of Panchayat Raj Institutions, the Self-Help-Groups, Peoples' Participation and Partnership, *et cetera*. Since development is a continuous process and change is inevitable, it is the conceptual clarity and sound strategy behind the philosophy of Rural Development that matters the most in ensuring sustainable as well as equity in development. Given the high incidence of poverty in rural areas, as well as existence of typical social atmosphere, ensuring sustainability and equity in development may gain further importance. The task is formidable, and is of unprecedented magnitude, innumerable challenges and possible failures, but there is no redoubled vigorous passion and professionalism to realise our dreams come true in Rural Development. Alternative to this, we cannot postpone this agenda except pursuing with dogged determination.

The Government has success rate in implementation of family welfare, pulse-polio programme, anti-malaria campaigns, and control age-old practices as '*sati*', animal sacrifice, and even to some extent in formal education. The failure of implementing agencies to adopt outcome of the evaluation studies, research observation, and also lack of political and social will on the part of the people's representative and educated persons were responsible even today.

HRD could be considered as an effective tool for transformation of ideas, values, behavioural change, conventions, and more specially as an agent of change. Hence, if the HRD programme is organised on set objectives, change the task according to the needs of target group, creation of congenial environment then the attitude of the learner is to be changed towards positive participation. Only then the sustainable development of life could be achieved.

In a democratic society people cannot remain silent spectators to the vast changes taking place around them; they have to participate effectively not only in the decision-making process, but also in the formulation and implementation of the developmental programmes. To achieve this objective, the citizens need to be developed for desirable participation and reap the benefits of rural development programmes.

Put simply, Human Resource Development is the Road to Rural Development.

References

Chambers, Robert (1983), *Rural Development, Putting the Last First*, London: Longman.

Chambers, Robert and Gordon Conway (1992), *Sustainable Rural Livelihoods: Practical Concepts for the 21st Century.* IDS Discussion Paper 296, IDS, Brighton, UK, February.

Cox, David (1998), "Toward People-Centred Development: The Social Development Agenda and Social Work Education" *Indian Journal of Social Work,* 59(1), pp.513-30.

Planning Commission, *Five-Year Plan Reports*, Government of India, New Delhi.

Todaro, Michael P. (1977), *Economics of Developing World.* London, Oxford Printing Press.

Uphoff, Norman, and Milton J. Esman (1983), *Local Organisation for Rural Development; Analysis of Asian Experience*; Rural Development and Social Organisation Asia-3; South East Asia, Macmillan India Ltd., Delhi.

Vivekananda, Swami, *Complete Works of Swami Vivekananda*, Vol. IV, p. 358.

46

Impact of Modern Technology on Agriculture

Channabasavaiah H.M. and Jayaraj M.

Introduction

Agricultural technology helped to increase the farm productivity in developed nations as well as underdeveloped nations like India. Most of the people in under developed countries depend upon agriculture for livelihood, *i.e.*, earning their bread from agriculture and allied activities. In India, the share of agriculture in GDP has declined from 51.88 per cent in 1950-51 to 29.02 per cent in 1990-91 and further declined to 17.39 per cent in the year 2012-13. At the same time, the agricultural production increases, that's why we are able to feed the growing population. Agricultural modernisation has two faces, one of that is modern technology helped to increase the productivity of the land holding and production as well, second one is, it reduced the employment opportunity of the marginal farmers and landless labourers. In this paper, we are going to discuss the pros and cons of agricultural modernisation and its impact on the rural economy.

Issues with Modern Technology

There is really little mystery about why agriculture is important—it is the physical foundation of human energy, health, and physical well-being—all key components of every important human activity. Agriculture is an art, science and industry of managing the growth of plants and animals for human use. Agriculture includes preparation of soil for cultivation of crops, harvesting crops, breeding and raising livestock, dairying and forestry. The two major types of agriculture are: traditional agriculture and modern or industrialised agriculture. There is no question of technology with traditional agriculture. Question arises when it comes to the modern agriculture. Modern agriculture used modern method of cultivation, hybrid seeds, advanced pesticides, chemical fertilisers, harvesting machines, threshing machines etc., to improve the productivity and reduce the cost of production. Herewith, I am going to explain the pros and cons of agricultural processes, one by one.

Tilling or Ploughing

The very first task of the farmer is to till the land with the help of plough, hoe, or cultivator. In traditional agriculture, our farmers use the wooden plough or hoe made up of wood and iron. In modern agriculture, the machine driven cultivators are being used broadly. It prepares the land for sowing the seed correctly in the depth and to absorb the rain water. Tilling the land by cultivators helps the farmer to increase the productivity of land. It loosens the soil better than the traditional plough or hoe. No doubt it helps the farmer, but in the countries like India, it leads to another problem, soil erosion. There are so many schemes introduced and implemented by the government to construct the bunds in the field. Our illiterate farmer unknowingly remove that bund to sow the seed. He doesn't know the importance of bund. When there is no bund, rain water flow with the soil. In the drought times, government provide employment opportunities by making bunds in the fields. But those bunds were destroyed by the peasants after one or two years.

Selecting and Sowing of Seed

Sowing is the next important work in agriculture. Before sowing, good quality seeds must be selected. Here we find traditional varieties and high yielding varieties. In the traditional varieties productivity is very less. High yielding varieties are beneficial for farmers. In India, along with indigenous producers, there are so many multi-national companies supplying high yielding variety seeds. Here our farmers are being cheated by the seeds companies. Due to this cheating, farmers themselves in some areas of Karnataka, Andhra Pradesh and Maharashtra. Governments are unable to check this menace to help the farmers. Now-a-days, genetically modified seeds are gaining momentum. The Monsanto provide GM Seeds to the farmers, here also company has cheated the farmers by selling spurious seeds. In Karnataka, there were so many demonstrations held to protest the greediness of the Monsanto company.

After selecting the seed, farmer has to sow the seed with the help of a tool into the soil. Before sowing, it must be treated by the Rhizobium. This bacterium helps the plant convert atmospheric nitrogen to ammonia. But our farmers are unable to do this. For sowing work we find two tools, first traditional one and second seed drill. Most of our farmers are using the traditional method of sowing and not modern seed drill. Seed drill saves the time and labour, but it is costly to our marginal farmers.

Use of Manures and Fertilisers

To increase the fertility of the land, a farmer has to add the manure and fertilisers to the soil. These substances help the plants to grow healthy. When farmers are growing a crop repeatedly, the land becomes poor in the sense of fertility. We can get rich manures from the decomposition of plant and animal wastes. In these days due to the modernisation effect, cattle rearing becomes difficult and rare, due to the paucity of green staples. Hence, farmers are substituting fertilisers to the manures. Excessive doses of organic residues (fertilisers) in agricultural fields could be dangerous for plants, invertebrates and micro-organisms living in the soil (Micro-nutrient imbalance, Nitrate pollution, Eutrophication). This is the finding of a study carried out by the Autonomous University of Barcelona (UAB), which has shown that the use of appropriate levels of fertilisers would prevent this toxic impact on the soil biota. "If farmers overuse chemical fertilisers for a long period, the fertiliser residues will affect water quality. When the nitrogenous fertiliser is washed away or carried into the air, it will influence air quality," Xu Mingang, vice-director of Institute of Agricultural Resources and Regional Planning, Chinese Academy of Agricultural Sciences (CAAS), pointed out in an interview with the ND TV.

Irrigation

Irrigation refers to the supply of water to the agricultural activities. In India, irrigating agricultural land is a major problem. After the green revolution, need for the water for agricultural purpose increased rapidly. In India, sources of water are: rivers, tanks, wells, canals and other artificial projects for the purpose of cultivation and agricultural activities. Agricultural irrigated land (per cent of total agricultural land) in India was last measured at 35.12 per cent in 2009, according to the World Bank. In India, irrigation system is dominated with the canal irrigation. But the most severe problem facing Indian canal irrigation is not so much the slowdown in growth, but the rapid deterioration of systems that have already been created. Maintenance is being woefully neglected, leading to poor capacity utilisation, rising incidence of water-logging and salinity and lower water use efficiency (WUE). On the whole, large canal-based irrigation is threatening to become unsustainable physically, environmentally as well as financially. We are unable to maintain the canal system to help the farmer; most of our canals are filled with shrubs and mud. Contractors are unable to maintain the quality needed. Farmers in the end of the canal are unable to get the water because of these problems.

Most of our farm lands are rain-fed and we are unable to provide water to those lands. In these lands, crops depend on the monsoon, that's why government provide subsidies to the sprinkler and drip irrigation. Here also were we find loopholes in the system. Our farmers cheated by the companies, using the spurious instruments. Companies are trying to eat the subsidy of the government, cheating the farmers.

Research has not been done to help the farmers in the arid zone. Crops which are able to sustain in the less water are not invented. In this area, we need research.

Weeds and Pests

Undesired crops growing with natural plants are called weeds. In traditional agriculture, removal of weeds done by the labouer and with the help of plough, labouer used *khurpi* to remove weeds, manually it was removed. Technology helps the farmers in this regard there are so many weedicides available in the market. These weedicides are sprayed in the fields to remove the weeds, but at the same time weed may develop resistance to the weedicides, it will become another mess with the environment.

Insects are beneficial and harmful to crops. Insects which are harmful to crops are called pests. Major insects are aphids, fruitfly, fungus gnat, leafhopper, leafminer, mealybug, pea weevil, pepper maggot, scale, spider mites, thrips, whiteflies etc. We use pesticides and insecticides to remove these pests. In the process, beneficial pests and insects are also killed, it is the major cause of concern.

Harvesting

Harvesting is cutting the crop after maturity. It may be done manually or mechanically. In manual harvesting traditional sickle is used, in the modern agriculture harvesting machines are using abundantly. It helps the farmers to save the time and labour, it also helps to dump the produce in their yards as early as possible. But this machine has its own drawbacks, it increase unemployment level in the rural India. The staple of the crop is used as animal fodder. When the machine cuts the staple in the middle of the plant, half of the plant remains in the earth, this is the major concern. The discretionary use of machines ruin the entire landscape resulting in ecological imsbalance.

Storage and Marketing

In the final leg of the agricultural activities, we find storage and marketing of the produce. Due to the lack of storage facilities, our farmers are pushed to sell their produce at the market rates. In the harvesting season, the rate of the produce is very low because of supply. By keeping this produce in the scientifically constructed warehouse, we can get good price after some time. Here is the main hurdle to the farmer. Due to the lack of finance, farmers borrow some loans from commission agents. When produce comes to the market, the farmer has to sell his produce in the commission agent's yards. Commission agent imposer, arbitrary interest rates and the farmer has to pay commission which is not in the rules. Sometimes this commission may be around five to 10 per cent of the bill. Government must provide fair rate to the agricultural produce and must provide grading and standardising facilities in the market yard.

What is the Future

Most of the agricultural research is done by the public institutions in India. We have to rationalise the research work done by the public institutions. Here are some suggestions to improve the condition and maintain the balance between the modern agriculture and traditional agriculture.

- In our country, agriculture is the most neglected sector when compared to other sectors. Our government must increase the funding to those promising institutions to develop them as international institutions.
- There are so many departments working for the welfare of the farmer. Government must co-ordinate the departments to co-operate with each other.
- Quality education is must to bring up the farmer to accept modern technology, and he must be trained using modern technology.
- Competitive research funds help direct towards well-defined targets; provide incentive for participation of a wider range of technology providers and encourage links between NGOs, farmer groups and research organisations
- A study was conducted in the Kenya by the Wilfred Nyangena and Ogada Maurice Juma. Findings of the study are in organic fertilisers and improved varieties which are indeed yield-increasing. When farmers work efficiently yield increases greatly.
- Consider the agriculture as an industry and provide research and development facilities.
- In these days, public and private partnership gains momentum. Consider the agriculture in the PPP module.
- Present Agricultural Produce Marketing Committees must revamp according to the present needs. There are so many advancements in the technology. APMCs must use this technology to help the farmers.
- Our policy makers don't know the ground reality of agriculture. They must come out of the offices and study the original problems of the farmers.

- Must educate the farmers to use the water judiciously to overcome the problem from salinity and water-logging problems. It is the uphill task before the government.

Conclusion

No doubt, technology plays very important role in the development of agriculture, but it must be pro-poor. Without technological advancement, we are unable to provide food for increasing population. Hence, we have to use the technology to remove the disparities between poor and the rich in rural India. There are so many gaps in the government departments and ground reality; we must fill the gap to improve the condition of the farmer. We have to use information and communication technology for the welfare of the farmer.

References

Competitive Grants in the New Millennium Reifschneider, F.D. Byerlee and F. de Souza (eds) (2000), Brasilia, Brazil: Empresa Brasileira de Pesquisa Agropecuaria (EMBRAPA), Inter-American Development Bank (IDB) and World Bank.

Data-book for use of Deputy Chairman, Published by Planning Commission, New Delhi on 10th March, 2014.

From Top Down to Bottoms Up: Institutional Reforms in Indian Canal Irrigation, Gulati, Ashok, Ruth, Meinzen - Dick, Raju. K.V., 1999, Delhi: Institute of Economic Growth.

http://mjcetenvsci.blogspot.in/2013/10/effects-of-modern-agriculture.html.

http://www.sciencedaily.com/releases/2008/10/081030194236.htm.

http://www.theepochtimes.com/n2/china-news/fertilizer-overuse-damages-agriculture-and-environment-in-china-62671.html.

http://www.thehindu.com/news/national/karnataka/krrs-threatens-action-against-monsanto/article5254628.ece.

http://www.tradingeconomics.com/india/agricultural-irrigated-land-percent-of-total-agricultural-land-wb-data.html.

Impact of Improved Farm Technologies on Yields – The Case of Improved Maize Varieties and Inorganic Fertilizer in Kenya, by Wilfred Nyangena and Maurice Juma. Discussion Paper, published in the Environment for Development, January 2014.

Technology and its Contribution to Pro-poor Agricultural Development - Agriculture and Natural Resources Team of the UK, Department for International Development (DFID) in collaboration with Rob Tripp of ODI, London.

47.

Issues and Challenges in Mahatma Gandhi National Rural Employment Guarantee Act [MGNREGA]

Damodaran K.

Introduction

This paper examines the issues and challenges of MGNREGA to be addressed to mandate the objectives of the act. In order to alleviate rural poverty by generating employment and creation of sustainable assets in Rural India, Government of India brought MGNREGA in 2005. MGNREGA is the largest employment providing scheme in the world. The main objective of the Act is to enhance livelihood security in rural areas by providing at least 100 days of guaranteed wage employment in a financial year to every household whose adult members volunteer to do unskilled manual work. In India, implementation of NREGA has led to both positive and negative impacts. This Act has brought economic changes in the rural belts. Simultaneously, the objectives of the NREGA are undermined by the local authorities to execute. Besides, corruption has exclusively damaged the Act and the eight duties of the NREGA are mandated for the name of records. People are still not empowered to use their right to demand and ensure transparency in the implementation of the scheme (Thomas, Bigi and Ruby Bhatia, 2012). Thus, the long-run benefits of the programme are questioned and the present study makes an attempt to address those challenges and issues.

Inefficient Planning

According to the MGNREGA guidelines, *gram panchayat* is the responsible authority to implement the scheme and plan the works. Annual plans made by the GP, are consolidated first at the Block and then at the district level to prepare the district plan/labour budgets. The budgets of the *gram panchayat* may picture the estimation of employment to be generated and form the basis of funds to be allocated to states. The Comptroller and Auditor General (CAG) audit 'however' found a number of inefficiencies with this planning process. Annual plans at the GP level were either not prepared or prepared in an incomplete manner. District labour budgets were not prepared and the projected employment generation wasn't included. Many plans also did not include the shelf of works or list of assets to be built. The CAG also noted significant delays at every level in the submission of annual plans (Kapur, A. 2013).

Lack of Focus

Though Schedule One of the MGNREGA referred to conservation of natural resources such as rainwater, land, forests, this was not reflected in the works floated for the scheme. In most cases, the MGNREGA works are mandated for namesake and to complete the transaction of funds rather the objectives of the Act.

Inadequate Manpower

At the Block and levels, the administration suffers from inadequate manpower for administrative and technical works. In particular, programme officer, technical assistants and employees for assisting the Act. The lack of manpower has adversely affected the preparation of plans, scrutiny, approval, monitoring and measurement of works, and maintenance of the stipulated records at the Block and GP level. The CAG report points out that besides affecting the implementation of the scheme and the provision of employment, this also impacted adversely on transparency (Kapur, A., 2013).

Discrimination

The major focus of the MGNREGA is to provide opportunity to the rural people of India to earn income. Also, it aims to reduce the inequality among the people in terms of gender and caste. The most important feature of the Act is it gives equal salary for both men and women, which shows the strength of the Act in reducing gender inequality. But, caste and gender discrimination is reported in most of the parts of the country. In most of the states, the women registration in MGNREGA is very low percentage while Kerala and Andhara Pradesh alone support the female through the Act. In some states, the political and powerful groups dominate at local level and get more number of job cards, which affect the opportunities for the poor rural people.

Absence of Worksite Facilities

As per Section-27, Schedule-II of the MGNREGA, the local government has to provide facilities at work place. That is, they have to provide safe drinking water, shade for children, periods of rest and first-aid box at the work site for workers. But, in most of the states, these facilities are not provided to the MGNREGA workers. Small children suffer without any shelter and the healths is affected. As a result, the female who have kids avoided working in MGNREGA. It also forces them rethink about applying for work in the first place. For the rural people, trees are the only source of shelter and the workers cannot find trees at all sites. Thus, temporary shelters must be built for those doing NREGA labour.

Transparency and Accountability

Transparency and accountability are important factors that may helpstrengthen the Act to a large extent. As per guidelines of the Act, District Project Co-ordinator will be responsible to ensure transparency and accountability under the scheme (Singh, 2008). For ensuring transparency, some steps like display of the list of works and persons employed on the *panchayat's* notice board and prominent places are undertaken but still transparency remains within red tape.

Monitoring

The NREGA evolves a strict monitoring-cum-concurrent evaluation mechanism for successful implementation. The Act provides variety of monitoring activities at various levels of implementation, *i.e.,* from village to central level. But, from many studies it is reported that standard operating procedures is at the central level while at local level there is no standard monitoring system, which may affect the livelihood of the rural people and leads to corruption at wider level.

Corruption

In India, corruption has negative impact on various programmes and it stands as *virus* in the developmental activity of the country. As a result, the various Acts to remove poverty and unemployment remain as an Acts and have as not solved the issue, regard to MNREGA, the local government involves in corruption and reported they claim that more people have received job cards than people, who actually work in order to generate more fund than needed, to be then embezzled by local officials. For issuing job cards, the local authorities' get bribe and the salary is also not given as per the Act. Therefore, corruption plays a major role in affecting the objectives of the Act, which stands as a major issue and challenge to the Act.

Delay in Wage Payments

Delays in wage payments have always been a matter of concern in previous employment programmes, and this issue continues to plague the MGNREGA. Wage payments are delayed for weeks, sometimes months. The time lag varies from state to state. For instance, in Jashpur district, Chhattisgarh, month-long delays were noted. In some areas like Barwani district, Madhya Pradesh, the delay was for a period of 15 to 30 days. Delays were also noted in Manika and Manatu Blocks in Jharkhand (Sood, 2014).

Lack of Awareness

The rural people are unaware of the provision of the MGNREGA. Due to this, the people are unable to get the benefits as per the regulations of the Act. The receipt of the application is the record for claiming their unemployment allowance. But, the rural people are unaware about the unemployment allowance and they do not apply for the same. On the other hand, the local officials deliberately never reveal about the unemployment allowance due to fear for which they will be punished for not providing jobs to the people. Poor awareness not only affects the rural people to attain benefits from the scheme but also leads to corruption. The government must arrange intensive training to the rural people and officials, so that the Act may serve its duty. If the local people understand the rules and regulations of the Act, then they can raise an opposition themselves if the authorities fail to serve the Act. With addition, the people must be aware of the RTI Act, and they must learn the need of the Act for attaining their needs.

Social Audit

A social audit is an ongoing process through which the potential beneficiaries and other stakeholders of an activity or project are involved at every stage – from planning to implementation, monitoring and evaluation. This process helps in ensuring that the activity or project is designed and implemented in a most suited mode to the prevailing conditions, appropriately reflecting the priorities and preferences of those affected, and most effectively serving public interest. To ensure transparency and accountability, social auditing and inspection of NREGA work for proper assessment along with measuring of appropriateness, some steps are to be taken as per the Act of NREGA. The success of social audit still remains questionable. The social audit process has a long way to go before it can claim to have contributed to transparency, empowerment and good governance.

Conclusion

Like other public programmes this has raised many eyebrows, all of which are not to be ignored. Claw of corruption is one of the major issues in the scheme. However, they require close local supervision, and the assets are poorly constructed, or simply not useful to the poor. Close vigilance is required to see that NREGA should not become just another plethora of poverty alleviation schemes that India has had since Independence (Sjoblom and Farrington, 2008). Besides, Government and NGOs have to analyse the outcome of MGNREGA in order to verify the objectives targetted in terms of social and economic development. The NREGA addresses itself chiefly to working people and their fundamental right to live with dignity. The success of NREGA, however, will depend on people's realisation of the Act as a *right*. Effective levels of awareness and sustained public pressure are crucial to ensure that the implementation problems are addressed and the objectives met.

References

Bidyut Mohanty, (2009), "Working of NREGA -- Voices from Panchayats," *Mainstream, 22 (15)*, http://www.mainstreamweekly.net/auteur206.html.

Centre for Science and Environment, (2008), "NREGA, Opportunities and Challenges." Centre for Science and Environment, New Delhi.

Feroze1, A. Roy, R. Singh, (2012), "Some Issues of NREGS: Review of North Eastern States of India with Special Reference to Meghalaya," *Indian Journal of Hill Farming*, 25 (2) pp. 27 - 32.

Kapur, Avani, (2013), "Highlights from the CAG Performance Audit of MGNREGA." http://www.accountabilityindia.in/.

Shah D, Mohanty S. (2010), "Implementation of NREGA during eleventh plan in Maharashtra: Experiences, challenges and way forward," *Indian Journal of Agricultural Economics*, 65 (3) pp. 540 - 51.

Siddhartha and Vanaik. A, (2008), "GAG Report on NREGA: Fact and Fiction." *Economic and Political Weekly*, 17 (25), pp. 39 - 45.

Singh, Puran, (2008), "National Rural Employment Guarantee Scheme - A Task Ahead." In Berma, Sawalia Bihari; Upadhya, Yogesh and Sant Gyaneshwar Pd. Singh (Ed.), *Rural Employment*, Sarup and Sons, New Delhi.

Sjoblom, D. and Farrington, J. (2008), "The Indian National Rural Employment Guarantee Act: Will It Reduce Poverty and Boost the Economy?" *Project Briefing*-7. London: ODI.

Sood, Tanushree, (2014), "NREGA: Challenges in Implementation." http://infochangeindia.org/.

Tanushree Sood, (2014), "NREGA: Challenges in implementation." Info Change India, http://infochangeindia.org./

Thomas, Bigi and Ruby Bhatia, (2012), "Impact of NREGA Scheme: A Study on the Overall Quality of Life of Its Beneficiaries," *Asia-Pacific Journal of Social Sciences*, 4(2) pp. 213 - 27.

UNDP, (2010), "A Study on the Performance of NREGA in Kerala," Ministry of Rural Development, Government of India, New Delhi.

Vijayanand S.M. (2009), "Performance of NREGA in Kerala," Ministry of Rural Development." Government of India, New Delhi.

48

Mobile e-Governance in Agriculture and Rural Development

Gayathri A. and Yuvaraja P.

Introduction

Information and Communication Technology (ICT) has increased the services for rural citizens. The efforts of improving the delivery of government services for the citizens though e-Government are focussed in the rural area. The e-Governance applications have made an attempt to offer services in terms of Government to Citizens (G2C), Government to Business (G2B) and Government to Government (G2G). These services help the rural people in terms of Agricultural, Health, Education, etc. Besides, ICT applications visualise the government schemes transparently. Most of the Indian rural farmers, literacy is low and they on 'depend others help' in accessing the PC (Personal Computer) based ICT applications. Also, it is twice expensive to operate an internet services in rural areas, because of power back up (poor power availability in rural areas), maintenance of computer hardware, lack of broadband connectivity, insufficient trained computer operators etc.

At present, mobile service is an alternate mode of delivery of e-services in rural area. In India, the rural population is about 72 per cent of the total population. India has 55.48 crore mobile users as per our India Mobile Landscape (IML), 2013. More than 29.8 crore, about 54 per cent of the mobile users are in rural areas as compared to 25.6 crore in cities and towns. The study found that 93 lakh people access Internet from mobile phones using data connection such as GPRS or 3-G and around 77 per cent of users are in rural areas. Most of the rural citizens below literacy rate also use mobile services. These services are becoming versatile (radio, camera, large storage, high data transfer rates), affordable and penetrative. In general, the e-services that to the stakeholders are G2C, G2B and G2G . But, the mobile services can potentially deliver and receive G2C2G (Government to Citizen to Government). Given this backdrop, the present study examines the role of mobile e-Governance in agriculture for rural development.

Database and Agriculture

The main phases of agriculture includes crop cultivation, water management, fertiliser application, pest management, harvesting, and post-harvest handling, transport of food products, packaging, food preservation, food storage, and food marketing etc. The above mentioned services are unique and performed at different point of time. A farmer may need direction to attain good agricultural output, wherein mobile services can guide him to a large extent. It may be a voice communication (Kisan call centre), SMS-based queries (pre-defined) and data transferring (using mobile applications). The mobile phone application is a structured software in terms of local language customisation, and remote transaction services; recent geopolitical information, social network interlink for sharing information and motivating. Therefore, these features can support the farmers for attaining agricultural development. For this, the government has to develop a mobile application in order to support the agricultural activity.

At the first level, the farmers have to register their mobile number and upload/install the application in his/her mobile. Besides, the government has to maintain the farmer's database regarding layout of land area, recent geographical information, soil nutrition, climatic conditions etc. With this information, the software has to integrate the features of the land and has to suggest farmers regarding improving agriculture. With addition, the software can provide some advisory services related to government schemes, seeds (an analysis report of demand seeds for that season), fertiliser, irrigation of water and time to harvesting. This mobile application provides crop insurance, seed companies, a real time system to intimate the farmers on market prices. To eliminate the role of middleman in agricultural marketing, the mobile application can mediate between the buyer and farmers. The forthcoming section examines the role of mobile application and agriculture in detail.

Natural Resources Information

Agricultural production is influenced by many factors such as climatic factors, soil nutrition (soil health card), water resources, pest management and government schemes. The mobile application has to maintain these factors in farmer's database. Integration of these factors is more complex, the structured application has to get more information from the research centre for the analysis.

Based on this information, the application has to suggest best possible solution to improve agricultural production.

Government Schemes

The mobile application has to provide the details of the government schemes to the farmers very clearly and transparently. Overall forecasting, agricultural marketing, crops, extension activities and new technology innovations are to be listed as like menu. The application designed should be user-friendly and has to support local languages. The mobile application has to provide loan particulars, lists of documents for applying loan, availability of loan, bank details, rate of interest, crop insurance (insurance depends on seed selection), and landmark of the bank and government subsidies.

Crop Selection

For crop selection, the mobile application has to compare the market price and demand. The details of government's crop subsidies, budget required to cultivate the crop (crop loan and insurance), climatic factors, water resources, suitable land properties, and cropping season etc., have to be supported by the mobile application. These details would give confidence to the farmers in execution of the agricultural activity at all levels. At the next level, the farmers can select a crop and has to store the same in the database. The mobile application would give suggestions according to the crops selected in a regular manner.

Land Preparation and Crop Use

The mobile application has to support the farmers in land preparation with the database regarding soil test result, effects of any disease from the previous cultivations (reduce that impact), layout of agricultural area and crop selection. With these key factors, the mobile application has to suggest the methods of land preparation. The suggestion of the mobile applications has to be in respect of efficient irrigation, sowing of different seeds, fertiliser and pesticide usage (type and quantity), inter-cropping etc. The mobile can also support the farmers by giving the list of seed companies, seed price and quantity needed per acre, select different seeds (depends on layout of field area), appropriate time to sowing (climatic factor) and seed sowing with suggested depth and distance.

Water Management

The mobile application has to enable Geographical Information System. Besides, the availability of water bodies has to be updated with the help of government water authorities. A real time system has to forecast the climate change, weather pattern, temperature, soil moisture levels, rainfall, level of rivers and ground water. The mobile application has to provide the available information to farmers regularly for the decision-making towards efficient use of water. With addition, the application has to suggest irrigation needs of a particular crop at all periods of the crop tenure.

Crop Growth and Harvesting

The mobile application has to help the farmers in understanding the crop density per acre for healthy crop growing. Using mobile camera, the images of plant growth, leaf size and crop colour can be compared with expected growth. This would help the usage of irrigation of water and fertiliser. Images of pest, disease affected leaf and stem of the plants can be compared with the service provided by the mobile application. Based on the facts, the application (interconnection with experts and research centre) can give suggestions in pesticide use accordingly. The mobile application can give videos of integrated and organic farming, which can educate the farmers to adopt the same. In the last stage, the mobile application can give the details of harvesting of a selected crop for reaping maximum yield.

Customer Care

A customer care centre consists of a complex of tele-communication infrastructure and computer support. The human resources and real time system in the customer care would help the farmers by answering queries raised instantly in the local language. It will interact with farmers to understand the problem and answer the queries; it may be predefined SMS code or a voice call. The mobile application can also divert the queries to agricultural universities (subject matter specialists), or research centre or history of previous farmer experience (information from database). Call centre can send their suggestion as a SMS (local language) or documentary videos or replayed by the voice call. It will also provide market prices, market demand of the farmer's produce.

Market Access and Pricing

The most common ICT intervention for the agricultural value chain is a pricing service in which commodity price information is pushed out to customers on a regular basis. The mobile application services comprise any service that provides beneficiaries; farmer's access information on pricing of his/her product. It would give links of buyers list and demanded price. The farmer can directly sell his/her product without any mediators. The most common advantages to such services are price transparency and improved negotiating leverage for the often disempowered seller (farmer). The mobile application can provide pricing data on agricultural produce. The provision of pricing services is also a relatively easy market to enter, so these services are often bundled with other services.

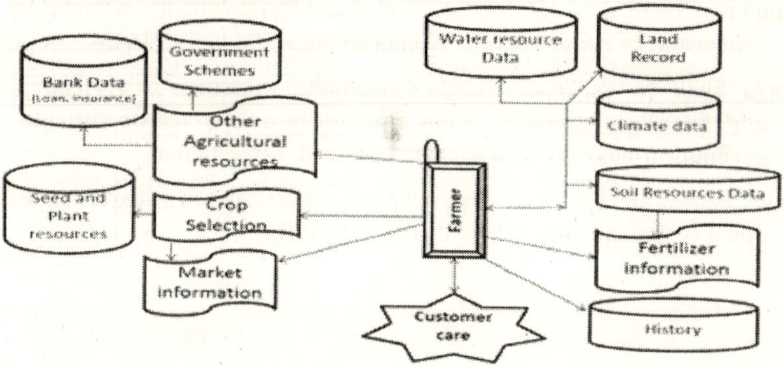

Conclusion

The proposed mobile application memory ship into mobile handset provides better service to the farmer for improving the agricultural productivity. The application keeps in touch with the farmer, government, research specialist and markets. The history of farmer's database provides a key-book of other farmers with in same categories. The model provides services through single window to the rural farmers. Instead of using PC-based ICT application, the mobile application would provide additional facility like handy, video, audio, image services with local language support. The farmers can directly connect with market access; pricing and can get expert suggestions (call centre). The advanced trained neutral network architecture model can also improve the services to the farmers. That is, based on the research institute and market status, the trained model would take decision by its own and give suggestion to the farmers. Therefore, an agricultural production is a complex process, but it has many successful stories. The proposed mobile application model is a bridge between farmer and e-Governance applications. With a simple training to the farmers, it is an easy way to utilise the mobile application. Mobile application provides a complete set of services in an integrated manner, which guides in improving the livelihood of farmers, agricultural production and rural development ultimately.

References

Baumuller, Heike, (2012). "Facilitating Agricultural Technology Adoption Among the Poor: The Role of Service Delivery through Mobile Phones" *Working Paper Series 93*, Centre for Development Research, University of Bonn.

Bhatnagar, Subhash, (2009), "Exploring Conditions for Delivery of Successful M-government Services to the Bottom of the Pyramid (BOP) in India," International Development Research Centre, UK.

Malhotra, Charru. *et al.,* (2009), "ICT for Rural Development: An Inclusive Framework for e-Governance," Computer Society of India, 216-26.

Meera, Shaik N., *Technology and e-Governance initiatives in Agriculture and Rural Development*,www.cips.org.in/public-sector-systems-government-innovations/documents /dr-shaik-n-meera.pdf.

Romit, Pandey and KS Vijaya Sekhar, From e-Governance to m-Governance: The way forward. http://ebookily.org/pdf/web2py.

49

Multi-national Companies and Rural Development—Opportunities and Challenges

M.L. Geetha and Jayadev K.A.

Introduction

Mahatma Gandhi once said, "The true India is to be found not in its new cities, but in its seven hundred thousand villages. If villages perish, India will perish, too." For Gandhi, villages represented true India, which has 6,42,000 villages, some with populations as low as 500. According to the 2011 Census, there are 316.5 million people in rural India. Some of them travel to larger towns, even metropolitan cities, to study, and many others, to work. Rural India is a scattered over a large area with different cultural, social, educational and economical development. A research by IMRB International found that some markets in India are big, but not affluent, such as markets of Uttar Pradesh, Bihar etc., and some markets are affluent but very small like Himachal Pradesh and Goa. Therefore, strategy for development of rural India should be flexible and adaptable. After liberalisation, rural India is slowly transforming itself from agriculture-based economy to service-based economy. In other words, non-farm sector is providing employment to rural youth. During 1983 to 1993 i.e. in rural India, six out of every 10 people were employed in agriculture whereas during 1994 to 2004, six out of 10 people in rural India were employed in non-farm sector.

Indian rural market is increasingly becoming the economic powerhouse of the country. The hinterlands, accounting for about 50 per cent of India's Gross Domestic Product (GDP) and housing nearly 70 per cent of the country's population, are showing remarkable multiplier effect and thereby excite policy makers and business leaders. Moreover, rural areas, where 12 per cent of the world population is residing, are witnessing enormous growth in incomes and crucial shift in consumer behaviour. Companies have realised this enormous opportunity and are tuning their strategies largely to attract the rural population through products and services.

Hindustan Unilever Limited (HUL) chairman, Harish Manwani, while addressing shareholders at the company's 79th Annual General Meeting (AGM) held at Mumbai spoke about the exciting growth opportunity in Rural India, and how it is becoming the epicentre of India's growth story. In the speech titled '*Rural India – An Emerging Powerhouse*,' Mr Manwani said, "It is often said that there are two India's – Bharat which exists in the villages and India which thrives in the urban areas. If our country has to have real progress and make its mark on the global stage, then these two India's must converge. Prosperity will have to come to our villages, towns and cities."

Need for the Study

- Rural India accounts for around 55 per cent of the manufacturing GDP; rural areas were host to nearly 75 per cent of new factories built in the last decade, and rural factories account for 70 per cent of new manufacturing jobs thereby increasing their income level.
- Rural consumption per person has increased by 19 per cent yearly between 2009 and 2012; two percentage points higher than its urban peers. In incremental terms, spending in rural India during this period, increased by US$ 69 billion, significantly higher than US$ 55 billion by urban population.

Literature Review

Vladislav Valentinov, Sabine Baum (2009), examined and compared institutional arrangements addressing market failures in rural areas. They found that rural market failures cannot be satisfactorily addressed by profit-oriented trading organisations and stressed the need for third sector organisations such as NGOs, co-operatives and associations. They concluded that further research is needed on developing the institutional economic theory of the rural third sector. Fatimah Hassan, Siti Masayu Rosliah Abdul Rashid (2012) made a study on extent of information and communication technology and its contribution to development of rural areas of Malaysia. They studied challenges, faced during the implementation of information and communication in rural areas. The study concluded that the introduction of information and communication is a driving force to economic development of rural areas, but still these areas were exposed to challenges and constrains. Nicoleta, Paun Ion Otiman, Teodor Mateoc, Camelia Manescu (2013), studied ageing population in rural areas of Romania, decrease in birth rate and subsistence on agriculture and scarce income resources and its implication on their quality life. Based on the analyses carried out and on study cases, the authors present the main aspects of the rural areas in the region, pointing out fact that local authorities should be concerned with the development of their own localities and implement successfully development projects. The authors have reached the conclusion that the development of non-agricultural activities determines the diversification and increase of jobs, increase of life quality in rural communities and socio-economic aspects development of the rural areas. Beata Skubiak (2013), studied risk of loss of relationship between urban and rural areas because of disproportionate growth in two areas and decreased territorial cohesion. The purpose of the study was to find the reasons for difference in economic and social development in urban and rural areas. They concluded that there is a need to strengthen a strong regional policy to fight these inequalities.

Objective of the Study

- To study the present scenario of MNCs operating in rural areas;
- To examine the results of penetration of MNCs in rural areas; and
- To offer suggestions and recommendations.

Research Methodology

The present study is descriptive in nature. It makes an attempt to study and analyse some of the multi-national companies operating in rural India and its results on rural economy. The study uses secondary data. The secondary data was collected from journals, periodicals, electronic data base, published and unpublished research studies.

Products Sold in Indian Rural Markets

Television Sets

The advent of satellite TV connections has accelerated the spread of television in rural India. For the first time, more than 50 per cent of the increased rural spending is on non-food products and services— and mobile phones and television sets top the list. Data from Consumer Electronics and Appliances Manufacturers Association show that as many as 16.4 million television sets were sold in rural India in 2012-13, of which 5.6 million were LCD sets. By 2025, India would rise from the twelfth to the fifth largest position in the consumer durable market in the world; the market is expected to reach USD12.5 billion by 2015. By 2020, the electronics market in India is expected to increase to USD 400 billion from USD 69.6 billion, currently India is one of the largest growing electronics market in the world. By 2017, the total number of TV sets sold in rural areas may reach 17 million units by the end of the financial year, while

LCD units sold are expected to increase to 7.8 million. Recent data shows that Dish T.V. Ltd. has 11 million connections, TaTa Sky Ltd. has 11.5 million subscribers, of which nearly half are in rural India.

Mobile Connections

Mobiles are the vehicle for biggest change among Indian consumers. Mobile phone penetration in India is noteworthy, it leaped from 1.4 units per 100 people in 1995 to 51 units currently. According to the Telecom Regulatory Authority of India, as of June 2013, India had 873 million mobile connections. Of these, 522 million were in urban areas, with the remaining 351 million in rural areas. Nokia Company was the leading mobile company till Samsung introduced android software. Rural India now accounts for 40 per cent of Nokia India's US$ 5 billion annual revenue. Along with Samsung, LG Sony Ericsson and Motorola, there are a number of handset-makers not only from China selling cut-price handsets, but also from India's home-grown companies that are chipping away at Nokia's market share lead with cheaper handsets, more practical or both. Mobile producers, in collaboration with various partners try to offer mobile banking and other services along with handsets.

According to Anupam Vasudev, chief marketing officer of wireless service provider Aircel India Ltd., although rural consumers buy mobile phones largely for communication, they are increasingly viewing these devices as their "window to the world". Mr Manu Sharma, General Manager, mobile products, Samsung Electronics Co. Pvt. Ltd. explains that low-cost phones such as Celkon, China Mobiles, Intex and K-touch are popular in rural markets.

Internet Facilites

According to the Telecom Regulatory Authority of India, as of June, India had 873 million mobile connections. Of these, 522 million were in urban areas, with the remaining 351 million in rural areas. There are 46 million active Internet users in rural India, according to a report, titled *Internet in Rural India,* published by lobby group Internet and Mobile Association of India and IMRB, a market research firm. Internet penetration in India is driven largely by mobile phones with some of the cheapest and most basic hand-sets today offering access to the internet. India has 110 million mobile internet users of which 25 million are in rural India. The growth of Internet penetration in rural India is driven largely by the mobile phone; 70 per cent of rural India's active internet population accesses the web via mobile phones. Forty-two per cent of rural India's internet users prefer using the internet in local languages. The high prevalence of content in English is a hurdle for much of rural India.

Marketing Strategy of Some of the MNC Companies

Hindustan Unilever Ltd. (HUL):

Hindustan Unilever is one of the India's largest consumer products companies, owned by Anglo-Dutch Uniliver. It penetrated Indian rural market in the year 2001. It started *Shakthi* project which is a self-helpgroup with network of women members coming from low income households selling HUL products in baskets from door to door. After ten years of efforts, there were 42,000 women entrepreneurs involved in selling HUL products in more than 1,00,000 villages in 15 states. Now, HUL has started selling products in small, cost effective sachets to rural masses. With 6.3 million retail outlets catering to the needs of rural India accounted nearly half of HUL's revenue.

Hindustan Unilever Ltd., (HUL)'s decade-old project *Shakthi* received a technology boost in 2012. About 40,000 *Shakthi Ammas* were equipped with a basic Smartphone. These smartphones had specifically designed software enable them to take and bill orders, manage inventory and receive updates on promotional schemes run by the company. This has improved their efficiency. The Shakthi work force rose to 48,000 in 2012, up by around 3,000 from the year before. Project Shakthi equips women with the basic entrepreneurial skills and facilities needed to set-up and market FMCG products.

LG Company Ltd.

The South Korean, LG Company entered rural Indian markets in the mid-1990s, when numerous television companies produced different models of televisions keeping in mind Indian urban population. But LG Company developed two models of colour television sets specially meant for rural market called as *Sampoorna* means complete in Hindi and *Cine Plus*. These TV sets priced slightly higher than black and white televisions became hit with rural India. Realising the potential of rural markets, LG produced refrigerators, washing machines and microwave ovens. All the products produced for rural population was a hit and contributed to 40 per cent of its revenue.

Dabur India Ltd.

Dabur India embraced the idea of getting rural folk to sample products and experience the benefits for themselves. The idea was to get word-of-mouth advertising of product benefits. The company made the most of fairs and *melas* during the harvest seasons when purchasing power is high. It also conducted school health camps to boost a toothpaste and chyawanprash portfolio and beauty pageants, to showcase its ayurvedic beauty products. Dabur's rural sales force used mobile phones to report sales. Phones were equipped with maps showing the demographics and market potential of each locality, to improve rural coverage. Over two years, Dabur's rural strategies saw it doubling the village sale under its coverage to 30,091.

Coca-cola and Pepsi Company

In soft drinks market, 2012 proved to be a year of brand revival, especially among the leading players such as Coca-Cola and Pepsi Company. A revamp of old brands started with Coca-Cola, when it revived its Citra brand in lime carbonates. In August 2012, the company also revived its RimZim brand. Similarly, Pepsi Co revived its Duke brand in India. Tough competition between Coca-Cola and Pepsi Company continued not just in carbonates but in other categories, such as bottled water as well as fruit and vegetable juice. Both companies are strengthening their non-carbonated drinks portfolio as carbonates are slowly losing their market to fruit and vegetable juice in urban India.

Pepsi Company with US $43.2 billion capital came to India 20 years back. There is increase of revenue through sale of soft drinks by 40 per cent and volume by 32 per cent. Because of Indian contribution out of which Indian rural market contributes 20 per cent for Pepsi companies business. Pepsi overtook Nestle as the top food and beverage company of the country. In order to expand its distribution infrastructure, Pepsi Company is planning to invest US$ 500 million in the country. To make those investments pay off, Pepsi Company is making arrangements to enhance marketing of products in rural market.

Havells India Ltd .

Havells India Ltd., marketing electrical appliances projects in housing sector, particularly in rural areas, is set to see a boom in coming years. As higher demand for houses automatically give rise to greater demand for lighting and other domestic electrical goods, the fast moving electrical goods and power distribution equipment manufacturer plans to enter rural India market with newly-launched 'Rio' switches.

Hero Motors Ltd.

Marketeers focussed on rural markets adopt new and unique approach to reach the rural fragmented markets. They apply various permutations and combinations of strategies to attract the rural consumers. One of the leading two-wheeler manufacturers, Hero Motors, added authorised representative dealers to the existing *hub-and-spoke* network. Appointed by the authorised dealers, the representatives facilitate easy purchasing and servicing of bikes for locals. This step added more than 5,000 touch points to Hero's channel strategy, enabling the company extend its reach to 20 per cent of India's 6,00,000 villages.

Titan Company Ltd .

Indian jewellery major-Titan is aiming at ambitious 20 to 25 per cent growth in its rural gold jewellery market in the country. The company plans to touch a turnover of Rs. 1,000 crore this year, by promoting the sale of jewellery through its retail gold chain 'Gold Plus'. Titan, for the first time plans to boost the store sale through extensive mass media marketing. The company intends to promote Gold Plus as a stiff competitor to traditional jewellers in the semi-urban areas of the country. The Gold Plus, being branded jewellery is currently priced above those offered by traditional jewellers. However, the company claim's that there are many instances where the local jewellers fail to conform to purity standards. Titan plans to lower the making charges on jewellery, which will make the jewellery less costlier and affordable for general public in India. Earlier, Gold Plus jewellery was five to 10 per cent costlier.

Suggestions

- For the fear of lack of infrastructure, many companies may not enter rural market. To attract MNCs to rural areas, the government should try to develop basic infrastructure facilities in rural areas.
- Before MNCs entering rural market, care must be taken against environmental pollution.
- MNCs operating in rural India should ensure employment opportunities to local rural people.
- Care must be taken against decline of values and culture of that land.

Conclusion

Consumer preferences in rural markets have shown a paradigm shift over the last few years. Rural consumers are gradually attracting major MNCs to spread their services to rural areas. Their consumption pattern looks very similar to that of urban counterparts. Premium products are replacing basic versions and brands are making their presence felt. Nielsen estimates that the FMCG market in rural India will mark US$ 100 billion by 2025, from the current level of US$ 12 billion. Moreover, the government's efforts to improve the efficiency of welfare programmes with cash transfers will further boost rural consumption; it plans to deposit US$ 570 billion in the accounts of 100 million poor families by 2014. With rural India getting empowered with computers, smart phones, and Internet is definitely going to make its way very soon.

Despite their obvious attraction, rural markets pose their own set of challenges, mostly related to distribution and logistics. The initial cost involved in building presence in rural markets is very high and many companies may not be able to make those investments. According to Dharmakriti Joshi, chief economist at Crisil Research, "A sharp increase of seven to eight per cent in rural wages in the recent past has spurred demand for consumer durables, automobiles, etc." Joshi also warned that, if the overall economy doesn't expand in the near future, "it is unlikely that rural India will continue to grow as it is not isolated".

References

Beata Skubiak, "Socio-economic aspects development of the rural areas", *Journal of Agri-business and Rural Development*, June 2013, Vol. 2, Issue 28, *pp.* 215-24.

Fatimah Hassan, Siti Masayu Rosliah Abdul Rashid, "Information and Communications Technology Development Products Towards Strengthening Rural Communities in Malaysia", *Canadian Social Science,* October 2012, Vol. 8, Issue 5, pp.-91-98.

Knowledge@Wharton, University of Pennsylvania, 2010.

Nicoleta Mateoc-Sirb, PauanIon Otiman, Teodor Mateoc, Camelia Manescu, "Analysis of development opportunities for rural entrepreneurship in the development region West Romania, Management, *Economic Engineering in Agriculture and Rural Development*, Vol. 13, Issue-1, pp 231-34 (2013).

Vladislav Valentinov, Sabine Baum, The Institutional Economics of Rural Development: Beyond Market Failure, *Journal of Central European Agriculture*, March 2009, Vol.- 9, Issue 3, pp. 457-62.

50

Promoting Inclusion and Participation of Marginalised Groups in Rural Development

K. Mohan Das

Introduction

The concept of Deprived or Marginalised Groups is generally used to analyse socio-economic, political, and cultural spheres, where disadvantaged people struggle to gain access to resources and full participation in social life. In other words, marginalised people might be socially, economically, politically and legally ignored, excluded, or neglected, and, therefore vulnerable. Marginality is debasing, for economic well-being, for human dignity, as well as for physical security.

Marginalisation or deprived is generally described as the overt actions or tendencies of human societies, where people, who they perceive to be undesirable or without useful function are excluded, *i.e.*, marginalised. The people, who are marginalised are outside the existing systems of protection and integration. This limits their opportunities and means for survival.

There are no general laws to understand and comprehend the complex nature of marginalisation. Marginalisation can be due to class, in relation to specific social, cultural, economic and political conditions, as well as ideological systems, social awareness, and human action.

Marginalised Groups vary in different settings. The religious, ecological system, patriarchy, political economy of a country, and the overall social system have an impact on the marginalisation of specific groups or an individual.

The marginalised groups existing in society have historically suffered from deprivation in all walks of life in general and in education in particular. Exclusion in developmental process has led to backwardness of economic, social and educational progress of the marginalised people of India. The reforms have been suggested right from the time of independence by various committees set up for the purpose.

Protecting the rights of marginalised and vulnerable persons is probably the most overlooked and disregarded area of human rights law. Marginalised groups are generally marginalised by society, making them easy to ignore. Since they ever represent small percentage of the population, they lack the critical mass that is often needed to successfully assert human rights claims. Furthermore, marginalised themselves are often antagonistic towards each other.

The marginalised and Rural development has always been an important issue in discussions pertaining to economic development, especially in developing countries, throughout the world. Although, millions of rural people have escaped poverty as a result of rural development in many Asian countries, a large majority of rural people continue to suffer from persistent poverty. The socio-economic disparities between rural and urban areas are widening and creating tremendous pressure on the social and economic fabric of many developing Asian economies. These factors, among others, tend to highlight the importance of rural development. The policy makers in most of the developing economies recognise this importance and have been implementing host of programmes and measures to achieve rural development objectives. While some of these countries have achieved impressive results, others have failed to make a significant dent in the problem of persistent rural underdevelopment scope and importance of rural development.

Despite participatory development the process is given prominence in rural development policies, people-centric development culture has not yet been institutionalised in rural India. Development practitioners, however, see decentralisation as necessary but not a sufficient condition for involving cross-section of local people into development intervention. Because of influential domination, a few powerful customarily overshadow the powerless mass, the poor and the marginalised and successfully block their meaningful integration in local government bodies in rural India.

People's participation is and essential for the developmental process. The notion of people's participation in their development has been gaining momentum in the process of human empowerment.

Since rural development is a dynamic process, mainly concerned with the rural areas include agricultural growth, putting up of economic and social infrastructure, fair wages as also housing and house sites for the landless, village planning, public health, education and functional literacy, communication etc. Rural development is a national necessity and has considerable importance in India, because of the following reasons.

Firstly, three-fourth of India's population live in rural areas, thus rural development is needed to develop nation as whole.

Secondly, some part of country's national income is derived from agriculture, which is the major occupation of rural India.

Thirdly, seventy per cent of Indian population gets employment through agriculture.

Fourthly, bulks of raw materials for industries come from agriculture and rural sector.

Fifthly, growing disparity between the urban elite and the rural poor can lead to political instability.

The main objective of the rural development programme is to raise the economic and social level of the rural people, which have been discussed below

Rural development is a national necessity and has considerable importance in India in order to develop rural area as whole in terms of culture, society, economy, technology and health, to develop living slandared of rural mass, to develop rural youth, children and women, empowering the human resource of rural area in terms of their psychology, skill, knowledge, attitude and other abilities such as infrastructure facility of rural area, providing minimum facility to rural mass in terms of drinking water, education, transport, electricity and communication.

Developing the rural institutions like *panchayat*, co-operatives, post, banking and credit, providing financial assistndent.

To develop the artisans in the rural areas, farmers and agrarian unskilled labour, small and big rural entrepreneurs to improve their economy. To develop rural industries through the development of handicrafts, small scale industries, village industries, rural crafts, cottage industries and other related economic operations in the rural sector, to develop agriculture, animal husbandry and other agricultural related areas, to restore uncultivated land, provide irrigation facilities and motivate farmers to adopt improved seed, fertilisers, package of practices of crop cultivation and soil conservation.

In order to initiate such developments, there can be different methods to be brought in such as developing entertainment and recreational facility for rural mass and leadership quality of rural area, improving the rural marketing facility and minimise gap between the urban and rural in terms of facilities availed, improving the rural people participation in the development of state and nation as whole, improvement in scopes of employment for rural mass for the sustainable development of rural area eliminating rural poverty and finally to solve the problems faced by the rural mass for their development.

To bring different skill development programmes, employment guarantee programmes such as the MNREGS , NREP etc., which are some of the flagship programmes initiated to develop the rural youth.

The Constitution of India categorically emphasises the need for establishing local governments with a inclusive character in form of panchayats. To this end, the representatives of the local governments are popularly elected. Though this guarantees political participation, the present local governments structure hardly provides any scope for participation of common people in decision-making process. As a result, inclusive development through Local Governments is still a dream only. Local people see development projects being implemented but they have hardly any stake in those. Projects are the backbone of local development. Development projects are undertaken to improve the livelihood of the community. Effective management of development projects depends primarily on proper project selection, project design, project implementation, monitoring and evaluation. Moreover, values, norms, social belief and opinions of the marginalised people which are affected directly or indirectly by development interventions should also be considered. Otherwise, sustainability of development projects may generally be questioned.

Participatory Development seeks to engage local populations in development projects. Participatory development has taken a variety of forms since it emerged in the 1970s, when it was introduced as an important part of the 'basic needs approach' to development. Most manifestations of Participatory Development seeks 'to give the poor a part in initiatives designed for their benefit, in the hope that development projects will be more sustainable and successful if local populations are engaged in the development process. Participatory development employed in particular initiatives often involves the process of content creation. For example, UNESCO's Finding a Voice Project employs ICT for development initiatives. Local content creation and distribution contributes to the formation of local information networks. This is a bottom-up approach that involves extensive discussions, conversations, and decision-making with the target community. Community group members create content according to their capacities and interests. This process facilitates engagement with information and communication technology (ICT) with the goal of strengthening individual and social development. This participatory content creation is an important tool for poverty reduction strategies and creating a digitally inclusive knowledge society, which can further emphasise for the better scope of rural development.

The most popular and widely adopted strategy for ensuring marginalised people's participation in local development is identified as inclusion. There is perhaps no other institution like local government bodies to provide a wide scope for marginalised people's participation at the grassroot level. In India, ever since decentralisation has become a major policy concern, the political masters have exploited it as means of gaining their political goals. As a result, despite numerous reform initiatives in this field by the successive governments, local government institutions have not yet emerged as autonomous and self- governing units. This, in turn, limited the scope of the marginalised people's participation in the local decision-making process as well as development process of rural India.

The grassroots reality shows that the local power structure in states like Karnataka is concentrated in the hands of local elites. These local elite under the patronage of central and local political leaders of the ruling party mostly controlled the local development programmes. The local political leaders are often labelled as an 'exploitative class' who control the destiny of the rural people by remaining close to the bastion of power and they often manoeuvre people's participation to their own benefits. As a result, despite huge external and internal pressure, the elusive phenomenon of marginalised people's participation in local development projects is ignored and exclusive, and have remained only in papers as a striking slogan.

Incompetence of Centrally Administered Local Development Programmes

Since the 'trickle down' effects of economic growth take too long to reach the poor, governments in the region have relied on centrally administered support programmes and planned interventions to raise living standards in the rural areas. These shortcomings have led to the realisation that poverty alleviation programmes cannot be effective unless the poor have a voice in the planning and implementation of schemes meant to help them. This, in turn, necessitates decentralisation of key government functions in order to make better rural development programmes in India through:

(a) contribute in decision-making that affects rural lives;

(b) appraise the outcome of their own decisions;

(c) reduce chances of misunderstanding;

(d) recognise the difficulties and complexities of administration, planning and management;

(e) believe responsibility for failure; and

(f) develop sense of belonging and commitment to civil society.

Rural Development through Top Down Initiative can be Brought Through

- Political and administrative autonomy to local bodies.
- Devolution of revenue to local bodies and empowering them to levy taxes to fund part of their expenditure.
- Periodic local body elections. Reservation of seats on local bodies for weaker social sections.
- Local database on administration.
- Local voluntary and private sector organisations collaborate with local governments in addressing development issues.
- Build local human capacities through improved access to health care, education and productive assets to ensure that decentralisation empowers the poor.

A great majority of people in the rural areas in India are under the line of poverty. They are deprived of adequate access in the basic needs of life such as health, education, housing, food, security, employment, justice and equity. Issues of sustainable livelihood, social and political participation of the vulnerable groups exists as the major problem in the rural India. Governments have failed to guarantee people's rights in the implementation level. People who belong to the vulnerable groups are unable to acquire and use their rights. In this background, the International Covenant on Civil and Political Rights (ICCPR) and the International Covenant on Economic, Social and Cultural Rights (ICESCR) have guaranteed the rights to sustainable livelihood, social, political and economic development for all especially those disadvantaged. Many countries have ratified these covenants. In 1979, the Government of India acceded to the International Covenant on Economic, Social and Cultural Rights (ICESCR).

Since India is a country of villages. *Panchayati Raj* system has influenced the village life extensively as one of the most important units of democratic decentralisation for rural development. Decentralisation of powers is nothing but transfer of powers from one tier of governance to another and, in same way, from one segment of population to another. Power moves from the dominant to the oppressed, men to women, caste Hindus to Dalits, upper castes to lower castes and bureaucrats to people's representatives. Power will not move on its own. It has to be made move. So, a driving force is needed. The task is not so easy as may be envisaged, particularly in an extremely weak to the margnialised society.

Affirmative Action

Reservations have been provided to the excluded and marginalised groups. With these developments an impression has been created that the whole representative democracy has been transformed into participatory democracy and the hitherto excluded have been included in governance and administration through the device of reservation of seats in local bodies. However, there are still several problems when we examine the issues of substantive inclusion of the marginalised in the functioning of elected bodies and in what they are able to achieve for their constituents in terms of promoting inclusiveness in the rural development. By merely creating institutions or providing formal training to people who hitherto lived and continue to live at the periphery of society and economy does not guarantee their entry into local governance and participation in the developmental process. The forces of patriarchy and caste are the two socially powerful forces that deter the marginalised respectively. Bringing such marginalised groups into the political sphere requires addressing the issues of dominance and exclusion both at the level of institutional structures and processes as well as at the larger social setting which the marginalised groups inhabit.

Secondly, panchayats are engaged with service delivery diverting their attention to the provisioning of developmental goods and services such as water, electricity, housing, education, sometimes at the cost of promoting social justice.

Thirdly, the rapid economic growth agenda of the state, particularly under neo-liberalism and globalisation has unravelled a new set of questions on role and mandate of *panchayats* relating to the governance of commons on which people's survival is dependent. Inthis fast changing context, the state efforts have mainly focussed on capacity building, primarily through training. Civil society effort has largely remained confined to capacity building. In recent years, the role of *panchayats* has gained prominence owing to their role in the implementation of the National Rural Employment Guarantee Programme which is out of sight from the marginalised group since they are socially discriminated. Thus 'Inclusion of the marginalised groups in rural development has been a serious problem in our civil society. 'Inclusion' in this context means the inclusion of the marginalised sections - women, Dalit and tribals -- in Rural development. However, 'inclusion' cannot be understood, without having any reference to 'exclusion'. Exclusion needs to be countered to promote inclusion. Since exclusion and inclusion are inter-related, new insights on inclusion through sincere analysis requires on both: causes, consequences and means of exclusion as also the ways in which marginalised groups work towards their inclusion.

Minorities, Women, Dalit and Tribals have suffered social and economic marginalisation for a long time and therefore are measured for affirmative action. Particularly, in the rural setting, the socio-economic hierarchies are inter-related. Hence, the groups, who occupy low position in social hierarchy such as Dalit, women, and tribal also invariably, occupy low position in economic hierarchy. While the focus on exclusion – inclusion has largely centered on how they take place within local governance institutions, an important area needing further solution relates exclusion of *panchayat* institutions in situations of political conflict or economic contestation. More study needs to address this field to generate insights on what happens to inclusion when panchayat institutions themselves get excluded from the processes of development and governance. From the above discussion, it is clear that there are two aspects that have significant implication for inclusion of the marginalised in the rural development.

Marginalised groups are now frequently questioning their exclusion and clash for mobilised towards inclusion. Efforts are underway in recent times to address the 'power and politics' played out in the spheres of local governance. Such mobilisations in recent times are visible in several ways. These include:

1. Building collectives by discriminated groups such as federations of women elected representatives;
2. Aligning politically;
3. Inhabit alternate spaces available for local development such as water users group, village education committees, self-help-groups micro-finance groups etc.

Hence, most of the marginalised groups are uneducated, untrained, and the power equation is still in the hands of higher castes. Nevertheless, a process of political socialisation has to begin within the society. The bureaucratic resistance is not visible in many matters. The stereotype and routine mindset of local bureaucracy has understood that the panchayat will remain forever and the bureaucracy has to work within the changed scenario. Political decentralisation does not mean participation only in the electoral process. Therefore, it calls for active involvement of marginalised groups in the functioning of rural local self-government institutions and pursuit of collective decision-making process, and their own transparent governance. *Grama sabha* is the only direct democratic mechanism in India for effective planning at the grassroots level envisaged, if a large number of *grama sabha* members actively participate in the planning process. At present 50 per cent of members especially the women are virtually outside the *Grama Sabha* meetings because they are not allowed to participate by their male family members and another big chunk mostly SC/ST and other weaker sections do not attend due to some social compulsions. These members are less motivated to attend meetings, because they do not expect any gain from such meetings but lose their one-day wage. Participation cannot be imposed on the marginalised from above; it should be voluntary and based on good will to participate among themselves forcefully.

By participation in this paper, I meant direct involvement of people and not indirect involvement through representatives. An equitable sharing of benefits of development by marginalised groups is possible only when there is equitable participation by them in the process of development. By doing so, marginalised groups can influence the decisions at the higher levels through their joint efforts and common voice. This may be termed as 'bottom up approach to integrated rural development.' The process can be accelerated only when the marginalised groups become conscious on their rights and privileges and build up strength to achieve justice for themselves in the sharing of benefits of development.

Conclusion

At the outset, this paper has enabled to show that a decentralisation reform in India is an ambitious process that seeks to empower local communities to engage in the rural development. This is a departure from most past decentralisation efforts which were geared only in the direction of administration. The objectives of decentralisation in India give decentralised governance a development mission and call up on local communities including the marginalised to shape their destiny. Decentralisation has enhanced participation in decision-making, enabled local communities to determine their local leadership through democratic elections, provided institutionalised structural arrangements for participatory development planning, and for involving marginalised groups such as women, SCs and STs in decision-making. Through decentralisation, the vast majority of civic bodies hitherto excluded from the development planning and implementation process would become actively engaged with formal governmental institutions.

Hence, promoting inclusive participation, when well-structured, provides institutional infrastructure - representation and meaningful powers - for sustained inclusion. The inclusion of disadvantaged sections has in principle ensured equality of political opportunities. In India, a movement towards democratic decentralisation has to be driven by the need to deepen the process of democracy by giving citizens a greater say in matters which impact more on their daily lives. The creation of institutions like *gram sabha*, accountability mechanisms, people's planning etc., lead to establishment of inclusive self-governance. And the main goal of inclusive participation is to include those, who have traditionally been excluded from political action and reduce disparities in society. The success of democratic decentralisation depends largely on the achievement to include all the marginalised groups in local decision-making and power structures effectively. Previously, many people on the basis of their social positioning - according to caste, ethnicity or gender - are excluded from certain social, economic and political opportunities.

However, the decentralisation efforts in the country since early 1990's, created an opportunity to all and enabled all disenfranchised and disadvantages groups to emerge as empowered participants in local democratic processes. Decentralisation through the process of democratisation created an enabling environment and act as a tool for social inclusion through enhancing the participation of the disadvantaged groups in local governance.

References

Dhadave, M.S., (ed.), (1996), *Rural and Urban Studies in India*, Rawat Publications, Jaipur.

Misra, Yatish, (2002), *Empowering People - Grassroots Organisations and Rural Development*, Kanishka Publishers and Distributors, New Delhi, 2002.

Sangita, S.N., "Self-employment Programme for Rural Youth - The Role of Non-governmental Organisations", *NMB Management Review*, Vol. 5, 2, July-December 1990.

Srinivas, M.N., (ed.), (1993) India's Villages, Media Promoters and Publishers, Bombay, Second Revised Edition, Reprinted.

The Hindu, Financial inclusion must for social change, February-7, 2009.

The Hindu, August-15, 2006.

The Hindu, January 18, 2008.

The Hindu, October 24, 2013.

Vyasulu, Vinod (1998), *Decentralisation From Above: Panchayati Raj in 1990s.*

51

Role of Panchayati Raj Institutions in Rural Development

H.K. Nataraj and A. Lakshmikantha

Introduction

Democracy is the most fascinating form of government and the most sought after one. The modern age, being the democratic age, has witnessed ever-growing and ever evolving aspects of never ending essence. We all claim to be democratic, and yet we are always short of it. We hold free and fair elections, the only characteristic of democratic system found in other forms of government and yet we find the government we constitute is not ruled by the will of the people. We grant liberties and rights to citizens, not bestowed in any other forms of government, and yet we find the freedom we enjoy is hardly exercised to influence our ruler; we speak but we are not heard. We are made equal through law and the constitution, having been assured of non-discrimination, a quality not found in any other form of government, and yet the system we evolve makes some are privileged than others. Democracy is never a perfect system of government and yet is the best of all systems known to the mankind.

Decentralisation is a key feature of any domestic policy. Federalisation ensures vertical decentralisation giving the federal government function of national importance to the provincial government regard importance and to the local government function of local importance. Such a division of power is an essential element of democratic system. Horizontally, the functions at every level of government are exercised by legislature, executive, judiciary. This is what usually referred to as the separation of powers. To avoid centralisation, which eats away the vitality of democracy, decentralisation is usually resorted to. Decentralisation ensures democracy, but it is only one factor and not the only factor and then the existence or absence of the separation of power is no guarantee that there exists democracy. India lives in villages, unless were reconstructed and develop them, India will perish. Gandhiji said, "If India is not to perish, we have to begin with lower rung of ladder. If that was rotten, all work done at the top or at the intermediate rungs was bound to ultimately fall. In the approach to rural development, the city village antagonism becomes the over-riding issue exploiting the villages itself is organised violence". The same feelings have been echoed by Rabindranath Tagore, when he said that the status of mother India has been reduced to that of the maid servant , due to draining of resources from village to cities. Gandhi's plea was for radical decentralisation and liberalisation of the villages from exploitation. The village is the fundamental unit for the development of our country and the state, because the root has been strong for the growth of the tree.

Panchayati Raj bodies are looked upon as instruments of rural development. As such, it becomes relevant and meaningful to evaluate the working of these institutions. Contributing to economic development and social welfare is the core strategy of *panchatyati raj*.

Objectives of the Study

The study is broadly an attempt to analyse the emerging scenario of women leadership at local politics by focusing on the elected women representatives of local self-governments of India compared to their counterpart in *gram panchayats* of Dakshina Kannada. More specifically, the study will focus on the views, opinions, activities and training of the local government representatives in the following areas:

1. Understand the grassroot level democracy, the decentralisation of power and women's political participation;
2. Examine the role of gender in the functioning of local political institutions and focus on a comparative perspective on the experiences of India and mainly Dakshina Kannada;
3. Constraints and problems, faced by women and men in the electoral process and as representatives in the local bodies;
4. The extent of devolution of power and active participation in the various committees;
5. The role of family networks, political parties and government and non-governmental organisations in their attainment of power;
6. Their participation in developmental works and programmes;

7. Gender-related obstacles encountered by women and men while undertaking development programmes;
8. Strategies to overcome the barriers need, level of awareness and training as well as initiatives taken by the government and non-government organisations in Dakshina Kannada areas;
9. To find out whether the *panchayati raj* institutions have served as instrument of rural development in general and with special reference to the sample of *panchayat* and *panchayati unions* selected for, as case study;
10. To analyse the change and growth in the pattern of institutional bodies over the period;
11. To evaluate the achievements in regards to development the minimising the problems and relevant aspects;
12. To measure the extent of public participation and co-operation with these bodies in the developmental efforts.

A Conceptual Clarification

Before we get into the debate, the paper needs to frame a conceptual clarity, so that the issues get focussed, accordingly, the major concepts are; 'The Concept of Development'; 'Rural Development in India'; and '*panchayati raj* System in India'; '*Gram Panchayat*' and 'The Role of *Panchayati Raj* Institutions in Rural Development'.

The Concept of Development

The concept of development has numerous definitions, and, therefore, has somewhat different, through inter-related meaning. Esman says, "Development is the rational process of organising and carrying out prudently conceived and staffed programmes or projects as one would organise and carry out military and engineering operation". To Colm and Greiger, development means change, change coupled with growth. Weidner holds the view that when a process is directed toward nation-building and socio-economic progress, that process of growth is development. For Hahn Been Le, development is both a process and a purpose. He, therefore, says that development is "a process of acquiring a sustained growth of a system's capability to cope with new, continuous change towards the achievement of progressive politics, economic and social objectives".

It may however, be pointed out that development is a multi-dimensional process involving changes in structure, attitudes, and institution as well as acceleration of economic growth, reduction of inequality and eradication of poverty. It is a transformation from a traditional society to a modern society. The political dimension of development includes, among other things, rationalism, secularism, participation, the social dimension of development includes for example, elimination of social evils, all distinction and all types of discrimination, equality of status, increase in social mobility its economic dimension means for instance, provision for social security, absence of exploitation, sustained economic growth, attainment of plenty and prosperity. All these dimension, of development are so closely related to on another that it is difficult to separate them: the development of one dimension or one of its aspects is bound to influence and get influenced by the other dimension or it's on any other aspects.

Development, in the context of under developed or developing countries, means the transformation of society from its traditionality to modernity, from its crude ways of doing things to sophisticated ways, its features and implications are:

1. Development is not static concept. It's dynamic, and hence, an ever-changing and ever evolving concept. One cannot imagine anything in a 'developed' form, for very 'developed' forms still needs some improvements. Development is thus, a continuing process.
2. Development is not uni-dimensional, but, is a multi-dimensional process. This means that development is not only economic development; it is also social development as also political or any other. It's goals are not confined to but merely economy : they touch very aspects of human and societal life: they may, to mention a few, include economic growth, social, progress, and political development, nation-building and the like.
3. Development implies growth. What it means is that all societies keep growing, expanding, advancing and therefore, are in the process of change-ever changing. The present society of a country is different from such a society of another country: Today's society is not what it was yesterday, in the past: likewise the future society would be substantially different from the society we find around us.
4. Development is closely related to technology. In essence, a technologically advanced society is a developed society. Technology has changed and in fact, is changing and in fact, is changing our life, each aspects of our life. Technology has made the world very small.
5. Rationality constitutes yet another component of development. What it means is that a developed society is not tradition-bound or religion-laden, but is one that stands up to reasoning and rationalism.

6. Development has yet other feature or requisite as well. Order, stability, security and the like prepare a ground for sustained growth. Countries have grown in years of peace rather than in years of wars. As development means change with growth, it implies substantial changes in infrastructure as well. You cannot run an import-export business without a developed banking system. How can you have a democracy with the institution of a dictator as the executive head?

It's best to begin with an examination of the concept of development. Development is no longer identified with a mere increase in GNP or even per capita national income. The increased incomes are expected to be so distributed as to result in a significant dimension of inequalities of income and wealth. Thus, less unequal distribution also is the abolition of obsolete poverty with employment minimum level or remuneration to all, who seeks employment and enough of increase in productivity to ensure minimum levels of income to all who are self-employed. Public distribution of goods and services for supplementing market supplies or what are termed as welfare and developmental services also constitute a part of the goal of development. Development is also expected to include the areas of health, education, culture, values and welfare. In short, all aspects of life and activity, which are subject to manipulation and controlled change, come within the sphere of development? The goal of development thus becomes the enrichment of the total quality of life and its availability at minimum levels to all sections of the population. In recent years, environment has also come within the scope of development in terms of maintenance, balance and harmony and added to the dimension of the concept of development. The concept of self-reliance or diminishing, if not dependence on external sources, whether at local, regional and national levels, has also now been included in the goal of development. Development is also their actual utilisation by the people for whom they are intended and involves the creation of the facilities necessary for such utilisation.

Rural Development in India

In India, since the Independence, there has been a concerted effort to reconstruct the rural India and the rural sector of the economy. Prior to this Tagore and Gandhi have suggested the development of villages in their natural surroundings where nature could best attract the people with its beauty. Gandhi wanted total transformation of villages by developing them from within into viable units. Pt. Nehru tried to give practical shape to these ideas through urbanisation, industrialisation and modern technical knowledge without breaking the old foundation of the country. As a result, several pilot projects were initiated all over the country which were concerned with the problems of housing, transport, communication, marketing and other infrastructural facilities like irrigation, school and health, etc.

A review of rural development programmes and their strategies in India reveals that its concept has substantially changed with the passage of time. For long, rural development meant 'expansion, development and modernisation of agriculture' and it was deemed to be synonymous for agricultural development. Perhaps, this idea was based on the assumption that agriculture is the prerequisite of rural way of life. However, this concept changed with the Community Development Programme launched in 1952, which aimed at transforming the traditional way of life for rural communities and assisting people to improve their way of life to meet the constitutional commitment of equity and justice.

In real sense, planned effort to rural development was initiated with the launching of Community Development Programme in the early fifties; although programme was not very successful, but it had promoted the growth of a network of basic extension and development services at the grassroot level in village, thereby creating awareness in the rural communities of the potential and means of development which made quicker adoption of major technological advances later in the mid 60's in agriculture possible. The benefits that accrued from these programmes were felt more by the better placed farmers and better endowed regions. This increased the regional disparities and the gap between the rich and the poor. Hence, the need was felt acutely to direct the development programmes towards the backward regions and towards the weaker section of the society. The Fourth and Fifth Plans initiated a number of programmes with a view to achieve economic equity and social justice.

The Five Year Plan included following features aimed at rural development. These are:

- Clear cut agricultural development state;
- Animal husbandry, dairy and fishery development;
- Forestry including development of social forestry;
- Agricultural research and education;
- Co-operation and credit;
- Rural development and poverty alleviation;;
- Irrigation, command area development, flood control,
- Village and small industries, and
- Employment, manpower planning and poor policy.

On April 1, 1978, Integrated Rural Development Programme was introduced not only to integrate ongoing programmes pertaining to areas but to launch a rigorous drive for eradicating rural poverty and providing economic benefits landless labourers, marginal farmers and village artisans.

The major thrust of the Fifth Five Year Plan (1980-85), was on strengthening the socio-concurrent infrastructure of development in the rural area alleviating rural poverty and reducing regional parities. The Ninth Five Year Plan has focussed four important dimensions of State Policy–quality of life, generation of productive employment, regional balances and self-reliance. With the multi-pronged approach adopted by the Ministry of Rural Areas and Employment through a wide range of programmes, it is hoped that adequate productive employment will be generated to eradicate rural poverty which would lead to significantly better living conditions. Rural development, thus, implies both the economic betterment of people as well as greater social transformation.

Increased participation of people in the rural development process, decentralisation and greater access, better enforcement of land reforms and greater access to credit and inputs go a long way in providing the rural people with better prospects for economic development. Improvement in welfare measures like education and health etc., constitute the social aspect of the rural development. Eradicating rural poverty, increase in rural employment and productivity constitutes the main tasks of such development.

The term 'rural development' is used in a wider connotation which implies the integrated development, of rural areas. Here, the emerging focus is the human development which strikes a harmonious balance between the individual, the community and the country and carried the planning to the grassroot level into the hands of rural people, the beneficiaries, can meaningfully contribute to its formulation and implementation.

The rural development is also area culture specific which provides for alternative regional strategies for spatial, functional organisation. The goals of the economic equity, social justice and self-reliance demand that man should be considered as the focus of development and the poor and the deprived should get the top priority. It is well-reflected in the *World Bank Policy Paper* (1975) which states: "Rural development as a strategy designed to improve the economic and social life of a specific group of people – the rural poor. It involves extending the benefits of development to the poorest among those, who seek livelihood in the rural areas. The group includes small scale farmers, tenants and the landless" (World Bank).

Local Self-Governments or Panchayati Raj Institution (PRIs) of India

The different countries in South Asia followed different paths towards political, social and economic development. India became a republic, a democratic and secular nation with a mixed economic set up that was overtly centralised, top-heavy and bureaucratic, besides taking recourse to import substitution and state sponsored industrialisation. The institutions of *panchayati raj* in the rural areas and *nagarpalikas* in the towns and cities represent local self-government and real decentralisation of power. They proudly represent the grassroot of India's democratic governance.

The Janata government appointed a high-level committee on Panchayati Raj Institutions under the chairmanship of Ashok Mehta in 1977 to evaluate the institution and its functioning over the past decade and a half. The report observed that the *panchayati raj* Institution has failed to transfer the fruits of democracy to the weaker sections of society as they were dominated mostly by the socially and economically privileged people of society.

The cause of democratic decentralisation received a boost during the tenure of Rajiv Gandhi. His government brought into the Parliament, the *Panchayati Raj and Nagarpalika Bills*. But, this move was defeated in the Rajya Sabha. The measure was revived by the government under Narsimha Rao and both the Houses passed the Bill in December 1992. The Act was brought into force by a government notification in April 1993 as *the Constitution (73rd Amendment Act 1992)*.

The 73rd Amendment marked a watershed in the history of the evolution of *panchayati raj* institutions. At present, the constitution provides for a three-tier system of *panchayati raj* for all states or Union territories except those having a population of less than 20 lakh.

Dakshina Kannada

Dakshina Kannada, also known as South Kannada , is a coastal district in the state of Karnataka in India. It is bordered by Udupi district to the north, Chikkamagaluru district to the north-east, Hassan district to the east, Kodagu to the south-east, and Kasaragod district in Kerala to the south. The Arabian Sea bounds it on the west. Mangalore is the headquarters and the chief city of district. Dakshina Kannada district has an area 4,866 square kilometres, and a population density of 390 persons per square kilometre. There are 354 villages and 203 *gram ppanchayat*, five *Taluk panchayats* in the district.

The district is divided into five *talukas*, Mangalore, Bantwal, Puttur, Sullia, and Belthangady. It used to include three northern talukas, Udupi,

Kundapur and Karkal, but these were separated in August 1997 to form Udupi district. Dakshina Kannada. Udupi and Kasaragod *taluk* are often called Tulu Nadu, as Tulu is the majority language in the region. The Alupas, who ruled this region between the eight and fourteenth century CE as a feudatory of all the major Kannada empires of those times and it is for this reason that the *Tulu* speaking districts are a part of Karnataka state.

The Gram Panchayat

The first formal democratic institution under the directive principle in the Indian Constitution is the *Gram Panchayat* or *Panchayat*. It is the primary unit of local self-government. *Panchayat* is a cabinet of the village elders, directly elected by the adult citizens of the village. *Gram Panchayats* are constituted considering their income, population and area. The income varies from mere Rs. 500 per annum to more than Rs. 2.00 lakh. The population varies from 500 to 25,000. The panchayat membership varies from 5 to 17. There is provision for reservation of seats for women, SC and STs. The panchayat has tenure of five years and is directly elected. The meeting is to be convened at least once in six months. It has income through taxes to perform functions. The main functions of *Panchayats* are:

- Representative function, where the main role is to voice and represent the opinion;
- Regulatory and administrative function, which consists of regulating the conduct of individuals and institutions and also collection of taxes;
- Service or developmental function, such as promotion of education, health, agriculture, etc.

The Role of Panchayati Raj Institutions in Rural Development

Panchayati Raj Department is an important department of Karnataka related to the rural development. The main objective of this department is to strengthen the *Panchayati Raj* System in the state according to the 73rd amendment of Indian Constitution so, that *panchayats* can realise the dream of rural administration and rural development with complete co-ordination and transparency. For this purpose, the department has provided a Citizen Charter. For the sake of public convenience and knowledge, this charter has been divided into seven subjects:

1. Financial aid to Gram Panchayats;
2. Rural Cleanliness Programmes;
3. Responsibilities of the Panchayats —(Transparency in work, rural Administration and development).

4. Responsibilities of public towards Panchayat;
5. Decentralisation Programme;
6. Control over the Gram Panchayats; and
7. Arrangement of *Panchayati Raj helpline.*

Citizen Charter is a continuous process, which will change periodically according to the feelings, recommendations, experiences and reactions of the public.

The various rural development programmes conceived and introduced at different points of time have been CDP, DPAP, SFDA/MFAL, MNP, IRDP, NREP, RLEGP, TRYSEM, DWCRA etc., at every stage the programmes with the same objective of poverty reduction have been recast to inculcate, the experience and the past failures. The presently working programmes are SJGSY, PMRY, EAS, TRYSEM and DWCRA. The schemes are operative both in urban and rural areas under different names. There are rural and also other programs to benefit specific section like SCP, Ashraya, Neralu Bhagya, Indira Awas Yojana and Ambedkar Yojana etc. However, not all of the programmes are implemented at the same time. Hence, the programmes being implemented in 203 *gram panchayatis* in Dakshina Kannada area during the last five years are— SJGSY, JRY, EAS housing schemes like Ashraya, Neralu Bhagya, Indira Awas Yojana, Ambedkar Yojana and Supply of power to weaker section (Bhagya Jyoti). In addition to the aforesaid functions, the *gram panchyat* is involved very much in the implementation of special economic programmes/schemes sponsored by both the Central and the State governments.

It is quite interesting to see the likely change in the structure of rural community. As a result of poverty alleviation programme to support the income and employment of the household in the lowest strata of the rural society for a long time, these households were with the victims of exploitation by the elite which had taken deep roots in the rural economy. Now, the question is whether the poverty alleviation programmes have weakened these roots and created any favourable atmosphere for the rural poor to improve their conditions. Another equally important change that we have witnessed in the rural scene after poverty alleviation or rural development programmes are that the poor people, who never had any voice in the functioning of the village institutions. Now, they are taking active part in these village institutions. This shows the confidence, gained by the poor in framing the programmes and policies meant for them. This change is predominantly due to the PRIs and their functioning.

Thus, the rural development programmes implemented through the *Panchayati Raj* institutions in selected area have provided more employment opportunities for village landless people, artisans, small and marginal farmers and handicrafts. These programs have also provided good social and economic positions for the rural people. The SC/ST people are getting more facility of rural development programme compare to other caste people, because they were socially and economically backward than their counterpart. And the rural development programmes also become a good instrument for infrastructure development of rural area. The *panchayat* providing more facilities like drinking water, sanitation, health services, school buildings, adult education, roads and bridges, street lights and etc., these facilities provided by *panchayati raj* institutions like a *Gram Panchayati's* in Dakshina Kannada as a agency of state government.

In rural development, Dakshina Kannada has its own footsteps as well as its own problems like naxalism, endosulphan tragedy, anti-special economic zones movements, party politics, caste politics, etc. Particularly, some rural people did not recognise with any rural development aspect because, of their literacy level, stereotype mind-set, negligence by local politician, lack of information about rural development policies and programmes. They did not have any exposure to accept the truth while women also participated in the election, and take a lead role. They had traditional mind-set which it thought of earlier traditional society.

Presently, we had reached some of achievements, but still we have so many challenges to solve which is regarding rural development or *panchayati raj* institution developments. From all these aspects, we have to learn understanding the actual problems, accept it. We should put real efforts to solve them, if it can possible, rural development in Dakshina Kannada will reach higher most.

Conclusion

To conclude therefore, policies and programmes ultimately find expression at the grassroots level and their success is determined by their effective implementation. The feedback from various evaluations of the programmes, while noting varying degrees at their effectiveness in different region, has brought to the forefront, the issue of institutional set-up and arrangements for the formulation and implementation. It has been recognised that local variations condition needs and potential considerable flexibility which could be utilised with advantage only in decentralised system of planning and responsibility. It is under such a system better integration of anti-poverty programmes in the overall development planning is feasible strengthening of the local level *panchayati raj* institution and decentralising the planning process would, therefore, have to form the central part of the planned efforts for poverty removal and rural development in the remaining part of this century.

References

Ambedkar SN, (2000), *New Panchayati Raj at Work*, Jaipur: ABD Publishers.

Ambedkar SN, (2004), "Panchayati Raj and Grassroots Politics: Issues and Perspectives", *Journal of Social Development and Justice.*

Ambedkar SN, (2006), *New Panchayati Raj at Work.* Jaipur: Gyan Publishers.

Bhagat N, (2004), *Women in Grassroots Democracy.* New Delhi: Gyan Publishing House.

Bhaktapada Sinha Roy(2009), *Panchayati Raj and Rural Development*, Neha Publisher and Distributers.

Bhaskar K, (1997), "Women Panchayat Members in Kerala: A Profile". Economic and Political Weekly.

Bose A, (2000), *"Empowerment of Women: How and When Economic and Political Weekly"*, 36 (51).

Chandrashekhar A, (1991), "Profile and Participation of Women Zila Parishad and Mandal Members". *Journal of Rural Development,* 10 (6).

Gowda G, (1998), "Political Linkage of Women Leaders of Panchayati Raj Institutions: Empirical Evidence from Karnataka". *Administrative Change,* 25 (2).

K.K.Singh, S.Ali (2011), *Specification of Role of Panchayati Raj Institution for Rural Development*, Sarup Book Publishers (P) Ltd .

Mohd Ajam Khan (2011), *Financial Decentralisation, Panchayati Raj Institution and Rural Development,*-Neha Publishers.

Sanjay Prakash Sharma(2006), *Rural Development and Panchayati Raj*,-Vista International Publishing House.

Tulsi Jain(2013), *Panchayat Administration and Rural Development,* - Neha Publishers.

Vijandra Singh (2003), *"Panchayati Raj and Village Development (Studies in Public Administration"*, Vol.1 and 2. Sarup Book Publishers (P) Ltd.

52

Analysis of Women Empowerment through MGNREGA in Karnataka

B. Sobha Rani.

Introduction

Empowerment refers to increasing strength of individuals or communities in the different spheres of life such as economic, political, social, spiritual etc. It also refers to instilling confidence in people in their own capacities. Empowerment is a process aimed at changing the nature and direction of systematic forces, which marginalise women and other disadvantaged sections in a given context. A large segment of Indian womanhood still suffers deprivation and discriminatory attitudes. It is necessary to mobilise the vast women power, if the country has to progress in all spheres of development. Empowerment of women is a long and difficult process, which is to be promoted with full public support and this could be successful only when those women living at the lower strata, who have been suppressed by the male-dominated society taking undue advantage of their lack of education and poverty can rise up to claim their empowerment, rightful place in their own society. In spite of the drawbacks in the implementation of legislation, significant benefits have already started t through better access to local employment, minimum wages, with relatively decent and safe work conditions.

Gender is the inevitable push factor for growth and development of a nation like India. In India women constitute a major share of chronically poor population. The government has framed different programmes/schemes to uplift women from poverty and vulnerability of life. One such women friendly programme is *Mahatma Gandhi National Rural Employment Guarantee Act* (MGNREGA) which was enacted in 2005, and the scheme (each state was expected to design its own scheme-based in the National Guidelines) designed under the Act was implemented in 200 districts on India in February 2006. The coverage of the Act was expanded gradually and since 2008-09, MGNREGA covers the entire rural India.

MGNREGA has provided unique opportunity to people from rural India to earn their own income without any discrimination of caste or gender. Most remarkable feature of NREGA is that it pays women the same as men, something that was virtually unimaginable in rural India. However, some states have registered high percentage of women workers getting enrolled in the scheme, whereas others have registered a very low percentage of women availing benefit under MGNREGA.

Mahatma Gandhi National Rural Employment Guarantee Act (MGNREGA): The MGNREGA guarantees 100 days of employment in a financial year to any rural household whose adult members are willing to do unskilled manual work. It is envisag in the Act while providing employment, priority shall be given to women in such a way that at least one-third of the beneficiaries shall be women, who have registered and requested for work under the Act. During the year 2012-13, total employment of Rs 134.76 cr person days were reported to have been generated. The employment generated for women were reported as 71.88 cr person days which is 53.34 per cent of total employment generated under this programme.

Women's Empowerment Under MGNREGA

Women's empowerment essentially refers to changing power relations between men and women in favour of women. The unequal power relations are reflected in different spheres of life such as, labour and employment, health and nutrition, education and skills, asset ownership, political and social participation etc. Unequal power relations denote that women enjoy limited power of decision-making in multiple spheres of life as compared to men. MGNREGA has facilitated increase of women's participation in the labour force. In this context, it is vital to assess whether women's participation in MGNREGA has instrumentalised change in the power relations between men and women, thereby increasing women's empowerment.

Women through MGNREGA

MGNREGA plays a significant role to meet the practical as well as strategic needs of women's participation. It has become a beacon of light in the empowerment of rural women and contributed substantially for the increased living and economic conditions by creating equal wages to male and female workers. The role of MGNREGA on women's participation can be examined through the following parameters:

1. **Income-consumption Effects:** By income-consumption effects, we mean an increase in income of women workers and as a result, their ability to choose their consumption baskets. MGNREGA empowers women by giving them a scope of independent earning and spend some amount for their own needs.

2. **Intra-Household Effects:** Women play a major role in raising the economic resources for their family but their contribution remains uncounted because they perform a significant amount of unpaid work. In rural areas, the dominance of males in intra-household decisions has been seen. MGNREGA has significant impact in converting some unpaid work into paid work and widen the scope of decision-making role of women in household matters.

3. **Community-Level Effects:** Women's participation at the local and district level of governance process is low in spite of 73rd Amendment of the Constitution. But women participation has increased after the implementation of MGNREGA in many areas. A large number of women workers attended the *gram sabha* meeting held in connection with MGNREGA . Community level empowerment of women is one of the great achievements of this Act.

Women's Participation under MGNREG in Karnataka

There are various factors which encourage the women workers' participation under this scheme include nature of work, which do not need skilled worker, the limited hours of work, availability of work locally, reduction of migration of male member, substantial jump in the wage rate etc. Participation of women varies widely across states. Women, participation under MGNREGS is measured in person days. At the national level, women ,participation has increased significantly to 53.01 per cent in 2012-13 (till January, 2013). Although, women work force, participation under the scheme has surpassed the statutory minimum requirement of 33 per cent, the Act stipulates that priority shall be given to women. In terms of implementation, it mandates that a minimum of one-third of the beneficiaries are women who have registered and have requested for work. However, ideally, there should be gender equality in participation in MGNREGS. That means, women proportion should be around 50 per cent both in terms participation and person-days of work. These are some issues which hinder women participation in MGNREGS in the state.

Achievements

- Ensuring livelihood for people in rural areas.
- Large scale participation of women, Scheduled Castes and Scheduled Tribes (SCs/STs) and other traditionally marginalised sections of society. SCs/STs account for 51 per cent of the total person-days generated and women account for 47 per cent of the total person-days generated.

- Increasing the wage rate in rural areas and strengthening the rural economy through the creation of infrastructure assets.
- Facilitating sustainable development, and
- Strengthening PRIs by involving them in the planning and monitoring of the scheme.

PROBLEMS RELATED TO WOMEN'S PARTICIPATION IN MGNREGS

1. **Non-availability of Child Care Facilities:** One of the major shortcomings of the Act is non-availability of proper crèche facilities at the work site, even though the Act includes this provision. Different studies show that women remained worried about their children while they are working at MGNREGA worksite even some women do not accept the job facilities of MGNREGA because of non-availability of proper child care facilities.

2. **Low Level of Awareness:** In many states 'women' participation is low because of low-level of awareness about the process and entitlement of the programme.

3. **Nature of Work:** Most of the studies reveal that nature of work is also not helpful for women workers. In most of the projects selected being related to rural connectivity and renovation of local water bodies involving earth work requiring application of physical force, male workers were preferred to women workers.

4. **Poor Worksite Facilities:** MGNREGA funds have been allocated for the provision of safe drinking water, resting place and first aid. But most of the studies reported that except drinking water facility all other facilities are generally absent.

5. **Delay in Payments:** Delay in payments is also responsible for poor participation of women particularly in case of single women if they are the main earner in the family. Because the Banks are far from the village, it becomes difficult for the women to open Bank Account and draw cash which discourage women participation.

6. **Policy Issues:** The effectiveness of MGNREGA crucially depends on what type of schemes it gives priority to lack of focus of social, gender inequality in creation of productive assets has been a major reason for limited success of wage employment programme. Compared to men, the proportion of unskilled, subsidiary workers among women is much larger under MGNREGA. Given poor health and literacy as well as the pre dominant responsibility of house work and caring, women have recourse only to work that is available.

Conclusion and Suggestions

MGNREGA has positive impact on employment pattern of women. Women have benefitted both as individual and community. Women are benefitted individually, because they are able to earn independently, spend some money for their own needs, contribute in family expenditure etc. The gained benefits of women as community can be understood by increased presence in the *gram sabha*, increasing number women speaking out in the meetings, increasing capacity of interaction etc. But the poor implementation across the nation (such as lack of child care facility, worksite facility and illegal presence of contractors) accrued the gender sensitiveness of this act mainly in north-eastern state. Certain initiatives and changes should be taken to remove these barriers. The valuable gains should not be derailed for poor implementation.

Suggestions

To increase participation rates of women workers in MGNREGA, the Ministry has suggested that individual bank/post office accounts must compulsorily be opened in the name of all women MGNREGA workers and their wages directly credited to their own account for the number of days worked. This Ministry has also advised the states:

- To identify widowed women, deserted women and destitute women who qualify as a household under the Act, to ensure that they are provided 100 days of work.
- To ensure that pregnant women and lactating mothers (at least up to eight months before delivery and 10 months after delivery) are given works which require less effort and are close to their houses.
- To conduct time and motion studies to formulate gender, age, level of disability, terrain and climate sensitive Schedule of Rates (SoRs) and to ensure accurate capturing of work done by women at worksites.
- To ensure that at least 50 per cent of the worksite supervisors (mattes) at all worksites are women.
- To ensure that worksite facilities such as crèches, drinking water, shade etc., are provided through convergence with Women and Child Development Schemes like ICDS.
- To encourage participation of women groups, including Self-Help Groups in awareness generation, capturing demand, planning, implementation, monitoring and maintenance of works.

Generally, women lack any productive assets other than their own labour. Often they do not even possess a homestead within which they could raise livestock or set up a shop to meet daily food requirement. There is thus the need to maintain to inform and assist public policy to institute implementation of programmes for a gender responsive political economy, with adequate measures for building women's ownership and control rights to productive assets. Needless to say, such measures are compatible with development needs of the country. That equal rights to productive assets of women with those of men, can lead to greater economic activity, change in the perception of dependence on men, and thus results in substantially reducing exclusion of women from social processes and promote development of diverse capabilities, thereby enhancing productivity and reducing inequality.

References

Dutta, S. (2009). "NREGA in West Bengal: Success and Challenges", *Kurukshetra,* 58 (2), 31.

GoI (2006), *"NREGA 2005 Operational Guidelines,"* Ministry of Rural Development, New Delhi.

Government of Karnataka, (2005), *"Karnataka Human Development Report 2005, Investing in Human Development"*, Planning and Statistics Department, GoK, Bangalore.

Hazarika, P.G. (2009), Promoting Women Empowerment and Gender Equality through the ....,

Hazra, A. (2009), "Transforming Rural India", *Kurushetra*, 58, pp. 7-9.

http://nrega.nic.in/netnrega/home.aspx.

Khera, R. and Nayak, N. (2009). "Woman Workers and Perceptions of the NREGA", *Economic and Political Weekly,* 44, pp. 49-57.

Pankaj, A. and Tankha, R. (2010). "Empowerment Effects of the NREGS on Women Workers: A Study in Four States", *Economic and Political Weekly,* 30, pp.45-55.

PRIYA (2008), *National Study: Phase-III*. "Role of Panchayati Raj Institutions in Implementation of NEREGA," New Delhi.

Ramesh, G. & Kumar, T.K. (2009). "Facet of Rural Women Empowerment: A Study in Karimnagar District in Andhra Pradesh". *Kurukshetra*, pp. 29-30, 58.

Right to Decent Work: Implementation of National Rural Employment Guarantee Programme (NREGP) in Assam State (India): A Case Study.

53

Human Resource Development and Rural Development

Subhaschandra D. Rathod and Shridevi J. Darabare

Introduction

India is the second largest populous country in the world, having more than one billion people.[1] As per 1991 Census, more than 700 million of its people are living in rural areas.[2] This fact shows that, the availability of human resources are residing in rural areas but the living standard, education, health, level of skills is high among the urban people than the people residing in rural areas. By realising this fact, the respective state governments and Union government have taken initiative by formulating policies, programmes for rural development as well as human resources development.

An educated and empowered population is the result of proper implementation of human resources development programmes and policies. This statement makes it clear that rural and human resources development is possible only by effective implementation of policies and programmes formulated for. Further, the policies and the programmes formulated by government contributes to increase productivity and thereby increase sustainable economic growth and development of nation. The human resource development is often referred to as the engine of growth and development of nation. One of the overriding objectives of a country's policy and planning is development of country by raising living standard and enhancing the productive capabilities of its people. Among various factors of production, human resources are only active resources which play an important role in economic development.[3] The development of country depends on availability and quality of resources, and the method of using the available resources.

Human resource constitutes the ultimate basis for the wealth of nation, therefore, human resource is the most important and vital factor for the overall development of any country.

Human resources hold a key position in the economic development of any country.[4] The real strength of the country and its institutions depend upon the capabilities of their people. Capital and natural resources are passive factors of production and human beings are the active agents, who accumulate capital, exploit natural resources, build social, economic, and political organisations and carry forward national development. Development of persons to their maximum potential and the conservation of talent is the gist of the concept of human resource development through health, education, skill, productive capacity, employment etc.

It is realised by past experience that, rural poverty is inextricably linked with low productive and unemployment. To overcome from these problems the government of India, and respective State governments have formulated number of policies and programs for providing health, education, employment, shelter, and so on. After the implementation of these policies and programmes there are positive outcome in the nation's rural development as well as human resource development, but not to the expected level.

With this background, the present paper has made an attempt to explain the contribution made by the rural development schemes, policies, programmes towards the human resource and rural development. Further, this paper seeks to examine the processes of human resource development in the rural context.

Object of the Study

The object of the study is to examine the origin and development of concept of rural and human resource development and to examine the relationship existing between the human resource development and rural development.

Conceptual Clarity

(a) Resource: Generally, the term resource denotes both renewable and non-renewable natural resource-something which is useful including land, water, air, or minerals as oil or coal etc. Resource is a sweeping expression. Material resources of the community in the context of reordering the national wealth embraces all the national wealth and not merely natural resources, all the private and public sources of meeting material needs, not merely public possession. Everything of value and use in the material world is material resource and the individual, being the member of the community, his resources are part of those of the community.[5]

(b) Human Resource: The working population of a country engaged in various types of productive activities or wanting to get an opportunity to do so is called human resource. There was lot of ambiguity about the meaning of the term Human Resource.[6] One school of thought says that all the human beings are not the resource. If all the human beings were resources, the poorest countries in the world would not be the countries with the maximum number of human beings. Human beings can be resources only when they have productive uses. In a broader sense, human resource denotes, energy, skill, talent, knowledge and attitude of human beings.

(c) Development: The term development is very elusive concept. In a technical sense, development refers to qualitative and structural changes in the state of economy. Development is a subjective and value-loaded concept, and hence there cannot be a consensus as to its meaning.[7] The term is used differently in diverse context. It basically means 'unfolding', 'revealing', or 'opening up' something which is latent. When it is applied to human beings, therefore means unfolding or opening up their potential powers. Development means the act, process or result of developing or growing or causing to grow; the state of being developed; happening.[8]

(d) Human Resource Development: Generally, the human resource development is a continuous process of promoting quality of life for all. Human resource development aims at the promotion of well being of individuals, families and societies. It deals with creating conditions that enable people to get the best out of themselves and their lives. Development is never ending process. As people develop in a new direction, new problems and issues arise and loop continues.[9]

Human resource development is a continuous process, which matches organisational needs for human resources and the individual needs for a career development.[10] It enables the individuals to gain their best human potential by attaining a total all round development.

As per United Nations Development Programme, the term human resource development refers to the policies and programmes that support and sustain equitable opportunities for continuing acquisition and application of skills, knowledge and competencies, which promote individual autonomy and are mutually beneficial to individuals the community and the larger environment of which they are a part.[11]

It is implied in the above conceptualisations of human resource developments, are the many facets of developments of people including their physical, intellectual, emotional, social, moral, political, and spiritual and all other forms of development.

(e) Rural Development: The term rural development is a sub-set of the broader term 'Development'. Author Khatar Singh in his book on 'Rural Development'[12] defines the term rural development 'connotes overall development of rural areas with a view to improve the quality of life of rural people' in this sense, it is a comprehensive and multi-dimensional concept, and encompasses the development of agriculture and allied activities, village and cottage industries and crafts, socio-economic infrastructure, community services and facilities, and, above all, the human resources in rural areas. As a phenomenon, rural development is the end result of interactions between various physical, technological, economical, socio-cultural and institutional factor.

Origin and Growth of Concept of Human Resource Development and Rural Development in India

(1) **Origin and Growth of Concept of Human Resource Development:** The concept of Human Resource Development is as old as human civilisation.[13] In early days, the term Human Resource Development was not prevalent but the academicians, business executives, corporate and bureaucrats in the society practised it.

The Human Resource Development as a function has evolved in India very indigenously from the year 1975, when Larcen and Turbo 'Company Conceptualised Human Resource' Development as an integrated system and decided to separate from personnel. Since then, most of the organisations have started new Human Resource Departments are redesignated their personnel and administrative departments as Human Resource Departments. Today, there are high expectations from Human Resource Development.[14]

By realising the fact that the development of human resource is a key to the development of a nation and education is the first step to the development of human resource, in the year 1985 by 174th amendment to the *Government of India Act*, the Government of India created new ministry called Ministry of human resource development. Ministry of human resource development is responsible for the development of human resources. The ministry is divided into two departments. First one is the department of school education and literacy which deals with primary and secondary education, adult education and literacy. The second department is department of higher education, which deals with university education, technical education and scholarship etc.

Human resource development in short means, investment in human capital, human capital means human can act as capital assets which yield a stream of economic benefits over their working life. An improvement in the mental capability, skill, and physical capacity of the people constitutes an increase in human factors to produce more.

Education is the first step for the development of human resource. Considering this fact, the Government of India formulated policies from time to time to provide education to the people. On the basis of the recommendations of Health Survey and Development Committee and the health survey and developing committee, the Government of India made its programmes for raising the health standards of the people in the country.

Despite efforts of improving health and nutritional status of the people, educational level of the people, by the government, the intended objectives have been not achieved because of improper implementation of existing policies.

(2) **Goals of Human Resources Development:** There are some universal goals towards which all-human resources development efforts should aim to achieve at the national level, human resources development aims at ensuring that people in the country live longer, live happily, free of diseases and hunger; have sufficient skill base to earn their livelihood and well-being. At the organisational level, the goals of the human resources development is normally to have competent, committed and motivated employees, to ensure higher levels of productivity, profitability and growth of organisation.[15]

Human resource development should be treated as an integrated concept. It promotes the development of all people and is not limited to any section or sector.[16] It deals both with the process of competency development in people and creation of conditions (through public policy, programmes and other interventions) to help people apply these competencies for their own benefit and for that of others.

Human resource development has been one of the major thrust areas in seventh, eightth, nineth and tenth five year plan.

(3) **Origin and Growth of Concept of Rural Development:** The concept of rural development is not an entirely new idea in India.[17] It has been in existence in various forms for many centuries prior to the launching of official programmers.

The several serious efforts approximating to what is now known as rural development were made only in the nineteenthth century.[18] Mahatma Gandhi started his constructive programme of rural development in an entirely different fashion, first at Champaran in 1917, and later at Sevagram in 1920, and at wardha in 1938.[19] His action plan involved the rebuilding of every aspect of human life *i.e.,* economic, education, and social and political, and envisaged a society based on self-supporting and self-governing villages.

If the villages perish, India will perish. On the other hand, if all Indian villages would come up to the Gandhian ideal, the country would be free from most of its worries.[20]

Our economy is developing fast, industries and big corporate are going globalised, with liberalisation tremendous changes are being felt in information technology, manufacturing, service sector, but nobody thinks about rural development to make it as fast as in these sectors. Visiting villages, we find even today houses made of mud, bamboos, and grass have no protection against storms, moisture and fire. The government realised the gravity of the situation and has taken some important measures to develop infrastructure in the countryside.

Despite these policies and programme, by the government for rural development, the rural India is still short of basic amenities, like drinking water, electricity, housing, food, health center, school buildings etc.

(4) **Basic Elements of Rural Development:** Whatever the geographical location, culture and historical stage of development of a society, there are at least three basic elements which are considered to constitute the 'true' meaning of rural development. They are as follows:[21]

(a) **Basic necessities of life**: People have certain basic needs, without which it would be impossible for them to survive. The basic necessity includes food, clothing, shelter, basic literacy, primary health care and security of life and property. When any one or all of them are absent or in critically short supply, we may state that a condition of 'absolute underdevelopment' exists.

(b) **Self-respect**: Every person and every nation seeks some sort of self-respect, dignity, or honour. Absence or denial of self-respect indicates lack of development.

(c) **Freedom:** In this context, freedom refers to political or ideological freedom, economic freedom and freedom from social servitude. As long as a society is bound by the servitude of men to nature, ignorance, other men, institutions, and dogmatic beliefs, it cannot claim to have achieved the goal of 'development'. Servitude in any from reflects a state of underdevelopment.

The rural areas with three-fourth countries, population have much low-level of income and consumption per head as well as much poorer access to education, health, transport and other essential services as compared to urban areas.[22] Removal of object poverty and unemployment are the twin objects of rural development with ultimate goal of improving the quality of life of rural people. The Government of India and respective state governments have formulated and implemented many rural development policies, programmes relating to education, health, shelter, employment, food, drinking water etc., accompanied with Ministry of Rural Development and Human Resource Development. Some of the important programmes are:

(1) Community Development Programme, 1952,

(2) Intensive Agricultural Development Programme,

(3) Small and Marginal Farmers and Agricultural Labour Development Programme,

(4) Training of Rural Youth for Self-employment,

(5) Integrated rural development programme,

(6) Rural Education, sanitation, development of women and children in rural areas.

(7) Indira Awas Yozana, Swarna Jaynthi Swarozhar Yozana, and

(8) Mahatma Gandhi National Rural Employment Guaranteed Programme etc.

The community development programme launched in 1952 for proper utilisation of the vast unexploited resources,[23] to encourage village people to become self-reliant, responsible citizens, to inculcate the spirit of self-help etc., but this programme could not bring prosperity to the rural masses up to the expected level, yet considerable development took place in the country side. The integrated rural development programme launched in 1976-77. The object of this programme is to alleviate rural poverty. Twenty selected districts were extended to cover 2,300 Blocks in 1978-79. It was further extended on October 2, 1980 to all the 5,011 Blocks in the country. All the program intended to rural and human resource development, but after the implementation of these programmes there are positive outcome in the nation's human resource as well as rural development but it remained unsatisfactory both in substance and speed. The past experiences on rural and human resources development signs of changes are quite conspicuous in many areas. But, if we have a closer look at the existing situation, we discover that there has not been any perceptible change in the equation of rural poor *vis-à-vis* the rural well-off. In spite of various measures initiated for the betterment of life style of the population as a whole, it has become evident that in most areas, the poor have become poorer and the rich have become richer. Further, although there has been some improvement in the communication system, production of agriculture outputs, animal wealth, public health and sanitation, etc., yet human population as a whole appears to have drifted away from their relatively harmonious relationship with the nature and the gulf of disparity between the rich and the poor appears to be on the increase.[24]

Rural development is not only economic development. It is the enrichment of the total quality of life in rural areas and its availability at minimum levels to all sections of the rural people.[25]

Human Resources Development *versus* Rural Development

Man, who has always lived in a society of some kind.[26] Man influences society and society influences man. The rural development is not a mechanical development, it is a human process. It requires hard work, dedication, responsiveness and accountability of both officials and non-officials to make rural development a success[27]. This statement shows that the rural development and the human resources development are interrelated phenomenon. Therefore, the process of human resources development and rural development go hand by hand. The development is both cause and consequence of change.[28] There is two way relationship between them, *i.e.*, development influences, and is influenced, by change. The change implies physical, technological, economic, social, cultural, attitudinal, organisational or political change. Whereas all manifestations of development can be traced to some change somewhere, sometimes not all changes lead to development; a change may be either for the better or the worse.[29]

Human beings are both the cause and consequence of development; it is the human factor that is the pivot of the process of development.[30] Therefore, the human resources development is impossible without rural development and *vis-a-vis*. Though, the study of human being is basic to the study of development, it cannot be of a human being in isolation, but rather of human beings in relation to their fellows, or of humans in society and in their environment.

There is close relationship between human resources development and rural development. Country develops if the human resource is developed to enhance economic development. State constructs roads, buildings, bridges, dams, power houses, hospitals, etc., and to run these units doctors, engineers, scientist, teachers, are required. Therefore, if the state invests in a human resource then it pays dividend in response.

The former President of India, Dr APJ Abdul Kalam, renowned scientist projected a vision for India in 2020 as a strong democratic country. He primarily believed that his vision of a strong country will be fulfilled building up on the contribution of each individual citizen. This statement clearly demonstrates the significance of human resource development of the country.[31]

The subject of rural development has always posed a challenge to the planners, implementers and the prospective beneficiaries.[32] For the last sixty years, we have been toying with the idea of '*Gram Swaraj*' or self-relient rural India. With utmost sincerity and concern, we have been experimenting with different policies, programmes and institutions, expecting success through hit and trial method.

Conclusion

It emerges from foregoing discussion that the initiatives taken by the both the Center and the State governments for rural and human resources development have not brought about the desired impact. The root cause might be the low-level of literacy, low-level of understanding capacity, lack of peoples' co-operation or participation in various development programmes, practice of political influence, and practice of corruption and lack of accountability of officers responsible for implementation of the programmes in case of failure in effective implementation or misadministration of the programmes. Further, there are some lacunas and weaknesses in the existing programmes and policies, which intended to provide basis for human resources and rural development. Therefore, even though there is positive outcome in the quality and quantum of development till it remained unsatisfactory both in substance and speed. Therefore, it is suggested that there is need for formulation of comprehensive umbrella programmes for sustainable rural development and human resources development.

Further, it is suggested that, an independent responsible authority shall be created for effective implementation of programmes formulated by the government for sustainable rural and human resources development. This way may be useful in solving the complex problems of rural and human resources development in India.

Notes

1. S.L. Goel, "Rural Development Administration in India: Some Observations", Cited in '*Rural Development Administration in the 21st Century*' (Surat Singh and Mohinder Singh eds.), Deep and Deep Publications Pvt. Ltd. New Delhi, 2006. p. 3.
2. Katar Singh (1999) *Rural Development*, 2nd Ed. Sage Publication, New Delhi, p. 23.
3. B. L. Mathur, (2000), *Rural Development and Co-operation*, 3rd ed., Deepak Parngi, RBSA, Jaipur, p. 167.
4. Dr. T. D. Tiwari (2000), *Human Resource Development: A New Prospective*, Shanti Prakashan, Delhi, p. 22.
5. *State of Karnataka v. Ranganatha Reddy*, AIR 1998 SC 215.
6. *Supra note*-4, p. 19.
7. *Supra note*-2, p.19.
8. P. Ramanatha Aiyar (2005), *Advanced Law Lexicon*, 3rd ed. Vol. 2, Wadhwa and Company, Nagpur, New Delhi, p. 1360.

9. *Supra note-* 4, p.16.
10. Shalini Singh (2006), *Human Resource and Managerial Development*, 1st Ed. Global Vision Publishing House, New Delhi, p. 3.
11. T. V Rao (1997) , *Human Resource Development*, Sage Publications India Pvt., Ltd. Delhi, p. .27.
12. *Supra note-* 2. p, 20.
13. *Supra note* -4. p, 16.
14. *Ibid. p.* 18.
15. *Supra note* - 4. p, 29.
16. *Supra note* - 4. p, 20.
17. Kishore Chandra Pandhy, (1986) *Rural Development in Modern India*, B.R. Publication Corporation, p.1.
18. *Ibid.*, p. 4.
19. *Ibid.*, p. 41.
20. *Ibid* ., (rear) p. 44.
20. *Supra note* - 2. pp. 21-22.
22. Government of India, Planning Commission, *Approach to Eighth Five Year Plan* (1990-95), New Delhi, May 1990, p. 12.
23. Mohinder Singh, (1992) "*Rural Development Programs in India*", cited in '*Rural Development in India*' (Mohinder Singh ed.), 1st ed. Intellectual Publishing House, New Delhi, p. 1.
24. *Supra note,* 1. p. 6.
25. *Ibid.*
26. Geeta Mehta, "Individual and Society: A Sarvodaya Point of View", cited in '*Gandhi Marg'* Vol. 9, No. 5, Journal of Gandhi Peace Foundation, New Delhi, 1987. p. 281.
27. *Supra note*-1, p. 1.
28. *Supra note* - 2, p. 24.
29. *Ibid.*
30. *Ibid.*, p. 25.
31. Mala Dutt, "*Development and & HRD in India*", Tokyo, March 2010. p. 2.
32. *Supra note*-1, p. 3.

References

Aiyar P. Ramanatha, Advanced Law Lexicon, 3rd ed. Vol. 2, Wadhwa and Company Nagpur, New Delhi.

Dr. Tiwari T. D., Human Resource Development- A New Prospective, Shanti Prakashan, Delhi, 2003.

Dutt Mala, "Development and HRD in India", Tokyo, March 2010.

Gandhi Marg' Vol. 9, No. 5, Journal of Gandhi Peace Foundation, New Delhi, 1987.

Government of India, Planning Commission, Approach to Eighth Five Year Plan (1990-95), New Delhi, May 1990.

Mathur B.L., Rural Development and Co-operation, 3rd ed., Deepak Parngi, RBSA Jaipur. 2000.

Pandhy Kishore Chandra, Rural Development in Modern India, B.R. Publication Corporation, 1986.

Rao T.V., Human Resource Development, Sage Publications India Pvt. Ltd. Delhi, 1997.

Singh Katar, Rural Development, 2nd Ed. Sage Publication, New Delhi, 1999.

Singh Mohinder, 'Rural Development in India' 1st ed. Intellectual Publishing House, New Delhi, 1992.

Singh Shalini, Human Resource and Managerial Development, 1st ed. Global Vision Publishing House, New Delhi, 2006.

Surat Singh and Mohinder Singh, 'Rural Development Administration in the 21st Century', Deep and Deep Publications Pvt. Ltd. New Delhi, 2006.

Index

B

C